# SOCIAL
# DISORGANIZATION

*By*

## ROBERT E. L. FARIS

PROFESSOR OF SOCIOLOGY, UNIVERSITY OF WASHINGTON

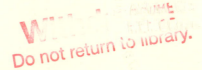

## THE RONALD PRESS COMPANY · NEW YORK

Library of Congress Catalog Card Number: 48-7569
PRINTED IN THE UNITED STATES OF AMERICA

# PREFACE

The present work is intended for use as a text in college courses dealing with the subject of social disorganization. Although the fundamental body of knowledge is far from complete, there does exist a valuable amount of sociological knowledge on this subject, and it appears timely and desirable to assemble it in an objective and organized presentation.

The primary concern is not with "social problems" or "social pathology." It is assumed that the various afflictions included in such categories are to some extent consequences of social disorganization and that an understanding of the basic sociology of disorganization is a requisite for intelligent solutions of such "social problems."

There is wide interest in and concern about the possibility of progressive disorganization and decline or downfall of our civilization. Many of the indications of such a development are the symptoms of disorganization which are analyzed in the present volume. In view of popular apprehension on this subject it has seemed appropriate to deal with certain processes of reorganization, in order to show that the course of civilization is not necessarily a one-way progress toward extinction.

The author has drawn upon the whole field of sociology and several of the related disciplines in preparing this book and he wishes to acknowledge aid from many of his teachers and associates. His most immediate obligation is to Professor Harvey J. Locke, whose able and conscientious examination of the manuscript added much to its clarity. Any blemishes which remain are, of course, the responsibility of the writer.

ROBERT E. L. FARIS

Syracuse University
    May, 1948

# CONTENTS

# SOCIAL
# DISORGANIZATION

# Chapter 1

## THE NATURE OF SOCIAL ORGANIZATION

### Importance and Nature of the Inquiry

Western civilization appears at the present time to be passing through some kind of major transition, a change so fundamental in character that it unsettles our basic institutions. Established procedures are giving way to uncertainty, confusion, individuated styles of behavior, so that the unity of the whole society becomes affected. Individual demoralization follows this social disorganization, with consequences so disturbing in appearance that some observers have been led to predict the downfall of this civilization.

Sociologists and scholars in related fields, however, have carefully examined the processes of social disorganization and have accumulated much useful knowledge of the mechanisms involved. While the great underlying cause appears to be the transition from pre-industrial folk society to modern industrial civilization, the details of the disorganization process operate not merely in a general disintegration of behavior standards, but through many specific mechanisms. These are separately analyzed in the present volume. Certain processes of reorganization which may in time bring a degree of new order and stability are also described.

Throughout the inquiry on the nature of disorganization, the interdependence of man and society remains impressively evident. Man has become, in the course of organic evolution, as dependent on his society as the fish is dependent upon his ocean. If worldwide social organization were to become totally disintegrated, it could only result in rapid extinction of the human race. It is in fact possible that, in the course of the long millennia of prehistory, local social organization in certain instances turned out to be inadequate, with the result that the populations perished without issue or trace.

Unlike the ocean environment of the fish, the society of man is a product of man's own activities. But man did not will nor plan the development of the principal structures of social relations upon which he came to depend. These structures evolved slowly—so gradually in fact that until a relatively advanced stage of develop-

3

ment was achieved, men were not aware of change nor of the arbitrary character of social organization. Their customs and institutions appeared, as Cooley has said, in the guise of nature.

In recent centuries, however, we have at last turned our attention to the subject of social organization and have learned of the many ways in which it involves our happiness and survival. At times we have even tried to gain control of the processes which had hitherto operated automatically. This effort, expressed through legislation, reform movements, revolutions, and in other ways, has not always been without effect, but the outcome is seldom exactly as foreseen or desired. It has become evident that efforts at control have the possibility of becoming effective only if the sciences of human behavior and social organization achieve advanced development. Progress toward solution of the major problems of society becomes more rapid when scholars abandon impatience and undertake the slower task of construction of an objective science.

Just as the physician must know the anatomy and physiology of the human body before he may be considered qualified to administer treatment to a victim of disease, so must the sociologist undertake the careful examination of the nature of social organizations before he can make a successful analysis of their pathological conditions. The sociologist's task is far less convenient than that of the physician, for he cannot bring his society into a laboratory for dissection, nor perform experiments on living examples. Methodical research is not impossible, however, for social life is all about us. While we do not perform experiments by action of will, history does it for us, and we may learn from events by careful and systematic observation. There are many distinct societies in the world today, and much change is taking place. Processes of organization and disorganization are there to be studied, and objective scientists are constantly at work, gathering and organizing the knowledge. Although it is in the very nature of sociology that it will be one of the last of the sciences to approach completion, there has already been accumulated sufficient material to be highly useful to the plans of men. It is first necessary, however, to have a fundamental acquaintance with the organized body of theoretical knowledge in order that the application be sound.

## General Characteristics of Successful Social Organizations

A successful society achieves a relatively stable system which is adapted to the physical surroundings and which enables its members to survive and to carry on the generally accepted tasks of the group. Other social organizations within a society are successful if they achieve systems which allow the groups to perform their implicit functions and to perpetuate themselves.

**The Functions of Custom.**—Man's first necessity, as Sumner has pointed out, is to live.[1]  Some time before the adequate survival instincts of his presocial stage were lost, man had to develop customs which were retained in habit and memory and transmitted through learning.  Presumably the folkways developed slowly in a process of trial and error, with little or no real foresight.  It was necessary that man develop not only the technical knowledge for such tasks as getting food and avoiding dangers, but also that man solve the fundamental problems of living with other persons in organized society. In response to the necessities of cooperative life several things were required: language for communication, division of labor for efficiency of operations, a system of distribution of products of labor, a body of techniques for minimizing friction (courtesies, gifts, etc.), solutions for quarrels (trials, ordeals, judges), mechanisms for making decisions of importance to the society (chiefs, wise men, magicians), systems of responsibility for persons needing care (family), methods to insure full transmission of the culture to younger generations (informal apprenticeship, specialist teachers, etc.), and various other basic systems.

It is not possible to make a complete list of the necessary social mechanisms of a society, for it is not agreed which of the virtually universal practices are indispensable.  Murdock, however, has suggested a list of universals, based on a survey of all known cultures.[2] He lists: age-grading, athletic sports, bodily adornment, calendar, cleanliness training, community organization, cooking, cooperative labor, cosmology, courtship, dancing, decorative art, divination, division of labor, dream interpretation, education, eschatology, ethics, ethnobotany, etiquette, faith healing, family, feasting, fire-making, folklore, food taboos, funeral rites, games, gestures, gift-giving, government, greetings, hair styles, hospitality, housing, hygiene, incest taboos, inheritance rules, joking, kin-groups, kinship nomenclature, language, law, luck superstitions, magic, marriage, mealtimes, medicine, modesty concerning natural functions, mourning, music, mythology, numerals, obstetrics, penal sanctions, personal

---

[1] William Graham Sumner, *The Folkways,* Boston: Ginn & Co., 1906, Ch. 1.
[2] George Peter Murdock, "Common Denominator of Cultures," in *The Science of Man in the World Crisis,* Ralph Linton, ed. New York: Columbia University Press, 1945, p. 124.

names, population policy, postnatal care, pregnancy usages, property rights, propitiation of supernatural beings, puberty customs, religious ritual, residence rules, sexual restrictions, soul concepts, status differentiation, surgery, toolmaking, trade, visiting, weaning, and weather control.

The above list is not completely intelligible without clearer definition of the categories, but its length furnishes an indication of the complexity of the problem of survival of even the most simple of human societies. Since these practices are stated to be found in all living and historical peoples, it may be suspected that even the more trivial of matters, such as luck superstitions, greetings, and decorative art, may have important functions, however difficult it may be to specify them.

**The Integration of Culture.**—Sociologists and anthropologists in general hold that in a stable, isolated society a slow and unrecognized process takes place by which the customs and institutions change in the direction of efficient adjustment to the conditions of life, and also change in the direction of consistency of the different practices with one another. If sufficient time is available, and if there is no change of environmental conditions or external interference, there is a tendency to approach a nearly perfect integration. In such a situation every common object and experience is socially defined, the alternatives and conflicts available to each member are few, the language and customs are organized, consistent, and regular, and the culture is so unified that no element can be disturbed without altering the whole system. A modern "functionalist" school of thought in anthropology has emphasized the value of such integration and has suggested that colonial officials who administer native peoples use extreme care in requiring alterations of native customs in order to avoid shattering the entire structure of the society.

In a stable and unified society the mores and institutions function with such success that serious deviation from conventional standards of behavior is rare. When a real crime, such as a killing, is committed, it may happen that nothing is done about it because there is no precedent in the memory of the people. Gutmann reports, for example, that among the Chagga an attempt was made at an unprecedented crime (a man undertook to destroy a pregnant wife by magic), with the consequence that the community knew of nothing that could be done about it. The oldest man in the country was called in, and the whole situation was presented to him. After enough questioning to bring out the details, the old man said confidently: "Nothing of the sort ever happened before." With this pretense that such things were hitherto unheard of, and presumably could never happen again, the incident was closed.[3]

The customs control nearly all of the behavior of the members of the society. Minor departures from correctness are dealt with by hints, light ridicule, and other informal means. There is no conflict here between individual and society, for the person is a product of an integrated and consistent social organization, and his tastes, attitudes, and habits are developed in his experience with his tribesmen. All the parts of the society fit in with one another and function smoothly, and the members conform naturally to the conventional standards. In Cooley's phrase, " 'society' and 'individuals' do not denote separable phenomena, but are simply collective and distributive aspects of the same thing."[4]

## SOME OBSERVED FEATURES OF SUCCESSFUL SOCIAL ORGANIZATIONS

The attention of sociologists has been directed more frequently at what are considered to be the pathological aspects of modern civilization than at the normal features, partly because of the urgency of the need for some wisdom in the handling of emergencies. In such a heterogeneous, shifting, and changing society as we live in today, it is not entirely obvious what it is that constitutes the normal or nonpathological, for standards are confused. The most fruitful sources of material, therefore, on the traits of successful societies are to be found in ethnological materials on isolated primitive or semiprimitive societies, for these are the social organizations which have had the long undisturbed periods which allow consistent and integrated cultures to develop.

**Cultural Harmony in Samoa.**—The observations by Margaret Mead on the experience of adolescent girls in Samoa constitute a classic contribution to the literature.[5] The central problem in the study is the comparison of the "stormy" experience of adolescence in twentieth century American society with the course of adolescence among the girls of a simple and homogeneous society. The investigator found that the experience of the Samoan adolescent girl was

---

[3] B. Gutmann, *Das Recht der Dschagga*, 1926. In William I. Thomas, *Primitive Behavior* (New York: McGraw-Hill Book Co., Inc., 1937), there are a number of lengthy excerpts from Gutmann's work.
[4] Charles Horton Cooley, *Human Nature and the Social Order*, New York: Chas. Scribner's Sons, 1902, p. 37.
[5] Margaret Mead, *Coming of Age in Samoa*, New York: William Morrow & Co., Inc., 1928.

lacking in the conflict and uncertainty that prevailed in the American system, and that she made a smooth transition into adulthood without the symptoms of mental disturbance formerly reported to be common in our society. There is apparently no physiological necessity for a period of "storm and stress," or for any other maladjustment, where the society contains no mechanism to produce it. In fact, custom in Samoa appears to have the power to overrule powerful physiological inclinations. It is a standard practice for some two dozen relatives of a mother to be present in the house at the time of a childbirth. While they laugh, joke, and play games, it is expected that the mother will not writhe or cry out, nor object to the lack of privacy.

Children in Samoa acquire the essential knowledge and behavior traits largely through an informal apprenticeship relation with slightly older children. There is only a continuous, gentle, indulgent pressure to conform to general expectations which impels the learner to make an effort. When boys approach young manhood, a competitive element enters their lives. Each is expected to try for distinction in some activity, such as house-building, carving, fishing, or oratory. But at the same time there is a demand that he should not be too efficient. To excel his fellows by more than a little is disapproved, and competition does not develop to a cut-throat stage.

Selfish, calculating individuality is not honored in Samoa, for one of the highest virtues is deemed to be human kindness. Particularly within the large circle of his own relatives the Samoan is expected to be helpful and generous, and to make no claims for definite repayment for any assistance he has given, or for donations of food, clothing, and shelter. It is, however, a matter of propriety for the person receiving the benefits of such help to make some equivalent return gift as soon as he is able. Individualism is far less developed in Samoa than it is in American civilization.

Personalities are never identical, even in the most uniform of societies, and differences, clashes, and quarrels are always possible. In Samoa, however, these are uncommon, and when they do occur it is only seldom that the consequences are serious. There are conventional methods of smoothing feelings after quarrels. When young persons differ with adults so that outbursts of wrath follow, conciliatory measures are quickly taken and prolonged discipline is avoided. If two young people of the same age in the same household engage regularly in conflict, the difficulty may be easily resolved by changing the household of one of them, for each person is welcome in a number of households. There is sufficient flexibility, both in the society and in the typical personality, to absorb the light conflicts that inevitably occur.   Mead found only two girls who could be referred to as delinquent in the sense of delinquency in our society, and in those cases there were special aspects of their experience to account for their behavior.

**The Continuity Principle Among the Chagga.**—The extreme emphasis on the welfare of the individual is not universal nor even typical of peoples where there is a strong social unity.   Here there is frequently a sentiment that the interests of the society predominate even if it requires some sacrifice of the interests of the persons. Gutmann, in his study of the Chagga peoples of Africa, has shown how powerful is the motive of continuity of the kinship group, or sib.[6]   Maternity and the symbolic and sacred character of mother blood are so important that nothing threatening to the principle is permitted.   The strength of the sentiment is shown by the reactions to any expressions of disgust or even levity in this connection. Gutmann reports that on one occasion some young people used the term "bark skirt" in a derogatory sense to ridicule a woman who had been soiled by a nursing child.   The offenders were brought before a court and sentenced to three days' imprisonment without food, and each was fined an ox or a goat.   If a girl committed such an offense, it was her father who was fined.   But a most drastic penalty was inflicted on a girl who ridiculed a school for brides and called the teaching lies and nonsense.   The chief called the women together and gave them permission to destroy the banana groves of her nearest relatives.   As the penalty was being carried out, the women sang a song on the theme of the insult, after which they pronounced in unison a curse against anyone who should ever again betray or deride the bride instructions.   The force of such a public expression is so great that the offenders are no longer able to remain in the community.

The Chagga conceive that the continuity of life and blood must go on in an inviolable order, and they enforce strict sanctions against departures from this order.   Thus if a daughter is married while her mother is still bearing children, it is believed that an essential unity of the blood stream is disturbed by simultaneous reproduction in two generations of the same family.   There is a saying: "If you are overtaken by your child you will die," meaning that disaster befalls a man or woman who is bearing children at the same time his children are also bearing.

---

[6] B. Gutmann, op. cit.

Although there is a normal love for children among the Chagga, the emphasis on sib continuity is stronger. If there is some symbolic defect in an infant, it may be disposed of in the interest of the group. A child is killed, for example, if the mother menstruated during pregnancy, if it was imagined that the child's voice was heard within the mother, if a foot or finger protruded first at birth, if the breast of the child was red, and in several other circumstances.

But even normal children were sacrificed for the welfare of the group. A method of defense against neighboring peoples bent on plunder was to bury small children alive at the points of entrance to the country and on the council ground at the court of the chief, in the expectation that these children would issue a warning noise before a hostile attack. The children chosen were without physical defects and had to be free from ever having had a cut on the body. They had to be from one of the old sibs whose feeling of descent was firmly rooted in the ground of the land. Such children were removed secretly without asking for the consent of parents, but later every attempt was made to appease the parents for their loss. As long as the parents were in a resentful state of mind, it was believed that the children would not give the warnings.

In such simple and smooth-functioning societies the recurring situations of life are clearly defined, and explicit mechanisms exist to deal with difficulties. Ambiguities are rare, and personal choices are far less frequent than among members of advanced civilizations. By far the greatest amount of control of persons is through informal means. Even where chiefs are theoretically in possession of great arbitrary power, they are expected to use it sparingly, and to operate as much as possible through personal influence.

**Integration and Social Control in Folk Cultures.**—In recent years social anthropologists have been turning attention to societies which they designate as "folk cultures." These are not primitive or preliterate, but are relatively isolated segments of modern civilization which have many of the aspects of primitive cultures.[7] Continuity of tradition and folk knowledge, strong development of kinship relations together with low emphasis on formal institutions and government, and the force of custom and informal social control are among the sociological features of these cultures.

---

[7] See for example R. Redfield, *The Folk Culture of Yucatan* (1941); H. M. Miner, *St. Denis: A French-Canadian Parish* (1939); and John F. Embree, *Suye Mura: A Japanese Village* (1939), all published by the University of Chicago Press.

Redfield has shown in a study of a series of Mexican villages and cities that the degree of remoteness from the influences of civilization is related to such features, and related to the extent to which the society may be said to have consensus or symbiosis as its basis of unity.[8] In the simplest of these folk societies the round of life is so well regulated that any trace of what a sociologist would regard as social disorganization is rare or absent. Even in the capital city of Yucatan, Merida, the folk elements are even yet so strong as to preserve a stability which offers strong contrast to the disorganization of industrial cities of the United States.

**Isolation and Cultural Continuity in Quebec.**—Isolation facilitates the preservation of the continuity of a folk society, and in some cases the interest of the society in continuity leads them to seek to preserve their isolation. An illustration of this is furnished by rural Quebec, where the French-speaking peoples have maintained a separate folk-society for three centuries in spite of the proximity of the rapidly changing American industrial civilization.[9] An important factor in their resistance to assimilation was, of course, their insistence on their right to maintain a language separate from the dominant English-speaking peoples. A Quebec *habitant* has the right to his own language in the schools, as well as in court proceedings, and in all official dealings with the government. In so far as it has been possible, legal handicaps resulting from ignorance of the English language are eliminated, and, while commercial disadvantage can not be completely removed, the abstention from commerce as far as possible and the concentration on agriculture are a part of the mechanism of isolation. The religion and other aspects of the folk culture of these people further promote their separation and preserve continuity.

The most important social groups in rural Quebec are the household family and the larger kinship group, within which affection and personal responsibility are highly developed. Pictures of ancestors hang on the walls, and knowledge of the exact blood relationship to each is kept fresh in the memory of living generations. Knowledge of the exact relation to living kin is also well developed. Kinship here, as in many preliterate societies, is much more than a set of names for biological relationship—it is a system of reciprocal rights and obligations and of definitions of modes of behavior.

---

[8] R. Redfield, *op. cit.*
[9] H. Miner, *op. cit.*

Behavior toward persons who are not kinfolk may be quarrelsome, and toward persons outside of their society hostile or even brutal, but within the sphere of their kinship group persons are expected to be friendly, responsible, frugal, conservative, and industrious. Serious departures from such standards are not common in Quebec villages, though emigrants from this culture are of course capable of undergoing all forms of disorganization when they reside in the industrial cities outside of their province.

**Folk Society in the United States.**—In view of the widespread public concern with social disorganization in our modern industrial civilization, it may be well to remember that not all of the population of the United States has been fully drawn into the urban social organization.   The rural and small town culture is still relatively stable.   In the most remote settlements, away from the principal streams of commerce and communication, there may be found surviving examples of the folk cultures of the eighteenth and nineteenth centuries.   Among the best known of these are the settlements of the Ozark Mountains and of the Appalachian Mountains, particularly in Virginia, North Carolina, and Tennessee.   The following description of the features of social life in an Appalachian village in a northern state illustrates the folk nature and the successful social organization in such communities:[10]

Creekville is a tiny village of sixteen houses, stretching for a distance of a half mile along a mountain stream.   The narrow valley has an elevation of about a thousand feet and is surrounded by mountains reaching to over three thousand feet.   There is no railroad, and the only road is a secondary highway that leads to no other town but turns around a mountain and connects with another highway which leads out of the mountains.   Twenty miles away there is a town of 8,000 population but the inhabitants of Creekville do not consider themselves within the circle of its influence.

The residents of the village are culturally homogeneous.   Most of them are or have been farmers, and the rest trade with farmers or sell services to them.   Their families have lived in the vicinity for many years.   Nearly all are Methodists or Baptists.   They share a rich heritage of folklore and folk customs.

It is characteristic of the members of any small community to be interested in one another, and to express this interest in continuous gossip.   The people know one another well, and have known all about each other for all their lives together.   Any new development is immediately common knowledge.   Young people who spend more than two or three evening engagements together, for example, will find that they have unofficially announced an expected wedding.

---

[10] From an unpublished study, contributed by a student who grew up in the village.

A resident, contending that there had been no unhappy marriages in the last fifteen years or so, offered as evidence the proposition that "If there had been an unhappy marriage in Creekville everyone would have known about it."

In such a situation there is little privacy or individualism, and little desire for it. When neighbors come for a brief visit they do not knock on the door, but simply walk in. There is also a custom of dropping in for a visit at mealtime without an invitation, and it is expected that the host and hostess will in time pay a return visit. When there is illness or other trouble, word spreads and people come to aid without being called. When the physician's car goes up the road, people say, "I wonder who's sick," or "Maybe John is worse." When they find who is ill, the neighbors come in with baskets of food, and, if necessary, help in the chores and the care of the children. The stream of visitors bringing cheer and aid may exhaust the sick person until the physician deems it desirable to intervene.

In such a community, where everyone is either a friend or a relative of nearly everyone else, selfish competition for property is at a minimum. There is very little pressure to "keep up with the neighbors," but rather it is considered a disgrace to live beyond one's means. Quarrels about property may occur, but often situations which elsewhere might evoke bitter lawsuits are allowed to endure without causing tension. One local family occupied for twenty-five years land belonging to some one else, paying neither taxes nor rent. There was some discussion at the beginning of the affair, but the owner decided to let them go on living there, partly because he had no need for the land at the time and nobody else wanted it. In another case a family occupied land for fifteen years, paying no rent to the owner. The latter never got around to insist that they pay, and beside, they were related to him, and he knew them too well. The situation ended, however, when the owner sold the land and the purchaser occupied it.

Social control is of course very strong in Creekville. A man may drink a little beer now and then, unless he is a member of the Baptist church where total abstinence is required, but women are expected never to touch alcoholic beverages. If a man ever becomes intoxicated, his reputation is permanently damaged. It is practically impossible to keep people from finding out about this; according to a resident, a man cannot even get quietly drunk in his own home without everyone in town finding it out. Once a minister's son drank too heavily, and from then on no "nice" girl in Creekville would consider going out with him.

Even laziness is something of a sin in Creekville. The nicest thing that can be said about a person, according to one resident, is that he is a good worker. A prospective bride is inspected by the relatives of the groom for qualities of physical strength and energy. A cruel reflection was pronounced on the laziness of a resident who died at the unconventionally young age of sixty, "You can rust out as well as wear out."

There are no illegitimate children in the community, and such sex irregularity as does occasionally occur furnishes material for conversation for some years. Serious crimes practically never occur in Creekville. Suicide is also unknown in the community, although there are two cases of strange deaths of farmers in the nearby hills.  One of these men, unhappy because his obese wife was too attractive to other men, climbed to the top of a high rock tower and shot himself.  After two decades the town is still horrified, and the story is a legend among the children.

The development of family and kinship relations promotes continuity of the local culture.  There are many who live with relatives, and those who do not do so make a practice of visiting often if relatives live nearby.  If the relatives live at a distance, they make a pilgrimage at least once a year.  The continuity of generations is strong, and old people usually live with their children.  Harmony between old and younger generations is the rule, but even in the rare cases in which some tension develops, it is never possible to send the old people to the poorhouse.  It would be a disgrace that no family in Creekville would want on its conscience.  One of the most shocking things a grandparent could say when he encounters insolence of youth is "I suppose you would like me to go to the poorhouse."  Parents deal with such rebellious children by saying, "I suppose you're going to treat me that way when I get old."

Old persons are much respected and, far from being regarded as obsolete, are admired for their vigor and for their wisdom.  The aged live up to this reputation.  One grandmother celebrated her eightieth birthday by repairing the pig pen.  When an old person dies it is a calamity, and his wise sayings may be quoted for several years afterward.  Children are characteristically at ease with old persons—one child remarked to a grandparent, "When you talk to me you are my own age."

**Folk Knowledge.**—Successful cultures are never the product of a few outstanding leaders, but have gradually been achieved in the slow crescive process described by Sumner.  It is not sophisticated science that builds customs and social organizations, but the unwitting mass trial-and-error activity of ordinary people who pursue their daily practical tasks.  Folkways are the creation of the folk.

Long before the emergence of science, man required a rich body of collective knowledge for meeting common situations of life.  He needed to know what foods were edible, what animals were dangerous, and how to manipulate the materials about him in order to have clothing, shelter, and protection.  He also had to know many principles of human nature and social interaction in order to be able to live in society and cooperate effectively, for no man has been able to survive alone.  All primitive societies, no matter how simple, possess a large and valuable mass of such "folk knowledge" and depend on it for their survival.  Not all of it is consistent with modern scientific knowledge, but the mass of it is obviously efficient in the cultures which survive.

Folk knowledge differs from scientific knowledge in several respects. By any living generation it is experienced as old, stable, and noncontroversial. Its origin is too far away and its discovery too gradual to be known. If reference to source or authority is ever made, it is in such terms as "it is written . . ." or "it is well known that. . . ." The issues that are common in scientific thought and the fads that flourish on the borderline of science and pseudo-science are not found in folk traditions.

The transmission of folk knowledge from generation to generation does not take place through such channels as technical academic training, nor through the printed word, but rather by means of informal apprenticeship in daily life. Young persons absorb knowledge from the old for, in the folk society, age is associated with experience and wisdom, rather than with obsolescence.

Despite the abundance of erroneous belief and even wasteful or dangerous knowledge in all cultures, there probably is, as Sumner pointed out, a long-run "strain toward consistency" in the elements of a culture, and a strain toward adaptation to the nature of the physical world. Folk agriculture has fed most primitive and all civilized peoples for long centuries, and, while it is clearly inferior to scientific agriculture, it is far better than none at all. Few urban dwellers, ignorant of farm lore, would be able to make a success of agriculture on the basis of their common sense alone. The wartime experience of apartment-house dwellers of the metropolis in their attempts to grow "victory gardens" furnished abundant illustration of the importance of folk knowledge. There were thousands of futile attempts to grow food in mixtures of clay, brick fragments, and old bedsprings, and in filled-in land formerly used for parking trucks. Corn was planted in single rows, preventing adequate pollination, beans were grown in unfertile soil, and tomatoes were tried in the shade of the north walls of buildings.

The philosopher and poet Emerson is said to have paid tribute to the folk knowledge of a milkmaid. He had been trying without success to persuade a calf to enter a barn, and when the power of his reason and imaginative ingenuity were exhausted, the milkmaid showed him the folk technique by dipping her finger into some milk and allowing the calf to lick the finger as she gently withdrew into the barn.

It has been observed that the American Negro has had little record of success in commerce. The interpretation offered by E. Franklin Frazier is that the Negro possesses no folk experience in buying and selling. Even the young Negroes who study in business colleges are unable to acquire there the rich and essential wisdom of commerce that is found in the folk traditions of such peoples as the Jews, the Scots, or the old Yankee traders of New England.

Folk knowledge lives only in situations where there is strong cultural continuity, and therefore much of it is lost in the modern urban populations which live in apartment houses with no local heritage, and in which the average number of children is small, the age gap between generations large, and the apprenticeship relation of child to parent virtually absent. But in the simple folk society the relation between generations is rich and the respect for age and experience so great that young persons spontaneously seek wisdom from the elders. The transmission is most effective where there is a rich consensus, a sense of likeness and affection which is particularly strong where the familism and wide development of kinship is prevalent.

**Teamwork and Morale.**—In addition to the consensus aspect of any society, there is a division of labor teamwork—a symbiotic basis of unity. Persons specialize in different tasks and exchange the benefits of the differentiation. Only a small part of such exchange is direct person-to-person reciprocity. In most teamwork each member contributes his activity to the whole organization and draws his reward or benefit from the whole. In situations where the task is important, the members of the organization are competent, and the mechanism is functioning well, each member may experience a sense of satisfaction that is magnified by the fact of organization. The satisfactions of the total achievement are also his own, and he may have an exhilarating sense of the total power of the group. When such a condition of high morale is obtained, the relatively individualistic satisfactions, the comforts and personal pleasures, become of secondary importance and may be put so far aside that they are indulged only at the times when they could not interfere with the general purpose of the organization.

A journalist observing the activities of the Army Air Forces in the Pacific islands describes the disappearance of formalism and of minor concerns with self among the members of a bomber command at the time when their activity reached the stage of successful operations :[11]

"Now we're in business," the B-29 people said to one another after the first of the low-level incendiary strikes, which burned out about seventeen square miles of one of Tokio's most congested industrial areas. The people of the Twenty-first Bomber Command had reached a state in which there

[11] Reprinted by permission from an article by St. Clair McKelway in *The New Yorker*. Copyright 1945. The F-R. Publishing Corporation.

were certain ingredients that I find indefinable but in which I do know that there was a certain kind of fatigue brought on by sleeplessness, undereating, and hard, uninterrupted concentration on the performance of a task.   There was a calmness, almost a lassitude, which was not laxness or laziness.   There was also a tenseness, a quickening of tempo, that was neither youthful nor nervous nor feverish.   The mind, the body, the spirit, the whole being seemed free and ready for anything and confident of success.   It was not elation so much as it was a knowledgeable acceptance of maturity.

Whatever their jobs were, officers and men did not want, and seemed unable, to sleep more than three or four hours at a time.   They ate irregularly, sparingly, and hurriedly.   They worked almost incessantly and, when they felt like it, played or relaxed completely, knowing they had it coming to them.   Even airplane commanders and their crews, back from a fifteen-hour mission to Japan, usually hit the sack for not more than five or six hours and were up and around again, attending classes, studying tactics, bombardment, navigation, and ordnance, and forming little groups in Quonset huts, talking flying, talking fighting, using their hands as airplanes, the way fliers do, flying the latest mission over again, perfecting it, and flying the next mission once or twice in advance, before the takeoff.   Good men were better.   Men who had seemed mediocre became good.

At the headquarters of our Twenty-first Bomber Command, on Guam, and in the B-29 wings and groups and squadrons on all three islands, staff people who had felt uncertain about how to do their jobs and had been inclined to stick to the book, to take the safest course, became confident, aggressive, eager to think of short cuts, eager to show that they could take them.   Assistant adjutants and their clerks, in military sections devoted to red tape, suddenly broke through the system they had themselves created, got out complex orders and directives by new, swift methods, and performed a thousand other worrisome and necessary drudgeries with an undreamed-of simplicity and speed. Messengers walked faster and took an interest in seeing that the right message got to the right man at the right time.   Jeep drivers took care of their jeeps and never ran out of gas.   A supply officer at headquarters, after all sorts of wangling both in and out of channels before he left the States, received an icebox for his tent and never got around to opening the crate and installing the precious mechanism until it had sat in a corner of his tent for five weeks. This unused icebox just sat there, like an unopened Christmas present in a child's room.   As a symbol of tantalizing self-denial, it got on everybody's nerves.   Finally, the supply officer's boss took him aside during one of the inspired moments of those delicious, smooth-running days and nights and said to him, "Listen, son, you go fix up your goddam icebox in your tent right now, and don't come back here until your beer is cooling in it, see?"

Everybody seemed to realize that everybody else was working his head off. Requests were made, commands were given, in quiet voices.   Everybody seemed almost miraculously full of tolerance and understanding.

Such experiences associated with high morale are well known to members of athletic teams, theatrical troupes, construction crews, and other small teamwork organizations at times when all is progressing well in their activity. In larger causes, such as that of a nation at war, similar processes may operate. High morale of the civilian population in wartime is expressed in the same sense of enthusiasm and dedication and in indifference to personal comforts and pleasures. The purposes of the society become the aims of each person, and the members derive their rewards from the general achievement. It is not necessary that the individual exist merely for the purpose of the society, but that he find his greater satisfactions in helping to achieve the general purpose.

## SUMMARY

Man's survival has always depended upon his preservation of an effective social organization. The knowledge he requires, both technical and social, is contained and transmitted in a collective process. The major needs are cared for by institutional arrangements. These elements of society tend, in isolated and stable societies, to fit into a closely integrated system in which no part can be altered without causing general disarrangement of the society.

Since each generation is born into a working system, the existing practices of the society appear to be the natural and right way. And since these are the ways of parents and ancestors, they also come to be regarded as sacred. Continuity thus becomes valued for itself, and the society is defended against radical change. Personal satisfaction tends to be high in the members of a group which possesses such a high degree of solidarity and in which the functions are being carried on successfully.

## SELECTED REFERENCES

Angell, Robert C. *The Integration of American Society.* New York: McGraw-Hill Book Co., Inc., 1941. See especially Ch. 2, "The Integration of a Society."

Cooley, Charles H. *Social Organization.* New York: Chas. Scribner's Sons, 1915. A classic which has lost no value since the time of its publication.

LaPiere, Richard T. *Sociology.* New York: McGraw-Hill Book Co., Inc., 1946. See Chs. 8 and 14, "Structural Dynamics" and "Social Organization."

Malinowski, Bronislaw. *The Dynamics of Culture Change.* New Haven, Conn.: Yale University Press, 1934. Ch. 4, "The Functional Theory of Culture."

McIver, Robert M. *Society: A Textbook of Sociology.* New York: Farrar & Rinehart, Inc., 1937.

Ogburn, William F., and Nimkoff, M. *Sociology.* Boston: Houghton Mifflin Co., 1940. Chs. 18 and 23, "The Organization of Society" and "The Interrelationship of Institutions."

Park, Robert E., and Burgess, E. W. *Introduction to the Science of Sociology.* Chs. 3 and 6, "Society and the Group" and "Social Interaction."

# Chapter 2

# THE NATURE OF SOCIAL DISORGANIZATION

## Definition of Social Disorganization

Social disorganization is disruption of the functional relations among persons to a degree that interferes with the performance of the accepted tasks of the group. Failure of a social organization to achieve a goal is not in itself disorganization, or a disorganizing factor, for if it results from circumstances beyond control and is not the fault of any member, the failure may be accepted without weakening the solidarity of the group. Financial disaster resulting from crop failure characteristically is endured by farmers in a philosophical spirit, but hardships resulting from deflation and mortgage foreclosures are regarded as the fault of a class of persons, and thus weaken the bond of loyalty the farmer has for the socio-economic organization as a whole. In this latter case there is someone apparently to blame, and the fabric of mutual confidence which is important to a teamwork organization is weakened.

**Disintegration of Roles.**—One of the most general characteristics of social disorganization is that the separate functions of members are not being successfully performed. In the simplest cases of teamwork, such as an athletic organization, this result is easy to perceive. A disintegration of the pattern of roles in a football team has an immediate and obvious consequence in the failure to gain ground, to score, and to prevent the opposing team from scoring. It is, of course, possible to lose a game without disorganization when faced with a superior opponent, but failure to achieve the aims of the game is inevitable if there is disorganization, unless there is also great weakness or failure in the opponents as well. In a football team the distinction between individual ability and effective teamwork can be seen clearly. A team consisting of players each of whom is individually brilliant may nevertheless function poorly and be defeated by a smoothly functioning team of less able athletes. If members do not all play their parts in the action, and if these parts do not coordinate into an effective pattern, the individual skills lose much, or in some plays all, of their utility.

A football team provides a useful analogy and example for the study of social disorganization, for here can be seen in simple form many of the failures of coordination that also occur in more elaborate social organizations. The necessity for each member to find his personal satisfaction in the achievement of the whole group rather than merely in his individual performance has already been mentioned. A football quarterback who placed his personal glory ahead of the collective purpose would be tempted, when his team is in scoring position, to call for a play in which he would be the one to make the score, even if another player might have a better chance of success. A halfback receiving the ball from center on a passing play may be subject to the temptation to carry the ball on a run and thus be the center of attention during the entire play. When such considerations enter into the actions of football players, as they occasionally do, the coach usually recognizes that harmony and morale in the team are inadequate.

The highest individual skills in a football performance are most effective when the coordination with other skills is perfect. When the coordination is weakened and each player loses confidence that his teammates will perform skillfully and on time, the individual player must divide his attention between his own duties and those of the others and modify his performance to a variable timing. A pass-receiver may be drilled to run to a prearranged spot to receive a pass, which should arrive there at the same moment. Where coordination is effective and confidence is high, the receiver will run to the spot without looking behind him until just as he is about to arrive, and thus gain an advantage over the defense by the swiftness and smoothness of the play. If, however, he lacks confidence in his teammates, if he fears that the line may allow opposing tacklers to break through and hurry the play, or that an awkward pass from center may delay the timing, or that the passer may have a poor aim, he may feel required to look frequently over his shoulder, thus slowing the play and betraying the coming pass to his opponents.

Such defects of coordination are not as easy to perceive in the teamwork that constitutes the whole social organization. The complexity is so great that the goals and the individual roles are not as clearly specified, but the processes of disorganization are of the same general character as those in a small and tightly integrated group. There are also, however, some complications that do not enter into the relations of members of an athletic team. For one thing, the aims of a society as a whole are not only not made explicit

at any one time, but they are not even understood to be the same
by all of the members. Furthermore, in modern times they are in
constant process of alteration and redefinition.   The consensus
among citizens of the United States is incomplete on such questions
as whether it is the proper function of the political order to control
prices or whether prices should be determined by interaction in a
free market.   There is also disagreement on whether it is the function of government to prohibit racial and religious discrimination
in employment, on the responsibility of government to provide
economic security and health protection to all, on whether it is the
responsibility of the family to assume care of aged relatives, and
on many similar issues.   When some of these controversial functions are being only partially achieved, there is disagreement on
whether the failure is to be thought of as social disorganization.

On the other hand there are many functions which are clearly
understood to be the responsibility of the whole society, or of
separate institutions within it.   Children are to be cared for and
given an essential part of their cultural education in the family.
Churches have the responsibility of preserving and transmitting
their particular religious heritages, although additional roles are
being assumed by certain modern churches.   The economic order is
assumed to provide for the production and distribution of goods and
wealth.   The political order has many clear-cut responsibilities—the
prevention of crime and disorder, the provision of many essential
services to communities and to larger areas, the resolution of conflicts of policy, the defense of the nation, and many others.   When
any of these functions or others of the same order are being inadequately fulfilled, there is clearly a situation of disorganization in
the society.[1]

**Ambiguity.**—Uncertainty of role may in itself be regarded as
an aspect of social disorganization.   Lincoln Steffens, during his

---

[1] There has been theoretical criticism of the concept of social disorganization, and some
avoidance of its use, on the ground that it is not an objective concept.   It is stated that
arbitrary moral disapproval of a condition enters into the judgment of whether it is to be
regarded as disorganization.   But even if we accept the idea that all mores are arbitrary and
that the aims of a society are undefined and changing, there is no reason to be hesitant about
employing a term that is relative in character.   All concepts referring to human behavior
necessarily have this relative aspect; if we had to avoid them, we could not even converse
about or study behavior.   It is necessary to recognize that social disorganization denotes
imperfections in whatever interaction systems we have, and that in many cases neither the
aims nor the mechanisms are defined so clearly that all can agree on whether disorganization
is present.   At the same time, however, it is clear that many situations involve no serious
amount of controversy.   When the police of a city, for example, turn aside from their conventional duties, cooperate with criminals, and fail to enforce the local laws, the public as
well as the scholar knows that some aspect of society is not working as it should, and the
"should" is objective enough for both practical and sociological purposes.

investigations of the nature of urban political corruption in the early years of the twentieth century, discovered that some of the corrupt officials were actually uncertain of the nature of their wrongdoing.[2]   One man who was prominent in such a scandal asked Steffens, the reporter, just what it was that had been bad in his actions, what was his crime.   Steffens told him that his crime was loyalty—the political official had been too loyal to his unofficial political organization and had neglected the conflicting responsibilities of his governmental role.   He had chosen to overemphasize the wrong virtue.

In any teamwork activity there is necessary an integration of roles and a unity and harmony of purpose among the members of the society.   Perfect agreement and harmony are necessary only in situations where the utmost in smooth coordination is vital, as in athletic teams, a team of surgeons, assistants, and nurses performing an operation, a military or naval engagement, and the like.   In less critical situations a social organization may tolerate some disagreement; normally it will contain a mechanism for resolving internal conflicts.   But when there is a serious decline of unity and harmony to the degree that the performance of the primary functions is affected, the condition may be regarded as disorganization.

**Contemporary Disorganization.**—In our modern urban civilization, which has been partly though not necessarily dangerously disorganized during the years of the present century, there are a great many instances of internal disharmony, which in their totality interfere with the proper functioning of the mechanisms of the economic organization, the political system, and the moral order in general.

There is at the present time a serious separation of major divisions of the population—a conflict of interest groups, of socioeconomic classes, of racial groups, and of cultural groups within the society.   An earlier equilibrium, essentially an accommodation, which held conflict to a low level, gradually underwent a process of disintegration before any new systems for resolution of conflicts could evolve.

Although the class organization of the population of the United States is not the same as the earlier fixed class system of many European countries, there are nevertheless some differences of culture, some contrasts of loyalty, and a certain amount of antagonism.

---

[2] Lincoln Steffens, *Autobiography*, New York: Harcourt Brace and Co., 1931.

For example, Roosevelt's attacks on "Wall Street" and the "money-changers" had an appeal to the low-income classes, and at the same time the high-income levels of the population expressed a certain political solidarity by their accusation against the President that he was a "traitor to his class." During and following World War II there was a class resentment of the standard relation between officers and men in the military services which was essentially an assault on the principle that any special privileges may be permitted to a class.

The principal cultural divisions of the United States population are based on European origins (and to a certain extent on origin in Asia and other regions), on sectional bases, and on rural-urban contrasts. Though most of the time conflict between these cultural divisions is slight, the tendency to withhold certain types of cooperation is occasionally visible, and there is often a marked disposition to form political divisions along these cultural lines. The division between North and South in national politics is at least in part a matter of culture contrast and hostility, although there are other bases of conflict as well. In many states and localities the distrust between urban and rural sections finds expression in political schisms. Illinois, Rhode Island, New York, and other states have a condition of near balance between the political power of the cities and that of the rural sections, and on occasions the hostility between the divisions is great enough to interfere with the proper functioning of political processes.

Racial hostility occurs not only between Negroes and native whites, but also between the latter group and Orientals, between Jews and non-Jews, and between Indians, Mexicans, and native white Americans. The relative scarcity of intense overt conflict is partly a result of the overwhelming predominance and power of the native white American. On the occasions when riots between Negroes and whites have occurred, their desperate character has revealed the intensity of the hostility. Extreme minority factions among the Negroes were reported during the second world war to have expressed racial sympathy with the Japanese, although this did not in all cases imply that a military defeat of the United States was desired. Some Negroes expressed hope that the United States would win in the end, but only after some humiliation at the hands of Japanese.

Racial and nationalistic cleavage within a country is disorganizing even when there is no expression in riot or disorder, for each minority racial group characteristically expresses its aims by voting for candidates according to their support of the racial policies. This process tends to produce politicians who place the aims of such a minority above the national interest, at least on matters where the racial policies come into conflict with national policies. This practice, coupled with the widely-observed political trading device known as "log-rolling," has at times so interfered with the ability of the United States Congress to deal efficiently and equitably with national problems that the clamor has arisen, and has found response, for greater powers to be placed in the executive branch of the government. Such a demand is in effect a recognition of serious disorganization in the legislative arm of the government.

The effect of conflicting interest groups on political processes is similar to that of conflicting racial groups. The insistence of western mining interests, for example, that their senators and representatives protect them is so great that on all issues in which such interests are involved, or on issues in which a trade or deal has been made for the ultimate benefit of such interests, the congressmen have characteristically shown a disposition to represent the mining group first and the national interest later. Not even the crisis of the greatest war in history was adequate to persuade the western silver bloc to allow the government to abandon its artificial support of silver prices.

Similarly, western cattle-raising interests have insisted on barring Argentine meat from local competition, even though the humiliating rationalization that all such meat was polluted by hoof-and-mouth disease was a serious disturbing factor in international relations, a hindrance in the pursuit of victory in a great war, and a threat to peace and stability in the postwar world. The so-called "cotton senators" show similar vigilance in protecting the interests of southern agriculture, even to the extent of blocking all activity of the upper house by a filibuster, when they consider that these interests are threatened.

The conflict of interest groups is also expressed in the determination of labor unions to achieve certain of their aims, regardless of public inconvenience. During and immediately after World War II a series of strikes in the steel, coal, automobile, and other key industries hampered war material production and delayed the process of reconversion to a peacetime economy. The coal strike of 1946 had the effect of curtailing the use of electric power, made necessary the rationing of gas in some areas, forced limitations on railroad services, and closed manufacturing plants of many kinds. The most disastrous effect of this strike was to delay the shipment of grain to starving populations abroad.   It is impossible to estimate the number of deaths by starvation caused by this one strike alone, but the true figure may be large.   The striking coal miners had no intention of producing such an effect.   They were, as were many other divisions of the population, merely considering their own immediate interest above all others.

The tactics of employers during the course of industrial conflict often reach a stage where it is clear that their interest is being put above the general welfare.   Employers have used lockouts, company police, hired strikebreakers, controlled company unions, propaganda, political influence, and other devices in a manner which has intensified the conflict and disturbed the internal harmony of the industrial order.

**Decline of Unity and Harmony.**—The decline of unity and harmony in a society, a primary condition of social disorganization, is visible in many other aspects of contemporary American civilization.[3]   The most important primary groups, the family and the neighborhood, are showing indications of increasing disharmony by the rising divorce rate and the virtual disappearance of neighborhood life in certain districts of the large cities.   In urban society there is a general tendency for the proportions of social contacts that are of a primary character to diminish, while secondary contacts are increased.   There is further an elaborate differentiation of interests that functions to limit the range of possible primary friendships each person may have.   In so far as persons seek companionship within their own occupational classification, the division of occupations into ever smaller specialties narrows the range of friendship opportunities.   The specialization of recreational interests has a similar effect—poker players select their friends from the poker enthusiasts, bowlers seek the company of one another, the "horsy" set forms an exclusive ring, and lovers of fishing, bridge-playing, rose-growing, skeet-shooting, and many other recreations prefer to gather with their kind.

---

[3] Some of the discussion in this and the following chapter may be regarded as controversial.   It is not universally agreed that an increase in the divorce rate represents an actual disintegration of social control, or merely a change in the value placed on permanence of marriage.   A system of permanent marriage, however, is still deeply imbedded in customs, mores, and law, and the rising divorce rate at least represents a willingness to act counter to these general principles.   Similarly the specialization of interests is sometimes held to be merely a change of personal tastes, but here again it can be claimed that this change is functionally related to disorganization, for our basic primary group life operates on the basis of consensus.

There is also some indication that preferences in politics, religion, and general philosophy of life are becoming increasingly specialized, and perhaps increasingly a basis of segmentation of primary relations. New Dealers, for example, felt uncomfortable at social gatherings in which loyal Republicans were in the majority. There has been some decline in the tolerance and casual friendship between Catholic and Protestant. Social gatherings of friends have an increasing tendency to be homogeneous with respect to attitudes regarding internationalism vs. isolationism, attitudes toward Britain and Russia, and attitudes regarding domestic political policies. In so far as each person is unacquainted, or only slightly and formally acquainted, with those who hold views opposing his own, he tends to exaggerate and oversimplify the position of the others, and to experience a greater hostility than would be the case if the understanding had the benefit of a primary friendship. Thus the division of social relations on the basis of such interests operates to increase the seriousness of the disagreements themselves, and therefore to increase the consequent social disorganization.

**The Failure of Functions.**—In postwar Europe and Asia there have been areas in which many of the major functions of society were for a time completely suspended. In China there were regions in which government almost completely ceased to operate, in which money became useless, and production and distribution of food and other economic goods virtually ended, so that large populations perished. Nothing approaching the severity of this experience has been observed in the United States. There has been a widespread partial failure of many functions in this country, but it is not inevitable that such disorganization should continue to the point of disaster. However, if some of the trends should persist indefinitely, it is difficult to imagine how the society could survive.

The functions of the economic system are to produce and to distribute goods and services. During the depression of the 1930's the system was disorganized to the extent that it only partially fulfilled these purposes. There were millions of persons who desired to work but were unable to find employment. There were industries ready to produce but without purchasers to pay for their operations. The social mechanisms which normally coordinate the wishes and activities in this sphere of life were in a state of disorganization. A somewhat similar condition exists in a period of inflation, a moderate instance of which took place in the United States during and immediately after both world wars. Either of these experiences, if prolonged and intensified, is capable of leading a nation into revolution.[4]

The experience in this country regarding political, religious, moral, and other functions, has also been that of a general but only moderate failure, tending to increase during the first half of the twentieth century, but not, by the late 1940's, approaching the disintegration point.[5] While the national administration has failed to get the utmost efficiency in mobilization of national power, it has done well enough, with the aid of allies, to win wars. It has not held the price level nor eliminated industrial stoppage, but has been able to contain both the inflation and the labor conflict within bounds which in other circumstances they might have disastrously exceeded. Similarly churches have been falling short of their goals without failing utterly, mores have been disintegrating without destroying the moral order, and the family has been losing ground without disappearing. The birth-rate dipped in the early 1930's below the replacement level, but turned up during the war period to delay the arrival of the time of population stability or decline.

## SOME GENERAL SYMPTOMS OF DISORGANIZATION IN A SOCIETY

When the essential conditions of disorganization are present—the disruption of roles and the failure of functions—there tend to arise a number of symptomatic expressions, not always in themselves contributing to disruption and in some cases possibly even anabolic, which betray the fact that established ways have been breaking up and that the social order is in an unstable condition. These are such familiar conditions in America and Europe during the twentieth century that they tend to be regarded as normal, and to the extent that it is normal for a changing society to be in a fairly constant state of partial disorganization, this may be so. Such symptoms do, however, for the most part find their clearest expression in the most disorganized aspects of society, and are less prominent or completely absent in the more stable sections.

Formalism.—Old, established, rigid institutions often contain rules and procedures whose origins, if not forgotten, have lost some

---

[4] During the middle and late 1940's it became evident that economic disorganization in Europe had reached a critical point. Food from the United States was required to keep people alive in many countries. An important aspect of the failure was the refusal of European farmers and peasants to deliver enough of their produce for the use of urban dwellers. There was little to buy with the inflated currency they received in exchange. In so far as they were able, many farmers first tried to accumulate something like a year's hidden supply for their own families, and then to dispose of any surplus on the black market. An essential for recovery appears to be restoration of the faith of the peasant in the market system—a system which had been deteriorating for many years.

[5] Analysis of these aspects of disorganization appears in later chapters.

of their importance in the minds of present generations, and yet which are observed by the force of personal habit or of institutional rigidity. The adherence to such rules, without regard to the meanings which are attached to them, is known as formalism. The mechanical aspect of the observance of religious rites in some instances may be regarded as an example. The prayer flags and prayer wheels in use among some of the peoples of Tibet operate automatically, each flap of the flag or each turn of the wheel constituting a prayer, working in the absence of the supplicant and during the times when his mind is otherwise occupied. Such rites have the appearance, at least, of formalism to peoples of European civilization.

Survivals of medievalism in nineteenth and twentieth century American universities are sometimes considered to be examples of formalism. Where a classical curriculum with emphasis on Latin and Greek, mathematics, grammar, rhetoric, and logic, is employed as the basis of educating young people to take their places in modern society, formalism is sometimes held to be present.

It must be remembered that an ancient practice may acquire a new meaning and function and thereby persist and serve a useful purpose. This is not regarded as formalism. It is also obvious that few persons would be willing to admit that their own behavior is properly classified within that category. It is always possible to rationalize and justify behavior which appears to others as formalism. Traditionalists in higher education claim that the classical curriculum trains the mind and is therefore well adapted to modern times. In a sense, then, the decision is not one of pure objectivity, or at least it is frequently difficult to establish the objectivity of any particular identification of formalism.

When a general sentiment spreads among the members of a society that an institution is pervaded with formalism, however much or little objectivity there is in their decision, the ground is prepared for some kind of reform or revolt. The hundreds of new religious sects that arose in the eighteenth and nineteenth centuries were, to a considerable extent, rebellious against the formalism of existing churches. [Formalism is the brittle condition that precedes drastic forms of violent disorganization and reorganization.

**Decline of Sacred Elements in a Society.**—Social organizations do not arise as the result of a rational process, but evolve so slowly that the origins of the old and central features of a society are unknown—lost in prehistory. They also acquire a sacred status to the members and are accepted and followed on this basis.   Change is resisted not on considerations of efficiency, but because of the emotional resistance to altering sacred ways.   When new features do enter and become of central importance to a social order, they also in time become sacred, even though their adoption involved most practical considerations.   The Constitution of the United States had a secular birth, but in time has gathered enough sacredness so that it is increasingly difficult to amend it, and even more difficult to criticize or attack it.   Such sacredness operates to preserve continuity in a society and therefore to preserve the integration. A decline of sacredness opens the way to disorganization.

In addition to religious elements and symbols of nationality, there are many other aspects of modern culture which have a sacred character.   Home, motherhood, the monogamous family, the basic moral system, and even language are within this classification, but not necessarily all to the same extent.   During the depression of the 1930's, when constitutional arguments were presented in opposition to certain reform and relief measures, a secular attitude toward legality in general was expressed by the advocates of change in the statement, "You can't eat the Constitution."   Similarly, during the 1920's postwar disillusionment found expression in secular attitudes toward morals and family life.   Free love was advocated by a few radicals, and monogamy and the general morals of family life were subjected to rational and secular discussion by prominent intellectuals.   At the same time the falling birth rate may be considered to represent a questioning of the idea, essentially sacred, that it is desirable to leave the land peopled with one's own descendants.

The sort of folk wisdom and morality conveyed in proverbs and the sayings and deeds of national heroes and legendary figures, often preserved in such publications as the McGuffey readers, have possessed a degree of sacredness.   Children were taught, at home and in school, that "honesty is the best policy," and that "early to bed and early to rise, makes a man healthy, wealthy, and wise."   George Washington was seriously described as a boy who would never tell a lie, and Lincoln became so transformed by legend that he became almost superhuman.   The "debunking" phase of history in the twentieth century, however, in correcting history has also secularized the legends.   The Farewell Address of Washington could not function with such mystical authority when Washington became understood as a normal human being as it had possessed when he was a semideity.   The "Poor Richard" formulas for success through hard work, honesty, and other sacred virtues were directly challenged by a prominent lecturer when he advised college graduates who sought success to "marry the boss's daughter."

It is obvious that modern trends of secularization in the United States have not reached a degree that imperils the existence of the social order.  For all the secularism about nationality, there was at least an adequate dedication to the national purpose during the second world war.  Monogamous family life continues as the preferred pattern, and departures from it encounter moral reactions. Children continue to be produced in large numbers, voluntarily, and without secular advantages to be gained from their production.  It is probable, in fact, that the secularization trend was checked by the second world war, and perhaps at least temporarily reversed.

Not all secularization is in itself disruptive to a society, except to the extent that changes in one aspect of a functionally interdependent system tend to upset the whole organization.  If the peoples of India would learn to adopt a secular attitude toward the cow, a valuable source of food would become available.  In a changing world, secularization makes possible a smoother adaptation to new conditions.  Because of this, the United States may have some advantages over many nations that have experienced general secularization to a lesser degree.  In the loss of order there is a gain in adaptability.

**Individuality of Interests and Tastes.**—Associated with the decline of the sacred and traditional is an emergence of individualism.  While the most sacred societies, such as newly formed religious sects, minimize individualism through communal ownership of property and uniform clothing and hair styles, there emerges in a secular order an individualistic competition in fad and fashion. No two women like to be found within the same field of vision wearing the same design of hat.  Among the high-style fashion leaders there is an almost savage contest to exhibit new and different designs of dresses, shoes, and accessories, and new tricks of hair styling and facial decoration.

Even for such durable possessions as homes, and in the face of such pressures for standardization as efficiency in construction and consideration of resale, there is a preference for houses that differ from those in the immediate vicinity.  In the furnishings and decoration of the interior, there is at one extreme a style competition much like that of clothing.  High-style decorators restlessly seek new and different colors and patterns for walls, and novelties in furniture design.  It is not enough merely to differ from others, at least for the style leaders—they must also make at frequent intervals fairly complete changes from previous schemes of decoration.

In traditional and stable societies recreation as a rule is social and almost ritual in character. The whole community gathers to dance, sing, or even work together. The individuation of tastes in modern urban society calls for different expressions of the recreational interest. Neighborhood groups do not often assemble for common play, but rather each person makes his own choice and pursues it alone or with the few others who are in the same mood at the time. Commercial facilities for recreation make such separation convenient. The members of a family may go entirely separate ways for an evening of recreation—one to the motion pictures, another to a billiard parlor, another to a dance hall. While such scattering characteristically meets with disapproval in a small and unified social order, there has arisen a spirit of acceptance and tolerance of individualism among modern peoples, and, in some quarters, a degree of respect that puts a higher value on the expression of individual and personal interests than upon conformity.

Although morality is entirely social in origin and has little meaning apart from the standards of a society, there may be found a point of view that justifies departures from conventional morality, provided that the person doing so has some private morals of his own. Among such persons, right itself is a matter of individual point of view.

**The Concepts of Rights and Freedom.**—Individuality in tastes flourishes in the same environment with emphasis on personal freedom and individual rights. These are not characteristics of the stable and traditional sacred society. In this latter environment the individual is not of great importance, and behavior of persons is defined in such details that personal liberty is at a minimum. Where traditions are breaking up there are to be found alternatives and undefined situations, and it is in these areas that personal liberty is tolerated. Instead of specifying a strict and dominating set of duties for each person, the society permits a claim of rights by each of its members.

The specified rights to "life, liberty, and the pursuit of happiness" in the American tradition are not universally claimed by man, nor are they paramount over all other considerations today. There is a varying degree of each of these rights—a definition of how far one has the right to life, how much liberty is to be allowed to each person, and within what bounds one may engage in the pursuit of happiness. Living among other persons in cooperative life necessarily limits the range of activity that can be allowed to each person. If unlimited pursuit of happiness were to be allowed, it would be possible to only a few members of a society. At the approach to one extreme, then, the emphasis on personal rights and liberties is in opposition to the unity and cohesiveness of a social order.

It is not known what degree of development of individual rights can be permitted without endangering the solidarity of the society. There can be little doubt that most of the traditional liberties that emerged from the Magna Charta, the French Revolution, and the American Revolution can easily be permitted in modern society. It has of course been found desirable to place some limitation on the right to bear arms, in order to reduce the facility of obtaining weapons for criminal purposes. In times of crisis certain civil liberties are suspended and martial law is applied. But most of the time there has been little difficulty in maintaining these principles.

In a time of increased individualism and the decline of responsibility toward the whole society there emerge expressions of new rights which are sought, some of which may be in serious conflict with the general welfare. The right of workingmen to strike has received official recognition in the law of the United States, in an act which has sometimes been called the "Magna Charta of labor." As a device for the correction of specific local injustices there is little dispute about the desirability of toleration of strikes. It is a matter of policy which will probably be for some time in a process of definition, however, as to how far this right can be applied. Because of the increased integration of the economic order, strikes tend to have an ever wider effect on the general public. A strike in a strategic industrial establishment does not merely affect the parties to the dispute but also stops the flow of products to other manufacturers and thereby stops the flow of a wide variety of supplies to the general public. Strikes in the electric power plants of a metropolis have the potentiality of being an immediate menace to the health and safety of the inhabitants. Economic life cannot function at more than a slow and inadequate pace without the elevators which are powered with electricity. Water is pumped to all but the lower buildings by electric power, and the cessation of this flow is an almost immediate health menace. Power stoppages without warning have caused particularly sudden danger in hospitals, where operations have been in progress, and where the mechanisms of the "iron lungs" are powered by electricity. In such a case, the victim of paralysis may be said to have a "right to breathe" which is encroached upon by someone's "right to strike."

Somewhat more extreme and possibly pathological expressions of "rights" are sometimes uttered in justification of criminal actions. Occasionally an embezzler or a thief will justify his lawbreaking by appealing to the right of happiness, or even the "right to live," although it may be argued that the old common law denies the right to live by theft, in that it permits a citizen to kill a thief in defense of property. The widespread attitude of putting rights above law is exemplified in the opposition to the prohibition act during the years when it was in force. Regardless of the Constitution and the laws of the various states, many citizens claimed a right to drink what they pleased, and by their insistence they in time defeated the law itself.

Where the emphasis on individual liberty is strong there is also observed a wish for privacy and for independence from some of the supervision and informal social control of the primary community. Privacy is not universally sought by human beings—many preliterate peoples live in small camps or villages in which the dwellings are so close together and so open in design that there is virtually no privacy. Even the early towns of New England consisted of houses placed very close together, often facing others across a narrow street—this in spite of the abundance of forests which presented the opportunity for complete privacy. These persons undoubtedly dreaded the dangers and the loneliness of the wilderness far more than is possible today, and they looked upon the presence of friends and neighbors as a protection and a comfort, rather than as an intrusion upon their privacy.

**Hedonic Behavior.**—In the most integrated and harmonious social order, the most dominant motives appear to be social. Group approval is sought more than any other good, and condemnation is dreaded more than any other disaster. The pleasures of social life, songs, dances, games, conversation, have the strongest and steadiest appeal, and the more individualistic physical pleasures are secondary. These latter gratifications become important primarily as persons become more and more individualistic and are therefore partially deprived of the opportunities to know and enjoy the pleasure of social activities. Although these persons do not necessarily realize it, the individualistic pleasures are enjoyed *faute de mieux*. The satisfaction they provide is less complete and less durable than that furnished by the group recreations—this at least is the inference that seems necessary in view of the choices made by those who are able to engage in either type.

The modern expressions of such hedonism, while not necessarily developed to a degree that threatens destruction of society, show a general tendency to increase, particularly among the urban populations.   The motion pictures and the pulp magazines constitute for a part of the population an almost obsessive interest, for they furnish what little romance and interest there are to be found in dull and lonely lives.   Hedonic eating, drinking, and cafe life may be considered a similar expression for another group, and for the more extremely individuated and disorganized, there are the commercialized vices.

To a certain extent the character of the daily press may reflect the degree of emphasis of its readers on the hedonic aspects of life. In rural and small town society there is an adequate primary group life which is satisfying to most of the residents.   The people live close to one another, are more interested in one another than in impersonal matters, and enjoy activities that are performed together.   The small town newspaper reflects this interest by giving most of its space to personal news.   The readers are apparently endlessly interested in knowing who has been ill, who has been away on a visit, what parties have been held and who attended and what they wore, what weddings are in prospect, and other topics of this kind.   Many of these rural newspapers carry very little national or international news and often none of the comic strips or human interest features used by the metropolitan press to build circulation.

There is a class of persons, eager to know and understand the affairs of the world, large enough to support serious newspapers, like *The New York Times,* and to call for a certain amount of general news and comment in many other leading newspapers.   But it is the judgment of the commercial publishers, those who have a strong financial interest in knowing the matter with accuracy, that the greatest mass circulation is built upon the comic strips, the special features of magazine sections, movie reviews, sports columns, and the like.   It is claimed that a majority of newspaper readers turn first to see what has been happening to "Little Orphan Annie," or to "Dick Tracy," before looking at the headlines dealing with world affairs.

During the decade of the 1920's, a period of postwar reaction when many indications of a spirit of hedonism were visible in the population, the metropolitan newspaper coverage of international affairs was superficially done and for the most part given a minor emphasis by assigning it a secondary location and by giving a meager amount of editorial content to it.   The "great stories" of the 1920's were the human interest events—things that occur all the time, but which take first importance in the public mind when the emphasis is on stimulation and pleasure, rather than on the serious matters that threaten the world.    During the decade when the world was reorganizing after the greatest war to that date, and when the process of generating an even greater war was developing, the front pages gave their greatest attention to such stories as the Loeb-Leopold murder case, the boxing contests of Jack Dempsey against Georges Carpentier, Luis Firpo, Gene Tunney, and others, the affairs of "Daddy" Browning and his blonde girl friend, "Peaches" Heenan, the "Fatty" Arbuckle scandal in Hollywood, the death and funeral of Rudolph Valentino, and the clowning campaigns of Mayor William Hale Thompson of Chicago.

In the 1930's and 1940's the depression and the war sobered the populations enough so that at least the front pages of the leading papers returned to matters of more general concern, and libraries reported that this change of attitude was also indicated by an increased number of calls for books on matters of general importance. But even then, it must be remembered that the tabloids held their enormous circulation with little other than feature material in their pages, and that during the serious wartime paper shortage of the 1940's there was no movement among newspapers to eliminate the comic-strip sections.

The war effort of the American people was sufficient to carry the country past the crisis, but there were indications of unwillingness to dispense with trivial luxuries and pleasures.    When electric power was so scarce that drastic conservation measures were necessary, an order was given to curtail many uses of electricity.    Among the economies required was the closing of night clubs at 1 A.M. The protest in New York City was so great that the mayor at first announced that the city would not agree to conform to the order. There was similar public objection to deprivations of such luxuries as nylon hosiery, liquor, coffee, and ice cream.    Even the vital necessity for quantities of gasoline for war use did not persuade the public to voluntary limitation of pleasure driving, and when rationing was introduced, a large proportion of automobile users obtained gasoline illegally and used it for purposes of pleasure.

**Semantic Difficulties.**—Within the heterogeneous population of the United States there is a common English language, but within this language there is a multitude of special vocabularies.    There is a separate universe of discourse for each of the different sections of the country, for income and occupational groups, national and religious groups, and for various interest classifications of the population. Linguistic barriers operate to add misunderstanding to the existing conflicts among such classes, and thereby increase the hostility among them.

The language shared by youth and age is in general inadequate for a complete understanding between generations. Words employed by the elders gained their meanings in a context which is inaccessible to young persons. The latter often have a sense that their elders are living and thinking in an unreal world. The linguistic aspect of this misunderstanding becomes evident when the old and young have the opportunity to engage in some long and confidential talks, the result of which is to dispel a large amount of the confusion.

The slang employed by young persons is perhaps even more mysterious to their elders, for the terminology is so idiomatic and eccentric that nothing short of actual participation in the group evolving the slang will permit adequate comprehension of it. In some cases young persons spend such a large proportion of their time with their own age group that they become almost unable to be articulate in terms other than slang discourse. Where this development approaches an extreme, the elders are mystified and often disturbed by the speech of the young, and the latter may be impatient at their elders' inability to grasp meanings, or, in other cases, amused at the blunders made by old persons who attempt to employ a vocabulary that they do not understand.

When employers and laboring men come into conflict, there is often a semantic aspect to their dispute as well as a clash of interest. It has been the experience of students of labor relations that a large part of the hostility between these groups can be reduced by long and sympathetic conversations which overcome this gap of communication and understanding. Similar results are often experienced following such extensive conversations between persons of different nationalities, religious groups, and other divisions of humanity.

**Mutual Distrust.**—Among the consequences of such individuation and segmentation of the population is the tendency of persons to distrust the members of groups other than their own. When affairs of the nation or world are in a troubled state, there is also an added disposition to blame some one or more groups. In an extreme form, such an attitude is analogous to paranoia in a person, and may lead to similar unjustified hostility and persecution.

In the modern world these mutual suspicions are numerous. Among the most menacing is the political and economic schism between conservatives and radicals, which has become involved with international tensions.  It is the conviction of some of the more alarmed conservatives that all radicals are deliberately in league with an international communist organization which has as its purpose the violent overthrow of government, confiscation of property, execution of those who are loyal to the old order, and the establishment of a proletarian dictatorship.  Persons who support such measures as a national housing program, extension of social security, and legislation favoring labor unions or the consumer are suspected of participation in a fully developed conspiracy.  For many years the House of Representatives Committee on Un-American Activities listed as "radicals" or even as "dangerous radicals" persons who signed petitions in favor of moderate reforms, or even persons who merely subscribed to liberal periodicals.

On the other hand extreme radicals tend to hold an equally distorted image of the conservative, holding him to be a fascist who seeks to maintain his property through holding the working peoples in a state of subjection and who is determined to maintain his power by any means, including collaboration with fascist nations. Objective statements by scholarly economists who advocated the rescinding of certain New Deal legislation in the interest of quicker recovery from the depression of the 1930's aroused accusations of fascism from some of the more excitable radicals.  Each party to the conflict extends and distorts the position of the other, thus altering technical disputes into irreconcilable moral conflicts.  Indications of this tendency are frequently shown in letters to the editors of newspapers or other responses to a controversial political speech or editorial.  It frequently happens that there are many letters accusing the speaker or writer of fascism, and others finding the same person to be a communist.  Such intense suspicion betrays the touchy distrust that exists between the parties that divide on the controversial issue.

In racial conflicts similar tension is often evident.  It often happens that an objective Negro scholar will publish an article on race conflict and as a consequence be accused by other Negroes, who have not been aware that he is one of them, of being a prejudiced southern white man.  Similarly, in the conflict group among the Jews, there is a tendency to find anti-Semitism in an impartial statement made by a Jewish writer who is loyal and sympathetic to his people.  Persons with extreme anti-Semitic views, on the other hand, claim to see evidence of elaborate conspiracies among Jews. There is a suspicion that Jews seek to control the economic life of the nation, that they plan to infiltrate the government in the interest of their group, and that they are in league with international communism for the purpose of overthrowing existing governments. The paranoid suspicions of this extreme group lead them to search for indications of Jewish ancestry in persons who appear to be radical. It is by such persons that false claims have been circulated that prominent figures in the national government were Jewish or had altered their names to conceal Jewish origin.

There are many other expressions of such a tendency in American life. Employers frequently accuse union leaders of attempting to take over the business, while the latter accuse the employers of trying to destroy labor unions. The more touchy Southerners accuse the northern people of trying to destroy their traditional way of life. Extreme feminists claim that men conspire to deprive women of their rights. Catholics and Protestants misrepresent the intentions of one another. Such conflicts are potentially paralyzing to national life. They have fallen short of causing paralysis in the United States principally because the extreme points of view have been held by small minorities. A movement of the attitudes of the mass of the members of each of these groups toward extreme distrust and hostility would constitute a severe menace to the general welfare.

**Unrest Phenomena.**—In periods of general disorganization there arises among the people a sense of awareness that something is wrong, even though there is no clear analysis of the trouble. Affairs are not going as smoothly as formerly, and dissatisfaction spreads. There tends to be a period which is analogous to the milling of a herd of cattle before a stampede occurs. It is behavior expressive of concern, of tension, but which does not make any direct contribution to the solution of the difficulties.

Wandering is sometimes interpreted as an expression of unrest. If conditions at home are not as pleasant as formerly, some persons decide to look elsewhere for happiness. Some travel at random in the fashion of hobos, or the wandering youth of Germany in the late 1920's. Others seek a promised land, which in the United States is symbolized by California. For many persons in Europe, it is the United States itself. Similar to wandering is the frequent change of employment and residence, in vague pursuit of a more satisfactory life.

The spread of rumors appears to be easy and rapid in times of general tension and unrest, particularly among populations that

are uninformed, or at least uncertain of the accuracy or complete-
ness of their information. Under conditions of wartime censorship
the situation is favorable to the spread of rumor. During the recent
world war tension about shortages prepared the ground for a series
of rumors about prospective rationing of various goods. In some
cases the rumors spread from a leak of true information, as in the
case of the prospect of shoe rationing, but the persons spreading
the rumor did not know the source. The rumor functioned, as did
other rumors of the sort, to stimulate a wave of panic buying at the
stores. It was reported in the press that many persons bought
any shoes they could obtain, regardless of size, style, and price,
in the general excitement of the panic. Similar rumors and consequent rushes on various other goods took place during the war,
and persons mobbed stores to buy canned foods, various articles of
clothing, tires, and in some localities even such items as electric light
bulbs.

**A Concrete Illustration: Prewar France.**—A nation that is
not under severe stress can apparently hold together in spite of a
considerable occurrence of such symptoms of disorganization as
have been mentioned in the above discussion. In times of intense
crisis, however, internal weakness may render the nation subject
to conquest or collapse. In the example described below, the role
of such factors as formalism, individualism, mutual distrust, and
other indications of structural weakness in the nation can be seen
in their interrelations.

The sudden fall of France following the German invasion of
1940 was unexpected by most persons who followed the news of
world developments and who had read in the press of the large and
supposedly efficient French Army, said by some writers to be the
best army in the world. Apparently this army never had an adequate opportunity to engage the Germans, however, but rather
seemed to disintegrate from lack of support behind the lines.
The nation fell more from internal disruption than from enemy
power.[6]

One of the serious divisions in the French nation was the gap
and conflict between generations. The effects of a falling birth
rate and the losses of men during the first world war were to create
a deficiency in the young adult age group in the 1930's, although
there remained a high proportion of advanced ages in the population.

---

[6] Most of the information in the discussion of France is taken from Georges Gurvitch,
"Social Structure of Pre-War France," *American Journal of Sociology*, Vol. 48, March, 1943.

There was as a consequence an unusual degree of discontinuity between the old and young generations.  France has characteristically, in spite of its revolutionary and democratic traditions, remained a traditionalistic country, and has been to an exceptional degree gerontocratic.  There is not the willingness that appears in the United States and elsewhere to trust important matters to young men.  Civil servants may remain in office up to the age of seventy or seventy-five years, thus slowing the upward climb of the younger men.  In the universities it was unusual for a French scholar to become an assistant professor before the age of forty.  In the great crises, the leaders who were given control of the nation were such old men as Clemenceau, who was in his seventies when he led France during the first world war, and Pétain, in his middle eighties at the time of the fall of France in 1940.

It is possible that the control of the aged is responsible for such conservatism as the rejection of the mechanization project offered in 1934 by de Gaulle, who was then only forty years old, and the adoption of the Maginot Line plan of defense.  It also led to a sense of rebellion among the youth of the nation.  In the years before 1939 there were a number of youth groups with political aims: young radicals, young socialists, young Catholics, young rightists. Some of these reacted against democracy partly because it was the political faith of their elders, whom they no longer trusted.  An appeal of the fifth column in France was put into the slogan, "The elders who did not participate in the last war, but sacrificed the younger generation, want to repeat it a second time; after their sons, they are now ready to sacrifice their grandsons."  The success of this appeal could scarcely have been so great had the age groups in France not been so greatly separated.

The immigrant groups which poured into France after 1919 furnished a further condition of divisiveness in the country.  France had hitherto been a traditionally hospitable country for political refugees, but had not until that time had experience with large-scale immigration.  The people were unprepared for the Polish miners and peasants who arrived in the northern part of the land, and for the Spanish and agricultural workers in the south.  The Russian anti-communist population and the remnants of the White armies also came into France in large numbers, and after 1933 a large migration of refugees from Nazi Germany—principally Jews— found refuge there.  In 1939, just before the beginning of the war, the immigrant population in France was the largest in Europe, and its seven or eight millions constituted about one sixth of the population of the country.

The greatest part of the immigrant group consisted of unskilled workers who would accept the lowest standard of living and the poorest working conditions. By the time of the depression of the 1930's their competition began to be resented. Slogans such as "France for the French" and "Down with the foreigners" gained popularity. Restrictive measures were taken—even naturalized immigrants were prevented from occupying public office or from practicing as physicians or lawyers before a lapse of ten years after naturalization. The growing hostility toward immigrants was fostered and exploited by fascist organizations.

Some of the political and social instability of France may be ascribed to the changes in the occupational structure of the country between the two world wars. There had been a decline in the proportion of farmers during this period, as the population flowed toward the towns and cities for employment, in some regions leaving farm villages entirely abandoned. The French farmer is said to have been the greatest supporter of the French Republic and of democracy. He supported the Radical Socialist party, which, despite its name, was a party of moderation, of mild social reform at most, and which has been considered the cornerstone of the Third Republic.

The division of France into economic and social classes was complex and disintegrating in its effects. The Catholic factions had become divided into liberal and reactionary wings, and there were divisions among the intellectual and professional groups and others. But the most serious conflict was between the industrial and financial magnates on the one hand and the revolutionary and socialistic laboring classes on the other.

The magnates were a small and well-organized group, joined by membership in the Comité des Forges and the French Employers Federation. They were the "two hundred families" which held control of the Bank of France, the autonomous institution issuing money in France, and they had great influence on economic matters in general and, through this, on political life. This circle owned and controlled most French newspapers, including the most influential, *Le Temps*. The members were involved in many partnerships with German heavy industry, especially in organized exchanges of the abundant French iron ore for German coal. Their power was so great that when Léon Blum, during the early days of his Popular Front government, tried to cut off the ore shipments to Germany, they frustrated him, threatening a stock exchange panic and the closing of many factories, thus insuring the flow of French ore to Germany until the actual outbreak of the war in 1939.

After the rise to power of the Popular Front, the magnate group
split into moderate and reactionary sections, the latter constituting
the defeatists, appeasers, and collaborationists who preferred the
defense of their vested social positions and economic interests to
the defense of France and who, headed by Flandin, congratulated
Hitler after Munich. A few went further and supported such
fascist groups as the Cagoulards.

At the other end of the economic order, the organized French
laboring groups were characteristically progressive or radical and
traditionally pacifistic and antimilitarist. During the early war
years the communist influence was exerted against cooperation with
the war, and met little resistance among other working groups, thus
playing a part in the weakening of the nation.

France had long been divided into many intense and mutually
hostile political factions, but during the 1930's there grew up a large
and powerful group of fascistic parties which played destructive
roles in the national life.

The Croix de Feu was founded in 1927 by François Coty, the
perfume manufacturer, for the purpose of directing France into
the fascist pattern of Mussolini's Italy. In 1928 Colonel de la
Rocque became its leader and directed its influence toward opposing
the leftist movements in France in the interest of French military
strength. With such broad aims it attracted not only the outright
fascists like Ybarnegaray, who was later to become a minister of
the Pétain government for Jewish persecution, but also organizations
of Jewish veterans, and such well-known persons as Mermoz, the
aviator, and Jean Borotra, the tennis player. Its slogan was *Travail,
Famille, Patrie,* which was later adopted by the Pétain government
to replace the revolutionary *Liberté, Egalité, Fraternité.* In 1934,
during the Stavisky scandal, the rightist elements of the Croix de
Feu joined with the Action Française to try to storm the Chamber of
Deputies and overthrow the government. The failure of this assault
virtually ended the movement. It was later revealed by Tardieu, a
rightist, that de la Rocque had for years been receiving secret government funds to keep the Croix de Feu quiet.

In 1936 Jacques Doriot, a former communist, obtained financing
with the help of Flandin and some industrial magnates, and founded
a fascist group which was called the Parti Populaire Français. He
acquired an evening paper *Liberté,* and issued fascist propaganda
with anti-British and anti-Semitic themes. He advocated the abandonment of Czechoslovakia during the Munich crisis, and opposed
the war later. After the French armistice he pledged allegiance to

Pétain.  His party became the most energetic advocates of collabor-
ating with the Germans and he was held to be a leading candidate
for the fascist dictator of France.

The extreme example of all the fascistic groups was the secret
organization known as the Cagoulards ("the hooded ones"), which
was actually a conspiracy against the Republic.  It was organized
by an engineer named Métenier, contained on its advisory board
some prominent industrialists and high military officers, and had as
sponsors General Weygand, Pierre Laval, and perhaps Pétain.  Two
bombings of buildings of employers' unions were attributed to the
Cagoulards, but an investigation into the matter was stopped on
the insistence of the general staff of the army and of the president
of the Republic, since it threatened to compromise many high-
ranking officers in the army and many powerful politicians.  The
investigation uncovered the fact that a large quantity of arms made
in Germany and Italy had been found, possibly as aid from Hitler
and Mussolini for a fascist revolution in France.  The leader of
the investigation against the Cagoulards was killed after the armistice in 1941.  Members assumed important positions in the Vichy
government and in the Legion, which was the only party permitted
in France during the occupation.

The history of France in the few years preceding the outbreak
of the second world war presents an instructive example of the
paralysis and the ineffectiveness of a nation which is split into many
sections by such divisions as those described above.  A nation in
such condition might have been able to pass through the milder
difficulties of peacetime, but the severe trial that sudden war imposes
was too great for the strength of France.  Under comparable stress
Britain abandoned her internal conflicts and went through the war
a unified and effective nation.

## The Relation of Social Disorganization to Catastrophes

Disaster may strike a social organization at any of a number of
points, and may severely interrupt the coordinated functioning of
the members.  In the most extreme instances there is a temporary
appearance of total social disorganization.  The fall of Atlanta
during the Civil War, the Boston police strike of 1919, the Florida
hurricane of 1926, and other similar crises have involved a general
breakdown of essential services, the outbreak of violence and looting,
and a general panic among the population.  Natural catastrophes
may put a social organization to a severe test, and an extreme disaster is able to wipe out the society itself.

**Distinction Between Catastrophe and Social Disorganization.**—It can be shown, however, that a natural catastrophe is not inevitably connected with social disorganization, and that in some cases even extreme hardships of this category may strengthen certain aspects of a social organization. Where the social organization is previously in sound condition, the outbreak of disaster may cause only a small amount of disorder and may call out a much larger amount of spontaneous altruistic or at least cooperative behavior for the general welfare. In the New England hurricane of 1938, for example, the notable response, even while the storm was at its height, was of unselfish and even heroic aid to others. Men appeared while the wind and rain were at the height of their fury and used axes, saws, and ropes to open the main routes. Even for days afterward they continued to do useful work for the general welfare, although there was no organization of this activity, nor any wage paid for it. There were many stories of daring rescues made during the storm and instances of courageous self-help.

Inquiries regarding the small number of looters picked up revealed that they were, for the most part, persons with previous records of larceny. They were not persons who were corrupted by the catastrophe, but persons who were trained by experience to be alert for opportunities for theft. The general population showed no inclination toward larceny, although the opportunities for it were abundant. Many houses were damaged, and in the business districts a large number of buildings and stores were open to pilfering without danger to the thief.

The essential services such as electricity, telephone, delivery of food and other goods, repair work, and the like were resumed with difficulty. Although it was many weeks before all of these were in a normal condition, the immediate reaction of delivery men, repair men, and others was for the most part a willing acceptance of greater than normal effort. Milk deliveries, for example, required a great deal more walking than usual because of the omnipresent obstructions to traffic, but the extra efforts of the men brought the milk around each day without interruption. Such was the general response of the population to the disaster—public responsibility and cooperative activity were heightened, and the degree of social disorganization that may normally be found in such populations was if anything decreased.

Disasters on shipboard may involve panics which virtually wipe out all cooperation, leaving each person to save himself. In the summer of 1934 the pleasure ship *Morro Castle,* returning from a scheduled cruise between New York and the Caribbean, caught fire as it neared port. According to reports in the press, the discipline aboard was far short of the expectations of marine traditions. There was said to be poor handling of the ship, some panic among the passengers, and lack of discipline among the crew. The ship was beached at Asbury Park, and many were saved, but many others were needlessly burned to death because of lack of organization for disaster. An explanation offered during the inquiry that followed was that, since the *Morro Castle* was a pleasure ship, the operators were negligent in their responsibilities in training the crews and passengers for emergencies, for they did not wish to remind the vacation-seekers of the possibility of danger.

Where the traditions of the sea remain strong, and where the crew and passengers are properly drilled, it is possible to avoid all panic and disorganization. When the British liner *Athenia* was torpedoed in the night early in the second world war, everyone behaved in a quiet and orderly fashion, according to the statements of persons aboard. Most persons were able to get into lifeboats and were saved. This was not primarily a vacationing or pleasure-seeking crowd. The danger of making the crossing was well known before the ship left port, and all persons aboard undoubtedly were mentally prepared for such an event.

On ships of the United States Navy, particularly during battle, discipline reaches a high development. Calmness, order, discipline, and efficiency normally prevail even when the danger is great and a ship is crippled and sinking. At the time of the loss of an aircraft carrier in the South Pacific it was reported that, before abandoning ship, the crew left their shoes lined up in perfect order on the deck. It was also stated that among the last to leave were some crew members who took time to eat some ice cream before the stores were lost in the depths of the sea.

Disasters that strike at the biological condition of man have similarly varying effects. They may, as in some disease epidemics, evoke conditions of panic. But here again, such catastrophes, even when extreme, are not the same thing as social disorganization and are not inevitable causes of it. In 1918 a severe epidemic of influenza swept the world, including the United States, and caused a heavy loss of life. The reaction of the American population was not one of panic, but rather of submission to extraordinary discipline. Soldiers were kept quarantined in restricted areas and endured an irksome loss of liberty. Civilians avoided public gatherings and conformed to such inconvenient regulations as the wearing of gauze face-masks in the presence of others.

When the arrangements for the Greely arctic expedition of 1882 met with failure, a group of the men faced a polar winter without food, except for the insufficient bits that could be gathered from the tidewater. The men lay in their shelter starving for many months with only one break in discipline. One of the men stole and furtively ate an extra quantity of the meager food, but his nausea betrayed him and he was at once executed by general consent. The others waited patiently for death, alloting the small amount of food equally, except that a slightly larger ration was given to preserve the strength of those who went in search of the small sea insects which they euphemistically called "shrimp."

## Quasi-Disorganization

It is sometimes observed that, in societies which apparently are in a sound condition of organization, there may occur some practices which are contrary to the ordinary rules and which appear to be at least temporary states of disorganization. In some cases, however, it becomes apparent that these suspensions of the mores are recognized and tolerated under specified conditions, and thus are not to be thought of as true disorganization, but as quasi-disorganization.

**Preliterate Saturnalia.**—Examples of quasi-disorganization may be furnished by the saturnalia which occur in many societies. On traditional occasions the members of the society may gather for a celebration during which many forbidden pleasures such as orgiastic dancing, drunkenness, fighting, and sexual license may be freely indulged in. For this behavior there is no penalty or disapproval, although the same behavior at other times might call out stern penalties. Among the Fijians there is a ceremony which has as its ostensible purpose the securing of the intervention of spirits for the recovery of a sick chief. Following the magic ritual, however, a feast takes place, and it is accompanied by "indescribable revelry." [7] All of the customary distinctions of status based on property are suspended. Men and women dress in fantastic costumes, employ toward one another language which is ordinarily considered indecent, and practice "unmentionable abominations" openly in the public square of the town. In their own phrase, they behave "just

---

[7] From a report by L. Fison, quoted in W. I. Thomas, *Primitive Behavior*, New York: McGraw-Hill Book Co., Inc., 1937, p. 265.

like pigs." Not even the strict taboos of brother-sister avoidance are observed. But after several days the feast is over, and the mores are again in force. The rights of property are again respected, married couples remain faithful to one another again, and brothers and sisters avoid speaking to one another.

Many other preliterate societies have occasions for similar wild celebrations, with almost total suspension of ordinary morality, and such behavior was also prevalent in ancient societies ancestral to our own civilization. Modern American culture does not contain a provision for any such total suspension of mores, but there do exist temporary states of toleration for certain classes of people and on certain occasions. Sumner has applied the term *conventionalization* to this practice of providing exceptions to the ordinary rules. Soldiers, for example, are not held to the same standard of morality that is expected of the rest of the population, particularly during wartime. Intoxication, sex delinquency, and disorderly behavior in the streets are tolerated to a degree which ordinarily could not be allowed to a civilian.

**Contemporary Conventionalization in the United States.—** University students, in the United States and elsewhere, have long claimed and received partial immunity from conventional standards of enforcement. In Germany, duelling persisted after it was outlawed, and students scarred with wounds were honored not only by their fellow students but also by persons outside of the university. The student whose scar happened to be located at an inconspicuous place, such as the top of his head, sometimes took the trouble to have his head shaved so that the mark of honor would be visible. In England schoolboys and university students have long made a game of evading rules and outwitting authorities and have enlisted a certain amount of public approval of this behavior. Oxford students, for example, engage in the forbidden pursuit of "night-climbing." Certain walls of buildings or bridges are scaled in the dark, not because it is difficult or even desirable to reach the top by ordinary means, but for the excitement and honor of breaking the rules of the university.

Such conventionalizations for students are common in the United States, and many are connected with athletic celebrations. A typical expression is the annual football riot at a mid-western university. The celebration follows the victory over a chief rival, and it is expressed in mob vandalism, looting, and spontaneous horseplay. A motion-picture theater and an adjoining soda fountain establishment are the conventional targets for damage. The police are unable to hold the large mob of students in check and make no effort to do so, and the town residents and merchants grumble a little but take no action. The university pays for the damage after the adventure is over.

Harvard University is the home of a traditional rioting custom which is uncontrolled by the university officials and the local police. There is no fixed time for the action to take place, but on a mild evening in springtime, a cry of "Hey, Reinhart" may be heard on the campus, to be repeated by other voices until a crowd of students gathers, works up a pitch of excitement, and sets forth on a night of revelry and vandalism. Few arrests are made, and even in these cases it has been customary to dismiss the matter quietly after a few days have passed. Somewhat similar customs have been observed at a great many educational institutions, including high schools, and have come to be regarded as something of a special privilege of the student. The participants are not necessarily persons with previous habits of delinquency, nor are they troubled with a sense of guilt. On the contrary, those who took a prominent part in such unlawful behavior may, during many years of respectability in community life, nostalgically boast of their part in student pranks. Such conventionalization is not social disorganization, nor does it cause disorganization, but is a temporary or local suspension of the rules by common consent, although the consent is often somewhat grudging in character.

Many other expressions of this process, varying in extensiveness and meaning, are to be found in American life. At weddings, men may kiss a bride openly when it might have been both immoral and dangerous to make an attempt to do so earlier or later. In certain localities a wedding is followed by disorderly conduct of a degree that would on other occasions call for police suppression, but the newly wedded couple who are being honored by a "shivaree" are not expected to object, but rather to submit in good humor to noise, tricks, and discomforts. The whole public is called upon to endure noise, pranks, and minor damage on such occasions as Hallowe'en and the Fourth of July, when children are excused from many of the requirements for neighborly conduct.

Annual conventions of many business, social, and political organizations are often accompanied with a certain amount of tolerated revelry which would in other circumstances call for police action. News reports of the behavior of men attending conventions of the American Legion in the years before the second world war describe such activities as taking charge of traffic direction and purposely creating the greatest tangle possible.   Other men are said to have amused themselves by dropping bags of water from hotel windows, attempting to drench persons passing on the sidewalk.   Some others are reported to have employed a portable electric device which they used to shock passing women.   Much other noise, nuisance, and damage typically accompanied these gatherings, but the public acceptance of such behavior for convention attendants and the revenue that such meetings bring to a city deterred the police from taking severe action.

## SUMMARY

Social disorganization is a disturbance in the patterns and mechanisms of human relations.   There are other kinds of difficulties that societies have to contend with—famine, epidemics, and other catastrophes—but these do not inevitably produce social disorganization, and it is clear that successfully integrated societies may maintain their functioning up to the very point of extermination.

A society experiences disorganization when the parts of it lose their integration and fail to function according to their implicit purposes.   Disagreement on the goals of the common effort may lead to a confusion in the duties of institutions and officials, and out of this there grows a sense of uneasiness and distrust of the whole organization.   In the general atmosphere of unrest there appear many symptomatic and often unrecognized expressions of discontent in the behavior of populations.   As the parts of the society continue to work at cross purposes, and as the important functions fail to be fulfilled, the tension increases until it brings about severe internal conflicts, as illustrated by the experience of France.   Such a general national disorganization may so weaken a country that a severe shock may cause its fall, but even in the cases in which total failure does not occur, disorganization may have such broad general effects as the reduction of productive efficiency and therefore of the standard of living, the frustration of political processes so that action is delayed or halted, and the production of discontent and unhappiness among the members of the populations.

Disorganization may be local as well as general.   It may occur in a small area, or in particular institutions, without national disintegration, although there is probably always some connection between the specific and general manifestations.   In the following chapters the forms of disorganization that are found in specific aspects of social life are analyzed. This material furnishes detailed applications of the general principles stated in the first two chapters.

## Selected References

*American Sociological Review,* Vol. 5, Aug., 1940. This issue contains a number of articles on the topic of social disorganization.

Blumer, Herbert. "Social Disorganization and Individual Disorganization." *American Journal of Sociology,* Vol. 42, No. 6, May, 1937.

Bossard, James H. S. *Social Change and Social Problems.* New York: Harper & Bros., 1938. Contains a good statement concerning the nature of social change and its relation to disorganization.

Brown, Lawrence G. *Social Pathology: Personal and Social Disorganization.* New York: F. S. Crofts & Co., 1942.

Dawson, Carl A., and Gettys, Warner E. *Introduction to Sociology,* revised edition. New York: The Ronald Press Co., 1935. Chapters 10 to 19 inclusive contain material related to social disorganization.

Elliott, Mabel A., and Merrill, Francis E. *Social Disorganization.* New York: Harper & Bros., 1941. A popular and influential work.

Kramer, Ralph. "The Conceptual Status of Social Disorganization." *American Journal of Sociology,* Vol. 48, Jan., 1943.

Mowrer, Ernest R. *Disorganization: Personal and Social.* Philadelphia: J. B. Lippincott Co., 1942. Contains a considerable amount of urban ecological material.

Queen, Stuart A., Bodenhafer, W. B., and Harper, E. B. *Social Organization and Disorganization.* New York: The Thomas Y. Crowell Co., 1935.

Thomas, William I., and Znaniecki, Florjan. *The Polish Peasant in Europe and America,* second edition. New York: Alfred A. Knopf, Inc., 1927. In an extensive methodological note the authors furnish a valuable statement of the nature of social disorganization and its relation to personal disorganization.

# Chapter 3

## THE NATURE OF PERSONAL DISORGANIZATION

### PERSONAL DISORGANIZATION RELATED TO SOCIAL DISORGANIZATION

**The General Relation.**—If, as Cooley stated, personality is the subjective aspect of culture, it is to be expected that in a disorganized society personalities would tend to be heterogeneous, individuated, disintegrated, and demoralized, and that in a harmonious and successful society, personalities would tend to be stable, sociable, and cooperative with others. Such a thesis finds general support in the observations available. Although accurate statistics are not available, the impressions, often systematically gathered, of ethnographers working with the simple, integrated, harmonious preliterate peoples in the main indicate that extreme deviations of personality among such peoples are less common than in our industrial civilization.[1] There are of course various diseases and injuries that cripple the nervous system and thus disable the personality, but instances of such disability would not properly be classified as personal disorganization. But there are many societies where individualism, extreme selfishness, personal eccentricity, functional insanity, suicide, alcoholic addiction, criminal behavior, and similar deviations from normality are all but unknown. It is true that in many primitive societies some of these do occur, but in most cases it is possible to show a reason for them in the partial disorganization of the society (often resulting from the disrupting influence of contact with civilization) or in some such inherent maladjustment within the culture as the extensiveness of black magic among the Dobuans, who possess a virtually paranoid personality pattern.

Although there may be found some relatively isolated communities in the remote rural sections of the United States—villages of the "Tobacco Road" type—in which special circumstances have so demoralized the population that personal abnormality is common, the characteristic personality of the dweller in the small village is that

---

[1] See Robert E. L. Faris, "Some Observations on the Incidence of Schizophrenia in Primitive Societies," *Journal of Abnormal and Social Psychology*, Vol. 29, April-June, 1934; and Ellsworth Faris, *The Nature of Human Nature*, New York: McGraw-Hill Book Co., Inc., 1937, Ch. 26, "Culture and Personality among the Forest Bantu."

of a conventional, sociable, emotionally stable, contented person. The great range of personalities that may be found in a metropolis is not ordinarily found in the typical rural village in which the social organization is sound and in which the processes of social control are functioning effectively.

An earlier theoretical viewpoint on the relation between personal and social disorganization—one still popular in some quarters but no longer widely held by sociologists—is that it is the addition of individual defects which eventually interferes with the effectiveness of a social organization. The causation is presumed to be from the individual to the social. However, observations of societies in the process of change from primitive to semicivilized, or from rural to urban, reveal indications that the disruption of social relations appears first and that the deterioration of the behavior of persons comes as a result of the breakdown of the processes which hitherto had operated to produce conventionality and normality of behavior.[2]

**Social Generation of Normal Personality.**—In a successful social order there is a sufficient content of folkways and mores to define all of the common situations that recur in social life and to leave a minimum of alternatives and decisions to each member. Normally each person requires little in the way of individual invention of behavior patterns but habitually and automatically performs in the standard manner prescribed by his culture. He confidently expects the persons he encounters in the routines of his life to behave in similar fashion, to perform the culturally expected actions. Such confidence becomes generalized into a feeling of ease, of being at home among his fellow men, and, while curiosity or impulse for adventure may on occasion lead a person to seek out new company, the preference is on most occasions to be with and talk to the persons whom he knows well and to converse in a fashion which has more of a ritual than an exploratory character. In a typical gathering in a primary community the men will tend to collect on one side of a room and discuss agriculture, politics, and business conditions, while the women take up such subjects as personalities, costumes, and the behavior of children. There is little demand for real novelty in either conversation. The comfort of being among friends, the sense of being at ease and without problems to decide—these are the pleasures of the evenings of conversation here.

There occasionally arises in a group in which the teamwork and

---

2 The May, 1937, issue of the *American Journal of Sociology* (Vol. 42, No. 6) is devoted to the topic "Social Disorganization." The question of causation is there extensively treated. See especially the article by Herbert Blumer, pp. 871–877.

harmony are exceptionally successful a sense of exhilaration and pride, an individual reflection of the esprit de corps, which further reduces the desires for individuality.   Members of an expert military organization or a crack athletic team are proud to submerge their individual styles of appearance in a uniform and in standardized patterns of behavior.   Groups of chums will often refer to themselves by names suggesting the strength of their unity—names such as the Four Horsemen, the Inseparables, the Three Musketeers, and the like.

Persons involved in homogeneous and unified social groups experience a satisfying confidence in the structure of mutual affection in the group, and in the essential similarity of one to the others. This feeling makes possible matter-of-fact assumption of strong and confident claims on one another, claims which in a more individuated population would be regarded as extreme impositions, and which make possible the development of such collective representations as private symbols, memories, and language.   The members derive their satisfactions through the group, their recognition is through the achievements of the whole organization, their individuality and possessiveness are expressed within the collectivity if at all.[3]

**Cultural Unity and Conventional Behavior.**—Unity of such a character is necessary, at least in some degree, for the production of conventionality in behavior.   It is not enough merely to be supervised by others if there is no interest whatever in what the other persons think, or if there is a conviction that all other persons are so different that there is no possibility of mutual understanding.   One reason for difficulty not only in influencing through primary social control, but even in communicating with, the older migrants who are to be found in the hobo districts of large cities is that through their long isolation from community life they have become indifferent to the opinions of others.   They do not feel embarrassment because of a dirty and ragged appearance, nor are they hesitant to perform actions which for a conventional person would normally be too humiliating—actions such as picking up the stubs of discarded cigars and cigarettes.

To a lesser degree normal persons may show similar detachment and unconventionality when they are in a position in which they can

---

[3] One need not be troubled by the thought that such behavior is illogical. The members of such groups may indeed be committing the "group fallacy" which has been so thoroughly discussed by Floyd Allport in his *Institutional Behavior*, Chapel Hill, N.C.: University of North Carolina Press, 1933, but it is not and never has been the fundamental disposition of man to base his social organization on logical principles. The above is a description of the way persons act, and on that basis they have had highly successful teamwork.

be somewhat indifferent to the expectations and judgments of others. It is common for persons who are away from home, and in a different kind of cultural surroundings, to care less for the reactions of the people about them.   Thus the American tourist abroad may point and laugh, even realizing that some resentment may be aroused, in a situation in which at home he would be inclined to be tactful.   Even the lesser excursions to large cities set free the behavior to some extent, for hotels are not homes and hotel employees are neither neighbors nor friends.   While few persons are utterly indifferent to the reactions of strangers—few for example are willing to create a noisy scene in a Pullman car even if they are among total strangers —-there is in most cases some release of the bonds of conventionality when there is no one about, other than strangers.

The sense of difference from others, of the impossibility of being understood, is observed among some mentally abnormal persons and among others who, while not entirely psychotic, have nevertheless lived through such unconventional experiences that they became convinced that no others could comprehend their point of view.   In an interesting case known indirectly to the writer, a farm youth, last of a series of sons in his family and separated from the next older by some years, was so indulged by all the members of his family that he came to conceive of himself as a person different from all others, and more delicate and valuable.   At times he even had the thought that there was some miraculous or divine purpose in his existence. As a result he pampered himself as others pampered him and failed to take responsibility for his own actions or for any self-development or improvement.   His lightest whims and fancies became to him as fixed laws.   At the same time, this sense of special destiny caused him to conclude that he was so different from all other living persons that it was utterly useless to try to explain himself to them. When he became deeply troubled about certain aspects of his behavior, he mentioned it to no one and experienced great loneliness in what seemed to him hopeless isolation.   Such an experience occurs in lesser degrees to many normal persons, and one of the valuable consequences of intensive interviews with advisors is that one learns that the troubles are known to others and that the experiences in connection with them are communicable.   The person is therefore less isolated and so is able to take a balanced view of his situation.

**Isolation and Eccentricity.**—It is an established principle in sociology that without social life the human being does not develop the traits that constitute a personality.   Complete isolation from birth onward leaves a human being with a psychological development that is essentially animal in character.   Complete isolation at any age, for any extended period of time, apparently results in some deterioration of the human nature in man.   Such information as is available on the experiences of prisoners held for long terms in solitary confinement and on other cases of extreme isolation indicates that after a period of loneliness, with perhaps some attempts to find substitutes for human companionship in pet animals, vermin, or imaginary companions, the sociability of prisoners deteriorates to the extent that they prefer their solitude and, in some cases, even dread the moment of release and try to return to their cells.[4]

A physiologist, C. L. Lundell, reported the beginning of such a process during two periods of isolation in a jungle in Honduras.[5] His duties as a scientist for the chewing gum industry required his presence in the forest alone, except for a few natives with whom he had little intercourse, for two periods of about six months each.   He reports that in his intense and desperate loneliness he turned to nature for comfort, "drawn by an inward force to harmony with the world about (him)."   His animal pets came to mean more to him than human contacts, and the nearby alligator and the rising palm above the treetops were nearer than friends.   Both times, as he left the camp to return home, he experienced a feeling of leaving something behind, and when he reached home he avoided people, even his friends.   Although he met with some reproach for not talking and mixing with people as had been his prior custom, he remained quiet and longed for the isolation of the jungle.   He further reports that his fluency of speech was temporarily impaired and his mental processes appeared to be somewhat dulled; he thus became convinced that further isolation might result in gradual intellectual and mental degeneration.

Even briefer isolation permits some deviation from conventionality of behavior, although established habits do not necessarily begin to deteriorate at once.   Persons who find themselves alone in a closed room frequently relax some of their manners and behave as they would not in the company even of their close associates. Many persons are willing to confess that when alone they spend a certain part of the time studying themselves in a mirror—an act which meets with ridicule or mild disapproval when observed by

[4] R. E. L. Faris, "Cultural Isolation and the Schizophrenic Personality," *The American Journal of Sociology*, Vol. 40, pp. 155–164, Sept. 1934.
[5] C. L. Lundell, "Isolated in a Tropical Forest," *Studies in Sociology*, Dallas, Southern Methodist University Department of Sociology, pp. 10–11.

others. Observations through one-way vision windows of persons who believe they are alone confirms the frequency of this behavior.

There is a form of isolation other than complete spatial isolation that also permits the development of extreme eccentricity. It is the separation from intimate, sympathetic, personal human relations. A person who is in a crowd of strangers is isolated in this respect and may suffer from loneliness that is virtually as severe as that of the jungle. The stranger, the migrant, the foreigner separated from his fellow nationals, the abnormally egocentric, and the extreme cultural variant all find communication on the primary level difficult and inadequate and so tend to suffer from isolation. In cases where this separation is maintained for years, deterioration may progress to an extreme stage.

### CHARACTER AND LIFE-ORGANIZATION

**Goals of Life.**—Life begins, for each person, before there is any consciousness of a reason for living or of any goals of life. Living is normally automatic. It is death that is discovered in childhood ages and that presents a possible alternative to the continuation of existence. But, since death is culturally and almost universally defined as undesirable, as an inevitable but sad event to be deferred as long as feasible, there is no necessity for each person to seek a personal justification for living. It is perhaps fortunate for the human race that this is so, for there are many persons whose lives are so dull, routine, and uncomfortable that they would find it difficult to rationalize their existence. But there are few suicides resulting from mere dullness of life—suicide is for the most part a response to a more drastic and exceptional crisis. Any society which endures necessarily contains mechanisms for defining and enforcing for its members motives to continue living and to carry out routine duties set by convention.

Even without being able to formulate a satisfactory definition of happiness, it is possible to differentiate between satisfactory and miserable lives and to examine some of the conditions which affect the type of life each person has. Assuming absence of physical sources of misery, of the hunger and pains which can impair the happiness of human lives, there is still a range of social experiences which is related to degree of satisfaction with life. In integrated and successful cultures conditions tend to produce normal personalities with fairly happy life experiences. Specific types of dissatisfaction may result from certain abnormalities in the culture.

**Status.**—The status a person has is no mere quantitative level of prestige.   It is a definition, or an organized set of definitions, of the character of actions expected of him and those he is to expect from others.   In all but the most relaxed and aimless activities of primary groups, there is a problem of order of actions, of ranking of influence, and of manner of communication.   Where efficiency is vital, as in a business organization or in an army, it is essential that not only the duties of each person but his rank with respect to others be explicitly defined.   No human society is without systematic status differentiation.   It is probably rare that any group of persons above the number of three or four is able to cooperate without some status distinctions emerging, however informally.   Status considerations enter so thoroughly into the quality of our common social actions that it is a virtual necessity to have an explicit understanding of one's own status if actions are to be efficient and without confusion.

In the more formal and institutionalized parts of a society, status is usually satisfactorily defined.   A schoolboy knows his relation to his teacher, a sergeant understands his relation to a lieutenant, and a court clerk knows how to behave toward a judge.   Within a conventional family the roles of father, mother, child, grandparent, aunt and uncle, and the rest, are clear enough for ordinary intercourse. But in less organized groups, and in new situations where persons gather without precedents, status is undefined.   Until some working system emerges, conversation and activity are awkward and often inefficient and the members of the group are in many instances uneasy.

In an established primary group, where the members have long known one another, status tends to be based on fairly accurate knowledge of the true character of each person.   But when strangers form a group, lacking such a basis for the ranking of one another, they can only make use of the information that most readily comes to their senses—the appearance and bearing of one another, the tone of voice and sound of authority or friendliness, and clothing and other possessions that may indicate status.   These indices are used because they have, in the long run, some relationship with personal qualities, although they are far from infallible indications in any particular person.   But the result of their use in sizing up one another furnishes a motive in persons to compete for these external badges of status. Thus, while in such a small town as Creekville it is reported that there is no use in trying to "keep up with the Joneses," it is of some importance to do so in urban life.   In this latter environment, where most persons are partial strangers to the majority of those they meet and deal with, there is an urgent competition in the indications of status—in showy and correct clothing, in jewelry, in manners, in the make of automobile owned, and in the residential address, as well as in a variety of minor matters.

Status is not an inherent property of a person; it is a relation of that person to others or, more accurately, a relation of his behavior to the behavior of others. It is relative, and therefore indeterminate and subject to continual change. There is no method of introspection and no psychological instrument which will tell a person his status. The mirror in which he may know this aspect of self is the reaction of others. But this is a variable and distorted mirror. Not all persons react in the same way. The same person does not respond in identical fashion on different occasions. It is necessary to discount the readings of one's own status in the behavior of others because of distortions introduced by tact. There are few persons so brutal that they will offer a frank judgment of another in a face-to-face conversation. Even our best friends, according to common knowledge, withhold comment on our worst shortcomings. Therefore, the discovery of a reasonably accurate working knowledge of one's own status is a performance of skill which requires time and study, and which becomes increasingly difficult in a heterogeneous and changing social environment.

It is then a condition of mild personal disorganization for a person to be unable to achieve a satisfactory general concept of his own status. His actions lack assurance, and his cooperation with others tends to be of low efficiency. In extreme cases, social intercourse is virtually paralyzed and the person is isolated, with the consequence that further eccentricities are developed.

**Familiarity with Roles and Customs.**—In simple societies there is no difficulty involving lack of familiarity with custom, for the social organization tends to be relatively easy to apprehend, internally logical and uniform, in the range of territory normally inhabited by any one person. In modern civilization, however, regional variations in customs and the alterations that accompany general processes of change result in a confusion of customs that make it difficult for persons who are separated from their familiar social groups to act gracefully and to avoid social blunders.

A few examples, falling well short of actual personal disorganization, may be presented. A resident of the western part of the United States may find, on moving to New England, that the ready and informal friendliness of the people of his former region is not

the style of the New Englander.  He may find that he is committing
mistakes and offending the latter when he brushes aside formalities
soon after being introduced and employs first names in addressing
his eastern acquaintances.

Young women, faced with a certain amount of drift in the customs of chaperonage and courtship, reveal their confusion by
requests for advice in this field.  One of the topics most frequently
treated in contemporary newspaper columns of advice is the question
whether or not a girl should allow a young man to kiss her after an
evening together.  Earlier mores barred the practice, except for
those who had agreed to marry.  Departure from the old standard
is not uniform or universal, however, and the confusion of folkways
presents a matter of individual decision which often may be troublesome or embarrassing.

Immigrants to the United States, even from so similar a country
as England, frequently encounter difficulty in finding their way about
in the new and strange ways of Americans.  They may address a
policeman as "Constable," tip the wrong persons or fail to tip when
expected, and find themselves at a loss in railroad car conversations
that spring up among strangers.

The above illustrations present problems that are in most cases
not too difficult to overcome as time brings familiarity with new
ways.  In other cases a person may feel so much uncertainty about
the standard ways of a new community that he may abandon the
effort and keep to himself.  In doing so he drifts further away from
conventionality, and his ability to adapt himself to the ways of others
tends to undergo deterioration.  It is in this class of persons that
confusion of customs may in time produce serious personal disorganization.

**Harmony Between Expectation and Achievement.**—There is
no standard of living or level of achievement which marks off the
contented from the discontented.  It is a commonplace that men may
accept without unhappiness a very humble level of existence if they
have never had reason to expect better.  The contentment with which
many traditional English people accept their "station in life" in full
view of others who enjoy great wealth and power is an impressive
illustration of this state of mind.  On the other hand there occurs
intense competition and dissatisfaction among persons with a high
standard of living who seek to outdo others of their level.  We
observe that a private soldier who never expected to advance may be
delighted at his promotion to the rank of corporal, while a United

States senator may be permanently embittered at his failure to achieve the Presidency.

In an agricultural society of the simpler kind, differences of wealth tend to approximate the relative amounts of energy and ability which different persons give to their farming. There is no expectation of gain other than that obtained through the farmer's own labor, and therefore no incentive for generalized resentment toward those who have accumulated greater possessions. In simple societies it is generally true that the mechanisms which differentiate the population according to amount of possessions and influence are well understood, so that unreasonable expectations and disappointments are not generated. The paths to wealth in modern civilization, however, are of many kinds and are not always adequately known to those who attempt to climb. Failures evoke dissatisfaction that is hard to endure because the reasons are not understood. Unhappiness, bitterness, cynicism, which may in many cases so transform a person that he is permanently maladjusted, are the typical results.

Young men whose conceptions of the operations of the business world are based on the reading of dime-novel success stories in childhood may enter the industrial order at the bottom and expect, by virtue of hard work, loyalty, and occasional brilliant flashes of inventiveness, to progress rapidly toward the top. When they fail to get ahead, while they observe the rapid progress of others, they are unable to perceive the reasons and become disillusioned and discontented.

In the American legend of rags to riches, of log cabin to White House, which is supported by many true examples of such progress, there is a lack of recognition of some other highly important factors which, though not indispensable, constitute part of the hidden mechanism that governs the degree of success achieved by various persons. The extent of the importance of personal influence, for example, is generally concealed in a mannerly silence. There are, of course, conspicuous instances of sons taking over their fathers' businesses and fortunes—these are well understood. But the less apparent network of friendships and personal obligations is extensive in the economic and social system. In times of hardship many a young man finds employment through the aid of some relative such as his mother's brother-in-law, or through an old college friend of his father, and during the period of this employment his opportunity for advancement is likely to exceed that of fellow employees who do not have the advantages of such a connection.

In addition to, and distinct from, the matter of influence or "pull" there is often a hidden advantage that is possessed by persons who have learned some of the ways of an occupation from a parent or close friend or relative.  A young man who enters a career of salesmanship may excel those about him because of a certain amount of knowledge absorbed from a father who deals in merchandise of a different character.  This knowledge, or skill, often unrecognized by those who have acquired it, operates as a form of capital to give a competitive advantage that may be permanent.  A son of a physician may acquire in his childhood and youth the traits of inquiry, organization of knowledge, and seriousness of purpose that give him an advantage over his fellow students in medical school, and he may also learn sympathy, tact, and other personal qualities which may make him superior in his medical practice.  The children of college professors often acquire some efficiency of mental organization, a vocabulary and ability of expression, and a habit of reading which aid them in training for and carrying on a profession.  If these persons are seldom fully aware of the nature of their advantage, acquired so gradually and unintentionally, their competitors who lack it are far less likely to know of it.  The latter are therefore mystified by their inability to perform as effectively.  In such a situation suspicions of injustice, favoritism, or discrimination may arise, producing a cynical reaction.[6]

There is furthermore, in many lines of competitive endeavor, an inadequately recognized functioning of traits of personal skill. Seldom is the economic relation among men who have business relations with one another so pure that the character of personal interaction is without significance.  A buyer often has nearly equal choices among salesmen and, whether or not he recognizes it, personal friendliness or antagonism enters into his decisions to purchase. Employers who know their employees by name, deal with them in an engaging manner, and permit them full self-respect may find that their difficulties with labor unions are far less than those experienced by rival firms with less pleasant personalities in management.

Sometimes the expectation falls short of the achievement because the persons involved are ignorant of the ways in which others achieve success.  Techniques which are well known to some are utter mysteries to others.  This is particularly true in certain applications of practical knowledge of human relations.  During the period of wartime shortages of materials and labor, persons with a supply of

---

[6] This point is more fully discussed in Robert E. L. Faris, "Interaction of Generations and Family Stability," *American Sociological Review*, Vol. 12, pp. 159–164, Apr., 1947.

either had wide ranges of choice as to which applicant would receive priority. Apart from government regulations and from bribery and black market operations, there were many allotments that were governed by personal considerations, not necessarily explicitly recognized by either party. A butcher with a limited supply of meat or a grocer with a small amount of butter often simply held back these goods for persons he happened to like—often for the housewife who always smiled, waited patiently, and never complained of the service. Similarly the handyman whose services were desired in dozens of households would first accept jobs in houses where it was pleasant to work, where the members treated him as a person and an equal and refrained from annoying him by criticism and suggestions concerning his work. The more aggressive, inconsiderate, unpolished persons suffered penalties which they did not understand, and to an extent that they could not realize.

Such misunderstanding and disillusionment are fostered by the unequal emphasis in our society on different classes of virtues. There is of course a value placed on agreeableness, consideration, tact, and friendliness, but somewhat stronger praise of such traits as integrity, honesty, frankness—traits which in extreme form are in partial opposition to personal effectiveness. In almost any profession there may be seen persons of ability who are less successful than their talents would appear to justify and whose failures result from having made too many enemies—nearly always many more than they realized. Minor failings of their competitors they may have denounced in terms which imply moral transgression, thus producing permanent injury to harmonious relations not only with these persons but with their friends, and often with the entire class of persons who are subject to similar failings. Such overemphasis on one kind of morality at the expense of another leads to a particularly disappointing class of failures, for the persons who do this are often conscious of superiority and of moral excellence, and are unable to perceive any proper explanation of the superior progress of their less moral competitors.

It is of course possible for persons to suffer disappointments in their careers without demoralization. Frustration can be endured if some reason for it is clear, or if there is an adequate acceptance of the factor of chance in life. Many politicians, for example, understand that the career of the elected official is in part a gamble and are thus able to wait out the years of defeat in good grace and when the time seems ripe to try again with a spirited campaign. Disillusionment is more common in the world of industry and in the professions, where traditional assumptions about the nature of success are not entirely in harmony with the processes that actually occur.

**Life-Organization.**—It is normal for persons to organize the principal objectives of their lives into some degree of unity which forms a core of activities in general. When such a life-organization is well integrated and when successful progress is made in the essential features of it, the person has one of the most important requisites for general happiness. When crucial aspects of the life-organization are threatened, on the other hand, the person faces an important problem. If no solution can be found, demoralization may be extreme.

A college student, for example, may have an intention to study medicine, to become the same kind of specialist that his father is, to become established in practice so that he can eventually succeed his father, to marry the girl he has been interested in, and to take a position of leadership in his home community as his ancestors had done. About such a cluster of aims his minor activities may be loosely organized. He may take an interest in persons who are also working toward a medical career and thus select friends partially on that basis, he may find golf an appropriate recreation for this kind of life, and in other ways he may shape his affairs to fit in with the central pattern.

An event which threatens to block the principal feature of such a plan is a menace to the entire structure. If the medical student fails an undergraduate course in chemistry, the pattern of his premedical education is broken, his entrance to medical school is in jeopardy, and consequently many other aspects of the integration of his plans are endangered. He may entertain other possibilities and construct a new life-organization, perhaps trying to take up another profession such as law, which will permit him to work toward a position of prominence and to marry the girl, though not to assume the career of his father. Or he may be forced to take less than this—to leave college and go to a city to find a low-paying position as a salesman or clerk, thus losing the possibility of local leadership and perhaps his chance to marry. Many persons are forced to make such drastic reorganizations in their plans, particularly persons who are at the beginning of their careers. The experience is painful, but the normal human is adaptable and often is able to find sufficient happiness in the revised life-organization, even if it is a less ambitious project.

When to the organized expectations of the person there is added the rigidity of the organized wishes and expectations of his family, relatives, and neighbors, the acceptance of a major revision is more difficult.  A complete shattering of a life-organization of this sort may result in the more extreme reactions—disappearance to another region, taking up the aimless wandering life of the hobo, or even suicide.

## MIGRANTS AND STRANGERS

**Mobility and Emancipation.**—Personal normality is related not only to membership in some sort of society but also to stability of relations in primary group life and to depth of integration with an organized community.  Any weakening of stability and integration has an emancipating effect on character and allows in varying degrees the development of irresponsibility, unconventionality, and disorganization.  Those whose lives involve a considerable amount of mobility and who thus are forced to spend a large proportion of their time among strangers are subject to this effect.[7]  They are not controlled by an organized society to the extent that settled peoples are and are thus free to express individuality to a greater extent.[8]

The completely detached wanderer, the hobo, tends to develop the minimum of responsibility and sociability.  He develops an indifference to the organized opinions of members of stable communities which sets him free from the requirements of their customs and, to a considerable extent, from their laws.  He tends in time to lose all desire for involvement in a community, perpetually seeking new territory and usually avoiding more than temporary companionship.  The itinerant peddler has been largely replaced by other types of sales people.  New transportation facilities have made it possible for the traveling salesman to spend more time at home and to lose the true migrant status, but in earlier times his reputation was somewhat similar to that of the hobo.  People bought his goods, but they did not trust him.  He had a disposition toward theft, swindling, and other transgressions and was dealt with in an atmosphere of suspicion.

The tourist is a temporary migrant, but even his relatively brief status as a stranger tends to have a similar, if less marked, emanci-

---

[7] A useful treatise on this subject is Margaret Mary Wood, *The Stranger* (New York: Columbia University Press, 1934).

[8] If a whole organized society, such as the Mormon group during their westward movement, travels together, the members are not strangers to one another and are not, at least within the community, sociologically migrants.  The community may, however, develop unconventionality in the eyes of nonmigrant peoples and even become, as in the case of the Mormons, a hostile outlaw group.  Such perpetually migrant peoples as wandering Gypsy bands, or traveling carnival groups, are described as irresponsible and dishonest in their dealings with the peoples they pass on their way but are also said to be as a rule well organized among themselves.

pating effect. He does not necessarily turn into a criminal, but the folkways and mores of his home community lose some of their power to control him when he is away from home. Hayner has described the characteristic behavior of hotel room occupants, who reveal many indications of this emancipation in their behavior.[9] Though the destructiveness displayed by hotel guests usually stops short of deliberate vandalism, the consideration shown for the equipment of a hotel room is far short of that exhibited for similar objects in the home. Standing full shod on beds, using towels to clean shoes, and crushing out cigarettes on carpets are actions not customary in homes, but they are common in hotels, in spite of the preventive strategy employed by some managers.[10] The taking of souvenirs, an old established practice, merges into outright larceny. The desire to take home a hotel spoon to remind one of a pleasant holiday is understood by the management, and in recent times has been countered by the provision of table silver that is not sufficiently attractive to constitute desirable souvenirs. There do occur incidents, however, in which an enthusiastic souvenir hunter attempts to appropriate the entire silver and linen service of his table. Towels are almost universally a conventional souvenir, but the occasional guest removes equipment of greater value from his room. Even more serious than the individual depredations against hotels, however, is the collective damage that sometimes results from the celebrations of persons who attend conventions. Experienced hotels have learned to make a practice of removing all furniture of value and as much of the breakable equipment as possible before entertaining the groups that hold boisterous conventions.

In residential areas of high mobility, such as rooming-house districts of the metropolis, most members of the population are strangers to one another. No integration of community life can form in the face of rapid turnover of residence. Persons who do remain in the same house for an extended period are unable to establish a permanent circle of friendships because the persons in adjoining rooms come and go in such rapid succession that there is rarely time for full acquaintanceship to develop. Many persons acquire a sense of isolation and loneliness, and of detachment from the general organization of humanity. The rooming-house population

[9] Norman S. Hayner, *Hotel Life*, Chapel Hill, N. C.: University of North Carolina Press, 1936.
[10] One of the most effective methods of prevention of damage and removal of equipment has been found to be a device which partially restores the personal relation. Some hotels place a small sign in each room, listing the equipment of the room and stating that the housekeeper, Mrs. Blank, is responsible and that any damage or removal will be charged to her. Thus the guest is made to feel that he will be hurting, not an impersonal corporation, but a live human being, possibly a needy widow.

shows many indications of personal disorganization, as later chapters indicate more fully. The recreation available is largely of the individual and commercialized type—the poolroom, the taxi-dance hall, the saloon, houses of prostitution, and gambling resorts. The rates of many phenomena indicating extreme personal disorganization are high. Among the high rates are those of divorce, certain types of criminality, several forms of mental abnormality, venereal disease, and suicide.

**Bohemians.**—In many of the larger cities of the United States and Europe there may be found areas inhabited by small and self-conscious aggregations of persons who affect a defiance of convention.[11] Many of these are artists, musicians, or writers, who have not yet reached the point of success in their careers. Their flouting of established customs is, however, less individualistic than that characteristic of rooming-house district residents. It becomes in some cases doctrinaire and even partially disciplined. The costumes of inhabitants of the Left Bank of Paris, however individual they may have been with the first wearer, eventually assumed a conventionality within the group, so that for a struggling artist the beret, the velvet jacket, the broad tie, and the little black moustache became established in the bohemian folkways.

The ideal of the bohemian is to depart from the traditions of the larger societies in a manner which may be called "creative nonconformity." The differences and the novelties are valued in themselves, and among the most earnest members of this class of radicals a lapse into conventionality is regarded as a betrayal of their collective ideals. In one instance a woman of this type who had been living in an unmarried state with a man finally decided to marry him. She soon received letters of reproach from her bohemian friends, who accused her of abandoning their ideals.

## Summary

Human personality is formed by the experience of living in organized society. It consists of an elaborate internalization of the system of relations to form an organization of wishes, attitudes, habits, and knowledge which is a unique combination within each

---

[11] The phenomenon of bohemianism is only marginal to personal disorganization. The conflict with the community and separation from it are often simply conflict with and separation from the larger and conventional society. Within the small, sometimes primary, group of fellow bohemians there may be effective social control and personal integration. But as the size of the rebellious group becomes small and the separation from conventionality extreme, there is an approach to the kind of personal disorganization represented by *folie à deux.*

person, not merely a replica of the social organization.  It is no more self-sustaining than it is self-generating, and in a situation of isolation or partial isolation it will deteriorate.  Furthermore the organization of personality is more difficult if the society is in a state of partial disorganization, and an adequately organized personality will also undergo some disorganization if the social organization that supports it loses some of its integration.

In the extremes of personal disorganization man loses all responsibility and conventionality, becomes criminal or insane, or even loses the desire to live.  Such disastrous results to an entire population might flow from a complete and enduring social disorganization, but no such condition is found in our modern civilization.  In the cases we observe, the causal condition is not complete social disorganization but a partial breakdown of the system.  This breakdown operates to isolate certain persons to an extreme degree, or to put them in a situation of extreme conflict with society, so that their actions are no longer subject to control by the organized social forces that govern normal persons.

Although the problems of criminality, suicide, and insanity are the more conspicuous and spectacular exemplifications of personal disorganization, the more widespread minor flaws in personalities may in their totality constitute as large a weakness in the stability of a society.  When there is a widespread disposition in the population of a nation to act in an individualistic manner in crises, to join in panics and to engage in hoarding; when there is a general failure of family life to produce children who are adequately trained and responsible; when large groups of citizens fail to cast ballots in important elections, or cast them selfishly or frivolously; when the majority of people show no general concern for the public welfare but rather pursue their individual interests to the point of menace to the interests of the whole—under such conditions their society is put in a weak state and, if subject to an extreme test, as was France in 1940, may meet with disaster.

Within the general organization of a society there are processes and institutions which, while interdependent with the whole, may be subject to particular defects and may result in specific consequences. The economic order is not separate from the rest of society, but there are types of disorganization which largely originate within this sphere and which have fairly standardized results.  There is also a degree of separateness in family disorganization, political disorganization, neighborhood disintegration, and various defective institutions; each of these types of failure has a result on the integration and effectiveness of personalities.    In the following chapters these specific processes and institutions as they have been observed in the United States will be subjected to sociological analysis.

## SELECTED REFERENCES

Brown, Lawrence G. *Social Psychology.* New York: McGraw-Hill Book Co., Inc., 1934.   Ch. 15, "Collapse of the Social World."

Ogburn, William F., and Nimkoff, Meyer. *Sociology.* Ch. 8, "Personal Disorganization."

Sherif, Muzafer, and Cantril, Hadley. *The Psychology of Ego-Involvement.* New York: John Wiley & Sons, Inc., 1947.   Ch. 7, "Breakdowns of the Ego."

Stonequist, Everett. *The Marginal Man: A Study in Personality and Culture.* New York: Chas. Scribner's Sons, 1936.

Thomas, William I., and Znaniecki, Florjan. *The Polish Peasant in Europe and America.* Vol. 2.

# Chapter 4

# REACTIONS TO ECONOMIC DISORGANIZATION AND POVERTY

___

## THE NATURE OF ECONOMIC DISORGANIZATION

Production and distribution of the necessities of life has been achieved by social organization rather than by individual effort alone since early prehistoric times—probably as long as *homo sapiens* has existed. Over the course of the millennia these systems of common effort have been in a continuous process of change, and for most of mankind, in a process of elaboration. The enormous gain in productivity that has resulted from the complex organization of specialists, and from the use of machinery and power, has made it possible for many more people to occupy an area than had been possible in simple food-gathering stages of economy. It also brought about the reduction, except for such times of disruption as war and postwar periods, of one of the greatest perils to human life—that of shortage, famine, and starvation. Hunting societies faced the risks of exhaustion of the game in their territory and other disasters—forest fires, drought, abnormally severe winters, and the like—that reduce the food supply. The increased efficiency of production, the defenses against perils, and the exchange of the goods between regions of the world have made men nearly independent of local catastrophes that imperiled his existence in the era of food-gathering.

This reduction of an ancient menace has been of enormous benefit to man, but there has emerged in its place a difficulty of a new kind, and one which increases in seriousness as the organization of economic life becomes more elaborate. The new peril is the fragility of the complex organization itself. The social machine of production is subject to the spurts and the stalls that constitute booms and depressions, and as the decades pass these appear to become more violent and possibly less subject to control. The general standard of living maintains an upward trend, but the distribution mechanism appears to develop in such directions that goods are shared with ever less equality and justice, and with some consequences of extreme hardship to certain sections of the population.

The modern economic peril is a matter of the failure of the system of human relations—it is social disorganization.[1] When men suffer from its effects they are not required to submit to an external and uncontrollable set of natural forces; rather they have the possibility of finding some human agencies to blame. For this reason conflict and demoralization are much more closely related to the conditions of shortage in modern times than they formerly were.

### INDUSTRIAL DISCONTENT AND CONFLICT

Since the beginning of the factory system, persons have remarked upon the contrast between the spirit exhibited by the farmer or craftsman who controls the conditions of his own labor and that of the employee who takes his place in an assembly line and becomes a collaborator with, and almost a part of, a machine. The craftsman, it is held, works willingly and long and often finds a certain amount of pride and satisfaction in his accomplishment, while the factory worker finds his work dull and fatiguing and without inherent satisfactions.[2] Later research has necessitated some revision of this viewpoint.

**Fatigue.**—An early and popular explanation of labor discontent was made in terms of monotony and fatigue. The character of the steady work of keeping pace with a machine was presumed to be more exhausting than the dawn-to-dusk labor of the farmer, for example. This viewpoint has led to much study of industrial fatigue and its consequences. Some of this research has been instrumental in showing how to improve certain specific types of discomfort in factories and thereby to remove production and to offer some relief to the discontents of workingmen. But this inquiry has not provided the principal key to labor unrest. Probably the most important effects of variations in the physical conditions of work in general— speed, muscular effort, temperature, humidity, and such conditions— are of significance only at the extremes of variation. Between these extremes, complaints about these matters may be only symptomatic of dissatisfactions that arise from sources of an entirely different character.

---

[1] Analysis of the causes of such disruption is not attempted here. This enormous task is primarily the responsibility of the economist. The material so far available is incomplete and at the same time so technical that it is hardly appropriate for inclusion in the present discussion.

[2] This topic is given an excellent sociological treatment in Wilbert E. Moore, *Industrial Relations and the Social Order*, New York: The Macmillan Co., 1946. Chapter 13, "The Worker and the Machine," furnishes part of the material that follows. See also Elton Mayo, *Human Problems of an Industrial Civilization*, New York: The Macmillan Co., 1933.

A famous experiment conducted at the Western Electric plant brings out the manner in which morale and fatigue become intertwined and become involved in the production rate.  In the investigation of such symptoms of discontent as strikes, high turnover, grumbling, nervousness, boredom, fatigue, and muscle cramp, the investigators chose a small group of workers to subject to a series of experimental conditions, while keeping records of the weekly output of each one.[3]   The experimental group consisted of five women whose tasks involved repetitive assembly of small electrical relays, each operation requiring about one minute to perform.

After a pre-experimental period in which the normal weekly output was observed, the five women were separated from the main body of workers and allowed to operate behind a partition.  This produced little change in their output, but the following series of changes produced in nearly every case a gain in productivity, in a few cases almost spectacular: paying by output as members of five-person teams, rather than as members of 100-person teams; introduction of five-minute rest pauses at 10 A.M. and 2 P.M.; increasing the rest pauses to ten minutes each; introduction of a system of six five-minute rests (in this case the constant interruption was unpleasant and the worker productivity declined slightly); establishment of two ten-minute pauses with light refreshments provided; ending the day at 4:30 instead of 5 P.M.; ending the day at 4 P.M. (causing a slight reduction in daily output but a rise in hourly production) ; returning to the conditions of an earlier experimental situation which involved working until 5 P.M. and two ten-minute pauses with refreshments; abandonment of Saturday work (reducing the weekly but increasing the daily production) ; returning to an earlier set of conditions which involved no rests, refreshments, or shortened day or week (resulting in the highest output of any condition so far) ; and finally returning to the stage involving two ten-minute rest pauses for refreshments (resulting in even higher production).

The obvious inference to be drawn from these experiments is that the physiological aspects (fatigue, hunger, and the like) of the tasks do not control the rate of performance.  In altering the conditions of work, the experimenters had also changed the social-psychological state of the team of workers.  It is apparent that these latter factors are of importance in the morale of the worker, and it is probable that the subjective experience of fatigue and other discomforts of the job are in large part consequences of disturbances in the social relations

---

[3] This study is presented in full in F. J. Roethlisberger and William J. Dickson, *Management and the Worker* (Cambridge, Mass.: Harvard University Press, 1939) and in Mayo, *ob. cit.*

of the worker.  The experimenters learned from interviews with the employees in the above study that the latter felt a sense of appreciation and enthusiasm at being a part of an activity of some general importance, and that they were stimulated by the feeling that their employers had taken a personal interest in them.  The employees reported a great increase in contentment with their jobs, and their absences decreased by 80 per cent.  Even the "sick absences" declined to a level only one-third that of the employees not in the experimental group.  Above all, the workers appreciated the sense of freedom, the release from continuous supervision, which so altered the atmosphere that they found themselves actually eager to come to work in the mornings.

It is probable that most of the complaints of monotony, fatigue, and some other physical discomforts that accompany factory labor are symptomatic of an unsatisfactory state of morale.  It is not that the physical sensations are imaginary, but that they can be and are endured or even ignored by persons who perform their actions by choice and with enthusiasm.  Athletes in training accept a grind of muscular effort that in some cases approaches a stage of torture, and yet, because it is their chosen pathway to fame and to other satisfactions, they often find themselves eager for the daily drills.  Music students, training for a concert career on the piano or violin, are required to undertake routine exercises by the hour, for day after day and year after year, accepting a monotony and a physical effort that surpasses most of the tasks on a production line.  Factory labor, on the other hand, yields no reward in personal glory or pride.  The laborer seldom sees and often does not understand the final result of his work—he cannot sense it as his own.  There is no incentive for him to put his heart in such work, and so the machine becomes a resented taskmaster instead of an instrument to serve his own abilities.

The general character of the relations of the worker to his employers is also a factor in labor morale.  If there is a sense of conflict or discrimination, or of unfairness on the part of the employer, or even an irksome social distance, the resentment of the employer may develop into a general dislike of his job, which may find expression in the minor complaints of fatigue and monotony as well as in union conflict strategy, slowdowns, and strikes.[4]

---

[4] Herbert Blumer, in a stimulating paper entitled "Sociological Theory in Industrial Relations" (*American Sociological Review*, Vol. 12, June, 1947), contributes the interpretation of much tension and conflict as consequences of a political struggle between two large organizations—big business and big labor.

**Rebelliousness.**—When the tension that grows out of minor dissatisfactions accumulates, it prepares the ground for organized conflict behavior. It is not, however, an inevitable outcome of hard working conditions that rebellion will develop. The situation has to be defined as one in which conflict is appropriate, the enemy has to be identified, and the persons must be organized. The labor movement is far from being a spontaneous affair—the conspicuous thing about industrial workers is the amount of effort it requires to organize them into conflict groups.[5]

A clear and extreme illustration of the principle that economic hardships do not inevitably result in protest or conflict is supplied by the pattern of relations between Negroes and whites in the southern states. Although in recent years, encouraged by labor organizers, representatives of certain agencies of the federal government, and various other public figures, the Negro even in the South has begun to express his desires by forming conflict organizations, there was a long period when hardships were great and the Negro's share of the goods of life was very small, but widespread expressions of antagonism did not occur. A large proportion of Negroes, particularly in the cotton states, accepted their status as natural and right, and held no resentment toward their employers or toward white people in general. There was no sense of injustice, and relations with white employers were often friendly in character, even though social distance was maintained and hard work brought only low pay.

The following observations, hitherto unpublished, were made by the author in a southern city in the depression period of the 1930's. They illustrate the degree of acceptance and rationalization of a status that is ordinarily considered intolerable:

The most extreme example of the accommodated Negro, often referred to as the "Uncle Tom" type, is not only contented but happy in a low status, and proud rather than resentful of his relation to the whites. One old man observed by the writer claimed to be able to remember his early childhood, when he was still a slave. He spoke of scrambling with other Negro children for the pennies which his white master scattered on the ground for amusement. The old man took obvious pride in the lifetime relationship he had with the same white family, and derived a feeling of personal prestige from the high status of "his" white family. In conversation he magnified their abilities and virtues to the extent that they appeared almost superhuman. Without indicating any dissatisfaction with his present circumstances, he stated that "slavery times was the best." It can be presumed that the content and manner

[5] E. T. Hiller, *The Strike* (New York: Harper & Bros., 1933), contains a detailed analysis of the natural history of this conflict process.

of his statements were influenced by the fact that he was addressing a white man, but the white family to which he was attached agree that his real attitude is reflected in these assertions. He is spoken of as a "good nigger."

A similar attitude is shown by an old woman who had been attached to a white family as cook and general servant for many years. Her pride in her white family leads her to exaggerate their virtues beyond any plausibility, and her actions correspond to these expressions, for she devotes herself to their welfare and convenience without regard to her own interests. If she were ill and unable to find a substitute to send to work, she would appear for her duties as usual. If exceptional demands were made, such as extra duties at odd hours, she considered it only right to fulfill them. In addition, she kept a responsible eye on the family in order to be of help in any emergency whether or not she was summoned. If she observed from her alley shack that smoke was coming from the chimney of the white family's house at four o'clock in the morning, she would at once dress and go over to see if someone were sick, departing on a trip, or in need of help, an early breakfast, or any other service.

Although her pay was extremely low, she did not ask for more. On one occasion she was given an extra dollar. She spent most of it at the ten-cent store, and became ill from the excess of candy and soda fountain products. The next day she told her employer, "It don't do to give niggers much money. They just spend it on trash and get sick."

One day when the white family was invited out to dinner, special circumstances required that they take her along. The hostess had no domestic servants and had prepared the meal herself. Consequently the colored woman refused to eat any of it, even alone in the kitchen, on the grounds that it was not proper—it meant that a white person had worked for a Negro.

It is from such a basis of apathy, resignation, accommodation, and actual rationalization and justification of their lot that industrial workers entered the long movement toward organization, conflict, and improvement. The active minority that takes the initiative succeeds by defining the problems of labor, indicating the nature of their enemy, developing a degree of solidarity, and educating them in the ways of mutual cooperation and of the discipline required for conflict. When, after a long period of such organization, the workers have achieved detailed definition of their aims and of the character of their opposition, there may be an almost constant atmosphere of hostility between management and employee, with reactions of conflict breaking out spontaneously on the most minor of issues. The contemporary disciplined organizations for conflict are by no means automatic expressions of human nature subjected to unpleasant conditions but are the products of long processes of social organization. However disorganizing to the economic welfare of a nation a series of strikes may be, they are not to be regarded as symptoms of chaos in the laboring class, but of integration.

### Conflict Reactions to Deprivation

In certain situations of poverty and perhaps injustice that are chronic, there may grow, in a gradual process of organization, a movement which prepares for actual conflict. This is not, however, an automatic development in all situations where people are in states of discomfort or need. There is required a degree of intelligence in the population, a certain amount of social integration, and a long period of active leadership and organizing activity. The mature labor union which conducts disciplined and successful strikes is far from being a spontaneous product of popular frustration. Furthermore, the conflict activity, once developed, may continue on the basis of a kind of institutional inertia supported by rising ambition long after any reasonable basis for a sense of poverty or oppression can be found. Some of the most effective strikes are conducted by old, well-drilled unions of well-paid workers who reach coolly for even more favorable pay and conditions of work.

During times of depression, when economic need is greater and more widespread, membership in labor unions does not increase, but declines. Fewer persons are employed and in a convenient position to maintain union membership. Union bargaining power declines in this period so that the advantages of unionization are reduced. The periods of large-scale strike activity are primarily those of prosperity, or at least the periods when production increases so that there is a movement toward prosperity. There is pressure for strikes during the prosperous periods of wartime, which pressure is held in check somewhat by the pressures of government and the sentiments of patriotism, but in the boom periods that follow wars the patriotic motive no longer interferes. At this time, when the standard of living of workers is higher than at any other time, and therefore when the pressures and frustrations of poverty are most remote, strikes are most numerous and protracted. In the timing of this activity, then, the organized labor conflict appears to be more closely related to ambition and hope than to desperation in the face of extreme poverty.

**The Desperation Strike: Pullman in 1894.**—In spite of the general relations between strikes and the recovery phase of the business cycle, there have occurred strikes which have been apparently desperate reactions to extremely unfavorable conditions. One of the great labor conflicts of American history, the Pullman strike, occurred at the time of a sharp business depression and in consequence of a drastic reduction in wages. Even in this instance, however, the action is far from being a simple response to the immediate unpleasant conditions. The background had been laid in a history of unusual conditions of paternalism and autocracy, and the process of mobilization for conflict was in the hands of active and able leaders.[6]

George Pullman, a self-made inventor and industrialist, built a huge and successful company for the production of railroad cars. He took pride in the company, in the high and steady dividends paid to stockholders, in his control of the affairs of the company, and in the model town he built, which he considered to be an ideal community and an important experiment which would lead to the solution of nearly all of the problems of labor.

In order to carry out his aim, Pullman maintained a tight control over the community. All of the buildings, including the church, were owned and controlled by the company. Political control was maintained by such powers as that of appointment of the town manager and other town officials. Opinion was influenced through the newspaper owned by Pullman, and outside ideas were discouraged by refusing unwanted speakers the use of meeting halls, and also, in the belief of many workers, by the use of spies and "spotters." Even the conduct of workers in their homes, rented from the company, was regulated in detail. The tenants were required to agree to observe many rules governing noise, loitering, care of equipment, and even places of smoking.

The collection of rents was for a time made by deductions from pay checks. After the state legislature outlawed this practice, strong pressure was put on each worker at the time his pay check was received to pay his rent at once. During the panic of 1893 wage rates were so reduced that some employees were able to earn little more than the amount required for rent, but reduction or delay of rent payment was not tolerated by the company.

There were also troubles with the management in the factories, for in addition to persistent attempts to prevent unionization, the company was accused of nepotism, favoritism, tyranny, and blacklisting. Furthermore, during the periods of reduced worker income, officials of the company had no reduction in salary. Pullman himself was criticized for maintaining his salary at its high level. His response was merely to indicate that it made little difference in the cost of a single railroad car.

It was in the face of such mounting irritation and tension that a new labor organization, the American Railway Union, founded to represent railroad labor of all classifications, was started and grew to a membership of about

---

[6] See Almont Lindsey, *The Pullman Strike,* Chicago: University of Chicago Press, 1942. The following material is paraphrased and condensed from this thorough and valuable historical treatment.

150,000.  Its leader, Eugene Debs, was an idealistic and thoughtful man who devoted his life to the cause of labor, and who preferred gradual and peaceful means to striking and fighting.  The provocations were too great, however, and the temper of the railroad workers too hot to hold in check, and, against the advice of their leader, the Pullman workers began the strike.

During the months preceding the outbreak of the conflict, the railroad officials had found an effective instrument for combining against their employees in the General Managers Association.  Through this organization they were able to present against the workers a united front of twenty-four powerful corporations, and to maintain a strikebreaking mechanism ready for instantaneous action.  Thus were ranged across a labor battlefield two large organizations, one representing management and the other the laborer.

The incident that set off the strike was trivial, as is so often the case in situations of great social tension.  In the spring of 1894 attempts by Pullman employees to obtain concessions from George Pullman were failing.  The representatives of the workers who conferred with a vice president of the company to present their demands had been promised that no discrimination would be made against them, but on May 10 three of them were discharged.  The company's explanation, that the only reason was that work was slack at the time, was not accepted by the employees.  That night during a protracted meeting, the grievance committee, acting against the advice of Debs, decided to hold a strike, but set no date for its beginning.

The following morning a rumor, now said to be groundless, went through the plants.  It was to the effect that the Pullman Company, having heard of the decision to strike, had decided to close the plant at noon.  Spontaneously the employees abandoned their work, and the strike was on.  That evening the company posted a notice that the plant was closed until further notice.

The following weeks were witness to a mounting flame of excitement and fury.  After the initial period of quietness, the Pullman workers persuaded union men on the railroads to refrain from handling any Pullman cars.  Since the railroad officials refused to separate these cars from their trains, the effect was to hold up a large amount of traffic.  The near paralysis of transportation threatened food supplies of cities, outlets for farm produce, and flow of commerce in general.  There was much public sympathy for the cause of the workers, but many influential newspapers and public officials took a position against the strikers.  The railroad managements employed strikebreaking workers, importing some from eastern states, and deputizing many so that they could carry weapons.  Eventually federal troops were called in to help maintain the flow of traffic and to put down disorders.

The greatest disturbances of peace occurred in Chicago.  In the orgies of rioting, destruction, and vandalism the Pullman employees are believed to have had no part and, according to the General Superintendent of Police in Chicago, a considerable part of the crowds was composed of hoodlums, tramps, and semicriminals, who joined in the activities with no purpose, and destroyed in wanton spirit.  On the evening of July 4th crowds began to gather on railroad property and demonstrate their aggressive feelings by such actions as turning over cars. The next day larger groups roamed over the tracks of the Rock Island lines, obstructing trains, overturning cars, and setting cars on fire. Half-grown boys joined in to throw switches, change signal lights, and throw stones at trains for the excitement of it. Women and children joined the crowd, which grew to about 10,000 and which continued in its activities all day, in spite of some efforts of federal troops to drive it away with bayonets.

The mob activity and car-burning continued for the next few days, and on July 6th $340,000 worth of railroad property was destroyed in a great fire in the freight yards. In the evening 700 cars were burned at one yard in South Chicago alone, by a mob of 6,000 described as mad with frenzy. On the following day a train, guarded by a company of militia, was confronted by a mob of several thousand people and was assaulted with stones and bullets. A bayonet charge was ordered; some members of the crowd were wounded, and others fled. But many returned, and the fight continued. Another car was overturned, and stones and bullets were exchanged again. After several soldiers had been wounded, the commanding officer ordered his men to fire at will into the crowd. Four rioters were killed and about twenty were wounded, and the crowd was eventually dispersed.

After these events the disorders waned. By the end of another week, all rioting was over and train schedules were beginning to return to normal. The strike had collapsed, under the pressure of public opinion, the power of management, and a combination of more than 14,000 armed men of the local, state, and national governments. During the period from July 19th to August 7th the militia was gradually withdrawn and the fight was over.

**Underground Violence: The Molly Maguires.**—In the Pennsylvania coal fields during the 1860's and 1870's there flourished a pattern of violence that was not in the standard pattern of labor conflict. Sudden and secret destruction, beatings, and murders of officials, done by small gangs of disguised men, occurred in a series, and there grew up the legend of the Molly Maguires, thought to be a conspiracy of Irish coal miners who were disloyal to the northern cause during the Civil War.

It cannot be denied that the conditions of coal mining at that time were even more dangerous and difficult than at present, and of such a nature as to generate a feeling on the part of the workers that treatment of them was unfair. When conditions were at their best, a miner could earn more in a day than most other laborers, but his work was unsteady, and often the competition of a surplus of labor drove down the wages. The charges for powder, which each miner had to bear himself, could amount to as much as one sixth of the miner's earnings, and other charges for supplies sold by the company further cut into his standard of living. Company stores were a source of irritation, as were company houses, which were cheap, bare, and uncomfortable.

The Irish immigrants entered the system, as immigrants customarily have to do, at the bottom, and their competition was resented by earlier resident miners. The usual patterns of prejudice arose, having the character of present-day race prejudice, with an added hostility toward those of the Catholic religion. In the face of such conditions and discriminations, a conflict organization was a normal sociological development. The men who were later tried for the violent deeds of the Maguires all admitted to being members of a fraternal organization called the Ancient Order of Hibernians, but this order, while raising money for the legal defense of its members, denied any direct connection with the lawlessness.[7]

A series of early disorders was attributed to the resistance the Maguires offered to the draft in the Civil War. After these, however, there followed a long series of attacks on officials of the coal companies, all in a generally uniform pattern. In February, 1863, a crowd of miners attacked a man named Verner, who had recently purchased a colliery. Verner had a revolver in his possession and was able to defend himself successfully. In November of the same year, a mineowner named Smith was murdered by a gang of about 25 men, who had blackened their faces to prevent recognition before they broke into his house. Several men were arrested for this action, but were released from the jail by a mob.

In August, 1865, David Muir, a superintendent of a colliery, was killed in daylight near his office. No one was arrested for this murder. There followed some months of outbreaks of lawlessness, robbery, assault, and rioting, by persons assumed to belong to this Irish group. In January, 1866, a Pottsville man, superintendent of a coal company, was killed on a main highway as he was returning home from work. These killings were typical of a whole series of murders of mine officials, sometimes involving robbery and often not. In Schuylkill County alone, in the first three months of 1867, there were five murders, six assaults involving serious injury to the victims, and 27 robberies. These activities persisted in a wave of crimes which did not subside until 1870, after which outbreaks were sporadic. One explanation of the inactivity of the disaffected group at this period was that their energies were turned toward political pursuits.

The public reaction to the long history of the Molly Maguire dis-

[7] J. Walter Coleman, *The Molly Maguire Riots*, Richmond, Va.: Garret & Massie, Inc., 1936. The following account is adapted from this study.

orders eventually reached a point where organized effort to counteract them was all but inevitable.   The initiative was taken by Franklin
B. Gowen, president of the Philadelphia and Reading Railroad Company.   He sought the cooperation of the Pinkerton Detective
Agency, which assigned an Irish Catholic detective to take residence
in the coal districts, join the Ancient Order of Hibernians, learn the
secrets and the membership of the organization, and prepare material
for legal action against those who had participated in the violence.

The detective, James McParlan, succeeded in making himself
immediately acceptable to the miners and even, in an advisory role,
in participating in some of the crimes.   When his true identity was
eventually discovered by the miners, he left the community and, in
the series of trials of the principal members of the Maguires, became
a highly important witness.   By early 1879 the long series of prosecutions, convictions, and executions was completed and the organization was essentially destroyed.   The occasional crimes in the coal
areas from that time on were attributed to individual persons and
not to the Molly Maguires.

**Sporadic Collective Expressions of Hostility.**—In periods of
economic hardship there grows among the lower-income population
a sense of worry and irritation that prepares the ground for organized action.   It is not necessary to assume that leaders are generated
by depressions; there are at all times a great many insignificant persons who enlist small followings with platforms of extreme and
unconventional aims.   It is in the periods of unemployment, however, that large numbers of persons so lose their confidence in the
established order that they are willing to join as a protest an organization whose purposes they would not in other times approve.

During the depression of the 1930's there emerged such movements as the National Union for Social Justice, led by the Reverend
Charles E. Coughlin, the Detroit radio priest; the Old Age Revolving
Pensions, Ltd., organized by Dr. F. E. Townsend; the political
movement created by Huey Long, sometimes known as the "Share
the Wealth" movement, which was partially taken over after Long's
death by Gerald L. K. Smith; and a series of minor and sometimes
eccentric social movements, some of them fascist in character and
others merely novel and harmless, like the Technocracy organization
which promoted a form of benevolent scientific dictatorship by
engineers.[8]   Much of the popular support of these movements was
given by persons who did not fully understand their purposes, but

---

[8] Movements of this character are discussed more fully in Chapter 14.

who sought in some collective action an expression of their desperate feelings.

In the pattern established by Coxey's Army, an aggregation of the unemployed led by "General" Jacob Coxey in a march on the United States Capitol in 1894, a loosely organized group of veterans of the first world war undertook in 1930 to gather in Washington, camping on public open spaces, including the grounds of the Capitol, in order to put special pressure on Congress and the administration for extraordinary relief in the form of a bonus. When requested to abandon their demonstration, they refused and were eventually dispersed by soldiers using tear gas, bayonets, and fire. Although this affair did not result in immediate success, it may have been an important factor in aiding eventual bonus legislation. Neither Congress nor the next President, Franklin D. Roosevelt, felt willing to incur the bitterness which the 1930 incident caused to be directed toward President Hoover, who had insisted that the veterans be sent away.

A different sort of direct and illegal response to desperate conditions developed in the coal mining regions of Pennsylvania during the same depression years. In the towns where mines were shut down, nearly all the income of the population was cut off, and conditions of life became very hard. There was thus no strong objection on the part of mineowners when some families dug out from some minor outcroppings a small amount of coal to heat their homes. In some cases it could be done easily with a pick, shovel, and basket, and from deposits that were hardly economic to mine commercially in any times. Soon, however, miners began to cooperate, using larger tools, and filling trucks with the coal. Eventually illegal alliances of some size grew up, not only to dig coal from the ever-expanding pits and shafts but also to market it, until this activity became of sufficient importance to compete with legal mining of coal. The efforts of owners to stop it, however, met with little success. Local public opinion was largely miner opinion, and local officials were necessarily sympathetic to the miners and made little attempt at effective enforcement of the law. In a few cases efforts by police to interfere with "coal bootlegging" met with organized violent resistance. The illegal mining was not stopped by law enforcement but by the opening of the mines in the years of return of prosperity.

## RESIGNATION TO STATES OF POVERTY

A low standard of living, rather than economic comfort, is the older and more nearly universal condition. Most primitive peoples

are and always have been in a state of poverty, without being particularly aware of the concept.    Shortage and famine may be
familiar, but not poverty in the sense that some persons have less
than others or that there is injustice in the distribution of goods or
that there is a class of persons expected to be inferior in possessions
and privileges.    Until recent historical times, wealth or even moderately comfortable economic status was available only to an extremely
small proportion of any population.    Poverty in the world is general
—until recently, almost universal—and so could only appear as a
natural condition, the way of the world, and not a matter subject to
control nor even particularly a source of discontent.

**Appalachian Mountain Peoples.**—Among the most primitive
residents of the United States are the mountaineers of the southern
Appalachian highlands, in Tennessee, North Carolina, and Virginia.
They are a part of our own civilization, although the most isolated
of them have been out of contact with the modern world for nearly
two centuries.    They have worked out their own methods of survival
in the interior hollows of the Blue Ridge and nearby ranges, so that
they are independent of the industrial revolution.    They raise their
food on small farms and in gardens, make their own clothes, construct rude cabins from the mountain timber, and produce virtually
all their other needs by their techniques of folk craftsmanship.    The
standard of living achieved by this style of existence is extremely
low—in many respects the comparison with the most extreme of the
metropolitan slums is unfavorable to the mountain environment—
but there is little or no subjective experience of poverty.

In the course of an investigation made in 1929 of some mountain
villages in Virginia, some attention was given to the characteristic
desires and worries of the residents.[9]    There were desires for possessions, particularly for tobacco and more adequate clothing.    The
investigators asked a number of children what they would have if
they were to be granted three wishes and found that their desires
were virtually all for immediate and personal needs.    There was no
expression of any desire for the future.    None of the children
expressed a wish for a better house, or a wish to travel.    They were
contented with their environment.

Other indications of a lack of ambition and of satisfaction with
their general conditions of life are revealed in the answers given to
the inquiry, "What do you want to be when you grow up?"    Most

---

[9] Mandel Sherman and Thomas R. Henry, *Hollow Folk*, New York: The Thomas Y.
Crowell Co, 1933.

of the children did not at first grasp the meaning of the question, but on fuller explanation gave such answers as, "I want to be what I am." Some of the girls said they wished to be "women" when they were grown.

Investigations of worries among the adults of the mountain villages revealed that they were at a minimum. There were no bills to pay or jobs to lose. Social inequalities did not exist. There were not enough ambitions to permit worry over frustration of ambition. Conscience did not bother them. Even sickness and death were unimportant as sources of worry, for they were common and familiar and were accepted with an attitude of fatalism.

Attempts to penetrate the inner life of the young people led to results similar to the following:[10]

Harry, eighteen, was sitting on the porch of his house in Colvin Hollow. The nearest description of his action was "just settin'." He showed little curiosity when he was approached. Because of his appearance of contemplation it was assumed that he was worried about something.

"What are you worried about?"

"Dunno."

"What's troubling you?"

"Nothing."

"Well, you want something and you can't have it. What would you want if you could have anything you say?"

"My pappy done gi' Richar' all the chaws. He done gi' me none. He allus gi' him all."

"Anything else you want?"

"Nothin'."

Harry was dressed in rags—a cast-off jacket and torn overalls. No shoes. But he failed to mention that he might want clothes—or anything else. He was worried only about "chaws" of tobacco.

**Temporary Deprivation.**—The sting of poverty, short of extreme misery, derives less from its physical aspects than from disappointment in the expectation of something better, resentment at injustice, and humiliation at the comparison with those who are more fortunate. If these latter aspects are not involved, poverty may be borne with no great amount of unhappiness.

Many of the pioneers who settled the American West spent the first years in a condition of extreme need and discomfort. The rude log cabins inhabited by some compare unfavorably with the worst of modern urban slums, but not all pioneers lived this well. Some had only a dugout—an excavation with a roof of sticks and mud,

---

[10] Sherman and Henry, *op. cit.*, pp. 108–109.

small, dirty, ill-ventilated.   Food was not always abundant, clothing
was far from elegant, and luxuries of any kind were, for most of
the pioneers, completely lacking.   But these were the conditions that
were to be expected on a frontier and did not for most of them
constitute a disappointment.   The opportunities for improvement
were there, and for the most part the pioneers expected to work and
elevate their conditions.   The discomforts were temporary and the
lot of all pioneers, and they carried no implication of failure or
disgrace of poverty.

It was widely reported that temporary poverty during wartime
was endured with good grace by large populations.   In England,
for example, during the second world war, virtually the entire
nation was thrown into a state of poverty.   The shortages of food
were so severe that the national diet, though adequate, was below
the standard normally considered proper at the relief level in American cities.   But the condition was borne with little complaint and
no disorganization because it was understood as a necessary consequence of war and of the efforts toward victory.   It was recognized
as temporary and as a hardship that was distributed with equality
by means of a fair rationing program.   Clothing was subject to
equally severe shortages, and the rations allowed were so scanty
that the population in general assumed a ragged and patched aspect
before the end of the war.   But it is not such a humiliation to be
shabbily clothed if the comparison with others is not unfavorable.
The rationing rules applied to all, even to the King and his family.
Women who normally would resent having to wear the same costume
for a long period of time were comforted by the sight of the familiar
suit worn interminably by the Queen.   Because of the bombing of
the cities, housing became extremely scarce, so that in this aspect of
life too, the mass of the population was subjected to conditions that
are ordinarily those of extreme poverty.   These and other hardships
were endured, however, with no sense of injustice and no indications
of social disorganization.   On the contrary, the national hardship
and dangers of war appeared to produce a spirit, at least for the
time, of increased dedication and responsibility.

## Resignation of a Community: The Case of Rivertown[11]

In times of economic hardship there may occur, in addition to
the various individual reactions mentioned previously, a general
adaptation of the community as a whole.   This may be either active

---

[11] From an unpublished study made by the author in 1936.

or passive—there is no inevitability about bitterness and conflict if the circumstances that produce such reactions are absent in the community. In the case of Rivertown the reaction was one of almost utterly passive resignation. The people did not understand the reason for their condition, did not know how to place the blame, and had no general conception of what might be done about it. They waited, and perhaps in certain respects deteriorated, but without sudden or violent tendencies to social disorganization.

Rivertown is a settlement consisting of a string of six villages which are spread along the highways that parallel both forks of a small river. The river is dammed at intervals to furnish power for textile mills, which constitute the main support of the economic life of the town. The total area of the township is about ten square miles. It is located about fifteen miles from one of the large cities of New England, but has the appearance of being hidden in an old and out-of-the-way corner. The roads are well-paved, but hills and curves discourage through traffic, so that there is an absence of bustle in the community.

The majority of the 18,000 or so persons in Rivertown are first or second generation foreign-born, and of these, about half are of French-Canadian origin, and about one seventh of Italian extraction. There are smaller proportions of English, Irish, Slavic, Portuguese, German, and other nationalities. A large portion of this population earns its living by working in the mills, of which there are about eighteen in the town. The main activities of the others are in connection with the local retail stores, several restaurants, two hotels, and two motion picture theaters.

The standard of living in normal times, when all the mills were operating, had been low, but there developed little sense of poverty or discontent among the people, for there are no great contrasts of wealth, and furthermore the immigrant populations know that they have improved their standard of living above that of their native lands. Since the depression, when unemployment and hardship has altered their conditions, they have even regarded the predepression years as times of plenty and happiness.

In spite of the proximity to the large city, Rivertown has an aspect of isolation from the contemporary world. Although many inhabitants read the urban newspaper, they apparently do not absorb the information and attitudes that are current among urban dwellers. References to well-known persons and news events are not understood by Rivertown readers. In the winter of 1936 the investigator found persons who had never heard of some of the principal issues of the day—Father Coughlin, the Townsend Plan, communism. In one case a resident stated his intention to vote for Hoover at the next election on the ground that Hoover would be more generous with money for relief.

In view of this isolation it is not surprising that efforts to organize labor unions had met little success. The workers did not have the organizing habit. They had no feeling of discontent—they had in fact nothing to fight for.

The insularity of Rivertown is a product of the way of life in mill villages. Virtually all the activities of the people center in local activities. Typically all the working members of a family are employed in the mills—often in the same mill—and live nearby. The mothers take time off to bear children and return to work when they are able. Children attend school as long as the law requires, then go to work in the mills. Young men usually marry girls who work in the mills, and both keep their jobs. Nearly all of the younger workers were born in the town and have never known anything but the mill life.

The recreational life centers for the most part in the villages. Inhabitants engage in church activities, dancing, visiting with friends, driving their cars, and attendance at motion pictures. The city is visited on occasion, but city life is not a part of the experience of Rivertown people. Their life is local, and most of the people know no other way to follow when the mills cease to provide them with support.

The closing in 1934 of one of the largest mills was a hard blow to Rivertown. It did not find the town in good condition for trouble, for there had been a period of general decline of the industry for more than a decade, with layoffs and closings. The permanent shutdown of the Rock Mill added 900 persons to the ranks of the unemployed and was one of the largest of the disasters of this kind. And yet the town did not go to pieces—there was no disorder, rioting, crime wave, or any other serious indication of social disorganization. There was discouragement and anxiety, but it did not destroy the normal fabric of social relations.

One reason for the absence of desperation is the manner in which the hardships were absorbed and distributed. The greatest burdens naturally fell upon the unemployed workers and their families, but these were shared by others—by friends and neighbors, by grocery and milk dealers who carried them on credit for a time, and by aid from private relief agencies, and from the town, state, and federal governments. The savings of families constituted a negligible factor—over 200 of the Rock Mills families were on town relief within a week after the closing, and within a short time this number increased to over 400. Debts, particularly installment purchase obligations, were virtually as frequent as savings in the Rivertown population.

Not all of the families involved in the Rock Mill closing received relief aid—in some cases members were employed at other mills, or were doing homework for a lace mill. But a year after the shutdown there were about 530 of this group receiving money from governmental sources—230 on WPA jobs, and about 300 receiving direct relief. Since only one member of each family is allowed relief or a WPA job, this 530 may represent as many as 800 or more of the former workers. The annual governmental relief bill during this period was about $160,000, of which about half went to former Rock Mills families.

The private relief which supplemented the government aid was in much smaller amounts and went principally to those families whose needs were particularly great. Most of it was given in goods rather than in money.

The contributions of grocers, milk dealers, and other merchants were involuntary. Many families bought on credit and accumulated large debts, which the merchants carried in the hope of collection in better times. When the grocer stopped credit on the largest accounts he often found that he had only a bad debt and that he lost trade, for the workers were then forced to buy with cash, and cash customers found the chain stores to be cheaper. One grocer, whose store is located in a community of former Rock Mill workers, stated that he had extended about $45,000 credit in one year to these families. He believes most of the debt will never be paid. He suspended credit and lost the trade of some of the workers, but, since he is a member of the community and a friend to many, he is unable to refuse food to some who need it even though they are unable to pay. The grocers themselves are saved from failure by the circumstance of being carried along by the wholesalers, who thus make an unintentional contribution to the support of the unemployed mill workers.

A similar cushion to the economic shock is furnished by the owners of the houses rented by the workers. Payments in many cases fell many months behind, but the owners usually prefer to allow the tenants to remain, in the hope of eventual recovery and collection of past rents due to them.

The close dependence upon a single paternalistic employer had so narrowed the initiative of the textile workers that there were very few who conceived of finding their own way out of the difficulty. Although it was not put in such terms as "the world owes us a living," it was clear that the people expected to be cared for by someone. Few thought of going elsewhere to search for a job—they did not know where to go or how to find one. Most of them could not afford to travel about, much less to move the family to another town. There was also the fear that if they moved they would not be eligible for relief in the new location. Most simply resigned themselves to waiting for re-employment, and in the meantime they expected that some agency would provide for them.

No organized conflict grew out of the frustrations of unemployment and poverty in Rivertown. There was a small amount of grumbling directed at the owners of the mill. Some workers held that it was not necessary to close it—one even stated that the owners were unwilling to operate unless they received 200 per cent profit.

Their experiences with relief and WPA work brought out more irritation than gratitude. The amounts received were at best barely sufficient, and there were humiliating inquiries by social workers, irksome lines to stand in to request a pair of shoes or overalls. On one occasion a group of over a hundred workers gathered at the work relief office when pay checks were delayed. There was no action, merely angry grumbling at the local representative of officialdom, who was unable to act otherwise, not having possession of either checks or money. One worker, asked by the investigator what he would do if he had neither work nor money, said that he did not know, "maybe shoot somebody," but he appeared to have no idea of whom he should shoot, or why.

Political radicalism, which might be considered an appropriate development in such frustrating conditions, found no support in Rivertown. The town government is normally in the control of members of the Democratic Party, but few of the workers know the differences between the major parties, except that this one is presumed to be more favorable to them. Coughlin, the Detroit radio priest, directed his appeal to this class of people but found no following in Rivertown—the appeal was too intellectual for them to follow. Socialism and communism are completely unknown to most members of this predominantly Catholic population. The most radical organization which had a following here was the Townsend Plan, of which there was a local club in the town. Its primary feature, a pension of $200 a month for elderly persons, was intelligible to all and appealed not only to old people but also to young ones who had elderly relatives to support. Even the grocer said, "We're all for that."

### Active Exploitation of Poverty

**Beggars.**—Since the beginning of history there have been persons who have learned not only to accept poverty but to capitalize on the contrast between their conditions and those of more fortunate citizens. These persons accept with mental comfort the gap between their status and that of the rest of the society. The normal sense of shame at being unable to carry their share of the labor of society deteriorates, and instead of avoiding display of their hardships while working to overcome them in conventionally approved ways, mendicants display and exploit the signs of their misery. They put themselves, then, in the status of outcasts, but from that low social position they achieve a relation toward the conventional populations that permits them survival and in some cases comfortable or even somewhat luxurious existence. Having failed, not only in their economic activity but also in social relations, they accept failure and exploit it. They constitute symptoms of a condition of social disorganization but have achieved a personal adjustment to it.

Gilmore has presented an illustration of the process by which a family drifts into the pauper status and achieves a begging technique which becomes an active family specialty, transmitted by apprenticeship to succeeding generations:[12]

The Jed family has been known among the residents of a southern community as a begging family for several generations. The first member to

[12] Reprinted from *The Beggar* by Harlan W. Gilmore by permission of the University of North Carolina Press. Copyright, 1940, by the University of North Carolina Press. Pp. 171–176. Some of the material in the following discussion of beggars is taken from this sociological monograph of Gilmore's in paraphrased and condensed form.

enter the community was Thomas Jed, who migrated alone to the region in the latter part of the nineteenth century. Little is known about him, except that he came alone, that he was unsuccessful in his work, and that he was a heavy drinker.

Not long after his arrival, Thomas Jed married a woman who was a member of a large and well-known family of low economic and social status in the community. This family, however, had no record of pauperism or dependency. The men worked at low-paid occupations, but supported their families, and gave to relatives whatever aid was necessary, so that it was never required to obtain aid from a social agency.

Eight children were born in rapid succession to Thomas and his wife, and, because of his low earning ability and his drinking, Thomas was almost from the beginning partially dependent upon his wife's family. For more than 20 years this support was maintained. Little gratitude was aroused in Thomas, however, who considered that his wife's relatives were interfering in the rearing of his children—a duty to which he himself gave no attention. These children grew up with the minimum amount of schooling, and with no experience in working.

All of the six children who survived married early. Two sons and one daughter moved to a nearby city, where they were eventually joined by Thomas and his wife, and by the other daughters, who had lost their husbands by death or desertion, and who had children to care for. This city kinship group then consisted of the aged couple, four widows with a total of 13 children, and two younger men with families. One of the men had a large and increasing family, and the other had acquired his father's drinking habit, so the group quickly fell into dependency. This time, however, they were no longer able to obtain aid from Mrs. Jed's relatives, and so became public charges. Their cooperation within their group was such that the social agencies could not deal with any family separately, and no agency felt able to reconstruct the entire tribe.

In time the family was abandoned by the social agencies, and after some efforts at aid from churches, and from distant relatives, they began to turn to begging. Thomas Jed begged on the streets, and his wife worked from house to house. One of the widowed daughters became an accomplished house-to-house beggar, while another became a habitual church beggar, and others followed this activity from time to time.

In time the adults learned to make efficient use of their children in begging. Children were taken along, or sent alone, to obtain aid from social agencies or churches, or were sent out to beg alone on the streets. The woman who was most skilled in residential begging often took one or two of her children along as a sample of "other sick children at home." Another widow took a daughter along on her begging until the girl was married, at the age of nineteen, after which she made similar use of a granddaughter. In such a manner the status of dependency and the technique of exploitation of their need and appearance was passed on to younger generations, so that during five generations nearly all branches of the descendants of Thomas Jed have been public charges.

Just as techniques of criminal activity have been perpetuated in unbroken traditions that have endured over many centuries, so have the methods of begging been culturally preserved. Many different types of begging approach have evolved—the religious motive is exploited by those who accept charity for the benefit of the soul of the giver (in the Near East such beggars have been known to threaten a strike) ; the pity motive is appealed to by those who exhibit their deformities, or who deliberately deform themselves or their children to produce an aspect of horror; embarrassment is the target of some modern beggars who employ strategy to humiliate the non-giver before the eyes of onlookers.

In the United States the religious appeal is less effective than elsewhere, but is exploited by such organized collections as those made by Salvation Army workers, the Volunteers of America, and others. The horror approach is more suited to regions of such misery as is found in Asia and is little used here. The most effective modern begging is a developed and skilled art, which borders on criminal activity or fraud. It is commonly acquired through apprenticeship with others who are experienced, and often involves cooperation of a group—in some cases a fairly widespread organization. Where the more advanced skills are employed, begging may bring such returns that it may be considered a career that is reasonably satisfactory in most respects, except for social status.

For this highest development many kinds of knowledge are useful. There are the best places, and the best times—known by experience. Crowds are necessary—crowds in motion, preferably composed of persons in search of pleasure. Thus the downtown section of a city, near the theaters and dance establishments, is a particularly favorable location, as are the streets near a carnival, circus, or large sports event. For a stationary street beggar, a corner location is not as good as a stand in the middle of the block, for in the former place the pedestrians are too busy watching traffic and dodging one another. A location by a very attractive store window is not considered favorable, since the contents of the window will claim all the attention of those who pass by.

While the stationary beggar has to depend on the appeal he can make by the quick glances turned in his direction and perhaps by two or three words such as "Help the blind," the panhandler has the opportunity of making a more elaborate campaign, and requires talents somewhat resembling those of the salesman. A common technique is to walk along with a victim, pressing upon him a story of hard luck and asking for a small amount of help. There is much judgment required, however, on such matters as whom to approach and where, and what to say.

A research worker furnishes an illustration of the process of acquiring such knowledge:[13]

As I was going into one of the shelters a man stopped me, saying, "Could you stake me to a dime? I got to get a dime to get started on." "Started on what?" "On the stem. But before I go out, I got to get a drink. I'm shaky as hell. Soon as I get myself together I'm going to quit drinking." In a few minutes the man came back and said, "Would you like to go out with me on the stem? You've got a pretty good front and you should be able to get a tumble." "O.K., Bud. I'm kind of new at this. You'll have to wise me up as to what kind of people can be stemmed and where to go." "Stick to me and I'll show you how it's done."

Walking down Halsted we picked up a couple of transfers punched an hour later. We boarded a north-bound car. "We'll get off at Fullerton. That ain't a bad spot and we'll work north from there." As we got off at Fullerton he said, "Now watch me. I'll nail that guy coming down the street." He had no success. Walking about ten feet farther he asked a middle-aged gentleman and I believe he got a nickel.

Coming back to me he said, "Now the main thing to do is to watch out for these flatfoots (police). You've got to be pretty careful. Another thing, young guys are best stemming. What beats them is women sitting in cars. When you approach these people you've got to have confidence in yourself as though you expect to get it, but don't demand it otherwise they get tough with you, and don't give them an argument. With these guys, tell them you're a married man with children or that you're waiting for your grocery and rent order to come through. Meanwhile you haven't got enough to eat. The same goes with the dicks (detectives) if you get gustled. Tell them you can't live on that $15 a month order. Another good line is to tell them you just got out of the County Hospital or out of the county poorhouse, or some place like that. Or you might tell them that you expect to get a job in a couple of weeks. If they take you to a restaurant, order something light that don't cost too much and ask them for the difference and say you need it for a flop for the night."

My tutor went on hitting them and then I saw him talking to a middle-aged woman. She seemed to be asking him a lot of questions and after about five minutes of conversation she handed him a nickel. He came back to me and blustered, "That cheap lousy broad. She asked me more questions than a bank would about lending a million dollars. I felt like throwing the nickel in her face." After he had made a few more touches he said, "Hell, this is enough for today. I've got enough to get a couple of jugs and some over for cigarettes. Let's get going back."

[13] E. H. Sutherland and H. J. Locke, *Twenty Thousand Homeless Men*, Philadelphia: J. B. Lippincott Co., 1936, pp. 137–138.

A research worker, posing as a homeless vagrant, obtained from another beggar the following advice :[14]

"Being a cripple I have to bum most of my money. Now today I made fifty-five cents. I got up at four o'clock and by six I was at work out at 71st Street, working the people going to the train on their way downtown. Sometimes I do not go out to these outlying places. I have regular routes along Jewish streets, such as Roosevelt, Kedzie, Division, Lawrence, and Sixteenth. I work one side of the street one day and the other side the next. I'll go into a store on my crutches and, if there are customers, I'll take off my hat and hold it out, generally picking up a few pennies. If there are no customers, I do not take off my hat and I don't say a word. Generally if the man is a foreign-born Jew, he will give me a penny or two. American-born Jews and American business men are the hardest to touch. They never tell you they won't give you anything, they simply say, 'The boss isn't in.' Before the depression it was a lot easier to bum than now, for people don't give as large amounts and there are a lot more bumming. For instance, over on Roosevelt Road the other day I passed six or seven working the same street and the stores undoubtedly get tired being bummed so much. Just like every other business, bumming suffers when there is too much competition.

"Sometimes I work depots and once in a while I work the Loop, but the police watch the Loop too closely. Some of the police are pretty good people, simply telling you to move on; others carry you away in the wagon. But in ten years' experience I have only been picked up two or three times. They have given me many bawlings out and orders to move on and stay out of the Loop. But they seem to be more lenient with cripples."

Another beggar adds to the above advice :

"The idea is to hit younger people, particularly the man with the pretty girl, for the man is unwilling to let the girl think he is a cheapskate. Another good type to touch is the man who gives you 'the brother eye,' for he is liable to be some sort of a religious nut who is in the habit of giving dough to people. I like to ask old women Sunday morning near churches, for this is the time when they are at peace with the world, feel holy and good, and feel that giving alms to the beggar is the religious thing to do.

"I use all the regular stories, but the one that works the best for me is when I ask the man for a quarter for the price of a meal. I never make the mistake of asking a man for a nickel for a cup of coffee, for people have heard that story too often. People like to hear something different and sometimes a man will give you something just because he knows that you have given him a new story which he can tell at the office.

"I believe that the dirtier the man is the better for the street make. If I am dirty, a man will give me a coin rather than have me walk with him down the street and have people think I might be one of his friends. I always walk along with the man I might be bumming. Of course, I get bawled out for it,

---

[14] *Ibid.*, pp. 139–141.

but this is all a part of the day's work.  And a man that can't take a bawling out has no business to go out on the stem.  I think the best method a man can use in stemming is to walk along with a couple.  Women are sensitive to the presence of a dirty bum going along with them and are very likely to give a coin to get rid of him.  It often helps to turn from the man to the woman saying, 'Sweet lady, you know how it is, for the love of Jesus won't you spare a bum the price of a drink of whiskey?'  This is apt to arouse the amusement of the couple and make them come through.

"In the long run the ability to beg is the ability to take the cussing the public hands you.  That is the reason junkers (drug addicts) are the best beggars; they are usually so hopped up with dope that they don't mind if they are bawled out every time they put the 'b' on a man.  There are a few men in the shelters that are on marijuana, and they, together with the alcoholics, make the best beggars.  I do not know of any drug addicts in this shelter, but if there were, they would be the birds to show you the fine art of begging. I learned what I know of the racket from an old bird that was on the junk and had to have more money than he was able to earn."

An even more active and social adaptation to the mendicant role is made by those who form cooperating teams for begging activity. Gilmore reports a business alliance of an urban beggars league.[15]

An organization of beggars formerly had their headquarters in the rear of a saloon run by Joe Thomas on a side street just off the central business section.  In this back room the beggars kept a supply of old clothes, crutches, false legs, collodion to put in the eyes to make "blind men," acid to make "jiggers" on the arms, and other articles needed in their make-up.  They would come here in the morning dressed in their regular street clothes and would change to their "begging togs."  At the end of the day, they would return to headquarters and change back to their street clothes.  There were usually about 70 members of this gang, including 10 or 12 women.  They were in charge of a precinct captain for an alderman who was a political friend of a state senator.  For protection each paid $1.50 to $4.00 per day depending on his "stand."  This protection consisted of security from police interference and assurance that other beggars would not be allowed in the loop area.

A still more advanced form of business arrangement may be found in enterprises in which a man hires and manages beggars, furnishing them with the make-up and equipment they need, and, if necessary, teaching them the art of begging.  Beggars are assigned stations, working hours, and paid wages or a percentage of their collections.  This type of begging, however, could hardly be considered as a reaction to poverty or need—it is simply the acceptance

[15] Reprinted from *The Beggar* by Harlan W. Gilmore by permission of The University of North Carolina Press.  Copyright, 1940, by the University of North Carolina Press.  P. 117.

of unemployment and substitution of a fraudulent enterprise, one more closely allied to the phenomenon of crime than to ordinary begging.

### DEMORALIZATION: SHELTER INHABITANTS

The pauper is one who no longer accepts responsibility for his share of the burden of daily work and who sinks into a status of dependency which is conventionally considered a disgrace. The pauper status is not merely a matter of not working—children, disabled persons, retired persons, are not regarded as paupers—but is a condition of a disapproved kind of dependency, one which is considered unnecessary or improper and cannot be assumed without loss of self-respect.

To those such as the members of the Jed family described earlier who have never known any other status, this outcaste role is not intolerable. In cases where the reduction of status is sudden, however, it may be very painful. While it is possible for a man who has failed to accept with good grace his lower status and to remain cheerful, it is in most cases so humiliating that a break with former life is made, sometimes through suicide and sometimes through migration. It is a characteristic of experienced hobos that as a class they avoid using their own names or telling where they came from or who their relatives are. A man's past is his own secret. An investigator of homeless men in an emergency government shelter reports that while it is easy to join in a general and friendly conversation, it is seldom possible to know the names of the men.[16] Although there was daily mail delivery at the shelter, few men received mail or wished to do so. They took the attitude that they did not want anyone at home to know they were there, some saying that it is bad enough to be there without everyone finding it out.

The same investigator, reporting on the conversation among the inhabitants of a shelter, states that intimate conversation is rare because of barriers of race, nationality, occupation, and the like, as well as the desire for anonymity. There is some grumbling about bankers and big business ruining little men and a certain amount of boasting of past, and largely imaginary, achievements. The principal topics, however, are related to adaptation to the way of life of a homeless pauper. The men discussed begging, snipe-shooting (picking up stubs of cigars and cigarettes), jackrolling, and ways of getting temporary work to earn a few dollars. At the same time hostility against the nonhobo world is shown in the condemnation of

---

[16] Sutherland and Locke, *op. cit.,* pp. 10ff.

case workers, of government, business, and the capitalist system. Sometimes rumors spread among them—that a hundred men at another shelter were poisoned and the administration tried to hush it up, or that there was a riot in a nearby street over the bad food given to hobos.

Just as personality deteriorates according to the length of time spent in isolation, so do certain traits of character decay when men no longer take an active part in the organized life of some society. The gradual adaptation to permanent uselessness and dependency results in the kind of demoralization which is referred to as being "shelterized":[17]

The monotony of the thing at first weighs on one's mind, but with the passing of time this condition slowly changes, and only at infrequent intervals, which become more widely separated, does this monotony bother him. It is not only the monotony of shelter life but the absolute aimlessness of the things one does. There is no end to accomplish, nothing to look forward to, no reason why one should even do the things he does. There is no reason why one should walk fast, so one learns to walk slow; there is no place to go. There is no need to look for a job, so after a bit one doesn't even think of it. There is no reason why one should go to the library when he can get a book at the shelter and go over to the McCoy Hotel and read. There is no reason to think independently, so one agrees with the group. A man's life becomes narrowed to a limited sphere of action, and after a few months his independence is broken down, his individuality disappears, his identity is lost, his personality becomes reorganized, and he becomes shelterized.

The only noticeable change is the change in oneself. With each succeeding day one feels himself pushed down into a hopeless maelstrom—getting farther and farther from the outer edge, into the middle of the vortex from which there will be no escape. The absolute uselessness of attempting to improve one's condition is soon a part of his thoughts and actions. Though the men may not entirely abandon hope, they talk always in terms of tomorrow. Tomorrow they will get a job and get out of the shelters. It's always tomorrow, never today. One man explained why he remained in the shelters, as follows: "Those men who do leave, I watch with envy, wishing I were in their boots. However, I know that they are going nowhere; that they are walking in a circle; that after a few months they will wind up in some shelter, possibly in another city. As far as I am concerned, I do not perceive how I am going to get out of the shelters and if I do get out how I can stay out. So I just stay on, thinking that perhaps things will be different later."

Of course, some of the men are hoping that something will break and they will get out. "Something is bound to happen soon; it can't go on like this forever. Either the government or the big industries will have to do something soon or the country will be all shot to hell. Just don't let it get you

[17] *Ibid.*, pp. 15–16.

down." It's always someone else, and especially the government, who has to do something to help. In the meantime the men wait and wait and wait, and if the shelters are open until the day they die, they will still be waiting for someone else to move them out.

Sutherland and Locke have made, on the basis of data on more than 8,000 shelter occupants, a composite description, or typical picture of the homeless man in the shelters: [18] "He is a man who secured a meager education, became an unskilled laborer at an early age, and continued that type of labor throughout life. He has been a hard and relatively steady worker but during the greater part of his life has been largely isolated from normal social contacts. After this career he finds himself, at the age of forty-five, beyond the age of employment in competitive industry, a dependent in a shelter." There is, of course, some variation· from the general type in the individual cases.

It may be of much significance that a high proportion of these men had a history of less than average involvement in conventional family and community life and more than an average amount of mobility. For example, before the age of fifteen about a third had lost their fathers by death, and about a third had lost their mothers. About one sixth had left their parental homes by this age. Approximately half who left home had little or no further contact with parents, and an additional 30 per cent had only occasional contacts with them. Only one third of them ever married, and practically all of these were isolated from their wives through divorce, desertion, or death. Few of them ever kept contact with any church after leaving home, and few acquired personal friends. Over half of them had been during their independent period either transient or engaged in seasonal occupations such as harvesting or railroad labor, which themselves require a certain amount of mobility.

These men were not, however, conspicuously at variance with the general population with respect to mental health and intelligence. The psychological deviations that appeared to be somewhat characteristic were lack of initiative and a tendency toward quickness of temper. The temper appeared in many cases to have a relation to the mobility, for many left jobs or abandoned their wives because of trivial incidents which irritated them. There were also indications of a deficiency in the traits of considering the future and of self-control. These latter are reflected in the inclinations of the shelter men to indulge in common vices: drinking, gambling, and irregular sex behavior.

[18] *Ibid.*, pp. 34–35.

It is further shown by Sutherland and Locke that the depression did not account for the hobo status of most of these men of the shelters.[19]  In an inquiry regarding residence both before and after the depression period, they found that only a small percentage of the men changed the type of urban district they inhabited.   There was movement within the areas of high mobility, but only a minor net movement from stable residential districts to the areas ordinarily inhabited by homeless men.   Rates of residence of these men were computed for each of the seventy-five local communities of the city of Chicago, and comparisons were made between the rates for the depression and for the predepression period.   The two sets of rates have a correlation with each other of $+.88$, revealing a high correspondence.   Presumably the majority of the shelter men were in the hobo classification even before the depression.

The investigators, in fact, found that the life-histories they were able to gather revealed that many of the shelter men had begun the process of deterioration and demoralization years before and had found various "long roads to dependency."   For some men there was apparently a direct, though slow, route through low-paying migratory labor to the hobo life.   As one man put it, "Sometimes I think that from the day I started work as a harvest hand until now there has been a straight line leading to this government flophouse." Other men with some trade or white-collar work had followed for a time a stable occupation, but through restlessness began to change from job to job.   The moves increased in frequency, until their labor began eventually to be casual in character.   The depression made it more difficult than ever to provide for oneself by this kind of work and so forced many of the casual laborers into dependency.

Other pathways to the shelter life were through marital difficulties, sexual maladjustments, or other factors which broke up family life and disorganized the lives of the men.   One man put it as follows, "I lived with my wife for ten years.   We had no children, but we got along very well together.   We were exceptionally happy.   After she died I kind of went to hell.   I didn't give a damn whether I worked or not.   Then after I lost my job I started hanging around North Clark Street, mostly around the cheap dance halls and taverns." [20]   Others, having divorced one or more wives, were so burdened with alimony payments that they took to the anonymous life of the hobo as an escape from this responsibility.   In some cases men left home because of difficulties which primarily affected other

---

[19] *Ibid.*, pp. 29–34, 70–93.
[20] *Ibid.*, p. 75.

members of their parental families. One man, working regularly at a job in his home town, found the scandal of his unmarried sister's pregnancy so hard to bear that he departed for a city, where he was unable to make a living and eventually deteriorated to the shelter life.

Alcoholism was a prominent factor in the process that led some of the men to dependency. In certain cases it was both a cause and an effect of family dissension and disorganization, and in others it was a factor in occupational failure—discharge for being drunk on a job or for being inefficient after spells of drunkenness. In the more serious cases of alcoholism the intensive drinking became so frequent that the men could not engage in other than casual work. Furthermore they allowed their appearance to deteriorate and their social ties to weaken and eventually drifted to the hobo areas and the shelter life.

Physical defects—injuries, lameness, poor health, and the like— played a role in the shelterizing process for some of the men. Finding difficulty in supporting themselves, these handicapped men lost faith in themselves and in their value to others and allowed themselves to deteriorate until they reached a condition of dependency.

The investigators found that the majority of the shelter men were reared in rural communities—some in foreign countries—and that they came to the urban industrial regions with hopes of acquiring wealth, and then perhaps of returning home with new high status. In the face of the inevitable disappointment after a trial, some became disillusioned and demoralized. The road to shelterization was further opened by the fact that they were separated from friends and relatives of their home community and perhaps by the bewildering experience of having to live in a large city. One man said, " 'Too much run in my head when I come here; too much people; too fast a life. I never be in a big city before. Here everything seemed upside down.' " [21]

The theme that runs through the backgrounds of these homeless dependents is detachment—from friends, relatives, home community, or any stable social life. In the process of demoralization some of them acquire acquaintances and some of them marry, but in most cases their associates during this period are also of unstable character and do not lead to integration in any general community life.

The decision to accept relief and enter the shelters is itself something of a crisis. It is an admission of failure and an acceptance of

[21] *Ibid.,* p. 84.

a status that separates the person from the larger, conventional, self-supporting community.  Furthermore the dull, inactive, regimented life in the shelters allows a process of deterioration to set in which in time renders the person increasingly dependent and helpless.  It is this that is meant when one speaks of a man becoming "shelter-ized."  He gets into a rut from which it is ever more difficult to escape.  Sutherland and Locke have examined in some detail this aspect of the process of deteriorating into dependency.[22]

The period of failure prior to the acceptance of relief or shelter-ization had involved humiliations which caused the men to lose con-fidence in themselves and in their social world.  Some of them had delayed the crisis by borrowing from friends, by pawning their possessions, and even by going without food or shelter.  The accept-ance of pauper status was a moral crisis to be resisted to the last.  One man put it this way:[23] " 'I had slept in Grant Park for a few nights; I was cold and hungry.  I went to one of the shelters and looked it over and said to myself, "It will be hell to be identified with that group of bums, but you will either have to go to a shelter or jump in the lake."  After two or three more nights in the park, I went to the shelters.' "

The routines of induction into shelter life are almost inevitably such as to increase the humiliation.  The entrant observes that he is one of a class of dirty, rough, pathetic failures, and comes to realize that in the eyes of other persons he is not differentiated from the typical "shelter bum."  The questioning to which he is subjected by the officials in charge is irritating and depressing in its effects.  His first resolve is usually to regard the shelter as only a temporary place to fall back on until he can re-establish himself in some kind of normal employment, but as time goes on this expectation weakens and ambition fades away.

As the new inhabitant of the shelters gradually comes to view his residence there as a matter of long duration, he learns to accept his status there, to identify himself with the shelter group, and to acquire the customs and mannerisms of his fellow shelter men.  He also begins to resemble his fellows in the loss of pride, self-respect, and confidence.  The passing of time comes to mean less to him, and he allows himself to be controlled by the circumstances of his pro-tected life.

In the special culture that is generated by the conditions of shelter life there are many reflections of the unsatisfactory character of this

[22] *Ibid.*, Ch. 7, "The Process of Shelterization," pp. 144–165.
[23] *Ibid.*, p. 145.

existence.  Neither the routine of the life nor the company is of choice quality.  The men are not inspired by one another—some in fact find the general table manners nauseating, and compare their fellows to hogs at the eating trough.  This animal-like atmosphere at mealtimes, together with the monotony and cheapness of the diet and the irritation of standing in lines, causes the men to have a special complex about shelter food.  The cursing and grumbling about food constitutes one of the typical aspects of shelter conversation.

Antagonism toward the shelter staff and toward case workers is partly a matter of the shelter man's sense of inferiority.  Abruptness and inconsiderateness are common qualities of lower-paid staff workers, and the shelter man tends to interpret this as an expression of contempt for himself.  There is a common belief that the workers keep the men waiting in lines for intentionally long periods, out of sheer spite.  The resulting antagonism is reflected in the epithets the shelter men employ—the watchmen are called "flunkies, boot-lickers, dog-keepers," and case workers are called "case makers" or "graveyard buzzards."  The shared sentiment against the staff is one of the factors which tends to unite the shelter men.

In institutions which have little or no provision for work or activity, the idleness itself is deteriorating to men who have been accustomed to working and other active functioning.[24]  After initial emotional disturbance, there occurs discouragement and finally complete loss of morale.  The men reach a state which is similar to that known in prisons as "stir crazy," and the term "shelter crazy" is sometimes used to refer to it.  An inmate described the changes in his mental states in the following words:[25] " 'At first I kept looking for work, but when I found nothing, I became discouraged and felt that there was no way out.  I came to the position where I felt that I was an outcast and a person whom society wanted to forget.  When I couldn't get work I felt afraid.  In time I began to fear for my reason.  I became timid, shy, and bashful.  I tried to get over my

---

[24] E. Wight Bakke, in his *Citizens Without Work* (New Haven, Conn.: Yale University Press, 1940) presents evidence that the conventional social services dealing with unemployed workers operate on the whole in such a manner as to produce more demoralization.  The services do not preserve, in most cases, the worker's opportunity to function in socially respected roles.  In some cases there is a necessity to abandon possessions which are to the family the symbols of self-reliance.  It has been difficult to provide relief which permits the worker to retain his skill and work habits and thereby to preserve his employability.  As a consequence his self-reliance may deteriorate and he may lose hope and initiative.  Furthermore, the services sometimes fail to keep the worker and the institutions of the community together and to maintain the worker's relationships to his customary associates.  Men who are on relief, or even those who because of failures have to earn their living by odd jobs and low-paid work, may avoid their former friends because of embarrassment and may acquire a sense of isolation in their own communities.  Bakke concluded that those who are able to maintain their friendships, their club associations, and other social relations, are provided with a strong protection against the deterioration of unemployment.

[25] *Ibid.*, p. 154.

fear, for when I went to a place to apply for a job, I knew that my whole attitude was against me.  I came to the conclusion that the only road to peace with myself was to say to hell with everything, to quit looking for work, and to resign myself to living in the shelters.' "

The nature of the life, and the atmosphere created by their inter-action, spreads a sense of distrust and suspicion among the men and produces discouragement and cynicism.  There is, for example, a belief that deception is preferable to honesty—the men hold that it does not pay to be honest, and exchange tales of experiences which support this view.  There are also expressions of hopelessness and deep pessimism, such as, " 'Not one man in ninety-nine who has passed forty years and has lived in these flophouses will ever make a come-back,' " or " 'I do not think I will ever leave the shelters except for the poorhouse,' " or " 'A sign should be hung on the front door of each shelter : "All hope is lost to ye who enter here.' " [26]

There is little confidence in religion, government, or business among the shelter men.  Religion is considered a "racket," in the class with such charity organizations as the Salvation Army, the Red Cross, the Y.M.C.A., and the various missions, which the men believe are involved in activities for the money to be gained from them.  Politics is held to be graft, and all politicians are considered crooks.  The men have had contact with politicians who have been willing to buy their votes.  They are often willing to sell on the grounds that everyone else is profiting by some kind of dishonesty, so they might as well get their small share.  Business is held to be a rapacious game played by clever and dishonest men who never give the little man a fair chance.  The capitalist system is believed to be a major source of general evil.

Sutherland and Locke find that a few men are able to resist the deteriorating influences of shelter life and remain for some time unaffected.  In this classification are some of the intellectual radicals, who find in their reasoning, study, and propaganda activity an organ-izing function.  There is also a group which avoids the typical despair and cynicism, but which is "shelterized" just as fully in another way—a group of contented men.  They have given up all struggle to maintain an independent life outside, and they find rest-fulness and peace in the shelter.  Some of the older men in particular are disposed to take this view.  One man stated, " 'I'm seventy-two years old.  I look pretty young, yet seventy-two years is a lot of years.  But after all what's the use of worrying?  It won't give me

---

[26] *Ibid.*, p. 157.

a job and it might give me wrinkles.' " [27]   Occasionally an experienced shelter man will warn a newcomer against allowing such a feeling of satisfaction to develop, on the grounds that this is a sign of permanent dependency.

The end products of the extreme demoralization process are the old, ragged, dirty, indifferent bums who make no effort to work, to care for themselves, to keep up any appearance, to cooperate in any way, or even to converse with others.   Except for the mild effort of shuffling along, seeking a shelter for the night or a food line, and occasionally picking up cigarette stubs, they take no responsibility for keeping themselves alive.   If a mission offers food or shelter on condition of undergoing religious conversion, they may become converted for the moment but relapse into individualism and indifference as soon as they are out of supervision.   In appearance and in personality they are so unattractive and unsociable that they often appear as objects of horror or disgust to persons who are unfamiliar with their type.   In their functions they are often so deteriorated that they are classified as mentally abnormal when subjected to psychiatric examination.

It occasionally works out that the very repulsiveness is turned to profit.   Anderson tells of a tramp whose reputation is so bad and whose appearance is so unattractive that his family prefers to keep him at a distance.[28]   His relatives pay him a small amount each week to stay away from them.

## REACTIONS OF URBAN POPULATIONS

A general examination of the behavior of urban populations in the depression of the 1930's, for the purpose of identifying symptoms of revolutionary activities, resulted in the finding that with all the "mass misery" there were few indications of serious rebellion.[29] There were local riots that stemmed from specific situations and had limited objectives, but the notable fact about the behavior of the American population during this painful era was its essential stability.

The city which had the closest approach to violence was Chicago, but even here there was nothing to indicate the danger of revolution. There were many factors which contributed to an unusual degree of vigorous protest in this city.   For one thing, Chicago had grown too fast ever to achieve an equilibrium similar to those of the older

---

[27] *Ibid.,* p. 165.
[28] Nels Anderson, *The Hobo,* Chicago: University of Chicago Press, 1923, pp. 46–47.
[29] Mauritz Hallgren, *Seeds of Revolt,* New York: Alfred A. Knopf, Inc., 1933.

eastern cities. During a large part of its first century of existence the city had been in an almost continuous boom of growth, and had acquired a reputation for being a disorderly, brawling settlement. The "city of the big shoulders" took what amounted to a certain kind of pride in this condition, and when, during the 1920's, it led the nation in spectacular crimes and gang warfare, there was some thing of a public tendency to consider the underworld leader, Al Capone, as one of the local celebrities.

In this atmosphere neither strikers nor police were accustomed to meet opposition with finesse. When fights occurred, the action in certain cases, notably the steel strike of 1937, became desperate and bloody. On one occasion during that conflict, a great crowd of strikers was gathered in an open field, facing a line of police. The charge of the police and the battle that followed was warfare on a miniature scale.

A less violent but perhaps more unusual demonstration of collective anger was expressed by a crowd of teachers from the public schools. They were not, however, attempting to initiate a revolution; they were merely trying to collect their pay. They were the outstanding sufferers from an unusual state of disruption in the local government which resulted in long delays in the payment of their salaries. The governmental tangle began in the 1920's, when, under the political administration of William Hale Thompson, the assessments on real properties were so inequitable that a group of taxpayers succeeded in obtaining a court order for a reassessment and a delay of tax payments until the time the reassessment was completed. The process, however, took so long that a period of several years went by with no collection of real estate taxes by the city. When at last the collections were resumed, the depression was well under way and land values were down, as was the ability of owners to pay the accumulated taxes. In the meantime the city had been operating on borrowed money and was reaching the limit of its credit with the local banks.

In this period of poverty the city was often unable to meet all of its payrolls on time. Instead of treating all employees alike, the city paid some of them on time and delayed payments to others. Necessity and expediency apparently controlled these decisions—the school janitors, for example, having long had a powerful and effective union, were always paid promptly even when the salaries of teachers were many months in arrears. A wave of protests from the teachers appeared, first in letters to newspapers, then in public meetings and demonstrations. A system of payments was instituted in which teachers were paid not in money but in tax anticipation warrants, which certified that they were entitled to the stated amount at whatever time sufficient taxes were collected. A few stores were willing to accept these in payment for merchandise; some discounted them. Many stores would not accept them at all, and of course they were virtually useless for the purchase of automobiles, for traveling expenses, or for any expenditures outside of the city.

The greatest demonstration of impatience on the part of the Chicago teachers was directed not at city officials but at a bank. One of the large local banks which had been advancing money to the city for the purpose of paying teachers eventually refused to continue the advances. A large crowd of teachers gathered in the bank lobby and shouted angrily. Former Vice President Charles G. Dawes, then an official of the bank, appeared before them to explain the point of view of the bank, but was shouted down by the angry teachers. His temper grew short, and he made his locally famous retort, "To hell with troublemakers." No action by the teachers took place, however, and the crowd soon dispersed. The city eventually caught up with the salary payments, and the teachers, whose salary scale compared favorably with those in most other cities, ceased their demonstrations.

## Summary

In the modern industrial world, economic hardship (except during and after wars) is seldom the result of shortages of materials or of natural disasters, but is a consequence of the failings of men, or of their relations to one another. The intricate and fragile mechanisms of distribution of goods and money do not allot wealth evenly or with full justice and do not maintain the production system at a steady rate. Unemployment and poverty, then, are for the most part consequences of one kind of partial social disorganization.

In the long experience of our civilization as well as others, the necessity of almost constant work by all members has been so obvious and pressing that idleness has been disapproved except for certain persons or specified times. Achievement has been honored, and wealth has represented honorable labor and therefore has conferred prestige. Poverty, and particularly dependency, have been considered disgraceful, and penalties of low status, low privileges, and partial ostracism have become appropriate for paupers. Thus extreme inability to provide for oneself has become a source of partial separation from the normally functioning community and a condition favoring further social disorganization.

The disorganizing effects of poverty, however, do not follow from the physical consequences, even when these actually interfere with the maintenance of health and life.   There are innumerable demonstrations of the ability of men to endure extreme shortages, including famine that brings death, while maintaining discipline and morale in their relations with one another.   A sound social organization is potentially stronger than the so-called "instinct of self-preservation."

A traditional view of certain nineteenth century scholars was that paupers are a class of the most inferior members of the population, biologically speaking, and that this inferiority in intelligence, skill, and strength is interrelated with many other forms of personal inadequacy—delinquency, suicide, insanity, and the like.   Neither modern biology nor sociology now supports this extreme hereditarian theory, and in the following chapters the role of heredity in most of the forms of personal disorganization is shown to be minor, and the causation of the abnormalities is accounted for in rather separate and specific defects of the social order.   Poverty, as low income or low standard of living, is also for the most part a result of the inability of the economic order to distribute wealth fairly. There are, of course, a number of disabled persons who are physically incapable of earning their own living, but if they constituted the entire class of the poor, the relief burden upon society would be so slight that poverty would not be thought of as a major problem.

The great masses of almost permanently low-income peoples in the United States are those who are either only partially incorporated in the modern economic order, such as the isolated mountain peoples or the populations of backward agricultural regions, or the populations who are new to the system and who enter at the bottom—the unskilled masses of immigrant labor.   But even their poverty is not permanent.   Each of the major immigrant groups in time works its way upward, out of the unskilled labor class and into skilled trades, commerce, white-collar work, and the professions.   As these peoples leave the lower ranks, their places are taken by new immigrants, who become the new classes of the poor.   Poverty of this kind is not a general disorganization of the economic system, but merely a specific defect in its allocation of earnings to those who enter the system at the bottom.

Temporary poverty occurs for larger numbers in the population when there is serious malfunctioning of the system, that is, in the great depressions.   It is clear, however, that such temporary poverty is borne without disorganization by the majority subjected to it and that where disorganization occurs there is some additional reason beside the mere fact of a low standard of living.

This latter generalization can be applied to the interpretation of economic hardship in general—such hardship does not in itself cause social or personal disorganization, but may be a factor in the deterioration of social organization that is already weak and may contribute to the demoralization of persons who are in some way or another isolated from a stable and integrated community life. Furthermore, in cases where a class of people becomes convinced that they have been the victims of injustice, their hardships may form the basis of solidarity of groups which engage in bitter conflict with employers, representatives of the law, or the entire society. The bitter strikes and riots, the crimes of the Molly Maguires, the demonstrations of the Chicago schoolteachers, and the marches on the Capitol are expressions of this kind of internal warfare. On the other hand, such reactions are shown not to be inevitable by the examples of those whose hardships are as severe, but who have no conflict organization supported by a sense of injury. The southern Negroes endured for many decades a condition of life more severe than those of the conflict groups mentioned above, without disruption of their functional relationships with the whole society and without large-scale personal demoralization. The inhabitants of such communities as Rivertown met with disasters in the depression years, but on the whole without conflict or demoralization.

The dangers of extreme poverty, of starvation, exposure, and disease, are subject to control and elimination in modern civilization, and in the contemporary United States they should no longer occur except through accidental oversight. There are additional discomforts and frustrations connected with low economic status, however, which are sufficiently severe to form the basis of conflict and of demoralization. The most important of these are connected with aspects of social status. The Western Electric investigation reported in 1939 showed that fatigue, monotony, and consequent dissatisfaction and absenteeism are results not of the physical conditions of work but of the nature of the relation between employer and worker. The experimental conditions, which so improved both the productivity of the workers and their contentment with their jobs, operated through providing them with a sense of importance, a feeling that they were appreciated as persons. In the conflicts between labor unions and employers, even where the visible issues are matters of pay and working conditions, intensive and sympathetic investigation often reveals that the largest irritations are caused by certain aspects of the social relations between these two factions.   Strikes have behind them, often as hidden factors, provocations of arbitrariness on the part of management and minor humiliations which cause the laborers to sense that they are not regarded as persons.   Even where general conditions of standard of living have been high, as among the Pullman workers, and where the employer has acted from altruistic motives, the resentment of paternalism has been a strong and important factor in the intensity of strikes.

Status and demoralization are also interconnected in the transition of persons to dependency status.   There is a strong moral barrier that opposes the acceptance of charity, and persons whose need is desperate characteristically undergo a crisis before they are willing to cross the line that separates independence from pauperism.   To cross it is to undergo a serious loss of social status and consequently of self-respect.   Once the step has been taken, however, the barrier continues to operate to make difficult a return.   The inhabitants of the shelters for homeless men on relief have as a rule not wished to communicate with friends or relatives or to reveal their true identities.   They have tended to confine their relations to those of their class and have often revealed timidity in applying for a job.   Many have experienced a sense of defeat and resignation and accepted the outcaste status of the shelter inhabitant as a permanent condition of life, which, from both the social and psychological points of view, involved personal demoralization.

### SELECTED REFERENCES

Anderson, Nels.   *The Hobo.*   Chicago: University of Chicago Press, 1923.
Bakke, E. Wight.   *Citizens Without Work.*   New Haven, Conn.: Yale University Press, 1940.
Gilmore, Harlan.   *The Beggar.*   Chapel Hill, N. C.: University of North Carolina Press, 1940.
Hallgren, Mauritz.   *Seeds of Revolt.*   New York, Alfred A. Knopf, Inc., 1933.
    A journalistic account of certain reactions of the United States population during the depression years of the 1930's.
Hiller, E. T.   *The Strike.*   Chicago: University of Chicago Press, 1928.
Moore, Wilbert E.   *Industrial Relations and the Social Order.*   New York: The Macmillan Co., 1946.
Sutherland, E. H., and Locke, H. J.   *Twenty Thousand Homeless Men.*   Philadelphia: J. B. Lippincott Co., 1936.

# Chapter 5

## CRIME: DEFINITION AND THEORIES

Criminal behavior has not always been regarded as a matter for sociological study, nor even for scientific study. The theological view which has prevailed so extensively and so long in our civilization has regarded misconduct as the deliberate and sinful choice of a free will. It required no study or explanation other than that of the wicked natural character of man and no rationalized treatment other than expiation or penitence and an inner conversion to rightness of behavior.

In the modern viewpoint, crime is understood to be relative to the culture in which it exists, and to be a reflection of a certain amount of disorganization within the culture. This interpretation is presented at length in the following chapter. Before examining this statement, however, it is desirable to consider how crime may be defined and to review certain early and influential theories concerning its causation.

### THE DEFINITION OF CRIME

**Relativity of Criminal Behavior.**—It is impossible to provide a list of actions which universally constitute crime. Standards of behavior vary with culture, and it is well known that deeds which in our civilization are regarded as abhorrent are not only permitted, but in some cases even demanded, among other peoples. Intentional killing, except in warfare or legal executions, is among the most serious of our crimes, and murder of a member of one's own family is particularly bad, but among the Eskimos there are some who regard it as a duty to put to death an aged parent. These people lead a precarious life, and their able-bodied hunters can provide for only a limited number. If a son does not do his duty in such a situation, his old father may reproach him and urge him to carry out this principle for the welfare of the group.

Our traditional mores forbid self-destruction but, among the Japanese and the Hindus, suicide has been regarded as an honorable, and even a required, action in specific circumstances. Theft is prohibited by our mores and laws, and certain kinds of thieves, such as the frontier horse thief, have been treated with great severity. Among some of the American Indians of the Western Plains, however, the theft of horses from other tribes was an achievement of honor and a virtual requirement for the demonstration of manhood.

At the same time we perform without sense of guilt or danger of penalty certain actions which are regarded by other peoples with horror. The Hindu, looking upon cattle as sacred, cannot approve of the vast and business-like slaughter in modern packing-house industries, nor in the indignities that are suffered by these animals in the traditional entertainment of the western rodeo. Among the Trobriand Island natives, to mention another example, there is reported a moral prohibition against the admission that brothers bear any physical resemblance to one another; thus a commonplace remark in our society becomes a serious wrong in theirs. Missionaries have reported that various primitive peoples have been shocked at the sight of physical punishment inflicted upon his own children by civilized man.

Crime can only be defined relatively, in terms of the relation of actions to the culture in which the person lives. Crimes are universal only in the sense that certain cultural principles are universal. As was stated in Chapter 1, it is not an easy matter to state clearly the list of cultural universals, for the variation in detail of practices makes the classification task difficult. There is, for example, a universal principle of close cooperation in primary groups, of friendliness, loyalty, and harmony, but this is expressed in different ways, and definitions of the membership of the primary groups are greatly varied. There is also a universal principle that sex relations are of interest to and subject to the control of the community, but here again details vary. In some societies complete chastity is required until marriage, after which a large amount of sexual freedom is permitted. There are other societies, however, which allow license until the age of marriage, and thenceforth expect fidelity. There are special occasions for suspension of ordinary standards in some cultures, and provisions for sex hospitality, as among Eskimos, and even some commercialization, as reported among some southern Pacific island peoples. There are also the well-known variations of the general form of the family—monogamy, polygyny, and polyandry, as well as modified forms of group marriage.

However arbitrary these standards of conduct may be, they may be enforced with severity, and their violation may arouse the greatest inner revulsion in the members of the culture possessing them.

Conscience and the moral sense are products of culture, but they may possess the power of instinct where the uncontradicted force of the society is strong, and they may easily be mistaken for instinct. The universal prohibition against incest, for example, has been held by Freud and his followers to be an expression of instinct. More than any other specific sentiment that is uniformly held among all peoples, the incest taboo bears the closest resemblance to an innate prejudice. But even this interpretation is subject to challenge. W. I. Thomas,[1] in a careful study of the phenomenon among many peoples, finds much evidence against its instinctive nature. For one thing, the variation is great, and some peoples prohibit with equal force certain forms of behavior which are not regarded as at all wrong by others. Among some of the Solomon Island peoples, for example, a man must never name his sister, enter a house or garden she is in, laugh or play in her presence, or even speak to her at any time during his life. On the other hand, among some of the American Indians, cooperation between brother and sister is very intimate.

Marriage or sex relations between members of the same family is in a sense universally prohibited, but not, apparently, by an innate distaste, for there have been instances in which royal persons have been permitted to form brother-sister marriages in order to preserve the purity of the royal line. Furthermore, in modern society violations of the taboo by delinquent persons is not uncommon where social disorganization is extreme.

Although there is no certain basis for a conclusion concerning the origin of the incest prohibition, most of the evidence indicates that it exists because it plays some basic social function. Tylor suggested that exogamy began as a device for extending the sphere of interpersonal, interfamilial, and intertribal relations. The relations among the members of an in-group are warm, intimate, secure, the relations with outside peoples uncertain and potentially menacing; and the advantages of acquiring relations by marriage are perhaps both obvious and enormous among primitive peoples. A number of peoples in fact explain their customs by just such rationalizations. The Arapesh of New Guinea say that a man would be foolish to marry his sister, for if he did so he would lose the opportunity to gain two brothers-in-law—men with whom he could hunt, garden, and exchange visits. Other observations support this interpretation, and Thomas flatly concludes that the horror of incest is of social derivation. If this is true of one of the most universal and intense

---

[1] William I. Thomas, *Primitive Behavior*, New York: McGraw-Hill Book Co., Inc., 1937, Ch. 7, "The Incest Tabu."

of prohibitions, it is even more certainly the case with ordinary crimes.

**Crime and Social Organization.**—Crimes are violations of principles of a culture—principles which can be in part arbitrary. The laws that define crime represent the end products of long, slow, unintentional, and unwitting development of custom. Actions which are originally trial-and-error attempts to deal efficiently with the problems of living may in some cases lose their original utility and remain as folkways, which have the purposes of manners, social grace, or etiquette rather than of mechanical efficiency. Some of these folkways in time may acquire such a central position in the social organization that they appear to be essential to the preservation of the society or the welfare of its members and thus become transformed into mores. Mores are strict rules, but are in the class of unwritten and incompletely formulated principles, with no fixed or organized mechanism of enforcement other than the spontaneous reactions of horror, disgust, and aversion of members of the society.

It is a general principle that folkways and mores are adequate for social control in the integrated simple societies but that, as growth and complexity develop, some of the mores are weakened and require more organized support if they are to function at all. It is at this time that the machinery of law is gradually introduced to buttress the failing mores. This sequence is not uniform, for it is affected by borrowing or diffusion of law and by other circumstances, but even in contemporary American civilization we can observe instances in which failing mores are enacted into law. In the middle 1930's there occurred in Tennessee a marriage involving a girl only ten years old. The state law contained no bottom age limit for marriages in which the persons had the consent of their parents, as was the case in this instance. Child marriages are contrary to the mores of that section as well as of the rest of the country, but it had not been foreseen that parents would consent to such a violation of mores. In view of the fact, however, a state law setting an age limit, even with parental consent, was soon passed. Other states, among them Rhode Island, having hitherto also relied upon the mores to prevent such happenings, also responded to these events by putting the prohibition into law.

Laws are thus enacted in consequence of partial failure of mores. If the mores change completely, or are abandoned entirely, the laws are deprived of an essential form of support. Eventually they fail of enforcement and are repealed or, as happens more often, they are

merely disregarded.  The "blue laws" of many New England communities (laws forbidding many kinds of work and other activity
on Sundays) are examples of the many laws which remain on the
books but which there is no attempt to enforce.  It would be sociologically unreal to classify the activity of a bus driver working on
Sunday as a crime, even though there is an unrepealed law pro-
hibiting such work.

A crime can only be considered an action in violation of such
criminal laws (not traffic violations or other regulatory measures
of that class) as are supported by general consensus.  If such a statement presents a definition without clear limits, it can only be stated
that there are no clear limits to the classification of criminal activity.
The borderlines are controversial, and not subject to exact determination.  Since our processes for punishment require a decision as to
whether or not a crime was in each case committed, we adopt the
trial system for practical purposes, but no realistic student would
presume that the categorical decisions of juries and judges are
scientifically exact.

**Marginal Crimes.**—Theft, smuggling, and murder are, in the
language of the law, criminal actions.  The mores, however, allow
exceptions and extenuations which are often recognized as "unwritten law."  The souvenir hunter, if he practices moderation in his
pilfering, is not customarily treated as a thief, nor were the Pennsylvania coal field bootleggers so treated.  Smuggling activity as a business enterprise exposes a person to the danger of prosecution as a
common criminal, with consequent disgrace, but small-scale personal
smuggling is widespread and is regarded by many as an almost legitimate game to be played against customs agents.  Persons who do not
regard themselves as lawbreakers may even boast of their successful
evasion of customs regulations.  Murder is also extenuated, and the
perpetrator usually set free, in cases of outraged husbands who kill
adulterers, and in certain "mercy" killings of incurable and suffering
relatives.

The problem of defining crime has other borderline difficulties.
Mores change and decline, and they vary in strength in different
parts of the same culture.  Often the background of an action, the
degree of provocation and intention, and other circumstances must
be examined in order to make a decision regarding its criminality.
In the sociological study of crime, however, it is desirable to employ
a broad definition.  Sutherland has proposed, and has provided a
reasoned defense of, the definition of crime as behavior which would

raise a reasonable expectancy of conviction if tried in a criminal court or substitute agency.[2]

### EARLY THEORIES OF THE CAUSES OF CRIME

**The Lombrosian Approach.**—Only recently in the history of man has there emerged any attempt to find the causes of deviant behavior. The mystical or theological conceptions of free will and sin required no further examination of the causal circumstances, and thus offered no stimulation to science. Tradition holds that the scientific phase of criminology began with the investigations of Cesare Lombroso, whose *L'Uomo delinquente* was published in 1876. This belief has been sharply challenged, however, by Lindesmith and Levin, who show that a well-established line of investigation, essentially sociological in nature, antedated by years the publications of Lombroso.[3] These writers maintain, in fact, that the effect of Lombroso was to set back the progress of investigation by turning the interest, particularly in America, toward factors of a biological nature. Lombroso's theory was a part of the stream of emphasis upon and enthusiasm regarding biological evolution. He sought to show that the criminal was a biologically inferior creature, a throwback to a primitive type inferior in many respects to modern man. He pointed to a long list of observed anatomical and mental traits which he considered to be symptoms of such a reversion, among them such abnormalities as low forehead, asymmetrical skull, protruding ears, left-handedness, obtuseness of senses, vanity, violent temper, absence of remorse, and the like.

Goring is conventionally assigned the credit for the effective refutation of Lombroso, although this claim is also an oversimplification of the history of the investigations. In *The English Convict,* published in 1913, Goring presented the results of extensive physical measurements made upon English convicts. In this research he found no indication of systematic differences from the noncriminal population.

Although sociologists soon turned away from the kind of biological determinism supported by Lombroso, there persisted a preference for this type of conception among such specialists as biologists, eugenists, certain psychologists, and physical anthropologists. As late as 1939 a prominent investigator published a treatise which has

---

[2] E. H. Sutherland, "White Collar Criminality," *American Sociological Review*, Vol. 5, Feb., 1940.

[3] Alfred Lindesmith and Yale Levin, "The Lombrosian Myth in Criminology," *American Journal of Sociology*, Vol. 42, March, 1937.

such similar biological emphasis that it is sometimes referred to as "neo-Lombrosian." [4]

Hooton performed a series of measurements and observations on a large number of incarcerated criminals and compared the results with similar measurements on a much smaller number of noncriminal citizens selected as a control group. In about 40 of these observations or measurements there was found to be a difference in averages for the criminal and the control groups. Hooton concluded that these differences are reflections of an innate biological inferiority which is also causally connected with tendencies to criminal behavior. He reported indications that certain types of abnormalities of physique are related to certain types of criminality. On the basis of his findings he advocated a eugenics program which would eventually eliminate from the population those classes which possess such innate inferiorities.

Recent as the research is, it has found little or no acceptance among sociological students of the causes of crime. Critics have found so many statistical and logical defects that they conclude that Hooton failed to furnish a reasonable foundation for his conclusions, which are contrary to the evidence regarding the nature of crime accumulated over many years of sociological research. It is necessary here only to mention a few of the outstanding fallacious inferences and methodological weaknesses of this study. In the first place, there was no satisfactory basis for acceptance of the two noncriminal groups which Hooton used as controls. To be representative of noncriminal native Americans Hooton chose a group of 146 firemen from the city of Nashville, Tennessee, and 167 militiamen from the state of Massachusetts. The scientific objection to these groups as representative samples of a population is that in both cases the membership is originally determined at least partly upon a basis of physical superiority, while the criminals who are caught and sent to prisons represent a selection, if at all, of the physically inferior criminal. It is highly probable that an important part of the observed differences between physical traits of criminal and noncriminal groups in Hooton's study is a result of this selection.

It has also been pointed out that Hooton had no satisfactory basis for his contention that the differences between criminal and noncriminal physiques must be interpreted as physical inferiority of the criminal. Hooton simply contended that since the criminal is obviously the undesirable person, his differences from the normal must

[4] Earnest A. Hooton, *Crime and the Man*, Cambridge, Mass.: Harvard University Press, 1939. This work is a popular presentation of the two-volume research study *The American Criminal*, of the same author, press, and year.

be symptomatic of inferiority. The logic of this assumption has been severely attacked by Merton and Ashley-Montague, who present an analysis of the meaning of the physical differences by a more objective criterion.[5] Resemblance to existing anthropoid apes, the chimpanzee, and the gorilla, is interpreted as "primitive" while contrast with apes in the directions in which man evolved is interpreted as "advanced." By these standards, the robber group is "primitive" in respect to length of ear, but "advanced" in height of head. The first-degree murderers are "primitive" in the relation of the width of forehead to width of face, but "advanced" in breadth of jaw. In the total group of 51 indices in which differences were compared on this basis, the criminals were more "primitive" in 19 respects, more "advanced" in 22, and indifferent in 10. This examination, then, gives no support to a theory that criminals are reversions to a more primitive or apelike form. While it does not disprove inferiority of other kinds, it calls attention to the necessity of an objective criterion of inferiority.

One further deficiency of Hooton's methodology may be mentioned. It is assumed that the physical inferiorities reflect innate characters. A few of them clearly do not—Hooton listed weight as one of the observations. But it is also highly probable that even stature, though not in adulthood as subject to fluctuation as weight, is a partial reflection of the conditions of life. The criminals incarcerated on charges of burglary and larceny, for example, may contain a larger proportion than does the noncriminal population of men who spent their childhood and boyhood in the poverty of urban slums and who, because of inferior diet, higher disease rate, and other unfavorable conditions of life, may not have grown to full height, apart from any innate tendencies. It is also entirely possible, in the light of modern research in the physical anthropology of human development, that proportions in the skeleton and skull, presumed by Hooton to be stable indications of heredity, are also modified by living conditions.[6]

**The Eugenics Approach.**—A similar, though somewhat separate, tradition in the investigation of the causes of crime may be found in the eugenics movement. Early in the twentieth century a

---

[5] Robert Merton and M. F. Ashley-Montague, "Crime and the Anthropologist," *American Anthropologist*, Vol. 42, July-Sept., 1940. This excellent article contains one of the most devastating of the many criticisms that have been made of the research under discussion.

[6] Two of the foremost investigators of this matter are T. Wingate Todd, and Wilton M. Krogman, whose careful research on many thousands of growing children has shown how plastic and responsive to conditions of life are the human bones. See W. M. Krogman, *A Bibliography of Human Morphology, 1914–1939*, Chicago: University of Chicago Press, 1941.

number of studies of the "family tree" type were made in which it was shown that certain families had records, over many generations, of high achievement by many of its members, while others contributed generations of undesirables to the population.  The Jukes, the Piney Woods, and the Kallikak families were shown to have produced large numbers of persons who were paupers, insane persons, suicides, delinquents, and criminals.  These facts were interpreted as clear indications of a general hereditary weakness in the family line —a weakness which expressed itself in a number of different manifestations.[7]

This type of eugenics research, however, has been virtually abandoned, even by those who still have a hereditarian bias.  The criticism of the practice of using fragments of information, based on fading memories and hearsay, to discover the traits of past generations of persons, has shown the futility of basing any worth-while conclusions on such unsatisfactory evidence.  Even the observations on living persons in these studies were characteristically unreliable.  In the Kallikak study many of the observations were made on the basis of a most casual inspection by a field worker.  Her notes which were used as the basis of the conclusions give clear indication of both the prejudice and the carelessness with which snap judgments of inferiority were made.  She wrote of her emotions at the sights of misery and degradation that greeted her when she entered the houses of the poor and of her revulsion at the filth and ragged conditions.  Some ill-clad and unkempt children were diagnosed in a glance, as revealed by such phrases in her record as "a glance sufficed to establish his mentality, which was low," or "Three children, scantily clad and with shoes that would barely hold together, stood about with drooping jaws and the unmistakable look of the feeble-minded," or "The father, himself, though strong and vigorous, showed by his face that he had only a child's mentality."

In the light of modern knowledge, there is an equally serious methodological defect in the technique of the family tree study, as made by these early investigators.  There is no separation of influences other than heredity which perpetuate within a family and community the conditions of pauperism, mental abnormality, delinquency, and other types of disorganization.  Families which for some generations are caught in a community which is in a state of disorganization may be affected anew in each generation by the demoralizing influences that surround the members.  Furthermore, within the tradi-

---

[7] For a representative study of this sort, see H. H. Goddard, *The Kallikak Family*, New York: The Macmillan Co., 1912.

tions of such families, techniques of the pauper life, begging, minor thefts, and the like are transmitted through learning, and it is not necessary to call upon heredity for an explanation of traits occurring in a family for several generations.

**The Study of Twins and Adopted Children.**—More recently there has emerged a technique of studying the influence of heredity involving the comparison of traits of twins.[8] If it can be assumed that identical twins have the same, or almost the same, heredity, while fraternal twins are no more alike in heredity than ordinary siblings, a comparison of the behavior of the two types of twins should reveal something of the importance of heredity. In the research of both Lange and Rosanoff, it was found that identical twins are more alike in tendencies to delinquency and criminality than are fraternal twins, although the more inclusive study by Newman, Freeman, and Holzinger brought to light cases of identical twins which differed markedly in some of their mental and personality traits. Lange, for example, found that of 13 pairs of identical twins ten were alike in respect to delinquent tendencies, while three were unlike. The fraternal twins, however, were alike in two pairs, and unlike in 15 pairs. Lange's results are, in a sense, too good for plausibility, for all but one of the 30 pairs of twins grew up together, and it is thus remarkable that 15 of the 17 pairs of fraternal twins, whose heredity presumably should be somewhat similar, are nevertheless unlike in regard to tendencies to delinquency.

There are technical difficulties in the twin-research method of studying the interrelation of heredity and crime. For one thing, it is scarcely worth while to employ comparisons, as did Lange, of the behavior of twins living together, for it is a common practice for parents to treat both members of a pair of twins so much alike that there is no satisfactory means of distinguishing similarities resulting from similar experiences from those that result from similar heredity. It is also a possibility that identical twins, because of their very similarity of appearance, may be more often treated in identical fashion, thus producing results that parallel the findings of Lange. Furthermore, until some objective method is employed in the selection of identical twins from a population, there is a statistical bias in the sample under study. Such cases are for the most part gathered for study because they have been reported by persons who are not

---

[8] Among the most significant are Johannes Lange, *Crime and Destiny*, translated by Charlotte Haldane, New York: Albert & Charles Boni, Inc., 1930; A. J. Rosanoff *et al.*, "Criminality and Delinquency in Twins," *Journal of Criminal Law and Criminology*, Vol. 24, p. 929, 1934; H. H. Newman, F. N. Freeman, and K. Holzinger, *Twins: A Study of Heredity and Environment*, Chicago: University of Chicago Press, 1937.

experts in their identification, and for this reason those identical twins that are conspicuously alike in mentality, personality, and behavior have a higher probability of being reported than those pairs who differ in these respects. Thus it is possible that the cases which are gathered for scientific study are biased in such a manner as to produce a spurious conclusion regarding the importance of heredity.

A method for the study of heredity that is potentially more satisfactory is the systematic study of adopted children who have been separated since birth from their true parents. In these cases there is a connection of heredity only with true parents, and a connection of experience only with foster parents. The systematic examination of the degree of resemblance to each set of parents should provide a valuable measure of the relative importance of heredity and experience. This promising method has not yet been satisfactorily applied in the study of causes of crime, for two practical difficulties interfere. It is difficult, for one thing, though of course not impossible, to locate and subject to intensive observation the true parents of children who have been surrendered for adoption, particularly after the many years that must have elapsed before the children reach the ages of chronic delinquent behavior. The second technical difficulty is that of elimination of the sampling error that results from policies, sometimes intentional and perhaps often unwitting, of matching in certain respects at the time of adoption the traits of the foster parents and the true parents. That is, agencies which place children for adoption often prefer to give children to foster parents of racial or national characteristics, physical types, and often intellectual levels similar to those of the true parents. The result of such matching is to produce a similarity which might falsely appear to be the result of heredity. It is not impossible, however, to eliminate such difficulties. When this is done, some of the most valuable knowledge on the importance of heredity to behavior may be obtained.

At the present stage of knowledge, most sociological students of crime do not place great emphasis on the hereditary factor, partly because of the inadequacy of the direct research on heredity but more because of the impressive results of sociological researches showing the processes by which a person acquires delinquent and criminal attitudes and behavior revealing the general conditions of social disorganization which permit such activity to develop.

**The Low-Mentality Theory.**—In the early period of extreme enthusiasm over the techniques of mental testing many efforts were made to prove that low mentality was an important factor in delinquency and crime.   The basic technique of this research was simple. Standard mental tests were applied to inmates of institutions for the confinement of lawbreakers, and the average intelligence of the sample was compared with the general average of the population, or the percentage of delinquents that were feeble-minded was compared with the percentage of feeble-minded in the general population.   In most of these studies it was concluded that the general mentality of criminals was low and that therefore feeble-mindedness was an important part of the cause of crime.

Sutherland, reviewing the results of 341 studies of this type, performed during the period from 1910 to 1928, finds an enormous variation in the estimated percentages of feeble-minded among the delinquents in these studies.   The range includes as low as 1 per cent feeble-minded and as high as 96 per cent.[9]   The highest estimates prevailed in the early part of the period, and a distinct downward trend appeared throughout the eighteen years.   The median study in the first four-year period, for example, contained a feeble-minded percentage of 51, while the median study in the last three years contained a feeble-minded percentage of only 21.

It is apparent that the criteria of feeble-mindedness must have been quite different in the various studies.   It has also been realized, particularly in the years since these studies were made, that mental tests are at best imperfect indications of hereditary mental capacity and that the systematic disadvantages of members of the lower economic and educational classes—the groups from which most of the delinquents are drawn—are of a nature to affect their performances on mental tests.   The intention of those who devised the tests was to make them independent of cultural and educational advantages, but in recent years it has not only been shown that most tests are clearly deficient in this regard, but it is also coming to be recognized that the perfectly "culture-free" test may be an impossibility.[10]

Sutherland has further pointed out that a part of the apparently low ability of the criminal group may be attributed to the statistical bias that results from the examination only of those who have been caught and confined in an institution.   It is probable that the delinquents and criminals who are less than average in intelligence are caught more often than are the more intelligent ones.   Furthermore "the feeble-minded delinquent is more likely to be convicted if

[9] E. H. Sutherland, "Mental Deficiency and Crime," in *Social Attitudes*, Kimball Young, ed., New York: Henry Holt & Co., 1931, Ch. 15.   This thorough and detailed critical analysis of the research is one of the best contributions to the issue, and forms the basis for much of the present discussion.
[10] See George D. Stoddard, *The Meaning of Intelligence*, New York: The Macmillan Co.

arrested, more likely to be committed to an institution if convicted, and less likely to be paroled early if committed to an institution than is the nonfeeble-minded delinquent." [11]

Systematic study of behavior within the prison indicates little relation between good behavior and intelligence. Furthermore, good behavior on parole bears no consistent relation to degree of intelligence. The highest proportion of violations, as reported by Ernest W. Burgess from an examination of inmates of Pontiac Reformatory in Illinois, was actually among those of superior intelligence, although the next highest rate of violation was among those of very inferior intelligence. [12]

Other objections to the conclusions of the early mental testers are pointed out by Sutherland, who finds, however, that there is apparently some relation between degree of intelligence and type of crime committed. Certain types of crime require high intelligence and are not often attempted by those who do not possess it. Fraud is among the high-intelligence crimes, for it requires careful foresight and skill for the gaining of the objective, as well as considerable wisdom for the avoidance of detection. Sex offenses, on the other hand, are characteristic of a much less intelligent class of criminals. The evidence is inconsistent regarding other specific crimes.

One of the most valuable direct examinations of the intelligence of criminals is that published by Tulchin. [13] Tests were administered to over 10,000 prisoners in three Illinois institutions during a seven-year period. The scores were analyzed in various ways by Tulchin and compared with those of soldiers in the army draft of the first world war. A noteworthy finding is that in a comparison of the soldiers and the inmates of two of the institutions in a 1920 survey of intelligence, there was no inferiority whatever on the part of the criminals. The percentage of the criminals classified as inferior was 24.4, while that of the soldiers from Illinois was 25.9. This result is perhaps more remarkable in the face of the disadvantages which are presumably characteristic of the populations from which the prisoners came. Tulchin shows that among the prisoners there is a variation of intelligence test scores according to a number of conditions. An examination of the foreign-born whites, for example, shows that there is a far higher proportion of inferior scores among those who have been only a few years in this country than among those who have been here over 25 years. In the Illinois State Reformatory, for example, the percentage of inferior scores among foreign-born

[11] Sutherland, *op. cit.*, p. 364.
[12] *Ibid.*, p. 370.
[13] S. H. Tulchin, *Intelligence and Crime*, Chicago: University of Chicago Press, 1939.

whites of less than five years residence in the country was 39.3. With the increases by five-year periods of residence, the percentages reduce as follows: 36.1; 26.3; 19.6; and 0.0.[14]

The nationality of origin of the foreign-born prisoners shows an important relation to their intelligence scores.  Presumably because of linguistic and cultural similarity, the scores of those from Canada and England were far above those from other countries.  The median alpha scores of immigrants from these two countries were 87 and 85 respectively.  Sweden, Ireland, and Germany furnished an intermediate group, with scores of 57, 54, and 52, while Austria, Poland, Russia, and Greece furnished a low group, with scores of 28, 24, 21, and 20.  Immigrants from Italy and Mexico had the lowest scores of all—15 and 14 respectively.  These differences can be fully explained only by a complete examination of the local opportunities and circumstances of each of these nationality groups, but it is apparent that the relation of low intelligence to criminal behavior cannot be separated from the life experiences of the criminal persons.

Among some groups Tulchin found a relation between intelligence score and age.  This relation was most marked for Negroes, whether born in the North or South.  The youngest age group of northern-born Negroes, for example, those between the ages of fifteen and twenty, had a median alpha score of 54, while the oldest group, over forty-five years, had a median score of only 31.  The corresponding scores for southern-born Negroes were 28 and 16. On the other hand, the native whites of native parentage had only slight variations between intelligence scores by age groups.  Possibly it is the fact that the Negro's exposure to educational opportunities is so recent that accounts for the lower scores of the older members of that race.

Tulchin's data also support the observations previously cited regarding the relation of intelligence to type of crime.[15]  In a separate examination of the characteristics of native whites, foreign born, and Negroes, he found that in each case the lowest proportion of inferior scores and the highest proportion of superior scores were found among criminals convicted of fraud.  At the other extreme, the highest proportion of inferior scores, with one exception, and the lowest of superior were found among those convicted of sex crimes.  Robbery, larceny, and burglary were intermediate and varied somewhat among the three types of population.  Murder constitutes the exception noted above, for among the foreign born the

---

[14] *Ibid.*, p. 27.
[15] *Ibid.*, pp. 39–41.

criminals of this type had the highest proportion of inferior scores. In all of the groups murder is related to low intelligence, though not as closely as are the sex crimes.

An examination of intelligence scores by sex indicates clearly an inferiority on the part of women prisoners.[16]  Women had more than half again as high a proportion of inferior scores, and less than a fourth as many superior scores as did men prisoners.  It should be borne in mind, however, that the type of crime and the nature of criminality differs somewhat between the sexes.  There are fewer of the active professional criminal pursuits among women, and a higher proportion of the crimes which require less initiative and intelligence.

The early theory, then, which held delinquency to be in large part a result of low intelligence, was based on observations too simple to show the true causal connections.  In the first place, it could not account for the delinquency of those whose intelligence was not low. But even in the case of criminals of low mentality, it is probable that the influence of intelligence is only great enough at most to disqualify such persons from the more skilled types of crime and therefore to direct them into crimes with less reward and probably more risk of capture and imprisonment.

**Mental Abnormality and Crime.**—Although the conception that crime is essentially mentally pathological behavior has never been as widely held as have the theories already mentioned, there have been scholars who have advocated such a theory. In some cases this is supported primarily by so extending the ordinary conceptions of mental abnormality that it includes all delinquent and criminal behavior.  The contention is sometimes made that the fact of criminality is itself sufficient evidence of a psychopathological condition. Such reasoning, however, does not constitute a contribution to knowledge but is merely an arbitrary attempt to alter the meaning of words which are well established in conventional language.

As Reckless points out, the diagnosis of psychopathic personality is widely employed by those who seek to account for crime on the basis of mental abnormality.[17]  This diagnosis refers to such traits as exceptional instability, egocentricity, and other behavior which involves departure from normality without assuming any of the more standard patterns of ordinary psychoses or neuroses.  This conception, however, is so indefinite and unreliable that much inconsistency is found in its application.  Reckless points out that the

---

[16] *Ibid.,* p. 139.
[17] Walter C. Reckless. *Criminal Behavior,* New York: McGraw-Hill Book Co., Inc., 1940, pp. 210–216.

percentages of inmates of various prisons receiving such a diagnosis vary from as low as 3 to more than 45. It is safe to say that the same psychiatrists who find nearly half of the convicted criminals to be psychopathic in this sense would also find a high proportion in the noncriminal population.

Healy and Bronner undertook to show the role of mental abnormality in delinquency through intensive examination of delinquent children and comparison with nondelinquent children of the same families.[18] For the 153 delinquent cases which constituted the main object of the study, there were only five cases in which the examination revealed a definite diagnosis of "mild or early psychosis." Of the 36 definite diagnoses of "personality deviations," the largest group was that of "neurosis or psychoneurosis" and the remainder were scattered among an assortment of abnormalities, none of which contained more than three cases. In the control group definite diagnoses of such conditions were rare. It must be remembered, however, that some three quarters of the delinquents were without a definite diagnosis of abnormality. The most conspicuous differences between the delinquent and the control groups in this study were in matters of relatively minor importance—food idiosyncrasies, nail-biting, speech defects, smoking, restlessness, feelings of inferiority, and the like. While it is not to be denied that these are considered undesirable traits in American culture, they are hardly serious enough to be thought of as mental abnormality, nor is it certain that they constitute important causal factors in the delinquent behavior. The same conditions of disorganization that isolate the delinquent from the control of family and community may be partially responsible for some of the personality deviations.

An examination of areas in Chicago in which the rates of delinquency and psychoses were high was made by H. Warren Dunham.[19] The finding was that the overlapping of cases was slight—that is, the 543 male persons committed as criminal and insane during a 13-year period constituted only 1.7 per cent of the total male insane committed from this population during the period and only 1.3 per cent of the male criminals sent to institutions.

Since the most frequent diagnosis of mental disorder associated with serious male criminality is that of schizophrenia, Dunham made a special examination of a sample of this type, using two common subtypes, the paranoid and the catatonic. Of the former, a series of

---

[18] William Healy and Augusta F. Bronner, *New Light on Delinquency and Its Treatment,* New Haven, Conn.: Yale University Press, 1936.
[19] H. Warren Dunham, "The Schizophrene and Criminal Behavior," *American Sociological Review,* Vol. 4, pp. 352–361, June, 1939.

345 included only 8 per cent who were charged with crimes, and of the 525 catatonic schizophrenics only 5 per cent were criminal, minor violations being excluded in both cases.

The research material on the subject of mental abnormality and crime, therefore, suggests that there is no strong connection between the two. The psychoses are not common among criminals and delinquents, and the milder types of personality deviations, which may be somewhat more common than among nondelinquent persons, are probably not significant as major causes.

## SUMMARY

Criminality is the evasion or violation of the more important and explicit rules of a society, whatever these rules may be. Some personality deviations may occur in any society, and some accidental transgression of rules is to be expected anywhere, but the more common and persistent forms of habitual criminality are prevalent only in a society which is in some degree disorganized. Early theories and research which attempted to link criminality with some kind of biological defectiveness have not been supported by modern findings. The defectiveness apparently lies not originally within the individual, but in the social organization of which he is a member.

## SELECTED REFERENCES

Reckless, Walter C. *Criminal Behavior.* New York: McGraw-Hill Book Co., Inc., 1940. Ch. 2, "The Nature of Criminal Behavior."

Sutherland, Edwin H. "White Collar Criminality." *American Sociological Review,* Vol. 5, Feb., 1940.

Tannenbaum, Frank. *Crime and the Community.* Boston: Ginn & Co., 1938.

Reckless, Walter C. *Criminal Behavior.* New York: McGraw-Hill Book Co., Inc., 1937. Ch. 15, "Primitive Law."

# Chapter 6

## CRIME AND SOCIAL DISORGANIZATION

Lawful and unlawful behavior are defined by the arbitrary rules of society, and the commission of acts of either classification is in most cases the result of individual learning. Cooperative behavior is produced by a social organization and must be maintained by a system of social control. If the social framework of a society weakens, there is a deterioration of the mechanisms of control and a consequent freedom of the actions of persons. This freedom is not always, or necessarily, directed into positive acts of criminality, but if there are influences in that direction, it allows criminal behavior to develop unchecked.

### Relative Lack of Criminality in Stable Cultures

It has frequently been observed that preliterate peoples who formerly lived in orderly fashion with little violation of their own principles of conduct have, following the shattering of their social organization by contacts with civilization, undergone experiences of disorganization which have been expressed in various ways, including marked increase in criminality. Among various American Indian tribes, for example, the abandonment of earlier custom has in most cases produced a large number of demoralized persons, inclined to pauperism, drunkenness, and various forms of delinquency and criminality. Hayner finds, for example, that in recent times there has been a relation of Indian disorganization and demoralization to proximity to white settlements and to the amount of individual income—money appears to add to their corruption.[1] Among those Indians of the Southwest who are some distance from a highway or a railroad, the native culture continues to function effectively; "theft is rare, and murder is unknown." On the other hand, the two pueblos near Albuquerque, Laguna and Isleta, are sources of a law-enforcement problem of considerable magnitude. The Quinault Indians of the coast of Washington received rich amounts on their

---

[1] Norman S. Hayner, "Variability in the Criminal Behavior of American Indians," *American Journal of Sociology*, Vol. 47, Jan., 1942.

timber claims, but now are among the most poverty-striken and demoralized of Indians.  Hayner asserts that the wealthier the tribe, the greater the offending, for money attracts predatory whites, and it furnishes the means for liquor and for mobility.

Such has been the history of the transition of the American Indian from native culture to civilization.  The crimes that have been most common are drunkenness and sex offenses, but various kinds of theft, as well as murder, are not uncommon among the Indians without a culture.  Radin has collected the autobiography of a member of such a group—a descendant of the Winnebago tribe, named Crashing Thunder.[2]  This Indian was almost a classic example of the "bad Indian" type.  He led a wandering, aimless life, never working if he could help it, and supporting himself by gambling and theft.  His customary life consisted of "chasing the payments"—going from village to village in order to be present on the days when government payments were made to the Indians, in order to be present when revelry made gambling and theft more profitable. Eventually Crashing Thunder committed a murder, for which he served a term in prison.  The murder was an act in which influences from earlier tribal life were mingled with the disorganizing influences of his present.  In aimless conversation with a similar Indian who was a companion of the moment, he observed that he had never killed an enemy.  In the old custom this meant that he had not fully achieved manhood.  His companion was similarly inexperienced, so they agreed to make up for their deficiencies.  One of the Indians was personally acquainted with a carpenter, a law-abiding man who was a descendant of a former enemy tribe, and so it was decided to kill him.  They entered his shop, asked him to come into his back room, and Crashing Thunder allowed his companion to kill the unsuspecting and defenseless carpenter.  In an additional act of perfidy, Crashing Thunder quickly touched the victim before his companion did, and thus, in "counting coup," appropriated the moral credit for the achievement.

In a study of the relation of crime to social disorganization in China a situation similar to that of the American Indians is revealed.[3]  Where contact with western civilization has been slight and the old culture functions, there is stability and adequate social control.  There are criminal bandits and thieves, but these are persons who live apart from village and family life.  The family system, with its mutual aid, ancestor worship, filial piety, and emphasis on

---

[2] Paul Radin, *Crashing Thunder,* New York: D. Appleton & Co., 1926.
[3] Ching-Yueh Yen, "Crime and Social Change in China," *American Journal of Sociology.* Vol. 40, Nov., 1934.

continuity, is a strong agency of control.  The village life furnishes an additional basis of regulation of behavior, as do the occupation guilds, with systems of mutual aid and of settling disputes and disciplining members.  The ideal of this ancient culture is stated in a saying of Confucius, "If you guide the people by law, and control them by punishment, they may avoid crime, but they will lack shame; but if you guide them by virtue and control them by *li* (mores, principles of equity), they will develop a moral sense and become good."

When westernization has penetrated, the system is rapidly upset.  The traditions and the power of *li* are destroyed, and crime spreads with rapidity.  The most prevalent crimes of males are theft and the sale and use of drugs—these constitute 58 per cent of total male crimes.  Female crimes are predominantly in connection with the drug traffic or abduction and kidnapping for sex procuring.  The drug traffic does not represent a new form of behavior, but an old practice which under new laws has become a new crime.  The abduction practiced by so many women is largely an enterprise of widows, who are caught in a particularly difficult situation.  Under the old custom remarriage of widows is disapproved, and yet in the cities, where family life is weakened, the traditional family support is gone.  Thus many turn for support to this particular type of crime, which is virtually a widows' monopoly.

Reckless, in a survey of the literature on this topic, finds that there is a world-wide occurrence of disorganization, often expressed in criminality as well as other forms of demoralization, where an isolated culture has been destroyed or partially destroyed by contact with civilization.[4]  This is the case not only among former preliterate peoples, but also among peasant peoples of Europe and elsewhere, among the all-Negro communities in isolated sections of the southern United States, and among members of isolated religious sects.  Where the transition has been sudden, as in the case of rapid economic development of the resources of a region or a business boom, the disorganization appears to be particularly severe.

## MODERN URBAN DISORGANIZATION

The type of crime which is conventionally conceived to be the "crime problem" is primarily a phenomenon of urban disorganization.  This is the class of crimes which constitutes the basis of a means of economic support, a career, and an underworld organiza-

[4] Walter C. Reckless, *Criminal Behavior,* Ch. 3, "Social Disorganization and Crime."

tion of professional criminals who organize their predatory activities along businesslike lines. The cost of such crime is high, both in the damage inflicted upon and tribute exacted from the public by the criminal activity and in the machinery of police, courts, and penal institutions that is required for its control.[5]

The criminal career of the professional lawbreaker begins in childhood. The majority of adult professionals have a history of serious and repeated juvenile delinquency, beginning in many cases before the age of eight. The mechanism which generates such skilled and organized activity is complex and extensive. Its beginnings lie in the conditions of the social organization which permit the agencies of social control that normally should prevent wrongdoing to deteriorate and to fail to function. These are the conditions of disorganization of neighborhood and family life that are particularly characteristic of the slum districts of large cities.

**Association of Delinquency with Urban Areas.**—The general association of high juvenile delinquency rates with the slums—the deteriorated urban areas near industrial sites where low-income and unassimilated populations constitute a majority of inhabitants—has been thoroughly and methodically demonstrated.[6] Sociologists have examined the rate patterns in most large American cities, and without exception the findings are that the high delinquency rates are thus concentrated, almost regardless of the racial or nationality composition of the population. The few exceptions are furnished by small, self-isolated groups, like the Orientals in certain west coast cities, or members of religious sects, which are able to live for a time in the midst of a high-delinquency region and resist the disorganizing influences.

Skeptical suggestions have frequently been made to the effect that the pattern of high delinquency rates in slum districts is largely the result of the political inability of slum-dwellers to keep their children out of the hands of the police. The contention is that the true incidence of juvenile delinquency is virtually equal in all parts of the

---

[5] This is the type of crime which flourished during the postwar decade of the 1920's and which formed the basis of much of the reputation of Chicago during the "Capone Era." It is of interest to watch the trends during the late 1940's to see if this aspect of history is being repeated. Developments during 1946, as reported by the Federal Bureau of Investigation, suggest that the United States may be moving into another period of prevalent crime. Rates for 1946 of the major forms of crime were higher than at any time during the preceding decade and were moving upward during 1947 at a very high rate of increase. The most rapid increases were in the classifications of robbery, burglary, larceny, and auto theft. More than a quarter of a million automobiles were stolen in the United States in 1946.

[6] The leadership in these investigations has been taken by Clifford R. Shaw *et al.* Their *Juvenile Delinquency and Urban Areas* (Chicago: University of Chicago Press, 1942) provides an adequate sample of the evidence on this matter.

population, but that it appears to be less in the high-income population because of their differential influence in protecting their delinquent children from the interference of police. While it is true that some kinds of delinquent behavior are occasionally observed among children of well-paid and highly educated parents, there is no comparison between the heavy records of increasingly serious criminal actions of the slum delinquent and the occasional errors of the children of stable residential neighborhoods. This observation is confirmed by the reports of delinquents themselves. Many of them report repeated thefts, burglaries, and robberies, day after day without interruption, continuing in some cases for years.

The association of delinquency with slum areas is further shown by the facts regarding the place of commission of the delinquent actions. Though some thefts and other crimes are committed outside the neighborhood—shoplifting in downtown stores, for example —a large proportion of the actions take place in the parts of the city in which the delinquents live. This would appear to be illogical, since houses in high-income neighborhoods and suburbs contain more articles of value, and thefts presumably should be more rewarding there; but perhaps because he is not logical, because he prefers to range in familiar territory where he is less conspicuous to passing policemen, or because it is not necessary to go so far to find opportunities for rewarding criminality, the delinquent operates largely within his own section of the city. An urban dweller in such an area who turns his back upon an unlocked bicycle for a few moments is not likely to see his vehicle again. On the other hand, in the high-income outlying suburbs persons leave many articles loose in public with no fear of loss by theft.

One further confirmation of the real association of delinquency with slum areas is furnished by data on truancy. Truancy and other forms of delinquency are closely related, for the same children usually practice both. For material on truancy it is not necessary to use police records. School records contain this information without bias in favor of high-income families. The truancy distributions in cities are generally in close agreement with the distribution of rates of all delinquency.

**Characteristics of Slum Areas.**—In order to reveal the causal connections between slum areas and delinquent behavior, it is necessary to examine in some detail the nature of urban slums. These are, in the typical city, on the fringe of industrial and commercial areas, most often near the central parts of the city. They are inhabited largely by those population groups which are newest to the city and newest to industrial life. It has been the history in the United States that each large racial or nationality group that has entered the slums has in time been able to improve its status and move out, but through immigration from abroad and migration from rural areas—particularly that of southern Negroes—the cities have maintained their large supply of new unskilled labor for work in industry which populates the slums.

The physical deterioration of the slums of the largest cities is extreme and is dangerous to the health and safety of the inhabitants. The buildings are for the most part old, in a bad state of repair, and inadequately supplied with facilities. Many are dark and lack proper ventilation. Some are dangerous firetraps. In such buildings the slum families typically live in overcrowded density, with no opportunity for privacy or for pleasant home life. Although suggestions are often made to the effect that the physical aspect of slum housing is a direct or important cause of delinquency, no proof of this theory has been forthcoming. Unpleasant as these quarters are, they are no worse in equipment or in crowded conditions than the peasant or tenant farm shacks from which many slum-dwellers came and in which they lived without criminality. The lack of privacy may furnish conditions that develop precocity of sex knowledge on the part of children, but probably no more than does farm life. It may be thought that a sense of bitterness at the necessity of having to spend life in such miserable quarters may impel some children to undertake crime as a protest or as revenge, but, as will be shown, there is little or no operation of this motive in the typical gang delinquency of urban slums.

Although it is a favorite cliché of many public officials, social workers, and amateur philanthropists that it is the lack of adequate recreational facilities which drives slum children into delinquency, this factor cannot be considered as a direct or important cause. It may be true that crowded and unpleasant conditions within the home impel children to seek their recreation outside, but there is nothing in the physical unattractiveness of the surroundings requiring that this activity be of criminal nature. Children may be forced, for lack of better playgrounds, to play in streets and alleys, but they can and do play harmless games such as tag, baseball, and hide-and-seek. There is a more positive force or set of forces that turns the behavior in the direction of delinquency. Once this direction is taken, moreover, the provision of recreational facilities does not necessarily reverse it. The delinquent children may enter playgrounds or settlement houses and enjoy the activities provided for them, and then afterward seek the adventures of shoplifting, burglary, and the like.  The recreational facilities may provide competition for the spare time of the children and thus shorten their daily periods of delinquency, but they do not necessarily operate as a direct deterrent or as a moral force for the complete abandonment of criminality.

The aspects of slum life which are important in relation to the high development of delinquency are the general conditions of social life—that is, the social disorganization that is prevalent in the area.  The disorganization, while not a positive influence in the direction of criminality, is the most important permissive circumstance, for the two most important primary groups that normally control the behavior of children and prevent serious delinquency—the family and the neighborhood—are unable to function effectively.

**Neighborhood Disorganization.**—In a settled village where there is little or no social disorganization, the people of a neighborhood constitute an effective primary group which is a powerful agency of social control.  Most of the members have known one another all their lives.  Newcomers are subjected to inspection and exchange of information which soon assimilates them into the primary group.  There is little privacy—personal interest is strong, and through the natural channels of neighborly gossip any information known to one is as a rule shortly known to all others.  Each person knows that whatever he does that is in any way a departure from the conventional will inevitably be discovered by neighbors and will not only be spread to all but will be perpetuated in the unwritten history of the community.  Not only is his own reputation at stake, but also that of his family, including the wider circle of relatives.  For those who are not often subject to temptations to depart from established ways of acting, this enveloping supervision is not oppressive, but it does furnish a visible force in opposition to unconventionality.  Children are warned not to act in certain ways for various reasons, but among them is the consideration "What would the neighbors think?" [7]

---

[7] An informant recalls a childhood incident which illustrates the operation of this supervision.  A boy five years old, wondering what cigarette smoke would taste like, picked up a lighted stub from the sidewalk and tried it for a moment.  Hours later, at the supper table, his father mentioned that an acquaintance had told him that his son was seen smoking on the downtown streets.  Not only the "wayward" boy but also the other children in the family were impressed by the omnipresence of adult supervision of their behavior and so became increasingly conscious that each of their public actions involved the reputation of the whole family.

The mobility of urban slum neighborhoods operates against the establishment of such a neighborhood consensus. There is no local history—not enough persons remain long enough to preserve a collective memory. Before persons have an opportunity to build up a thorough acquaintanceship with neighbors, one or the other moves away. In a situation of such frequent moving, most persons abandon the attempt to make acquaintances on a basis of proximity, even when it occasionally becomes possible. Each family lives in a world of strangers and cares little for the opinions these strangers form of them, for there is no collective force of opinion and no public reputation to build up and cherish.

The heterogeneity of the residents of these areas also tends to discourage the formation of neighborhood life. Persons surrounded by a mixture of racial and national groups experience a sense of futility in the development of primary acquaintanceships. Normal ethnocentrism and traditional intercultural hostilities interfere with friendliness and mutual understanding. Members of one group do not seek the approval of peoples of whom they themselves disapprove.[8]

The collective life with which the immigrant peoples were familiar in their lands of origin is not subject to transplantation without a great amount of disruption. The life of the European peasant cannot be lived in the modern American industrial city, and when many central features of the old culture are necessarily abandoned, the whole fabric of the culture is weakened. The mechanisms of control of individual behavior are not sustained apart from a whole integrated culture, and thus general culture shock is a cause of some individuation of persons. These slum persons, especially children and youth, whose habits have not been set by years of experience, are thus left unguided by a stable social organization and are consequently more responsive to the surrounding influences of urban life.

**Family Disorganization.**—Patterns of delinquency develop most readily in the first generation of children born in the city. In most families the parents of foreign birth are not criminal and are in fact dismayed by the prospect of having criminal children. The typical foreign-born father attempts to prevent the delinquency of his children, often employing violent physical discipline, and is

---

[8] There do exist in some of the largest cities some small and relatively unmixed communities, as in the Japanese sections of west coast cities, or the pockets of highly orthodox Jews in eastern cities. In these it generally does occur that a primary neighborhood life is developed and social disorganization is avoided. Most of the neighborhoods inhabited by foreign-born populations, however, contain a mixed group of nationalities.

bewildered at his failure. The primary reason for the difficulty of control is the cultural gulf between Old World parents and American-born children.

Foreign-born adults seldom are assimilated to any great extent into American culture. They hold to many old habits, preferences, and loyalties. Their speech reflects foreign origin in accent and idiom if they acquire the English language at all. The atmosphere in the home, the furnishings, the diets, and the family customs, have a strong imprint of the land of origin. The children, on the other hand, acquire the new language without perceptible foreign traces and, through their playmates and school life, learn to prefer the American costumes and mannerisms and to hold in contempt the foreign aspects of their home life. They may even be ashamed of the apparent ignorance of their parents and may lose respect for their abilities and their judgment.

There thus grows such a split between the generations that there is little mutual understanding between them and little basis for the control of children through family sentiment and loyalty. Attempts at control by corporal punishment alone usually fail, producing hostility that increases the split between the generations.

Shaw and McKay have presented a case study which furnishes an admirable illustration of this form of intrafamily conflict and its relation to the loss of control of the behavior of children.[9]

Nick, a fourteen-year-old Greek boy, was brought to the Juvenile Court on a delinquency petition, charged with various forms of misconduct, including theft from his home, running away, use of abusive and obscene language, quarreling with parents and sister, and similar behavior. According to his mother, "Nick no wanta work. He big man, fourteen, and wanta play ball all day. Father say, 'You go today and work in restaurant and work with uncle, for he pay you and you learn the business.' What does he say? He makes faces, cusses, laughs, and runs out to play ball. . . . He tell me to 'go to hell,' 'shut your mouth,' 'why don't you holler all the time.' . . . He get up at noon and go out and play ball. That not right. I go out to the ball game and say, 'Nick come home with me from these bad boys and work.' He laugh at me, make a face, tell me to go home and to mind own business. He like nothing but ball. He gets very mad and breaks the chairs, smashes the house, and falls on the floor kicking and saying bad names to me. The father work hard. Have heart trouble. Nick ought to help. His father work hard when he was only eleven years old. That would be right way for Nick."

Nick did not share with his parents the expectation that his occupational career should begin at fourteen, for this was not the pattern among the boys

[9] Clifford R. Shaw and Henry D. McKay, *Report on the Causes of Crime*, Vol. 2, No. 13, Washington: National Commission on Law Observance and Enforcement, 1931. The following material is adapted and condensed from this report.

he knew. In the culture with which he was familiar, this was an age for playing baseball with other boys, and he resented the efforts of his parents to deprive him of this phase of his life. He put his position as follows, "I've had a lot of trouble at home. They all fight me and hate me. They don't want me to play or have any fun with the fellows. They say I ought to work all day and then only play a little at night. The other fellows my age don't work, and I don't see why I have to if they don't. My married sister always has her gab to say. She can't keep her nose out of my business. She tells my mother what to do with me, that I ought to work and never play and that I ought to be put in jail. She's always fighting me. I can't help but curse her. I can't hold myself. She'd make anybody sore.

"My uncle tries to boss me all the time and make me work. He sticks with my sister against me. They both hate me. My mother makes me mad when she won't let me play baseball. She always goes out to where we play ball, and she whips me, and then the boys laugh at me, and when she goes away they say, 'You've got a heck of a mother. Our mothers don't make us stop playing ball.' She always whips me out there and then scolds me and the other fellows. That's what makes me sore, and then the fellows have the laugh on me. . . .

"They kick me and say they are going to put me out of the house. My father puts pepper in my eyes and hits me with an iron or anything when he gets mad. They're all against me except the guys on the street. They all like me.

"All was going well until I stole two dollars from my mother and bought a baseball glove. When my mother found out she gave me a beating and sent a note to my eighth-grade teacher, stating that I had robbed two bucks. She asked me why I robbed them. I told her the reason and I never robbed again. . . .

"The other night when I was playing ball with the guys out in the street my ma came out, began scolding me, broke up the game, and made me come in. Then she whipped me with a big stick. The next time I met the guys they made fun of me and asked me if I asked my ma if I could come out. I whaled into Irish and beat him up, but I got a black eye. Then my dad beat me for fighting and for not asking my ma if I could go out and play.

"That's the way they are all against me. I feel like I don't belong there. They tease me and nag me and I get mad and feel like I could kill them. That's why I hit them with a chair or anything. I can't have any fun. If I work hard they still fuss at me and don't give me any money. I get filled up with mad feeling and tear into them, I can't help it. They all think I am a liar and thief. I get blamed for everything. I wish I wasn't living with them. They don't want me to have any fun. I don't tell the guys I have to work all the time."

The population of the neighborhood in which Nick's family lived was pre-dominantly of Irish and German-American extraction. There were no other Greeks in the vicinity, and thus there was little basis for understanding between Nick's parents and the neighbors, who spoke of Nick's people as

"foreigners" and even "dagoes," and regarded them as outcasts.  One neighbor stated, "Say, that's the worst family in this neighborhood.  I don't want
to knock them but they're poor stuff.  They're some foreign nationality and
when you've said that you've said a mouthful.  I don't have nothing to do
with them, but I can't help but hear their family feuds.  They have a lot of
trouble with the boy called Nick.  They beat the life out of him.  You can
hear him for three blocks.  I know the brother-in-law; he's a pretty rough
customer.  He's a cocky sort of guy."

A second neighbor stated, "That's a foreign family.  I don't do nothing
with them.  They're a bad set.  They quarrel from morning till night.  Why,
we can't sleep sometimes because of the way they fight around there.  They
beat the kid something awful.  Come around some night when they're all
there and you'll find what kind they are.  They're a bad lot.  The kid's not so
bad.  They beat him almost to death.  The way he screams is a fright.  I
guess the foreigners fight a lot, anyway, don't they?"

A third neighbor said, "That's a dago family or some other foreigners.
They fight most of the time.  The oldest girl has a sharp tongue.  You can
hear her all the time laying somebody out.  The kid seems purty nice; he'd be
all right if they wouldn't beat him all the time.  I guess they are like all
foreigners, just fighting all the time.  They have a madhouse all night.  They
pound Nick around, want him to work and support the family, I guess.  I
don't blame the kid.  I told him he didn't have to work and that it was against
the law for him to work yet.  These foreigners want their kids to work before
they're out of the cradle.  You ought to throw the old folks in the pen instead
of the kids.  They don't belong in this country; they don't know how to live
here.  I wish they'd move out of here, but they own those houses so I guess
they are here to stay.  We don't have much to do with them, only I side with
the kids.  I like the boy.  He's a nice chap.  Too young to work.  I told him
I'd leave that dump if I was him."

Nick's parents reveal their alien culture and their failure to comprehend
American ways in their statements of their points of view.  The father stated,
"I was born in Europe.  My father was a strict man.  He beat his kids if
they did not mind.  At the age of eleven I started to work as an apprentice in
a machine shop, for I didn't want to go to school.  All boys there except
the rich ones begin to work.  I worked hard, but I didn't get no pay.  That is
the way things are there.  The boy works and learns a trade to make a living;
that is a good way, that is the only good way.  In America things are not
good for a boy.  He don't learn a trade, nothing else; just wants to bum
around.  It is good for a boy to work hard.  He is some good then and knows
lots when he gets big and can make his own living without stealing.  I had
to mind my father.  I couldn't do anything else; if I didn't I got beat up.
Many time I got beat up.  The father whips lots in the old country.  That is
the reason their kids mind and don't get into bad things.  He was the boss,
and I couldn't argue him.  Here in America the kids don't have to mind.
They only laugh at the father and fight him and play all day.  I came to
America nineteen years ago and worked in a machine shop all the time.  I

work hard and give my kids good to eat, clothes, and everything.  My oldest
kids are good, but Nick want to play ball and run around with Irish kids and
not work.  I say, 'Nick, work in your uncle's restaurant and learn the business,
for that is good for you.'  He just fights and curses and runs away.  I whip
him and send him to work, but he calls me bad names.  He fight all of us and
steals.  His uncle give him good chances in restaurant, but Nick no care; just
want to be thief and bum.  He worst boy I ever saw.  I can't make him be
good.  Won't you scare him hard, maybe have him arrested and put in jail to
scare him and make him work and not fight and not steal any more?"

Nick's mother is less articulate, but takes the same view as the father.
"I was born in Europe.  My father and mother poor people, no nothing to
eat and have to work hard.  I no went to school.  They keep me home and I
work hard with my brothers and sisters.  If I want to be bad my father lick
me hard and make me work harder.  We no never did much bad like kids in
America.  The father he boss and lick kids hard.  Over there when kid come
eleven years old they stop school and work for father and learn job.  All kids
give money to father and he spend it for them.  That is the right way when
children mind father and mother and know something and have something to
live on and for his wife and kids.  In America kids curse father and call him
'old man' and make faces at him and gets mad and fights when father licks
him.  That is not right.  Kids are bad and need licking, lots licking.  But
father can do nothing, just lick and lick, but kids only fight."

While the culture conflict between generations, as illustrated in
the case of Nick, is common among immigrant populations of the
slum areas, there are other aspects of family disorganization which
also involve loss of control over the behavior of children.  Absence
of a parent, dissension between parents, parental demoralization and
indifference to children, and even in some cases actual criminality
of parents may be found.  But except in the relatively uncommon
cases in which parents actually send their children to steal and to commit other delinquencies, such family disorganization is not necessarily
a direct impulsion to delinquent behavior.  In spite of severe conflict
with his parents, Nick did not engage habitually in the serious forms
of delinquency which lead into professional criminality.

**Positive Influences toward Delinquent Behavior.**—Criminal
behavior is as old as history, and has been transmitted culturally in
unbroken streams of tradition.  Tricks of burglary, robbery, and
theft known to ancient Roman criminals have been preserved in a
succession of European thieves, together with methods of cooperation and with rationalizations, and are preserved in underworld life
in America today.  Not only the more developed skills of the adult
professional criminal, but the elementary crimes of the beginning

juvenile delinquents are thus contained in a partially separate and seemingly immortal branch of culture.

In communities in which children are free of control by law-abiding elders, they do not automatically become delinquent, but they are easily subject to assimilation into the cliques of delinquent children that survive in such regions.  The boy gangs that may be found in the slums of all large cities are the cultural bearers of juvenile delinquency, and virtually all of the beginners acquire their first techniques in the normal process of adapting to the standard ways of the group.  Thrasher and Shaw, among others, have given close attention to the characteristics of these delinquent gangs, and have shown how they function to transmit patterns of delinquency.[10]

The most conspicuous fact about such delinquency is its thorough-going group character.  The gang boys possess a partially separate culture of their own, and delinquency is a part of this way of life.  Once the patterns are learned they are followed in a matter-of-fact spirit much as other standard ways are observed in any society.  Boys who are new to the behavior observe its universality, and soon partake of it in a simple spirit of social conformity.  There is no sense of guilt about the delinquency, though all of the boys know that the majority of citizens and officials regard it as wrong.  The attitude is comparable to that of soldiers, who, however sociable and sympathetic they may be to their own people, can kill enemies without experiencing any feelings of remorse.

The nature of this behavior, and the matter-of-fact participation, are revealed in accounts written by the boys themselves.  Shaw and McKay have published the following personal documents:[11]

As far back as I can remember . . . when I was about five years old . . . we were always playing tricks, going junking, and stealing from morning till night.  We would get some milk bottles in front of the grocery store and break them in somebody's hallway.  Then we would break windows or get some garbage cans and throw them down someone's front stairs.  After doing all this dirty work and running through alleys and yards, we'd go over to a grocery store.  There some of the boys would hide in a hallway while I would get a basket of grapes.  In the meantime, if my basket of grapes would be a handicap for me in running, I would throw it away.  The grocer, getting his grapes, would give up the chase, but on returning to the store he would find about ten baskets of grapes were missing.  He would cuss the day that he fell for the old, old trick.  Many times I would double back and

---

[10] Frederic M. Thrasher, *The Gang,* Chicago: University of Chicago Press, 1927. Clifford Shaw and Henry McKay, *op. cit.,* Ch. 6.
[11] *Op. cit.,* p. 117 ff.

reach the store before the keeper did, just to see the expressions on his face. When he'd see all the stuff gone that the other boys had taken sometimes he would spot me and give chase, but that was like a turtle trying to catch a rabbit because I was considered the fastest boy in the neighborhood. In the meantime the other boys had gone to our hangout and we would all meet there. While we were eating the grapes, we'd talk about the grocer and the trick we played on him. "Say, you guys, wasn't that an easy one and don't these grapes taste good? I've a mind to go and buy some more."

There were 12 or 15 boys in the gang and if it wasn't getting grapes, we'd be getting cakes out of the bakery by sticking long poles with nails tacked to the end and putting them through the windows. We'd stick the cakes and pull them out and eat them right there in front of the bakery. Sometimes we'd bang on the front door. The man would come out and chase us, while the other boys would go to the rear of the bakery and carry out a lot of cakes and pies. Then we'd climb on the doorsteps across the street and eat the things in front of the baker. . . .

I cannot remember when I first started stealing. It was as soon as I began to play around in the streets and alleys with my older brother and his pals. They were stealing junk, lead pipes from buildings in the neighborhood, shoplifting, stripping cars and strongarming drunks. We would go into a building and cut out the pipes and haul them to our hangout or a back yard. When we got a big pile we'd sell it to a junk man and then maybe break into his shed that night and steal it back and sell it to another junk dealer. . . .

I can't remember the first crime I committed. When I was a kid I used to fight. If you know anything at all about Chicago, you must understand that we were always fighting in that neighborhood. First we fought for the championship of our block. Next we fought to see which kid would be the king pin of his school. We had gang fights and had all kinds of trouble keeping leadership over the different neighborhoods.

In our block we shot craps for money. Some of the kids would steal from news stands on the corners, and others would steal money from their mothers' pocketbooks and from their sisters and brothers. Some of the kids bought candy with the money they stole, and some would buy cigarettes, chewing gum, tobacco, and snuff. These fellows were supposed to be tough guys. I never used chewing tobacco or snuff, but I smoked cigarettes when I was very young. . . .

I would play hookey from school with a couple of kids and go scouting for coal along the tracks of some railroad. We would get tired of picking coal from the tracks and would climb on some coal cars that were passing by and throw the big lumps of coal off and then later on pick them up and load our sacks. When we had all our sacks loaded we brought our wagons and put what we could in them. We then put a kid there to watch the rest of the coal until we came back. He was supposed to look out for the railroad detectives and if any of them came around the kid would tip us off and where the detective was located at, so we wouldn't get pinched. . . .

The first things that I remember are the good times I had playing with my chums in the prairie near the settlement and in the alley and street. We liked anything that had a thrill in it and it didn't make any difference what it was. Shooting craps, playing coppers and robbers, making raids on news stands, bumming from school, junking, snatching pocketbooks, and playing games in the prairie. I always liked anything that gave me a kick and was always looking for thrills.

I cannot remember when I started to steal, but it was about the age of seven. I always wanted to be in the midst of any excitement, whether it was stealing, breaking windows, breaking in schoolhouses and tearing up the furniture, or playing a ball game. Nothing thrilled me more when I was a kid than to try to break some windows in the settlement or school with the other fellows or help raid a fruit peddler cart and take all of his fruit, or make a raid on a junkman's wagon. Being chased by somebody was the thrill of the stealing. Sometimes the whole bunch would go into a store and one fellow would steal something, and while the man was chasing the fellow to get the stolen orange or apple the rest of us would raid the whole store, run out of the back door and into the alley.

We traveled all over the city by bumming rides on trucks or sneaking into street cars. We never paid for anything because the guys razzed you if you couldn't get by without paying. It was smart to sneak into a crowded street-car without paying. . . .

Almost all of my pals went robbing and stole everything that was loose. The older guys were called "big shots" because they were in the racket. They went in for big jobs like stealing cars and stickups. They looked down on us little punks but we heard their braggings of their doings. One would say, "Well, I pulled a job for a grand today." When asked how he did it he would say, "Oh, that was a soft job, I had that spotted for the past month, so I knew when to do the job." I listened to these "big shots" when they gathered on the corner or shot craps in the alley. They told stories of their doings that thrilled me.

While solitary delinquency does occur, particularly among children with abnormal personalities, it is a relatively rare thing among boys in the delinquency areas of the city. The first delinquency each boy commits is virtually always performed in the company of others, and at their instigation. There are no indications of inner motives of protest or revenge or of pathological wishes of any sort. The motives are clearly social in origin. Each boy is shown how to perform the action, and it is implied that he will not be able to associate with the gang unless he proves himself to be adept in their standard activities. Although these boys are from poor families and in many cases are undernourished, the hunger or need motives are not apparent in the early delinquencies. If food is stolen, the main reason is excitement or adventure. Some stolen food may be eaten, but all of the boys are explicit about the nature of the enjoyment. The typical statements are, "We did everything in the gang, anything for a thrill and excitement" or "It wasn't the eating of the food, but the taking of it, that was the fun." In the following example the degree of apprenticeship and of social motivation required is well illustrated:[12]

> Joseph started to walk past the fruit store, and as he came to a box of fruit he took some fruit and walked on. He motioned me to do the same thing. I would walk behind him and as soon as he would pick up a piece of fruit I was supposed to do likewise. It took lots of practice and he had to set many examples before I could at last gain enough courage to follow suit.
>
> Never a thought occurred to me as to whether it was right or wrong. It was merely an interesting game. The apple or orange didn't make as much difference as the getting of them. It was the taking them that I enjoyed. On subsequent afternoons we made it our habit to pass this fruit store many times and steal various things. I found as much fun and enjoyment in grabbing a potato or an onion as to grab anything else. The proprietor soon discovered what was going on and in his endeavor to curtail further depredations on his stock began to keep a sharp lookout for our approach and to watch us closely as we passed. This only made the game more interesting and it began to require real skill to get away with anything. Often after this he would chase us for a block or two in order to teach us a lesson but he never did. This is when it started to get real good, and you couldn't keep us away after that. The chases added spice to our little game.

Ambition and pride operate not to cause the boys to seek success in a legitimate career, but rather to advance to more skilled and remunerative crimes. In the gangs there is a strong disapproval of the boy who fails to grow up to the proper stages of a criminal career. The easy, low-income crimes are held in contempt by the more advanced criminals, and disdain for those who commit them is freely expressed:[13]

> In my racket, which was the auto racket, we wouldn't have a sneak thief of any kind. It takes guts to steal cars, and we wouldn't trust our lives with a low piker like a petty thief. The way we looked at it was that if a fellow didn't have enough guts and ambition to do anything but jackroll a poor old drunk man or snatch an old lady's purse he was a coward and no good in a hot racket. A sneak thief is looked down on by all real criminals and is not trusted. Stealing junk and vegetables is all right for a kid, but it's not a man's job. . . .
>
> Billy, a hardened criminal from Chicago, was eight years my senior, and was in [the prison] on a five-to-life sentence as a burglar and stick-up man. Billy took a great liking to me, mostly out of pity, and gave me instructions on how to get on in the prison, and how to get by with the police outside. He indelibly impressed two things upon my mind. First, never to trust anybody with your affairs in crime. You never know when a partner will rat

---

[12] *Ibid.*, pp. 223–224.
[13] *Ibid.*, pp. 247–248.

you if he gets into a close pinch and finds it an advantage to "sell his soul" to
the police. . . . Secondly, Billy chided me for petty stealing.  His idea was to
"do a big job or none at all."  Of course, he considered that I was just a kid
and wasn't old enough to "do a job" like him.  He figured that the dangers
and penalty were about the same whether you did a little job or a big one, so
you just as well choose the best.  Besides, he said that there was some satisfaction in doing a real man's job, and that it was easier to pay the penalty for
a big haul.  That sounded reasonable to me, so I thought if I ever pulled
another job it would be a big one or none.

On the other hand, the successful gangsters, the "big shots," have
the inspiring influence that heroes have to nondelinquent persons :[14]

How would you feel toward the King of England or the President of the
U.S.A.?  Well, the young crook feels the same toward the "big shot."  The
"big shot" is the ideal—the ultimate hope of every forward-looking criminal.
So he is held in awe and respect. . . .
Every boy has some ideal he looks up to and admires.  His ideal may be
Babe Ruth, Jack Dempsey, Al Capone, or some other crook.  His ideal is what
he wants to be like when he grows up and becomes a man.  When I was twelve
years old we moved into a neighborhood where there lived a mob of gangsters
and big crooks.  They were all swell dressers and had big cars and carried
"gats."  Us kids saw these swell guys and mingled with them in the cigar
store on the corner.  Jack Gurney was the one in the mob that I had a fancy
to.  He use to take my sis out and that way I saw him often.  He was in the
stick-up racket before he was in the beer racket and was a swell dresser and
had lots of dough.  He was a nervy guy and went in for big stuff.  He was
a mysterious fellow and would disappear sometimes for several days but
always came back.  He was looked up to as the leader of his mob and anybody
would be glad to be in his place.
He never talked to me about crime, but I secretly looked up to him for his
daring and courage.  He was what a fellow would call a big hit to me.  I
liked to be near him and felt stuck up over the other guys because he came to
my home to see sis.

When the assimilation of a delinquent boy into the gang and the
acquisition of the techniques of criminality are complete, it is usual
for a boy to find the life so much more fascinating than the daily
routine of school and play that he throws himself into this new life
with high enthusiasm.  In the typical case there is virtually no deterrent effect of arrests or commitment to institutions.  These interruptions are simply endured with a shrug, and in some cases
imprisonment increases both the prestige and the opportunity to
learn new techniques and to form new alliances.  Shaw has presented
a number of intensive case studies which illustrate this frequency in

[14] *Ibid.,* p. 249.

the face of activity of officials.  The following example is typical—
James Martin's official record contained 71 entries between the ages
of six years and eight months and twenty-four years and three
months.[15]  The first arrest occurred at ten o'clock at night, when
James was found by the police to be wandering in the streets with his
three brothers.  Within less than two years he had been reported or
arrested, in most cases for begging, but with an occasional truancy
or theft, as many as 26 times.  At the age of eight years and four
months he was arrested on a charge of burglary, which he admitted
to performing in the company of a boy nearly thirteen years old, and
was placed in a home for dependent children.  A year later he
escaped, and apparently returned at once to his former activities.
The following year contained 13 entries on his record, of begging
and burglary activities and three commitments and three escapes.
When, at the age of ten years and seven months he escaped again
from the home for dependent children, the superintendent asked
that he not be sent back there again.  The begging, burglary, commitment, and escape pattern continued with regularity until the age
of sixteen years and seven months, when James was arrested for
theft of an automobile.  He asked the judge not to send him back to
the reformatory, hoping for a chance to go free, but the judge sent
him to a different one, from which he escaped within the month.
The following month he was arrested again while attempting to steal
a car.  He was returned to the reformatory, from which he promptly
escaped again.  The pattern of automobile theft continued without
interruption other than brief commitments to institutions until at
the age of seventeen years and nine months he was arrested with two
boys of about the same age, again for car theft, and sentenced to the
state reformatory for a one-to-ten-year term.  He remained here
for six and a half years, and his release constituted the seventy-first
and final entry on his record.

Although the indications are that the enforcement machinery,
and the institutions for correction, can claim little credit for prevention of crime, it does happen that for some reasons a number of
delinquents drift out of criminal activity during their late teens or
early twenties and learn to support themselves by lawful employment.  Those who continue in crime, however, may specialize in
various directions.  Those with high intelligence and special skills
often undertake the practice of fraud or confidence games, or of
picking pockets.  Others may continue their comradeships of the

---

[15] Clifford R. Shaw, *Brothers in Crime*, Chicago: University of Chicago Press, 1938, pp.
23–34.

gang life and enter systems of organized criminal enterprise. For these adult criminals, predatory activity becomes a way of life, more interesting and rewarding than any other path that is open to them, and in fact the only way most of them know. There is a whole social organization in which they fit, and there is even in many instances a certain stability in their relations with the noncriminal community. The life-organization is built about criminality, and so criminals of this type are virtually inaccessible to influences of reform, particularly those conventional influences of courts and institutions. Severity of enforcement has the effect of driving them underground, or even away from a vicinity, or into different crimes, but seldom of effecting an abandonment of the criminal life.

## COOPERATION AMONG CRIMINALS

**The Lone Criminal and the Small Gang.**—Pickpockets and skilled thieves, confidence men, and other skilled specialists often work alone, or in twos and threes. No large organization is required, but some cooperation is in most cases useful. A pickpocket, for example, can work most effectively if he has two or three partners. One distracts the attention of the victim and another actually removes the wallet from the victim's pocket. One or more stand in such a position as to conceal the action and often to receive the wallet from the active thief, so that if an outcry is raised the actual thief can safely submit to search. The nature of the professional wisdom that is accumulated through experience in this skilled form of criminality is illustrated in the following statement by a young practitioner of the art :[16]

If the victim hasn't a pocketbook in his pants pocket or a roll of money, whenever the occasion may be, if it is on a train or at a convention, and the man looks prosperous enough, you would know that he had money some place. So it is then that they try what is known as an "insider," meaning that the man has his wallet in his inside coat pocket. This work, to take a poke from the inside pocket is altogether different. The "wire" (the actual pickpocket) has to be facing the victim. It is known to be a fact by pickpockets that if the victim will stand for what is known as a "throw" he can be beat. By a "throw" I mean putting a newspaper under the man's chin or by having a topcoat or short coat on your arm and holding that under his chin. The "stall" is directly behind the "mark" in the position otherwise occupied by the "wire." The "duke" man is standing behind the "wire," bracing him with his body, if it is on a subway or a car or train, and a newspaper or coat shades his hand

[16] Shaw and McKay, *Report on the Causes of Crime*, p. 238. See also E. H. Sutherland, *The Professional Thief*, Chicago: University of Chicago Press, 1937.

from working. He can unbutton three buttons on a "mark's" coat and reach in and take a man's pocketbook from inside his coat or even vest. The same thing goes for a stud or a diamond pin. I myself and several others that I have talked to find an "insider" as easy, if not easier, than a "prat poke" if the man will stand for a "throw." The average man, when you put a newspaper under his chin, he will brush it away, but anyone that will stand to have that paper laid under their chin can be beat, and most generally are.

Among pickpockets they always stay spread out, no matter where you may be. On a train, you stand by yourself, never "connecting." Working in a city, you never "connect," never stand talking to each other. While standing on a corner waiting for a street car to pull up, one of the mob sees a "dick." Then we have what is known as a "works office." He reaches up and pulls with his right hand on the lapel of his coat—gets one of his companions' eyes, and then does this. That signifies that there is "heat." The other fellow passes that to the third, and so on, and when the car pulls up, you get on that "natural"—that is, you don't work.

In some cities larger rings of pickpockets have been reported. One of these possessed a particularly effective defense organization. At a central office a person remained on duty at a telephone, receiving hourly reports from the active pickpockets. If any operator failed to report, it was assumed that he had been picked up by the police. Since it was a common practice of the police to move the thief from station to station without booking, to prevent his being found and set free on bond, the organization merely sent their own lawyers, armed with writs, on a station-to-station search. These lawyers were prepared to furnish bail, or, if the victim were present to make a complaint, to offer a settlement at once. By this means the organization was able to keep its members free and working, with little time lost in the jails.

The confidence men often work with one or more partners. There are a number of old and much-used techniques, which are employed with various refinements and adaptations. If a victim appears to be somewhat dishonest himself, having, in the criminal's phrase, "larceny in his heart," he may be persuaded to enter into an arrangement to cheat a third person who is in fact a confederate of the confidence man. There are also various devices, in most cases requiring skill, poise, and plausibility, used to persuade victims that by putting up a large sum of money they are certain to gain a fortune. For example, a man may, after friendship has apparently been well established, be allowed to wager on credit, and to win, on paper, a fortune. This, however, is to be made available to him only if he demonstrates that he would have been able to pay if he had lost, and so he is required to furnish a large sum of such "good faith" money, with which the confidence men then disappear.[17]

**The Organized Professional Underworld.**—A number of forms of criminal enterprise are handled more efficiently if they are performed by a large organization. During the period in which the national prohibition of liquor was in effect, the profitable manufacture and distribution of illegal beverages required an organization which was as extensive as many large business or industrial organizations. The organization of vice and gambling enterprises, of rackets, and of various other illegal activities tends to develop into a large-scale, centralized, and efficient affair. When fully developed, it becomes entrenched in the political and commercial life of the city and can be eradicated only with extreme difficulty. Its leaders possess wealth and often, through their connections with politicians and business leaders, a considerable amount of political power. Crusades sometimes remove a few key figures, or drive the organization temporarily underground, but the large body of personnel usually survives and rises again when conditions are favorable. The costs to society of such a criminal organization are incalculable, for they include not only the direct income from illegal enterprises but also the political inefficiency and the commercial waste that is involved.

Landesco has made an unusually thorough and close-range study of the underworld organization in Chicago during the 1920's, when that city was known over the whole world for its spectacular crime and corrupt politics.[18] His principal conclusions were: (1) The underworld organization of Chicago, containing interlocking activities in commercialized vice, gambling, bootlegging, and gang crimes

[17] The amount of erudition required to trap intelligent victims may be large, as is illustrated by a case known to the writer, in which the confidence man failed because of inadequate general knowledge. A Professor Blank received a research grant to visit some primitive peoples in a distant part of the world. The criminal, reading the newspaper publicity telling of Dr. Blank's prospective departure from a seaport, made his plan to obtain money from the professor's wife. A few days after the ship sailed, he placed in the mail box of the professor's family a telegram reading "MADE ARRANGEMENTS FOR SHIPMENT OF ITEMS COMING THROUGH TO YOU WITH MR. COLLINS AMOUNT TO BE PAID NINE HUNDRED AND TEN DOLLARS ARRANGE FOR CASH HOLD INTACT NO QUESTIONS ASKED HANDLE STRICTLY CONFIDENTIAL REGARDS. Signed JOHN BLANK MD.

The message was immediately recognized as a fake, for the professor was not a medical doctor and would never sign his name with an M.D. But any of a number of other errors would also have destroyed the apparent authenticity of the message. Not many professors make sudden and confidential deals and require their wives to furnish large sums of money in haste. Few husbands close their telegrams to their wives with "REGARDS" and with their full names. Telegrams are usually either telephoned or delivered by a messenger, and not merely placed in a mail box. This confidence man attempted a most difficult task: to defraud an educated person and to fabricate a message from a husband to a wife—a feat which very few criminals if any could have performed.

[18] John Landesco, *Organized Crime in Chicago*, Part III of The Illinois Crime Survey. Chicago: Illinois Association for Criminal Justice, 1929.

and enforcing its decrees by bombs, murder, and other violent and illegal methods, had a long continuity in the history of the city; (2) the extralegal government had no formal organization, but was held together in a kind of feudal system by powerful leaders, personal loyalties, alliances, and agreements, and even a code of morals; (3) during a 25-year period the overlordship of the underworld was held by only three men in succession, and there was a persistency of minor personalities in their organization, while during the same period the continuity of the police organization was far inferior— there having been thirteen chiefs of police, only one of whom served for a full term; (4) there was an extension of activities into fields ordinarily controlled by other interests, such as labor unions and the distribution of liquor; (5) there had grown up certain alliances and friendships between leading gangsters and politicians, involving mutual benefits at the expense of the public welfare; (6) the leading organizers of the underworld were able to avoid direct or detectable criminal actions, and were able in other ways to protect themselves, so that they enjoyed virtual immunity from prosecution.

A similar situation was found by Steffens to exist in most of the leading American cities some years earlier, and from time to time the outbreak of unusual activity, or the revelation of the workings of such an organization as "Murder, Incorporated" of New York City in the 1930's, shows the persistence of these patterns.[19] It is obvious that the large expanding industrial city in this country uniformly suffers from a disorganization that permits highly organized criminality to flourish. Not until the 1930's, when the depression slowed the growth of cities and ruined legitimate businesses, did reform crusades and drives against crime and political corruption in the cities show a tendency to endure beyond the few months of the brief flurry of public enthusiasm.

In Chicago the technique of bombing was developed into a specialty by an organization which made the bombs and which on order would undertake to bomb a home or a business establishment. Bombing was extensively used in the organization of rackets. In the typical situation, a series of independent business establishments, such as dry cleaners, would be visited by two or three rough-appearing men, who would inform the proprietor that an association was being formed, that his initiation fee and dues would be a certain amount, and that a specified scale of prices would be maintained. If he refused, a veiled threat was made, and in cases of persistent refusals, bombs would be thrown in the night to wreck the shop.

---

[19] Lincoln Steffens, *The Shame of the Cities.* New York: McClure, Phillips & Co., 1904.

The services of the criminal bomb specialists were also purchased for political violence and for commercial purposes. In 1928 the homes of United States Senator Charles S. Deneen and Judge John A. Swanson were bombed as a political maneuver in the primary elections of that year. The commercial rivalry, in 1922, between certain building trades unions and other workers and employers involved a series of bombings, presumably at the instigation of the unions, which sought to prevent the employment of labor under a scale known as the "Landis award." Another use of bombing was made in the course of an attempt, largely by real-estate interests, to check the expansion of the Negro district into neighborhoods previously occupied exclusively by white people. Houses newly occupied by Negroes and churches and commercial buildings purchased by them were bombed in a long series of incidents between 1918 and 1924. In 1919 alone there were 14 bombings of this nature on the southern fringe of the Negro area.

There is a tendency for all of the important illegal enterprises of a city to be consolidated into one unified organization, with a single head. The prostitution, gambling, bootlegging, and racketeering organizations may for a time be separate and even local in character, but ambition drives the bootleggers of one section of a city to expand their territory by encroaching on other districts or by driving out or taking over their rivals, until in time there is a single bootlegging organization in the whole city. It is during this period of rivalry that the gang wars flourish, involving many spectacular murders of gangsters by rival gangsters. Landesco classifies 30 incidents, in each of which one or more men were killed, in the "South Side Beer War" of Chicago between 1923 and 1927, and 27 incidents in the "West Side Beer War" during the same years.[20]

When the city-wide integration of bootlegging or other criminal enterprises is complete, gang warfare ceases and peace brings efficiency into criminal business. The integration process continues, however, until all of the important types of organized crime are gathered into one great organization with a single overlord. When this stage is reached, as it was in Chicago during the reign of Al Capone in the late 1920's, the more spectacular disorders no longer are common, and the underworld functions more quietly and efficiently, in the manner of a large business organization.[21]

---

[20] Landesco, *op. cit.*, pp. 924–928.

[21] Capone's organization, in his most prosperous period, is estimated to have taken in about $100,000,000 a year, of which he kept as personal income about $20,000,000. When it is taken into account that he paid no income tax until prosecuted by the United States, it is obvious that there were few higher incomes in the entire nation.

**Interrelations of the Underworld with Politics.**—It is virtually impossible to carry on stable operations in such enterprises as gambling, prostitution, and bootlegging without the knowledge of the police.  Where police organizations are honest and efficient from top to bottom, only a sporadic and disorganized criminality can be carried on.  One of the first necessities of the underworld is to prevent interference by the police.  This is done through bribery of the policeman on the beat, or through corruption of the police department up to the top, and even through relations with the political administration of the city.  It is not necessary that each individual policeman be bribed—the honest officer can be transferred to an outlying district or can be simply discouraged when the persons he arrests are invariably set free.  Corruption at the top is more efficient and is sought by the underworld.  Heavy tributes are paid to politicians and officials for protections from raids and from political interference.  The criminal organization may also render service at the time of elections, by frauds, intimidation of voters, and other devices which insure the election of those who cooperate with them.

**Interrelations with Business Interests.**—A stable underworld organization may find various ways to penetrate into the fabric of commercial life.  As in the case of the real-estate bombings, it may have services to render to desperate businessmen who believe they cannot meet their crises in any other way.  Employers have had occasion to employ gunmen of the underworld organization as strikebreakers or for the protection of strikebreakers in major industrial disputes, and union organizations, as mentioned above in the "Landis award" bombings, may also use gangster services in retaliation.

The boundary line between legitimate trade associations and labor unions on the one hand and criminal rackets on the other is not sharply defined.  The rackets are those organizations in restraint of trade which are forcibly organized by and for the benefit of a few officials, or even one head official.  Some of these have membership in large national labor organizations, however, and are on the fringe of respectability.  At the other extreme, however, are the extorting rackets which invade small businesses by violence and rule them with arbitrary power for maximum exploitation.  The gang racketeer then operates a business organization, using the same principles and methods that are employed by many labor unions, but solely for his own benefit.  In some cases businessmen have called upon gangsters for protection against racketeers—possibly the same ones.

When, in Chicago, an owner of a chain of dry-cleaning shops refused to join the association and was subjected to a series of bombings, window-smashings, and the like, he sought protection from Capone himself by presenting the latter with stock in his business. This device was successful, and his shops were no longer molested.

## INTERRELATIONS WITH NONCRIMINAL CITIZENS

Much of the income, and therefore the power, of organized crime comes from the unlawful patronage freely given by persons who do not support themselves by crime. The vast bootlegging organizations depended upon the purchases of many citizens who knowingly contributed to the strength of the criminal underworld, placing their immediate wants above the public welfare. The purchasers often rationalized their actions in the name of liberty or on the principle that the actions of one person are of little importance in the mass. The same is true of prostitution, organized gambling, black market activity, and other enterprises; none of these would have the size or power they have enjoyed without widespread patronage by the general public.

**Atlantic City—an Example of Entrenchment.**—Although large industrial cities are notorious for criminal organizations, perhaps the most thoroughgoing penetrations of the life of a city by such a machine are to be found in the resort cities which must be "wide open" if they are to attract crowds of pleasure-seekers. Cities like Reno, Las Vegas, Miami, and Atlantic City derive their major support from such sources and therefore concentrate on supplying the utmost in pleasures as well as on deriving high profits. The domination of Atlantic City by its local boss, Enoch L. Johnson, was brought to light by the investigations of federal treasury agents, who worked for five years before they could obtain his conviction.[22]

Johnson was the Republican boss of southern New Jersey, and the head of the illegal enterprises of Atlantic City. These enterprises constituted a larger business than the hotels—the principal legitimate source of city prosperity. In 1936, for example, while the Boardwalk hotels failed to make a profit and a number of banks failed, the illegitimate activities under Johnson's control took in $10,000,000, of which $250,000 went to his personal income.

Along with the control of this commercial life, Johnson also had complete domination of the local government—picking personally the county board and the judges, and through his brother, who was sheriff, controlling the choosing

[22] Jack Alexander, "That's How They Got Nucky Johnson," *Reader's Digest*, May, 1942, pp. 79–87. The following paragraphs are adapted from this article.

of jury panels and even the policemen in the city. Rival racketeers did not have to be fought by gang warfare—Johnson's police simply drove them out of town and cooperated in the workings of the local rackets. An under-sheriff, for example, did the work of collecting the tribute from the houses of prostitution—from each $50 a week in winter and $100 a week in summer. Even non-criminal operations brought tribute, for public road and building contracts contained provisions for alloting sums to Johnson.

Because of the size of Johnson's machine and the depth of its penetration into the life of the city and because of his wealth and ability to protect his underlings, the treasury agents had great difficulty finding anyone who would give evidence that Johnson received graft. Income tax prosecutions usually depend on ledgers and cancelled checks, but these were lacking in Johnson's case, for his racket industry operated on nonwritten orders and with trans-actions in cash. Johnson had no bank or brokerage account, and the gam-bling racket preserved no records of their business. Furthermore, there was a general conspiracy in the city to protect Johnson—his underlings accepted jail sentences rather than give information about him. The agents encoun-tered perjury, deceit, and jury-fixing and even found respectable citizens unwilling to cooperate with them. Only after five years of most thorough and difficult work and the conviction of 46 other persons, did the agents succeed in building up a case that secured a ten-year conviction for Johnson. Even this result was achieved only because of certain accidents of internal conflict within his organization. A reform administration eventually came into power and virtually closed down the vice and gambling activities of the city.

**Circus "Grifting."**—Sutherland, in an investigation of the minor forms of predatory cheating known as "grift," formerly an impor-tant source of revenue of small traveling circuses, states that these practices could flourish only under conditions of general cooperation by presumably noncriminal persons. The principal types of opera-tions of this grift consist of short-changing and sure-thing gambling. Sutherland states:[23]

As a behavior system circus grift has developed techniques, methods of fixing cases, a language, traditions, cooperations among grifters, business arrangements with the circus management and the public officials. The grifters form a somewhat exclusive group. The technique of execution of the racket includes mechanical gadgets or manual dexterity through which the outcome of the gambling is controlled so that the grifters take no chance.

Four elements must be present to make possible circus grifting on an extensive scale: a dishonest circus management, dishonest public officials, grifters, and victims who are either dishonest or anxious to get something for nothing. The decrease in circus grifting during the last forty years is due principally to the changed attitudes of the circus management because of

[23] E. H. Sutherland, "Circus Grift," *Bulletin of the Society for Social Research*, Dec., 1939, p. 11.

the increased size and permanence of a particular circus.  The mobility of the circus is an important factor in the four elements which have been listed.

**Prestige of Gang Leaders.**—Another form of public cooperation with organized crime is the granting of respectable status to gangsters who achieve wealth and power, and sometimes political importance.  When John Oberta, a young protégé of the leaders of a large Chicago bootlegging gang, undertook to campaign for political office, a testimonial banquet was given in his honor by a local post of the Veterans of Foreign Wars.[24]  A number of prominent racketeers and allied politicians were among the crowd of some 500 friends, relatives, and neighbors.  The leading speaker was Tim Murphy, who was prominent in Chicago politics.  He made no attempt to conceal or even to apologize for the gangster background of the guest of honor, but even referred to his own criminal history, evoking loud applause.  Murphy stated in this connection, "You probably know us from the newspapers.  I have been picked up, many's the time, for 'funny larceny' and concealed 'ideas.'  I even served three years in Uncle Sam's boarding house.  And I want to tell you that even there the men are 90 per cent good."

In the course of the festivities, further distinction was granted to Oberta by the president of the Post, who awarded him an honorary medal, against the background of a mounted guard and a fife and drum corps.  At the close of the affair a priest spoke briefly, referring to the good deeds of Oberta.[25]

In a discussion of the spectacular funerals of gangsters, characteristic of Chicago in the 1920's, Landesco points out that many of the obligations of prominent citizens and politicians come to the surface in connection with these ceremonies.[26]  When, for example, James (Big Jim) Colosimo, a powerful chief of the vice industry, was shot and killed in May, 1920, he was borne to his grave with great pomp.  Included in his cortege were many prominent politicians.  An alderman and a state senator were among the active pallbearers, and among the honorary pallbearers were eight more aldermen, three judges, several men who were later to become prominent judges, and two congressmen—Thomas Gallagher, and J. W. Rainey, who later became speaker of the United States House of Representatives.

---

[24] John Landesco, *op. cit.*, pp. 1008–1010.

[25] Landesco (*op. cit.*) added in a footnote that since the description of the banquet was written Big Tim Murphy had been assassinated.  After Landesco's footnote was written, it may be added, Oberta married Murphy's widow, and some time later Oberta himself was assassinated.

[26] *Ibid.*, Ch. 25.

Differing attitudes were shown in newspaper editorials of the day, but it was agreed that the funeral was an impressive and significant affair. The Chicago *Tribune* stated,

A cavalcade such as moved behind the funeral car of Caesar is to pay homage to the memory of the man who for more than a decade has been recognized as the overlord of Chicago's underworld. Such tribute from men set up to make and enforce our laws, to a man who in much of his life was a law unto himself, is more than the tribute of friendship. It is a tribute to power, regardless of the source or justice of that power. Jim Colosimo ruled his world. Out of his rule came sudden death to him. Raised to the throne of the half world, he was a maker and breaker of political aspirations. His methods were ruthless, considering the law only in so far as to avoid its penalties. The penalty which came to him was not of the law but of the kingdom which he had built up, yet it brings to his grave a concourse notable for its lights and shadows. It is a strange commentary upon our system of law and justice. In how far can power, derived from the life of the underworld, influence institutions of law and order? It is a question worthy of the thoughtful consideration of those dependent on and responsible for such trust.

The Hearst paper, the Chicago *American,* expressed itself with less sternness and with more sentimentality:

"No matter what he may have been in the past, no matter what his faults, Jim was my friend and I am going to his funeral." These and similar words were heard today from the lips of hundreds of Chicagoans. They were to be heard in the old Twenty-second Street levee district, over which Jim for so many years had held undisputed sway, they dropped from the mouths of gunmen and crooks, while many a tear ran down the painted cheeks of women of the underworld. They were heard from many a seemingly staid business man in loop skyscrapers and from men famous and near-famous in the world of art and letters, who had all mingled more or less indiscriminately with the other world, which walks forth only at night. All these classes, hundreds of each, will be present at the funeral.

Among other notable gangster funerals of this pattern were those of Anthony D'Andrea in May, 1921, "Nails" Morton in May, 1923, and Dion O'Banion in November, 1924. The O'Banion funeral was the most spectacular in some respects. The casket was said to have cost $10,000 and to have come from Pennsylvania in a special express car that contained it alone. Truckloads of flowers were sent, among them a basket of roses from Al Capone. Although funeral processions are ordinarily not permitted to pass through the central business district, O'Banion's cortege held up loop traffic for twenty minutes shortly before noon. Thousands of persons stood on sidewalks, fire escapes, and roofs to watch.  At his wake, though not at the funeral, were six judges and a prominent alderman.  After this occasion, newspaper publicity on the presence of prominent men had the effect of causing them to avoid further displays of this type, and subsequent gangster funerals took place without lavish display.

Living gangsters, however, continued to be regarded as celebrities, and numerous prominent and respectable visitors to Chicago sought introductions to the most famous of them, particularly Al Capone, whom they considered a fascinating rogue and, in view of his services in supplying liquor in a dry age, a useful one.

## Social Disorganization and Rural Criminality

The preceding discussion has shown the nature of the relation of professional crime to urban conditions.  There are also criminals who originate in rural or small-town areas, although they are less frequent in the population and do not produce such large and powerful underworld organizations.  Their criminality, while not a result of the same sequence of experiences as are undergone by urban delinquents and criminals, is connected with a situation that may be considered partial social disorganization.

Clinard has examined 60 inmates of an Iowa reformatory, all young white males from rural localities in the state.[27]  Their principal crimes—forgery, larceny, and auto theft—were in most cases characterized by crude and amateurish technique.  These criminals did not possess, as do urban professionals, the characteristics of a definite criminal social type defined by (1) an early start in criminal behavior, (2) progressive knowledge of criminal techniques and crime in general, (3) crime as the sole means of livelihood, and (4) a self-conception of being a criminal.  They were rather somewhat detached, mobile, and reckless young men who committed their crimes almost casually.  They referred to themselves as being "fast" and had come to engage in migratory labor, trucking, construction work, or work with a circus or carnival—occupations which loosened ties with the home community.  They enjoyed their emancipation, and some expressed a certain amount of pride in it.

Criminal techniques in each case were, as among professional criminals, acquired from more experienced persons, but among the rural criminals much less study was undertaken.  Clinard quotes one as follows:[28]

[27] Marshall B. Clinard, "Rural Criminal Offenders," *American Journal of Sociology*, Vol. 50, pp. 38–45.
[28] *Ibid.*, p. 41.

We couldn't thresh for a couple of days, and so I went to town the next day and ran across some boys, and they asked me if I wanted to go to a celebration with them. I said I didn't care, for I couldn't haul bundles because it rained. And that is how it started. They wrote some checks out that day. Then we went to another one the next day, and then I got started to write some. [He continued to forge checks until he was caught.] Well, I never did know how to write a check until the gang showed me how to write the checks, for they wrote most of them and cashed them, too, for I was a little bit scared to cash them. Then after a while I thought it was a pretty good idea of getting a little money on the side, so I wrote two or three of them and tried it out myself and they cashed them every time. So that is how I got all the information about writing checks.

Auto thefts are equally crude, and do not involve the special techniques employed by urban car thieves. Rural criminals do not have alliances with "fences" who receive the parts stripped from the car. The rural thief steals principally for his own use and simply drives the car away, not necessarily searching for any particular brand of car.[29]

The crime I done was a few miles from home. Perhaps I would have done it anywhere, as I had to be at a certain place at a certain time. I wanted to go to a dance, and my folks would not give me any money, so I really didn't care what I done. I had a car, but it was getting fixed and I didn't have the money to pay for it, so I stole my neighbor's car, just to show my folks I was not scared. I told them I was going to do it, but they didn't think I would. I have never thought about any crime as far as that goes. Like breaking into a place is way out of my line. I always was honest. My father is one of the best citizens. I consider him one of the best in that county. The boys I went with never stole anything. I never had any experience stealing cars. Guess it don't take any practice. When a boy I would use dad's car without asking him, but he didn't care. Sometimes he didn't like it very well, but he always got over it somehow.

It is obvious that the problem of reform of the rural offender is less difficult than is that of the urban professional criminal, whose entire experience and life-organization are constructed about a criminal livelihood. As one of the rural offenders put it, "The farm boy as a rule had just made a slip and intends to go back to the farm."

## WHITE-COLLAR CRIMINALITY

**The Extent of White-Collar Criminality.**—Sutherland has examined the nature of the crimes and of the offenders in cases where there are backgrounds not of slum life but rather of respectability

---

[29] *Ibid.*, p. 44.

in legitimate business or professional life.[30]   This "white-collar criminality," however, is causally related to social disorganization, and it is shown to involve great cost to society.  Sutherland finds that it is accounted for by "differential association"—the criminal acquires his patterns of behavior from the more experienced persons with whom he associates.

Within the classification of white-collar criminals are persons of various kinds.  Among these are the "robber barons" of the last century and similar characters of the twentieth century—Ivar Krueger, Alexandre Stavisky, Richard F. Whitney, Philip Musica alias F. Donald Coster, Albert B. Fall, and Harry F. Sinclair.

The most frequent forms of white-collar criminality consist of such things as "misrepresentation in financial statements of corporations, manipulation in the stock exchange, commercial bribery, bribery of public officials directly or indirectly in order to secure favorable contracts and legislation, misrepresentation in advertising and salesmanship, embezzlement and misapplication of funds, short weights and measures and misgrading of commodities, tax frauds, misapplication of funds in receiverships and bankruptcies." [31]

Sutherland cites many crimes that flourish in the medical profession, which he holds to be less criminalistic than some other professions.  Among the offenses of physicians are "illegal sale of alcohol and narcotics, abortion, illegal services to underworld criminals, fraudulent reports and testimony in accident cases, extreme cases of unnecessary treatment, fake specialists, restriction of competition, and fee-splitting."

In support of his contention that the costs of white-collar crime are probably several times as great as the financial costs of all the crimes which are customarily regarded as the crime problem (urban professional crime), Sutherland cites an embezzlement by an officer of a chain grocery store which involved in one year a loss of $600,000.  This amount was six times as great as the annual losses from 500 burglaries and robberies of the stores in that chain.  He further points out that "public enemies numbered one to six secured $130,000 by burglary and robbery in 1938, while the sum stolen by Ivar Krueger is estimated at $250,000,000, or nearly 2,000 times as much."  An investment trust, attracting investors by advertising the importance of diversification, actually had 75 per cent of the values in the portfolio in the securities of affiliated companies and lost for its investors an estimated $580,000,000.  A city sealer in Chicago,

---

[30] Edwin H. Sutherland, "White-Collar Criminality," *American Sociological Review,* Vol. 5 (1940), pp. 1–12.
[31] Sutherland, *loc. cit.*

granting immunity from inspection to stores which gave charity to his constituents, caused householders an estimated loss of $54,000,000 in two years. But Sutherland holds that, great as is this financial loss, the damage to social relations is more important. "White-collar crimes violate trust and therefore create distrust, which lowers social morale and produces social disorganization on a large scale."

**The Nature of the Violations.**—In most of these crimes, the nature of the dishonesty is either a misrepresentation of asset values or duplicity in the manipulation of power. In both of these types there is an indefinite borderline between ordinary commercial prac·· tice and improper or criminal behavior. Misrepresentation is respectable in the world of advertising; the truth that sells is at least "warm." Business interests have fought with indignation, using moral arguments, against government prohibition of various misrepresentations in advertising and labeling. The whole truth has never been considered a normal part of the intercourse between buyer and seller. No simple formula can define the distinction between what is to be permitted and what is unlawful; there are infinitely small degrees of variation along the borderline. At the same time there is a strong competitive pressure to push as far into the borderline as similar companies are doing. There is no clear point, in many cases of misrepresentation, at which one may say that the behavior suddenly passes from legal to criminal.

Duplicity, or double-crossing, as it is popularly known, is a situation in which a man holds two antagonistic positions, one of which is a position of trust. Sutherland illustrates this principle by reference to a football game in which the coach of one of the teams playing the game acts as referee. Corporation directors who, acting on inside information, purchase land which the corporation will need in order to sell it at a profit to the corporation, are committing this form of crime. In this case again, however, it is hard to establish a clear boundary between common practices that are not regarded as improper and illegal forms of duplicity. In modern complicated business structures a certain number of antagonistic functions are inevitable among businessmen, and there is no agreement about the propriety of certain degrees of such duplicity. In the spring of 1946 newspapers reported controversies regarding the right of a justice of the United States Supreme Court to take part in a case which was argued before the court by his former law partner and regarding the right of United States senators from cotton states to speculate in cotton futures when, by virtue of their committee positions and their official influence, their public remarks affected the fluctuations of cotton prices.

**Conditions Favoring White-Collar Criminality.**—The zone of life in which white-collar criminality flourishes, then, is that in which the commercial life is complex and in which definitions of proper behavior are impossible to state in perfectly clear terms. The condition which produces the pressure that drives men into such illegal behavior is the intensity of competition. Presumably most physicians would prefer to obey the regulations of the profession and the laws of the states and refrain from such practices as fee-splitting. In depression years, however, when they like nearly all other income-earners suffer reduced income, there is a desperate temptation on the part of some to crowd close to the borderline of such regulations. The principle can be violated in such slow and easy stages that a sudden moral crisis of decision may be avoided. Physicians may, without explicit agreement, fall into the custom of calling in one another for consultations, the necessity of which may be increasingly questionable. By gradual stages such reciprocity may develop into outright fee-splitting. Sutherland mentions a report that two thirds of the surgeons in New York City engaged in fee-splitting in the 1930's.

The close resemblance of white-collar criminality to legal and approved standard practices and the competitive pressure to push against the borderlines allow the offender to retain, in the eyes of many who experience the same competition, a respectable status. Businessmen often feel sympathy with a white-collar criminal who is caught in actions which are closely similar to those they themselves are performing. They also are often aware that the same kind of competition operates on such moral leaders as presidents and athletic directors of colleges and universities and impels many of these officials to tolerate or even actually encourage evasions of intercollegiate agreements regarding the eligibility and the amateur status of athletes.

John R. Tunis, in an exposé of such evasions in American institutions of higher education, reveals the close similarity of such behavior to white-collar criminality.[32] The competitive pressure is present in the necessity of maintaining football gate receipts to support large athletic programs, to pay for mortgaged stadia, and, in some cases, to contribute to the general funds of the institution. During the prosperous period of the 1920's a large number of edu-

---

[32] John R. Tunis, "What Price College Football?" *American Mercury*, Oct., 1939.

cational institutions expanded their athletic programs and built large stadia and field houses in order to enter the big business that was developing in intercollegiate competition.   Tunis states that the foot-ball budget of a university in the "Big Ten" conference of the Mid-West ran to $212,000 a year in the late 1930's.   Successful teams are necessary if this budget is to be met.   In another case a university paid almost $100,000 yearly for interest on its stadium alone and was therefore committed to making a large profit.   Winning teams are also virtually necessary to some institutions which depend for their income on the state legislatures, which are often more favorably inclined if their university has a winning football team.   Even endowed institutions are subject to pressure from alumni, who con-tribute large sums each year and who express themselves insistently on the importance of athletic victories.   Administrators are therefore under great pressure to win, and, since they compete against institu-tions equally bent on victory, the necessity of making great efforts is continuous and increasing.

The problems of defining eligibility and amateur status of players are similar to those involved in business and professional life.   While rules may be written in explicit form, possibilities of evasion and of gradual crossing of the borderlines are many, and progressive viola-tions under the pressure of competition are extremely difficult to control.   A rule of the "Big Ten" conference, for example, provided that no scholarships, loans, or remissions of tuition should be awarded on the basis of athletic skill, and that no financial aid should be given to students by individuals or organizations, alumni or other, with the purpose of subsidizing them as athletes or of promoting the athletic success of a particular university.   These provisions are evaded in numerous indirect ways, however, and in some institutions the pretense of adherence to them almost entirely falls away.   One device for evasion is the summer camp, often operated by a football coach, in which players are employed as counselors but allowed to spend most of their time practicing football.   Other jobs on the campus often involve only nominal duties, such as functioning as watchman at the stadium one night a week, or some light work in a dormitory.   Loans are often extended with no effort at collection, indirectly constituting salary payments.   Enthusiastic alumni, work-ing through fraternities, often find inconspicuous ways of paying the tuition and other expenses of athletes who show promise.

Eligibility rules also require that a member of a college athletic team be a bona fide student, which usually involves a year of resi-dence before competing (to discourage tramp athletes who shift from college to college in search of higher income) and the maintenance of a minimum standard of grades.  Professors in some institutions have been subjected to pressure to award passing grades to football stars.  Where this is not feasible, special courses are sometimes available, taught by easy-going faculty members who are known to require little work, to give high grades, and to favor athletes.  Institutions having departments of physical education normally have little difficulty with eligibility rules regarding grades, for it is not usually considered that courses in "Principles and Practices in Football Coaching," "Advanced Swimming and Life Saving," and "Organization and Administration of Camping Activities" have either the difficulty or the educational value of courses in mathematics, languages, or sciences.  Often free tutoring is available to the few athletes who do happen to find it difficult to pass their courses.

Under such conditions and using various methods of evasion, many educational institutions have eventually drifted into an almost purely commercial activity, bidding for athletes, maintaining them with salary, easing their studies, and often preparing some of them by "farming" them to preparatory schools at the expense of the college—all this in spite of solemn agreements in writing.  It is virtually impossible for a college president to be ignorant of such practices in his institution, though it is usual for the actual dealings to be handled by a minor athletic official so that the presidents and the athletic directors may maintain a fiction of innocence.  The analogy with white-collar criminality is very close.  Football is referred to by Tunis as "an unsavory racket" which favors "the few with brawn rather than the millions who need instruction" and which "determines the conduct of college presidents, deans, and administrative officers."

**Demoralizing Effects of White-Collar Criminality.**—The temptations arising from scarcity of various goods during the second world war increased the prevalence of rule-violation and lawbreaking among the general population.  Rationing and price control created enforcement difficulties by defining as wrong certain practices which had not hitherto been disapproved in the mores.  Governmental agencies approached the problem of regulation with extreme caution and perhaps by this fact lost the chance of getting adequate control.[33]  It is clear that, in many respects, the problem got out of hand.  For

[33] A journalistic account is available in *Wartime Racketeers*, a book by two Washington newspaper men, Harry Lever and Joseph Young (New York: G. P. Putnam's Sons, 1945).  A sociological study has been made by Marshall B. Clinard, who served in the Office of Price Administration for a period.  See "Criminological Theories of Violations of Wartime Regulations," *American Sociological Review*, Vol. 11, pp. 258–270, June, 1946.  A volume by Clinard on the O.P.A. and the black market is in preparation.

example, during the late war and early postwar period, a major part of the supplies of gasoline, meats, butter, and other products were in certain areas being sold outside of legitimate markets, in spite of continuous efforts at enforcement.  As late as 1946, a raid on a black market in automobiles in the village of Leesville, South Carolina, brought to light an organization that had handled some $100,000,000 worth of business, in which a typical sale was $2,150 for a new Ford coupé.

It is impossible to measure the extent of general cheating practices, but there are indications that such practices are increasing and that they are penetrating into new types of activity.  During 1946 and 1947 there were news stories of cheating by college students,[34] corruption by a United States congressman, and many other forms of general corruption.  In some areas the black market had so disrupted the legitimate market that money became an inadequate means of obtaining goods.  There were news reports of the required ways of "playing the angles" to keep supplied with daily wants.  To obtain a car, one had to trade in a used car for something like $9.00; to buy a bottle of Scotch whiskey it was necessary to buy a quantity of wine, gin, or rum.  Housewives organized reporting systems to inform one another of the arrival of chain-store trucks, in order to be first in the lines.  Tipping and gift-bestowing became popular methods of staying on good terms with butchers.  Many transactions were a kind of barter—a car could be traded to obtain an apartment, and vice versa. A butcher was reported to have entered the construction business, trading meat for unpurchasable nails, flooring, and plumbing fixtures.  Other media of exchange were football tickets, good liquor, soap, sugar, and automobile batteries.

It is the prevalence of such practices among the general public that supplies men like Capone with such a rationalization as this one (attributed to him in earlier years) : "All I ever did was to supply a demand. . . . They talk about me not being on the legitimate. *Nobody's on the legit.* You know that and so do they."[35]

When minor graft and bribery become virtually universal and are carried along for a number of years, they eventually become an established part of the social organization—a sort of legitimate graft.  This is illustrated by the practice of the "squeeze" in China, which involves behavior which would presumably be subject to crim-

---

[34] A study revealed that 53 per cent of the students at one university cheated in examinations.

[35] Capone's illegitimate business, however, was no small menace, for it involved some 500 murders.  Likewise, the illegitimate business of such persons as wartime black market slaughterers endangered the population by wasting dangerously short supplies of by-product materials, including many essential drugs.

inal prosecution in the United States, but which has become a "right" among the Chinese. Similarly, in parts of Mexico, including Mexico City, there has grown the practice of *mordida* (bite), which can be characterized as "more of a custom than a crime." [36] In this action, a policeman extracts a small bribe from minor violators. A part of the bribe may be turned over to superiors, if the latter are aware of the action. At certain traffic intersections the police have been expected to turn over some 20 to 30 pesos a day to superiors, thus requiring them to "bite" at least ten drivers at two pesos each before they could begin to make money for themselves. Tourists are, by stricter regulations, exempt, for they are too important to Mexico to be offended in this fashion.

Other government officials also extract the *mordida*. Hayner mentions the practice among inspectors, whose requirements may run as high as 1,000 pesos. Even office secretaries have in some cases learned to require a fee from a visitor who needs a conference with the chief. In general the *mordida* may be said to be a well-established and deeply rooted practice which would not be easy to eliminate.

## Summary

Criminality is generated in a collective process. The kinds of criminal practices which form the basis of a professional career are seldom invented but are the products of processes of collective invention which began in prehistoric times. The delinquents of each new generation learn the techniques and the rationalizations of crime and acquire from more experienced criminals the motivation for a career of crime. While a portion of the criminal population is mentally abnormal or deficient, the majority are defective in neither way, for no personal abnormality is required in the processes that generate criminality. The process is social in character and psychologically normal.

The essential feature in the social disorganization that underlies criminality appears to be failure of the normal mechanisms of social control. In a modern secular civilization this control is not as strong as in isolated and homogeneous primitive or peasant societies, or as in such religious societies as those of rural Quebec or the early Shaker or Mormon communities. In cities, and particularly in urban slums, the weakening of family and neighborhood controls may be so extreme as to constitute complete failure. In such a situation

---

[36] Norman S. Hayner, "Crimogenic Zones in Mexico City," *American Sociological Review*, Vol. 11, pp. 428–438, Aug., 1946.

children who have not already acquired life-organizations based on habits of conventional behavior are, though not inevitably delinquent, at least easily subject to the positive influences of the boy gangs, the "fences," and the organized rewards of the underworld criminal organizations.

The weakened defenses of modern society are also revealed by the occurrence of rural criminality. The typical offender appears to be somewhat detached from parental and community influences, so that a mere example of successful forgery is often enough to induce him to try it with a casual or matter-of-fact attitude toward the outcome.

Generalized confusion of standards in our changing contemporary society is also a factor in the encouragement of criminal behavior. The underworld organization of professional criminals is provided with important support by the noncriminal citizen who vigorously insists upon his right to consume prohibited beverages or drugs, to engage in illegal gambling, to purchase goods in evasion of rationing and price regulations, and the like. "Rights" of different kinds and of different origins have come into conflict, and no unified code is accepted by the mass of the population. In this confusion it becomes easy to make and to rationalize moral decisions on the basis of individual interest. In the case of white-collar criminality, such decisions are particularly prevalent because of the competitive pressure which makes partially true the rationalization that "everyone is doing it."

The record of various efforts at prevention and treatment of delinquency and criminality is for the most part one of complete failure. There have been cases of criminals who have been reformed by persistent and skilled effort, but the amount of attention that is apparently necessary to this process is so great that there is little possibility of a general solution to the crime problem by direct application of such individual skills. The histories of recreational programs for the prevention of delinquency cannot be interpreted without technical analysis. Where such analysis has been carried out, little justification has been found for the claim that these programs succeed in their purpose.[37] The penal institutions have a record that clearly indicates failure to reform, revealing rather a tendency to educate inmates in advanced techniques and to stimulate cooperation among criminals and a spirit of revenge against society.

---

[37] The most thorough study is that by Frederic M. Thrasher, "The Boys' Club and Juvenile Delinquency" (*American Journal of Sociology*, Vol. 42, pp. 66–80, July, 1936). Thrasher found that a new and expensive club in New York City not only was unimportant as a factor in the prevention of delinquency, but that the boys showed a tendency to be even more delinquent during their membership than either before or after.

## SELECTED REFERENCES

Clinard, Marshall. "Rural Criminal Offenders." *American Journal of Sociology*, Vol. 50, July, 1944.
Hayner, Norman S. "Variability in the Criminal Behavior of American Indians." *American Journal of Sociology*, Vol. 47, Jan., 1942.
Hayner, Norman S. "Social Factors in Oriental Crime." *American Journal of Sociology*, Vol. 43, May, 1938.
Landesco, John. *Organized Crime in Chicago*. Part III of the Illinois Crime Survey. Chicago: Illinois Association for Criminal Justice, 1929.
Reckless, Walter C. *Criminal Behavior*. New York: McGraw-Hill Book Company, Inc., 1940. Ch. 3, "Social Disorganization and Crime."
Shaw, Clifford R. *Juvenile Delinquency and Urban Areas*. Chicago: University of Chicago Press, 1942.
Sutherland, Edwin H. *Principles of Criminology*, revised edition. Philadelphia: J. B. Lippincott Co., 1947.
Taft, Donald. *Criminology*. New York: The Macmillan Co., 1942.
Thrasher, Frederic M. *The Gang*. Chicago: University of Chicago Press, 1927.
Yuen, Ching Yueh. "Crime in Relation to Social Change in China." *American Journal of Sociology*, Vol. 40, Nov., 1934.

# Chapter 7

## THE VICES

### THE NATURE OF VICE

Most of the forms of behavior which constitute the vices are not in themselves necessarily to be regarded as abnormal. The abnormality lies in excessive use—in the tendency to depend upon vices for the principal satisfactions of life, and to be enslaved by them. Conventional and normal sources of satisfaction become for some reason unavailable, so that temporary stimulations or comforts are sought for diversion, for relief from boredom or suffering. They enslave partly because the relief is only temporary, and because the habit of seeking stimulation in such temporary methods allows the person to abandon his efforts to achieve a satisfying life on a more conventional and constructive basis.[1]

Human happiness is not yet subject to precise definition, nor is it possible to arrange, in the order of their power to satisfy, the various pleasures available to human beings. It does seem clear, however, that ordinary physiological pleasures—eating, drinking, sexual pleasure, and the like—are not in themselves sufficient to provide a happy and satisfactory life. Where opportunities are available for persons to engage in complex projects, extending over periods of time, involving cooperation with other persons, and yielding demonstrable results at the end, the preferences of most persons are for these, and physical pleasures usually take a minor place. Indulgence in sensory stimulations in such cases tends to occupy spare or leisure time, and is not allowed to interfere with the main business of life.

---

[1] There is not general agreement among sociologists on the definition of vices. One point of view is that certain forms of behavior are classified as vice only because of general disapproval. In this view, the vices of today may become the conventional behavior of tomorrow. To speak of vices at all is seen as mere expression of arbitrary value judgments. It is the argument of sociologists holding another view, however, that vice may be objectively defined as behavior which has strong appeal, has some tendency to be habit-forming to the point of enslavement, and reflects and perhaps in some cases partly causes a condition of detachment from social integration and life-organization. The fact that some of the forms of vice, such as alcohol and drug addiction, may be destructive of health is incidental to the definition, but not without significance in its effects on social organization. Viewed from this standpoint, vice is an objective concept apart from conventional value judgments, and remains vice even if it becomes convention—as had drug addiction in China.

Projects involving great importance and high intrinsic interest may even so dominate the lives of the persons undertaking them that such persons regard physical pleasures and even necessities as bothersome competition for time and attention.  Even the normal comforts of eating and sleeping may be neglected—sometimes to a harmful degree—in the periods when rapid and absorbing progress is under way.  Edison, for example, begrudged the time conventionally taken for sleeping, and would often make out with brief cat naps in his laboratory, taking up his work again as soon as he felt a little refreshed.  The Curies pursued their radium research with extreme indifference to comforts and pleasures, and undoubtedly with danger to health.  There is no reason to think that such disregard for ordinary pleasures indicates abnormality—such absorption is not uncommon even in the lives of ordinary persons during the periods when their lives are fully occupied by activity in complex and interesting projects.

In other circumstances, when there is no integrated activity to claim the attention and to make time pass rapidly, the aimlessness of life becomes oppressive and the minor stimulations achieve a greater importance.  Old people, for example, who have completed their responsibilities and have no further work to occupy their time find the periods between meals to be dull intervals that are largely occupied with impatient thoughts of the next meal to come.  In residential hotels populated by pensioned widows, such persons may be seen daily fidgeting in their chairs, edging toward the doors of the dining room some minutes before they open.  Unemployed persons, unused to inactivity, often experience an almost desperate necessity to kill time by gambling, drinking, or other diversions of the kind.  Childless married women who reside in apartment hotels and who are without employment or housework often find relief from their boredom in alcohol, eating, gambling, motion pictures, and such activities.

These activities become vices when the person becomes dependent upon them.  It is in the nature of such pleasures that the gratification is of very short duration and that their power to stimulate diminishes, so that ever increasing amounts are required in order to provide constant pleasure.  Some of them are also in varying degrees incapacitating in their effects, so that opportunity for satisfaction from normal organized activities becomes always more remote.  A vicious circle thus involves the person, and the possibility of escape from such habits continually declines.

## ALCOHOLISM

**Motives for Consumption of Alcohol.**—The drinking of alcoholic beverages is a practice followed over most of the world and during all of the centuries of written history. Drunkenness and addiction do not, however, occur wherever alcohol is consumed. The use of table wines in France and other European countries and of beer in Germany has not been associated with widespread tendencies to addiction. The Jews have used wine for many centuries, but have successfully maintained a tradition of moderation, as have many other peoples. Excessive consumption, therefore, is not inevitable in the use of alcohol but requires some explanation other than the nature of the drug.

The motives for taking alcoholic beverages vary with the person and the social situation. A sip of wine is a routine requirement in many religious ceremonies, and no personal preferences are required to account for the conformity with such customs. There are other ceremonial usages which are equally routine and arbitrary—the drink a host extends to an arriving guest, which can scarcely be declined without rudeness; the toasts at formal dinners; and the stirrup cup of the hunter. Although an addict may enjoy drinks taken in connection with such occasions as much as he does a solitary drink, other persons may have no motive except the normal desire to conform to the folkways.

Like the first cigarette of the teen-age youth, the first alcoholic drink is often merely an effort to assume a more adult status and may involve no sense of physical pleasure at all. During the period of national prohibition in the United States, the quality of the intoxicating beverages available to most persons was so poor that, except for true addicts, the pleasure of drinking had to be simulated. It was fashionable in some circles to take a swallow of raw gin or of a mixture based on laboratory alcohol, and to control the grimace, substituting an expression of pleasure and an exclamation over the "delicious" taste.

There are various other social occasions which virtually require the taking of alcohol—ordinary conviviality, business courtesy, entertainment of buyers, and the like. In many situations it is difficult to avoid taking a drink without causing offense to other persons. Such social pressure is a large factor in the consumption of alcohol, although it cannot be said to be a general cause of either intoxication or addiction.

Some of the motives for drinking are more individual in character. Persons with poor appetites sometimes acquire the practice of taking a small amount of liquor before a meal to stimulate desire for food. There are others who use liquor to get relief from exhaustion after hard work, or from physical discomforts and pains. In some such cases a minor form of addiction may be acquired unwittingly. Many of the proprietary remedies of the pre-prohibition age achieved their relieving effect largely through the unacknowledged inclusion of alcohol as a principal ingredient. It is probable that a considerable number of women in those times became mild alcoholics as a result of becoming dependent upon a popular remedy for periodic discomforts.

**The Nature of Addiction.**—None of the above motives, however, accounts for the craving exhibited by the extreme addict. The latter is truly a slave to liquor and devotes a major part of his attention to the pursuit and consumption of it. He does not seek the milder beverages but demands those with high alcoholic content, placing potency above quality in his preferences. He deliberately undertakes to become intoxicated, and he seeks this state often. While intoxicated he dreads and postpones his emergence from the state of drunkenness. His goal appears to be to make the periods of intoxication as frequent and as long as possible, and to keep the sober periods at a minimum. His desperation to maintain this condition is such as to allow him to abandon other considerations that are important to normal persons—his career, his reputation, his obligations to his family, and his moral integrity. The addict of long duration becomes indifferent to his appearance, to his long-term welfare, and to ordinary standards of conduct. General deterioration of personality and mind eventually set in. Medical warnings, even of certain death if the behavior is continued, are in many cases disregarded.[2]

The motives of the addict are obviously individual in character—he does not demand company in his drinking. Ordinary relief from pain or exhaustion will not account for the desperation of the behavior of the addict. It is in fact probable that the motives in the early and in the advanced stages of the process are not the same.

An indication of the possible motive for the beginning of addiction is suggested by the nature of the principal psychological effect of alcohol. The drug acts as a depressant on the nervous system, although there is a period in which the subjective feelings are those of stimulation. The effect is gradual, and the nervous processes of

---

[2] Although a work of fiction, the case study of a drunkard in Charles S. Jackson's *The Lost Weekend*, New York: Rinehart & Co., Inc., 1944, is so sensitive and accurate that it is possibly the best description of its kind currently available.

highest complexity are the first to be affected. The lively process of self-consciousness, involving the interaction of imagination of appearance to others, of their reciprocating judgments, and of one's own reactions—as described in Cooley's "looking-glass self" concept—is early subdued. As a result the person feels free and confident and has a sense that his conversation is more entertaining and his humor is more effective than he does when his faculty of self-criticism is functioning. It may be added that, when sober persons are present, they do not always share this judgment of the high quality of the alcoholic's conversation.

It is probably this dulling of the more lively processes of thought that appeals to persons who are in the process of becoming addicted. There are unpleasant or unbearable thoughts—intrusive worries, keen embarrassment, attacks of conscience—that cannot easily be thrown off. Persons differ in their ability to resolve such mental problems. Those who are able to think their way through to some satisfactory conclusion would not ordinarily find the thoughts as painful as would those who face persistent and endless mental torment. For this latter type of person, escape through forgetfulness is a tempting relief. If the obsessions are of a mild character, harmless diversions such as movie attendance, recreational activity, minor gambling, and the like may be sufficient to occupy the mind, but the more intrusive thoughts can be temporarily eliminated only by a drug. During the period of intoxication alcohol offers relief from worries or attacks of conscience, and it is therefore a welcome form of escape.

The temporary character of the relief may itself be one of the factors in addiction. Nothing automatically takes place during the intoxication to solve the problems that underlie the obsessive thought —on the contrary, by virtue of having run away from the problems the alcoholic is further than ever from a solution. He is weakened in more than one sense by having taken the path of the drug; when his unpleasant thoughts return, they are made all the more unbearable by this realization. If alcohol offered the most convenient relief the first time, it increasingly becomes virtually the only possible relief, and so the addiction habit takes ever firmer hold.

Another probable factor in the more advanced stages of addiction is dread of the discomforts associated with the emergence from a prolonged spell of drunkenness. The experienced alcoholic knows, even while in a state of partial intoxication, that acute distress, sickness, and mental depression await him in the hangover period to come, and in order to postpone this phase he prolongs his drunken-

ness as much as possible.  This means that, when the drunken spells
do take place, they tend to be intense and protracted and to have an
accelerating effect on the processes of addiction and deterioration.

**Causes of Addiction.**—The literature on the general theory of
alcoholic addiction is at present in an incomplete and confused state.
The early enthusiasm for a hereditary explanation of alcoholism has
been declining, and in its place there have arisen a number of psychological theories which account for the behavior on the basis of such
traits as homosexual inclinations or mother attachment.[3]  There is
also an increasing interest in the study of social factors associated
with alcoholism.

It has long been observed that, at least in the United States, there
is an association of alcoholism with poverty.  Drunkenness among
the wealthy is not unknown, but the large mass of addicts is found
among the lowest income classes.  In the city of Chicago, the spatial
distribution of the residences of persons whose deaths were attributed to alcoholism shows an extreme concentration of cases in the
central slum areas.  The distribution of cases of alcoholic psychoses in
the same city is virtually identical.  An examination of the economic
status of all of the types of mental disorder in the city reveals that
alcoholic psychoses come from the communities with the lowest
monthly rentals.[4]

The Chicago data reveal that most of the first admissions for
alcoholic psychoses occur at an older age than for many of the common mental disorders.  The majority are committed between the
ages of thirty-five and sixty-four and the peak age group is that
from forty-five to fifty-four.  This suggests that it takes a number
of years of drinking to reach the degree of deterioration that calls for
commitment to a mental hospital.  A study in New York State furnishes data which agree with such a conclusion.[5]  From a statistical
examination of over 1,500 first admissions in 1936–37 it is possible
to construct a description of the experience of the typical patient
with an alcoholic psychosis, using modal figures from each tabulation.  Since more than three fourths of these patients are males, the
typical addict will be referred to as a man.  The figures show that
he acquired his drink habit sometime around the age of twenty-four

[3] For a recent careful psychological explanation, see Harriet R. Mowrer, "A Psycho-
cultural Analysis of the Alcoholic," *American Sociological Review*, Vol. 5, pp. 546–557,
Aug., 1940.
[4] R. E. L. Faris and H. W. Dunham, *Mental Disorders in Urban Areas*, Chicago:
University of Chicago Press, 1939, pp. 112–113.
[5] Horatio M. Pollock, *Mental Disease and Social Welfare*, Utica, N. Y.: State Hospitals
Press, 1941, Ch. 14.

and, since his first admission came at about the age of forty-six, he had experienced 22 years of steady drinking. Hard liquor furnished the large part of his consumption, with whisky by far the favorite beverage. His drinking had been regular rather than periodic, and intoxication had occurred once a week or oftener, but, since week ends were the principal times for this, there was in most cases no great loss of time from employment.

The Chicago study earlier referred to found indications that strong social integration may be an important factor in protecting persons against alcoholism. In two of the communities of low-income population there are large numbers of Russian Jewish people. Although these people contribute their quota of cases to the schizophrenic rates, they include far less than the expected number of persons with alcoholic psychoses. One of the communities had only one alcoholic psychosis patient in 30 who was Jewish, and the other community one in 37. This tendency of the Jewish people to abstain more than the general population from intensive alcoholism has also been noted elsewhere.[6]

The Chicago data further indicate a relationship of high alcoholic psychosis rates to social instability. There is a negative correlation of the psychosis rates in the various urban areas with rates of home ownership, and a positive relation with the percentages of lodging-house and hotel residents. There is also a positive relation with the percentages of foreign born and Negroes in the population. These groups are new to city life and are only partially assimilated to the conditions of modern industrial civilization. The rates are particularly high for white persons who reside in areas predominantly occupied by Negroes, and for Negroes living in areas largely inhabited by whites—suggesting that detachment from one's own people and consequent social isolation may be a factor in the personal disorganization of alcoholism.

It is not possible to make a confident interpretation of the relation of alcoholic addiction to low-income populations, but a few possible mechanisms may be suggested. It may be that difficult conditions of living furnish a more constant source of worry than is found among persons of higher incomes. Not only the lack of money but also the responsibilities of family life are matters of concern, for approximately two thirds of the patients are married, and presumably many have the large families characteristic of their income group.

At the same time the intellectual equipment of these people is relatively low, so that the ability to think through and solve problems

---

[a] See Faris and Dunham, *op. cit.*, 114.

is more likely to be deficient than would be the case among persons of higher income and education. It may be that the relatively extra-verted Irish, for example, tend to develop far less of the mental power to solve personal problems than do the Jewish peoples, with their traditions of learning and intellectualism. If so this would partially account for the contrast between the extremely high rates in the areas of Chicago populated by the Irish immigrant groups and the low rates for the Russian Jewish populations.

It appears highly probable that some personality factor is involved. It may not be necessary to search for mother fixation, homosexuality, or other deep-seated complexes. The trait of the alcoholic is that he runs away from his problems rather than accept responsibility for their solution. There are other forms of escape also—migration, suicide, simple dependency—but perhaps these are also associated with the same personality trait that is involved in alcoholism. The overlapping of alcoholism with these other forms of behavior suggests that this is so. In any case, the search for an explanation of the disposition to alcoholism may require the exam-ination of various experiences in family life. There may be many ways in which a family can fail to instil personal responsibility into children. Among the common faults are indulgence of whims, too easy forgiveness for breaches of conduct, and display of concern over minor ills, injuries, and discomforts. Out of such treatment may grow a weakened character which, when confronted with occa-sions which involve mental torment, finds retreat or escape the easiest or the only acceptable way out. Whether alcohol or some other form of escape is chosen may be determined by factors that, so far as the personality type is concerned, are accidental.

In addition to being an expression of personal disorganization, alcoholism is associated in various ways with other forms of social disorganization. It is apparently a causal factor in some family disorganization, for one thing, since a number of divorces are granted because of drunkenness. The saloon has been considered a focus and a partial cause of a certain amount of community dis-organization, and an indirect factor in industrial disorganization, particularly where the customs of a drunken week-end spree after payday and a Monday hangover holiday have prevailed. When and where drinking has been prohibited, there has been a tendency for illegal supplies to be furnished by organized criminal interests, which at times have found the bootlegging income to be an easy source of wealth and power.

## Drug Addiction

The phenomenon of drug addiction is different in several respects from that of alcoholism.  While alcoholic liquors have wide use in social ceremonies and are familiar to most adult members of modern civilization as well as many preliterate societies, the opiate drugs are not in common use except in certain Oriental regions, and their use in Europe and America is approved only for medical purposes. Therefore, while a large part of the population of the United States is exposed to the influence of alcohol, only a very small proportion acquires any familiarity with the opiates.  There is thus inevitably a much larger element of accident in the fact of exposure to these latter drugs than in the case of alcohol.

When, however, for any reason a person takes drugs repeatedly and reaches the stage of addiction, he finds the habit exceedingly strong and all but impossible to abandon voluntarily.  Those who are determined to cease using drugs are able at best to place themselves in the custody of agencies that will take responsibility for control and cure, thus abandoning their freedom for the time being and assuming the status of prisoners or hospital patients.  During this period of voluntary commitment it is common for the addict to lose his resolution in the face of the discomforts that follow withdrawal of the drug.  Only because he has yielded control over himself to other authorities does he escape a change of mind and behavior and a return to the habit.

Conventional explanations of drug addiction place emphasis on personal abnormality similar to that involved in addiction to alcohol. The addict is presumed to have an unstable disposition and to yield to a drug because it will replace his tormenting mental conflicts and fears with a relieving sense of euphoria.  Among the abnormal types reportedly found among drug addicts are paranoid personalities, homosexuals, criminals, neurotics, nomadic personalities, and inadequate and emotionally unstable personalities.  Not all addicts are found to be abnormal, however, for even in a study in which "carefree individuals, devoted to pleasure, seeking new sensations" were classified as abnormal (constituting 38 per cent of the sample), there were 14 per cent for whom no abnormality could be found.[7]

Lindesmith, on the basis of a careful and thorough research project, involving intensive life-history interviews with fifty opiate

---

[7] A presentation and critical review of such theories may be found in A. R. Lindesmith, "The Drug Addict as a Psychopath," *American Sociological Review*. Vol. 5, No. 6, December 1940.

addicts, has formulated a theory which accounts for the behavior of this class of addicts in somewhat different terms.[8]  He found that, although some users do experience a sense of euphoria following the first few uses of the drug, euphoria does not account for addiction.  The experienced user does not report such a feeling, but on the contrary claims that the effect of the drug is to make him feel "normal."  Lindesmith accounts for addiction on the basis of conscious fear of the distress that follows abandonment of the use of the drug.  This fear causes the addict to seek further drugs to avoid the discomfort and to maintain "normal" feelings.  Relapses, after long periods of abstention from the drug, are accounted for by the desire of the addict to control his "feeling tone."  While in the phase of constant use of the drug, he has learned that he could regulate his moods at will, but without the drug he is a passive victim of his environment or of other uncontrolled factors.

Lindesmith supports his theory by a carefully organized presentation of evidence.[9]  He cites examples indicating that the grip of the drug is so strong that even apparently normal and strong-willed scientists and medical men who have tried, for one reason or another, to use the drug and then abandon it seldom avoid being enslaved by the habit.  On the other hand, he finds that many persons have, under medical administration, become habituated to the drug without becoming addicted.  The reason, in these latter cases, is that they do not realize the connection between the discomforts of the withdrawal and the drug.  The distress begins a few days after abandonment of the drug, but ordinarily does not become severe until two weeks or more, when discomfort is accentuated, involving persistent nausea, general weakness, aching joints and pains in the legs, diarrhea, and extreme insomnia.  In one case obtained by personal interview, Lindesmith found that a man who had been severely injured and who had been receiving medical administration of morphine for many weeks for the relief of his pain developed withdrawal distress after his release from the hospital.  His irritability and discomfort were intense, and when violent nausea developed during the night he summoned his physician, fearing that he was about to die.  The physician suspected the nature of the discomfort and administered morphine, without informing the patient of the nature of the drug.  This measure produced temporary relief, but not until the physician revealed the next day that he had given a drug did the

[8] A. R. Lindesmith, "A Sociological Theory of Drug Addiction," *American Journal of Sociology*, Vol. 43, January, 1938, pp. 593–609.
[9] A. R. Lindesmith, *Opiate Addiction*.  Bloomington, Indiana.  The Principia Press, 1947

patient know of the causes of his discomfort. After the physician withdrew the drug, the man bought a hypodermic syringe, used it himself, and became an addict.

The strength of addiction is great, partly because the addict ordinarily does not want to be cured. Lindesmith states that, when the Japanese government in 1929 permitted unregistered opium-smokers in Formosa to register, giving them the choice of applying for either a cure or a license, only 30 addicts out of approximately 25,000 asked for the cure.

In the United States, where governmental efforts to eliminate the trade in and illegitimate use of drugs are persistent, the addict finds it a difficult matter to obtain a constant supply. Not only is he forced to deal with criminal agents, but he finds it necessary to pay high prices, and in desperation he is sometimes driven to criminal practices himself. In many cases the desire for company in addiction, and perhaps the desire to create a larger demand and a steadier supply, leads the addict to introduce his acquaintances to the drug.

Drug addicts admitted to mental hospitals from the city of Chicago have had records similar in several respects, though not in all, to those of alcoholic addicts.[10] More than three fourths are males, and the most common ages at the time of admission are between thirty-five and forty-four. The highest rates of incidence are in the hobo, rooming-house, and hotel areas in the central parts of the city, where the population is highly mobile and individuated. The foreign-born and Negro areas which have high rates of alcoholic psychoses do not have high rates of drug addiction. The highest rates of drug addiction are among native-born whites, the incidence among foreign-born whites being only about one tenth as high. The majority of the addicts are unmarried and are presumably detached from any community life. It is not known whether conditions in which such mobile and detached populations live are causal factors in addiction, or whether the fact of addiction impels persons to seek residence in areas of the city where their habits and activities are subject to minimum scrutiny and where they are near sources of supply and cooperating addicts.

Since the drug traffic in the United States is not as great as the liquor traffic, the underworld mechanisms of supply are not as large. There is, however, a certain amount of international traffic that is well organized and that involves secondary corruption in the same manner as do other illegal forms of commerce.

---

[10] Faris and Dunham, *op. cit.*, pp. 119–123.

GAMBLING

**The Relation of Gambling to Social Disorganization.**—Gambling, like the consumption of alcohol, has had nearly world-wide distribution since prehistoric times. In most cultures it is approved or tolerated, and in some cases it actually plays important magical and social functions. In view of its general popularity, it is desirable to inquire how gambling ever came to be regarded as immoral and to be classified with the vices. One possibility is that, in regions where continuous hard work of a highly responsible character was necessary on the part of each individual if the community were to survive, there arose a moral disapproval of idleness, of frivolous pleasures, and of the desire to get something for nothing. At the same time, where large-scale gambling does take place, it easily becomes a tempting spot for the gatherings of cheats, who there find rich opportunities for obtaining easy money. Race tracks, gambling casinos, and the card rooms in hotels and on ships have long had the reputation of being gathering places of predatory thieves who lie in wait for their victims and in various illegal ways extract money from them.

There is also a reaction within stable communities against the diversion of funds and energy that takes place when gambling establishments are allowed to flourish. Banks, department stores, and other local business establishments often oppose the establishment of horse-racing in their vicinities because of the resulting diversion of money from the normal channels of trade and the removal of money from the community itself.

It is often observed that, just as certain persons are unable to handle alcohol with good judgment and responsibility, there are those who are corrupted and enslaved by addiction to gambling. Some persons whose routine lives are dull and whose minds are perhaps unpleasantly obsessed with worries and other bothersome thoughts find unusual stimulation and relief in the diverting activity of gambling and become dependent upon the activity for mental comfort in somewhat the same way that others depend on alcohol. Although such addiction to gambling is seldom as severe as alcoholic addiction and is lacking in the harmful secondary effects to health, it does in some cases lead to the neglect of occupational and family responsibilities and is in other ways demoralizing. Thus there is a tendency for those affected—employers, relatives, and friends—to oppose gambling when carried to such an extreme.

**The Appeal of Gambling.**—The nature of the appeal of gambling is illustrated by the following case in which temporary addiction accompanied a disruption in the occupational, family, and community life of a professional man.[11]

Frank H., a college instructor about thirty-five years old, was engaged in study for his doctor's degree and earned his income by teaching elementary courses. His wife worked half time and contributed her earnings to their common funds. While his work and academic standing were advancing successfully he was a happy and contented man, and the couple were harmonious in their relations with one another and popular in the college community. A conflict arose, however, between Frank and the professor under whom his thesis was being written, and Frank became discouraged about the possibility of completing his work for the degree. In this state of partial frustration his studying deteriorated and his thesis work ceased to progress. Partly on this account he was not asked to continue in his teaching position, and thus at the close of an academic year he found himself without employment and with little prospect of continuing in his profession.

Frank's wife then undertook full-time employment and became the sole support of the family. Frank accepted in return larger responsibilities for housework, but his time was far from fully occupied in the care of their small apartment. He planned to continue study toward the completion of his thesis, but his restlessness prevented concentration, and he soon abandoned his books for other activities. He sought employment elsewhere, first by listing his name with teachers' agencies and then by looking for other forms of employment, but it was a time of business depression, and he failed to find anything suitable. In desperate restlessness he began to kill time by frequent attendance at movies, partially concealing this activity from his wife and friends out of embarrassment.

One day Frank and his wife celebrated an anniversary by attending a local race track. It was his first sight of a horse race, and he found the horses, the crowds, and the gambling highly diverting. He and his wife placed a two-dollar bet on each of the races, and came out only a little behind on this first day. From this moment on, Frank was a race-track addict and attended the races at every opportunity. His ability to pick the right horses was poor, and he nearly always lost. One afternoon he lost his spending money for the entire month, as well as that of his wife, which he had borrowed. On their return from the track the couple had to borrow money from friends in order to eat. By one device or another, however, Frank continued to obtain sums adequate to get to the track and make small bets. Virtually all other interests and responsibilities were abandoned. In conversations with his friends Frank spoke with enthusiasm about horse racing and tried to induce some of them to accompany him. Efforts to study or to find employment were virtually abandoned.

---

[11] From material collected by the writer.

It soon became apparent to his wife that their income could not endure a continuation of this behavior and that Frank's demoralization was becoming a serious matter.　Although the couple had always been harmonious, she spoke firmly to him, insisting that he discontinue the track attendance and gambling entirely, and find a suitable job, as otherwise she would leave him.　This ultimatum shocked Frank to his senses, and he shortly found employment as a salesman—an occupation which had hitherto been unacceptable to him.　He resumed a steady mode of life, and his self-respect returned, as well as harmony with his wife and satisfactory relations with their friends.　Not long after he found an opportunity to resume academic work and from that time on continued to have a happy life, with no necessity for the stimulation of gambling.

The problem of the control of gambling is complicated by the fact that the mores are not clearly defined in our society, and also by the fact that it is difficult to distinguish pure gambling from related forms of behavior.　Sales and purchases of stock on the exchanges may be pure gambling, although more often they are legitimate and essential commercial activity.　A large part of commerce involves some degree of speculation.　There are also various forms of contests, arranged for publicity and other commercial purposes, which come as close as the law allows to being lotteries.　Mild amusements such as games of chance with prizes flourish in churches and social organizations, and, since they are often employed to raise money for a good cause, they have the moral support of the community.　Even the larger lotteries, such as the Irish Hospital Sweepstakes, are offered on behalf of charitable causes and, though against the law in the United States, they thus encounter little moral resistance.　Proposals are frequently made that the government use the lottery device for raising general funds, as has been done in certain European countries, in order that taxes may be lowered.

The appeal of gambling to many of those who indulge in it lies in the artificial excitement.　For those who have acquired a taste for stimulation and excitement, dull periods become hard to bear.　Ordinary games and contests that do not involve gambling furnish some diversion, but when these become stale, interest may be added by introducing hazards of gaining or losing money.　There is a tendency for the gambling addict who is able to afford it to increase the stakes from time to time in order to counteract a decline in the element of excitement.

The association of gambling with spectator sports—horse and dog racing, baseball, football, jai alai, cockfighting—and with such sedentary amusements as card games, dominoes, backgammon, and the like illustrates the tendency of such games to become dull in themselves and to require the element of monetary hazard in order to hold the interest of a large mass of enthusiasts. It is generally held that many of these sports could not be continued at all without gambling. This is of course clearly demonstrated in the case of horse racing; tracks appear in the United States only where gambling is made legal. Horse racing without gambling does not attract sufficient crowds to pay the expenses of the activity.

Excitement is only one of the attractions of gambling, however. It furnishes the motive for the amateur, while others are attracted by the lure of getting something for nothing. These latter may fall into two types—the superstitious and the dishonest. In games of pure chance, virtually all players realize that the long-run probability provides for no gain. In the forms of gambling provided commercially, such as roulette, other casino games, and slot machines, only the entrepreneurs have a statistical probability of winning because of the intentional loading of odds in their favor. Nevertheless, there are many who believe in luck, who play hunches, who fabricate systems to beat roulette wheels, somehow entertaining the magical conception that they are protected from the impersonal operation of pure chance and from the intentional loading of odds. The numbers game capitalizes upon the wider prevalence of superstition among the less educated than the well educated and, with its small stakes and easy availability, flourishes in the urban slums.

**Exploitation of the Gambling Interest.**—The class of gamblers that actually achieves something for nothing, or perhaps something for a moderate amount of applied skill, is the dishonest group. In a sense these individuals are not gamblers at all, but rather the fraudulent exploiters of gamblers. They are attracted to virtually every place where gambling flourishes, for there the opportunities for cheating are always abundant. The gamblers are characteristically in a stimulated state and are therefore inclined to be somewhat reckless with their money. At the same time, their superstitious hopes of winning put them off their guard, while their avarice makes them easy prey to some of the baited schemes of the cheat.

The most profitable activity of the dishonest exploiter of gamblers is to obtain control of the facilities for gambling—to operate the horse race betting establishment, the gambling casino, and the numbers game. He can thus set sure and high odds in his own favor, and can obtain enough wealth and political power to make prosecution difficult. Enoch L. Johnson, the Atlantic City boss in the 1930's, sold numbers tickets through 800 retail stores in that city. Costs and profits were deducted from the gross income from sales, and the remainder was returned to the purchasers in winnings. The system was so arranged, however, that the most probable percentage of winnings paid out could be no higher than 46.4, and government investigators discovered that even this low percentage was not actually paid out. Somehow a method was discovered to decrease the actual winnings to only 35 per cent of the gross income. The resulting enormous returns constituted an important part of the source of Johnson's power and immunity in Atlantic City.

Where gambling is illegal, it can only be provided by criminal entrepreneurs. And since it is potentially big business, there is a tendency for the organization of illegal gambling to become large, centralized, efficient, and expansive. In the first quarter of the present century, the gambling enterprises of Chicago came under the control of an underworld character named Mont Tennes. The process of acquisition of the control, like that in the bootlegging enterprises, consisted in taking over by force and thus inevitably involved much violence. Eventually Tennes gained control of the wire services which supplied information from the race tracks, not only in Chicago, but in a number of other cities as well, and was referred to as the "czar of all the race track gambling in the United States and Canada." [12] His 90 poolroom gambling establishments in Chicago paid him $3,600 weekly, and 70 in New York City returned about $4,000 a week. His weekly returns from San Francisco were about $1,800, from St. Louis and Albany $1,000 each; and from nearly 20 other cities he received smaller amounts. Not until 1923, when a reform mayor and an efficient chief of police drove him out of business in Chicago, was the power of Tennes seriously threatened. Even then, Tennes was never arrested, for he represented himself merely as the dispenser of sporting news.

The expansionist habits of criminal gamblers impel them not only to acquire control of the conventional forms of organized gambling but also to invade other promising fields. When betting on major league professional baseball became popular on a large scale, the gamblers not only sought to conduct their regular business, but, in order to increase the income, engaged in bribery. The "Black

---

[12] From John Landesco, *op. cit.*, p. 881.

Sox" scandal of 1919, when a number of the leading players of the Chicago White Sox team were bribed to lose the World Series, illustrates the degree of penetration of this criminal influence. Even amateur college sports have reached such a degree of popularity that attempts at bribery by professional gamblers have recently begun to take place, as in the case of members of the Brooklyn College basketball team in the middle 1940's, who were approached with the promise of a sum of money if they would contrive to lose an important game.[13]

It is in such ways that a form of behavior such as gambling, apparently harmless in itself, particularly when the stakes are small, may become a factor in social disorganization and personal demoralization. As an essentially unproductive activity, it is somewhat analogous to the presence in the animal kingdom of parasites which in small numbers may do little harm, but which have the potentiality of becoming numerous and highly destructive. It is a form of vice which often operates to produce more harm than becomes immediately apparent.

## PROSTITUTION

**The Extent of Prostitution.**—The prevalence of sex delinquency among youth and of extramarital sex relations among adults is impossible to estimate with any approach to accuracy, for by far the larger amount of it is almost certainly successfully concealed. In itself such behavior represents a weakened state of the mores, since it is contrary to the explicit principles of our society and occurs in spite of social mechanisms to prevent it—especially mechanisms to maintain the virtue of women. A trend during the present century has developed in the direction of some toleration or extenuation where it can be assured that no harmful secondary effects occur, such as pregnancy, disgrace, or infection, but the

---

[13] Two prominent cases that occurred late in 1946 revealed the persistence of the interest of gamblers in the corruption of athletic contests. An operator named Alvin Paris was indicted for attempting to control the outcome of a professional football game between the Chicago Bears and the New York Giants. Paris had offered parties, women, and sums of money to two of the prominent Giant players, who, though refusing the bribes, remained silent at this attempt to "fix" the game. One of Paris's associates, Harvey Stemmer, was found to have been operating by telephone from jail, where he was serving a year term for bribery of college basketball players.

In the other case, a prizefighter known as Rocky Graziano was offered a bribe of $100,000 to lose a match. Graziano did not accept the bribe, but he got in trouble by failing to report it and by having the fight called off on the excuse that he had a back injury.

It was further reported in news magazines that bookmakers were even accepting bets on teams in the Louisiana Evangeline baseball league. California gamblers were accepting bets on the outcome of the Academy Awards. Numbers operators even approached the Secretary of the Treasury of the United States, offering a large sum if he would alter the figures in the Treasury Department statement on which numbers winnings are based.

strength of the mores in opposition to such behavior is still indicated by the degree to which parents attempt to protect their children, especially their daughters, and by the strong reactions against persons who publicly advocate greater sex freedom outside of marriage.

Professional prostitution indicates the more severe conditions of social disorganization and has consequences that are damaging to individual health and to the social structure. According to the United States Public Health Service, the wartime incidence of syphilis in the nation was estimated at over 3,000,000, and it is believed that gonorrhea attacks three times as many people a year as does syphilis. It is further stated that the annual cost, in the early 1940's, of care for the syphilitic insane and blind alone is more than $41,000,000, which is six times the 1940 cost of the national control program. In war time the infection rate may constitute a serious handicap to military efficiency. It is claimed that 7,000,000 man-days were lost to the United States Army in the first world war as the result of venereal diseases.[14]

In addition to the menace to the health of patrons and the damage to the lives of professional prostitutes, the industry has the tendency to become organized by criminal agencies, to become large and powerful, and thus to have the same corrupting effects on the political and social order as do other underworld activities.

**The Prostitute.**—The embracing of a career in prostitution does not in itself reveal mental abnormality. In the literature of half a century ago it was often assumed that prostitutes were women who were "oversexed" or in some other way mentally unbalanced. Case studies of girls who become sex delinquents and prostitutes, however, fail to indicate any such general state of abnormality. The motives for undertaking such activity are apparently the same as those which impel normal persons to undertake many conventional forms of behavior.[15] Girls learn sex delinquency from other persons, in the same apprenticeship relation in which other forms of delinquency are transmitted in juvenile gangs. In typical cases the exploitation of sex as a means of support is not planned or chosen; rather the girls drift into the profession with little foresight. There are indications that the average intelligence of these girls is somewhat low, and presumably that the career opportunities available to them are largely of the low-paying drudgery type. Those

---

[14] A news report of September, 1946, stated that the United States occupation forces in Germany had by that time a venereal disease rate of 305 cases for every 1,000 soldiers, which was at the time a record high rate.

[15] See the studies in William I. Thomas, *The Unadjusted Girl*, Boston: Little, Brown & Co., 1923.

who work as waitresses or barmaids in cheap restaurants or beer halls would not necessarily find that prostitution represents either a degradation in the social scale or a loss of income. Reckless offers a generalization, based on interviews with a number of prostitutes detained in a workhouse, that the actual idea of entering this career in most cases came from other girls who were already in it.[16] The "white slavery" form of procuring, apparently, and the pattern of resorting to prostitution following a fall from a high and respectable position are not common. Prostitution is apparently merely another opportunity to earn a living for those whose abilities, resources, and opportunities are low. There is in most cases little or no moral crisis, since virtually all have had previous experience in sex delinquency, and there is no conception of being criminal, even though they realize that they are subject to arrest and punishment from time to time. According to Reckless, difficulties with the law are simply regarded as among the normal risks of the trade, and these, together with the other standard hazards—beatings, infections, and the like—tend to harden rather than to demoralize them.[17]

The typical career in active prostitution, however, lasts for only a few years. Competition from younger girls reduces the earnings of the veterans. In some cases, also, the association with criminal elements, the pariah status, and other aspects of the career tend to turn the girls into such criminal activities as shoplifting and picking pockets, and to lead some to become addicted to alcohol or drugs. These, of course, often undergo extreme personal demoralization.

The general conditions that furnish candidates for this activity, then, are the same ones that generate juvenile delinquency—the weakening of family and neighborhood controls and the persistence, and transmission from person to person, of traditional delinquent activities. The disorganization in the general society which makes possible an organized criminal underworld also makes possible the organized prostitution industry.

**The Patrons.**—Although sex delinquency is widespread and not confined to any class of males, there is considerable evidence that the bulk of the patrons of organized prostitution are unattached, mobile, individuated men—particularly the residents of urban hotel and rooming-house districts. This evidence is of several types, but all point to the same conclusion. In Chicago, for example, the distribution of deaths attributed to venereal diseases, the distribution

---

[16] Walter C. Reckless, "A Sociologist Looks at Prostitution," *Federal Probation,* Vol. 7 (1943), p. 13.
[17] *Ibid.,* p. 13.

of cases of general paralysis, and the distribution of addresses of men arrested in vice raids all show the same pattern of concentration in these areas of high mobility and nonfamily life.[18] The men who fall into these classifications are not necessarily completely demoralized, but their behavior reflects deficiencies in their lives, which lack not only family but local community controls and satisfactions, leaving them to find substitutes that are provided commercially in the houses of prostitution, taxi-dance halls, gambling resorts, and the like. The forms of behavior adopted in such circumstances may in some individuals function as vices.

A study made in Dallas, Texas, revealed a form of sex promiscuity entirely independent of commercial prostitution, and flourishing among the higher income classes of the more stable residential areas of the city.[19] The patrons made use of tourist camps or auto courts located along main highways in the vicinity of the city and brought their own girls, presumably nonprofessionals, posing as tourists and registering under false names. It is estimated that about 2,000 couples from the city employed the cabins for this use on a typical week end. Since the income from such couples was greater than that from bona fide tourists, because the former stayed as a rule less than two hours and permitted the cabins to be used several times in an evening, the owners often preferred to admit the couples, and many even refused to take tourists at all on week-end nights.

By checking license numbers the investigators obtained the names and addresses of a sample of 100 owners of local cars seen at such tourist camps. The distribution was city-wide, but with a distinct deficiency in the central slums and rooming-house areas in which most patrons of commercial prostitution are found. In the outlying high-income residential communities the scattering was as dense as anywhere. Among the occupations represented were ten owners of large firms, nine professional men, seven executives of large firms, four owners of small businesses, thirteen clerical workers in large firms, thirteen salesmen, and other assorted occupations. These are of course the occupations of the registered owners of the cars and not necessarily in each case of the users of the cars at the tourist camp, though undoubtedly in most cases the latter were at least members of the same family.

Although the above development does not represent the degree of disorganization that accounts for commercial prostitution, it

---

[18] See Walter C. Reckless, *Vice in Chicago*, Chicago: University of Chicago Press, 1933, p. 166, and R. Faris and H. W. Dunham, *op. cit.*, p. 126.
[19] Elbert L. Hooker, "The Urban Tourist Camp," *Studies in Sociology*, published by the Department of Sociology, Southern Methodist University, Dallas, Texas, Vol. 1, No. 1.

must be concluded, in view of the ease with which the couple trade in the camps could have been stopped, that a sense of apathy about the mores had become locally prevalent.  In such developments, exposés in newspapers often bring a successful drive for control; if not, there is a tendency for underworld commercial interests to acquire control of such successful enterprises.

**The Entrepreneurs.**—[Although a few urban prostitutes independently manage their own businesses and a few persons operate small independent establishments with several girls, the larger part of the industry tends to become organized by the same criminal interests that control other illegal enterprises.]  When the police defenses of a city are weak and inefficient, the income from prostitution may constitute an important source of income to the underworld, and often to the corrupt political organization that allows it to flourish.  In Atlantic City, for example, the red light district contributed an important part of the $10,000,000 gross annual income of Enoch L. Johnson's illegal organization.  In other resort cities such as Miami, Reno, and Las Vegas, and at one time or another in most of the large industrial cities in the United States, there have been powerful organizations obtaining large sums from such enterprise.  During the wide open days in Chicago in the early part of the present century, Minna Everleigh, proprietor of one of the most notorious and luxurious resorts, claimed that she had paid over $100,000 to the city vice chiefs in her day, and furthermore that she had contributed $3,000 to the "Kenna-Coughlin fund" which was used to defeat in the legislature a bill which would forbid the sale of liquor in disorderly houses.[20]

[The prevalence of organized prostitution is probably always evidence of corruption of the police and often of the whole political organization.]  It is extremely difficult to conceal the location of resorts from police for any length of time, and it is probable that most policemen know the location of virtually every resort on their beats.  Often it is the policeman who collects the tribute that purchases immunity from raids, although when corruption reaches up through the whole police organization the tribute may go directly to the top, in which case the policeman gets less graft or none for himself.  An honest and diligent policeman who insists on raiding a protected organization may simply be transferred to an outlying beat where there is no opportunity to embarrass the arrangement.

[20] John Landesco, *op. cit.*, p. 850.

During the administration of Mayor William Hale Thompson, Chicago was known as a wide open city. Without ever making an outright admission of tolerance of the vice resorts, the administration nevertheless made only the most ineffectual efforts at control. The impossibility of a pretense of ignorance is illustrated by the public knowledge revealed in the following frank discussion of conditions, published in the *Chicago Daily News* of August 2, 1927:

Harry Cusick, convicted panderer, who was snatched from a "stretch" in the penitentiary by a gubernatorial pardon, is operating a disorderly hotel at 516 South Wabash Avenue. This hotel, despite the repeated and vigorous protests of businessmen in the neighborhood to Chief of Police Hughes, continues to run without serious interference. Male "ropers" on the street ballyhoo the place like a barker at a street carnival. Dennis Cooney is the undisputed overlord of the ward, the right-hand man of Kenna. No matter which political party has been in power, at no time during the past seventeen or eighteen years have Cooney's political connections interfered with his control of vice, booze, and gambling. His influence reaches into the South Clark Street and Cottage Grove Avenue police stations as well as the detective bureau. His payroll includes professional reformers, prohibition agents, and politicians of high and low standing. The underworld salutes him as "Duke."

Cooney's immunity is definite, investigations of the records in the Morals Court reveal. After a busy session chopping up disorderly houses and putting vice to rout in the West Madison Street district, where there is no overlord with Cooney's political affiliations and business system, the City Hall vice squad has frequently moved back into the First Ward to spend the early morning hours celebrating at Cooney's expense. While in other wards the Capone-Cusick mob, by the exercise of a reign of terror, has been able to "muscle in," the Kenna-Cooney combine, with its strong political and police connections, has presented too sturdy an opposition.

Cooney's headquarters are at 2138 South State Street, better known as the "Rex," one of the worst dives of its kind in Chicago. On the first floor is a saloon at which intoxicating liquors are dispensed openly. One flight up is a cabaret in which entertainers mix congenially with the patrons. Gunmen, dope peddlers, and hunted criminals frequent the place, yet it is here that the city police, plain clothes and uniform, do their celebrating. Arrests are never made at Cooney's. In connection with the cabaret is a disorderly house that never closes. On the busiest of three eight-hour shifts, upwards of forty girls are to be found in the place. Outside in the street are two police sergeants, Coleman and Benniecki, who have been assigned to the corner of Twenty-second and State Street for many years. It is their assignment to humor and protect any City Hall politician who might get unruly in the place, but to bounce a black-jack on the derby of any stranger who might complain about the service.

It is during the prevalence of such "wide open" conditions, when corruption spreads through the enforcement machinery, that the underworld operates efficiently and peacefully. The gang disputes and warfare tend to be associated with periods of disruption when no dominant person rules the whole city, leaving open conflict as the only method of settling differences among rival factions.

It is not necessary for corruption to involve every part of the police organization. Not only can patrolmen be transferred, but zealous officials high in the organization can be frustrated. Surprise raids on resorts may be carefully planned, only to find an empty house—because of advance warnings to the vice operators from some one who had knowledge of the plans. Successful raids are sometimes made in the "wide open" city, but often these are merely disciplinary measures taken against resorts that have been established outside of the organization rather than indications of a true determination to enforce the law. One resort that flourished during the 1920's in Chicago had an unusually favorable location for immunity from raids. The building it inhabited lay across the state boundary, part of it in Chicago and part in the state of Indiana. A raid from either side was met merely by moving for the time being into the other end of the building. Apparently simultaneous secret raids were difficult to arrange.

**The Neighborhoods.**—The most favorable location for prostitution resorts is near the central parts of the city, convenient to transportation and in neighborhoods in which many persons come and go and the visitor does not feel conspicuous. It is preferably a disorganized area, where there is little community life and where neighbors do not know or take an interest in one another but mind their own business. Residents of a stable residential neighborhood are disposed to organize to expose and to eliminate any resort openly operating in their vicinity. Since the larger part of the patronage is among unattached men of the hotel and rooming-house areas, the most favorable location for resorts is in the rooming-house district or in near-by slum regions. When nothing interferes with free choice of location, most of the resorts locate here. It is in times of reform crusades and zealous enforcement that the resorts are scattered, driven underground into small and frequently changing locations, or driven outside of the city boundaries, where they flourish along the highways, disguised as roadhouses and saloons.

Lohman has shown that, even where public opinion in the slum neighborhoods is against the operation of houses of prostitution in the vicinity, economic factors operate to maintain them there. Few residents of such neighborhoods own their own dwellings. In most cases the ownership is in the hands of persons of higher income who live in remote residential areas, and who have nothing but a financial interest in the slum neighborhood.[21] The impersonality of control, often operating through agents, serves to divorce the sense of moral responsibility from ownership.

Lohman states that his examination of the total police blotter for the year 1936, seeking information concerning every instance in which a woman was arrested in a flat or apartment on a morals charge, indicated a striking divergence between the places of residence of offenders and of owners of the premises. "With but few exceptions the buildings were owned by persons living in the more conventional communities of the city, persons usually of upper middle-class social position. A not inconsiderable number of property holders were residents of the Lake-Front community, which epitomizes of course the conventional moral order. The impersonal business relationships which prevail between the owners of such property and the renters is quite dramatically expressed in the large proportion of such properties owned or managed by banks, building corporations, charitable foundations, religious organizations, colleges, and other educational institutions. Two such properties, notorious for the number of occasions on which they have been raided, are owned, humorously enough, by a prominent university and an orphan asylum."

The impersonality and the freedom from a sense of moral responsibility are achieved by the common practice of entrusting the administration of such property to renting agents. These latter seek the highest return, without reference to moral considerations. Commercial prostitution is often able to pay much higher rentals than mere residential use and so constitutes an economically advantageous use of the buildings. Without necessarily informing the actual owner, the renting agents often seek to rent for such purposes, knowing that the owner is unlikely to make inquiries as long as income is returned at a satisfactory rate.

Lohman found that agents were often willing to admit such a preference. One agent, who handled much of the property in the

---

[21] Joseph D. Lohman, "A Note on Vice and the Local Community," *Bulletin of the Society for Social Research* (University of Chicago), December, 1938.

slum area at the instance of a large and reputable bank, stated, "I know this district as good as anybody, I ought to after thirty years. The bank gives us all their property to manage in this district, buildings they hold in trust and others their clients have them take care of. I'll tell you why we get their business—it's because we get the best returns. I know who to rent to. Give me a *hooker* all the time. She pays regular and she pays good. You never have to wait for the rent. There's only one thing can beat her and that's a bookie. I get three times as much out of that property as it's worth. The bank don't ask questions and neither do I. I just bring in the rents."

Even an owner, who no longer lived in the neighborhood, justified his preference for such tenants on the ground of high returns. "I'd rather rent to the street-walkers any day. I'd hate to have to invest any money in the property, which I'd have to do in order that respectable people could live there. Some of the Italians kept stoning a place I rented to some Negroes but they got tired of it after a while and it didn't bother me as long as they stayed there. I didn't even have to fix the broken windows but once, they patched them themselves. But for a while I had some private detectives down there to watch the place. Nobody's going to tell me what I can do with my property."

**The Persistence of Organized Prostitution in the Face of Control Efforts.**—The ancient status of the "world's oldest profession" and its tendency to flourish in cities over the world and to rise again after being wiped out or driven underground by local crusades have so impressed some officials and scholars that they have entertained the conception that it is impossible to eliminate the practice. This belief is further strengthened by the conviction that the practice is fundamentally based on unchangeable human instincts, especially the demanding wish of the male for sexual variety. In response to such ideas, a policy has been favored in certain quarters of allowing in each city a segregated vice district, in which prostitutes would be licensed and given frequent medical examinations. In this way it is believed that the industry could be kept under control, and that the spread of venereal diseases could be eliminated.

Present knowledge, however, supports neither the above beliefs nor the policies based on them.[22] Controlled and inspected vice

---

[22] A compact and authoritative argument against tolerated prostitution may be found in Philip S. Broughton, *Prostitution and the War*, Public Affairs Pamphlet No. 65, New York: Public Affairs Committee, Inc., 1943.

areas have been tried in various European countries for many years, but venereal diseases have not been eliminated. It is reported that in the first world war during a dispute between American medical authorities of the A.E.F. and medical officers of the French army, Clemenceau objected to the American practice of placing houses of prostitution out of bounds and defended the French system of regulation. General Pershing, however, was able to show that the American army, despite its high rate of venereal infection, still had a better record than any other army in France. American army medical corps statistics showed that many of the cases of venereal infection among American soldiers were acquired in regularly inspected French houses of prostitution.[23] It is, of course, well known that inspection systems are inadequate for the prevention of disease transmission. Even a prostitute who shows no sign of infection may transmit the germs. Flexner has reported that under the inspection systems used abroad the prostitutes were not free of disease, and that tolerated vice areas did not end the conditions of corruption and inefficiency.[24]

Broughton, arguing that police toleration in the United States has not only not lowered the venereal disease rate, but has actually increased it, presents the following experience.[25] A large American metropolis was running wide open in 1917, with no police interference except arrest and isolation of the diseased prostitutes. The venereal disease rate among the troops in the city was 168 per thousand per year, and prophylactic treatments were being administered at the rate of 826 per thousand. Then, late in 1917, the resorts were closed down; a little over a year later the disease rate had declined to a little more than 5 per thousand per year, and the prophylaxis rate to 53 per thousand.

A reverse experiment, mentioned by the same author, is described in Haiti in the same year. The venereal disease rate among the Marines stationed there had risen so high (170 per thousand) that the Navy Department tried the policy of a segregated and inspected district. Within less than a year, however, the rate increased to over 243 per thousand and the trial was abandoned. The conclusion to such experiments has been that the tolerated and segregated vice resort is far more efficient in serving large numbers of patrons than is clandestine prostitution under conditions of enforce-

---

[23] H. H. Young, *Hugh Young: A Surgeon's Autobiography*, New York: Harcourt, Brace & Co., Inc., 1940. Cited in Public Affairs Pamphlet No. 65.
[24] Abraham Flexner, *Prostitution in Europe*, New York: The Century Co., 1914. Cited in Public Affairs Pamphlet No. 65.
[25] Philip S. Broughton, *op. cit.*, pp. 14–15.

ment, and that it can therefore vastly increase the number of exposures and the probabilities of infection. Since, in some prosperous foreign resorts, the average prostitute may serve more than 40 customers a day, it is obvious that even daily inspection would be futile as a means of controlling infection. Prophylaxis of the male, in theory a satisfactory method for preventing the spread of venereal diseases, is actually often inadequate because of carelessness, delay, and drunkenness. It has been the experience of military officials that most men employ prophylaxis only when it is compulsory. Presumably few civilians bother with it.

Suppressive measures diligently applied apparently can greatly reduce the operations of organized prostitution and can reduce the disease rate. An efficient red light enterprise requires not only a number of professional prostitutes but an organization of other functionaries—operators of the resorts, suppliers, procurers, lawyers—which cannot endure determined and persistent disturbance by enforcement officials. In some cases it is not official corruption but only public apathy that is primarily responsible for the failure of police to destroy the illegal organization. An instance is reported in which conspicuous public demand broke through such inertia:[26]

The president of a western university located in a small city was apprised of the existence of a brothel in the neighborhood of the university. This resort was visited by students in search of novel forms of excitement. The president called the attention of the county prosecutor to the existence of this brothel but without satisfactory results. One day the mother of a student came to ask the president what could be done about this vicious resort. He worked out a plan with her and other women of the community. The next day two women called on the prosecutor and demanded the closing of the brothel. The second day four women called making the same demand; eight women on the third; on the fourth sixteen women demanded the closing of the resort. When on the fifth day thirty-two women came to see him, the prosecutor could stand the pressure no longer. He caused the closing of the disorderly resort and warned other officials that "when a bunch of women get started there is hell to pay if you do not let them have their own way."

## MARGINAL AND MINOR VICES

It is not possible to draw a precise distinction between recreation and the vices. Not only the nature of recreational activities but also their meaning to the individual and the amount of

---

[26] Walter Clarke, "The Community's Part in the Battle Against Prostitution," *Federal Probation*, Vol. 7, p. 39, April–June, 1943.

indulgence are involved in the differentiation. Eating, for example, is wholesome and necessary, but after a certain undefined amount the consumption of food becomes gluttony. Certain types of abnormal eaters apparently consume food far in excess of their needs, with serious detriment to health, in response to some general restlessness or dissatisfaction in their lives, thus making a vice out of a necessity.

Mores regarding amusements and pleasures have, in the United States, undergone much change, and this change has taken place at different rates in the various sections of the population. The mores are thus far from being stable and integrated on the matter of recreation. Puritanical mores have opposed most of the directly sought amusements and pleasures. Although these mores have greatly declined in strength, traces of such sentiment remain today. Not only are Sunday amusements disapproved in certain conservative localities, but such traditional recreations as dancing, card playing, and theater attendance are held to be wrong. Tea and coffee, now almost universally accepted as staple elements of diet, have in some quarters been classed with alcohol and tobacco as immoral drugs, and young people have been solicited to pledge abstinence from them as well as from the stronger intoxicants.

A distinction is sometimes drawn by welfare workers and other writers between recreation that somehow builds up the person, restores his energies, and in other ways improves him, and amusements which tear down, damage, and perhaps enslave him. It has been stated that modern urban culture, for example, is so complex and makes such demands on its members that there arises a necessity for change and relaxation during leisure moments, but that urban dwellers instead tend to engage in highly mechanized recreational activities, which waste their time and energy and cause mental and physical damage.[27] One also hears that the recreational pursuits of the city dweller are too passive. Reading, theater-going, card playing, radio-listening, and the like involve little physical exertion except for the expenditure of "vicarious emotional energy" and provide only an unwholesome "release and escape."[28] It is unlikely, however, that statements of this character are entirely free of prejudices that remain from the mores of an earlier period.

There apparently are, however, definite changes in the recreational preferences and activities of the American people. These involve a decrease in the element of sociability and an increase in com-

---

[27] Mabel A. Elliott and Francis E. Merrill, *Social Disorganization*, New York: Harper & Bros., 1941, p. 865.

[28] Niles Carpenter, *The Sociology of City Life*, New York: Longmans, Green & Co., 1932, pp. 255–256.

mercially provided recreation that can be supplied to individuals who live alone. Commercial recreation can thus more conveniently be indulged in to the excessive degree that may be regarded at least as marginal or minor vice.

In the period preceding the motion picture, the automobile, and the radio, the prevalent forms of recreation in the conventional small community were largely social in character. A favorite summertime practice at the end of a working day simply consisted of porch-sitting, chatting with neighbors and friends who passed by or stopped in, discussing local events and personalities, and the like. For special occasions, similar activities were organized on a larger scale, with visits to relatives, family reunions, and community picnics. Such patterns remain even today, in many areas, and it is not without significance that most of those who have the opportunity for such tranquil and friendly visiting find it more appealing than the less social forms of recreation. Listening to the radio, playing bridge, and such diversions are, in such circles, indulged in only *faute de mieux* and are immediately and gladly abandoned if interesting company arrives. It is possible that the same preference holds everywhere, in the sense that when people are familiar with and have the opportunity for rich social recreations, they value them more than individual stimulations. Even in many urban communities today there are many persons who refuse to play bridge, not on moral grounds but because they disdain to spend an evening in such a pursuit when there are available more interesting and satisfactory things to do.

The mobility of city life, the heterogeneity of the population, and the absence of physical facilities for visiting and porch-sitting have been factors in the modern decline of the pattern of neighborly visiting. Many inventions of the past fifty years have provided an abundance of new types of diversions. The automobile introduced the recreational driving pattern, the touring vacation which isolates the family from neighbors during the vacation period, and it brought within range of the car-owning family a much larger number of motion-picture theaters, restaurants, amusement resorts, sports events, and the like. The motion picture and the radio also compete with visiting, and they entertain each person individually even when people join together in such recreation. The effect of nation-wide standardization of entertainment through such devices is to reduce the variety of conversational material; apart from expressing their judgments on the entertainment, there is little that persons who have seen or heard the same shows can tell one another about them. Furthermore, in view of the increasing amount of time spent in such forms of entertainment, information about persons, which in rural communities conventionally furnishes so large a proportion of the interesting material for conversation, is not gathered in great abundance. The art of general conversation is also adversely affected by the circulation of mass literature. The person who reads *Time,* the *New Yorker,* the *Reader's Digest,* and other current periodicals and who subscribes to the Book-of-the-Month Club, finds that most of his acquaintances read the same things and that he finds few to whom he can tell the new anecdotes and jokes or relate the new and interesting knowledge gleaned from his reading. Recreation thus increasingly becomes pluralistic rather than collective behavior.

The individual character of recreation and its immediate and artificially stimulating effect are most perceptible in commercial amusements catering to the relatively disorganized and individuated populations of the city—the residents of the hotel and rooming-house areas. These people have little or no opportunity for social recreation and thus must find their amusement in solitary forms of behavior or artificial substitutes for social relations, for the most part of a commercial character. Most large cities contain one or more amusement parks of the Coney Island type, in which persons may eat, drink, swim, dance, watch various forms of entertainment, be tricked, jostled, spun, whirled, and cheated, in each case on payment of the proper charge. Physical pleasures and elements of excitement and fantasy are the principal sources of stimulation here.

There tends to gather along the streets where the homeless men congregate a typical cluster of appropriate commercial amusements, also of the immediate and stimulating type of appeal. Among these are burlesque shows in which the humor is so standard and inexpert and the dancing and other performances of skill are so inferior in quality, that there remains only the sex stimulation of the strip dancers to account for their ability to survive commercially. There are, in the same areas, amusement device houses in which shooting galleries, pin-ball machines, fortune-telling scales, peep-show movies, and wax museums constitute the entertainment.

In or near the rooming-house areas are to be found numerous poolrooms and gambling resorts, as well as "closed" or taxi-dance halls in which men who are unable to provide themselves with dancing partners may, on payment of the moderate charge, dance with girls provided by the management. An interesting study of this form of entertainment has shown how closely dependent it is

upon the patronage of detached males of the rooming-house population.[29]   Paul G. Cressey found that in Chicago no dance halls
could survive commercially for as much as a year outside of the
central business area or the principal rooming-house areas, although
the trial of other locations was repeatedly made.   By presenting a
door prize to the holder of a ticket drawn by chance, Cressey con-
trived to have the patrons of such a dance hall leave their addresses
(so that the money could be sent to the winner).   He found that 48
per cent of the patrons lived in the rooming-house area, and most
of the others near-by.[30]

The patrons of the taxi-dance hall represent a selection of men
who are unacquainted with women, lonely, unattractive, or otherwise handicapped.   For those who do have feminine acquaintances
it is more pleasant and cheaper to patronize the large conventional
dance halls that are abundant in the city, but among the rooming-
house dwellers are many men who are strangers to the city and who
do not have opportunities to make quick acquaintanceships, men
who because of age or some deformity find it difficult to make
themselves attractive to young women, and men with other assorted
handicaps.   Because of the racial color line drawn against them,
men from the Philippines are not welcomed in large dance halls
where white men may often meet girls and find dancing partners.
These Philippine men are proud and romantic and are unwilling to
accept classification as members of the dark races.   Since there are
virtually no women in the city from their home islands, they turn
to the taxi-dance halls where they are not only permitted to purchase dances but can even find a certain acceptability in friendships
with the girls.

The dark skin color of the Filipinos, constituting something of
a social handicap, is compensated for by their Latin courtesy and
romantic attitude and by their generosity to the girls.   A girl who
has accepted a Filipino for a friend may be slightly apologetic in
the company of the other dancers, but at the same time she tends
to enjoy the frequent gifts and the considerate attentions received
from her "fish"—attentions which are not characteristically received
from other patrons of the taxi-dance halls.   For these men, isolated
by social distance, lacking in normal opportunities for family and
social life, such dance halls furnish an important substitute which,

---

[29] Paul G. Cressey. *The Taxi Dance Hall,* Chicago: University of Chicago Press, 1932.
[30] Cressey further noted an interesting commercial limitation on the sites favorable
for these halls in the late 1920's.   He found that the successful dance halls—those enduring
for more than a year—all were established on land that was valued at $400 to $500 a front
foot.   Those established on either higher- or lower-priced land all failed within a year.
Convenience to cross roads of city transportation lines was also an important factor in success.

though helpful, is only partially satisfactory. The friendships do not ordinarily lead to marriage, they tend to be expensive, and there is some degree of exploitation of the men. Clearly this behavior is engaged in only because of the lack of something better.

## SUMMARY

Throughout most of his life on the earth man has led an active and a cooperative life. Apparently discontent and restlessness are at a minimum in such conditions, for it is largely among idle and socially isolated persons that we find the tendency to seek happiness in temporary physical stimulations. These stimulations have the power to give immediate relief in most cases, and they have the advantage of requiring little long-range planning or social coopera-tion. While it takes nine players to form a baseball team and many more to form a league in which team play becomes most absorbing, one may take alcohol or drugs alone, gamble with only one or a few other persons, or even alone with a machine, or purchase other physical pleasures from commercial establishments that exist to exploit his psychological hunger.

It is a characteristic of pleasures of this class that they do not provide any enduring satisfaction and that, in some cases at least, they intensify the craving after each attempt at satisfaction. This fact, together with the development of the habit of searching in these particular directions for satisfactions, thereby allowing the interests and abilities that lead toward normal social life to dis-integrate from disuse, apparently underlies the habit-forming nature of the vices. This may be true even of minor vices that involve activities ordinarily normal or even essential in character. Eating may become a vice when a person acquires the habit of turning to such activity during every moment of boredom, restlessness, or other psychological crisis, thus failing to develop any efficiency in dealing with his problems in a more conventional way.

The minor vices, then, may be harmful only in constituting a waste of time and a permissive factor in the failure of a person to develop himself as well as otherwise he might. The stronger indulgences of the victims of drug and alcohol habits, however, are physiologically harmful as well. Apart from the direct effects of the drugs on physiological processes, there is the factor that normal motivations are affected, so that appetite and therefore diet tend to be adversely affected. In the case of gambling, there are secondary dangers that involve loss of income and in many cases temptations to dishonesty. The heavy loser may be tempted to acquire a new stake through embezzlement or other illegal means, but the gambler, whether winner or loser, who becomes accustomed to the rapid and easy flow of money without much accompanying effort is in danger of losing his taste for relatively plodding conventional methods of acquiring income through steady work.

The vices are troublesome to the public well-being in other indirect ways. The commercialized prostitution industry is a principal source of venereal infection, which is a large public health menace and a burden to the economic order as well. But perhaps much greater is the damage to the social and political order resulting from the growth of the criminal underworld organization that provides the prohibited activities on a large commercial scale. The huge incomes taken in from such enterprise provide the source of much of the power and immunity of the organized criminal underworld and further furnish the means by which the latter extends corruption into police departments and political administrations, and to some extent into the general economic and social order.

The persistence of vices in the face of efforts to control them has suggested to some persons who are concerned with the matter that such behavior is instinctive, fixed in human nature, and therefore unchangeable. The policy favored then becomes one of open toleration and regulation, in the hope that harmful secondary effects may at least be minimized. Modern knowledge, however, does not confirm the instinctive nature of the motivation, but finds it rather in a disorganized state of society which produces demoralized persons. The persistence of vice is apparently the consequence of persistence of the underlying conditions of disorganization. Where these conditions alter, vice declines without organized effort; but where they remain, even the most fervent crusades often fail or have only temporary effect. While it appears that almost any control is better than none, there is no immediate prospect of the abolition of vice without a general stabilization of modern civilization.

## Selected References

Cressey, Paul G. *The Taxi Dance Hall.* Chicago: University of Chicago Press, 1932.

Dewey, John. *Human Nature and Conduct.* New York: Henry Holt & Co., 1922. Section 2, "Habits and Will."

Jellinek, E. M. *Phases in the Drinking History of Alcoholics.* New Haven, Conn.: Hillhouse Press, 1946.

Lindesmith, Alfred R. *Opiate Addiction.* Bloomington, Indiana: The Principia Press, 1947.

Reckless, Walter C. *Vice in Chicago.* Chicago: University of Chicago Press, 1934.
Sutherland, E. H., and Locke, H. J. *Twenty Thousand Homeless Men.* Philadelphia: J. B. Lippincott Co., 1936.
Vedder, Clyde. "The Taxi Dance Hall." Ph. D. thesis, University of Southern California, 1947.

# Chapter 8

## SUICIDE

### Cultural Relativity of Suicide

Suicide, like crime, has varying meanings in different cultures. The intentional ending of one's own life is, in our society, subject to moral disapproval and can therefore be regarded as an indication of social disorganization. This is not an inappropriate view, since the social organization contains fairly elaborate mechanisms to prevent suicide, and to instil in its members the will and the sense of obligation to live out the natural span of life. Suicide then necessarily reflects some kind of failure of that social mechanism and occurs only among persons who are in some way detached from the full influence of social control.

There is apparently no normal or universal human disposition to suicide. Presumably it is an invented device for the solution of misery, for it does not even seem to have occurred to some peoples. Cavan, in a review of the literature on suicide among preliterate peoples, finds the phenomenon unknown to many.[1] In the Caroline Islands, for example, the natives are reported to laugh at the idea that a man would kill himself. An early inquiry among native Australians similarly brought only laughter. The natives of the Andaman Islands had no knowledge of the act until they had come into contact with outside peoples—Hindus or Europeans. A study of about twenty sources dealing with the Bushmen and Hottentots of Africa failed to uncover any reference to suicide among these peoples, although it is found over the rest of the continent. There are also certain peoples in South America who, in their aboriginal state, lacked knowledge of the practice.

There is, however, widespread occurrence of suicide among preliterate peoples, some of it having about the same meaning that individual suicides have in our society—a personal means of escape from intolerable conditions. There are other types, however, which are not standard in western civilization. Many societies have a provision for suicide which is not only approved but is even expected

---

[1] Ruth S. Cavan, *Suicide,* Chicago: University of Chicago Press, 1928, Ch. 4, "Suicide in Preliterate and Oriental Groups."

and enforced.   In northern Asia and among some of the Eskimo peoples the aged and sick are expected, in times of food shortage, to take their own lives in order that others may survive.   Suicide is employed as a form of revenge among the African Bankundo; if one man owes another a debt which is unpaid, the creditor may take his own life, and the blame is laid on the debtor.   The Japanese sometimes perform their ritual suicides in a similar spirit, as a rebuke for an insult or disgrace; in order to make it clear who has offended them, they sometimes carry out the action on the doorstep of the person to be rebuked.

Suicide is often expected or required on the occasion of the death of an honored or high-ranking person.   Among some of the Indians of the Northwest Coast it was considered an honor for slaves to die with their masters and to be buried in the same place.   Among some Central American tribes it has been reported that the death of a chief required the voluntary death of wives, attendants, slaves, and friends.   The suttee custom in India apparently has a similar meaning; wives presumably had value only as they could help their husbands, and they were expected to follow their husbands into death willingly, usually by throwing themselves upon the funeral pyre.   The force of the mores is such as to impel the members of a stable and efficiently functioning society to do this without question and to resist efforts to abolish the custom.   The British outlawed the suttee practice in India, but such is the appeal of the sacred mores to the conservative members of the population that attempts to evade the prohibition have continued into recent years.   One widow, in spite of police efforts to prevent it, successfully carried out her self-immolation with her husband's body as late as the middle 1930's, according to newspaper accounts.

In parts of Malaysia there is found the custom of running amok, which may be regarded as a marginal form of suicide.   The Mohammedan faith prohibits the taking of one's own life, but not the murder of others, particularly persons of different religions.   Thus a convenient, and in fact glorious, method of ending life is to attack others until one is killed.[2]

---

[2] Cavan, *op. cit.* (footnote, p. 66) cites Cole regarding efforts to reduce the custom of running amok.   In the Malay States and the Dutch East Indies a man who feels aggrieved undertakes to kill people until he is himself killed, in a standardized pattern. The first method employed by the British and Dutch was to order that anyone who ran amok should be put to death, but since this was the desire of the native in question, it only increased the practice.   It was later discovered that running amok became less popular when the native was taken alive, put in chains, and made to work on the road.

The religious sanction for running amok is explicit.   Cole states that native Mohammedans of the South Philippines sometimes take a vow before the native local priest to kill a certain number of Christians before they themselves are killed.   Such a man is called a *juramentado* (one who has taken an oath), and shaves his eyebrows as a mark of distinction.

Certain other forms of suicide may be regarded as marginal. It occasionally happens in the course of war that men are asked to volunteer for missions which involve virtual certainty of death. The acceptance of such a mission, particularly if made by free choice, may be regarded as akin to suicide. But in the majority of cases it is unlikely that such decisions are truly a matter of choice—it is not a matter of wishing to be dead, but rather of facing the necessities of war and of resigning to fate in view of the importance of a task. Military traditions are such as to penalize those who refuse to volunteer when it is clearly appropriate to do so, and the force of such informal social pressure may be such as to allow the soldier little real choice. In some cases indoctrination with national spirit and personal adoption of the aims of the war are sufficient without further immediate social pressure. Newspaper reports during the North African campaign in 1942 told of a British soldier who was among the last to withdraw from a seaport which the Germans were entering. He chose to detonate a large supply of munitions abandoned on a dock by the British during their hasty retreat, so that they would not fall into enemy hands. The only method available in the time he had was to go out on the dock and set off the explosion, losing his life in the blast. His friends quoted him as remarking, "I'm only twenty-seven and too young to die, but we can't leave these supplies for the Germans."

It is certain that the pressure put on the soldiers of the Japanese army was far more explicit and strong. The squad that carried a bangalore torpedo to a street barrier in Shanghai, exploding themselves along with it, were widely celebrated and were commemorated by a statue which represented them in the action. Later the systematic and large-scale use of suicide airplane pilots, known as *Kamikaze* (divine wind) pilots, was successfully organized. These men loaded their planes with explosives and dived into the ships of their enemies, losing their lives in the attack but also inflicting far more certain as well as greater damage than they would be able to do by safer methods of bombing. Although some of these fighters were reported to lose their nerve and turn aside before the moment of crash, the Japanese were successful in indoctrinating a large number, and they thereby produced a form of attack that was difficult to meet. The element of free choice, however, in the *Kamikaze* pilot was so slight that his behavior can hardly be considered suicide in the ordinary sense. It was, rather, a marginal form which may more properly be called an assignment to certain death through strong social pressure.

## SUICIDE IN WESTERN CIVILIZATION

**Suicide and the Social Organization.**—The mores of the western world have long been in opposition to suicide. While there has been sympathy for persons who have willfully retreated from unbearable conditions of life, there are few occasions in which suicide is approved. The exceptions are found in subgroups within the society—secularized peoples who have developed a greater emphasis on rights as against traditions or responsibilities, and such groups as the military organizations of certain European countries, where an officer may be given the privilege of committing suicide in order to avoid official punishment for a serious transgression.

The force of social pressure against suicide in contemporary civilization does not lie merely in the traditional mores, but in a battery of influences which are intertwined in the social order. The Christian religion, for example, contains specific sanctions against suicide. In most countries there are also legal prohibitions as well, although enforcement of such laws is not usually systematic, since sanctions are usually possible only against unsuccessful suicides, and the sentiment is usually that such persons have already suffered and deserve no further penalty.

Other pressures against suicide may be less explicit but are nevertheless powerful in their operation. There is a general sense of admiration for one who fights back in the face of difficulties, who never yields if he is able to struggle at all; conversely, an atmosphere of disgrace surrounds the person who shows a tendency to quit. The implication of cowardice in the action of self-destruction, then, is among the general social forces that have a deterrent effect. The atmosphere of disgrace not only affects the suicidal person himself, but also tends to pollute the reputation of his immediate family and also of his family line. Where family continuity is strong, a whole line of ancestors may be symbolically betrayed by suicide.

Obligations to other persons are imperiled by suicide. A husband and father in most cases imperils the welfare of his wife and children when he deserts them in this way. He also injures the feelings of friends and, in many cases, abandons a number of projects and responsibilities in which he has become organically involved. Similarly in the normal case a wife and mother, or even a child, has involvements and responsibilities which contribute to a moral opposition to suicide. Among normal members of an integrated society, such integrated pressures undoubtedly deter from suicide innumerable persons who may have no individual inclination to live but who will continue to bear unhappiness or pain rather than inflict such broad and generalized injury on others.[3]

In highly integrated sections of our society, then, the suicide rate is very low. There likewise appears to be a very close relation between suicide and social disorganization. In any examination of the rates in various levels or conditions of society, there is revealed a marked increase in rates among those persons who are in a state of detachment, disintegration, or demoralization, and there is a relation in all modern countries in our civilization of high suicide rates to modernism, industrialization, and urbanization. However intimate and personal may be the decision to end one's own life, the statistics regarding suicide in the aggregate show evidences of highly regular principles that underlie the variations in rates.

**Variations in Suicide Rates.**—Halbwachs, in one of the most thorough statistical examinations of suicides available, has gathered evidence on a number of the regularities in the rates. For each country of Europe he finds a characteristic level of rate which tends to remain in somewhat the same relation to other countries over a period of many years, although in general these countries have a long upward trend that apparently reflects the transition to industrial civilization. Where industrialism has had the most rapid development, the rise has been most rapid, and while agricultural regions have also experienced increases in suicide rates, it has been a slower development.[4]

Two most conspicuous bases of variation in suicide rates are those of age and sex. Suicide is uncommon among children, and tends to increase with age through the entire life span of man. Cavan has presented the rates for the United States (except for non-reporting states) by age groups in 1920. The table below shows the regular rise of these rates for each age until the 90–99 period, when the numbers involved were too small to produce a reliable rate.[5] The relationship is virtually the same wherever useful figures are available for tabulation by age.

The probable meaning of the higher rates for old persons lies in their increasing detachment from social responsibilities and from

---

[3] Students of family life have shown: "The greater the degree of unity and intimate association in a family, the less is the likelihood of a member participating in behavior which will bring disgrace to the family." E. W. Burgess and Harvey Locke, *The Family,* New York: American Book Co., 1945, pp. 607–608.

[4] Maurice Halbwachs, *Les Causes de Suicide,* Paris: Alcan, 1930. Halbwachs, a distinguished student of Emile Durkheim, was requested to undertake a revision of Durkheim's famous research study of suicide which had been published in 1897. This was soon found to be impractical, so a new edition of Durkheim's work was brought out and Halbwachs made a new and far more substantial study, which he dedicated to his teacher.

[5] Cavan, *op. cit.,* p. 312.

SUICIDE RATES IN THE UNITED STATES BY AGE GROUPS IN 1920

| Age | Rate per 100,000 | Age | Rate per 100,000 |
|---|---|---|---|
| Under 9 | — | 60–69 | 26.0 |
| 10–19 | 2.1 | 70–79 | 27.0 |
| 20–29 | 9.5 | 80–89 | 34.0 |
| 30–39 | 13.7 | 90–99 | 27.5 |
| 40–49 | 18.5 | 100 over | — |
| 50–59 | 22.6 | | |

the other integrated deterring factors referred to at the beginning of this chapter. After their children reach adulthood, the family responsibilities of the parents decline; later, on retirement from occupational activity, other responsibilities diminish. With increasing years it happens also that the friends of elderly persons die off or move away, so that there is less of a sense of desertion of loved ones to prevent a contemplated suicide. Other factors that may be involved in the high rate for old persons are the increase of illness and infirmities, increase of economic failure, and perhaps a weary sense of personal obsolescence in a changing world. The low rate among children may be partly because the idea has not occurred to them, but probably largely for other reasons. Cavan has shown, however, that there is a form of suicide tendency among children. A study of children's responses to a questionnaire shows that the wish to die is not rare among children, and that a probably related thought, the wish never to have been born, is also not uncommon.[6] Most children who express such wishes have some indications of abnormality in their relations within their families. Among the typical situations, according to Cavan, are suffering from unjust punishment, bereavement, inferiority or jealousy regarding a sibling, thwarted wishes, and conflicts within the family. There are suggestions of a tendency for such reactions to be more common among children who have had less than the average number of playmates during their early years, but the evidence is not conclusive.

It has long been a matter of general knowledge that the suicide rate for males, in western civilization at least, is three to four times as high as that for females. Speculative papers dealing with the psychology of women have been written to account for their relative immunity to suicide. Some writers have gone so far as to assume that there is in the female a strong conservative principle that operates as an instinctive deterrent. Speculation of this character, however, has been based for the most part on the crude data from

---

[6] Cavan, *op. cit.*, pp. 315–317. See also Cavan, "The Wish Never to Have Been Born," *American Journal of Sociology*, Vol. 39, pp. 493–500.

our own culture.   The differential does not hold in Oriental cultures. Von Mayr presents figures to show that in Japan the female rate more nearly approaches that of the male, while in India it far surpasses it.   It must be remembered, however, that these observations make no distinctions between the different types of suicide, and that the Japanese *seppuku* and the Indian *suttee* are quite different in meaning from most occidental forms of suicide.[7]

Even in the United States, the sex difference does not hold constant throughout the whole age range.   Dublin and Bunzel show that for the ages fifteen to nineteen the female rate is even slightly higher than the male rate.   For later ages the female rates rise only slowly with increasing years, while the male rate rises rapidly in almost a straight line.   In the eightieth year, the female rate is about 11 per 100,000, while the male rate is about 78.

Not all persons who start out to end their lives make a success of it, however, and an examination of attempted suicides shows a somewhat different sex ratio.   Dublin and Bunzel cite three studies which indicate that women, though succeeding at suicide less often than men, have a higher rate of attempts at suicide that do not succeed.[8]   Donalies found in Germany, for example, that in a group of cases of successful suicides there were 56 per cent more men than women, but that in the attempted suicides there were 35 per cent more women than men.   The Peller study in Vienna contained a finding that during the years 1926–1930 there were among males 2,816 successful and 4,336 attempted suicides, and that among females there were 2,162 successful and 5,581 attempts.   If all attempts had been successful, more women than men would be counted as suicides.   In the Philippine study it was likewise found that a larger number of females than males attempted to commit suicide.

It is impossible to distinguish with certainty the *bona fide* attempts from those that are not really meant to succeed.   It is clear in some cases that persons who take too small an amount of poison to kill, who turn on the gas when other persons are near-by in the house, or who jump into shallow water or leap from a bridge in the presence of crowds actually expect to be rescued.   Their attempts are gestures to win sympathy or some other social advan-

---

[7] G. von Mayr, "Selbstmordstatistik," in his *Statistik und Gesellschaftslehre*, III, 298, cited in Cavan, *op. cit.*, p. 309.

[8] Louis I. Dublin and Bessie Bunzel, *To Be or Not to Be*, New York: Harrison Smith and Robert Haas, 1933, pp. 54–55.   The cited studies are: G. Donalies, "Statistical Observations on 3,000 Cases of Complete and Attempted Suicide," *Monatsschrift für Psychiatrie und Neurologie*, Vol. 69, Aug., 1928; S. Peller, "Zur Statistik der Selbstmordhandlung," *Allgemeines Statistisches Archiv*, 1932; and D. Anzures, "Analytical Study of Suicide," *Journal of the Philippine Islands Medical Association*, Vol. 7, July, 1927.

tage. It is possible that more of the attempted suicides of women
are of this type than are the attempted suicides of men.

A factor in the failure of more female suicides than male
attempts may be the different probabilities of success in the methods
employed. A classification of these methods by sex indicates
marked differences, and on the whole the methods preferred by men
appear to be somewhat less likely to fail than those used by women.[9]
Forty-one per cent of the successful male suicides of all ages in the
United States, 1926–1930, used firearms. Hanging was next in
popularity with males, with nearly 20 per cent employing this
method. Gas, poisons, knives, drowning, jumping, and other
methods were used by smaller percentages. Among women, on the
other hand, the most frequent methods were the use of poisons,
employed in 32 per cent of the cases, and gas, used in 21 per cent.
These methods are more subject to failure than firearms and hanging, the methods preferred among males. It may of course be that
they were to some extent chosen so that they would fail, but it is
not certain that this is the only or the principal explanation of the
difference. A more plausible explanation lies in cultural factors,
which make firearms less available to women and which make the
technique of hanging less familiar to them. From the feminine
point of view, also, it may be significant that poisons and gas do
not produce the horrible mutilation of the wound from a gun fired
close to the head, or of hanging. Women, having more concern
for their presentability of appearance even after death, may thus
be inclined to prefer the somewhat less certain methods of self-
destruction, and therefore to fail more often.

If suicide is related to detachment from social life and responsibilities, it is to be expected that marital status should be a basis
of significant variations. This is borne out by a number of studies.
The most conspicuous relationships concern the status of the
widowed and divorced, who everywhere have higher rates than the
single or the married, regardless of sex.[10] In Ohio, for example,
Frenay found that the suicide rate in the years 1911–1920 per 100,000
single men of fifteen and older was 22, while the rate for married
men was 26, for the widowed, 64, and for the divorced, 100.[11]
Cavan found a similar result in data for Chicago during the period
1919–1921; the male rates for single, married, widowed, and

---

[9] Dublin and Bunzel, *op. cit.*, p. 61.

[10] See Dublin and Bunzel, *op cit.*, Ch. 11, "Marital Status and Suicide," for a
review of the research on this point.

[11] A. D. Frenay, *The Suicide Problem in the United States*, Boston: Richard G.
Badger (The Gorham Press), 1927, pp. 82–83. Cited in Dublin and Bunzel, *op. cit.*, pp.
126–127.

divorced were 22, 27, 78, and 147 respectively.[12]　In each of these studies the relationship for women was similar, except that the contrasts were less marked.

Since the average ages of the groups being compared in the above studies are not the same, and since suicide shows marked variation by age, a more accurate conclusion may be drawn by examining age groups separately. Data from Canada for the period 1925–1929, analyzed in this manner, show that, over the age of twenty-five, the single have higher rates than the married. The high rates for the widowed, divorced, and separated are maintained, but the contrasts are not as great as shown in the studies in which there was no correction for age.[13]

Childlessness has been shown to be another important factor in the explanation of suicide. Bertillon made a study in France in 1879, in which he showed that married men without children had a suicide rate two and one-third times higher than that of married men with children. Similarly married women without children had a rate three and a half times that of married women with children.[14] This suggests that the presence of children protects women against suicide even more than it does men. Since these figures are not corrected for age, however, the effect of children may be somewhat distorted, for younger married persons have not had time to produce their quota of children. Durkheim made an adjustment which is the equivalent of such a correction, and all the contrasts remain except one. Single women of the same average age as married women with children actually have a lower rate than do the latter— the rate is only two-thirds that of the married women with children. Apparently, in the European population at least, the fact of marriage is not a protection against suicide in women at all unless there are children, although it is for males whether or not there are children.

Even the number of children appears to have some effect in certain regions. Halbwachs has cited figures from Budapest for the years 1923–1925, classified by the number of children. For both men and women the rate is highest where there are no children, and declines with the addition of each child up to five, with a slight increase in families in which there are six or more children. All available figures agree substantially that membership in a family where there are children operates as a deterrent to suicide.

---

[12] Cavan, *op. cit.*, p. 319.
[13] Dublin and Bunzel, *op. cit.*, p. 407.
[14] Cited in Maurice Halbwachs, *Les Causes de Suicide*, Paris: Alcan, 1930, p. 226.

**Comparison of Urban and Rural Rates.**—It is to be expected that the social disorganization associated with industrialization and urbanization will be reflected in higher rates of suicide for urban populations. In general this is true, both in European countries and in the United States, although there is not a perfectly uniform relation to size of city. A chart of urban and rural rates in the United States covering the years from 1900 to 1929 shows that both series rise and fall in roughly parallel fashion, but that the urban rate stays well above the rural rate in each of the years, running for most of the period approximately one third higher.[15] Age differences between these populations are not sufficient to account for the contrast in rates.

Within different regions of the United States, although the regional variation of suicide rates is great, the contrasts between rural and urban rates remain marked. In the cotton-growing states of the South, for example, the rates are very low, both for Negroes and whites, but city rates are higher than rural. The white suicide rate, 1925–1929, for Alabama, for example, was 8.3 per 100,000, but in Birmingham it was 23.1. The Negro rates in the same two regions were 1.8 and 3.1 respectively. In Georgia the white rate, 1928–1929, was 13.2, while in Atlanta it was 16.6, and the corresponding Negro rates were 2.0 and 2.7. On the West Coast, although suicide rates are among the highest in the country, the same contrast is found. The California rate is 26.3 per 100,000 population (1925–1929 data), and the San Francisco rate is 38.8. The Oregon rate is 20.0 and the Portland rate 27.0. The Washington rate is 21.0 and the Seattle rate 29.1.

**Variation of Rates in Urban Areas.**—There is a variation within large cities, however, which is greater than that between rural and urban rates. In New York State, for example, where the state rate, 1925–1929, was 15.7, the New York City rate was 17.0. But the rate for the Borough of Manhattan was 26.4, while the other boroughs all had rates below that of the whole state: the Queens rate was 14.4; the Bronx, 13.9; Richmond and Brooklyn, both 12.2.

Cavan computed rates for 72 local communities of the city of Chicago, thus providing a more precise and detailed comparison.[16] While the rate for the whole city was 15.2 per 100,000 in 1919–1921,

---

[15] Dublin and Bunzel, *op. cit.*, p. 78.
[16] Cavan, *op. cit.*, pp. 80–87.

only nine of the local communities had rates of over 20.  The highest rate was found to be in the central business district, which includes some of the hobo area on its fringes.  Here the rate was 87. The next highest were the areas adjacent, the Near North Side with a rate of 59, the West Madison Street district with a rate of 40, and the Lower North Side with a rate of 35.  These are also areas with populations of hobos, rooming-house dwellers, and other disorganized low-income populations.

In two areas which were not homogeneous in character, Cavan found it desirable to examine suicide rates for separate divisions of the areas.  In each case it turned out to be the more mobile rooming-house part of the area which had the higher rate.  In the Lower North Side district, for example, the western part, populated almost entirely by individuals of Italian descent, had a rate of 27, while the eastern section, a hobo and rooming-house district, had a rate of 37.  The Uptown community, with a rate of 20 for its whole area, was divided into two sections, one of which is residential in character and had a rate of only 14 suicides per 100,000, while the gay white light entertainment and rooming-house section known as the Wilson Avenue district had a rate of 25.

This association of high suicide rates with urban central districts, particularly those of high mobility and great disorganization, has been confirmed by observations in several other cities. Schmid has provided this information for Seattle and Minneapolis.[17]  In both cities he found that the highest rates were to be found in the central districts in which are located the hotel dwellers and the hobo and rooming-house populations, and in which the indications of social disorganization are prominent.  A similar conclusion is reached from an examination of suicide rates in the various sections of the city of Providence, Rhode Island.[18]

**The Influence of Religion on the Suicide Rate.**—In most areas where comparisons can be made there are differences among the suicide rates of the various religious groups.  In general the Catholic rates in Europe and America remain lower than the Protestant rates, even though in both groups there has been a marked increase during the past century.  The Jewish rate, which a century ago was low, has had the most rapid increase of all and has passed both the Catholic and Protestant rates in some areas.  The informa-

[17] Calvin M. Schmid, *Suicides in Seattle, 1914 to 1925: An Ecological and Behavioristic Study*, University of Washington Publications in the Social Sciences, Seattle: 1928; and "Suicide in Minneapolis, Minnesota: 1920–1932," *American Journal of Sociology*, Vol. 39, pp. 30–48.
[18] From an unpublished study by the author.

tion for Prussia supplies a typical illustration. From the period 1849–1855 to the year 1926 the Catholic suicide rate in this area rose from 50 to 148 per million. In the same period the Protestant rate rose from 160 to 294. The Jewish rate, which had been lower than the Catholic rate in the earlier period, rose from 46 to the highest of the three religions in 1926—505.[19]

While vigorous condemnation by the Catholic church may in part account for the generally lower Catholic rates, there are other factors involved that perhaps are more important. Halbwachs has suggested that such strong penalties as the refusal of Christian burial may motivate many Catholics to conceal the fact of suicide in the death of a friend or relative, thus distorting the rates for this group. He also points out that in Europe the Protestant group has generally had a larger proportion of urban peoples, while the Catholics were more numerous among the peasants, where the suicide rate is normally lower. Protestantism is in fact related in its origin to the rise of capitalism, and it is thus to be expected that secularization and disorganization would have spread within this group before it did among the peasant peoples. The importance of this factor is indicated by the fact that the contrast between Catholic and Protestant rates is far from uniform in areas of different degrees of industrialization and that in parts of Germany, notably Pomerania, Brandenburg, and Schleswig-Holstein, the Catholic rates have exceeded those of the Protestants.[20]

Religious groups differ not only in their positions in the industrial system but also in their degree of social integration. Cavan has suggested that social integration is the basis for the low rates of the two states, Utah and Idaho, in which Mormonism, an offshoot of Protestantism, is the most prevalent religion.[21] Suicide rates are also low in the South, where the Southern Baptists, a conservative Protestant denomination, are numerous. It is not necessary, however, to assume that religious traditionalism constitutes the force acting against suicide in these instances. It may be that the higher integration found among all settled agricultural peoples accounts both for conservatism in religion and for the low suicide rate. Halbwachs refers to England as an apparent exception to the general experience. Though industrial and Protestant, it has a low suicide rate compared to other European industrial countries. But the force of the Church of England is relatively strong in com-

---

[19] The figures for the earlier period are from Weichbrodt, quoted in Cavan, *op. cit.*, p. 38. Halbwachs supplies the figures for 1926.
[20] From Halbwachs, *op. cit.*
[21] Cavan, *op. cit.*, p. 43.

parison with other scattered and individualistic Protestant denominations, and furthermore England experienced the industrial revolution early and has had the time to find a new stability in an
industrial civilization.

High Jewish rates in modern times may reflect the industrial
position of people of this religion and the consequent secularization
and partial disorganization, but it may also be in part a consequence
of increase in sentiment against Jews and in actions of hostility
taken against them. In central and eastern Europe, following the
first world war, anti-Semitic activity greatly increased in intensity,
and, particularly in such places as Warsaw, waves of Jewish suicides
occurred.[22] Appeals to the Jewish populations by their rabbis and
sanctions taken against the suicides themselves by refusing permission for burial of their remains in the consecrated cemeteries were
of little effect.

**Occupational Status and Suicide.**—Crude comparisons of
occupational rates are misleading, for the principal occupational
categories are also related to other factors that are significant in
suicide rates. Agricultural occupations, for example, are associated
with the conservative and relatively integrated social life of rural
areas. Low-skilled urban occupations are associated to a certain
extent in the United States with the Catholic religion.

It is also not an easy matter to interpret rates for occupational
groups without information on the nature of the social life involved
in the different categories. In many cases classification of occupations groups together persons whose lives are different in various
important respects. Data from England and Wales, for example,
showing the standardized mortality from suicide for various occupational groups during the years 1921–1923, show that the highest
category consists of the "Never Occupied" with a rate of 37.7 per
100,000, which is far above that of "all occupied and retired civilian
males" (24.3). The "Never Occupied" group, however, is specified
as "Capitalists, etc., Inmates of Institutions, Tramps, etc." It is
virtually certain that if a distinction were drawn between tramps
and "capitalists" their rates would be very different, and that the
rates of inmates of institutions for penal reform would also be
different, and undoubtedly much lower, than those of inmates of
institutions for the aged and for the mentally abnormal. The
information from this study does yield the useful observation that
low rates, between 22 and 24, are found in the classes of "unskilled,"

[22] Dublin and Bunzel, *op. cit.*, p. 122.

"intermediate," and "skilled" workers; that a somewhat higher rate, 28.1, is found among the "professions and highest ranks of business life"; and that an even higher rate of 31.1 is found among "entrepreneurs, managers, retail traders, clerks, and teachers." Here again, however, the lives of entrepreneurs and teachers are probably dissimilar in important respects, and thus the classification conceals possible significant variations.[23]

From a table showing standardized mortality rates from suicide among males in England and Wales, 1921–1923, of specified occupations, it is possible to obtain more detailed information. It becomes immediately apparent that income and social class levels are not the principal factors that account for high suicide rates, for both high- and low-income and high- and low-prestige occupations are found to have high rates. At the other end of the rate scale, however, it is clear that low rates occur primarily among those of low or moderate income and prestige.[24]

The rates, expressed as a relation to the standardized mortality from suicide of all occupied and retired civilian males (taken as 1,000), are classified into three groups—high, average, and low. The high rates, with a mortality ratio of 1,200 or more, are found among a variety of occupations, but it is plausible to infer a certain amount of instability in the way of life characteristically associated with many of these. For example, the highest rate of all, 2,609, is found within the classification "Inn, hotel keepers, publicans." The world of the hotel-keeper is socially unstable in various respects. He is often not a member of any community, but has dealings largely of a commercial character with other people. The residents of hotels are a mobile population. If not themselves disorganized, they are often inclined to be enjoying something of a moral holiday, so that no moral stability results from such social relations with them as the keeper can have. It is probable that a considerable number of innkeepers are themselves somewhat mobile. The hotel business is subject to much risk, and failures, requiring moving elsewhere to try again, are common. Even managers who are successful may transfer at not infrequent intervals, moving to larger hotels and more rewarding positions. The association with high mobility shown by this rate for hotel-keepers provides an interesting agreement with the observation of the association of high rates of suicide, in cities of the United States, with hotel and rooming-house districts.

---

[23] The figures are from Dublin and Bunzel, *op. cit.*, p. 94.
[24] Dublin and Bunzel, *op. cit.*, Table XXXVII, p. 399.

The next highest rates are found in such occupations as registered medical practitioners, 2,012; auctioneers and appraisers, 1,712; solicitors (meaning lawyers), 1,654; barmen, 1,654; wholesale and retail dealers, 1,621; dealers in fish and meat, etc., 1,621. Nineteen other categories of occupation have rates above 1,200, and among these are such diverse trades as farmers, domestic servants, insurance agents, bank clerks, and commercial travelers.

At the low end of the scale are railway signalmen, with a rate of only 387. Next come chemical workers, 436; bargemen and boatmen, 453; locomotive engineers, firemen, and cleaners, 498; railway officials, station masters, etc., 547; railway porters and lampmen, 605; conductors, brakemen and guards, 654. Among the twelve other low-rate occupations are such as bricklayers, carpenters, civil service officials and clerks, printing pressmen, and building trades laborers. This low-rate group contrasts conspicuously with the high-rate group in one respect which may be significant. They are nearly all employees, while nearly all of the high-rate group are in some independent business for themselves. Furthermore, the railroad workers, conspicuously low in the suicide rates, are in Britain selected on the basis of careful inspection, and are strictly regulated in their conduct—the use of liquor for example is carefully controlled. Their unions furnish a further basis of both selection and social control, and possibly of general stability. In most of the low-rate occupations, also, it is probable that the income, while not high, is steadier and more certain than those in the high-rate groups, which can fluctuate between wealth and poverty in unpredictable fashion.

**Suicide and Economic Fluctuations.**—It has long been known that the rates of suicide tend to increase during periods of depression. This phenomenon has been observed in various areas of the United States and Europe. It shows up clearly in a comparison of a general business index and a suicide index based on death rates in ten cities of the Middle Atlantic region from 1910 to 1931. The two curves move roughly in opposition, one rising as the other falls. A coefficient of correlation between the two indexes, —.47, indicates the degree of relationship, which is fairly typical. An exact correspondence, with a coefficient of correlation of 1.00, is never to be expected, for other factors beside economic conditions are also of importance in their effects on variations in the suicide rate.[25]

---

[25] From Dublin and Bunzel, *op. cit.*, pp. 103f.

Halbwachs presents annual figures for Germany from 1881 to 1913, showing suicide rates and a wholesale price index. The price fluctuations may be grouped into five periods of steady decrease and four periods of increase. In the first period of decreasing prices, 1881–1887, the average suicide rate was 210 per million. In the following period of increasing prices, 1888–1891, the average suicide rate dropped to 201. The same contrast was found in all of the comparisons of adjacent periods except one. In the period of decreasing prices from 1908–1910 the average suicide rate was 219, and in the following two years of increasing prices it rose to 221. Since there was a trend of rapidly increasing suicide during these years, however, this rate of 221 was actually below the secular trend, and does not therefore constitute a true exception to the principle that suicide rates tend to fall during prosperity and rise during depressions.

The most plausible and obvious explanation of the observed relationship lies in the connection between business failures and unemployment, with consequent personal demoralization. It is to be expected that males would undergo this experience in greater numbers than females, and this is confirmed by an examination of the separate rates for males and females, in which the coefficient of correlation between the business index and the suicide index for males was −.51 while that for females was −.32.[26] Since the standard error of the latter coefficient was .20, it is not to be regarded as statistically certain that there is any actual relation shown here at all.

**The Effects of Wars and Political Crises.**—In all modern nations of the world for which data are available, there is observed a decline in the suicide rate during wartime. During the first world war, for example, the rates in England and Wales declined from 10.0 per 100,000 in 1914 to a low of 7.5 in 1918, thereafter rising until in 1922 they again reached 10.0. In Germany the decline from the 1914 figure of 21.2 reached its low of 15.3 in 1918, and then rose to 21.3 by 1920. A similar pattern is observed in other countries, although not all reached their minima in the same year. The United States, for one, had a lower rate in 1920 than in 1918.

It is an obvious possibility that some of this effect may be the result of a bias in the reporting of suicides among military personnel. Men who would otherwise commit suicide by ordinary methods may deliberately expose themselves to danger with the

[26] *Ibid.,* pp. 106–107.

intention to end their lives and thus be recorded as battle casualties rather than suicides. The decline in the suicide rate among soldiers is in fact very great. In the United States Army, during the first world war, the rate for white enlisted men declined from 53 per 100,000 in 1914 to a low of 12 in 1918 and 1919, after which it rose to 32 in 1920.[27] There are a number of observations, however, indicating that military bias in the reporting of suicides is not sufficient to account for the decline. For one thing, the effect was by no means limited to nations at war. Some of the neutral countries in Europe had greater declines than did the belligerent nations. Norway had a low rate in 1918 that was only 53 per cent of the 1913 rate in that country, and Sweden in the same year had a rate only 55 per cent of her 1913 rate. Denmark had its minimum rate in 1919, and it was only 49 per cent of the 1913 rate. These declines of course cannot be accounted for on the basis of unreported suicides of soldiers.

It is a possibility that the economic prosperity ordinarily accompanying war is the influence that reduces the suicide rate. There is no reason to doubt that this is a factor, and yet it does not account for the tendency, best shown by the careful examination made by Halbwachs, using data for France, for suicide rates to decline not only during wars, but also during intense political crises which involve no military action, and in some cases which involve no change in the level of economic activity or prices.

The suicide rates for France are more valuable for such a study than can be found in other countries, for several reasons. The French nation has had a somewhat more lasting unity than most other modern nations, and events which affect one part of France affect the whole with little delay. Furthermore, unlike the United States, which has been gathering data on deaths for a large part of its area for a relatively short time, the French have useful statistical information on the whole of France for more than a century. French statistics, being a responsibility of the national administration, have a uniformity of meaning and are protected from some of the distortions of local conditions and pressures that interfere with the reliability of statistics in some other countries.

From 1827 to 1927 the suicide rate for all of France has had a steady upward trend. When averages for three years at a time are computed, each successive period is as high as or higher than the last, with three exceptions. For the three-year period ending in

---

[27] *Ibid.*, p. 113.

1871, the time of the Franco-Prussian war, the average rate was
37.5 per 100,000, which was lower than the average for the preceding
period—41.0. After 1895 another decline is observed, from a rate of
73 for the years 1893–1895 to 72.5, 69, and 67, in the next three
periods, after which there was a rise. The other exception is found
in the period that includes the second world war.

When annual rates instead of three-year averages are used, there
are a few more periods of decline, each of which occurred during
a period of political crises. From 1829 to 1830, a period of revolution, the rate declined 8 per cent. A 9 per cent decline from 1847
to 1848 reflects the influence of another revolution. The coup
d'état of Napoleon III caused the rate for 1853 to decline 7 per
cent. In 1863 a decline of 5 per cent coincided with republican
opposition to the regime.

The most impressive material, however, showing the effect of
political crises is the presentation of the rates in France during the
Dreyfus *affaire* at the turn of the century. Halbwachs found that
the important developments in this exciting case were clearly
reflected in the suicide rates, causing reductions that in some cases
were equivalent to those of the first year of war. Since this was
not a period of economic abnormality, the pattern of rate changes
was not complicated by the fluctuations of a business cycle, but
apparently reflects with exceptional clarity the exciting political
developments of the day. This was a period of great political agitation in France and had many of the aspects of revolution. Out of
the anti-Semitism of the French army officers there developed, in
alliance with the clergy, a conspiracy against the Republic. The
French were divided into "dreyfusards" and "anti-dreyfusards,"
and over a period of six years the conflict took an irregular course,
with advantage going first to one side and then to the other. The
suicide rate for all of France began to decline in 1899 and reached
a low in 1902. Not until 1905 did it catch up with the trend, which
had been a typical amount of increase for each year over the preceding year.

Halbwachs made a more detailed examination of a part of the
period by means of a month-by-month examination of rates. In
order to obtain comparisons of adjacent months, the seasonal fluctuations were taken out by expressing each monthly figure as a relative
of the average rate for the same month over the six-year period
beginning in 1892. The result indicates a very close relationship to
the major developments in the case, beginning in 1899 with the

death of a president who figured importantly in the affair and the election of a new pro-Dreyfus president.[28]

Although the figures for France as a whole show these developments to be reflected in lower suicide rates, Halbwachs found that the effect was not even in the different parts of the country.  In the annual fluctuations the suicide rates diminished the most in the city of Paris.  The next most affected area was the southern part of France.  The figures for Brittany show no apparent decrease at all, but, since the normally lower rate in this area had been increasing faster than the urban rate in France, the slowing of the rate of increase in this period suggests that there was some effect of the crisis even here.

When annual data are examined in relation to the line of the trend of increase in the suicide rate, other French crises also appear to be reflected in temporary deficiencies of suicides.  Among these periods were the year 1875, when a constitution was adopted in the midst of a split among the supporters of the monarchy; the years 1879 and 1883, when there was agitation against the church and decrees were passed to curb the Jesuits and to secularize the school system; and the years 1889 and 1890, when an attempt by Boulanger to destroy the parliamentary regime was defeated.

The explanation of this apparently clear connection between intense political crises and a reduction in suicide rates is far from obvious.  It may appear that there is an inconsistency in the generalization that suicide reflects social disorganization when there is actually a decrease in the rate during periods of political disorganization.  At the other end of the scale, however, from intense controversy which divides a nation is the disorganization of political apathy, in which quiet corruption spreads.  Perhaps this latter is the real disorganization, while the crises are actually the painful concomitants of the processes of reorganization.

It may partially account for the suicide reduction to point out that in times of crises persons take an interest in such affairs which keeps their minds off their own troubles and allows them less time to brood over their personal misery.  It seems somewhat more plausible, however, to account for it on the basis of the social integration that takes place when persons are swept into causes and thus become integrated into social teamwork, acquire long-term goals that give their lives more meaning, and absorb a somewhat mystical hope and enthusiasm about the future in general.  Although

---

[28] Some of this material appears in Halbwachs, *Les Causes de Suicide*. The author had the pleasure and the valuable experience of taking a course at the University of Chicago in 1930 in which Professor Halbwachs presented this subject in somewhat greater detail.

the United States is less subject to such precise and intense controversies as the Dreyfus *affaire,* it is easy to remember the almost
religious fervor of the popular movement which sprang up to elect
Wendell Willkie to the presidency, and to observe the element of
sacredness in the cause of the members of the Townsend movement.
Such developments to some degree reorganize personalities, and
they are particularly attractive to those persons whose lives have
been somewhat deficient in purpose and who thus are somewhat
more susceptible to suicide than the average person.

**Suicide and Mental Abnormality.**—There is a certain proportion of suicides in which a clear diagnosis of mental disorder can
be made, and it cannot be disputed that in some of these cases the
mental abnormality is causally associated with the act of self-
destruction.    In many other cases, however, the association may
be accidental.    If between 10 and 20 per cent of the total population experience some insanity during their lifetimes, as is indicated
by modern estimates based on the study of mental disorders in New
York State, it is to be expected that by chance alone a somewhat
similar proportion should be found among suicidal persons.    Since
suicide as well as mental abnormality is more common among older
persons, the proportion might be even higher.    Cavan states that
approximately 20 per cent of the 291 suicides reported in the city
of Chicago in 1923 "may be definitely stated to have been insane." [29]
All doubtful cases were classified as insane, and not all of them
were necessarily insane at the time of the suicide.    The Metropolitan
Life Insurance Company reports a similar percentage, 18.8, among
the 2,211 suicides among its policyholders in its Industrial Department in 1923–1924.

Higher estimates may be found, such as that of Kraepelin that
"mental derangement is the cause of at least a third of the total
number of suicides"; in fact, there have been claims that all suicides
are committed by insane persons.    Apart from the ordinary difficulties of objective diagnosis of mental abnormality, however,
there is the further handicap in the case of suicides that there is no
living person to study and that the decisions regarding insanity
must depend only on the information available from persons who
remember the suicide victim.

Among the diagnoses reported with greatest frequency among
suicides is that of melancholia.    The symptoms associated with
this condition are not different in their essentials from normal

[29] Cavan, *op. cit.,* pp. 112–113.

behavior, but only in degree. The depression and mental unrest of melancholia are more than the psychiatrist would expect from a normal person in the same situation. A careful study by Stelzner, in which about a third of the cases of female suicide were diagnosed as melancholia, shows that in many cases there were actual events in the lives of some of the women which would justify some sense of depression on the part of normal persons.[30]  For example, one was a cripple and was concerned about the difficulty of earning a living. Another had made an unhappy marriage. There were also cases of justifiable fear of blindness, illness of husband, loss of position and family trouble, broken engagement and death of father, and other crises of like character. Some appearance of melancholy is inevitable in the more severe crises of life. It is not to be expected that the most normal person would maintain a cheery aspect during the weeks in which his suicide was being contemplated.

The theory that all suicides are the result of insanity is a mere fallacy, for such a statement can only be supported by contending that the very act of self-destruction is itself abnormal and therefore an indication of mental derangement. It is not in any case a helpful generalization, for it furnishes no basis for prediction or explanation. Even if all suicides could be shown to result from mental abnormality, it is far from true that all persons with mental disorders either commit or attempt suicide.

According to Maurice Halbwachs, one of the most careful case-study researches in motives for suicide is that made by Dr. Suzanne Serin.[31]  Of the 1,000 cases of suicide in Paris occurring between January, 1925, and October, 1926, Dr. Serin was able to get sufficient information on 420 cases. These were classified into three major groups: (1) 150, or slightly more than one third, gave indications of mentally pathological conditions, although only 78, or slightly more than half of these, had well-defined mental disorders. This figure is in agreement with the proportions found by Cavan and by the Metropolitan Life Insurance Company. (2) Another 130 cases were associated with alcoholism. (3) The remaining 169 had no indications of either type of abnormality—their suicides occurred as the consequence of intelligible and normal motives. Among these were intimate sorrow, poverty or failure, physical diseases, and the threat of disgrace or punishment.

---

[30] H. Stelzner, *Analyse von 200 Selbstmordfaellen.* Summarized in translation in Cavan, *op. cit.,* pp. 114–123.
[31] From the 1930 class lectures of Professor Halbwachs.

## The Suicide Process

Cavan has presented, on the basis of case study material, some evidence that the act of suicide has a long background of preparation and development and a close relation to the life-history of the suicide. From an early lack of satisfaction or happiness in life there develops in gradual stages a more specific idea of preference for death. Cavan refers to the early stage as the unidentified craving, in which there is only a generalized wish for death, or wish never to have been born, with no specific plans for suicide.[32] There may occur such expressions as the claim to be "disgusted with life."

In other cases Cavan found a recognized wish for something which is apparently unobtainable. It is not uncommon, for example, for elderly persons, particularly the widowed, to leave notes accounting for their suicide on the basis of loneliness. One man of sixty-five stated his need specifically as the need for a home and a wife. Others seek independence, security, or freedom from oppressive conditions. Disappointment in love is the motive for some others who have set their expectations on marriage to a specific person and are unwilling to continue living if this wish is frustrated.

In another class of cases Cavan observed that strong mental conflict made life too unpleasant to be continued. A Jewish man who married a non-Jewish American woman found himself torn between his mother and other persons of his own cultural group and his loyalty to his wife. His discomfort was such as to lead him to entertain the wish to die, although he made no specific plans for suicide. In still other cases, contrast between ideals and actual situations of life have furnished the basis of the conflict.

In many cases the crisis is precipitated by disruption of the life-organization. Among the occasions mentioned by Cavan are such things as arrests, illness, the breaking up of the home, fear of blindness, change of residence, and the like. When the new conditions appear to be intolerable and there does not seem to be any other way out of the unpleasant situation, suicide offers a certain means of escape.[33]

---

[32] Cavan, *op. cit.*, Ch. 9, "The Suicide Process," pp. 148–177.
[33] Popular presentations of psychoanalytic theories of suicide, omitted here, may be found in Dublin and Bunzel, *op. cit.*, Chs. 20 and 21, and in Karl M. Menninger, *Man Against Himself*, New York: Harcourt, Brace & Co., Inc., 1938.

## Summary

The type of suicide which prevails in European and American civilization, the individualistic desertion of responsibilities and of social relations, is contrary to mores and law and represents a failure of the mechanisms of social control. It may therefore be presumed to be some indication of a state of disorganization, and the times and places of high rates may be useful indicators of particular aspects of deterioration in the society.

In various ways statistical data bear out this association of suicide with social disorganization. The contrast between the low rates associated with peasant agricultural regions and stable isolated religious groups and the high rates in industrial urban regions furnishes one important confirmation. Another is the association of low rates with family life and the presence of children. Further confirmation is given by the increase of the suicide rate in all countries which are going through the process of industrialization. Occupational data, while not as easy to interpret with confidence, differ in suicide rates in such manner as to contribute to the same generalization. The decline of rates during wars and political crises is probably in harmony with these data. Perhaps the most important fact bearing on this point, however, is the association of the highest suicide rates within large cities with the most intensely mobile and detached populations, the hobo, hotel, and rooming-house populations. These peoples, as we know from the study of unconventional behavior, vice, and mental disorders, constitute the most disorganized population of any size that is to be found in modern cities.

The condition apparently reflected in the above observations is that of isolation, detachment, and freedom from social control, which allows the person to make his decisions primarily on the basis of his own inclinations and interests rather than of his responsibilities to others. This fact alone, however, is not sufficient to account for suicide, for it has been shown that other types of demoralization develop out of the same conditions. The study of motives and of the suicide process, as well as the information on the increase in suicides in times of depression, reveals that severe crises are present in the lives of many of the persons involved. Many of these crises are sufficient to break up the life-organization of the person and thus to require some drastic measures to get away from an unbearable situation.

Even with the combination of social disorganization and the presence of extreme crisis in the life of the person, however, it is not inevitable that suicide should occur. There are other common reactions—going away to make a new start in life, continuing to fight to conquer the problems, adopting the life of an irresponsible wanderer or idler, addiction to alcohol or drugs, or becoming dependent upon others through hypochondria or by embracing a psychosis. The act of self-destruction, then, is only one of the many possible ways out of an unbearable situation, and there remains the problem of accounting for the choice of this method by those who make it. There is presumably some trait or organization of traits in the personality of some persons which predisposes them to a reaction of this type.

Because of the particular difficulties involved in investigations of the sanity of suicidal persons—perhaps the greatest being the fact that few persons are identified as suicidal until after their deaths—there are fewer satisfactory data of a statistical character on this personality factor than on the other aspects of suicide. It is the impression of most psychoanalysts, as well as of Cavan and other sociological investigators, that the trait is a fundamental aspect of character, present in most cases in childhood as well as later. In some cases there are suggestions that pampering in infancy and overprotection by parents may develop a type of ego-centric irresponsibility which causes the child to seek aid from others in the solution of his minor crises, rather than to depend upon his own resources. This is the reaction that is the basis of the "quitter" type, who deserts in either play or work when he cannot have his own way and who uses his reaction as a gesture of reproach against others. Children of this type sometimes threaten their parents by saying that the latter will be sorry when they find the child dead, and they often have death fantasies which enable them to enjoy the sense of reproach.

While research on the personality factor underlying suicide is inconclusive, it is hardly to be disputed that the reaction of the suicidal person is not an approved trait in our society and that the infantile "quitter" reaction that appears to be related to it represents a departure from the general ideal of personality. To the extent that this is an abnormal development, it may reflect a degree of family disorganization, for it is a primary function of the family to produce in children normal and stable personalities capable of accepting the responsibilities of adult life in approved ways.

The theory relating the various observations of suicide in the most plausible explanation is that high rates of suicide are produced by the convergence of three factors: (1) a condition of social isolation which is usually the result of residence in an environment of social disorganization, (2) a severe crisis in the life of the person, sufficient to shatter his life-organization, and (3) a personality factor which leads a person in such a situation to choose the most drastic "quitter" path of escape. All three of these factors reflect different aspects of abnormal conditions of a social organization. The steady trends of more than a century, showing a rise in the suicide rates accompanying the development of industrial civilization, reflect the inevitable stresses and flaws that take place during such drastic and fundamental alterations of a social structure.

### SELECTED REFERENCES

Cavan, Ruth S. *Suicide*. Chicago: University of Chicago Press, 1928. An ecological and sociological study of much value.

Dublin, Louis I., and Bunzel, Bessie. *To Be or Not to Be*. New York: Harrison Smith & Robert Haas, Inc., 1933. Contains much useful statistical material on suicide.

Frenay, A. D. *The Suicide Problem in the United States*. Boston: Richard G. Badger (The Gorham Press), 1927. Useful for its statistical material.

Halbwachs, Maurice. *Les Causes de Suicide*. Paris: Alcan, 1930. A highly organized statistical and sociological study, based partly on European material not readily available in the United States.

# Chapter 9

## MENTAL ABNORMALITY

The human mind is not merely physiological in its operations. It is an integration which is built up in social experience and is sustained by interaction within an effective social organization. It is to be expected, therefore, that disorganization of a society would be reflected in deviation from mental normality among its members. While this conception is too new to have been the subject of extensive research, certain relations between social and mental disorganization are suggested by present knowledge.

### The General Nature of Unconventionality and Mental Abnormality

Mental abnormality consists of behavior which is in some sense defective. It may result from any of a number of breaks in the mechanism which is necessary for efficient and orderly behavior. These breaks may be in the physiological mechanism—brain, glands, nervous system—or in the social organization. They may result from injuries or infections of various kinds, or from overprotection and isolation. The particular set of symptoms that accompanies the basic maladjustment to society is usually the product of the life-history of the individual, the unique experiences he has undergone.

The problem of precise definition of mental abnormality involves difficulties similar to those involved in the definition of crime. Normality of behavior is, within limits, a matter of cultural relativity. Just as certain actions are considered to be criminal in one culture and are approved in another, so are certain forms of behavior and thought considered normal in some areas and abnormal in others. Furthermore, the same behavior may be normal or abnormal within our own society, depending upon the context in which it occurs. There can, then, be no universal and objective definition of insanity. It must be defined in relation to the cultural context.

For a broad but useful classification, behavior may be considered with respect to intelligibility and approval. Persons whose actions are both intelligible and approved are simply good persons, conventional and appreciated members of a community. If their actions are intelligible but not approved, they constitute breaches of custom, sins, or crimes.   There may occasionally occur instances in which actions are unintelligible but valued—this is the case with the genius and the mystical leader.   Finally, when actions are neither intelligible nor approved, the persons are held to be insane.

Interesting variations regarding both intelligibility and approval of certain actions may be found within our culture.   Uncertainty on either of these points often leads to confusion regarding the normality of the behavior of a person.   Residents of college towns, for example, are inclined to be tolerant of the public pranks that accompany hazing and the initiation activities of college fraternities. The same behavior, however, performed in distant places, away from the context of college life, is subject to being judged insane. The crucial point is often whether or not one can explain why he indulges in such actions—whether a social context is available to account for it.   When a person acts as if he were either "drunk or crazy," it is with a sense of relief that his friends discover that he has in fact been consuming quantities of alcohol.

Occasionally statements that are truthful and sensible are misunderstood by persons of limited knowledge, so that an incorrect suspicion of mental abnormality is formed.   During the first world war, a recruit, while undergoing the classification procedure, answered the sergeant's question regarding his occupation by stating truthfully that he was an anthropologist.   Presumably the sergeant had not heard of the term, for he handed the soldier a slip which called for him to report for a special psychiatric interview.

In another instance observed by the author, an elderly man who had been for some years confined to a wheel chair was brought to a psychopathic hospital for examination.   His neighbors in his home town had taken the initiative in arranging the interview because he had begun to call himself a philosopher.   Having known him for all of his lifetime, the neighbors knew he was nothing of the kind and presumed that his mind was failing.   What they did not realize, apparently, was that in his extensive reading, the principal occupation of his sedentary life, he had undertaken a certain amount of study of philosophical literature and had begun to feel at home in the subject.   The findings of the hospital staff were that he was not insane, and he was returned to his home.

It is not uncommon for a person to be taken forcibly to an urban psychopathic hospital because of a solo public display of great religious zeal or frenzy.   In most parts of the country this type of behavior is held to be so inappropriate that it could only be an indication of insanity. In parts of the rural South, however, particularly among members of the small and "primitive" religious sects, it is expected that religious emotions will be openly expressed, and it is often regarded as desirable that members should stand on public streets and attempt to enlighten and convert those who pass by. Such persons encounter little danger of being held for mental examination as long as they pursue this activity in the areas in which it is understood.

Boisen, in a study of prophets and other religious leaders and zealots, has shown that there are many persons who, because of their religious activities, have been held to be insane, while other persons who exhibited very similar traits and were able to gain a following became leaders and founders of sects. In some cases it appears that only the minor accidents which determine success or failure in drawing persons into a new organization were the determining factors in the fate of the would-be leader.[1] It may be that some unbalanced fanatics living in modern cities would even have escaped commitment and become prophets if they had had the fortune to reside in regions of less sophistication.

### THE EXTENT AND LOCATION OF MENTAL DISORDERS IN MODERN SOCIETY

Because of the indefinite borderlines of the definitions of mental abnormality, it is difficult to gather precise statistics on the prevalence of these conditions, and to make accurate comparisons covering different times and places. There has been a familiar item appearing in the press from time to time, pointing out that if the rate of increase in mental disorders continues without interruption, it will not be many decades before the entire population is insane. On the other hand, critical examination of the statistics has led to the questioning of whether these figures really prove that there is any true increase at all in the standardized rates.[2] The figures may only show improvement in diagnoses, increases in facilities for hospitalization, and perhaps aging of the population, which allows more persons who might otherwise have died young to survive long enough to have a mental disorder. The greatest difficulty in making accurate estimates is the problem of ascertaining the number of persons who have mental disorders but who are not hospitalized or put in the care of a physician.

[1] Anton T. Boisen, *Exploration of the Inner World*, Chicago: Willett, Clark & Co., 1936.
[2] Ellen Winston, "The Assumed Increase of Mental Disease," *American Journal of Sociology*, Vol. 40, January, 1935.

One of the most accurate means of stating the probable incidence of insanity in the population has been supplied by Malzberg, who has computed the expectation of mental disease in New York State by a technique similar to that used for stating the expectation of life from the life table.[3] For each year of age from one to one hundred, he presents, for males and females separately, the number developing a mental disease during the remainder of life of 1,000 alive and sane at the beginning of the age interval. At birth, the expectation for males in 1940 was 80.5, and for females 82.0. This meant that nearly one out of twelve newborn infants would develop mental disease at some time of life in New York State. This is a far higher expectation than had prevailed twenty years earlier, when figures for the same age for males and females were 48.1 and 48.2 respectively. In 1940 the expectation for males aged nine to fourteen was 85.4, slightly more than one out of 12; among older age groups the rate was progressively lower. For those males who reached their hundredth birthday sane, the expectation of developing a mental disease during the remaining years was only 39.2, or slightly less than one-half the expectation at birth.

Since the Malzberg study is based on figures for admissions to hospitals, it omits the unknown numbers of persons who are never committed. There is no basis for a reasonable guess concerning these, so it can only be stated that somewhat more than one out of 12 persons, as of 1940, might be expected to develop some mental abnormality during their lifetimes. This is of course an impressive figure in itself. Pollock has, in addition, made calculations concerning the economic loss resulting from this high rate of mental disease.[4] On the basis of 1931 figures for the United States as a whole, he estimates that the annual cost for hospitalization is approximately 208 millions of dollars and the annual loss of earnings 569 millions. The grand total therefore is about 777 millions for the cost of hospitalized cases alone. One reason for the heavy expense is that persons hospitalized for mental diseases occupy space for longer periods, on the average, than do persons hospitalized for other types of afflictions.

In general the hospitalization rates are higher in cities than in rural areas. Landis and Page, presenting the first-admission figures for 1933, show that for all ages the rate for urban males is the highest, after which comes the rate for urban females, and then

---

[3] Benjamin Malzberg, "The Expectation of Mental Disease in New York State, 1920, 1930, 1940," in *Trends of Mental Disease*, New York: King's Crown Press, 1945, pp. 42–55.
[4] Horatio M. Pollock, *Mental Disease and Social Welfare*, Utica, N. Y.: State Hospitals Press, 1941, pp. 83–84.

rural males, with rural females the lowest of all.[5]   The contrast is not the same, however, for each of the various classifications of disorders.   The greatest contrast is found in the rates for alcoholic psychoses, which were about three and a half times as high in urban areas.   General paralysis, psychopathic personality, cerebral arterio-sclerosis, paranoia, senile dementia, schizophrenia, involutional melancholia, and the psychoneuroses were found to have higher urban rates, the contrast being greater in those named earlier.   In the manic-depressive psychoses, throughout most of the age range the rate was highest among urban females, while in most of the same age range the next highest rates were among rural males. The urban male rates and the rural female rates were somewhat lower until the middle years of life.[6]

## THE RELATION OF MENTAL ABNORMALITY TO URBAN SOCIAL DISORGANIZATION

By far the greatest and most revealing contrasts of rates of mental disorders have been found in the various sections of large industrial cities.   Here the contrasts are not a matter of high rates being merely three times greater than low rates; the contrasts are on the order of ten to one or greater.   Furthermore, the study of variations in urban districts whose characteristics are already well known yields far more meaningful information than does the cruder contrast between urban and rural areas.

The most intensive study of urban insanity rates has been car-ried on in the city of Chicago.[7]   Studies of a similar character, though of lesser scope, have been made in Providence, Milwaukee, Saint Louis, Cleveland, and other cities.[8]   These latter studies, as far as they go, confirm the findings in Chicago.

The basis of the Chicago study consisted of 34,864 cases of mental disorder admitted to four state hospitals and eight private hospitals in the Chicago region during the years 1922–1934.   These cases were classified on the basis of the various subcommunities of

[5] Carney Landis and James D. Page, *Modern Society and Mental Disease,* New York: Farrar & Rinehart, Inc., 1930, pp. 44–55.

[6] Various persons have reported preliterate societies in which the social organization appeared to be in good functioning order and in which mental abnormalities were rare. See R. E. L. Faris, "Some Observations on the Incidence of Schizophrenia in Primitive Society," *Journal of Abnormal and Social Psychology,* Vol. 29, pp. 29–30, 1934.   Such observations are not universally accepted, however.   For a discussion and an extensive bibliography, see John P. Gillin, "Personality in Preliterate Societies," *American Sociological Review,* Vol. 4, October, 1939.

[7] Robert E. L. Faris and H. Warren Dunham, *Mental Disorders in Urban Areas,* Chicago: University of Chicago Press, 1939.

[8] Stuart A. Queen, "The Ecological Study of Mental Disorders," *American Sociological Review,* Vol. 5 (1940), pp. 201–209.

the city in which the patient lived before his first admission to a hospital, and rates were computed for each area, based on the population aged fifteen and over. The lowest average annual rate in the city during this period was 48 per 100,000 population in an outlying residential area. The highest rate, more than ten times as high as the lowest, was 499, and it was that in the central business district which includes a hotel and hobo area. The next highest rate of 480 was found in an adjacent hobo and rooming-house area. The ten subcommunities with the highest rates, in fact, were all located near the center, and were hobo and rooming-house areas or Negro apartment-house areas in the most deteriorated part of the Negro districts. In general, the pattern of rates in the city area consists of a sharp concentration of high rates in the central areas and a progressive decline in all outward directions, with the lowest rates arranged along the outlying stable residential districts. Where industrial zones are located in outlying areas, as in the Lake Calumet area on the southern edge, or along the western industrial fringes, the rates are somewhat higher than in nearby residential areas.

Because of intensive research in the characteristics of the local communities in Chicago, largely carried on by the faculty and students of the Sociology Department of the University of Chicago, the conditions in these areas are quite well known. It is precisely in these areas of highest insanity rates that other indices of social disorganization are most noticeable. In the hotel and rooming-house areas the rates of suicide, venereal infection, and family disorganization are extremely high, while in the foreign-born slum areas are concentrated the high rates of juvenile delinquency and crime. These are areas of high mobility in the population, of extreme poverty and demoralization, and of cultural heterogeneity and confusion of mores.

Mental disorders are not all alike, however, and it might be expected that their different causes would indicate different relationships to social disorganization. Examination of the separate distributions of the various types of disorders yields the expected variations in results, showing certain types to be related to particular forms of social disorganization, while other disorders are associated with entirely different forms. Some types, also, are apparently not very closely related to any social disorganization that varies systematically in urban districts.

Social disorganization may be a factor both directly and indirectly. With regard to schizophrenia, there is much evidence to indicate that social experiences related to the disorganization of modern life may be fairly direct factors in causation of the abnormal behavior. In alcoholic psychosis the direct cause presumably is alcohol, but behind that is the process of addiction which leads to the extended overconsumption of the beverage. In the case of general paralysis, or paresis, the direct cause is the syphilis germ, but, as has been shown in the previous discussion of vice, this disease is largely spread by the organized prostitution industry which flourishes as a result of social and political disorganization.

## The Relation of Separate Mental Disorders to Urban Conditions

**Schizophrenia.**—While definitions of schizophrenia and descriptions of the symptoms vary in the technical literature on the subject, it can be fairly stated that the essential character of schizophrenic behavior is its unreal, dreamlike quality—an appearance of being out of touch with conventional reality—for which condition no obvious physical cause can be found. Delusions and hallucinations are common, as are inappropriate emotional states, and in many cases a progressive deterioration of intellectual capacity.

The cases of schizophrenia in the Chicago series constitute the largest single group of disorders, including 7,253 cases or about 22 per cent of total cases of mental disorder. The distribution of these cases is quite similar to that of all types of mental disorders combined. Because of the importance of these cases in the total, this result cannot be considered surprising. The highest rate of schizophrenia, like the highest rate of all insanity, is in the central area, and the next highest rates are in the adjacent districts. The lowest rate, in an outlying area, is 14 (per 100,000 population of ages 15–64) which is less than one tenth as large as the highest rate of 150. The pattern shows the same gradation from the center outward, and the same local increases in the outlying industrial districts. Rates are high both in the mobile hobo and rooming-house areas, and in the foreign-born and Negro districts.

The concentration of cases in the central areas cannot be explained on the assumption that foreign-born and Negro people are more inclined to become insane and that therefore the high rates merely represent the large numbers of such peoples in these areas. A careful analysis of this matter eliminates such a hypothesis.[9] First,

[9] It has not been universally accepted that the distribution of rates represents any causal relation between the conditions of life in the areas of high incidence and the mental disorders. In the early stages of the study, when reports were based on data

the local communities were classified into eleven types: rooming-house (comprising all of the areas which are primarily rooming-house districts), hotel and apartment-hotel, Negro apartment-house, single-home and two-flat areas, and the like. For each of these eleven classes of areas the foreign-born schizophrenia cases were divided by the foreign-born population of the areas, yielding a purely foreign-born rate. If the principal explanation of the rate pattern in the city were the differential distribution of the foreign born, this device should even it out, and the result should be a fairly equal distribution of rates. Such is far from the actual result, however. The variation by areas remains as great as ever. The foreign-born peoples are apparently differentially subject to the development of schizophrenia according to the parts of the city in which they reside, for their rates in the rooming-house areas were 126 per 100,000 adult population, while in the areas that were predominantly single-home and two-flat, renting for over $50 a month, their rates were only 21—less than a fifth as high. The calculation of rates for foreign-born males alone shows even sharper

---

less adequate than were available in the complete study, a number of objections or alternative hypotheses were raised. These were considered with care, and information was sought to test them as far as it was possible. The authors of the Chicago study eventually rejected all of these alternative hypotheses as being inconsistent with the findings. The hypotheses, and the principal reasons for their rejection, are listed below.

1. *Significance of rates.* This question was raised when the rates were based on only one year of cases from the Chicago Psychopathic Hospital. Even on the basis of this smaller number, many of the comparisons were statistically significant, i.e., they could not be accounted for on the basis of chance variation. The later research, however, contained such an enormous number of cases that most of the comparisons upon which any argument was based were overwhelmingly significant. The appendix of the Faris and Dunham volume presents, where appropriate, information on the significance of certain differences between rates.

2. *The poverty explanation.* It has been suggested that, since the great majority of cases are committed to public hospitals, which are free, there is a selection of poor people in the sample, and, since the high rates are in areas of low income, the concentration merely represents a distribution of poverty rather than of the incidence of mental disorders. Patients from all of the private hospitals in the Chicago region were included in the sample, of course, but this addition, even though the spatial distribution of cases was somewhat different from those in public hospitals, made little difference in the total because of the small number of cases from private hospitals. Their unimportance is shown in the correlation coefficient between the rates based on state hospital cases alone and those which include the private hospital cases also. The coefficient is 0.99, almost a perfect correspondence.

There remain missing the cases which are not hospitalized at all, but are cared for in their own homes. No means is available to estimate the number of such cases or their distribution in the different parts of the city. In most of the hospitalized cases the behavior preceding the time of commitment was so extremely insane that it is difficult to imagine that there could be many families in the city, excepting possibly a few very wealthy ones, in which it would be at all feasible to care for anyone in such a state. Few families allow a member to be hospitalized until they feel that they must, and when this point is reached, few families are in a position to avoid it.

The most important failure of the poverty hypothesis, however, is that it does not account for the differences in distribution between the different psychoses, except possibly for the contrast of manic-depressive psychoses and of neuroses with the others. It supplies no basis for the clear contrast between the types of schizophrenia, and between schizophrenia, alcoholic psychoses, and general paralysis. If poverty were the principal reason for the concentration of cases, there would be no reason for such contrasts to occur.

3. *The transiency hypothesis.* It has been held that some of the appearance of concentration may be the result of a statistical illusion which follows from a failure to adjust the rates for transiency. That is, if the cases from an area taken during the period

contrasts.  The highest and lowest rates were in the same groups
of areas, but the contrast is between 129 and 14, the higher rate
being about nine times as great as the lower.  The next highest rate
in this latter examination was in the Negro apartment-house district,
in which the foreign-born rate was 128.  In the areas in which
foreign-born people were in the majority, the rate was 41, only
slightly higher than the city total rate of 36.

A similar examination of the variation of the Negro rate—i.e.,
Negro cases divided by Negro population—in the various classes
of districts, yields a similar conclusion.  The Negro rates varied
by area far more than the Negro rate for the city as a whole differed from white rates.  The variation of racial and nativity rates
for the city as a whole is shown by the following figures: native
white of native parentage, 26; native white of foreign or mixed
parentage, 28; foreign-born white, 38; and Negro, 41.  The Negro
rates, however, varied from 36 to 95 in the various classes of communities.  The Negro rate within the district which was predominantly Negro-inhabited was 39, which was actually less than

of a year are divided by the population as of a single day (the day the census count is
taken), the rate may be regarded as too high if during the year there had been enough
turnover of the population to make a significantly larger number than was present on the
one census enumeration day.  It could be conceived that, if the population of the hobo
and rooming-house areas turned over three times during the year, the rate would really
be three times too high, and should therefore be reduced to one third to adjust for
transiency.  This would be appropriate, of course, only if the persons who were present
in the area during only one third of the year were not subject to hospitalization in whatever
places they spent the other two thirds.  If they were equally subject to hospitalization
elsewhere, no adjustment of rates would be required.  Accurate figures for the determination
of the amount of the transiency distortion are not available, particularly since there is
no way of knowing the probabilities of hospitalization in the areas in which the persons
move when out of the area in question; but, on the basis of a study of mobility made in
Chicago in 1934, it can be estimated that the effect of transiency on the rates is slight
at most.  In the rooming-house areas, for example, there were only 36.6 per cent who had lived
less than a year in the area, while in one of the most stable areas, the single home and
two-flat area with rentals averaging over $50 a month, there were 21.6 per cent resident
less than a year.  The slight adjustment of the rates for transiency could not obscure
the great contrasts of rates between these areas, such as that for schizophrenia, in which the
rooming-house area average annual rate was 93, while the residential rate was only 21.

Again, the transiency hypothesis fails to account for the marked differences in distribution of the various types of mental disorder and could therefore be of only minor significance at best.

4.  *The drift hypothesis.*  It has been contended that persons who are mentally
abnormal tend to fail in their economic activities and as a consequence drift into the
slum areas, from which they are eventually committed.  The concentrations of rates, therefore,
would represent not the areas in which insanity develops, but areas to which persons drift
after they become abnormal.  An unpublished study of catatonic schizophrenics, however,
a group who were sharply concentrated in the foreign-born and Negro slum areas, found
that most of the patients were born and brought up in the areas from which they were
committed and had not drifted into them.  Rate computations were also made separately
for younger (twenty-nine years and less) and older (thirty and over) schizophrenics of
both paranoid and the catatonic types, and of first commitments and recommitments.  If
drift were important, there should be a sharper concentration of older cases and of
recommitted cases, for these have had more time to fail and to drift to the slums.  The
findings, however, were that the amount of concentration was approximately the same,
except for some indications of a drift of some of the catatonic schizophrenics from one
low-income area to another, that is, from foreign-born slum areas to hobo areas.

Once more, it may be pointed out that the contrast between distributions of different
mental disorders is inconsistent with the hypothesis that a drift to the slums as a result
of economic failure is the principal cause, for there is no reason to assume that the drifts
would be in such precise streams.

the Negro rate of 41 for the whole city.  It is within this area, however, that the rates were extremely high for the other groups— 88 for the native white of foreign or mixed parentage, 131 for the foreign-born white, and 138 for the native white of native parentage. The figures indicate not only a great variation within all nativity and racial groups by area, but also a tendency for the racial rates to be highest in the areas in which another race is in the majority.[10]

**Types of Schizophrenia.**—Although the belief is held among the staffs of many hospitals that the difficulty of accurately distinguishing the subtypes of schizophrenia makes it not worth attempting, such a separation is nevertheless made in the hospitals in the Chicago region.  When separate examinations of the spatial distributions of the rates for these types are made, it is immediately obvious that there are some significant distinctions.  The three principal types, paranoid, hebephrenic, and catatonic, had clearly distinct distributions, the greatest contrast being between the paranoid and the catatonic, with the hebephrenic somewhat intermediate.

The paranoid group contained a higher proportion of males and of older persons than did the other two types.  The high rates were sharply concentrated in the central business and hobo areas and in the adjacent rooming-house districts.  The rates in the foreign-born and Negro areas were above average but not as high as those in the districts of highest mobility.

The catatonic group, containing more younger persons than the other two and more females than males, presents a sharply contrasting distribution.  The highest rates were in the foreign-born areas and in certain parts of the Negro district, but not in the same parts that had the high paranoid rates.  The catatonic rates in the central district and the adjacent rooming-house areas were in the lowest classification, although it is here that the paranoid rates were highest.

The hebephrenic rates were high in the central business district, in the near-by Negro and rooming-house areas, and also in some of the adjacent foreign-born areas.  These appear to be somewhat intermediate between the extreme contrasts of the other two types.

Some additional statistical observations confirm the connection between mobility and paranoid rates and between catatonic rates and foreign-born and Negro areas and also agree concerning the intermediate status of the hebephrenic pattern.  Pearsonian coefficients of correlation were computed for each of these three sets of

[10] Details are available in tables in Faris and Dunham. *op. cit.*, pp. 50–55 and in the appendix

rates compared to the percentages of hotel and lodging-house residents in each community. The high paranoid coefficient, +0.82, indicates the high relation to mobility. The negative coefficient for the catatonic rates, —0.29, indicates that these are not associated with high mobility. The hebephrenic coefficient of +0.57 is intermediate.

The marriage rates in the different communities of the city may furnish a further index of stability, and therefore conversely of mobility. The correlation of paranoid rates with the ratio of married to single persons is, as expected, a high negative, —0.66. The catatonic rates are not correlated with this index, apparently, for the coefficient is 0.00. Again the hebephrenic coefficient of —0.52 is between the other two.

The correlation of catatonic rates with percentages of foreign-born and Negro populations in the different communities, however, yields a high positive coefficient of +0.86, while the coefficient for the paranoid rates with these percentages is only +0.11. Again the hebephrenic coefficient of +0.40 is intermediate.

The association of the catatonic rates with foreign-born areas does not necessarily mean that more of the persons having this disorder are foreign-born. The actual percentage of foreign-born is nearly the same as among the other two classifications—slightly less in fact. It merely means that these rates are high in the areas in which these populations constitute the majority.

**Nature of Schizophrenic Symptoms.**—Some of the traits of the schizophrenic have a resemblance to the symptoms that develop in persons who have been isolated for extended periods. These latter often develop a rich fantasy life, with inappropriate or unconventional emotions, and apparently in time also suffer deterioration of the mind. They also have, in common with the schizophrenics, a deterioration of the wish to associate with other persons—a decline in the sociability motive. The development of seclusiveness in turn contributes to further isolation where the preference of the person is a factor in social contacts.

It has been held that this trait of seclusiveness is a central aspect of the abnormality of the schizophrenic and that it may be a hereditary deficiency. It is not entirely necessary to assume a hereditary cause, however, for many persons appear to lose their preference for sociability after, and as a consequence of, a period of isolation which was not a matter of their own choice.[11] Observation of

---

[11] Some of the evidence on this point is presented in R. E. L. Faris. "Cultural Isolation and the Schizophrenic Personality," *American Journal of Sociology*, Vol. 40, September, 1934.

long-term prisoners held in solitary confinement, for example, has shown that many of these, though confined against their will, nevertheless in time lose their desire for freedom and social contacts with others. Sociability is thus probably not an inborn trait, but is acquired individually in the process of interaction with other persons. Apparently it is a trait that must be continuously nourished by social intercourse to avoid deterioration of the impulse to associate with others.

In studies of early experiences in the lives of patients diagnosed as schizophrenics, it is often possible to observe clear indications of a partial social isolation, in many cases not of the person's own choosing. This isolation is essentially a restriction of the person's social world to a very small group and a deprivation of the normal intimate primary relations with persons outside of the family. Such partial isolation weakens the social adaptability of the person by depriving him of the knowledge of how to deal with other persons. His partial failures cause discouragement and further isolation, in a process which can properly be termed a vicious circle.

A special examination by the author of 100 cases of schizophrenia which, in order to avoid a bias of selection, were taken consecutively from the records of a state hospital in New England, yields useful information on the factors involved in isolation. Approximately half of the cases (53) were older persons whose friends or relatives could not be located or could not supply information about the early life of the patient. Of the remainder, where sufficient information was available about childhood experiences, the case records revealed that more than half, 27 as against 21, had been definitely sociable in childhood. These were clearly not deficient by heredity, but developed their disorder as a result of abnormal social experience. In the typical case there were three stages visible: first, a stage of normal sociability, in which the child wished and sought for companionship; second, a process of exclusion by others, accompanied by a continued effort to gain their approval and comradeship; third, acceptance of defeat, involving a change of interests away from social intercourse and the construction of a system of rationalization, developing into an interaction between the growing preference for seclusiveness and further exclusion by others in the vicious-circle process.

While apparently any of a number of fortuitous conditions may start the exclusion condition—deafness, inability to speak English, physical deformities, and the like—by far the most common condition involved is the development within the family of the traits of the "overprotected child"—the pampered, egocentric, intolerant product of too much adoration by a parent—and the inability of such a child to gain acceptance into groups of normal children. Of the 101 cases in the series examined, there were 54 in which the factors producing isolation were apparent, and of these, 29 were unmistakably of this "spoiled child" type.[12]

While the overprotection or pampering of children appears to be a factor in the development of schizophrenia, it is not to be supposed that this is by itself sufficient. There are many children subjected to such influences who in time outgrow their egocentric and infantile traits, usually by means of participating in the activities of children who do not grant their pampered playmates exceptional status. They learn from other children that they are not in fact more precious, able, and important than any others, but that this is only a peculiar conception their mothers have of them, as other mothers often have of their own children. But, where there are special difficulties in the way of gaining entrance into activities of other children, there are possibilities of developing the isolation process. It is in the slum areas of the city, where delinquency rates are high and where juveniles have a tradition of toughness, that children are least tolerant of the pampered and egocentric weakling who cries for his mother when frustrated. Possibly it is this fact that accounts for the greater tendency for peoples in these areas to develop schizophrenia. Elsewhere, in stable residential neighborhoods, or in suburbs, there may be a greater availability of sympathetic playmates and a higher degree of parental and neighborhood cooperation which eases the process of assimilation of the spoiled child into play groups with other children.

The following condensation of information from a case in the author's files illustrates a typical beginning of the exclusion process:

In his early childhood, Jim had a smooth, round, attractive baby face, and long blond curly hair. His mother, an affectionate and sentimental woman, kept him dressed in fancy clothes and trained his hair into long curls of the "Lord Fauntleroy" type. Since the family lived in a slum, little Jim was unique in appearance among the neighborhood children, who were customarily allowed at an early age to run the streets and to develop independence.

Although tied to his mother's apron strings until five, Jim entered public school at the proper age. On his first day at school he was automatically subjected to teasing, pranks, and beatings by his schoolmates and returned home

---

[12] A member of the staff of the same hospital, examining a longer series of schizophrenics, found about 75 per cent to have had this experience in childhood. Since he had opportunities for fuller inquiry, it may be presumed that his percentage is more nearly accurate.

in tears to receive comfort from his mother.  The experience of persecution was repeated a number of times in the first weeks of school, each time resulting in crying and running to his mother.  Only after these experiences did Jim's father prevail upon his mother to have the curls removed.  It was apparently too late, however, to avoid the reputation of "sissy" and "crybaby," and the reaction of his schoolmates was not altered.  By returning home daily after school, Jim fell further behind the neighborhood boys in athletic skills and other conventional abilities and knowledge.  His father made attempts to teach him to throw and catch a baseball, but without succeeding in arousing a strong interest.  Jim did not prefer seclusion, however, but yearned for friendship with boys and often made ineffectual efforts to establish it; but since he did not know the conventions among boys of his age, he did not succeed.  He therefore had to spend much of his time at home. He developed an interest in reading, concentrating on pulp fiction, detective stories, and tales of success.

The importance of social life to normality of behavior, particularly of experiences in primary group interaction, is suggested by the special handicaps to which such isolated persons as Jim are subjected.  Success in most pursuits of adults requires a reasonably adequate familiarity with human nature, with the subtle and unwritten conventions that are acquired unwittingly in years of intimate association with other persons.  Formal and secondary social contacts are not sufficient to develop this knowledge, for they conceal the real feelings of persons, hiding emotions behind tact.  Nor is reading a satisfactory substitute, for too much of fiction and biography is distorted, simplified, and altered toward fantasy to improve the story.

The person who is isolated from primary contacts outside of his own family during the years of childhood and youth is too far behind to catch up in his adult years.  The direct and frank rebuffs which children give to one another, which enable each to acquire from others a reasonably accurate conception of his own status, are rarely given among adults.  The result of years of isolation is a great and socially incapacitating ignorance of how other people think, feel, and behave.  This is often complicated by misconceptions acquired in family life or from reading which lead further to disastrous mistakes in social interaction.

Incidents from two similar cases may furnish illustrations.  Jim, whose early life is described above, and Peter, who had a very similar experience in his childhood, both failed when they tried to deal with the relatively hard-boiled men with whom they had to work in their attempted occupations:

Jim left high school after two years and decided to seek his fortune in the world of business.  The best jobs he was able to obtain were the low-paid, routine occupations of shipping clerk, elevator boy, and the like.  After about two months in a job without a promotion, he usually quit and sought another, for his expectations of a career were formed by the success stories of pulp fiction, and he expected to get ahead rapidly.  In one position, that of office boy, he had some contact with men not much older than himself, and sought to establish friendships.  Not knowing any better technique, he bought boxes of candy and other gifts, which he presented to them.  Although the men accepted these offerings, they regarded Jim as queer and did not invite him to join in their social activities.  Jim's efforts only increased, but since the gifts required more money than he was earning, he began to embezzle small amounts from the firm.  In time this activity was discovered, and his employer called him in for an interview.  His tears and lack of explanation led the employer to advise Jim's father to consult a physician, who in turn brought about Jim's commitment to a mental hospital.

. . . . . . . .

Peter left high school in the middle of his course and sought one job after another.  He never stayed in a position for long, leaving either because of his dissatisfaction or through discharge.  The decreasing employment opportunities of the depression years discouraged him, and when one day he saw a recruiting poster of the U. S. Navy, he impulsively joined.  He was sent for training to a station in the vicinity of his home city, where at once he received shocks of disappointment.  The men were not of the type he had imagined or had learned from his fiction-reading to expect.  Instead of clean-cut, idealistic heroes, he found about him hard-boiled, vulgar-talking, unsympathetic men.  Peter made such blunders as objecting to the type of language the men used and to other aspects of their conduct.  The reactions varied from scornful laughter to fighting, and on one occasion Peter was knocked out.  His tearful complaints to an officer brought no sympathy, so Peter took the drastic step of threatening suicide.  He climbed to the top of the signaling tower but soon came down the ladder without winning concessions from the officer.  He became a favorite butt of pranks and mild persecution by the other men in training and began to develop exaggerated suspicions of the degree of persecution.  After a second incomplete suicide gesture the officials were willing to release him.  At the time of his discharge Peter was sent to a hospital to take care of minor ailments, but while there he expressed such suspicions of persecution that he was in time transferred to a mental hospital.

Status is an important aspect of social behavior and interaction in any society, and in our complex civilization it is intertwined with virtually all aspects of life.  Effective cooperation requires an accurate sense of one's own status and a reasonably good knowledge of the status of others.  And yet, because of our conventions which discourage frequent and accurate representations of the status of persons, and because of the sensitivity and tact which is involved in most adult relations, such accuracy requires a rich knowledge of human nature and a lively use of the imagination. The person who, through isolation, has failed to acquire this knowledge and who carries in his mind a number of misconceptions often fails in many aspects of his social relations. To make his troubles worse, he is usually unaware of the reason for his many failures.

Such a process develops not infrequently among overprotected children and produces one of the typical complexes of the schizophrenic—the paranoid reaction. While not all pampered infants develop exceptional abilities, or even the belief that they are more gifted than other persons, it is not uncommon for some of these to be mentally enriched by the large amount of intimate contact with the adult who does the pampering. Also, since a mother's pet often is also the teacher's pet, he frequently makes a good record in school, and therefore has some basis for a belief in his own superiority. The exclusion from the play of his schoolmates, furthermore, provides opportunities for more than the usual amount of reading, thereby contributing to the development of even greater mental precocity.

The extreme conceit of the paranoid child, then, has its origin not merely in fantasy, but in the words and actions of the parent who is most important in the life of the child. The conception is often supported by other adults, particularly teachers. The principal dissent from such admiration usually stems from other children, and their reactions are easily rationalized as the results of jealousy. Often the rationalization itself is supplied by the parent. The effect of such rejection of the judgment of other children is to make the conceited child increasingly indifferent to their opinion and therefore to cause him to lose contact with the one social group which could provide him with an accurate conception of himself and with the means of revising his personality and adapting his behavior to the expectations of others.

The paranoid character grows out of such childish egocentricity. The wisdom of his parents may appear cosmic to an overprotected child, and therefore the agreeable and never effectively challenged opinion that he is exceptional among children becomes a central and immutable fact of his life-organization. He expects special privileges as a matter of course and takes success in life for granted. The failures that he encounters do not alter his egocentricity, for he has a well-developed system of accounting for them. And yet failures in adult life are all but inevitable for such a person. On

rare occasions an individualistic creative artist such as Richard
Wagner may be able to make his own terms for dealing with other
persons, but in the ordinary career the necessities for being reasonable and agreeable to other persons are involved in the possibilities
of success and failure.  The paranoid personality does not even
know how or why he irritates and offends other persons, and,
because of the tendency of most persons to avoid direct issues when
possible, he is in many cases not aware of the consequences of his
inability to cooperate effectively.  He only knows that he is not
succeeding as he always expected to and that his failures are so
general and yet without visible cause that there could only be one
explanation—that there is a vast and secret conspiracy against him.
Having such a suspicion, it is easy for a person with an alert mind
to find supporting indications.  A strange stare on the part of some
person, a whispered conversation between two persons across a
room, friendly approaches and kindnesses on the part of others—
all these suggest the activities of secret plotters.

The paranoid complex—conceit and suspicion—may have every
degree of development.  The symptoms in minor form are common
among persons who are not regarded as abnormal.  The child who
drops a dish and says to another, accusingly, "See what you made
me do?" or the tennis player who misses a shot and conspicuously
examines the strings of his racket to imply that he was not responsible for his own failure is exhibiting this reaction.  A more severe
form, though without the extreme development that requires hospitalization, may be found among the highly intelligent but conceited students who not only cannot accept with good grace a low
or average grade in a course, but must blame the professor, or even
imagine a conspiracy involving several faculty members.

In the extreme form, paranoid reactions are bitter and dangerous.
The fullest development of delusions of grandeur occurs in cases
in which the person is convinced that he is the most worthy person
in the world.  If this is so, then it is obvious that there is a mon-
strous state of injustice, for the greatest person on earth should
surely have a more satisfactory status and should in fact be in a
position of great leadership.  The most logical inference is that the
plot to keep him down is one that is vast in scale, involving persons
of prominence and power.  The wrong involved is also so enormous
that measures of desperation against the evil persons are required.
Homicidal plans are thus frequently made, and in a certain proportion of the cases they are actually carried out.  In the case of the
paranoiac, such killings are not necessarily the result of sudden

bursts of uncontrolled rage but may be the outcome of a long process of study and planning. Though based on fantastic assumptions and motivated by abnormal resentment, paranoid plots are typically developed in a process of cool and systematic thinking.

The paranoid reaction in schizophrenia is thus clearly a development associated with experience in planning and executive action. This reaction has a lower frequency among females than among males and a relatively low frequency among Negroes (in the Chicago sample), particularly those of the lowest income and education group. A relatively late age at first admission is also exhibited by paranoid schizophrenics. In the Chicago sample only 26 per cent of the paranoid males were committed under the age of thirty, and only 14 per cent of the females. This is in sharp contrast to the ages at first commitment of the catatonic cases, in which 67 per cent of the males and 57 per cent of the females were under thirty. It takes more time and intellectual resources to develop the degree of organization of paranoid symptoms calling for hospitalization than it does to develop the catatonic reaction. A number of cases have been found in the Chicago sample in which an early first commitment involved a diagnosis of catatonic schizophrenia, while in the same case at a later age there appeared a diagnosis of paranoid schizophrenia.

**Complexes Involving Guilt.**—Within certain areas of modern society there may be found powerful and yet inconsistent influences regarding the nature of sin, particularly sex transgression, and the penalties for it. These influences inevitably have a confusing effect, and this would be far more severe and widely distributed among the general population were it not for the fact that most persons acquire, from their general primary relations with others, a balanced point of view which provides them with a *modus vivendi* for the complexities of moral beliefs.

The matter of sex morality is particularly confused by the general conspiracy of silence maintained traditionally by older generations toward the younger. From the formal influences of conventional society a youth would learn that there is such a thing as sex but would not know the subject in any detail. He would gather from many kinds of literature, ranging from tabloid newspapers to the Bible, that it involves a powerful force that many persons find irresistible, in spite of the many influences which society exerts to control it. At the same time there is a moral and theological tradition which holds that sex behavior, though tolerable in marriage, is essentially evil in nature and extremely sinful outside of marriage. Along with this view may be found accompanying folk beliefs which sometimes cause young persons to believe that even minor transgressions leave a visible mark which is apparent to others and which inevitably disgraces a person for the rest of his lifetime.

Until recent years, the principal source of sex education has been the informal exchange of knowledge and opinions that passes from child to child throughout the years of schooling. Though much of the information they transmit is crude, incomplete, and inaccurate, it does have the effect of reducing the sense of mystery and of putting the subject in a somewhat more balanced moral perspective. The terror and confusion are removed, and the normality of the interest and activity become understood.

The experiences of overprotection and isolation, however, may, just as in the case of the paranoid schizophrenics, so deprive the youth of this indispensable influence that he reaches adulthood with only the knowledge that he picks up outside of primary group communication. In most cases this means that he has lost his last opportunity, for conventional adult social relations do not have the character of the direct and uninhibited interaction of children and youths. He is without the proper equipment to deal with the many situations in which sex becomes involved and is subject to strong moral torment because of the inconsistencies he encounters.

The typical process that involves the extreme development of such a complex begins with the overprotection of the child, usually by the mother, and consequent isolation from other children. It is the mother who is particularly obsessed with sexual prudishness and who is intensely interested in religion who is most inclined to transmit to her child a special horror of the subject of sex. In these cases again, where the mother is the principal source of social influence and knowledge, her ideas tend to have a cosmic importance to the child, perhaps in many cases more than she intends. The child becomes a fanatic on the subject, and acquires the conception that sex is inexpressibly evil, dirty, and brutish, and that sexual transgressions can lead only to utter and final social disgrace and to theological condemnation. The normality of sex and its role in reproduction are often unknown to these persons, who see in it only an uncommon but powerful influence of the devil.

When such young persons approach adulthood, it becomes increasingly difficult to avoid encounters with sexual influences of some sort. Newspapers, magazines, novels, and motion pictures thrust the subject upon them. Popular songs concentrate their major efforts on celebrating by innuendo the place of sex in life. The subject of sex also becomes well-nigh inevitable in the normal approaches young persons make to one another in the courtship process. The sheltered and innocent youth eventually encounters sex with a shock. It may be only a trivial occasion such as a kiss or a caress which stirs unmistakable internal sensations. The result is often a crisis, a panic, which requires some drastic reaction.

The responses to such crises vary. One of the most extreme reactions is that of complete collapse. The person recognizes sex sensations and therefore becomes convinced that he is inhabited by the devil and is without hope of being saved from this influence. He not only is morally lost but is also totally disgraced among people and can only turn away and suffer the catastrophe. Such a person often reacts by abandoning all activity, taking to a chair or bed, refusing to talk or apparently to hear others, and turning his face away—totally defeated by his sin.[13]

Another response, less extreme and hopeless, is the attempt to deny to himself and to others the nature of the evil, and to deny that the impulses lie within his own human tendencies. A most common effort of this sort is the claim that someone is sending an influence of a mystical character—thought waves, electric waves— or that someone has been polluting his mind with poisoned food, or with gas. This claim disguises the nature of the problem and puts the responsibility upon someone else, usually an unknown person. Inquiry about the effects of the poison or the thought influence often reveals that it causes, in his belief, the sex sensations or fantasies.

The following excerpt from a case of this type furnishes an illustration of the reaction:[14]

Samuel Morton was committed to a state hospital at about the age of thirty, following an incident in which he assaulted an elderly university professor in the latter's office. When he was asked to give a series of interviews at the hospital, for research purposes, he willingly agreed and gave an explanation of his actions and a statement of his life history. He stated that he assaulted the professor because he believed that the latter had been poisoning his mind with a brain-wave machine, which made him have bad thoughts.

Samuel was the son of orthodox Jewish parents and was born and grew up in the slum sections of a large American city. He was attached to his parents, and he concentrated more on studies than on playing with other children.

---

[13] In mid-1946, when the venereal disease rate among the United States Army of occupation in Germany reached an all-time high, *Time* reported the following news item: "In Frankfurt, Army psychiatrists noted a growing total of mental cases, particularly among soldiers scheduled for return to the U. S. Symptoms: obsessions of 'shame and fear' as a result of 'sexual promiscuity.'"

[14] From an unpublished study by H. Warren Dunham.

He played the violin and studied various subjects, including such university subjects as medicine, philosophy, and law. As his parents were poor, he earned his expenses by playing the violin in dance orchestras.

While his childhood had been passed in surroundings that were pious, moral, and respectable, the company that Samuel associated with at the dance halls was very different in character. Since, however, he had avoided other boys, whom his family called "roughnecks" in his childhood, he had little understanding of the other musicians and the patrons of the hall and easily misunderstood their motives. Presumably many references to sex went unnoticed by him, but when the topic came unmistakably into the conversation, he usually reproved the other persons, or simply walked away.

On one occasion he arranged to call on a girl whom he had met at a dance hall, and when he arrived at her house she was taking a bath. She called out to him to take a chair and wait in the parlor. After a few minutes, she entered the room nude. According to his account, he merely laughed and told her to get dressed, and he took her out to have dinner. His sex interest was aroused, however, and he experienced a certain amount of conflict. He was bothered because he could not get his mind off the girl, and also because she was not the "intellectual type" and not suitable for him to marry. Obsessive imagination possessed him, and he frequently had images of nude women and of sections of the female anatomy. He began to claim that experimenters at a nearby university were responsible for these images. When he read in a newspaper an account of a brain-wave machine used by scientists at the university for psychological research, he boarded a streetcar and went to the university. Apparently he did not have accurate knowledge of who the experimenters were, for the man he assaulted worked in a different department and had nothing to do with brain research.

During the interviews, Samuel made frequent reference to the imagery which intruded upon his attention. "While I am talking to you these people who are communicating with me are continually interrupting us. Right now they are sending me a picture of the hospital. They send this to me by way of my retinal visual center. You understand this, do you not? (The interviewer asked the nature of the picture.) They showed me that I was ill and in bed and I saw the head nurse getting after me. She was probably interested in me because my father is a physician. Isn't it wonderful the mechanism they have by which they can send me these pictures? It is one of those famous inventions which will, no doubt, have its place, but right now it is being used for a very base purpose. This device is patented by Blank University. I think that in the future opticians may be able to make a great use of this device. I know that you understand that these are not hallucinations. What do you think about them?"

Later on, after describing a sexual approach that had been made to him by a stranger, he stated, "You know that I have been sick with a fever and a headache which are caused by these voices. They annoyed me last night. On the ward the attendants are forcing me to make a bed, and I do not believe that a man in my physical condition should have to do this. These

voices are in defiance of all law and morals. After I get out of here and find
out who these people are, I certainly intend to have indictments drawn up
against them. Last night they annoyed me continually with what I call their
continuity of attack. I am fearful that they will produce intra-cranial fever.
They talked about a wealthy lady that I met who is now in Baltimore. Before
I was sent out here, she had asked me to do some work for her, but I was
unable to do this because these people began to experiment with me."

In the later interviews Samuel became more frank and specific regarding
the content of these fantasies. "Last night I had experimental dreams and
also was shown some pictures. (He describes the highly erotic content of
the dream without disguise or euphemism.) All night long they annoyed me
with experimental seminal emissions, leaving me in a semi-exhausted condition in the morning. . . . In the last few days their talk has been much less.
Formerly it was nothing more than a fatigue study with apparently no therapy
involved. This morning they tried to arouse my anger against my father
by calling him dirty names. They would also show father in rather funny
and absurd costumes. When I was cleaning the ward this morning they were
continually annoying me by showing pictures of nude females. . . . These
experimental pictures which I receive at night are not dreams, they are
pictures. The picture last night of my sister showed her very ill and with
tired arms. She seemed to be frantic about being at home. Right now they
furnished a picture of her in the nude. Years ago I was wandering around
the house in a thoughtful mood and I accidentally walked into her room and
saw her lying on the bed nude. I was rather embarrassed and merely said,
'Pardon me,' and walked away. She also seemed embarrassed and said,
'Excuse me, Samuel.' "

The imagery often made only brief interruptions in the interviews, but
in each case he referred to the "pictures" as if they came from an external
source. "On ——— and ——— Streets once there was a dog attacking a
little girl. People started to throw things at the dog and finally drove him
away. This was a little Polish girl and she was very poorly dressed. Wait
a minute, please don't give me those pictures. They are trying to show me
how a certain girl looks. I was often moody because of the lack of brilliance
in school. It seemed like I always wanted to get out and to take long walks in
the park. I was shy and quiet, as old as I was, very abstract, and often
wanted to be by myself."

Samuel was asked at one point why he believed that he had been singled
out by the university scientists for these experiments. "It is because I have
innate courage and ability, and I am of an intellectual trend of mind. They
are making studies in poetry, music, form, color, psychology, esthetic sexual
responses, observations under sexual stimulation, and studies of sensuality;
in physiology, studies in sound, noise, and euphony."

While the claims of seeing images and hearing voices are often
referred to as hallucinations, it is not necessary to infer that the
schizophrenic always confuses these experiences with ordinary

reality. In many cases there are clear indications that he regards these as experiences having a special character. Furthermore, despite furious insistence when challenged, it is possible in some cases to draw out a patient sympathetically and find that he does not really hear, or see, these things in the ordinary sense. A schizophrenic patient who violently insisted that he was Christ explained to the author in a calmer moment that the latter could also take a role at will, illustrating the process of identification by referring to the way in which persons admire and partially impersonate the leading actor in an intensely absorbing motion picture. The same patient, on another occasion, claimed to have no memory before a certain recent date. Only a few minutes later, however, he answered questions about a trip he had taken to Florida some years before. His claims were obviously not to be accepted at face value—they were metaphorical expressions which he used for force in his language, for his feelings were too intense for ordinary terms. Others have observed the same principle. An investigator asked some children who "heard voices" to describe the character of the sound.[15] The children then spoke of the voices as being "quiet voices" or "not really a voice, nor even a whisper, but a sort of silent whisper." This appears to be very close to an unacknowledged, but perhaps not entirely unrecognized, action of conscience.

Similarly, certain schizophrenics of the same type as Samuel Morton report that they "feel electricity." It is not to be assumed that these persons could not actually distinguish their true sensations from the shock one obtains from an electric circuit. Further questioning often reveals that the sensation is "like electricity" and is localized in the head or the abdomen or genitals. Sometimes it is described as a "buzz" which appears at certain times only, and often the connection between such sensations and sexual stimulations is as clear as is the case of the "experimental pictures" of Samuel Morton. By denying, or attempting to deny, the true nature of the sensation, the schizophrenic is attempting to escape from the sense of horror, but the agitation that accompanies the statement suggests that in many cases, perhaps most, the effort is not completely successful. It is a desperate attempt to convince others, and as much as possible to convince themselves—an effort that does not fully achieve its purpose.

Another schizophrenic reaction to the shock of sex stimulation is that of cleaning up and reforming the environment—the home,

---

[15] Max Levin, "Auditory Hallucination in Non-Psychotic Children," *American Journal of Psychiatry*, Vol. 11, pp. 1119–1153, May, 1932.

the neighborhood and city, and even the world. The person, appalled at his thoughts and temptations which appear as "dirtiness" in his mind, inferentially ascribes his difficulties to his environment and seeks relief by cleaning it. Some spend their time incessantly washing their hands, dusting, or cleaning the floor. Others attack dirt and evil on a larger scale.

In the following case, Arthur J., a young patent lawyer, furnishes an illustration of the more frenzied and large-scale reaction of cleansing.

Arthur J. grew up in a home that had a strong Christian and moral emphasis. After college training he moved to the metropolis to live alone in a hotel for men, where the moral standards were in great contrast to those of his home. There he made some casual friendships, living quietly and studying law at night in addition to carrying on his work as a junior patent lawyer. His friends did not know the extent of his prudishness but were aware that he was somewhat more moral than the average city youth.

On one occasion Arthur became involved in an affair with a girl, the details of which are not known, and suffered in consequence a violent attack of conscience. He spent a sleepless night, during which he, in his own words, "fought the good fight."

The following morning, a Thursday, there began a period of frenzied and irrational activity, most of which had reference to reform, improvement, or cleaning. The first idea was to devise a rocket in order to travel to another planet. While he had no more than the idea of doing so, he took the inventor's attitude of worrying that some one might steal the idea and beat him to it. He did, however, mention the project to two of the men who worked in the same office, but they believed that he was joking.

Thursday night Arthur stayed up all night, "fighting." About two o'clock in the morning he wrote a letter to the president of a large university, volunteering to take charge of getting men to work on the rocket project and offering to be the man to ride the rocket. In contrast to his usual reserved and organized style of writing, the letter was florid and wandered to other subjects, giving high praise to Admiral Byrd, and ending with a tribute to President Roosevelt and the New Deal. Remembering that a man who had a room across the hall was a patent adviser, he attempted to wake him, but since the latter was a sound sleeper, he failed. He continued his "fighting" the rest of the night, and accosted the patent man in the morning, telling of his letter concerning the rocket project. The patent expert advised him not to mail the letter.

Friday morning he stayed away from his office, spending his time instead at the public library, looking up information on rockets. At noon he mailed the letter and then went to see the head of his department. The head persuaded him to stop the letter, and Arthur took the necessary steps. That evening he joined a group of his friends in a customary game of poker, saying at the start that he would play just one hour and then leave. His friends noticed that his mind was not on the game and asked him if he wanted to drop out, but he declined. His play, however, was listless, and he had to be reminded to deal, ante, and draw. Finally, with no excuse or apology, he left and went to his room.

An hour or so later he telephoned one of his poker group and told him that there was good music on the radio, then that he had noticed the steam pressure must be too high and that the floor was hot. Following other rambling remarks, he invited the friend up for a talk. When his friend came, he told him of the rocket idea and showed a draft of the letter he had written about it. The friend, recognizing that something was wrong, encouraged him to talk about his troubles and drew him out. Arthur's remarks were disorganized and became increasingly intense, as if he were working up to a subject that he could not quite bear to face. He spoke of his unworthiness, his sin, and confessed four or five "love affairs." He said that he had missed his calling and should have been a minister. He spoke of wishing to help people and expressed great idealism. On the other hand, he thought his sin made him unworthy, and he earnestly insisted that his friend give up liquor and tobacco.

The friend describes the next stage of the interview as follows. "Then his attention seemed attracted by the strange twists to ideas we were uncovering, and he saw that anything was possible (even a trip by rocket?). He told me about some strange visions he had once had, and that they came when he had had a nervous breakdown three years before. (He had then been working very hard and had been alone except for his landlady and the men who worked at his office, whom he avoided because they were not his own kind. He had been touched off by some experience with a girl.) At about the same time, I realized that he could not confess his worries and troubles, because he did not see any hope at all—he had been brought up with certain fundamental ideals, and he had violated them. The result was acute mental anguish—he went through several spasms of torture, tears, clenched jaw and fist, the worst of the kind I ever saw, and after each one for a moment was most rational. Then, of course, I realized that he was starting another serious breakdown, so I abandoned my efforts to reason his trouble out with him and merely tried to keep him calm, because after the last and most violent spasm he began to be hysterical. This started with ideas about the filth all over the city and the responsibility of the electrical company for it; the dirty washrooms at the public library; the look of appeal and need from the faces of people who turned to him as he passed. I almost had the notion at one moment that he thought himself a new savior, and he mentioned having dressed to try to be a minister as closely as his wardrobe would allow. But he rapidly began to wander in his speech, and to cover politics, Europe, and other subjects, with most unusual and brilliant connections between them."

The friend summoned another acquaintance, and the two continued to talk with Arthur, who carried on his excited discourse. At one period he shouted obscenely his disgust with big corporations, politicians, dirty streets, smoky air, and the like. He boasted about his adventures as an adulterer, and finally roared with laughter for ten minutes over one of his remarks. Then he suddenly became sick, and he went out to vomit. When he returned, he quieted down and became absorbed in quiet thought. Eventually he tired and was persuaded to go to bed.

The following day a relative came to get him, telling him they were taking him to his home town for a rest. He accepted the plan, and was taken to a mental hospital near his home, which he entered without protest.

In a number of schizophrenic cases, a series of life problems finds an apparent solution in a plan thought up by the patient. When his problems seem to him to be the same as those of others, he tends to believe that he has a solution of the world's difficulties. The magnitude of this idea also suggests that destiny chose him to be a savior of humanity. Hence there arises the thought that he may be a second Christ, and that he has the duty of putting over his new scheme for the benefit of the world.

Such a development is illustrated by the case of Albert, a young commercial artist, who was committed at the age of twenty-eight:[16]

Albert, the second of four sons in the family of a tailor, was the special pet of his father until the latter died when Albert was sixteen years old. He absorbed a greater amount of moral idealism than did his brothers and chose a career in painting, in contrast to the ordinary commercial careers his brothers preferred. He never achieved an entirely normal status with other children or with young men of his age, but always considered himself superior in talent and morality. His comrades considered him different but interesting.

During his early adult years, Albert became involved in a series of conflicts which greatly disturbed him, for he saw no solutions to them. These were conflicts of different types, moral, esthetic, economic, and psychological. He had formed in his childhood a strong homosexual attachment to his father and had come to have a sense of guilt connected with it. He had furthermore acquired in his childhood a violent anti-Semitic prejudice, only to learn in his adult years that his family was of Jewish descent. He had acquired a moral distaste for commercial art, and yet he could not earn a living by any other means. He had learned to consider himself as a romantic and tragic figure, like his literary idol, Poe, but could not persuade his acquaintances to accept him in the role—they presumed he was clowning. After a period of easy earning, the depression threw him out of work, and he came to hate the necessity of either asking his brother for money or going without pocket funds. He fell in love with a fragile and prudish girl, who did not find herself attracted to him. Finally, he became severely addicted to

---

16 The case is presented more fully in a paper by the author, "Reflections of Social Disorganization in the Behavior of a Schizophrenic Patient," *American Journal of Sociology,* Vol. 50, pp. 134–141.

alcohol and, after a period of absention and relapse, found himself unable to give up.

During the idleness of his unemployed period, Albert engaged in a considerable amount of serious reading, hoping to find some way out of these problems. He was fond of Poe because he recognized a parallel in the artist, addicted to liquor, and highly romantic in love, who led a tragic and short life. He sought for other examples, including John Barrymore, and certain French writers. He also read works on religion, philosophy, and science. One day his older brother handed him a cheap paper-bound book bought at a newsstand—*A Night in Luxembourg*, by Rémy de Gourmont. Albert read this with interest, and in the course of the reading he was so struck with parallels to his own life and problems that he decided that the book contained the key to his difficulties and also to those of the whole world. In a brief period of excited discovery, he found a resolution of his conflicts, and decided that somehow he had been chosen to restate the ideas of de Gourmont and to give them to the world, inaugurating a new utopian era.

He set out to write, in a series of books, the new system. His enthusiasm and excitement were so great that he wrote rapidly and threw the papers on the floor. Sentences were often incomplete, and much of the writing consisted of ideas and reminders that were to be treated fully when he could get around to it. He interrupted this work only to send letters to de Gourmont, to the newspaper, and to certain local celebrities, informing them of the new system he had discovered which would solve the difficulties of the world. He casually informed his landlady, who had called to collect the rent, that he was Christ.

The content of his writing, emotional and eloquent, consisted of an application of his new system of *Love and Clear Reason*. By adopting these new principles, all people would achieve complete peace and happiness. Countless miracles would result, and, in fact, Albert believed that some were happening already, for he claimed to see his father coming to him, to be free from pain, to have complete self-control, and to have the power of giving these benefits to others.

In the writing, he asserted: "This is the New Age of Reason and Thought in Man"; "The Secret of Life is Love. Nature has borne me so that I may forever enlighten the minds of men. . . . I am Jesus returned"; "This is the End of the Bloody Revolution of Thought"; "Everything and Everybody will be Happy. Everything and Everybody will be Beautiful." The contents contained many statements of the consequences of the adoption of the "new system." There would be no more ignorance, viciousness, vanity, greed, lust for power, or crime. There would be no immigration laws, no race prejudice. There would be no wars or depressions. There would be no fear, and no death.

After about two days of this activity, Albert's family tricked him into entering a mental hospital. While there, Albert continued to think out consequences of his system, and tried to explain it to other patients and visitors. He was frequently angered, however, by their obvious judgment that he was crazy. He knew where he was, and why, but held that "clear and perfect reason is not insanity," and asked to be set free. For a period he entertained an idea that "detectives" were responsible for his captivity.

The "hallucinations" and "delusions" displayed by Albert apparently had the character of the "quiet voices" experienced by other patients said to have auditory hallucinations. When he claimed to be Christ, he also knew well he was Albert. His demonstrations of exceptional powers, such as ability to disregard pain, were made by such means as striking his forehead with the open palm of his hand. The statements seemed to be completely sincere when he was doubted or challenged, for he insisted angrily that he meant what he said; but at other and calmer times, he would explain his statements. He thought his new system was good, was deeply impressed by his own discovery of it, and wanted to express it dramatically, *as if* he were Christ, or some other appointed savior.

Such cases as the above illustrate the general character of the schizophrenic reaction. Through their social isolation, schizophrenics are deprived of the important knowledge of the way of the world and of people that can only be acquired in many years of experience in primary group life. The inadequate views of status, morals, and the world in general that they pick up from parents or from reading merely confuse them in their adult years, so that they become increasingly involved in difficulties and are more perplexed than ever. They react in various ways, but in most cases, unless they can live sheltered lives as housewives or as workers in some quiet routine occupation, they fail so conspicuously as to require hospitalization. Commitment itself is usually a shock, since it is often arranged by deception on the part of friends or relatives who do not wish to tell the patient where he is going. This means to the patients, however, that their best friends have deserted them. In the hospitals the circumstances are usually such as to separate them even further from normal and conventional primary group life. The result is further discouragement, apathy, and in most cases a gradual and progressive mental deterioration. The social circumstances themselves operate to produce this vicious-circle process.

### THE RELATION OF OTHER PSYCHOSES TO URBAN AREAS

Distinct differences between the distributions of various psychoses in the city of Chicago may be found. While in some cases a plausible explanation of the connection between area and psychosis rate can be made, in others it is possible in the present state of knowledge only to suggest hypotheses. Such of these suggestions

as are of value to the study of social disorganization are presented
in the following paragraphs.

**General Paralysis.**—In the discussion of vice it has been pointed
out that the mental disease of general paralysis or paresis is caused
by the syphilis germ as it becomes lodged in the brain and damages
the tissue. Indirectly, however, this disease is clearly related to the
social disorganization of vice areas. Correlation of the rates of
general paralysis with figures for the rates of vice resorts in 1928,
and with the venereal disease rates for the same year, yield coefficients of +0.72 and +0.87 respectively, indicating a close correspondence in the distributions of these conditions. Presumably
a certain proportion of the syphilitic infections that occur in the
vice areas reach the stage of general paralysis, and so it can be held
that the principal reason for the persistence of the high rates is the
existence of commercialized prostitution.[17]

Racial and national traits are apparently of less importance than
is the state of the social organization. The national rate for Negroes,
for example, is much higher than that for whites, and the Chicago
rate for Negroes is also higher by almost three to one—the rates
being 11.9 for whites and 30.1 for Negroes. The Negro rates vary
considerably, however, in different parts of the Negro district. The
highest rates are in the parts of the Negro district nearest the central
business area, where the disorganization is most extreme. They
become lower in the more outlying Negro sections where the
standard of living is higher and disorganization is less. The general rate for Negroes, within the Negro areas as a whole, is, however, much lower than the rate for white persons in the same Negro
areas. The Negro rate here is 29.4, while the white rate is 77.9.

**Alcoholic Psychoses.**—The alcoholic psychoses are distributed
in a pattern which resembles that of schizophrenia, with the highest
rates in the central business area, and high rates in the nearby
hobo and rooming-house and slum areas populated by the foreign
born. These are also the areas in which other indices of alcoholism
are high. Possibly these cases represent the population that drinks
hard and long and survives long enough to acquire a psychosis.
As shown in the earlier discussion of alcoholism, it takes about
twenty years of steady and hard drinking in the average person to
build up an alcoholic psychosis. While it is not certain that alcohol

---

[17] The information regarding the vice-resort rates and venereal infection rates is
taken from Walter C. Reckless, *Vice in Chicago*, Chicago: University of Chicago Press,
1934, and the correlations are presented in Faris and Dunham, *op. cit.*, p. 131.

is the sole or even main cause of the mental abnormality in these cases, the evidence indicates that there must be some close relation between ordinary alcoholism and these psychoses. Possibly the social disorganization causes personal demoralization in the manner suggested in the chapter on vice, and the alcoholic psychosis cases merely represent an extreme.[18]

**The Old Age Psychoses.**—The distribution of high rates of senile psychoses and psychoses with arteriosclerosis in Chicago shows somewhat less concentration than do those previously discussed, but there is a similar clustering in the central Negro and rooming-house areas, and to a somewhat lesser extent, in the central foreign-born slums. Here again the observation is not inconsistent with the contention of some psychiatrists that senile psychoses are in reality late schizophrenia. Whether or not this is the case, the spatial distribution suggests a relation to urban social disorganization, and this is further confirmed by the fact that the rate for white persons living within Negro areas (159.8 per 100,000 aged 65 and over) is much higher than the Negro rate in the same areas (84.6). There are other aspects of social disorganization that may also be related to the occurrence of old age psychoses and to the hospitalization of cases. Among these are the isolation of elderly persons, sudden changes in the aged person's routines of living, disintegration of families, and dependency.

**Manic-depressive Psychosis.**—A significant fact about the important mental disorder known as manic-depressive psychosis is that its distribution in the city is far less concentrated and forms no pattern that indicates a relation to the characteristic forms of urban social disorganization. While a measure of the degree of concentration indicates that manic-depressive psychosis has as high a tendency to concentrate as does schizophrenia, the areas of high manic-depressive rates are not gathered together in sections of the city but are widely scattered. There are high-rate and low-rate areas in central regions, and many high-rate areas in outlying neighborhoods of different types. The lake-front apartment-house and apartment-hotel districts, of high rental classes, have some tendency to high rates, but there is little other indication of significance in the pattern.

---

[18] It is of course possible that some, or many, of these cases are actually schizophrenics with a history of extreme alcoholism. The similarity of the distributions is consistent with this hypothesis. There are points of disagreement in the distributions, however—the Jews of the low-income districts in particular have a very low rate of alcoholic psychoses, although their schizophrenia rates are high.

There are other distinctive features of the manic-depressive rates. The high-low range is much smaller than that of other psychoses. The rates of the 2,311 manic-depressive cases range from 0 to 13.38. The catatonic schizophrenia cases, only 711 in number, produced a rate range of 0 to 222. The correlation of rates with schizophrenic rates is +0.24, also indicating little resemblance between the distributions. The manic-depressive cases have about half again as many females as males, and they differ from schizophrenic cases also in having more married than single cases of both sexes, whereas the schizophrenic cases contained an excess of married women and of single men.

There are indications of higher income and educational status for the manic-depressive cases. Over half of the cases lived in communities where the median rental paid was $61.68, while half of the schizophrenic cases came from communities with a median rental of $33.45. A correlation of manic-depressive rates with an index of educational status yields a relation of +0.44, while the schizophrenic rates are negatively related, with a coefficient of −0.47. These relationships largely disappear, however, when a separation is made between the cases in private hospitals and an approximately equal number of those in public hospitals. It is in the former type, where payment is required for the care of the patient, that those of higher income and education are found.[19]

In view of the lack of a clear pattern in the manic-depressive distribution, no hypothesis is suggested to account for the disorder. It may be contended that this lack of evidence of a relation to social conditions bears out a popular belief that the hereditary factor is particularly important in this psychosis. The possibility remains, however, that manic-depressive psychosis is in part generated in experiences, but in those which do not have a relationship to urban community contrasts.

## Neurotic Behavior

In the Chicago study there were 977 cases of psychoneurosis, of which two thirds were in private hospitals. It is not clear whether

---

[19] It is possible that the diagnosis of manic-depressive psychosis does not have precisely the same meaning in private and in public hospitals. The author is informed by members of staffs of both types of hospitals that in cases of some doubt, the manic-depressive diagnosis—a more hopeful diagnosis than some others—is sometimes intentionally given in private hospitals in order to encourage the relatives to keep the patient there for treatment. If the more hopeless diagnosis were given, the prospect of lifetime expense might discourage the relatives. In many cases involving a transfer from private to public hospitals, the diagnosis is also changed from manic-depressive to schizophrenia. Many cases in the Chicago sample of manic-depressives, therefore, may be actually borderline well-to-do schizophrenics.

there is a greater exclusion of these lighter disorders from public hospitals due to crowded conditions or whether there is actually a tendency to higher incidence among people who are able to pay and who wish to avoid commitment to a free institution. The similarity of the psychoneurotic distribution to that of manic-depressive psychosis is indicated by the coefficient of correlation between the two sets of rates, +0.69.

The hospitalized cases undoubtedly constitute a smaller proportion of the neurotic population than of the truly psychotic group. The neuroses are less disabling in social and business life and do not as often require hospitalization. They constitute only about 1 per cent of the hospitalized population, have one of the lowest death rates of all disorders, and have one of the highest discharge rates. About 80 per cent of the patients hospitalized for psychoneuroses are eventually discharged, while the figure for schizophrenia is less than 50 per cent.[20]

Neurotic symptoms vary in the different cases, but there is an underlying core of dissatisfaction, unhappiness, and uncertainty in all of them. Some persons become highly nervous, with such symptoms as trembling, nausea, headaches and other pains, nightmares, memory lapses, loss of appetite and weight, dizziness, tension, excessive perspiration, heart palpitations, frequent crying, and fatigue. There is also in some cases the typical "anxiety" feeling, of being small, helpless, inadequate, deserted in a hostile world, which may produce reactions of immobility or of fleeing in panic. Such symptoms arise in persons who are facing problems or crises which are too great for their abilities and retreat from which is for one reason or another difficult. They constitute the reactions of persons who can neither win nor withdraw and who are thus suspended in a highly unpleasant state of conflict.

The life situations which may present such difficulties are highly varied. In wartime there occur many casualties which involve no physical injury but are the result of the trials of battle, which become too great for many soldiers. In the first world war such cases were commonly called "shell shock" because of the belief that they were caused by minute hemorrhages in the brain following the nearby explosion of a shell. The discovery that only a very small proportion of "shell-shocked" patients had such a condition, however, led to the change in conception.

---

[20] *Patients in Hospitals for Mental Disease, 1933*, Washington: Bureau of the Census, 1935. This period is used because it seemed desirable to avoid the disturbing influence of war.

A study of 276 cases of combat neuroses shows the typical conditions in which they develop.[21]  In most of the cases the symptoms arise gradually, although about 30 per cent develop their symptoms abruptly, following such experiences as a nearby explosion or artillery barrage, a fierce battle, or even the death of a close friend.  In a number of cases there are indications of some previous disposition or instability, though the proportions found by different observers vary considerably, with some finding as many as three fourths predisposed to neurosis.  Among those who appear to be predisposed, the breakdown comes somewhat sooner, and improvement comes more slowly.

Predisposition apparently involves a general inadequacy of character and personality and is the result of some deficiency in experiences in primary group life.  The person somehow missed a part of the influences through which other persons normally acquire strength of character to endure the harder trials of life.  Weinberg presents a good illustration in the case of a twenty-three-year-old infantryman who had been in the army two and a half years and had spent eighteen months overseas, and who was in or near combat for about three months before his breakdown occurred: [22]

My father is a welder, and he makes enough money to support us, but he didn't get along so well with my mother.  My mother said she was promised to him so she married him.  She wasn't in the house very much.  She went out with her friends, "women" friends, and drank a lot.  They fought a lot, and I didn't like to see them.  I went outside and took long walks.  When I was fifteen, my mother was operated for gall-stones, and after the operation she got pneumonia and died.  I began wandering around and didn't go to school for a week.  I wanted to be by myself.  I cried, too, but I didn't let anybody else see me.

I've always been alone.  I used to play with my sister, but I grew out of that.  I stuck around home or went for long walks.  There was nobody that I wanted to go with.  I never belonged to a club or had a real friend.  When I came home from school, I didn't play ball or other sports.  I didn't know how.  I did little jobs for my father or sat home and listened to the radio. There were three boys who lived on my street, and they wanted to know me. So one day, they started throwing snowballs at me and then tried to make my acquaintance.  I got to know them, but didn't have much to do with them. They came around only when they wanted something.  Money or something like that.  I got onto them, and I wouldn't give them anything.  People always wanted something from me.

[21] S. Kirson Weinberg, "The Combat Neuroses," *American Journal of Sociology*, Vol. 51, pp. 465–478.
[22] *Ibid.*, pp. 470–471.

I quit school in the eighth grade. I got into too many fights with other boys. They would start out of nothing. They would get on my nerves, and I would start throwing fists. I get hot-tempered easy. I got a job through my father in the factory, and the boss let me alone so I could do my work. When anybody lets me alone, I'm all right. When they start to bother me, I feel like fighting. I only know one girl. I got to know her when I was eighteen. She was fourteen, a neighbor. She ignored me, but later I began to talk to her; when I was twenty and was going into the army she said she would write to me every day.

In the army, trouble started. I was never with so many people all the time. Everybody telling you what to do. I said the wrong thing or somebody said the wrong thing to me, and we would fight. I kept to myself as much as I could. When I'm by myself I feel good. In real life nobody notices me or fights with me. I want people to like me. They will like me when I can be somebody. I daydreamed about people liking me—all the time. I went to town every week-end in the army and looked at the store windows or went to a show. When we finished training during the week days, I went for walks. I wrote letters home nearly every day and got two letters a week from home. I wrote a lot to my girl friend, but she was slow in answering, so I stopped writing to her. And she said something I didn't like. After five months of training they sent me to a P.O.E. I got scared and wrote my father that I was going overseas. He told me not to worry, that I wouldn't go. But I did.

In Africa I got so lonely, I could sit and cry. I missed my home, and was scared too. Then I tried to go with the others when they talked and put in a word here and there. I did my work so nobody would laugh at me. From Africa we went to Anzio and stayed there about three months. I was scared all the time. I wrote letters home while I was in the foxhole and things were quiet. During the shellings there were times when I wanted to run back, but I didn't. The other fellow got on my nerves, and I got on his nerves. I tried my best not to show it, and wanted to get along with him. I saw some men I knew get killed, and that made me angry and scared. I got shot in the arm. Then I got some fragments in my side, and that jarred me up so much, I wanted to get away. Then they had a shelling, and one landed near me and I fell unconscious. When I woke up in the hospital, I was shaking and nervous.

The sense of isolation reported by the above soldier is not without significance. His sense of fear was his own, and not shared with the other men. It is reported that nearly all soldiers have a sense of fear before a battle, but their knowledge that they are together decreases the loneliness for those who maintain rapport with one another. There is a sense of solidarity and collective responsibility in a military unit which leads the men to recognize that symptoms of anxiety may damage morale and mutual confidence, and which therefore leads them to keep themselves under control as much as possible. Each one realizes that the others are "taking it," so he cannot afford to be a "quitter" either. The quitter not only breaks the military tradition and the good record of the unit, but he also endangers the men in the battle with him.

In such cases, the conflict that produces the neurosis is a mental torment which reflects the external conflict of social forces. On the one hand there is a social process which, through isolation or other abnormality of social experience during the years of development, left the person in a weak and inadequate condition to meet crises. And on the other hand, there is the present social force of collective expectation which makes it extremely difficult to run away from the crisis, problem, or danger. The pressure is strong to remain loyal to the group, not let the other men down, nor desert one's friends and comrades and thereby increase the danger to them.

Panicky desertion thus represents a sharp break from the habits produced by military training and from the social control that originates in the collective expectations of comrades. Desertion is a disgrace of the highest order and involves such a severe sense of conscience that it is seldom allowed to stand as an isolated, calm, premeditated act. By his symptoms the deserter tries to imply lack of responsibility for the action. He claims loss of control. "I went haywire." "I went to pieces." He professes weaknesses, loss of memory, and other inabilities, which imply that he was not well and not himself, and therefore less to blame. Since his conscience is deeply involved, he usually wishes to convince himself as well as others that this is the case, that he is genuinely sick and not a true deserter of his comrades. Probably this self-deception is achieved to some degree in many cases, but usually not enough to be fully comforting to the patient. The true casualties—men who are so wounded that they are unable to move farther—do not have the symptoms of mental discomfort that trouble the combat neurotics. The latter prefer to avoid discussing the episodes of their breakdowns and often genuinely try to keep them out of memory.

The claim of amnesia may in some cases be exaggerated. It represents an effort to deny or to forget, but the uneasiness with which a patient approaches the subject of his troubles indicates incompleteness of achievement in forgetting. Organic ailments aid the rationalization and are thus sometimes claimed insistently in the face of denials by medical officers. Some of the neurotics, returned home for a rest, have a guilty sense of being talked about and express envy of those who have lost limbs, implying that the latter had undeniably legitimate reasons for being excused from further fighting.

The incompleteness of forgetting and the unsatisfactory state of the rationalizations stimulate dreams, in which the unpleasant battle experiences enter as elements. These often are so vivid and terrifying that some men are unable to move or speak on awaking, while others awake screaming, kicking, and falling out of bed.

There are somewhat similar processes of conflict between limited human abilities and the social pressures of expectations of others operating in ordinary life, with consequences somewhat like those of battle neuroses. Examples may be found where persons reach for a degree of success which is beyond their ability but are unable to abandon the effort because of the pressure of a parent or wife, or because of public commitment to achieve success which makes it too painful to withdraw to lesser goals. Ambitious self-made fathers may drive their sons toward goals which the sons are not adequately trained to achieve. In other cases, young men who have been leaders of their classes through school and dominant in extracurricular affairs as well, perhaps voted "most likely to succeed" upon graduation from college, may understandably choose objectives too difficult for their abilities and yet not be willing to abandon them because of the belief that all of their classmates and friends expect them to take important places in society. Uncertainties and conflicts subject such persons to almost constant torment as long as they persist in the unsuccessful efforts, and the symptoms of illness may constitute as welcome an excuse for withdrawal as those of the victims of combat neurosis.

In many cases, real organic disabilities apparently develop in consequence of the strain of such conflict and conveniently present a genuine excuse for slowing up and reducing the ambitions. Attention has been given in recent years to the connection between intensely competitive business activity and the development of peptic ulcers—the condition popularly known as "Wall Street stomach." A number of research investigators have concluded that such ulcers are most likely to occur in ambitious, hard-driving business men who are constantly meeting obstacles which they feel impelled to overcome.[23] Peptic ulcer is in fact sometimes stated to be a disease of the striving and ambitious men of western civilization.

Saul mentions a case in which the driving force came from an ambitious and capable wife.[24] "A 46-year-old man had been overindulged in childhood by his mother. He married a superior woman,

---

[23] See Leon J. Saul, "Physiological Effects of Emotional Tension," in J. McVicker Hunt, *Personality and the Behavior Disorders*, Vol. 1, Ch. 8, New York: The Ronald Press Co., 1944.
[24] *Ibid.*, pp. 276–277.

expecting that she would indulge him, but she devoted herself to her own career with such success that the patient felt impelled, out of self-respect, at least to equal his wife's position and earnings. It was when he drove himself to business activity that his postprandial stomach pains and chronic hyperacidity developed. After eighteen years this eventuated in an ulcer, with a hemorrhage two years later. After the hemorrhage he established a relationship with a soft, unambitious, indulgent, motherly type of woman and his symptoms disappeared. Unlike this patient, the majority of ulcer cases studied had an inner drive to responsibility and activity, which in large part they accepted and enjoyed, protesting against it only unconsciously."

A number of other symptoms may also develop in similar situations of conflict. Saul mentions a case of a young physician, "an only child, who had been overly protected by his parents and enjoyed his extreme dependence on them. When he graduated from medical school and faced the responsibilities of his internship he developed anxiety and diarrhea. He did not dare withdraw, however, because he felt that he must make restitution for all his parents had given him and sacrificed for him. The same constellation repeated itself when he stepped out into practice. He resented the new responsibilities and demands and, if he were settled down for a quiet evening and received a call to go out, he would feel glad to have the practice but resentful of leaving his comfort for exertion and responsibility and would react with diarrhea." [25]

Essential hypertension—elevated blood pressure without evidence of related kidney, vascular, or other disease, is another characteristic disorder of our complex and competitive civilization. It is reported to be rare among such peoples as the Chinese, Egyptians, the peoples of India, and the natives of Africa, though not among the Negroes in America, who are reported to have an incidence of hypertension two and a half times greater than southern white people.[26] The essential causal conditions, as reported in a study by Alexander, are (1) that the patient is caught in a conflict situation with which he struggles without adequate solution or escape and (2) that he sustains a chronic repressed rage.[27] Saul illustrates the process with a typical case:[28]

Mr. A. came with a complaint of anxiety. He was in his forties, with a hypertension fluctuating from 160 to 200 systolic over 110 to 130 diastolic,

[25] *Ibid.*, p. 279.
[26] *Ibid.*, p. 281.
[27] F. Alexander, "Psychological Aspects of Medicine," *Psychosomatic Medicine*, Vol. 1, pp. 1–18.
[28] Saul, *op. cit.*, pp. 282–283.

which had been increasing for the preceding ten years.  He was the only
patient of the series with marked arteriosclerosis and somewhat impaired
renal function.  He was one of a number of children, and had been spoiled
and dominated by his mother who also dominated the physically strong father.
His mother made him work from the age of six to contribute to the family
who lost their money at that time.  He reacted with lifelong bitterness to being
thus prematurely forced to work after the earlier extreme spoiling.  She forbade sports as dangerous, and later forbade the patient to see girls other than
those of his own faith.  He obeyed despite his envy of the boys who engaged
in athletics and in sexual play with girls.  She set him the ideal of wealth,
inspired him with excessive ambitions and great expectations, and forced him
into marriage against his will with a girl of her choosing.

   Thus his whole life, his work, his religion, his marriage, came to mean
submission to the mother—bending the knee, as he put it—and also being
forced out of the earlier situation of maternal spoiling and protection into
excessive ambitious activity.  He tried in vain for many years to escape or
rebel against this unconscious attachment to the mother.  Finally he actually
got a divorce and tried to indulge in sexual promiscuity and alcoholism.  He
even took a girl to the Orient in an effort to escape his fears and be free
sexually.  But the anxiety was too great and he was forced to give up the
rebellion.  The patient's hypertension always increased during these periods
in which anxiety frustrated his attempts at heterosexuality.  Apparently in
an effort to escape the conflict with his dominating mother, this patient turned
to his father.  But although on the surface his relations with men were less
acutely disturbing, the dependence and submissiveness toward them was even
more intolerable than toward women.  Again the patient rebelled, using
unconscious hostility as his defense.  This was most clear toward his boss
to whom again he would not "bend the knee."  Besides his hostility from
rebellion against his dependence and submissiveness, he would rage at not
getting the passive receptive satisfaction he demanded, i.e., at not being able to
be dependent on others, but being forced to ambitious independent exertion
and responsibility.  But his rage from rebellion and from frustration was
never directly expressed.  He was quiet and gentlemanly with all.

   Other suspected effects of emotional tension include asthma
and hay fever, laryngitis, skin disturbances, endocrine disturbances,
epilepsy, and genito-urinary disturbances.  Most of the research is
of recent date, and the hypotheses are not to be regarded in all cases
as having been fully confirmed, but the list of possible ways in
which social conflict and the resulting mental conflict may find
expression in physiological disorders is impressive.

   It is not necessary to assume that civilization is too complex for
the nerves of man.  There are many persons who meet crises continually and who surmount their difficulties.  There are other
normal persons who withdraw in sensible fashion from situations

which are too difficult and thus escape the torment of continuous conflict. The hardships come to those who are unable to withdraw —usually because of social pressure, and yet who do not have the equipment to win. The frequency with which the "spoiled child" situation is mentioned indicates that maternal overprotection is a common means by which the person comes to face the world with inadequate strength. Probably it is also the parent who would spoil a child who characteristically entertains impossible ambitions for his offspring and who drives him into efforts that are unreasonably strenuous.

There are many complexities and inconsistencies which entrap the more tender members of our civilization. In addition to the notorious strains of battle and of intense commercial rivalry, there are the heated passions of interracial and nationality conflicts, the tensions that arise within families where harmony is absent, and many other types of worry and strain. While some of these sources of conflict may in time be reduced, it is not a reasonable expectation that such strains will ever become uncommon in civilized life, for with changing times new uncertainties and inconsistencies will almost surely arise to take the place of those that may disappear. The hope for reduction of this class of nervous disorders must lie in the possibility of eliminating the maladjustments that produce the weaknesses in those persons who cannot endure the strain. Inquiries into the processes of family and primary group life in which the overprotected and isolated personalities are developed may provide some basis for a strengthening of the functions of these groups and for the production of a sturdier population which will be resistant to the conditions which now precipitate neuroses.

## SUMMARY

There is a general relation between the social disorganization of industrial civilization and some of the most important forms of mental abnormality. The incidence is not only greater in general in cities than in rural areas, but is by far the greatest in the parts of the large cities in which the social disorganization is most intense. The weight of the evidence is that in the central areas of the city—the hotel, hobo rooming-house, and low-income slums populated by the foreign-born—are to be found the principal breeding grounds of insanity.

The processes do not operate in a vague general way to produce mental abnormality, but in specific ways. General paralysis, for example, has its high incidence in rooming-house areas because of the social processes which locate there the prostitution traffic and which supply the patronage which becomes subject thereby to venereal infection.  Since the sources of infection are easy to locate, there is little scientific difficulty in suggesting a means of elimination of this particular disease.  The obstacles, however, are political and social, and our understanding and control in these fields has not so far been sufficient to produce universal abolition of commercial prostitution.  The principal barrier, and probably the last one which will be removed, is the general political corruption that exists in many large cities, permeating not merely the city administrations and police organizations, but also business interests and even a good proportion of the citizenry at large.

Alcoholic psychoses have been shown to develop in greatest frequency in those parts of the city where chronic alcoholism is greatest, and the explanation for this, as suggested in Chapter 7, possibly lies in the unsatisfying nature of the life available to residents of these areas, and in certain factors of culture and personality. Schizophrenia appears to grow out of a complex of family and neighborhood processes and to be complicated by confusions that exist within the culture.  The neuroses seem to be related to social processes producing soft personalities which are thrown suddenly against extreme hardships of life from which they cannot withdraw, usually because of social pressure.

Some psychoses remain at present unexplained by conditions of social disorganization, although it is possible that further knowledge will in time show connections not now visible.  Some have a clear-cut physiological basis that is related to sociological conditions only in the indirect manner in which are virtually all diseases, accidents, malnutrition, and the like.  Since, however, those which are clearly related to the extreme disorganization of cities constitute the great majority of cases and the major burden of expense, it is a reasonable expectation that any possible stabilization of society might also bring, for the first time since careful records have been kept, a substantial reduction in the incidence of mental disorder.

## Selected References

*American Journal of Sociology,* Vol. 42, May, 1937.  This entire issue is devoted to aspects of the relation between social disorganization and mental abnormality.

Boisen, Anton.  *Exploration of the Inner World.*  Chicago: Willett, Clark & Co., 1936.

Cameron, Norman.  "The Functional Psychoses."   In J. McV. Hunt, *Personality and the Behavior Disorders,* Vol. 2, Ch. 29.   New York: The Ronald Press Co., 1944.

Faris, Robert E. L., and Dunham, H. Warren.  *Mental Disorders in Urban Areas.* Chicago: University of Chicago Press, 1939.

Queen, Stuart A.  "The Ecological Study of Mental Disorders."  *American Sociological Review,* Vol. 5. Apr., 1940.

# Chapter 10

## FAMILY DISORGANIZATION

### The Family in the Stable Community

There is no society known to ethnography or history which does not make important use of the institution of the family. The family is in fact almost everywhere a central and indispensible nucleus of society, and, while it is conceivable that a society might be devised with no family institution, no such experiment has so far been known to succeed. Moreover there is so much convenience and logical appropriateness in the monogamous family, in which the married pair and their own children form the standard household group, that this is everywhere the most widespread arrangement, even among societies in which polygamy and polyandry are approved.

In a stable community, the functions of the family are usually so explicitly recognized that the formation of the family and the conduct of its members are far from being considered a private matter among those within the group, but rather are held to be the concern of the community itself. Custom and law specify which persons are eligible to marry, what kind of ceremony will initiate the union, what the household arrangements will be, and what the obligations of the members will be to one another and to other members of the community. The choice of mate, in fact, is in many societies made by parents rather than by the principals themselves, and in other cases the specified range of eligible persons is so narrow that the individual choice is severely limited. The ceremony often contains much instruction and admonition regarding the proper behavior of the partners and their responsibilities to the community and to ancestors and offspring as well.

Disruption of families is less common in stable societies. There is less expectation of a continuation of the "breathless" form of romance than is found among many modern peoples. The relatively homogeneous population also offers less opportunity for clashes of temperament and of conflicts of culture within the family. Even where unhappiness develops between the married pair, it does not necessarily mean the dissolution of the family, for the community emphasizes other functions more than that of the achievement of happiness by the couple.[1]

Burgess and Locke have stated the essential nature of familism by listing five characteristics.[2] These are: "(1) the feeling on the part of all members that they belong pre-eminently to the family group and that all other persons are outsiders; (2) complete integration of individual activities for the achievement of family objectives; (3) the assumption that land, money, and other material goods are family property, involving the obligation to support individual members and give them assistance when they are in need; (4) willingness of all other members to rally to the support of another member if attacked by outsiders; and (5) concern for the perpetuation of the family as evidenced by helping an adult child in beginning and continuing an economic activity in line with family expectations, and in setting up a new household."

Such traits are common in the traditional rural family in the United States, and are particularly well developed in the Ozark Highland region, where isolation has protected the communities from the disintegrating forces that accompany civilization. The family system in rural Quebec represents another example of a highly stable institution, so integrated with the community life and regulated in great detail that its members are highly conscious of their responsibilities to the whole French-Canadian society.[3]

In the remote village of Saint Denis, in rural Quebec, the culture reflects the unity of an isolated region which has been little influenced by the developments of modern times. The *habitants* have developed and preserved a harmonious culture that fits in with the circumstances of their agricultural basis of life, and which perpetuates itself successfully as long as external influences are excluded.

The religious, civil, territorial, and economic unit of rural Quebec life is the parish, but within the parish, the central social group is the family. It is

[1] An example, known personally to the author, of such a family in a relatively stable community in a medium-sized southern city illustrates a process which may be fairly common in such regions. A young man discovered on the day of his wedding that his bride did not love him, but had married him for security and because of the prestige of his family. Family pride, however, and the integration of his social and business life in the community made it virtually impossible for the young husband to consider obtaining a divorce or separation. The only approved pattern in the community was that of a conventionally functioning family. For about a third of a century, then, until his death in late middle age, the husband and wife lived together, bore and raised a child, and presented to their friends and relatives the outward aspect of a happy and loving couple. The husband employed terms of endearment and conducted himself with the conventional romantic chivalry in his relations with his wife, and she maintained the appearance of a contented wife. Their true feelings of misery were known to only a very few of their closest relatives.
[2] Ernest W. Burgess and Harvey J. Locke, *The Family*, New York: American Book Co., 1945, p. 69.
[3] The material on Saint Denis is condensed from Horace Miner, *Saint Denis*, Chicago: University of Chicago Press, 1939, Ch. 4.

a highly unified group, in which all members have their clearly specified traditional responsibilities.  The men, for example, attend to the principal farming work, the main crops and the animals, and they cut the wood, repair the houses, and attend to business matters.  The women do the vegetable gardening, the milking, the household work, and the washing, cooking, spinning, weaving, knitting, and clothes making.

The typical household contains three generations of members and constitutes a large family.  The short cultivating season and the relatively primitive methods of cultivation require, for the typical farm of 100 acres, two or three able-bodied males and the support of female labor.  Thus there may reside in the farm household, beside the married couple and their children, one or more younger brothers, and a retired parent or two.  The brief period when the younger brothers have left, and before the sons are old enough to do adult work, are the hard years in the life of the Quebec farmer, when he may have to call on some relatives for help.

The family is linked by sentiment and mystic feelings to a wide circle of relatives, and to its deceased members.  Kinship includes third cousins and all closer relatives.  Genealogy is kept alive by the interest of the members, and the walls of the parlors of the farm house are hung with the pictures of ancestors.  Children who have died are also remembered, and it is common for parents to use such expressions as "I have fifteen children, ten living." Prayers and masses are offered for deceased relatives.  When Miner asked a number of twelve-year-old children what they would do if they had a thousand dollars, all said that they would use part of the money for masses for the deceased relatives.

Although political differences and other types of factionalism may be found within a parish, it is uncommon for disagreement of this kind to exist within a family.  Political quarrels are often intense, and family dislikes may follow the same lines.  Marriages are usually within the political group.  As a result, even the women have had little interest in the ballot for their sex, for they hold that they are each represented by a man.

There is a strong bond between territory and family in Quebec.  One son, not necessarily or even usually the oldest, inherits the farm of the father at the time of the retirement of the latter, and remains on the land.  The other sons may leave if there is no room on a nearby farm, but the daughters marry in the locality if possible.  Only fifteen per cent of the girls in Saint Denis married outside of a range of twenty miles from the village, according to the observations of Miner.  Marriage is in fact related to property, and involves a contract, with dowries.  If one partner dies, the other is likely to remarry into the same family, if he can, in order to keep the lands within the family.

The attachment to the locality is such that travel holds little appeal, and the principal object of trips away from home is to pay visits to relatives.  A parish four miles away may never be visited if no relatives live there, according to Miner, and travel abroad holds no interest at all, except in the case of such persons as the man who stated, "I would like to visit the grave of my brother in France." The typical honeymoon trip is a journey to the city of Quebec, to visit relatives, and to the nearby shrine at Saint Anne de Beaupré. The religious institutions of Saint Denis are strong, and the sacred elements permeate much of the culture, including family life. There are sentimental feelings about the "earthly Trinity" of Jesus, Mary, Joseph, and about Saint Anne, the mother of Mary. The social system itself, including the family, has a sacredness that is maintained even by the threat of hell for nonconformers. The life cycle of each person, with its crises or transitions, involves sacred "rites of passage." The regulation of life from birth to death is so rhythmic that the elderly persons become aware of the repetitiveness—in one case an old man employed the figure of speech that life is like the turning of a wheel. The forms of the French-Canadian family life have thus been reproducing themselves almost perfectly for two centuries, only recently to encounter influences that threaten to disrupt the system.

### Disorganization of Family Functions in Contemporary Civilization

In the United States the disorganizing forces of modern times have had particularly great effects upon the principal institutions of the society. The family has been fundamentally changed by such developments as the industrial revolution, the tides of population movements to American shores, the mixing of different cultures, and the rapid transformations that follow the adoption of such important inventions as the railroad, the telephone and telegraph, the automobile, the motion picture, the radio, and the technological developments that lighten family responsibilities and free women from drudgery—the development of laundries, bakeries, canned and frozen foods, and the mechanization of housework through improved stoves, vacuum cleaners, washing machines, and the like.[4]

**The Transfer of Economic Functions.**—One of the important effects of inventions is to bring about the transfer of economic functions from the home. In contrast to the labor of the Quebec family, little altered by modernism, in which the food is produced and prepared, and much of the clothing made by old, simple, and inefficient folk techniques, the modern urban housewife who lives in a mechanized apartment building has very little work to do in the home. Unless she works outside to add to the family income, her economic importance is almost nothing. The children on the

---

[4] William F. Ogburn has conducted extensive research on this subject of the effects of inventions and social change on family life. A convenient source for the essential findings may be found in the volume, edited by W. F. Ogburn, *Recent Social Trends in the United States,* New York: McGraw-Hill Book Co., Inc., 1933, Ch. 13, "The Family and Its Functions." In Burgess and Locke, *op. cit.,* this material is brought up to a later date (see Ch. 16).

farm begin to constitute a productive asset at a fairly early age, when they are able to take on some of the chores, but the urban children not only do not contribute but constitute a fairly heavy expense, since they require costly additional rooms and are expected to have advantages of various kinds that are not available to rural children.    Even the productive activity of the husband is altered by these trends, for he tends to specialize in a more and more narrow type of occupation and to purchase all other services.    Unlike the farmer who cuts his own wood, fires his own stoves, pumps his own water, slaughters his own meat, and performs other similar tasks, the urban apartment-house dweller simply turns on his heat and hot water at will and telephones for his groceries.    His household is not an economic unit in the sense that the traditional farm family has been.    His economic activity is kept separate from his family life, and his wife and children do not participate in it.    One important type of interdependence is thus reduced or lost.

This does not mean that no division of labor remains.    The wife may have some importance as general administrator of the household affairs, even if the drudgery is taken off her hands.    She may also serve usefully as the custodian and trainer of the children, as a hostess on social occasions, and in other ways.    But while useful in such respects, she is not nearly as necessary as is the wife on the one-family farm, and this fact is significant in the matter of family solidarity.[5]

**Decentralization of Activities and Loss of Consensus.**—Not only have economic functions been transferred to nonfamily establishments, but so also to a great extent have the functions—largely performed by the family in traditional rural society—of education, religious observance, recreation, and protection.    The result is a great decentralization of activity from the family to the community and a corresponding loss of unity within the family.    The interests of the members are specialized and not shared within the group, and, in extreme cases, the members have little in common and only a minimum of activity which is performed together.    Thus not only is the family affected by the emancipation of women, which has received much attention in the last few decades, but by the emancipation of all of the members of the family from one another.

---

[5] It is said that the marriage proposal made by Tom Lincoln to his second wife, Sarah, was made in the direct and practical terms which show this necessity of a wife and mother on a farm.    It was put in such terms as, "Sarah, I'm a man of a few words.    You need a husband, and I need a wife.    I've come to take you back if you will marry me.    I must return today, so if you will, say so now and we'll put your things right on the wagon and start back."    Without delay, Sarah agreed to become the stepmother of Abraham Lincoln.

In the urban apartment-house culture, each family tends to occupy the amount and quality of dwelling space that it can afford. Apartments of all sizes and degrees of luxury are normally available, and increase of income therefore permits movement to a more desirable apartment. Each additional room is an increase in the cost of living, and so each child is a major burden to the family budget, on this account as well as for clothing, medical care, and recreational costs and other costs that affect urban dwellers more than farm families. This fact, together with greater familiarity with the techniques of contraception, tends to hold the urban family to a smaller size, both with respect to the number of children and to the presence of other relatives in the family.

In income and occupational classifications where there is a delay on the part of young men in reaching economic independence, as in the professions which require a long period of training and in other careers that ordinarily develop slowly, the age at marriage is relatively older. This delay in turn reduces the possibility of large families.

In small families, particularly those in which the age of marriage is somewhat advanced, the cultural continuity between the generations is affected. The child grows up with a long age gap between himself and his parents, with no intermediate members of the family to bridge the gap of generations. In the rural 12-child family, the oldest child is born to relatively young parents, who remember their own childhood in an environment which is little changed in the two decades since their own birth. Each later child has the advantages of the influences not only of parents, but of experienced brothers and sisters. The last child has siblings who are themselves of adult age, and in many cases are themselves bearing children. When the older or middle child of a family of this sort reaches parenthood, he is enriched by abundant experience with children of all ages, for he has spent many years in a family in which care of infants was a constant activity.

In contrast, the man and woman who have their first child in their middle thirties, and who scarcely remember their own solitary childhood, are seriously deficient in ordinary folk knowledge of babies. They often are in total ignorance of the simple techniques of infant care and are puzzled and frightened by the minor difficulties of handling their baby. If they attempt to follow instruc‑ tions in a book, they may misunderstand or overemphasize minor symptoms and may compound their difficulties by errors of control and by an atmosphere of tension and apprehension about all matters concerning their infants.  Throughout the growing years of their children, such urban parents, having grown up in a different kind of environment, tend to become increasingly bewildered by the nature of their own children and hence lose the kind of influence that grows out of mutual understanding.  The children then develop as best they can, and with little benefit of guidance from parents or from any older person whose concern for their welfare is great. They in turn reach the age of marriage with no memory of a successful family system and with no understanding of the nature of children, and thus suffer from the same state of ignorance and helplessness.

**Functions of Personality Development.**—It is largely within the interaction of family life that infants are expected to be transformed into human personalities.  It is here that they acquire the beginnings of the sentiments of sociability and responsiveness to the wishes of others, and of the general trait of cooperativeness. The beginnings of a conscience are also acquired in early life. Language is also here acquired, together with the special linguistic traits, dialect, modes of expression, and range of vocabulary that remain associated with families, social levels, and local regions.

Although folkways and mores, like language, are attributes of the whole society, it is within the family group that some of the most important of these are acquired.  The particular degree of sensitivity of a person to standards of etiquette, as well as to moral standards, is often considered to be an indication of the type of family life in which he was reared.

The family is also expected to inculcate in its younger members a general sense of responsibility to the social group.  This may begin with responsibility to the family group itself, so that children will feel obligated to conduct themselves so as to bring no discredit to their parents and siblings and also will develop their lives in such a fashion as to maintain the good standing of their family line—to pass on the family possessions, including a good reputation, to their posterity.  Such a sentiment is often expanded into a similar sense of responsibility to the community, to the nation, and even to humanity in general.  It is a necessary motive to prevent the kind of policy implied in *"Après moi le déluge."*

It is a further function of the family to develop in children the necessary strength, toughness, and resilience to surmount the hardships of life.  In a primitive hunting society such as that of the

Eskimos, no special mechanism is needed for this purpose, as the trials of severe cold, game shortage, and arduous work for all constitute adequate schooling in dealing with difficulties. Even the chores and the inconveniences of the family farm life are ordinarily sufficient to provide such induration. It is in the urban family, in which there are no traditional tasks for children to perform, and few hazards and hardships of which they become aware, that there is the greatest danger of escaping such training and of growing into the soft, delicate, overprotected, and inadequate personalities which appear to be so common among the persons who develop certain neuroses and psychoses.

It often happens to children of urban apartment-house dwellers that they are sheltered from all but the slightest discomforts. In the one-child family, the light bump of a fall to the floor may bring both parents to their feet expressing conspicuous solicitude. A cut finger or a slight fever arouses visible worry and alarm, which the child cannot fail to absorb. The requests on the part of the child for pleasure are readily granted, and gratifications come to be expected as the natural right of the child. Tolerance to frustration fails to develop, so that inability to gain an expected desire may be the occasion for a sense of panic. Tears and the threat of tears, as well as the display of symptoms of illness, operate so successfully as a means of control of parents that they are relied upon in crises to an increasing extent. As a consequence, there is a failure to develop the kind of strategy that is useful in adult life to influence other persons tactfully and a failure to acquire an ability to bear discomforts and disappointments and to summon the strength and resolution to persist and fight back in the face of difficulties.

**The Function of Control of Behavior.**—In addition to the development of the most important beginnings of personality, the family is expected to function as the principal guiding influence in the control of the behavior of children until they reach adult independence and to a certain extent after that, for it is expected that by such time the habits will be so developed, and such a concern for the family reputation will be acquired, that the parental influence will persist throughout the lifetime. Normally such a process of guidance involves a rich set of influences, largely informal in character, in which through apprenticeship, casual example, the pull of sentiment and affection, and occasional explicit instruction and correction, the child acquires over the course of his growing years a habit of conformity to the customs and rules of the community, and a sensitivity to the expectations of others, so that he is able at the proper time to take his place as a responsible and respected member of the adult community.

One of the most important elements in the process by which such cooperativeness is developed is the visible pattern that is set by parents and other older members of the household. The child learns principles of conduct by seeing them expressed in daily action. If the family is harmonious and unified, wrong actions will be avoided simply because, in the social world that is important to the child, such things are not done. Acts of generosity or of kindness become habitual because they have appeared as the customary mode of behavior on certain types of occasions.

The family normally derives important support in its task of guiding the behavior of children from the friends and neighbors, the primary group outside of the family itself. In an integrated community, these outside persons also by example reinforce the teachings of the parents. Furthermore, they constitute an important source of supervision, for the children soon learn that any misbehavior which is observed by neighbors is likely to be reported to parents. The concern of parents for good reputation in the community is absorbed by the children, and the latter acquire a sense of bearing responsibility on their shoulders.

Modern processes of social disorganization which weaken the harmony of family life also affect the ability of the family to control its members. The heterogeneity of urban populations, with resulting heterogamy among its members, results in families in which there is no uniform tradition of behavior and thus no simple example of harmony for the children to acquire. Undefined behavior dilemmas, inconsistencies of parental example, and tension and conflict between parents unpleasantly throw upon the child the responsibility of choosing or devising his own ways of behavior in the crises of daily behavior. This often is complicated by a sense of rebellion against the parents, whose failures are so obvious to the child that respect is replaced by irritation and contempt.

It has been shown that the relation between "broken homes"— homes with a parent missing—and juvenile delinquency has often been exaggerated. In urban slums, where neighborhood and family disorganization is extreme, even the unbroken families have great difficulty in controlling their children. Cavan, in a study of 435 delinquent boys and 155 delinquent girls in Rockford, Illinois, found that the majority of these came from homes in which both parents were present.[6]  In the case of the boys, 66 per cent came from homes that were not broken, and of the girls 51 per cent had both parents living at home.  Of the 34 per cent of the boys from broken homes, 11 per cent had lost their fathers through death, 7 per cent had lost their mothers, and 1 per cent had lost both.  There were 15 per cent, however, whose homes were broken by separation or divorce, which indicates that it may have been the conflict and dissension occurring before the divorce or separation that destroyed the control of the parents over the children.  In the case of the girls, the figures are even more striking, for of the 49 per cent of the delinquent girls from broken homes, 29 per cent involved divorce or separation, and only 10, 7, and 3 per cent involved death of father, mother, or both, respectively.  It thus appears that, particularly with girls, it is not so much the incompleteness of the home that is related to delinquency, but the manner in which the family was disrupted.  It is highly probable that much of the loss of control occurred while both parents were still in the home and developed because of their inability to live in harmony.

Some confirmation and additional information on this conclusion is supplied in a study of delinquents in the State of Washington by H. Ashley Weeks.[7]  Of the 414 males in the sample, 60.4 per cent were from homes that were not broken, and of the 39.6 per cent from broken homes the larger portion, 23.2 per cent, were from "voluntary" broken homes—those broken by divorce, separation, or desertion, and only 16.4 from "involuntary" broken homes—those broken by death of one or both parents or by the confinement of one or both in an institution.  Again, the females showed the relation more conspicuously, having 68.1 per cent from broken homes, of whom 37.2 per cent were from "voluntary" broken homes.  The types of delinquency committed by males were somewhat different from those of females—over 75 per cent of the male offenses were in the property, traffic, and misdemeanor classifications, while an almost equal percentage of the female violations, 74.7 per cent, consisted of running away, ungovernability, and immorality.  In further analysis of the figures, Weeks shows that the voluntarily broken home is most directly related to such types of delinquency as ungovernability, running away, and truancy for either males or females, although the relation is most close with

[6] Ruth S. Cavan, *The Adolescent in the Family*, a publication of the White House Conference on Child Health and Protection, New York: D. Appleton-Century Co., Inc., 1934.  Cited in Ruth S. Cavan, *The Family*, New York: The Thomas Y. Crowell Co., 1942, p. 340.
[7] H. Ashley Weeks, "Male and Female Broken Home Rates by Types of Delinquency," *American Sociological Review*, Vol. 5, pp. 601–609, Aug., 1940.

females.  Of the ungovernability type of delinquency, for example, among females, only 11.5 per cent of the delinquents were from unbroken homes, and 88.5 per cent were from broken homes.  Of the latter group, the great majority, 53.8 per cent, were from voluntarily broken homes.  Clearly this represents a kind of protest and rebellion of girls against the situation of dissension in the home, and shows how thoroughly the conflict of parents destroys their influence over the conduct of children.[8]

Cavan has placed the emphasis on the type of relation between parents and with children, rather than on the mere fact of presence or absence of a parent in the home, by employing the concept of the "psychologically broken homes."[9]  This term refers to homes in which the conflict and dissension are such as to destroy the effectiveness of the home in the control of children.  This concept she finds to be related to conditions of loss of social status, loss of family unity, and loss of emotional security.  On the other hand, she points out that a home which is technically a broken home may be psychologically unbroken if there are substitutes for the missing parents, or if such harmony is achieved with the one parent that there is no loss of unity and control.

There may be degrees of ineffectiveness in the relations of parents which produce a partial condition of the "psychologically broken home," with effects on the behavior of children similar in kind but less severe in degree than those produced by the more extreme conflict.  Where parents are self-centered, concerned with their own pleasures rather than with the welfare of their children, and indifferent in their attitudes toward one another, the children may be affected in such ways as the development of a sense of neglect and loneliness, resentment toward parental and other

---

[8] A contribution to our knowledge of the relation of certain types of behavior problems and states of family life is furnished by a statistical study of 500 case records at the Michigan Child Guidance Institute. (See L. E. Hewitt and R. L. Jenkins, *Fundamental Patterns of Maladjustment*, Springfield, Ill.: The State Printer, 1946.)  Employing the tetrachoric *r*, the authors computed the interrelations of many behavior traits and family conditions and established certain groupings or syndromes.  A pattern of *family rejection*, involving among other things unwanted pregnancies, post-delivery rejection of child by parents, unwillingness of mothers to accept parental role, open hostility of parents to children, or loss of contact of both natural parents, was found to be associated with *unsocialized aggressive behavior*, expressed in assaultive tendencies, malicious mischief, defiance of authority, cruelty, and similar traits.  *Parental negligence and exposure*, indicated by lack of parental supervision or harsh discipline, irregularities of home routine, unkempt interior of home, deterioration of neighborhood, and similar conditions, are associated with *socialized delinquent behavior*, as shown by gang activities in stealing and truancy, staying out late at night, and similar traits.  A third pattern, *family repression*, in which are involved inconsistency of discipline, unsociability of parents, sibling rivalry, and other conditions— is related to *overinhibited behavior*, characterized by such traits as seclusiveness, apathy, worrying, submissiveness, and the like.  A careful examination of the entire study will repay the effort expended by the reader.

[9] R. S. Cavan, *The Family*, pp. 361–363.

authority, and other undesirable personality characteristics. The essential aspect of the psychologically broken home is that there is a deficiency in the apprenticeship relation so that the child is handicapped in his social interaction with others and unprepared for the experiences of normal social life in the years of youth and adulthood. The following case, from the author's files, is a representative example of a mild form of such deprivation:

(The writer is a young man in his junior year at college.) First I shall give a brief account of my parentage. My father was born of a farm family which was large and poor. He was the only one of five children that got off the soil, and happens to be the most successful financially. He virtually ran away from home so that he could obtain an education. He then became a country school teacher.

My mother was born in a small village of old-fashioned Quaker-Baptist parents, in which such things as playing cards and Sunday amusements were prohibited. Her family was large and she was the youngest. She went through high school.

I came into the picture in another little village where my father was the young schoolmaster. During my first five years my family moved frequently as my father received promotions that took us to other towns. When I was six we moved to a small industrial town where my father became the principal of the high school.

I am the oldest child in the family. My sister, the middle child, was born at this time. What little of my boyhood days there that I can recall seem to have been normal and happy. After spending five years in Rumford my family moved to another part of the country, where my father became head of a state vocational school system. These schools were in their early stage of development and this meant that my father was on the road most of the time. He never was home except Saturdays and Sundays, for he traveled continually. For ten years we lived in that region and only just recently have we moved back near our old home.

I have always attended public schools, and in my early years I was a good student, but later I experienced much difficulty in getting passing grades. I believe that this was because I missed my father's help and discipline at homework time. Also it was hard for me to get accustomed to changing schools. I changed schools almost yearly until I entered high school. Because I was always slow to get acquainted with strange children I made a practice of going home immediately after school. There I remained until the following morning. Thus I missed taking part in sports and became tied to my mother's apron strings. At home I helped my mother around the house. During this period she was very sick and several times we almost lost her. I shall never forget how sad I used to feel for long periods of time. Eventually my interests at home turned to wood and metal work and I became quite a proficient builder. I remember that my chief response from others came from articles that I had made.

Several times when my father was home, I remember that he went out to play ball with the neighborhood boys. I never played, because I had never tried or dared to, and I felt hurt to think that my father should be more interested in other boys than in me. I got the idea that he did not like me and so I sought more of my mother's apron and attention.

When I was about ten years old, my brother was born. As I recall I did not think much about his arrival, but I do know that I liked him and accepted the task of watching him willingly.

I joined the Boy Scouts when I was twelve years old, but I was too afraid of the boys and their tricks to enjoy or to attend the meetings regularly. Just why I had this fear of boys I do not know. Until I was a junior in high school I made it a practice to cross the street in order to avoid approaching policemen. I also belonged to the Y.M.C.A. but never made use of the swimming pool or other "real boy" privileges. I did become proficient at billiards, and I read books occasionally. My main reading interest was in science and mechanics. I have ability in the mechanical line, but my father is very poor with tools.

I also had a love for nature, and often I stole away for hours to be alone. I am at home in the woods and to me nature is God's true and only religion. It, like my mother, sheltered me and gave me something to be interested in. On the whole, my pre-high-school days were without important experiences and they seem long as I look back on them.

When I entered high school I was strongly impressed by its bigness. I remember the first day too well, for it seemed to spell doom for me. I thought I couldn't last the year, to say nothing of the four years. I remember that I was alone while the others sought their familiar gangs and cliques from former schools. My choice of a future at that time centered about a trade, or forestry, and at one time my greatest ambition was to be a hermit. But this wish was only a pattern of self-vengeance and was slowly overcome by my innate love for associating with people.

At the time that I entered high school my voice was changing and of course it had that familiar trait of jumping from high pitch to low and back again many times in the course of a sentence. The other children laughed, of course. The result of this ridicule made me isolate myself further and even to the extent that I never spoke unless spoken to, and that was very seldom. The teachers apparently took pity on me and spared me, for they seldom called on me to recite.

My voice remained in such a condition for five years. I had some kind of nervous condition which increased the difficulty. Whenever I attempted to talk I would become nervous and my vocal cords would tighten, so that I could not speak for an hour or two afterwards. I was taken to voice specialists but none could seem to help me. The result of this handicap is most serious, for it came at the critical time of my boyhood. Even to this day I can trace a good many of my traits and peculiarities to this condition. In high school I was self-isolated from the other children, and this meant that I did not play with them or develop many friendships. In the classroom I was never called upon to recite but had to hand in written work. I sat in the corner while the class activities were carried on without me.

I never attended the class parties or dances and never was asked to any private affairs. Not until I was eighteen years old did I have my first "date." In general my high school activities and interests centered about my workshop to which I came home promptly each afternoon. The rest of my time was spent in the woods and around the house. As the oldest child I grew up with responsibility on my shoulder for household work. I always helped with the dishes, and I was the handy man.

I developed during this period of semi-inactivity and isolation an imaginary world of my own. I made a habit of retiring early to my room where I could dream day and night of my own world in which I was supreme. As I recall this imagination it was built on the idea of future rather than present supremacy. I would picture myself in the future, free from present handicaps and on equal grounds with all.

My voice condition continued until the end of the first semester of my senior year in high school. There had come to our church, in the meantime, a young minister who was very kind to me. We spent much time together and he always considered me as one of the others. It was he in whom I confided and to whom I carried all my troubles. He brought a new interest and hope into my life. One day he asked me if I had ever tried to do anything about my voice. I answered that I had not, and he told me that he thought that I could overcome my difficulty. We spent long afternoons in the church, practicing, and I supplemented this by speaking to the trees in the nearby woods, and by reading aloud evenings in my room. I finally was able to control the quality of my voice if I did not get nervous.

I remember the first day that I went back to school equipped with my "new" voice. I started in the first class by actually raising my hand and reciting. The surprised looks were plentiful. This success continued until the last class in the afternoon, which was an English class. We were enacting parts of plays at the time and I volunteered. I did fairly well for a while, but unexpectedly I lost control of my voice and someone laughed. The defeat was terrible and I remained silent for a week. Then the following Monday I repeated the attempt. This time the result was more successful and I noticed an attitude of cooperation among my classmates. Slowly I began to take part and interest in school activities, but this was just the beginning of the breakdown of my shyness and timidity. Three years, however, have passed and the pattern is broken, although I suppose that some trace will always be left with me.

So encouraged and strengthened by this success, I decided to take up oratory. Eventually I entered and won the extemporaneous contest. Not only did this great success crown my efforts, but I was immediately accorded higher status with my fellow students. This gave me greater confidence, and marked the beginning of my adventure into social circles.

The majority of persons with such a poor start do not have the good fortune to encounter such a skilled helper and thus to reach a happy ending. The longer such self-consciousness and isolation endures, the less is the probability of escaping from it, for the role of seclusiveness becomes accepted by other persons as well as by the isolated person himself. Here, in a milder form, is the same kind of vicious circle process of isolation as is found among schizophrenics.

**Other Functions of the Family.**—In addition to the central purposes discussed above—the development of personality and the control of behavior—the family in our civilization has historically possessed other functions of varying degrees of essentiality, some of which are also affected by modern trends of change and disorganization.

Although in time of war the Germans recently attempted to obtain an additional population supply from unwed mothers, at other times and in other countries the family is still presumed to be the means by which the society maintains its numbers. Except in cases where the married pair has been unable to bear or to care for children, the traditional attitude has been that they are expected to bear them freely. Where such a sentiment prevails, bachelors are considered selfish, and childless married persons are either resented or pitied. The recent decades, however, have brought a change in sentiment, along with an increase in availability of contraceptive techniques, resulting, in most modern nations, in a rapid decline of the birth rate. In many countries, including the United States, the rate has declined below the point at which a population with a normal age distribution would replace itself, so that, as soon as the excessive number of women of child-bearing age passes out of the population, the actual numbers are expected to decline. The consequences of a failure of this type, a declining population, are far-reaching. Whether they are regarded as desirable or undesirable depends on traditional sentiments, national purposes, and other conditions.[10] If the number of soldiers available is a factor in future warfare, such a decline could be disastrous. On the other hand, there are possibilities of an achievement of somewhat greater stability in society following the stabilization of population growth.[11]

[10] A popular and highly readable discussion of this matter is available in an article by Stuart Chase, "Population Going Down," in the *Atlantic Monthly* for February, 1939. See also *Problems of a Changing Population*, Washington: National Resources Committee, 1938.

[11] See Ch. 13 for some speculations concerning future stability.

The family institution has also traditionally been a mechanism for providing certain satisfactions to its members. The desire for comradeship and affection is gratified by a warm and harmonious family life, and those who live alone often sense the lack in this aspect of their lives. A "psychologically broken home" may, however, fail completely to provide such an atmosphere, so that members of the same family and household may have somewhat the same sense of loneliness as those who live among strangers. Even in families without dissension, the modern trends toward specialization of interests and individual and commercialized forms of recreation produce a condition in which the members of many families derive less of this type of satisfaction from one another. Each member pursues his own interests and sees the other members of his family at mealtimes but not often together at other times.

The family has traditionally also been a unit for much of the ordinary social life in a community. In the established customs, families visit other families as a unit, and in paying calls on a new family in a neighborhood a whole family makes the acquaintance of another whole family. In much entertaining and recreation, the units are married couples. At dinner parties or evenings of bridge, couples are invited together, and unmarried persons have less opportunity to be included, as they involve a problem of finding a dinner or bridge partner. In social circles in which divorce and remarriage are common, such arrangements become less convenient. It may be that this condition is a factor in the popularity of cocktail parties in sophisticated metropolitan life, for such parties involve little planning of activities and no necessity of arranging for compatibility as in the case of dinner parties, and they do not require that persons come in any particular numbers or combinations. If divorced and remarried persons appear in the same room with their ex-spouses, they can avoid one another or withdraw without crippling the party.

### Underlying Factors in Modern Family Disorganization

Rapid social changes that have accompanied the technical developments of the industrial revolution, the movements of population, and the alterations in traditions, have weakened in numerous ways the early and stable form of family life. They have so transformed the social order that the traditional forms of family life could not be maintained, and at the same time they have made it difficult for a new equilibrium to become established. Among the modern conditions that are involved in such family disorganization are secularization of attitudes, individuation of personalities, heterogeneity of population, and disintegration of neighborhood life.

**Secularization.**—Virtually all aspects of the traditional family system have been regarded as sacred aspects of the society. The basis on which the marriages were arranged, the ceremony of the wedding, the nature of the household arrangements, the duties of husband and wife, the obligation to bear children and to care for them until grown, and the obligations of children toward parents and of all toward both ancestors and posterity—these have all been deeply set in the mores. Any challenge of these arrangements or proposed alteration has met with intense emotional resistance on moral and religious grounds.

Although all of these early attitudes may still be found today in conservative areas, there has been in modern life a general trend toward secularization of many aspects of society, including the institution of the family. This has not destroyed entirely, but has reduced, the sacred aspects of the family. Monogamy itself is still virtually unchallenged in western civilization. An occasional publicist may question the desirability of this aspect of family life, but, if taken seriously, he is emotionally resented by the large mass of even modern peoples. But many considerations, such as the permanence of marriage, the status of the wife, the basis of choice of mate, the desirability of children, and the like, have undergone secularization.

Burgess and Locke have stated the revolution of family life as a shift from an institutional to a companionship basis.[12] In the traditional sacred family, a wife is chosen for her suitability in carrying on the institutional roles of being obedient and faithful, a good worker with clean and frugal habits, and a healthy and virtuous wife and mother. Since these traits are best judged by experienced persons, the sacred community typically places much initiative and responsibility for the arrangement of marriages in the hands of the parents of the couple, rather than leaving the matter to the inclination and judgment of the young persons themselves. In modern life, however, where companionship and love are the primary considerations, there is often little or no inquiry concerning the ability of a prospective bride to cook or keep house, and no thought of requiring obedience or others of the sacred virtues.

---

[12] *Op. cit.,* p. vii.

The historical development of the emancipation of women also meant the secularization of many aspects of family life. Women pushed aside the conception that they are weaker than men and need to be sheltered in family life, and in so doing they broke away from much of what was involved in the traditional roles of wife and mother. The growth of emphasis on careers and other outside activities—club affairs, recreation, education, and the like—further encroached on the traditions.

It has been held that in the traditional form of society a man desires a wife who will be the ideal mother of his children, and prefers one in the image of his own mother. In the modern desire for companionship, however, the maternal type of woman is not held up as the ideal for marriage, but rather the slender, sexy, and at the same time athletic type, popularized in somewhat exaggerated form in the "pin-up girl." There is little moral objection to drinking or smoking, dancing, and other pursuits of pleasure that have been regarded as unsuitable for the maternal type of woman in the earlier tradition.

There has been a change from the emphasis on the importance of children, regarded in the traditional family as a central aspect of a marriage, to an attitude that children are desirable if the parents enjoy them and if they can be cared for without too great expense or inconvenience. Women with careers, however, feel justified in deferring the production of children or even in avoiding this function entirely. Other couples whose tastes lie in the direction of travel or other activities that are not favorable to a settled home life, or who simply do not care to have the trouble of bringing up children, avoid childbearing with no sense of immorality.

The secularization process is also visible in the increasing frequency of civil marriages, in unions without legal ceremony, and in the increasing acceptance of separation or divorce as the solution for unhappiness in marriage. Among the more extremely secularized people, the unions may be entered into with no commitment of permanence, but rather with explicit agreement that the "marriage" is on a trial basis and is subject to being discontinued at the wish of either member. Such marriages have the secular purpose of providing gratification for the members and are not presumed to involve further responsibilities of the type involved in the older traditional marriages.

**Individuation.**—While the traditional form of marriage involved the joining of two entire families into a friendship and alliance, the modern trend is for the bridegroom to consider that he has married a woman without necessarily marrying her family. His ideal is not to live with his or her parents, but to establish a separate household and to seek his friendships within his own age group and on the basis of congeniality rather than of blood relationship. In such a custom it often occurs that the parents of the bride and groom never meet unless at the wedding ceremony itself, and after that they do not bother to maintain social relations with one another. It is obvious that divorce or separation is easier in such conditions, for it does not involve the embarrassing severance of the greater alliance of families or the intervention of relatives who wish to prevent the dissolution.

To the extent that the choice of mate becomes an individual matter, the conditions are favorable for the most elaborate development of the romantic complex, which is particularly highly developed in certain parts of contemporary American culture. The romantic tradition is not world-wide, but is an importation of European elements of some centuries of development, and has been defined, spread, and popularized by minstrels, poets, fiction writers, and others until it has reached in some areas an extreme, mystical, and individualistic form.[18] The complex involves many types of belief. Among the valued characteristics of the lovers themselves are physical attractiveness, personal charm, and masculinity and femininity. The couples are expected to have complete and exclusive involvement in their love affair, with much emotionality, daydreaming, undying hope and faith, as well as innocence and credulity. They are presumed to be young, impulsive, and jealous of rivals. The process of courtship is expected to contain such elements as a novel setting and auspicious circumstances of the first meeting, symbolic importance of trivial objects and events, and swings of emotional exaltation and depression. The man is expected to portray great chivalry in his actions and to be only further spurred by obstacles, disregarding custom and convention in his determined pursuit of the lady.

The romantic complex further involves a belief that the event of falling in love has much that is unique in it. True love may occur only once to a person (if it appears to happen more than once, one or more experience must have been illusory), and when it occurs there is presumed to be an unmistakable emotional signal that may even take place the first time the principals see one another. The two are supposed to be destined for one another and unable to escape

---

[18] See Llewellyn Gross, "A Belief Pattern Scale for Measuring Attitudes Toward Romanticism," *American Sociological Review*, Vol. 9, pp. 463–472.

their mystical fate, for true love is held to be imperishable and eternal.

Romantic love is also individualistic in its specific emphasis on disregarding wishes of other persons and conventional responsibilities. Disregard of the desires of parents is expected, and an elopement in the face of their opposition is held to be one of the most romantic forms of marriage. The honeymoon requires privacy and secrecy, and the special attentions afterward that are expected from each by the other have the effect of setting them apart from any company they may be in. Economic considerations are not to be taken into account, for they are incompatible with romance. True love is also presumed to be strong enough to overcome other unfavorable circumstances—differences in race, religion, cultural background, and educational and social status. No importance is given to the making of an effort to be harmonious, for this is believed to be unnecessary in the case of true love.

It has been well demonstrated that the conditions regarded as not significant in the romantic beliefs are in fact highly important in determining the happiness of modern marriages.[14] Marriages involving independence from parents, differences of status and background, detachment from community life and responsibilities, and other conditions approved by the romantic tradition actually have much less possibility of happiness. This knowledge, however, is not as widely distributed, and perhaps has less appeal in itself than the romantic mythology. Current fiction, both magazine and novels, radio programs, popular song lyrics, and, perhaps most important of all, motion pictures, present romance with great appeal. The songs earnestly declare the elements of romance by such promises as "I would climb the highest mountain, swim the deepest river, etc., to find you," "I'll be loving you always," and "We'll let the rest of the world go by." Crooners have publicly proclaimed themselves to be "vagabond lovers" earnestly seeking "the girl of my dreams." Operatic tragedies portray love as transcending all other loyalties, and as being stronger than the desire to live. The motion pictures present the process in close-up detail, with all of its fascinating variations, so that it is little wonder that the tradition spreads into even such alien cultures as that of China.

The romantic tradition may add to the interest of love and marriage and yet compromise with practicality, as it does in France, where dowries are negotiated in businesslike fashion by parents,

---

[14] See for example the two celebrated statistical studies of the factors involved in marital happiness: E. W. Burgess and L. S. Cottrell, *Predicting Success or Failure in Marriage*, New York: Prentice-Hall, Inc., 1939; and Lewis M. Terman, *Psychological Factors in Marital Happiness*, New York: McGraw-Hill Book Co.. Inc. 1938.

and in England, where persons fall in love, but in most cases take care to fall in love within their own social class levels. In a society that is somewhat disorganized, however, and which has a family system in transition, the romantic emphasis increases the number of marriages unlikely to succeed. It is among such groups as the actors of Hollywood, where individualistic romance constitutes the main product of the industry, and in which most of them believe sincerely, that marriages are particularly precarious and temporary. Even there, however, disillusionment comes slowly, and many a "great screen lover" has entered a third and fourth marriage with the publicly expressed conviction that "this time it is the real thing." Marriage itself is disappointing and disillusioning in many cases, for the romantic expectation is that the breathless stage of erotic excitement will continue indefinitely, but general faith in romance itself survives a series of such disappointments.

**Heterogeneity.**—Common backgrounds and expectations favor harmony in married life, and in a society in equilibrium marriages are customarily formed between persons who are similar in such respects. In Europe, peasants have married peasants from the same or a nearby village, guild members have married within their own occupational level, and nobility and royalty have married within their own ranks. The marriages of rural Quebec, and of farm peoples in the United States, have involved on the whole no great differences of culture or social class and have had only minor differences of personality and character to even out in the marriages. In urban areas however, there are far greater possibilities of heterogamy (marriage of unlike persons), and therefore of unsuccessful unions.[15]

Heterogamy operates in various ways as a strain on marriages. The relatives and friends of the two partners exert pulls in separate directions. If religious differences are involved, there is often a pressure on both sides to induce the unlike member to embrace the religion of the particular side, and in some cases this pressure becomes insistent with respect to the religion in which the children are to be reared. The family and relationship groups have conflict-

---

[15] This does not mean that some tendency toward homogamy does not remain. E. W. Burgess and Paul Wallin, in "Homogamy in Social Characteristics" (*American Journal of Sociology*, Vol. 49, Sept., 1943), present the results of an ingenious study of 1,000 engaged couples. They show that for this group there is a considerable tendency toward homogamy in respect to religious affiliation and behavior and, in descending order, in respect to family background, courtship behavior, conceptions of marriage, social participation, and family relationships. Even where homogamy was highest, however, in respect to religious affiliation, there were over 20 per cent who became engaged to marry outside of their own major religious group (Catholic, Protestant, Jewish, and none).

ing influences in other respects also, and these become reflected in
tensions between the married partners. The husband's family,
for example, may expect the couple to participate in social activities
to which a wife of lower income and social class origin may be
unaccustomed. She may try, but feel ill at ease and at the same
time suffer from a sense of snobbish desertion of her own people.
Her husband may at the same time be annoyed by her reluctance
and may also become highly conscious of her ignorance of the folkways of the upper status group and of her lack of poise.

   Persons who marry partners with highly different traditions of
family life often find that the contradictory expectations of their
own household arrangements produce disagreements and conflict.
A successful and self-made man who has been reared in a family in
which the father held strong authoritarian power may marry a
woman whose family had a strong and harmonious equalitarian
tradition. Each may expect as a matter of course that his own
married life will follow the pattern set by his parents. The husband
may begin by making the major decisions on where to live, what kind
of furnishings to buy, and the like, without consulting his wife.
She may, on the other hand, have expected to have a joint bank
account, to have an equal voice in major purchases and household
decorations, and to be a partner in decisions on important policies
of the family. Each considers his own way to be right and natural,
for it is the way in which he was brought up. Mutual feelings
that the other is unreasonable easily develop in such circumstances.

   Interracial and intercultural marriages also involve a necessity
for harmonizing contrasting tastes in clothing, household furnishings and decoration, dietary matters, recreational activities, and
matters of etiquette. These are matters which often appear trivial in
the period of excited love, but which tend to grow in importance,
so that certain mannerisms and desires of the partner become
increasingly irritating. In many cases there is involved a disparity
in status between two races or cultural groups, so that the habits
and preferences of the partner of the lower status group come to be
felt as a social handicap by the other. Such difficulties are not
insurmountable, for some married couples make a suitable compromise and learn to appreciate the differing tastes of one another, but
they do make the problem of accommodation greater and thereby
decrease the probability of a harmonious marriage.

   One frequent source of contrasts between the members of a
married pair is that which arises after the marriage is contracted,
through the change that occurs in one of the partners. This often

happens when two persons of low income, social, and educational status are married, after which the husband completes his education, becomes successful, and gains entree to circles of higher status than those to which he and his wife had been accustomed. By virtue of his achievements he may find that he can hold his own in the new social relations, but his wife, who had not the opportunity, because of housework, child-rearing duties, and the like, to improve herself to an equal degree, cannot follow or take part intelligently in general conversations and develops a retiring disposition as a result of her sense of inferiority. By contrast with other women who are better groomed, more sophisticated, witty, and informed, she feels plain and dull. Often the fear that she is a handicap to her husband develops in her a sense of guilt and insecurity. The visible disappointment of her husband may lead to nervousness which increases the personality difficulties, until the marriage becomes a failure.

Such a history is not infrequent among those who marry before completion of a graduate or professional education. Often the wife takes employment for a few years in order to assist in the financing of her husband's education. Soon after the completion of it, he may find that he has entered a new social world of highly educated and interesting persons. The break in the marriage may come as a result of his selfish decision that he now has more desirability and bargaining power, but it may also come as a result of the wife's initiative because of her unhappiness in her sense of strain, of inferiority and failure in the new social group. The process is also often seen in careers in which spectacular success comes suddenly— particularly film acting careers. The history of Hollywood has contained a large number of examples in which one member of a married pair experiences a rise to stardom while the other does not, and in which the famous member puts aside the old mate in order to marry a new one of approximately equal prominence and desirability.

**The Status of Women as a Factor in Family Instability.** —In the early preindustrial stage of our civilization it was a widespread practice to guard and shelter women and after marriage so to reduce their privileges and accessibility that little possibility of escape from unhappy marriages was available to them. Temptations to leave one husband in favor of another were infrequent, for the duties of a wife were so standardized that there was less difference from one home to another than is found in modern urban culture. Furthermore, on entering marriage, women have been expected in various ways to reduce their attractiveness—by adopting a dull and virtually uniform costume and hairdress, by confining themselves to household activities with a minimum of outside social life (except in the presence of their husbands), and by bearing children in fairly steady succession. The coquettish mannerisms of nubile young women were not permitted to married women.

Remarriage of young widows has in general been approved, and even expected and encouraged, and something of a place in the social system has been provided for the spinster, but the divorcee has had no proper place anywhere. The force of the social system operated to place adult women in families as much as possible and to tie them down with prescribed duties so that they had a limited amount of freedom and opportunity to escape from marriage.

For more than a century women of modern civilization have been engaged in a concerted and highly successful drive to gain emancipation from traditional restrictions and to gain equal opportunities with men. In the second half of the nineteenth century they succeeded in opening the doors to higher education on a large scale. During the same period many new careers opened up, some of them largely monopolized by women. Ogburn has pointed to the invention of the typewriter as an important step in the emancipation of women, in that it made available the careers of stenographer and secretary. Along with this process came the improvement of services and the lightening of household tasks through inventions, so that the manufacture of clothing, the making of soap, the baking, washing, and even some of the cooking came to be done commercially, outside of the home, and the care of the home itself came to be increasingly mechanized, thus releasing the time of the housewife and permitting outside activities. The movement has brought political and legal gains for women, granting for them the right to vote, to serve on juries, and to occupy important governmental positions. At the same time there has been infiltration of women into many kinds of occupations—the process being particularly rapid during times of warfare. Along with these gains in economic and political freedom, women have broken through many of the moral restrictions of the old order. Along with revolution in costume, from a traditional, unappealing, and hampering garb to more revealing and competitive dress, has come independence from many moral restrictions. Women in the United States acquired, largely during the decade of the 1920's, the privileges of smoking, drinking, and traveling alone without incurring moral disapproval.

In view of such a revolution, it is hardly to be expected that in contemporary marriages women would accept without question the kitchen status of the earlier system. In cases where income is low and no household servants can be employed, the modern bride induces her husband to bear a share of the drudgery, at least during times when he is not otherwise usefully engaged. Dishwashing becomes a joint affair, and in many cases modern husbands even learn a certain amount of the art of cooking. Also the modern wife may insist on taking active part in some outside activities, either through a part-time career or in political, club, or recreational activities. While she may tolerate an occasional "night out with the boys" on the part of her mate, she expects to participate with him in most social activities. She expects not only security from her marriage, but an interesting and happy life, and she is far less inclined than the wife of earlier times to accept a disappointment in this respect with silent endurance.

Such a higher expectation of the satisfactions to be gained in marriage, together with the emphasis on the romantic aspects, induces many persons to seek dissolution of marriage on increasingly trivial grounds, in order to try again with another mate.

It is a commonplace observation that legal grounds for divorce do not accurately reflect the reasons for the rupture. Persons who do not wish to remain married will, if they are able, either satisfy the requirements of the law in their own state or establish residence in a state in which divorce is more easily granted. The most popular as well as a highly elastic, legal ground for divorce is that of "mental cruelty." In actual cases this concept has been successfully used to obtain divorces for such mild torments as caustic comments on the wife's cooking, objection to her use of lipstick, criticism of her statements in the presence of others, and even refusing to take a bath. This reflects a tendency on the part of judges, with the approval of the community, to allow a divorce if one or both members insist upon it, and there are few families in which it would be impossible to demonstrate the occurrence of an occasional inconsiderate act.

**Deterioration of Community Support of Family Life.**—As stated earlier, the formation of a family, in the traditional society, was an affair of a large circle of relatives and of the community. Such a family established roots which penetrated widely and deeply in the community life. With the rich interchange of knowledge in back-fence gossip, found in integrated communities, there is little possibility of maintaining within the family any great degree of privacy. The behavior of husband and wife toward one another are matters of public knowledge, and often public concern, which may lead to intervention in cases where it appears to be appropriate. Behavior which is not approved by the community leads to penalties, often indirect and invisible to the family itself, but readily recognized by many others, who take a lesson from it. This supervision makes it difficult for a husband to abuse his wife, and penalizes a wife for becoming slovenly. It makes it all but impossible for a wife to develop an amorous relation with another man, and makes it dangerous for her husband to establish a clandestine romance. At the same time, there are deep and gratifying rewards that flow from a long record of good family and neighborhood relations, for the reputation of being "fine people" carries with it many pleasant aspects.

If marriages are not satisfying or happy, the pressure of a community is toward concealment of the fact, and toward maintenance of a durable union having at least the appearance of harmony. Desertion or divorce is penalized in a number of ways, and the total effect may be so severe as to make this outcome unthinkable. In many cases the church, which is a center of social activities as well as religious observances, does not tolerate a disruption of marriage, so that a divorce involves expulsion from this institution. In many occupations a good reputation is essential—a professional man would lose many clients after the disgrace of a divorce, a merchant would lose much of his patronage, an employee of a bank would be discharged. In addition the primary relations become awkward after a divorce. Some friends sympathize with the husband, others with the wife, and it is difficult for either to join a group without sensing hostility and resentment within it. Furthermore, in stable communities events of this class are never forgotten, and if the couple remains there the divorce will be the subject of comment even after decades have passed.

In the virtual anonymity of urban apartment-house life, however, there is a great degree of freedom from such supervision and control. Where mobility is greatest, neighbors do not know one another at all and pass in the halls and on stairways without recognition of one another. Unless behavior is scandalous and conspicuous, or in other ways obtrusive and objectionable, it is of little concern to others. The duration of such a marriage is not affected by the attitudes of neighbors, nor is there any constraint against infidelity.

The child-rearing function of the family also suffers from lack of neighborhood support. While in the conventional community there is a network of cooperation between the children who play together and their parents, such a social structure is lacking in the most mobile urban regions. The parents of a child often do not know the children he plays with, and almost never know anything about their parents. There is little possibility of organizing parents to maintain common standards of behavior for all of their children, as is often done by informal negotiation in small integrated communities. As a result the urban parents have much more difficulty in controlling their children and in maintaining over them the kind of influence that transmits to the child the largest amount of intellectual and moral capital.

It is among such persons as the urban apartment-house dwellers that individuation and secularization permit many women and mothers to conduct their lives with at most minor emphasis on the welfare of their children. Some, aided by rationalizations from certain schools of modern psychological thought, allow their children to develop with a minimum of influence and control—"doing what comes naturally"—thereby abandoning their welfare to the accidents of the various streams of urban influence. Others who are able to do so may conceive that they meet their obligation to children by putting them in the care of servants, buying them all the playthings a child could wish for, and sending them to good schools and summer camps. Children brought up in such fashion, however, lack the stabilizing motivations that are acquired in the warmth of primary group life and thus tend to be somewhat detached, individualistic, and lonely, and to be lacking in certain kinds of social knowledge so that they suffer from uncertainty in many situations, and are inadequately equipped to handle the normal crises of life. Such children often get into special difficulties that are easily avoided by well-balanced persons, particularly in affairs with the opposite sex, and in extreme cases are so bewildered that they see no way out other than suicide.

Such neglect of children on the part of career women and busy fathers is not penalized in the urban setting referred to above, but is the subject of community-wide discussion and criticism in a village. If such criticism does not alter the ways of the parents, the children may still obtain a considerable amount of helpful guidance from friendly adults and may also tend to follow the behavior standards of neighborhood children who are under the collective control of parents.

The extreme of neighborhood disorganization is found in highly mobile and heterogeneous slum populations, particularly those in which the first generation of migrants to the city reside. Here, as has been shown in Chapter 6, many children escape completely from the control of parents and other adults and authorities, to be subject only to the standards of the gangs of delinquent children that inhabit their area. Such children have such a small tie with conventionality that many conduct their lives in a manner that virtually constitutes warfare against their society.

### PROCESSES OF DISRUPTION WITHIN FAMILY LIFE

It is difficult to separate the disruptive forces that are present before a marriage takes place from those that develop afterward, for there is a considerable amount of interaction between them. The correlation studies of marital happiness by Burgess and Cottrell and by Terman, however, show that there is a considerable amount of predictability of happiness on the basis of characteristics of each partner present before marriage. In general it has been shown that persons of essentially similar backgrounds, having sociable, generous, cooperative personalities (instability in women, and inferiority and seclusiveness in men are particularly unfavorable), enjoying harmonious relationships with parents who themselves had a happy marriage, and living and participating in the life of stable communities have a high probability of happy married life together. In addition, according to Cavan, where they have formed a family which has a high degree of integration and flexibility in the face of new conditions, they are well equipped for meeting severe crises, such as those of business failure and unemployment.[16]

In view of the rapidly rising rate of divorce in the United States, it is clear that fewer couples marry with such ideal conditions. Those who do not have them all may still achieve a reasonably happy marriage, but, as the number of unfavorable factors present before marriage is increased, it is probable that only exceptionally good luck during the course of the marriage will allow the members to be happy. In a marriage that is made on an unsound basis, such misfortunes as the necessity of having a mother-in-law live with the couple, the loss of employment because of depression, a separation because of the absence of the husband in warfare, and others of the kind may be sufficient to pull the family apart, although

---

[16] Ruth S. Cavan, *The Family*, Ch. 12, "Social Crises and the Family; The Depression." See also Robert C. Angell, *The Family Encounters the Depression*, New York: Chas. Scribner's Sons, 1936.

more integrated and adaptable families, as Cavan and Angell found, may be even more unified by their hardships.

The observation that the probability of divorce is highest in the early years of married life further confirms the statement that most of such marriages were undertaken on a weak basis. The peak expectation of divorce is in the third, fourth, and fifth years of marriage, after which there is a steady decline, year by year. In most cases, the dissension and conflict begin earlier, possibly in the very beginning of the marriage, but do not immediately result in divorce.[17] There are several factors that cause the delay, such as the reluctance to admit defeat so soon, the desire to avoid comments by friends and relatives, the intervention of persons interested in holding the marriage together, and other difficulties related to support and the division of property. The following case illustrates the operation of such delaying factors:

Marjorie C., an attractive and vivacious young college graduate, had been "going steady" since early high school times with an attractive but somewhat indolent young man, who, following his graduation, failed to gain entrance to the graduate training he desired and began to resign himself to idleness in his indecision about what career to undertake. Marjorie lost patience with him and asked her friends if he were a good marriage risk. The consensus of their judgment was that his occupational success was so uncertain that she should waste no further time on him, so she told him that she would not go with him any more.

Shortly after this break, Marjorie met a young man, Clark S., who began immediately to pay her ardent courtship. He was lively, handsome, and carefree, and enjoyed spending money freely and having gay times. Marjorie enjoyed many activities with him—dancing, playing the piano, athletics— and was quickly fascinated. When they became engaged, some of Marjorie's friends tactfully approached her to warn her that Clark's reputation in the city was not good. Clark himself had told her, however, of a minor disgrace in which he had figured, and so Marjorie rejected the advice of her friends and maintained her confidence in him. The friends persisted and on one occasion asked an older man whose judgment she might respect to repeat the warning, but Marjorie held on to her faith in Clark and set a date for the wedding.

The ceremony was performed at a fashionable country club, and many persons attended. There were fashionable presents, stylish costumes, good music, and hearty congratulations. The couple told their friends of the new house, beautifully furnished, which awaited their return from the wedding trip. The rice was thrown, and Marjorie and Clark left for a two-week honeymoon at an expensive shore resort.

---

[17] T. P. Monahan, "The Changing Probability of Divorce," *American Sociological Review*, Vol. 5 (1940), pp. 539–545.

Clark's behavior and attitude altered the instant the wedding was over, as if a mask had been taken off his face. The gallant courtship attitude was replaced by truculence and cruelty. Apparently he did not love his bride, but had won her to show himself and others that he could. The stay at the beautiful resort was miserable for Marjorie, but she told no one about it at the time, and even posed for snapshots, simulating happy smiles.

Hoping that Clark's mood was temporary, she returned with him to their new house and tried to find a place in the circle of young married people. She entertained some of her friends in the new house, maintaining the pose of being happy in her marriage. Clark cooperated when they had guests, but on other nights often went out alone. In time Marjorie heard that other women were seen in his company, but she said nothing about it to him and remained silent with her friends. She sensed that they were all watching to see how long the marriage would last and stubbornly held to her course to show them she had been right. In time, however, wearying of the inconsiderate treatment by her husband, she went to see the minister of the Protestant church which she had attended all her life. His advice and plea was that she not get a divorce, but continue to try to make the marriage succeed, and his urging prevailed.

For a few months longer Marjorie maintained the appearance of a contented wife and homemaker, but new humiliations occurred to make the situation even more unbearable. She learned that Clark had greatly overstated his income, and that he had bought their furniture on credit and was unable to maintain the payments. It was her disagreeable task to stand off the creditors as they came to the house during the day while he was away. There was even uncertainty about his ability to continue the payments on the house itself. Clark, however, was unconcerned and made no effort to solve the financial difficulties, apparently being willing to live from day to day.

Clark continued to keep company with other women, often those of low reputation, and word of such behavior continued to reach the ears of Marjorie. One afternoon, as she returned from shopping, Marjorie found her husband, half-drunk, sitting on the living-room floor playing cards with one of these women. He remained there, said "Hello" to Marjorie, and continued the game. Marjorie then abandoned all expectations of making the marriage a success, and proceeded to get a divorce.

Not all of the marital dissensions are so one-sided—the above account represents an extreme. It is often true, however, that one partner contributes more than a reasonable share to the hardships of the family. Cavan presents a case in which an extreme attachment by the husband to his mother made the marriage an almost complete failure. The mother had dominated all of her children, so that when the second son married, he insisted on living near her and visited his mother every evening for a time, often lying on the bed weeping and saying that he wished to remain there to sleep in his old bed.   **The eldest son was** similarly dominated, and though he married against the wishes of his mother, the latter accompanied the newly wedded couple on their honeymoon.   When the couple settled in the home, the mother attempted to dictate many of the decisions, against the wishes of the bride.   The son always took the side of the mother in the disputes; and before long was joining his mother daily for lunch, and several times each week during the evenings.   When he agreed to divert money from his earnings to help his mother buy a house, his wife left him to secure a divorce.

Personal inadequacy may test a marriage in various other ways. A not uncommon difficulty is the use of illness by one of the partners to win a dispute.   An experienced hypochondriac may simply take to bed with symptoms of distress and demand care whenever it is called for by the domestic strategy.   Such a role is perhaps more often taken by women, and according to Mowrer, by one who is a youngest child, or who had the role of the youngest child.[18]   In some cases a resourceful woman may employ such a technique not only for the purpose of winning arguments but also for avoidance of household drudgery, sex relations, childbearing, and any other responsibilities which she considers unpleasant.   She may control not only her husband but also her children by such a device and may be so successful in its application that she may not need to develop herself in other ways and thus becomes dependent upon the use of illness as a means of control.   Since it is not a rare or difficult matter for persons to rationalize their own familiar defects, it can be understood that there is a certain amount of sincerity in the spells of the veteran hypochondriac, and often even a genuine illness or weakness that is nurtured and exploited.   While it is often difficult, and sometimes virtually impossible, for a husband to escape from such a wife, the temptation is strong to break away when it can be done.

A somewhat similar and infantile retreat from crises, more common among husbands than among wives, is the practice of becoming intoxicated.   This contributes nothing to the solution of the crisis and leaves the entire burden in the hands of the wife, together with the additional problem of managing a drunken husband.

There are a number of personality defects which may operate as a strain on a marriage, but which, if a partner of a certain type is chosen, may be tolerable.   A highly dominant or tyrannical husband is, for most women, difficult to live with, but there are women

---

[18] Harriet R. Mowrer, *Personality Adjustment and Domestic Discord*, New York: American Book Co., 1935, pp. 88–145.

of "mousy" dispositions who apparently do not resent it and who perhaps even prefer a role of submissiveness. A maternal and dominant woman may find a suitable husband in the meek and submissive male who wants above all else to be mothered. On the other hand, two dominant persons married to one another present a difficult problem of achievement of harmony.

The factor of sex adjustment is only infrequently significant as a biological difficulty but becomes involved in marital discord by virtue of its relation to the moral backgrounds of the partners and to the course of harmony in other relations of married life. Because of the traditionally greater protection of young girls and women, there is in our society a systematic difference in the amount and quality of sex knowledge on the part of men and women. In general, women acquire greater inhibitions and prudishness than men do. In the course of the normal marriage these are soon overcome, but in extreme cases such women are unable to overcome a sense of guilt and horror and so do not achieve a satisfactory sex experience. In such cases the dissatisfaction of the husband may lead him to seek experiences with other women and hence to weaken and perhaps terminate the marriage.

Although sex relations may in some marriages continue even through periods of intense quarreling, it is usual for dissension about other matters to be reflected in disharmony of sex relations as well, to the dissatisfaction of one or both partners, and thus to the further detriment of the family solidarity. A wife who is angry about other matters may refuse the sexual advances of her husband, and he in turn may withdraw with injured pride, stubbornly refusing to renew the overtures.

### PHASES OF THE DIVORCE SEQUENCE

Marriages that begin with a degree of success, only later to culminate in divorce, do not necessarily run a direct course toward the state of dissolution. Each sequence is individual, but there are developments that occur with some frequency and which may be thought of as somewhat typical.

There is a stage in the process in which it is common for vacillations to occur. After becoming dissatisfied with the union and contemplating a break, the members may experience an emotional reaction and make a strong effort to recapture their early love and harmony. The husband may bestow unexpected attentions, surprises, and gifts on his wife, and she may become increasingly demonstrative in her affections.  In one such case, in the middle stages of the development of disharmony, the husband, who had taken the initiative in the matter of the divorce, located and moved his family into an attractive new home in a better neighborhood than the family had hitherto inhabited and bought as surprises a new electric refrigerator and a fine piano for his wife.  The gesture did not call out the response expected, however, for through her expressions of gratitude it was evident that his wife was somewhat hurt that she was not allowed to express any choice in the selection of such major purchases, and furthermore she believed that the family income did not justify such expenditures.  Her attitude further chilled the enthusiasm of the husband, and the progress toward the divorce was gradually resumed.

In families in which there had been a period of harmony and success, the process leading to divorce often involves severe emotional strain.  Nervous ailment of some severity may develop, which may for a time be confused with physical symptoms.  A wife, whose husband was obviously drifting away from her but who had not yet definitely announced his intention to be divorced, developed abdominal pains so severe that she was examined for such conditions as appendicitis and pregnancy.  Her physician found, however, that the difficulty was nothing more than contractions of the pylorus resulting from the domestic tension.  In another case, general nervous distress led a wife to seek advice from a physician, who in turn sent her to a psychiatrist.  The latter could promise no relief unless she separated from her husband.  Following their divorce, the former husband himself went through a period of emotional strain, possibly from a mixture of guilt and residual love for his former wife.

In a few cases the termination of a marriage so destroys a life-organization that a considerable amount of personal demoralization results.  Some men, broken in spirit, lose ambition in their career activities, become apathetic toward former acquaintances, and sometimes become careless of appearance and manners.  In more extreme cases alcoholism may develop.  Divorced women may also become extremely disorganized.  Waller has mentioned a case in which the ex-husband, who had taken the initiative in securing the divorce, decided, on the date at which the divorce became final, to make a gesture of generosity to his former wife.  Although Waller himself, who had the confidence of the man, strenuously advised against it, the ex-husband sent her a generous sum of money.  Her reaction was to commit suicide.  Apparently she could endure being divorced from a selfish character, but not from a man of such chivalry.

Much tension within families develops silently and without explicit expression. Some couples may come to their termination without a single overt quarrel. It is believed by some students of behavior that a certain amount of frank quarreling may be beneficial, on the theory that it operates as a catharsis.[19] Duvall and Hill, for example, insist that the open and aboveboard way of expressing anger is probably the least dangerous form of domestic dissension. Not only does it prevent long-term misunderstandings from being built up, but, they hold, it satisfies a need that most persons have to fly off the handle periodically. They contend that in much of daily life, particularly in occupational activity, there are annoyances and conflicts which must be borne without free expression of emotions, and that these must find an outlet somewhere. Man needs a place where he can give vent to his annoyances, and according to Duvall and Hill that place is within the family. Quarrels to satisfy these needs are considered to be productive, if they clear the air and lead to a new and more complete understanding, and to be useful in strengthening the marriage. They produce a release of tension, and a good feeling that all is well and that marriage is a fine thing.[20]

A prominent investigator of family conflict, J. L. Moreno, has paid particular attention to the concept of catharsis and has carried out extensive research by use of a technique of dramatic re-enactment of family processes on a stage.[21] In such a process, called the "psychodrama," he concludes that the spontaneous expression of emotions clarifies and erases the causes of conflict.

As an illustration of the process of marriage conflict and the achievement of catharsis through psychodramatic treatment, Moreno

---

[19] Evelyn M. Duvall and Reuben Hill, *When You Marry*, Boston: D. C. Heath and Co., 1945.

[20] Duvall and Hill recognize that there are quarrels that are not beneficial—they speak of them as "destructive quarrels." These are "directed not at an issue but at the person." They lead to alienation and become progressively severe. One may question the soundness of such a distinction. Perhaps the classification is made after the results are known. If the couple becomes reconciled it must have been a "constructive quarrel"; if not, it was a "destructive quarrel." It has not been methodically proved that quiet, objective discussions may not arrive at solutions just as satisfactory if not more so than does the quarreling. Nor can one be certain without the most penetrating kind of experiment that even the best of "constructive quarreling" does not leave some residue of wound and disillusionment that more than counteracts the "cathartic" relief. In the middle 1940's the motion picture public was entertained by published accounts of open quarreling between a well-known Hollywood actor and his wife, both of whom expressed themselves openly and freely. For a time it was represented that this was no strain on the marriage, but, when the husband played a romantic role with a much more calm and poised woman, he divorced his wife and married the new leading lady. After that, no more stories of bickering were circulated about him.

[21] J. L. Moreno, "Mental Catharsis and the Psychodrama," *Sociometry*, Vol. 3, 1940, pp. 209–244.

presents the case of Mr. and Mrs. T., which he refers to as typical. The outcome of the process, however, indicates that "catharsis" has a broader meaning than his theoretical statement suggests and in fact covers even the acceptance of the termination of a marriage and not merely the termination of the quarreling and the resumption of harmony. The essential facts of the case are shown in the following condensation: [22]

Mr. and Mrs. T. had been finding their marriage less happy, and, presumably at the initiative of the wife, came to the Institute for aid in the preservation of their union. In the preliminary interview they gave no clue to the nature of their difficulties, so they were asked to go on the stage and to start acting as if they were at home, showing their typical interaction together, but with more spontaneity than they were accustomed to displaying, having no regards for the feelings of one another.

Within a few moments they were quarreling about the expense of the psychodramatic treatment. Mrs. T. justified it, however, as worth any amount of money if it would help make the marriage happy again. Thus her objective was made clear—she had come to eliminate the conflicts and to restore the happiness of the marriage. To her, the only success of the psychodrama would be to accomplish this aim.

Mr. T., however, who had not wished to undergo the treatment, burst out with the information, which was new to her, that he did not want to continue the marriage anyway, because he was in love with another woman. Mr. T. had the objective of terminating the marriage, and presumably would soon have done so if the psychodramatic treatment had not been undertaken.

An auxiliary actor, here designated as Auxiliary B., supplied by the Institute, was asked to take the stage with Mr. T. and enact a scene which was to represent the conversation to take place the next evening with the woman, Miss S., whom Mr. T. loved. Mr. T. informed Auxiliary B., who was taking the part of Miss S., that he had begun a treatment on the psychodramatic stage, and that in the course of the action he had told of his feeling for her. He said that he had begun to realize that he was carrying two persons as well as himself into difficulties, and that he knew he must come to a decision. He decided on the stage that he would divorce his wife and marry Miss S.

The actual dinner engagement with Miss S. was allowed to take place, and, at the second session on the stage, Mr. T. and Auxiliary B. were asked to re-enact the meeting on the stage as it actually took place. What had happened was that Miss S. had made a decision different from that of Mr. T. and had decided to end their relationship, returning a gift that he had given her. She stated that she was unwilling to rob another woman of her man. Her reaction caused in Mr. T. a feeling of guilt and a loss of self-confidence. Mrs. T., however, was pleased in the expectation that their marriage was saved.

---

[22] J. L. Moreno, "Psychodramatic Treatment of Marriage Problems," *Sociometry*, Vol. 3, 1940, pp. 1–23.

Mr. T., however, stated that even though he might not marry Miss S., he would separate from his wife. He realized that such a step would be cruel to her, but since the matter had come out into the open he was not going to continue the marriage.

In a third session Mrs. T. stayed away and the real Miss S. was called in to enact a series of scenes showing the history of the love relationship with Mr. T. She had come reluctantly to the theater, and with the intention of discontinuing her relations with Mr. T., but the dramatic representation of their history revived memories and sentiments to such an extent that both spontaneously recreated their desire to become married to one another. Mr. T. stated that he wanted to have a child, a boy, with Miss S. He had come to realize that although he and his wife had been compatible as lovers and that she was a good home maker, he had never been able to accept paternity in the marriage with her.

In the remaining sessions Mrs. T. was given the opportunity to try and re-establish the marriage. She and her husband acted out scenes showing their courtship, her sacrifices to aid in his career, their early childhood and old age. This had no effect on Mr. T., who was still determined to marry Miss S. It did, however, apparently show Mrs. T. the hopelessness of her situation, for she eventually came to accept the situation and her anger toward Miss S. declined. After some thirty hours of acting on the stage, covering a period of three months, the treatment ended. In the statement of Dr. Moreno, "A full catharsis for a separation and a divorce was attained."

The outcome of the conflict of Mr. and Mrs. T. was in this case essentially the same as it would have been without the treatment. Catharsis did not have the classical effect of reducing the tension and restoring the harmony, but merely consisted in reconciling the wife, to a degree, to an outcome which had seemed inevitable from the start. It is not certain that she would not have become equally reconciled within three months after a single declaration by her husband of his intention to secure a divorce. The nature and operation of "catharsis" in social relations will remain largely unknown until a large amount of additional careful research is carried out.

### Divorced Persons and Their Children

**Adjustment to Divorce.**—The organization of society about the institution of the family, which is presumed to be monogamous and permanent, is such that there is no standard role of the divorced person. The status of the latter is uncertain and awkward, and without conventional means of adaptation. He has to find his own place in his new social relations.

Burgess and Locke list several common types of adjustment to divorce, representing divergent individual efforts to achieve a new

sense of social equilibrium.[23]  The first is that of talking to others
about the divorce, which is presumed to have a cathartic value.  A
tendency is observed among some divorced women to live together
or in the same building, and for divorced persons to enjoy talking
about their problems.  It may be interpreted, rather than as a
catharsis, as an effort to rationalize their situation and to rebuild a
satisfactory status.

A second type of adjustment is a continuation of some association with the former mate after the divorce.  Some couples continue a relationship of affection and comradeship while living
apart, and some even maintain an association that involves quarreling.  Others live together again and become reconciled, or go
through a series of separations and reconciliations.  One man,
weary of being dominated by his wife, secured a divorce from her
but continued to reside in her house as a boarder.  In this new
relationship the difficulty disappeared, and he stated that he liked
being her boarder much better than being her husband.  In other
cases persons see their former mates occasionally and casually and
sometimes with diminishing frequency as they become reconciled
to the condition of being separated.

Another common type of adjustment is for one or both of the
former partners to move away from the community in which the
married life was spent.  Often the wife returns to her parental
community, or to the place where she had most of her friends before
she was married.  In this way many complications of social relations
are avoided, and objects and places that have unpleasant associations are escaped.

One of the most successful solutions to the awkward problems of
the divorced person is a second marriage.  In this status it is easier
to find a satisfactory role in community life and to rebuild a normal
family life, forgetting the unpleasant aspects of the earlier marriage.
As one woman stated, "Being a wife and mother of three healthy
children certainly gives one no time to dwell on the past."[24]

**Children of Divorced Parents.**—Among most preliterate
peoples, where large kinship systems predominate, divorce is less
common.  When it does occur, for reasons of barrenness of the
wife or other serious shortcomings, there is little hardship on the
children.  In patrilinear and patrilocal societies the children are
ordinarily the property of the father, and after a divorce they are

---
[23] E. W. Burgess and H. Locke, *op. cit.*, pp. 643–647.
[24] *Ibid.*, p. 645.

cared for by his other wives or by his close female relatives and continue to grow up in the same village and to associate with the same adults and children as before, except for the mother, who returns to her own people.  In matrilinear and matrilocal families, the father and ex-husband returns to his village, leaving the children in the community of the mother.  Their status and social environment are little altered by the fact of the divorce of the parents.[25]

In the small family system of western civilization, kinship has lost much of its importance.  When marriages are terminated, therefore, there is much less possibility of such kinship substitution.  The affectional bonds are more sharply concentrated within the small group, and are not easily terminated when the family separates, nor easily transferred to other relatives.  In the processes of dissension leading up to the divorce, children are typically tormented by divided loyalties and emotional confusion, which, in the opinion of some investigators, is more damaging to them than is the experience of living with a divorced parent.

The children of equalitarian families do not automatically belong to either parent, but to some extent are claimed by both of them. It is for a court to decide which parent will have the custody, or how custody should be divided.  While both parents often compete for the affection of the child, thus adding to his torment, the court attempts to decide the custody on the basis of the child's welfare. On the whole, judges have not developed or employed any systematic means of deciding, and in many cases they award custody by rule of thumb.  In some cases there may be seen a tendency to award the children to the plaintiff, presumably the "innocent" party, and in others there is a disposition to rely on the advice of social work agencies.  At the present time, in the United States, a majority of the children of divorced parents live with the mother.  While some provision is often made for visits to the other parent, there is evidence that a considerable number have little contact with the father after the divorce.[26]

Where the time of the child is divided between the divorced parents, the disputes of the ex-mates may continue to be carried on, in a sense, through the child.  Each parent tries to justify his own position to the child, and to discredit the other by inference and

---

[25] See Kingsley Davis, "Children of Divorced Parents: A Sociological and Statistical Analysis," *Law and Contemporary Problems*, Durham, N. C.: Duke Law School, Summer, 1944.

[26] *Ibid.*, p. 706.  Davis cites a study by Weeks ("Differential Divorce Rates by Occupation," *Social Forces*, 1943, pp. 334–337) in which it was found that 32 per cent of a group of high school students whose parents had been divorced did not remember their father's occupation, as compared with only 8 per cent of the students from nondivorced homes.

innuendo, if not openly.  In some cases the father uses the child to try to find out how his ex-wife is spending her alimony, or whether she is going out with other men.  Cases of bribery of children, in order to get them to seek such information, have been reported, and some children are taught to "lie, spy, and black-mail."[27]

In many cases the child is exposed to the difficulty of having *two* stepparents, which increases the awkwardness of his family rela-tions.  He must remember what things cannot be discussed in each household and must keep in mind certain limitations on his rights and claims in either family.  If the child shows a preference for one of the parents over the other, which is likely to happen in many cases, the mate of the parent who is less favored may develop a resentment toward the child, with complicating results.

Because of general moral disapproval of divorce, outspoken pronouncements of church officials, and the unpleasant atmosphere of the legal actions involved, the children become aware of a sense of disgrace and suffer from a sense of guilt by reflection from the actions of the parents.  They become self-conscious in the presence of their companions at school and elsewhere and sense that their status in society has an unnatural aspect.  The child of deceased parents can be referred to by a common word, *orphan,* but there is not even a standard concept for the child of parents who are divorced.  They can scarcely help acquiring a sense that society has no standard place for them and that their very existence is an embarrassment to a community.

## SUMMARY

The family is an institution of world-wide importance, for it carries important functions in all known societies.  Human nature requires a long and intimate participation in primary group life for its development, and the most convenient and widespread method of providing this is to have a married couple reside together in a household, caring for their own children.  The children have the benefit of highly interested and emotional care of a pair of adults, of association with one another, and usually of stable relations with a set of relatives whose interest in them is also strong.  In such rich human interaction the essential human traits are acquired—sociability, communication, sense of responsibility, toughness of character, and the most basic folkways and mores of

---

[27] *Ibid.,* p. 708.

the society.   At the same time, the family often serves as a convenient economic unit, forming the basis of production, division of labor
and sharing, and transmission of hereditary property.   It also
provides a basis of satisfactions for its members—affection, recreation, and the like, and serves as a social unit in other respects.

In most societies these functions are so well carried out by a
family system, and so integrated into the general organization of the
society, that there is some consciousness of the central importance
of the institution, and a strong moral emphasis on its maintenance.
Attacks on the family system are viewed as general threats to the
survival of the society itself.

In modern industrial civilization, a set of social trends that
constitute virtually a slow social as well as industrial revolution
has had fundamental effects on the family institution.   The transformation to a complex factory and commercial system, the migrations and vertical mobility of populations, the loss of continuity
with the past in many areas, the detachment from community life,
and the invention of many labor-saving devices for the household—
these and other developments have altered the family from a large,
settled, traditional, and sacred institution of kinship to a small,
isolated, secular household.   The trends of civilization have also
replaced many of the functions hitherto carried out by the family,
so that they are done more cheaply and efficiently elsewhere, thus
reducing some of the importance of the family, and some of its basis
of solidarity.

Other aspects of social disorganization, particularly frequent in
urban life, have the effect of weakening the basis on which marriages are formed and thus of contributing to the rapid increase
of unhappy marriages and of divorces.   The divorce trend had risen
at the end of the second world war to the point where approximately
one marriage in three was expected to be legally terminated.

The consequences to society, and to the persons involved, of high
rates of family disorganization are of various kinds.   In some cases
there is extreme personal disorganization or demoralization, resulting
in pauperization, alcoholism, or suicide.   In less extreme cases there
may be observed loneliness, inability to find a place in a community,
and perpetual discontent and unhappiness.   In the case of the
children of divorced parents, there is suffering from the general
atmosphere of guilt and wrongdoing in the matter, and from an
undefined status which involves awkward conflicts of loyalties, uncertainties of affections, and lack of a standard position in the community.

The rising divorce rate does not necessarily indicate a collapse of modern civilization, but it does reflect a fundamental change in the traditional organization of society. It is clear that some sort of equilibrium must be recovered if the essential functions of family life continue to be performed.

## SELECTED REFERENCES

Becker, Howard, and Hill, Reuben. *Marriage and the Family.* Boston: D. C. Heath and Co., 1942. A symposium.

Burgess, Ernest W., and Cottrell, Leonard S. *Predicting Success or Failure in Marriage.* New York: Prentice-Hall, Inc., 1939.

Burgess, Ernest W., and Locke, Harvey J. *The Family.* New York: American Book Co., 1943.

Cavan, Ruth S. *The Family.* New York: The Thomas Y. Crowell Co., 1942.

Locke, Harvey J. "Mobility and Family Disorganization." *American Sociological Review,* Vol. 5, Aug., 1940.

Mowrer, Ernest R. *The Family: Its Organization and Disorganization.* Chicago: University of Chicago Press, 1932. Contains urban ecological material.

Mowrer, Harriet R. *Personality Adjustment and Domestic Discord.* New York: American Book Co., 1935.

Nimkoff, Meyer F. *Marriage and the Family.* New York: Houghton Mifflin Co., 1947.

Zimmerman, Carle C. *Family and Civilization.* New York: Harper & Bros., 1947. A pessimistic view of present trends.

# Chapter 11

## DISORGANIZATION OF RELIGIOUS INSTITUTIONS

The concept of religion is so broad and variable that it is extremely difficult to achieve a definition of religious disorganization that will find wide acceptance. To members of an old and stable church, the behavior of new and radical sects appears to be disorganization of the most serious kind, while the latter groups often account for their break with older churches on the ground that these have degenerated into formalism and corruption. Different religions emphasize separate values—the worship of God, the saving of souls, the maintenance of morality, the reform of society—and each group disapproves of the variant views of the others.

Any one religious institution, however, contains implied functions which can be fairly objectively examined, and it can be observed whether the mechanism successfully carries out these functions or whether partial or complete failure develops. Disorganization of religious institutions, therefore, does not involve the methodological difficulties present in the more general question of religious disorganization. Religious organizations have definite origins, purposes, and experiences, and they change and sometimes die. They respond to circumstances about them and are affected by social disorganization. These are the processes which are examined in the present discussion.

### The Sectarian Cycle as Illustrated by the Methodist and Other Movements

**The Concept of "Natural History."**—The study of the history of social movements and institutions is not undertaken merely for the purpose of understanding one particular movement in all of its unique experiences, but in the attempt to reveal stages in the developments which are typical, and to represent the phases that all similar movements or institutions normally go through. Such an approach is referred to in sociology as "natural history." Religious movements follow different courses according to their nature and the society in which they are organized, but there are many that have gone through a series of well-defined stages that may properly be designated as the "sectarian cycle."

**Circumstances of Origin.**—In general it may be said that social movements arise when a large number of people conceive that existing institutions are not functioning properly. The institutions are believed to be corrupt, decadent, or disintegrating, allowing a situation to arise which is undesirable or intolerable. In the case of religious institutions, the conditions regarded as objectionable in existing churches have been such as a high degree of formalism in ritual and ceremony, the automatic or mechanical character of religious observances, the participation of churches and church officials in commercial and political affairs, the weakening of the relations between morality and formal religion, and the general failure of religion to penetrate throughout the affairs of the society. A number of sects have arisen in objection to the lack of personal spontaneity in religious activity, shown by such mechanical observances as attending a service without becoming involved in the proceedings and by paying for benefits in various ways and thereby accumulating religious and moral credit in order that daily life may be safely enjoyed with less scrupulous morality and less spiritual feeling. Often the lower, uneducated, peasant classes, disturbed at extravagances and departure from the traditional moral codes on the part of the wealthy and the nobility, constitute the large body of recruits for the new movement of protest and reform.

The typical course of such a movement is shown by Methodism, which was a reaction to the general conditions of disorganization in eighteenth century England. According to historians of the period, great demoralization spread over the country.

The court became a royal brothel. The play-house became the temple of England. The drama of the day could not now be exhibited, nor even privately read without blushes. Many of the most learned and devoted clergymen, whose writings are imperishable in our religious literature, were either silenced or displaced. The ministrations of the Church grew formal and ineffective. The Puritan churches themselves at last fell into general decay, while the masses of the people sunk into incredible vice and brutality. . . . The higher classes laughed at piety, and prided themselves on being above what they called its fanaticism.[1]

---

[1] Adapted from Abel Stevens, *The History of the Religious Movement of the Eighteenth Century Called Methodism*, 1858. Quoted in Carl A. Dawson and Warner E. Gettys, *An Introduction to Sociology*, New York: The Ronald Press Co., 1935, Ch. 19, "Change Through Social Movements," pp. 708–729.

**Leadership.**—The leader of Methodism, John Wesley, had come from a pious family in a conservative village to Oxford, where corruption appeared to have gained a strong foothold. He found a great emphasis on rank, with which was associated such privilege that the functions of the University were threatened. In order to gain preferment in the university, it was more important to know and to entertain the right people than to be assiduous in attendance at lecture hall and chapel. The atmosphere of life at Oxford was said to be dull, lazy, futile, and silly. The requirements for a degree were retained in form, but the degree of bachelor of arts, for instance, was conferred at a private examination at which the candidate could choose his own examiners. He naturally preferred to select his good friends, and the examination was often a perfunctory and meaningless affair. Money and the time spent at the university earned the degree, rather than intellectual effort and learning. Professors took their duties lightly, many making no pretense of teaching, and undergraduates employed much of their time drinking, smoking, bowling, and flirting with town women.[2]

**The Beginnings of Unrest.**—When persons become aware of disorganization and corruption, the first reaction is an undefined restlessness or sense of uneasiness. There is no clear articulation of what is wrong with the society or its institutions, but there are sporadic expressions of discontent, somewhat analogous to the milling of cattle in the uneasy moments before the stampede. The tension has a contagious aspect and calls out various symptoms of collective unrest—wandering, local disorders, agitation, and the like.

Collective action does not develop quickly. Agitators stir a population to a consciousness of the problems and arouse them to a degree of excitement. Usually various formulations and suggestions of the nature of the trouble are made, each attracting only a limited number of adherents, before a leader succeeds in presenting a convincing definition of the situation and a plan for action. When this happens and a group begins to gather about the leader and give him loyal support, the movement may be said to begin.

**The Stage of Collective Excitement.**—Although it is possible for social and religious movements, such as the Buchmanist movement in recent years, to avoid any fanatical or highly emotional displays, there have been in the past a large number of sects which began in a series of revival meetings of a highly excited and orgi-

---

[2] Elizabeth K. Nottingham, *The Making of an Evangelist*, doctoral dissertation, Columbia University, 1938, Gettysburg, Pa.: Times and News Publishing Co., pp. 77–81.

astic character. These may be highly spontaneous in the early period, the expressions of emotion being unplanned and uncontrolled. The interaction of the members of a crowd, brought to a pitch of frenzy by the eloquence of the leader, produces a circular or reciprocal effect, in which the excitement of each contributes to that of the persons beside him, and vice versa. Particular forms of expression of intense frenzy may spread among such people in a contagion, and in such meetings are developed the characteristic quakings, shakings, rollings, and jumpings that have given the popular designations to Quakers, Shakers, Holy Rollers, and Holy Jumpers.

About the year 1800 an epidemic of religious frenzy, known as the Kentucky revival, broke out in Kentucky and Tennessee, chiefly among the Methodists and Baptists, with accompaniments that far surpassed the wildest excesses of the ghost dance. Fanatic preachers taught their deluded followers that the spiritual advent of the kingdom was near at hand, when Christ would reign on earth and there would be an end of all sin. The date generally fixed for the consummation was the summer of 1805, and the excitement continued and grew in violence for several years until the time came and passed without extraordinary event, when the frenzy gradually subsided, leaving the ignorant believers in a state of utter collapse. The performances at the meetings of these enthusiasts were of the most exaggerated camp-meeting order, such as may be witnessed in many parts of the South, especially among the colored people. . . .

From another authority, endowed perhaps with less of fervor but with more common sense, we get a description of these "exercises" which has a familiar ring that seems to bring it very near home. "The people remained on the ground day and night, listening to the most exciting sermons and engaging in a mode of worship which consisted in alternate crying, laughing, singing, and shouting, accompanied with gesticulations of a most extraordinary character. Often there would be an unusual outcry; some bursting forth into loud ejaculations of thanksgiving; others exhorting their careless friends to 'turn to the Lord'; some struck with terror, and hastening to escape, others trembling, weeping, and swooning away, till every appearance of life was gone, and the extremity of the body assumed the coldness of a corpse. At one meeting not less than a thousand persons fell to the ground, apparently without sense or motion. It was common to see them shed tears plentifully about an hour before they fell. They were then seized with a general tremor, and sometimes they uttered one or two piercing shrieks in the moment of falling. This latter phenomenon was common to both sexes, to all ages, and to all sorts of characters."

After a time these crazy performances in the sacred name of religion became so much a matter of course that they were regularly classified in categories as the rolls, the jerks, the barks, etc. "The rolling exercise was effected by doubling themselves up, then rolling from one side to the other like a hoop, or in extending the body horizontally and rolling over and over in the filth like so many swine. The jerk consisted in violent spasms and twistings of every part of the body. Sometimes the head was so twisted round that the head was turned to the back, and the countenance so much distorted that not one of its features was to be recognized. When attacked by the jerks, they sometimes hopped like frogs, and the face and limbs underwent the most hideous contortions. The bark consisted in throwing themselves on all fours, growling, showing their teeth, and barking like dogs. Sometimes a number of people crouching down in front of the minister continued to bark as long as he preached. These last were supposed to be more especially endowed with the gifts of prophecy, dreams, rhapsodies, and visions of angels." [3]

The sense of external seizure, or penetration of the mind and body by a spirit, is such that the rolls, jerks, and other frenzied expressions are often interpreted as the possession of the body by Satan, which naturally inspires great terror, or by the Holy Ghost, which is grounds for impressive joy. In the Methodist movement, the eloquent preachings of Wesley and Whitefield were such as to stir crowds to this high pitch of excitement, and it is reported that many persons were thrown into "paroxysms of extreme, though usually transient, agony." Wesley, who believed in the existence of witchcraft, attributed the contortions into which many of his hearers fell to the direct agency of Satan, who tore the converts as they were coming to Christ. On the other hand, the Molokans, or "Holy Jumpers," the Pentecostal sects, and others, earnestly seek to achieve the seizures, believing that they are a sign of supernatural approval. [4]

A characteristic of the stage of collective excitement in the life cycle of the sect is the extreme fanaticism of the behavior of new members. In joining the new group, they desert the wicked world of ordinary people, following the new leader with whole-souled devotion. They break with an old way of life and take on a new one. According to Lecky, "In the intense religious enthusiasm that was generated [in the Methodist movement], many of the ties of life were snapped in twain. Children treated with contempt the commands of their parents, students the rules of their colleges, clergymen the discipline of their church. The whole structure of society, and almost all the amusements of life, appeared criminal. The fairs, the mountebanks, the public rejoicings of the people, were all Satanic. It was sinful for a woman to wear any gold

---

[3] J. Mooney, *Publications of the Bureau of Ethnology*, 14 (1892–93), Part II, pp. 942–943.

[4] From W. E. H. Lecky, *A History of England in the Eighteenth Century*, New York: D. Appleton & Co., 1882. Quoted in Dawson and Gettys, *op. cit.*, pp. 717–718.

ornament or any brilliant dress. It was even sinful for a man to exercise the common prudence of laying by a certain portion of his income. When Whitefield proposed to a lady to marry him, he thought it necessary to say, 'I bless God, if I know anything of my own heart, I am free from that foolish passion which the world calls love.' 'I trust I love you only for God, and desire to be joined to you only by His commands, and for His sake.' It is perhaps not very surprising that Whitefield's marriage, like that of Wesley, proved very unhappy."[5]

Dawson and Gettys have characterized the nature of leadership in these early stages of the cycle:[6]

Leadership in this stage is characteristically of the prophet and reformer types. The prophet feels a sense of possession. He has a sense that he has special and separate knowledge on the matter. He speaks with a sense of authority. He is a revealer of a message, a new philosophy of life. He uses the sense of authority to make articulate the hopes and wishes of the people and to add weight and prestige to their direction. There is a feeling that he is not himself; some one else speaks through him. The reformer leads in attacks on specific evils, and his program is more clearly defined than that of the agitator or of the prophet. He is determined to change conditions in conformity with the mores, and his enterprise is possible only if the mores are ready for it.

In sharply differentiating itself from the corrupt society from which it separated, the sect places great emphasis on minor symbolic expressions of the difference. If their movement is partly a reaction against overemphasis on pleasure, decoration, art, and comfort, they may impose most extreme restriction on their membership to abstain from virtually any trace of these amenities. The early Methodists not only forbade dancing and opposed theaters but, according to Lecky, banned even the pleasures of secular music. "A poor Kingswood collier was noted for his skill in playing the violin. He passed under Methodist influence, and at once consigned his instrument to the flames."[7]   Similarly, in their early periods, the Shakers, Quakers, Molokans, Amanans, and other groups emphasized simplicity in life, manner of dress, and activities, particularly ruling against decorations. The costumes were of the peasant types for the most part, uniform for all members, and totally lacking in ornament, even, in some cases, in minor decoration of buttons (hooks and eyes were used for fastening). Their meeting places

---

[5] *Ibid.*, pp. 717–718.
[6] *Ibid.*, pp. 720–721.
[7] *Ibid.*, p. 718.

were not decorated, and no instrumental music was allowed. The Dunker sect has at various times prohibited attendance at animal shows, the playing of the card game of "authors," the purchase of pianos, the use of sleigh bells, the wearing of neckties, the use of violins, the erection of tombstones, and even the taking of membership in the Y.M.C.A. In the early days of the telephone, the Old Order Brethren made a ruling that it was unscriptural for any of their members to have such an instrument.

It is to be expected that persons who have not been swept into membership would resent the assertions that much that they do is sinful. The normal reaction to the claims of the new sect by non-believers is one of hostility, often expressed in persecution. Neither faction of society is disposed to tolerate the other, and there is a period of virtual warfare in many cases. Such persecution tends further to unite the members of the new sect and to aid in the control of its members. It also in many cases furnishes the necessity of withdrawal to some remote or isolated place where there is a minimum of contact with other peoples, and where it is possible to build a new society with little interference. The Mormon society not only abandoned their original location in New York State, but were driven from Missouri and Illinois by gunfire, and even in their distant settlement at Salt Lake City were subject to pressure of the force of arms until they capitulated on the principal issues of the conflict.

**The Stage of Formal Organization.**—The group which originally meets in the spontaneous frenzy of the revivals and which continues to observe such exercises in time undergoes a certain amount of inevitable change. Spontaneity tends to decline and ritual develops whether planned or not, for the accidental practices of the early meetings always become standardized and routine. The behavior which occurs in early meetings becomes the expected behavior from thence forth. Organization develops in the very nature of human interaction. The group develops explicit aims, history, and traditions. A structure gradually penetrates the fabric of the collective life.

The leadership in this stage tends to change in nature. The fanatical agitator is not an appropriate person to construct a social organization, and, if the original leader is unable to change his relation to the group, he may be succeeded by a new kind of leader. Dawson and Gettys state:[8]

---

[8] *Ibid.*, pp. 723–724.

The leaders at this stage are usually of the statesman type. They are the ones who formulate policies and attempt to develop social policy into an art. It is they who gauge the forces in the current mores and perceive and evaluate their tendencies. They are the ones who endeavor to understand and voice the convictions which have become established, and to propose measures which will realize the interests of which the group has become conscious. The agitator of the period of unrest and the prophet and the reformer of the stage of popular excitement may become the statesmen of this more formal stage, but they do not commonly do so because they are unable, as a rule, to make the necessary adjustment to the changing order.

**The Institutional Stage.**—In time the structure becomes mature, and the new society contains a mechanism for enduring. Its leadership, policies, rituals, and way of life are organized, and the life of the group settles into a routine. The leadership now tends to fall into the hands of a man who is essentially an administrator— the agitator, prophet, and reformer have no place in such an organization. The new leader's control is less personal and conspicuous and is on the whole calm, settled, and orderly.

As the ways of the new group become stable, persons outside the sect become accustomed to them and observe them without shock. The conflict dies down, and a degree of toleration enters and in time increases. At the same time the hostility of the members of the sect toward other peoples diminishes, and with it some of the fanatical resolution to keep their ways entirely different. The ascetic regulations tend slowly to be relaxed as members perceive that other peoples can enjoy simple pleasures without any perceptible harm. Youthful members of the sect, noticing the interest and color of the costumes of outside youths, long for a certain amount of such decoration in their own clothing. Such influences are almost irresistible, and there arises in the sects a general movement toward conformity with the external world.

This development of the accommodation process, however, does not take place with equal rapidity among all of the members of the sect, and schisms easily arise on the basis of differences in rate of acceptance of modernism. The Mennonite peoples have split several times into orthodox, partially conforming, and highly adapted divisions. Sometimes the introduction of a single concession to modernism causes a split. The Disciples disagreed on the question of whether such an instrument of beauty and pleasure as an organ should be permitted in a church, and the organ party separated from the opponents who would not accept such a departure from old ways.

When such trends of accommodation to the ways of outsiders reach a point in which there is no real conflict remaining and in which there is acceptance on both sides that the other group is religious, the movement may be said to have changed from a sect to a denomination. The denomination prefers its own ways but has lost all fanaticism and is now able to cooperate with other religious groups. There is no longer an assumption that when the end of the world arrives, they will be the only ones to be saved.

In coming to terms with outsiders, the members of a denomination become increasingly responsive to their social surroundings and tend to adapt to the prevailing manners of the vicinity. Thus the Quakers of southern California, in spite of the tradition of quietness and restraint in their earlier traditions, tend to approach the style of the other evangelistic organizations of the Los Angeles vicinity, singing hymns and introducing touches of showmanship into the service. Such denominations as the Baptists, the Disciples, and others have held to a relatively fundamentalist tradition in southern regions, while becoming much more liberal in the North, particularly in the larger cities.

Denominations also respond to their times, and in a period of secularism and social disorganization they make many concessions to changing practices of the population. In their intensive study of Muncie, Indiana, in 1925, the Lynds report a large amount of such secular drift.[9] Although no accurate measurements were devised, numerous candid statements to the investigators by Muncie residents indicated a wide divergence from the sectarian spirit. One prominent man, when asked why he joined the church, answered not that he did it to save his soul, ". . . because who am I to buck an institution as big as the church, and anyway it seems necessary to conform, but I guess my pastor knows all right how little my heart is in it." A painter was asked if he believed in Hell, and he answered, "Sure I do—Hell on earth." The Lynds in fact concluded that, in Muncie, the belief in Hell was dying out.

The church affiliation of a newcomer was often made on the basis of instrumental considerations. Business and professional men sometimes confessed to joining a church because of the opportunity it gave to make good contacts among the leaders of the community. A young physician may join a church to become known and may seek a church office in order to increase his reputation for stability and responsibility.

---

[9] Robert S. Lynd and Helen M. Lynd, *Middletown*, New York: Harcourt, Brace & Co., Inc., 1929, Chs. 20–23.

Secular activities have been seized on by churches in order to maintain the interest of young people and to keep the church a center of general community activity. Thus many have organized club activities, Boy and Girl Scouts, athletic teams, recreational and educational programs, and social service functions. In many cases a large proportion of the beneficiaries of these efforts are not members of the church, although there is usually the hope that a certain number will in time be attracted to membership.

In contrast to an earlier tradition requiring that Sunday be entirely reserved for sacred activities, and even to legislation forbidding many forms of recreation on that day, there is reported an increasing disregard of such observance by church members, and something of a retreat of the church in the face of this growing secularization. In 1890, proposals that Sunday baseball games be allowed in Muncie were rejected, but as early as two years later, the religious authorities gave way and baseball was played, with the compromise that a band would be present to play sacred music at intervals during the game. It is of course obvious that such transitional devices as the band would soon disappear, and the game in time continued without music.

As Sunday became increasingly a day of active recreation, with emphasis on sports, motoring, and motion pictures, the churches retreated again by making such concessions as early services for golfers. Special extenuations may be found for the toleration of practices that have grown popular. At a summer camp maintained by a religious organization, a large group of visitors paid a visit on Sunday, a day on which ordinarily no swimming was allowed. At noontime, however, the yearning of the visitors for a dip in the inviting lake became so visible that the authorities proclaimed that a special swimming period would be held that afternoon "for hygienic reasons." In such ways the rear-guard action of the churches operates against advancing secularization.

The same trend is reflected in sermons. Instead of the earlier, fervent, hortatory sermons on sin and salvation, the denominations tend increasingly toward the general topical lecture, dealing with moral and social issues more than with theology itself. The audience hopes for a talk that will be interesting and short, rather than emotionally moving.

To members of more traditional and conservative churches, such trends appear to be disorganization. In time this may cause such a reaction as that in which the sect began—a state of unrest, followed by a series of revivals and the organization of new movements.  The cycle thus is repeated.  There is no certainty, however, that such reorganization must occur in every historical period or that traditions may not undergo permanent changes.

### ADAPTATIONS OF CHURCHES TO METROPOLITAN ENVIRONMENTS

Since isolation is difficult to maintain in the large modern city, nearly all sects and religious institutions are somewhat affected by the nature of the social life of the metropolis.  The social and economic pressures influence the sectarian to make concessions in the direction of making his peculiarities less conspicuous.  Many Jews become persuaded to trim or remove their beards and to adopt the external appearance and manners of other peoples.  While some continue in the orthodox observances, other groups adapt their customs to Sunday observance, and still others abandon the Hebrew faith and join denominations of the dominant Christian faiths.

Similarly the Molokan peoples, in the city of Los Angeles, find it difficult to maintain their religious customs of always eating together, of wearing peasant costumes, and of avoiding social relations with outside persons.  The young people who work in factories are not always able to go home for lunch, and they find it awkward to keep separate from workers who are not members of their group.  The men sense the amusement and disapproval of their custom of wearing a beard, and the women become weary of the head-shawl and yearn for the more attractive headgear and dress of the women they see at work and on the streets.  The children who attend school absorb some of the derision felt for their group by outside peoples and are thus weakened in their sense of allegiance.  Only extreme isolation and a strong internal discipline can allow such peoples to resist the intrusive influences of urban life, and few groups succeed for long periods in achieving such conditions.

**Adaptations to Population Movement.**—It has been recognized that, in the expanding city, populations flow in streams from central locations toward the outlying areas.  As a racial or national group flows out of one area, it is succeeded by another, with different culture traits.  The type of church preferred by the former group is often not appealing to the tastes of the succeeding population, and the existing church is thus involved in a predicament.  There are various possible courses that may be taken, of which the most obvious, and in most cases the one with the greatest probability of succeeding, is for the church to move out with its population, keeping up with its members in their progression toward the periphery of the city.[10]

In the city of Chicago, many Protestant churches have chosen this course of following their populations. As their membership gradually abandons the original neighborhood where the church building is located, a condition develops in which only a few members live near the church and most live at some distance and find it relatively inconvenient to make the long trip on Sundays. Often the crisis becomes evident as some of the more distant members begin to attend churches in their own neighborhoods. At such times, these churches have built or acquired a structure somewhere near the center of their population, abandoning their old building to other uses.

Such an adaptation, while usually successful, is only temporary as long as the city continues to grow, for the stream of population continues to flow outward, and in time the second location of the church is again far behind the majority of its members. The same course is again open to the church, and in many cases is taken—to move once more to a site close to the residences of its members. Kincheloe observed one case in which a church occupied seven locations in the city of Chicago as it moved to keep up with its migrating membership.

**"Climax Vegetation."**—Another possible reaction to the crisis of abandonment by the membership is to change the character of the church, adapting to the new populations that enter the neighborhood. In many cases this adaptation is not successful and the church eventually dies or federates with another church, only to die later. There are, however, in each of the principal types of urban areas forms of churches which are able to survive. Borrowing a term from botanical ecology, Kincheloe has spoken of these as the "climax vegetation" of the area. In the competition for space and survival in the city, other types of churches die, but those that have the essential features that fit in with the nature of each area are able to hold their place.

The conventional Protestant church of the type that flourishes in small towns can best survive in a stable residential area of middle-

---

[10] The material on the adaptations of the Protestant churches in Chicago presented in the following pages is taken from research by Samuel C. Kincheloe. The essentials may be found in two articles in *Religious Education* for November, 1928, and April, 1929. The titles are "Major Reactions of City Churches" and "The Behavior Sequence of a Dying Church."

class home owners. Near the edge of the city, and in the suburbs, where neighborhood life survives, a church may be a social center of a community and may require no unconventional features to hold its membership. The minister is typically a member of the community and is widely acquainted there. A certain number of secular features may be added to the activities, but they do not constitute the main purposes, nor are they necessary to recruit the membership required to sustain the church. The services are conventional and do not require exceptional speakers or music, nor any effort at showmanship. Such a church survives because it is lodged in the traditions of an integrated community.

The "downtown churches," however, are of an entirely different character. There is no community in the central business district, which is largely inhabited by transients and strangers. Kincheloe found that the "climax vegetation" church for this part of the city is the large hall to which strangers are attracted by speakers of fame and distinction. For this reason these services, which approach the spirit of popular lectures, are sometimes referred to as of the "great voice" type. They are often held in rented auditoriums, as it is expensive to occupy land in the business area and there is little need for the church there on business days in any case. There is not much continuity in the attendance at such churches—the audience is largely different each week—nor in the sermons, for there is a tendency to make use of different preachers. Some churches, however, are able to build a following around a man who is an eloquent and forceful speaker and who can attract many attendants week after week, as well as strangers who are in the city temporarily.

In the apartment-house districts of the city, there is a similar condition of mobility and anonymity of the population, so that the neighborhood churches that thrive in stable residential areas do not find conditions suitable. Again, however, emphasis on distinguished speakers and on quality of music, somewhat as in the downtown churches, assists a church to survive here. Kincheloe has observed also that the Christian Science churches are among those that find such areas favorable.

There are found, in and near the central business district, a few cults of the more extreme and unconventional type. These draw their clienteles from all over the city—the cult is not usually a neighborhood affair. National societies for healing often establish headquarters here. There are also lecturers on numerology, spiritualism, and other esoteric cults, who travel from city to city, renting halls in the central business districts and advertising in the papers for an audience. They are financed by "admission donations" collected at the entrance. They are largely attended by persons who have not achieved a satisfactory life and who have no allegiance to more conventional churches.

Not far outside of the central area, in the hobo districts, are found the missions and "night churches." These often occupy a store building with a plate glass front. They seek to attract and convert the wandering homeless men who pass by their doors. Signs, often illuminated, identify the nature of the place—sometimes merely by stating "JESUS SAVES." The interior is simple and rude, containing a platform with a piano and rows of folding chairs or benches. Signs on the wall urge the reader to "Come to Jesus" or to "Write to Mother." The services consist of emotional attempts to secure conversions, to save the souls of the forgotten wayfarers. This is often aided by the lure of coffee and doughnuts, or even in some cases of a meal and a night's lodging. Such institutions do not support themselves but are maintained by the Salvation Army and by other religious organizations. Their success in procuring permanent conversions is difficult to estimate, for their clientele is too migratory to follow. It is probable that many conversions are insincere or temporary, and that the food and rest are responsible for attracting a large proportion of the men who enter.

In communities inhabited by mainly foreign populations in which Protestant Christianity does not predominate, the Protestant churches adapt by providing a number of social services, largely secular in character, to the populations of the neighborhood in the hope of attracting them into membership. These services are principally aimed at young people and consist of educational and recreational activities, often presented in connection with a short and informal religious meeting. These churches are also usually unable to support themselves and are maintained by a larger church organization or by former members who have moved out of the district with the stream of population movement. As a rule, also, they do not have great success in attracting permanent membership from the children of Catholic and Jewish parents. Some of these children take part in the activities but continue also to retain allegiance to the churches of their own people. When realization of the hopelessness of its aim reaches its supporters, the financial backing of this kind of church may be terminated. It is thus often not a permanently successful adaptation to urban conditions, but rather merely the late stage of a dying church.

## The Behavior Sequence of a Dying Church

Kincheloe and his assistants have made a detailed study of the natural history of a Protestant church in Chicago to show the stages through which it went as it experienced its slow decline and death in the face of unfavorable changes in the character of its neighborhood. The church, which is referred to by the fictitious name of the Monroe Park Church, began about 1870 and rapidly obtained a satisfactory membership. The original Scotch membership drifted away, but the church successfully attracted young people from the German immigrants who entered the community in large numbers, and to a lesser extent other immigrant groups. While successful, the Monroe Park Church never became large or wealthy, for even in the early period its neighborhood was being invaded by working populations of the stockyards, lumber yards, and other industrial plants. Such of its members as became prosperous soon moved out of the neighborhood and were lost to the church.

The height of success for this church came in the late 1880's, when it had a large Sunday school and much influence in the community. At this time the building was improved by the addition of a new front. The minister was a man of magnetic personality; he filled the church to overflowing with his preaching, which was of an emotional and evangelistic character. During his period of ministry, however, a scandal broke out which dealt the church a severe blow, from which it never fully recovered.

The population movement and neighborhood changes were, however, the most important causes of its decline. A Bohemian invasion was met by adding a preacher of that nationality to conduct services in the native language. The device did not succeed, however, and in time the Bohemian group withdrew and met independently in a rented hall. In order to attract some of the Jewish population that entered the neighborhood a number of New Testaments printed in Yiddish were acquired, and a night school was established to teach them English, reading, and writing. The Jewish population enrolled in large numbers and studied with eagerness, but, since the Monroe Park Church was able to make no religious impression on them, the effort was finally abandoned.

A young man was then called to the pastorate. He was full of vigor and tried a semisocialistic work among the foreign populations of the neighborhood. He instituted a forum to which they would come to debate ideas and theories on religion and socialism. The experiment failed, however, and was given up.  He also developed a boys' club which lasted for some time and succeeded in building up the Sunday school.

The young people did not furnish sufficient support for the church, and early in the twentieth century the church came under the control of the local Missionary Board.  The leadership was thereafter furnished from a number of supply pastors or student pastors, who remained only a year or two and furnished only inexperienced leadership.  Although occasionally there would be as many as 50 persons at the Sunday morning services, it was usually more nearly 30.  The effort began to appear hopeless, and in 1910 the pastor said "let the old cat die."

Churches, like colleges and many other institutions, do not die easily.  There is something in the nature of their organization that tends to keep them going for some time, almost without visible means of support.  Although the death process of the Monroe Park Church may be said to have begun by this time, it was not until seventeen years later that the church was formally disbanded.  The discouraged remark of the pastor angered the lay leaders, who stubbornly got to work and kept the church going as before, for some time making no departure from the conventional church program.

In the early 1920's a new minister gave the church a brief period of hopefulness.  Without disturbing the ordinary program, he added some boys' work, redecorated and repaired the church building, and added a chapel.  The recognition that the church was in danger of dying was implicit, however, in the plans to pass from the conventional type of church "to one serving the community."  The new direction did not help, however, and some members of the congregation began to look for some one to blame.  They accused the minister of having "no push" and asked him to resign.  His resignation followed, and the affairs of the church soon assumed a critical shape.  The Mission Board decided that the church should be closed and, as it held the deed to the building by virtue of the support given for many years, sold it to another congregation.

The sale of the building over their heads made the members of the church angry, and they gathered together and resolved that their church should not be closed.  They entered a new stage of hopeful activity and rented the building from the group that bought it.  Shortly afterward they even succeeded in persuading the other denomination to allow them the use of the building rent free, or to provide them with an adequate place in which to meet.  The congregation obtained a pastor and paid his salary without aid from the Missionary Board.

The decline in the next three years was rapid. Once again, the church tried a program of community service in order to attract young persons to membership. But there were at this time very few American Protestant adults living in the community, and the children who attended did not become attracted into membership in large numbers. Many of the children of Dutch parentage attended the Holland church in the morning and the Monroe Park Church in the evening. Catholic children from Polish homes were even less affected by their participation in the Monroe Park Church activities.

As failure approached it was not acknowledged and perhaps not even recognized. The most active workers assumed that their efforts were important and rewarding and were not to be abandoned. The following excerpt from a statement by a worker from an institution that trains religious workers shows the tenacity of hope and loyalty:

It was not until February 17, 1924, that I was privileged to go to Monroe Park Church. . . . I shall never forget that first trip! I took a street car downtown and then over to Twelfth Street. It was bitter cold, a snowy night, and I had never been out in the city alone, to say the least down through this district and at night. I had no fear, for whom God sends He protects.

I felt that it was a definite mission God had privileged me to perform because it was so unlike any other experience I had ever had. At last I arrived at the church, and after peering around and rubbing the snow off the sign I was able to make out Monroe Park Church, so I decided I was right.

The door was not yet opened, and I waited some time before one of the men of the church came who ushered me in and built a fire. By that time the congregation had arrived. It consisted of six or seven people, the majority being children. Reverend Mr. Atwood gave an inspiring message, and I sang two or three solos.

Not much there to leave an impression, was there? No? Ah, yes! It will never leave me. How I realized anew that just as the Christians of that community were turning away from the church by not supporting it, just as the non-Christians were turning a deaf ear and blind eye to the symbol of His only hope for salvation, so too the cruel world turned aside and spurned the love of our Lord! The church was in that community and many knew it not. . . .

They invited me to come and sing for them again, which I promised to do. Now, for the term, I was already assigned to one church and was doing all the practical work I could do with my schedule and employment, but somehow I was drawn to the old Monroe Park Church and couldn't stay away. . . .

I decided that if God wanted me there, I'd be willing to go, and I prayed definitely for Him to show me—and He did.

The people called for me as a special worker from the Institute, and I was then "officially" assigned to work at the Monroe Park Church. . . .

As far as religious interests are concerned, I owe much to Monroe Park Church through the grace of God for my own spiritual development. Here it was I first served Him wholeheartedly in a consecrated service, where I saw the sinfulness of sin, the matchless mercy of the saving grace of God, wept and prayed, laughed and sang, all for the glory of God. Where I made my first confession of faith by rejoining the church as a Christian, and not as a mere human effort to be better. . . .

Monroe Park Church then and now!

Out of the dusk comes the dawn and out of the church comes Christian love and the message of salvation. A message the world needs, and Monroe Park Church is sending out in that community. God's word will not return to Him void!

Monroe Park Church, in my judgment, is doing more for the community than any other institution around there—but it can and will do more if permitted to remain. I believe Monroe Park Church will remain and will do a great, far-reaching service for God and for humanity. . . .

If ever a church claimed me and held me fast it is Monroe Park Church. Every experience and lesson learned in that beloved place has but proven to be a development of Christian character and faith in my Lord.

Monroe Park Church lives! She cannot die because God has her destiny in His Hands!

The author of the above statement, together with her husband, dropped out of the Monroe Park Church a few months after it was written. The church lasted about two years longer.

Another worker who was for many years one of the mainstays of the church expressed similar optimism and determination:

Having come to Chicago from a little village in the West when I was but nine years old, I became a member of Monroe Park Sunday school. My sister, brother, and stepmother were members of this church but not active workers. They and my father attended the services. My oldest brother had heard the call to enter the ministry from his church and had gone away to school to prepare himself for this calling. He is now a missionary in India.

A few days after my thirteenth birthday I united with the church, being at that time the only child who was a member; when the pastor wanted me to delay joining the church for a few weeks, I said I would not put it off. I know now that it was God calling me to His service, and I have never regretted for one moment that I said "Yes" to Him. I was very conscientious and felt that since I was a member it was my duty and privilege to attend mid-week prayer meeting, although no other child ever went. I was always there.

I became a Sunday school teacher shortly after I joined the church and have continued to teach in the Sunday school up to the present time. . . .

When I was in high school we moved out of the neighborhood about a mile and a half from the church, right near another church of our denomination. The rest of the family then attended this other church, but I would not leave Monroe Park. My heart and soul were in the work there. Our family tried their best to get me away, but it was not accomplished. . . .

I have never for a moment considered leaving the church I love. For one and surely the main reason, I feel that I am needed there. God still wants me to work for Him in that neighborhood. The missionaries leave their homes and travel far into unknown lands to carry the gospel to those who know it not. There are those in and about our church who need and want the gospel and need it just as truly as the so-called "heathen." Who would take my juniors, a group of thirty-five or more girls and boys under twelve years, and train them for future leaders, and encourage them to memorize God's Word, to let their voices be heard in prayer to Him, and testimony for Him, if I gave them up and left them? Sometimes when I have felt overburdened and as though I could not continue to do all I was doing, I have tried to get others to take my place there, but have not been able to find those who would do it.

Who would take my intermediates—that noisy, giddy, silly crowd? . . .

My faith bids me be assured that God will provide for Monroe Park Church to continue to serve the community. He has overcome obstacles for us that humanly seemed impossible, and He will continue to use His power on behalf of His church as long as we are faithful to the trust He has committed to us.

The desperate efforts of the final two or three years were largely aimed at attracting and holding children at any cost. The children of the neighborhood, however, were less interested in the religious than in the recreational aspects of the meetings, and therefore concessions to this latter basis of interest were made in increasing degree. The services became increasingly informal, and the religious content was made brief and dramatic. The following three descriptions of the junior church services show the grades of this adaptation at intervals during the last three years of the life of the Monroe Park Church:

By six-thirty a hundred or more youngsters have gathered and the service begins. One-half hour is given over to such songs as "Christ Arose," "The B-I-B-L-E," "Yield Not To Temptation," "Come into My Heart, Lord Jesus," and others similar to these. There is no lack of enthusiasm. The children sing at the top of their voices, and often the singing passes into wild shrieks and yells. A young man from the Bible Institute swings his arms and leads them on—using every trick in the leader's repertoire. Sometimes the boys sing one verse—the girls the next; then the boys are told to see if they can "beat" the girls—and they do—in yelling at least. The same songs are sung over and over again, and the children know them so well that at about the second note of the piano they all chime in, full force.

During all this time the leader and assistants do their best to keep order. A short prayer follows, after a long exhortation to keep heads bowed, and strictly quiet. Even after these exhortations, however, it is rather noisy. Then another young man from the Bible Institute follows with a Bible story. At this particular service he told them the story of the life of Jesus, going into detail, and ending with the Resurrection. He emphasized the saving power of Jesus's blood, and how Jesus died for our sins. He said that we could be saved by coming to Jesus and taking Him into our lives. He told the children that he believed that they were not always as good as they looked, and that they were not entirely free from sin.

This was followed by a definite appeal to get to know Jesus and lead a new life with Jesus in their hearts. He finally called for a show of hands of those who wanted to accept Jesus as their Savior. About sixty little hands shot up. This almost took the speaker's breath away, for evidently he was not sure in his own mind that the children knew what they were doing. He prayed, however, that these little ones did realize what they were doing.

After about sixty little folks had, as the speaker said "been washed in the blood of the Lamb," he sat down and a collection was taken. The final event was a more or less orderly grand rush for a handful of peanuts given to each child, after which the majority of them headed for home.

For a time a device was tried of separating the boys and girls, holding meetings consecutively for each group. In the following account, a meeting of the boys' junior church is described as it took place about a year and a half before the end of the institution:

In the front of the room were Miss Watson, Mr. Jacobs, Mr. Haven, a young lady who sang, and a young man who played the fife, all of whom were from the Bible Institute. There was a young Jewish girl present who had been converted to the church, and there were three or four men members of Monroe Park Church.

The people who had musical instruments were warming up in a rather informal fashion. Both pianos were going; the saxophone and the fife were both being tried out. Presently a hymn was announced, in which the boys all joined. After this hymn, Mr. Jacobs straightened up sharply before the crowd, and said; "Shut up! Be quiet there!" and pointed to a boy of about ten years of age. He walked around and placed his hands on the shoulders of various boys to keep them quiet. He insisted that they sit on the chairs in the main part of the room and not on those around the sides. "You must be quiet if you want to hear the music. You've got to be still. Be quiet, I say."

After several "sh-h-h's," Miss Watson announced a hymn in which they all joined. The musicians were playing their instruments, and the boys were singing at the top of their voices. They soon ceased singing and started yelling. The leader reminded the boys that they were singing, and that this was not a yelling contest; that it wasn't "smart" to yell. The first fifteen or twenty minutes was taken up in singing songs. The children all knew the words to these songs and began singing immediately when the musicians started. The leader attempted to keep them from starting until the musicians had played the first line through, but had no success— the minute the music started, so did the boys, and by the time the musicians were ready for the second line, the boys were there too. Mr. Jacobs, who played the saxophone, would stop in the midst of playing, go into the crowd, yank some boy out of his seat by the collar, and take him up to the front and put him on the floor. Even when he was playing a duet, a special number, he stopped to quiet some of the boys. Miss Watson's main business was to try to keep order among the boys, returning hats that they had thrown away, telling the boys to be quiet, to "shut up," not to act foolishly. In one case she thought a certain boy ought to sit up in front, but he decided to leave. Mr. Jacobs said, "Don't let a little commotion like that bother us. He'll be back soon." . . .

It came time for the story. Special precautions had to be taken in order to keep the audience quiet. There had been a contest going on between the boys and the girls. The winners were to have the banner on their side of the house. It was a contest of numbers. The device that they were going to use to keep the children quiet while the story teller was talking was to count "out" any boy who made a disturbance during the story. He started the story and suddenly yelled, "There goes one off." Then he put a mark down on the blackboard.

His story was the one about David's sin. He told in colloquial and slangy language, of David's numerous wives and children and his desire to have the wife of Uriah. He introduced his story by saying, "Once there was a king who was all powerful. Now the Lord loved David because David loved the Lord. David had several wives and lots of children. I don't think God liked that, but He doesn't say anything about it. Now, David was up on the roof of his palace in the hot summertime. He had a tent up on top of his house to keep cool. David's army was going away. He had two generals, Joab and Uriah. David looked over the palace wall and saw a good looking girl— Bathsheba. He sent his servants to bring her to him. Bathsheba hadn't been used to going before the king, so she powdered up. David fixed his tie. In came the girl. David said, 'You're a swell-looking girl.' Now Bathsheba was willing because she said her husband was a bloke anyway and he was getting old."

Then he told how David had Uriah killed and how the men took off their hats and put the flags at half mast because they loved Uriah so much. David merely said, "Well, in a battle you expect to lose a few, don't you?"

"Bathsheba was fond of rouge, fine clothes, and jewels. She liked her new place very much. David thought he had everything all fixed up. But the Lord found David out. He loved David but he had sinned and because he had He told him that he could keep his kingdom but that his sons would have to suffer. When anybody sins somebody always has to suffer. So David's little son was killed and that is the reason Jesus Christ had to die—he died for your sins and for mine. But now we can't be saved just because He died for our sin, but we must believe that He died for our sins.",

By this time Miss Watson had made the count of the children. She said, "Now when I tell you the results of the contest I want no whistling, no stamping, or no clapping. Just be quiet. There were seventy-eight girls and eighty-two boys, but the boys only won by one point because a number of them were ruled out."

At this stage of the decline there was no difficulty in getting large numbers of children to be present, but it appeared to be almost impossible to maintain a religious atmosphere. Some of the church elders insisted for a time on maintaining order, but this resulted in big drops in attendance. Some of the boys admitted that they came only for a good time, looking on the church as "just like a show." In the final description given below it is obvious that the ultimate concessions were made—the religious element reached a minimum and the recreational aspect became completely dominant.

The intermediate meeting was scheduled to be held at eight o'clock, but most of the boys and girls were there about seven-thirty. Before the regular meeting they began to play a few games. One game they like is "Spin the Bottle." Miss Watson had Harry popping corn for them to eat after the meeting. By eight o'clock they had nearly all arrived—about twelve girls and eighteen boys. This was the third week that they had attempted a combined meeting of boys and girls. They had been held separately simply because the boys ruined the girls' meetings. . . .

Before the meeting the rows of chairs were pushed back against the wall and just a small circle of chairs arranged for the group. The actual meeting itself was short—a few songs, a prayer, and then the "message," generally a Bible subject or some similar inspirational type of address.

Miss Watson stated that she had never been able to get them to play successfully together, except that the boys' first organized football team last fall had been quite successful. I tried to help her start several games before the meeting but the boys were too busy chasing each other around the room and over the chairs. After the meeting Miss Babcock was asked to teach them a new game. She arranged them into two groups, the boys on one side and the girls on the other. The game she wanted was "Black and White," where one side chases the opposite side. At first, regardless of which side was "it," the girls would run screaming to their wall, the boys pell-mell after them. The next time, the girls chasing the boys, one girl tagged a boy, and three of the boys caught her and deliberately pummeled her. That was the end of that game.

The next game used a number of target squares drawn on the blackboard to be thrown at with an improvised cotton ball. The boys were against the girls and I was quite surprised at the lack of chivalry. The boys would bump the girls, or trip them, or use any other ways of deliberate cheating. The girls (Miss Watson called them her gigglers) did not seem to mind it, but took it as a matter of course, and even in a number of cases retaliated. Then Miss Babcock asked that the portable blackboard be taken back. Six of the boys gathered it up and before Miss Babcock could get out of the way had bumped her on the head with it. Part of the boys wanted to go one way and part the other, and the blackboard was in danger of going to pieces. Miss Watson stopped them and made two of them carry it safely to its place.

Then the popcorn was served from the large pan with a cup into the hands of the kids. In five minutes there was popcorn everywhere in the room. The boys opened pockets, held caps for more corn, and kept moving their positions around the room until it was impossible to tell which of them had already had their helpings.

By this time it was after nine o'clock and Miss Watson announced that it was time to go. The girls, after considerable trouble in finding hats or gloves, which the boys had hidden, were sent in a bunch first, and the boys kept for a while. Then the boys had to be put out—at least most of them— for they kept finding excuses for coming back for more popcorn. Finally the last four or five were cornered by Mr. Jacobs and taken by the collars and put out! And then Miss Watson said, "Well, they are getting a little better— they are not quite as bad as they used to be."

In spite of the above expression of optimism on the part of Miss Watson, the church was finished, and in July, 1927, it was formally disbanded. A community center remained for a time, providing club and recreational work for children and other services to the local community.

Although the generalizations made in the Kincheloe studies are meant to apply only to certain Protestant denominations in the cities, it is probable that no church fully escapes its environment and that systematic differences may be found in both Catholic and Jewish churches according to the parts of the city in which they are located.

### SUMMARY

Religious institutions characteristically arise, not in the slow and unrecognized crescive process in which such institutions as Lloyds, the London insurance house, acquired its form, but rather in a highly self-conscious social movement which runs through a series of stages in its typical life cycle. It originates in a period which is believed to be a time of disorganization, corruption, or degeneracy. A sense of unrest becomes contagious and in time puts a certain section of the population in a keyed-up state in which there is susceptibility to dramatic leadership. When a leader arises who can stir these people, there follow the typical revival meetings in which large crowds reach a stage of collective excitement and display their feelings in spectacular orgiastic behavior. The actions acquire definition, and through repetition they become routine. In time the crowd becomes organized into a sect, with its characteristic traits of fanaticism, hostility to and isolation from the world of nonmembers, severe leadership and discipline, and reaction against the aspects of the surrounding society which have appeared to be symbolic of corruption.

Complete isolation is sociologically difficult to maintain, and without it the utter differentiation from the surrounding society becomes lessened. The sect undergoes a slow process of accommodation, in which concessions are made to the ways of other peoples, and the external symbols of hostility and differentiation are abandoned. When the members of the group reach the stage in which they are willing to grant that members of other groups may be said to be religious, the sect may be said to have evolved into a denomination.

Religious denominations, and the individual churches of which they are composed, continue to adapt to the society in which they exist. In the face of the secularization and the partial social disorganization of modern civilization, particularly as found in urban life, many churches have undergone drastic transformations, while others have dwindled and withered away. Not only does the form of the church adapt, but also its meaning in the lives of its members. Thus, as societies become increasingly secularized, men take part in church activities for increasingly secular considerations, and the church programs themselves are adapted to more and more secular activities. In some instances, as in the case of the Monroe Park Church, this evolution reaches a point where the institution can no longer be considered to be a church and, in spite of the intense reluctance of a small core of loyal members or workers, is forced to abandon this status.

SELECTED REFERENCES

Dawson, Carl A., and Gettys, Warner E. *An Introduction to Sociology.* New York: The Ronald Press Co., 1935. Chs. 16 and 19.
Faris, Ellsworth. *The Nature of Human Nature.* New York: McGraw-Hill Book Co., Inc., 1937. Ch. 5, "The Sect and the Sectarian."
Hertzler, Joyce O. *Social Institutions.* Lincoln, Neb.: University of Nebraska

Press, 1946. Ch. 14, "Change and Institutions: Disorganization and Reorganization."

Kincheloe, Samuel C. "Major Reactions of City Churches" and "The Behavior Sequence of a Dying Church." *Religious Education,* Nov., 1928, and Apr., 1929.

Lynd, Robert S. and Helen M. *Middletown.* New York: Harcourt, Brace & Co., Inc., 1929. Chs. 20–23.

# Chapter 12

## POLITICAL DISORGANIZATION AND CORRUPTION

### FUNCTIONING OF A POLITICAL ORDER

In a democratic society, a system in which the people govern themselves through their chosen representatives, there are involved several assumptions concerning the operation of the processes by which the collective will is expressed. Among these are: that reasonably clear issues will arise and become known to the people; that candidates, taking stands on these issues, will become known to the electorate; that discussion of these issues and candidates will occur, spreading knowledge and sharing judgments from person to person; that rational choices, largely based on "enlightened self-interest," will be expressed through the ballot; that through such a process of choice will be chosen the candidates most satisfactory to the general interest; and that these elected officials will be subject to continuous and critical scrutiny by the citizens, thereby being motivated to provide honest and efficient government.

The extent to which such assumptions are fulfilled varies with the nature of the social organization. In the town meeting system, which still survives in parts of New England, the conditions are often favorable for the operation of democracy according to the above theory. In the relatively isolated sections of rural Vermont, for example, there are towns in which virtually all of the population is native to the locality, and in which most families have occupied the same farms for generations. All persons are well known to one another, and all persons are well informed regarding conditions in the town. There are no complex problems or issues which are beyond the grasp of uneducated farmers and their wives. The business of a town meeting consists of choosing a few officials, discussing the tax rate, and deciding on expenditures for such matters as road repair, relief to needy families, purchase and maintenance of equipment, and the like.

In such regions most of the voters are well acquainted in advance of the meeting with the matters which are to be taken up and have discussed these with their acquaintances. In the meeting itself they discuss and arrive at decisions which they are well prepared to

330

make.   If there is a question of improving a dirt road, the citizens all know precisely the condition of the road in question and what the consequences would be of deferring the repairs.   They also have a fairly accurate idea of the amount of work necessary to make the improvement, and the proper cost involved.   If a matter of relief to a farmer who has had bad luck is brought up, nearly everyone knows precisely what has happened to the man, what his situation is, and how much money is essential to the basic welfare of his family. Disagreements arise, and factions develop on occasions, but these are on matters of policy and involve little misunderstanding of facts or conditions.   When officials are to be elected, the voters have little difficulty in making their choices among the persons they have known for a lifetime, for the shared knowledge of personal information is detailed and accurate in such primary communities.

Where such conditions prevail, town meeting forms of government operate satisfactorily, yielding essentially the kind of government desired by the persons who inhabit the area.   It is possible, of course, for conditions to change so that such a political method ceases to operate in the manner described above.   In an industrial and residential suburb of a large New England city—a suburb of about 30,000 population—the town meeting form of government is retained, but the town is actually dominated by a small political machine.   The officials are chosen by vote at a town meeting, but by a very small number of voters.   The time and place of the annual meeting are so arranged as to produce the minimum attendance. A small room in the town building is used, large enough to accommodate a hundred or so persons, and the meeting is scheduled for a mid-morning on a week-day in October, a time when most workers and business people are working at their livelihood.   Most of the citizens do not even hear of the meeting, in spite of the published notices, and do not know what is decided there.   The machine members attend, transact the necessary business briskly, and adjourn for the year.

In the State of South Carolina, an old system of election campaigning survives, providing for closer contact between voters and candidates for governor, congressmen, and other officials, than is available in other states.   The system provides that the candidates travel to the county seat of each county, where a meeting of voters is held.   Each candidate makes his speech from the same platform, in a lengthy and continuous performance.   There is often a certain amount of mixing between candidates and voters at the same time, and some informal discussion during and after the speeches, in

which judgments concerning the merits of the various candidates
are exchanged. This opportunity to see the candidates in action at
close range and to compare them side by side has the effect of putting
in office the official actually wanted by the voters. While these
winning candidates have not always had equally high esteem in
other states, there is little doubt that these elections have in general
satisfied the voters of the State of South Carolina. It is often
suggested, however, that the cost in money, time, and energy of
making the series of speeches is sufficient to discourage many
potentially valuable candidates from entering the contest.

The governmental system of the United States evolved in an era
which was preindustrial. The methods of expressing the will of
the voters are adapted to the early agricultural form of society, in
which the people lived in settled communities, in integrated social
organizations composed of homogeneous populations. As the industrial and urbanization movements slowly moved over the face
of the land, however, the society so changed that political mal-
adaptation developed.

In political disorganization there is no longer a condition of
institutional arrangements which efficiently express the collective
will. Instead there is a growth of processes which bear parasitic
or even predatory relations to the unorganized mass of citizens.
The corrupt governmental organization tends to fulfill only the
minimum requirements of the implicit governmental functions and
devotes the rest of its energies to satisfying the desires of segmental
interests—the enrichment of members of the machine through
graft, the granting of special favors to business interests and
criminal organizations, and the provision of benefits to such racial
or national groups as are helpful in times of elections.

An examination of the most extreme instances of political
corruption reveals their relationship to social disorganization. It
is particularly in areas of rapid industrial expansion, where many of
the indices of disorganization treated in this book are shown to
occur, that governmental institutions have deviated from their
theoretical ways of functioning. The methods of gaining office,
the means of holding power, and many of the actions taken while
in power are largely unconnected with the theory upon which
democratic government is founded and furthermore are in turn
destructive to the social organization in various demonstrable ways.

Corruption in state governments is somewhat less common and
less extreme than is found in the most disorganized cities, but
where it occurs it has similar characteristics. It is found in states

which are dominated by one or more large cities in which political corruption is highly developed and also in states in which there is a severe degree of economic disorganization—as in the cotton states during the 1930's.  Corruption in the federal government is even less common, but in times of general disorganization such as the postwar period of the 1920's conditions occur which allow marked inefficiency, distortion of functions, and even criminality to penetrate into the Cabinet of the President.

### DISORGANIZATION IN URBAN GOVERNMENT

The administration of a great city is far different from that of an agricultural community, for it involves problems far more complex and technical in character.  The decisions are for the most part not of a nature that can be submitted to the electorate as political issues.  There are in fact few issues, in the ordinary sense, in urban politics.  The great choices of national policy are not involved.  What is presumably desired is that the conventional services of a metropolis—collection of taxes, provision of police, water, fire protection, parks, and welfare services, and the like—be provided efficiently, at reasonable cost, and without corruption.  Except for such questions as the desirability of issuing bonds for a new boulevard, bridge, or park—a question which is often directly submitted to the voters in a referendum—there are no choices for the voters to make except between candidates for office.  These candidates do not often differentiate themselves on issues, but on other matters.  They often both claim to be both honest and efficient and infer that their rivals are somewhat deficient in both respects, but this appeal is so hackneyed in politics that it tends to be taken as a matter of course by voters and to be ignored in the process of choosing candidates.

**Bases of Candidate Appeal.**—Since elections tend to select the candidates of a whole party rather than to split tickets and choose some of each, the main emphasis in campaigns is on the person who heads the ticket—in urban campaigns, the candidate for mayor.  If he can gain the support of the majority of voters, he usually carries the rest of the candidates along with him.  It is therefore important for the party to choose a mayoralty candidate with maximum appeal.  Without issues, the emphasis tends to fall on personality and color.  Urban voters occasionally choose a dull speaker and colorless personality who is honest and able, but in the long run the political odds heavily favor the man with a radiant and appealing personality. An ideal candidate has an agreeable and conspicuous appearance, a hearty manner with people, and good rapport with crowds. He is a good showman with a knack of getting publicity. Mayor "Jimmy" Walker of New York City, who had had professional experience in entertainment as a dancer and song writer and who had a knack for staging spectacular shows of welcome for visiting celebrities and for appearing in public before happy crowds, gained and held office largely by these abilities.

In the spring of 1940, a candidate whose primary attraction was a colorful personality defeated the incumbent mayor of the city of Milwaukee, who had held office for twenty-four years and provided the city with one of the most honest and efficient administrations of any large city in the country in that generation. Mayor Daniel Hoan, a Socialist, conducted a campaign for re-election without glamor, simply speaking of his long tenure without political scandal, with model police and fire departments, with a city debt that was the smallest in the country on a per-capita basis, and with an exceptionally low crime rate. His opponent, however, the young, handsome, blonde son of a barber, Carl Zeidler, prevailed over Hoan largely on the basis of personal appeal. He joined dozens of fraternal and civic organizations and diligently attended meetings, often allowing himself to be prevailed upon to make a speech or sing a song. He learned the first names, according to his own estimate, of 50,000 residents of Milwaukee. During his campaign he appeared at numerous meetings, tossing his wavy hair, flashing a blinding smile, and singing songs such as "When Irish Eyes Are Smiling." At one meeting of 600 women, Zeidler is reported to have made his entrance arm-in-arm with a mannequin, beautifully dressed in a bridal gown, and to have sung "I Love You Truly" as he walked with her down the aisle.[1]

One of the most colorful American mayors of modern times, however, was William Hale Thompson, also known as "Big Bill, the Builder," who dominated Chicago for most of the 1920's. Thompson was a large, handsome man with an impressive ability for oratory and a great love for a spotlight. His appearance before a crowd had a magnetic effect, even on some of those who were unsympathetic to his policies. His speech was in the popular idiom, informal and full of slang. His clothes were loose and his gestures free, and his breezy manner was crowned by a large western hat, which he waved at appropriate intervals.

---

[1] *Time*, April 15, 1940.

Thompson's campaign meetings were carefully staged and spectacular in execution.  They were held in large auditoriums and
motion picture theaters, richly decorated for the occasion with ban-
ners and flags.  The central feature on the speaker's platform was
a large American flag which served as a background for the campaign performance.  The organization saw to it that the hall was
filled and that the supporters knew when and how to applaud—
which was at virtually every point of emphasis or pause, and as
loudly as possible.

The meeting began with a patriotic song, and, before Thompson
made his entrance, minor candidates made their speeches, often dull
in character but full of praise of Thompson as well as pleas for
support of their own candidacy.  A more gifted speaker sometimes
addressed the crowd specifically on the merits of "Big Bill."  From
time to time the speeches were interrupted by a courier who would
enter the hall, run to the stage, and announce that Thompson was
on his way; that he was two miles down the street; that he was
only a block away.

The actual entrance of Thompson was preceded by a final courier
shouting with high excitement that "Big Bill" is here, and accompanied by a fanfare of bugles.  A soldier, a sailor, and a marine
in uniform marched to the stage with flags flowing from staffs, and
behind them, out of a knot of scurrying men, strode Thompson
himself, waving his campaign hat, coming swiftly to the center of
the stage as the band broke into the "Star Spangled Banner."  The
men in uniform saluted, and as the audience sang Thompson grasped
the flagstaff and waved the flag above him.

The main address followed.  It was in simple language but both
humorous and dramatic in character.  Clear characterization of the
conditions in Chicago before or after he had held office were
contrasted with the more favorable conditions during his tenure.
He pointed to clear and well-known facts to support his claims,
however unreasonable the inferences were.  During the mayoralty
of Dever, generally acknowledged to be an honest and efficient
mayor, for example, warfare between members of criminal gangs
became spectacular.  Thompson compared this with the apparent
peaceful conditions during his terms of office, when organized
crime operated quietly and efficiently without need of competition
and conflict.  He related an experience that occurred during Dever's
regime, when he visited another city, where the other mayor opened
Thompson's coat and inspected it inside and out.  Thompson
inquired the reason for this action, and the other mayor said he was

looking for bullet holes.  The tale was told humorously and acted out for illustration.

The central theme of the campaign of 1926, however, was so apparently irrelevant and unconventional that it became the subject of national and even international interest and amusement.  It was an attack on Great Britain and international cooperation in general, with particular attention given to criticism of the World Court. Possibly to appeal to Irish voters, and certainly aware of the postwar reaction to Europe and the isolationist spirit, Thompson claimed that Britain was engaged in a great plot to get the United States entangled in foreign affairs, and ultimately, by way of insidious schemes, was planning to get the United States back to the status of a British colony.  This Thompson promised to prevent, and said that if he was elected he would go over and "punch King George in the snoot."  The following portion of one of his 1926 anti-British speeches on behalf of Congressional candidates illustrates the character of his argument : [2]

All this argument for the World Court is a lot of propaganda for the King of England.  They tell us that we ought to trust England—that she is our friend.  Well, the King got control of all the rubber, and raised the price enough to pay all their debt to us.  That shows they're pretty friendly, doesn't it?  Then the King got control of coffee, and is doing the same thing. I shouldn't be surprised if the King had something to do with slipping over the Volstead Act on us so that their distillers can make fortunes selling us bootleg liquor.  You are paying them a billion dollars on just these three items.

How do they do it?  By using our pro-British senators to vote down Old Glory.  I admit I never expected much of McKinley [Illinois member of the House of Representatives], with him running over to see the King every summer.  He likes it over there so well that with your help we'll fix it on April 13th so that he can spend his winters there too.

I helped elect Charley Deneen senator.  I thought he was an American. But he hadn't been in Washington a year before the King got him.  I apologize for what I did.

For the second time in the history of the United States of America they voted for gag rule.  They were afraid and ashamed to let anyone know what they were doing.  They won't tell you now—ask them about the court and they reply "watch me throw this hunk of mud !"  That bell-hop McKinley refused to debate with Frank Smith.  If the two had ever stood on a platform together, McKinley wouldn't get enough votes to know he was running. Smith looks, acts and talks like a senator.

---

[2] Carroll H. Wooddy, *The Chicago Primary of 1926*.  Chicago: University of Chicago Press, 1926 pp. 64–66.

That poor, miserable reprobate, McKinley, says "don't blame me—the party wanted me to vote for the court," and tries to hide behind that great American, Coolidge. I predict that Coolidge will before long announce that he wants us out of the court—he keeps his ear to the ground.

I hear McKinley is on his second million now [a reference to the heavy campaign expenditures of candidate McKinley]. . . . They say he's a good business man. What kind of business do you call it to spend a million to get a $7,500 job—unless there's some business going on we don't know about? You might expect anything of a man who voted to haul down the flag and destroy American institutions.

It's a lie to say they voted for the world court. There isn't any world court. What it is is the Permanent Court of International Justice of the League of Nations. One of the reasons they stopped debate was to keep us from finding out what their "world court" really is.

The international bankers put the world court planks in both party platforms. Let's hope that the people will find some new way to nominate a president and make a platform so we can get out of the clutches of the international bankers.

They say we are bipartisan because the Democrats are helping us keep Old Glory at the masthead, when thirty-one Democrats helped them pull it down!

Charley and Willie think it takes seven Yankees to lick a Britisher. Well, I'm pretty old and fat, but I'll guarantee to lick any Britisher my weight. If they are so good, why don't they send someone over to lick Jack Dempsey? Why couldn't they lick Jim Jeffries? It seems to me I remember that dear old John L. Sullivan used to go over to England and lick a couple of Britishers every night.

We'll get rid of one of our pro-British senators on April 13th.

I'm not in this campaign for anything for myself. I think there is great danger ahead. We stand at the crossroads. You always stood by Bill when he needed you. When they called me Kaiser Bill and the newspapers bribed with English money called me a traitor you re-elected me as mayor to prove I was right. When you need me I owe it to you, and I'll be here.

I see a picture in my mind of the nations gathered around the table at Geneva where John Bull has seven votes to our one. The different ones are telling about unemployment and distress in their countries. Uncle Sam says that everyone in America is happy and prosperous. They suggest that the American tariff be lowered so they can sell us goods and start their factories moving. Uncle Sam protests—that would throw American laborers out of work. "You object!" says John Bull, "Well, majority rules, *call the roll.*"

After the war, I saved Chicago from the bread line and the soup kitchen with my Pageant of Progress, and I don't ever want to see anything like that in America.

All this may happen if you're not alert. McKinley and Deneen will vote you into the league, the flag of internationalism will be raised above Old Glory, the Constitution nullified, all American institutions as laid down by the Fathers struck down.

They'll call the roll on the repudiation of all war debts, and what they don't pay, you've got to pay. Thirty billions—no wonder McKinley is willing to pay a million to save that much for the King.

They've had twenty-eight wars since the armistice, one for every ninety days. After they get Uncle Sam in they'll have one every sixty days.

The King wants it so—McKinley and Deneen are voting so—let's be rid of them at the first possible time.

I'm here to prevent you from suffering. I need not be in this campaign at all. I'm not running. I love our flag, and want nothing over it—I want us to be left alone.

In his attacks on Mayor Dever, Thompson brought to the stage a textbook used in the public schools and compared it with one used during his own administration. The pictures of patriotic heroes that formerly appeared had been dropped out, and Dever was accused of having been influenced by England to reduce the patriotism of school children.

One of Thompson's most notorious tricks was his "rat show," which he used to dramatize his break with two former political cronies, Fred Lundin and Dr. John Dill Robertson. He brought with him to the stage a cage containing two rats, one of which he addressed as "Fred" and the other as "Doc," reproaching them for their desertion of him. His remarks ran in part as follows: "Fred, let me ask you something. Wasn't I the best friend you ever had? Isn't it true that I came home from Honolulu to save you from the penitentiary? . . . I have learned, Fred, that you are going to try to flood Chicago with 500,000 copies of a newspaper called the *Bulletin*, full of lies about me. I think that justifies my saying that your political monicker ought not to be 'fox' but 'rat.' "

In the course of the campaign, as well as in the period building up to it, Thompson saw to it that his name was constantly in the headlines. If nothing else would achieve this, he would undertake pure publicity stunts. In one instance when affairs were dull, he announced an expedition by steamship down the Mississippi River to the Gulf, and on to the southern Pacific where on certain islands might be found some tree-climbing fish. He actually did board a yacht and traveled part way down the Mississippi, abandoning the project when it failed to hold newspaper space.

It is not to be assumed, however, that personal appeal alone accounted for the successes of Thompson at the polls. His organization made use of all the devices in common use for the winning of elections and even then did not win all the time. Thompson lost to Dever in the early 1920's, and again to Cermak when, in 1932,

Roosevelt carried the Democratic ticket into power in many normally Republican areas.

**Appeals to Races, Nationalities, and Interest Groups.**—In any body of voters there are groups which, because of their tendency to emphasize their particular interests, are regarded by politicians as blocs of votes. Special attention is given to techniques of appeals to each of these. Thompson often spoke of himself as a "friend of the Negro" in order to win the support of the large Negro community in Chicago. He spoke at their meetings, shook hands, and kissed babies. He appointed a few Negroes to city jobs. There were similar efforts to land the Jewish vote, the Irish vote, the Polish vote, the Lithuanian vote, the German vote, and others. Various means of appealing to these national groups were employed. The antiwar and isolationist stand was calculated to appeal to the German voters in Chicago, however irrelevant it might be to urban affairs. The protests over the removal of the pictures of the "great American patriots" Kosciusko and Pulaski from the public school textbooks were calculated to appeal to the Lithuanian and Polish groups, although it is said that on one occasion Thompson mixed up the nationalities of the two and was reproved by delegations from both groups.

Although the nation prohibited the consumption of alcoholic beverages by constitutional amendment at that time, Thompson was aware of the strong sentiment against prohibition and featured attacks on it during his campaign. Although the city had no power to disobey the federal laws in this respect, Thompson could by inference indicate that he favored a "wide open town," in which there would be little interference with quietly operating saloons and speakeasys. The toleration of illegal pleasures had an appeal to certain business interests also, for hotels, theaters, and stores gather in money from the many visitors who come to the city for pleasure.

The nickname assumed by Thompson, "Big Bill, the Builder," was also chosen to appeal to business interests and labor. During his terms of office a number of large construction projects were undertaken. However extravagant they may have been, and involved in graft, they did provide contracts and jobs, and the cost was spread widely and in part deferred to cause serious trouble in later days. Those who benefited from such projects knew whom to thank, while those who paid heavily had less understanding of the cause of the expense. Extravagance was a political virtue in such circumstances.

Even children were not overlooked. Once a year during his period in office Thompson had distributed, in his name, sets of tickets to the largest amusement park, including admission and coupons for a number of rides and concessions. Each child in the public schools was presented with one of these, to have a merry holiday by courtesy of the mayor.

**Benefits, Favors, and Special Services.**—Every successful city politician is called upon to perform a large number of personal services on behalf of his constituents. These are in fact important sources of support on election day, for a man who has been helped out of trouble is presumed to have enough gratitude to vote for his benefactor. Many of these services are trivial and involve no impropriety. They constitute the routine work of honest politicians as well as corrupt ones.

Salter, in a series of sketches of Philadelphia politicians, presents sample statements concerning this class of activities:[3]

Many of my voters come to my home to ask favors. You ought to come round some night. My father can tell you. Sometimes they sit there and I sit in the next room at my desk and take them one by one just like a doctor. My wife is not so much interested in all the people as I am, and I tell her that she must always smile at everyone. And I must be careful that my children avoid friction by not hitting other children. I must not let my children think that they are superior to any children in the neighborhood or the division. I must also watch out for arguments between neighbors. . . .

John R. needed a job. He wanted a letter of reference to the Sage Brush Oil Co. I wrote a letter on the stationery of the Philadelphia City Council and got Jimmie [the division leader] to sign it.

C. G. was in bad shape and wanted help from the Dodge committee [a charity organization for desperate relief cases]. I sent a letter to the committee for help.

I sent for the automobile license for two people. . . .

In summer I get a permit card every year to open a fire plug. Fifty or sixty children come under it. There are few baths in my division. The permit is from Chief Jones of the Bureau of Water. It authorizes me to open the fire hydrants and equip them with sprinklers.

Here is a family of three Italians who never voted. The boy is a garage mechanic. One night he started to fix a car at the owner's house, and had to take it to his garage. He was arrested on the way back. Police asked to see his license. He had none. His mother came to me. I said, "Why should I help you? You never vote. No, I won't help you." Then the father came, and he gave me a hard luck story. I told him that I would not run around

---

[3] J. T. Salter, *Boss Rule: Portraits in City Politics*, New York: Whittlesey House, 1935, pp. 78–80.

town to help him—he never did anything for me. Finally they both came. Then I told them that I would help. I got the boy out on a copy of the charge. The family said that they would always vote. . . .

Beno Cellani pays a $3.50 support order for a child that he thinks he is not the father of. He wanted to fight the order. I took him to Martin's office for free legal advice. Martin advised him to go on since he had pleaded guilty. He pays now and feels all right about it.

My people that own homes must pay taxes, of course. I tell them when the taxes are due, and in many cases I deliver the tax bills and try to get the people to pay in advance and save the three per cent the city gives those that pay their taxes before a certain date.

There are a great many types of such services, of every degree of importance and legitimacy. Politicians may send Christmas baskets to the poor, may get up at any time of night to try to get a man out of jail, see that a widow has her affairs put in shape, help a constituent get his assessment reduced, call off the police from raids on saloons and gambling houses owned by loyal supporters, and the like. These services are on the whole humanitarian, and must be performed by someone. They are a factor in political disorganization, however, in that they provide the political machine with a form of support based on gratitude and loyalty, thus decreasing the independence and alertness of voters and allowing the organization latitude for graft, corruption, inefficiency, alliance with criminals, and arbitrary decisions on policies that should be determined by the popular will.

When the efficiency of large-scale business is involved, the slow and uncertain processes of honest government may not be satisfactory to the businessman. He does not want to deal with a mayor and a council and judges and other officials—he wants to deal with one man who can decide and whose decision will hold. A political boss is almost an essential from this point of view, and many large industrialists or utility company heads have no wish to abolish the boss system. Even a certain amount of bribery and graft may be more acceptable to such persons than the slow uncertainties of red tape. In order to insure continuous favorable actions in their interest, large companies have made heavy contributions to the campaigns of candidates, often of rival political factions. Insull, the public utilities magnate of Chicago, is said to have done this during the 1920's. In 1926 it was shown that he made a campaign contribution of as much as $125,000 to Frank L. Smith, a candidate for the United States Senate, while the latter was still head of the Illinois Commerce Commission. This, together with other heavy expenditures on behalf of Smith's campaign, totaling over a million dollars, was too much for the Senate to tolerate, and it refused to seat him. The support of city officials by business interests is less conspicuous, however, and often goes unnoticed or at least unpenalized.

The benefits and favors performed by politicians arouse more gratitude than those which come as a matter of course or right through officials of professional relief organizations and other bureaus for general welfare purposes. The politician knows how to give with a smile, even though the gift tends to pauperize rather than rehabilitate the beneficiary, and he is appreciated in contrast to the efficient, punctilious, and irritating social worker. He can act at once, without inquiries about legality, and can go directly to the man most likely to help without going through the ordinary tortuous channels.

**Election Day Techniques.**—It is the traditional duty of the loyal party worker to get to work on election day and bring in the votes. The all-important thing is to win—methods are secondary. This is made crystal clear to the workers, together with the reasons for its importance. Wooddy quotes the characteristic remarks of a Chicago political leader to the precinct captains of the ward organization of which he was committeeman:[4]

I don't want applause; what I want first is pledge cards, but, more than that, votes. This is a real fight, and every man must do his share. Look at that chart—some of the precincts show no pledge cards at all. Who is the man from this precinct?

(A man rose in the audience and claimed that he had thirty cards to turn in as soon as he had time to copy them.)

You're expecting a raise in salary in your job, aren't you?

(The man signified assent.)

Carry your precinct or you not only won't get it, but you'll lose your job altogether.

I don't want to scold, but I believe I've been as good to this ward as it has to me. . . . I want to say to you that if any man does not carry his precinct on the thirteenth of April, he'll be fired on the fourteenth. If a man means anything in his precinct, he can carry it. If he doesn't mean anything in his precinct, he has no business in politics and holding a job. The reason that ———————— is on the ticket for municipal judge in spite of the fact that he is a new man in the ward is that he had the banner precinct. . . . I promised that whoever turns out the biggest vote in his precinct will be on the next county ticket, if I sit on the slate committee. and I think I will.

---

[4] Carroll H. Wooddy, *ob. cit.*, pp. 7–8.

What is more, any of you that don't get out the vote and have jobs, will lose them, and they'll go to those who do work and have no job. I'm looking at one right now that has no job, and he'll have one that someone else now has unless you get out the vote. Don't think I don't mean this. I've fired the ward committeeman and I've fired the president of this ward club, although he had a $6,000 job.

I believe that to the victor belongs the spoils. He who contributes most to winning the election ought to sit at the first table, and those who do less should sit at the second table. Any one of you who can come to me and show that he got out more votes than someone else who has a better job can have that job.

Such a speech explains the energy and application of the local politician in serving his constituents in order to secure their votes, and also shows a reason for the strength of the temptation to employ illegal methods to insure a heavy majority on election day.

There are many tricks in common use at the polling places. In general the safer ones are used, but if the election is important and the outcome uncertain every possible means may be used to insure victory. Votes are bought—sometimes from floating groups of hobos who go from precinct to precinct and collect a fee at each place for supporting the ticket. These men identify themselves by giving the name of a person who is registered and who is known to be in favor of the opposition. If and when the real person turns up, he is informed that he has already voted and is shown that his name is checked on the list. If he makes a sufficiently vigorous protest, he may be allowed to vote, but a way is found to nullify his vote after he leaves.

Although the law forbids it unless the voter requests aid, it is not uncommon for members of the organization to enter the polling booth to make sure that the voter supports the ticket. Protests of the voter are of no avail when even the policeman is dependent upon the organization for his job.

If the balloting itself does not yield a satisfactory victory, the majority can be improved in the process of counting. Where ballots are marked in pencil it is not difficult for judges to find most of the opposition ballots defective or to render them so by furtive markings with concealed bits of lead pencil. The presence of judges from both major parties, and of special watchers, is supposed to prevent this, but in districts where a machine has strong control the opposition officials are also in their control. In some wards of Chicago the Thompson organization actually designated certain persons to be Democrats, so that they could be the representatives

of that party in the polling places.  If outside and unsympathetic
watchers appeared, they were controlled by threats, by kidnapping,
or by such devices as physically crowding them away from the
table where ballots are counted.

In many cases where violence is useful, it is provided by roving
bands of gunmen who may be called upon to remove a protesting
voter, an annoying watcher, and, in certain cases, a threatening
candidate.  In the primary elections in Chicago in 1928, a Negro
candidate for alderman of the Twentieth Ward, Octavus Granady,
was shot and killed in midafternoon of election day—murdered
on the streets by hirelings of his political opponents.  In that ward,
known as the "Bloody Twentieth," the control of the Thompson
machine was so effective that many precincts turned in a larger
number of Thompson votes than there were registered voters.

**The Machine and the Boss.**—The political machine is a natural
growth in response to demands of various kinds from different
sections of the community.  To the politician it provides security
and advancement, to the gangster it provides the conditions in
which he can carry on his livelihood, to the businessman it furnishes
a convenient source of decisions—often favorable—and a supply
of opportunities, and to the general public it provides a variety
of appealing services.  The successful machine is a highly disciplined
organization.  It calls for, and for the most part gets, the utmost
loyalty from its members.  As Salter has put it:[5]

> The most striking single identifying quality of these division leaders (and
> the majority of the ward leaders too), who have consciously or uncon-
> sciously chosen politics as a career, is loyalty.  These men are loyal to their
> leaders just as their leaders are in turn loyal to their own leaders and the
> organization.  It is personal rather than civic loyalty.  This loyalty pattern
> is a habit of mind among the overwhelming majority of the members of any
> successful party organization.  It is so implicit in normal times that one must
> turn, in nature, to a highly trained bird dog to find its counterpart, or to a young
> child's faith in its parent.  In a free moment, these men unhesitatingly
> describe themselves as "order men."  They take orders and ask no questions
> (and neither do they answer any unless they are told to).  One of the Hon.
> Dick Weglein's men in the Twenty-ninth Ward told me he would go to hell
> if Sheriff Weglein told him to, for he knew that Weglein would not tell him
> to go to hell unless he had some good reason.  The sheriff, in turn, was a
> follower and friend of the late Tom Cunningham, and, in the summer of 1931,
> when Cunningham told Weglein that he was not the Republican party's
> candidate for mayor, the loyal leader of the Twenty-ninth was painfully dis-

⁵ J. T. Salter, *op. cit.*, pp. 36–37.

appointed, but thought no more of the matter.  He is now sheriff, and there is to be another mayoralty election in 1935.

Mr. Fred Lunt, who is now leader of the XYZ Ward and president of the ——————, is so much an order man that a prominent Philadelphia newspaper man recently remarked, "If Senator Vare were to tell Fred Lunt to set fire to Independence Hall, he would do it." Or, to put it in Freddie Lunt's own words, "My platform is short, sweet, and easy to say—I am for William S. Vare."

Salter goes on to say, however, that when the machine fails to deliver the usual results, the loyalty tends to decline—apparently it is loyalty to a winner.  But as long as the organization is a winner, the loyalty is strong, for it is an exceptional politician who has the ability to succeed independently of an organization.

The boss makes the decisions for the organization.  He may hold an office himself, but it is not necessary, and often he does not bother to do so.  He selects the men who are to be chosen for office by the voters and gives the orders for the conduct of the members of the machines.  His control is in a sense absolute and dictatorial, for his orders are followed as long as he produces success, but he does not have freedom to fail.  There are choices that he cannot afford to make if he should wish.  He must hold the support of his men, and of substantial elements of the community, for above all else he must win at election times.

If corruption is not in the essence of bossism, it is at least an easy condition to develop.  The necessity to win is a force in the direction of the use of methods sufficient to win, and the accessibility of power and wealth constitute further temptations to take what is easily available.  The greed of many bosses, in fact, has been responsible for their downfall, either at the hands of an outraged citizenry engaged in a reform crusade or through prosecution and conviction for lawbreaking.  Pendergast of Kansas City, Johnson of Atlantic City, and Tweed of New York City were among those put behind bars for their avarice, although in two of these cases it took the utmost skill and persistence of agents of the United States Treasury Department, tracing evidence of violation of the income tax laws, to secure convictions.  The Tammany organization of New York City survived many setbacks and was finally reduced to insignificance only by a generalized attack, including investigations, prosecutions, and a general crusade, in which there emerged a rare political personality—a reformer who was not only honest but also popular, humane, and a good showman—Mayor Fiorello LaGuardia. Not the least of his achievements was that he lasted more than one term.

The greed of Enoch L. Johnson of Atlantic City has already been related in Chapter 6. The degree of this eagerness for money is not unique. Richard Croker, a political boss in New York City in the late nineteenth century, explained his motives to Steffens without euphemism. "Like a businessman in business, I work for my own pocket all the time." [6]  He was successful in his efforts for a period but never matched the achievements of William M. Tweed and his ring, which had its beginning in 1869. By virtue of heroic efforts, which included arrangement for the naturalization of nearly 60,000 immigrants within 20 days in order to have them vote for him, Tweed and his men gained control of all of the offices in the city government, including that of mayor, and of the governorship of the state. Tweed had the most impressive political organization in the country, and his power and wealth—then estimated at from five to ten millions of dollars—was growing rapidly.[7]  This gang proceeded to loot the city treasury with no sense of restraint. Tweed personally obtained a block of stock worth $40,000 for permitting the City Council to approve of the construction of the Brooklyn Bridge. There were many other kinds of theft—from the state government and from business organizations. As a member of the board of directors of the Erie Railroad, for example, Tweed received bribes totaling $1,500,000 in a period of three years, for "legal expenses"—actually for having desired measures put through the state legislature and for having the governor sign them.

While in modern times such plunderers have learned the value of keeping out of the spotlight, Tweed and his many followers openly displayed their affluence. Some who had become wealthy over night began to display their new status by wearing silk hats and diamonds. Lacking experience in wearing silk hats convincingly, however, they became subject to a certain amount of public amusement—some newspapermen began to refer to them as Tweed's shiny hat brigade. The boss, sensitive about the matter, gave orders that these men must join a certain club, where they would observe how men who were accustomed to good things comported themselves.

On May 5, 1870, the Board of Audit of New York City, composed of Tweed and two of his men, authorized the payment of $6,312,500, of which more than $5,500,000 was paid fraudulently. The money was for work on the new County Court House, which in all cost over $12,000,000, of which about $3,000,000 was

---

[6] Lincoln Steffens, *op. cit.*, p. 238.
[7] Denis Tilden Lynch, *"Boss" Tweed: The Story of a Grim Generation*, New York: Boni & Liveright, 1927.

required to build and furnish the structure and the other $9,000,000 went to the members of the ring. All other bills rendered to the city involved a payment of two thirds of their face amount, and later of 85 per cent, to the ring. When such bills did not come in fast enough, Tweed had the County Auditor make out vouchers to imaginary firms and individuals in order to keep the flow of money going at a high rate.

**The Relation of the Machine to the Underworld.**—As shown in Chapter 6, organized criminal gangs often have cooperative relations with a political machine. This arrangement is of mutual benefit, for the gangs need protection and the machine requires various services. One important channel of cooperation is through the police department, in cases in which it is possible to operate the underworld efficiently and at the same time to keep its operations sufficiently under control so that the public does not become outraged. In fact, a corrupt police department may operate services that act like a safety valve to mollify public indignation.

Such were the circumstances in New York in the early 1890's, when Lincoln Steffens reported the political corruption existing in the great city.[8] The Superintendent of Police, Thomas F. Byrnes, had thoroughgoing knowledge of the activities of the professional criminals operating in the city. These men were in fact protected by him from the competition of outsiders—out-of-town criminals were subject to arrest and imprisonment if they were caught practicing their trade in New York City—and were subject to certain of his orders. The police also had the duties of collecting bribery payments from saloons operating at illegal hours and from other illegitimate enterprises.

Close relations with burglars and pickpockets are shown by the power Byrnes had to restore loot when it was advantageous to do so. A banker told Steffens of a time when a house had been robbed and valuable diamonds taken. Byrnes promised the victim that the diamonds would be returned to him in three days, and on the exact day specified two men appeared at the house to return the jewels "with the compliments of the inspector [Byrnes]." Steffens himself had his pocket picked, on a Saturday, losing an envelope with his week's pay, and made a personal complaint to Byrnes over the telephone. Byrnes asked a few questions—how much money was in the envelope, how it was addressed, what streetcar routes had been traveled by Steffens—and then promised to have the money on

---

[8] Lincoln Steffens, *op. cit.*, pp. 197ff.

Monday morning. At that time it was returned, in the original envelope. Byrnes had known what men were operating on each streetcar line and ordered his detectives to speak to them, saying that they had robbed a friend of a certain amount of money in an envelope which was described. The word went out that Byrnes wanted it back Monday morning, and it was promptly returned.

In general a victim of a theft does not insist on anything more than the return of his lost money. He avoids, if possible, the bother of appearing in court to press charges against the offender. Instead of a sense of shock and indignation at the implications of such a relation as Byrnes held with professional criminals, the victims felt simple gratitude at the restoration of their property. Byrnes made capital out of such favors and was able to perform many different kinds. A family of great wealth sought his aid in ridding them of a foreign nobleman who had won the love of their daughter. Byrnes agreed to see what he could do, and a few days later he informed them that they would see no more of the man and asked for enough money to pay the man's passage home, and perhaps a little more. Prominent persons who had become involved in some scandal and were subject to the annoyances of blackmail could come to Byrnes, tell him all about it, make one more payment, and end the whole matter.

If criminals were protected from police interference and from outside competition, so were some persons, and even whole regions, protected from criminals, if they arranged it with Byrnes. Wall Street men did not wish to be annoyed by pickpockets and other thieves of the underworld, and they gave Byrnes inside information from time to time, enabling him to make money in the stock market legitimately. In return Byrnes established a deadline on Fulton Street beyond which no thief could operate.

Late in 1894, in the face of a crusade led by the Reverend Dr. Charles H. Parkhurst and the Lexow Investigation, the system was temporarily broken. A confession by a key man, Captain Schmittberger, collector of graft from the Tenderloin District between Fifth and Ninth Avenues and Twenty-eighth and Forty-eighth Streets, brought to light and to newspaper publicity the operations of the corrupt arrangement, and in the next election Tammany candidates lost out, though not forever. Schmittberger, because of his reputation for honesty, had been given the duty of visiting the saloons and gambling and prostitution resorts to collect the monthly tribute, amounting in his district sometimes to over $20,000. The funds were then taken to the police station, counted in the presence of the captain, and divided according to an agreed system among the superintendent, the inspector, Schmittberger himself, and, in smaller amounts, a couple of ward men. Other ranks and men in the police force, not eligible for this particular graft, had their own sources of funds. Patrolmen often received tips, a five- or ten-dollar bill from time to time from the operator of a resort. Desk sergeants also often received tips from prisoners and made additional money by sending them food and by dealing in the business of bail.

The system was so universal in the zone of life known to Schmittberger, and his initiation into it was so easy and gradual, that he did not fully realize the serious wrong of it until the investigation and exposure. He had been honest within the system, never holding out more than his share in the graft, but after the breakup of the organization, he turned into a policeman who was honest in the general sense, and incorruptible. He was given a tranquil district for a time, where nothing of importance ever happened. On one occasion, however, he recognized a respect in which this new and strict honesty handicapped him, for it cut off all his contacts and information with the underworld and left him in the dark when he was called upon to find the persons who had committed a crime. A big river launch, owned by an acquaintance of Steffens, had been robbed at its moorings, and Steffens asked Schmittberger if he could find out who did it. Without underworld connections, however, Schmittberger was unable to find out. An honest policeman necessarily had a harder time finding out about such matters.

A truly honest policeman is of course a threat to such a corrupt system, but one, or a few, could be eliminated as menaces by means of transfer to outlying districts where little activity took place. These distant precincts are often viewed as penalty assignments. It is said that Lewis J. Valentine, the distinguished Police Commissioner of New York City for some years, was, in his rookie days, sent out to the remote regions as a penalty for his zeal in enforcing the law without favor.

In conditions of public apathy, such discipline is sufficient to discourage initiative on the part of police, for no influential persons appear to take an interest in their cases, and they perceive how the more cooperative men prosper. When public opinion reaches a high state of impatience with political corruption, however, a revolt of a few honest policemen may be more difficult to control. An incident in Central Falls, Rhode Island, in the summer of 1946, illustrates such a degree of instability. Four new policemen, war veterans, had been promised a 20 per cent raise in pay but were put off by the Chief of Police. They sought aid from the political boss, who suggested that they circulate a petition through the membership of the police force. This device, however, only resulted in retaliatory assignments—guarding city dumps, or traffic duty at empty intersections. At the suggestion of a newspaper reporter, they finally found a point of attack where they might inflict some hurt on their chief. They began to raid slot machines and gambling resorts that had been well known all the time and had been taking in something like $1,000,000 a year. The mayor met this threat by suspending them on the charge of "something they should have done, but failed to do."

The matter was reported in the papers, and a wave of public protest arose. A Good Government Club, several veterans' organizations, some prominent lawyers, and other groups of citizens took an interest. Mass meetings were held, and the four policemen became local heroes. The mayor gave in, and announced cancellation of the suspension hearings and restoration of the men to the force. The public was not appeased, however, for an independent organization composed largely of veterans selected a ticket for the fall elections and aimed to get rid of the entire administration.[9]

**Results of Urban Political Corruption.**—There is no way to obtain an accurate estimate of the financial cost of corruption in the political organization of a city, but it is certain that in some instances the amounts are impressively large. The outlay of funds for campaign purposes is impressive enough—Chicago machines are said to have spent as much as $150,000 between elections and $600,000 on election day for literature, picnics, dinners, liquor, hotel rooms for headquarters, and other measures that aid in victory, including the purchase of votes. These figures constitute only a small part of the financial burden imposed on the city, however.[10] Fortunes go into the pockets of the dominant members of these machines—invisible drains on the bank accounts of the citizens. Pendergast, the Kansas City boss, did not need to hold a political office to divert a stream of money into his pockets, for he could easily persuade the city to purchase cement from his own company at a good price, influence retail liquor dealers to buy from his wholesale

[9] *Time*, Aug. 19, 1946, pp. 22–23.
[10] Noel P. Gist and L. A. Halbert, *Urban Society*, second edition, New York: The Thomas Y. Crowell Co., 1941, p. 455.

establishment, and gain by supplying a garbage-removal service to the city at a good margin of profit to himself.[11]

Legitimate construction projects may produce income in great amounts, particularly when they are built at a greater cost than necessary. In the 1920's in Chicago, it was charged that a short cinder bridle path in one of the city parks, built during the Thompson regime, cost the taxpayers a quarter of a million dollars. The cost of the stadium on Soldier's Field in Chicago, the contract for which was awarded to Edward J. Kelly, who later became mayor, is said to have been $8,000,000—four times as much as a similar stadium in another city.[12] It is not a plausible supposition that a lower bid by an honest contractor who was without political influence could have anything like an equal chance at such projects.

Barnes, discussing methods of profiting from political office, states that some of these private companies were organized purely for the purpose of the efficient exploitation of political power. Coal companies, for example, were organized by persons who had influence with the assessors and the members of the board of tax review. Purchases of coal from such companies, not necessarily at the market price, carried with them the possibility of tax relief.[13] One company printed cards urging customers to "Buy your coal of us and cut your taxes." Persons who complained to the assessors about the size of their taxes were solicited later on the telephone and promised relief if coal orders were given. In the central business district, where tax pressure is great, Barnes states that at one time 90 per cent of the coal used there was purchased from such companies and that the assessment reduction in one year alone amounted to $500,000,000.

Many other devices are used. Barnes mentions a case in which the city of Chicago paid $2,250,000 to experts merely for their opinion on a city bond issue. Most of this presumably was "kicked back" to the Thompson machine. Offices and promotions were allotted to those who bid highest for them. Public funds were placed with bankers who returned benefits in one form or another. Payrolls were padded with many nonexistent workers at high profit. Something like one out of every eight names on the public payrolls in Cook County was at one time fraudulent, and in campaign years, according to Barnes, about $2,000,000 was paid out in this manner.

---

[11] *Ibid.*, p. 457.
[12] *Ibid.*, pp. 457–458.
[13] Harry Elmer Barnes, *Society in Transition*, New York: Prentice-Hall, Inc., 1939, pp. 509–510. Quoted in Gist and Halbert, *op. cit.*, pp. 459–460.

The cost of these and other forms of graft during the rule of Thompson in Chicago has been estimated at between 75 and 125 millions of dollars a year.

The visible cost in dollars, however, does not represent more than a portion of the damage to society inflicted by political corruption. Another important effect is the surrender of a city to the power of professional criminals. In view of the indispensability of the underworld organization to the corrupt political machine, the latter cannot afford to curb the criminal activities to any great extent; when matters are at their worst, it can only allow the power of the gangs to dominate much of urban life. The rackets sink their fingers deep into the economic life of the city, often operating openly and without fear of suppression. Even the more crude crimes claim a somewhat open place in the affairs of citizens. In Chicago, during the relatively lawless period of the 1920's, word was spread around by the men who performed holdups with a gun, that any man who failed to have at least fifteen dollars on his person would be subject to slugging. Newspaper publicity was given to a few cases in which men with funds insufficient to satisfy the robbers were knocked unconscious with the butt of a gun, and some cautious citizens thenceforth took care to have the required amount when walking along the streets at night. Some ingenious men followed the practice of concealing most of their money, but leaving something over fifteen dollars in their wallets in case of a holdup.

During the same period automobile thieves operated so steadily that few persons who parked their cars on the streets escaped having them stolen at least once. Most of these cars were recovered soon after, stripped of their disposable parts. Insurance covered the losses in most cases, and the principal cost to the owner lay in the inconvenience and in the high theft insurance rates. It was a matter of public knowledge that a certain chain dealer in used car parts was the principal receiver of the stolen goods, but for some years nothing was done about the matter, and the public was virtually helpless.

A common public reaction to such open criminality, unless it is carried too far, is a resigned acceptance and cynicism. The criminals, after all, are admitted to be engaging rogues—many prominent persons actually sought introductions to Al Capone while he was ruling the criminal organization of Chicago—and they did provide things which noncriminal persons wanted. Illegal liquor, felt by many to be a necessity, was supplied by the organizations, and most purchasers would not care to betray their supplier to enforcement officials, for they would prefer to have the steady supply of liquor and crime rather than go without the drinks. It is easy to rationalize such support of crime—one can say that a single person could have no effect on the system by his lone boycott anyway, and as long as others were getting some he might as well get his too.

By way of further rationalization it could also be said that it is impossible to be rid of underworld activities, for the folk belief claims that gambling is in human nature and that human nature cannot be changed, just as it is said that "Prostitution always has been, is everywhere, and always will be." The fact that many persons do not care for gambling and that there are communities without prostitution does not disturb the beliefs in such established generalizations, for these are supported by a persistent demand on the part of many persons for such services. It is easier on the conscience to justify support of organized crime on the grounds of its inevitability than on the grounds of a candid wish for its benefits.

The more it becomes known that persons are gaining riches by dishonest and illegal means, the more persons engaged in political activities and in business careers are tempted to cross the boundaries of legality in the search of fortune. The rationalization here is, "Everybody is doing it; why shouldn't I?" The more nearly it is true that everybody is committing sharp practices, the greater is the temptation for those who ordinarily prefer honesty to follow the custom. A state senator, practicing law in a New England city, was brought to court on a charge of collecting money on a fraudulent claim of application of political influence, but justified himself by claiming that competition is such that a lawyer cannot make a living by honest means. The atmosphere of easy and universal evasion of law thus spreads into other fields and is one of the contributing factors to the prevalence of white-collar criminality.

Apathy and cynicism on the part of the general public, generated by the sense of helplessness in the face of corruption and criminality, has other consequences as well. Part of the explanation of nonvoting by eligible citizens is that it is of no use, that the machine controls the result anyway. This might make little difference to the general welfare if the abstainers from the ballot represent a general cross-section of the public, but this is not the case. The machine gets out the vote in the districts which it has under control, and it does not suffer from apathy. The nonvoting behavior strengthens the machines and therefore contributes to corruption.

In general, when voting is light professional politicians maintain control—it takes a heavy vote to bring a reform.

Discouraged voters have a further tendency to preserve the power of machines by voting straight tickets. If politicians are "all alike" and "all crooks," the voter may prefer only those of the political party to which his people have traditionally considered themselves to belong. There is a further phenomenon of confusion among voters, reflected in the tendency to cast votes for frivolous considerations. If none of the professional politicians is any good, it is reasoned, why not have some good sport anyway and elect the band leader who is running for pure publicity—on a platform which promises hostesses and flower boxes on all streetcars. The man with a hillbilly band and the singing cowboy make their appeal, not on issues or any sensible consideration, but to the frivolity of the voters, and their successes in recent years suggest a reflection of a degeneration of political intelligence on the part of the electorate.

Where power is in the hands of machines, candidates can hold office only by means of machine support. To the extent that the machine is corrupt, the candidates must at least make their compromises with corruption, if not actually take part in it. It cannot be said that every candidate receiving the backing of a corrupt machine is necessarily dishonest—often the machine selects an honest candidate in order to stave off public revolt, hoping that in gratitude he will be reasonable after attaining office. But there is an expectation on the part of most backers that there will be continual cooperation with the machine. The price of machine support for a nonmember candidate is at least his support of their ticket. There are many honest, able, and public-spirited citizens who refrain from seeking political careers because they do not like to compromise with ideals and cooperate with corruption. Men of ability often are called upon to make sacrifices if they accept governmental positions, for the salaries are often considerably lower than their business incomes. While the corrupt politician may derive a $100,000 annual income from a $7,000 job by dishonestly exploiting it, this means is not open to a man of integrity. The prevalence of corruption, therefore, tends to bar many of the desirable kinds of men from candidacy for office and instead recruits the least scrupulous.

The interrelations of public attitudes, governmental corruption and organized crime are reciprocal in character and extend subtly throughout much of the fabric of society. Education, churches, literature, and other aspects of human activity become polluted in varying degrees and in turn weaken the defenses against further criminality and corruption. There are processes which work in the other direction—periods of reform and stability are possible—but in times of rapid movement, change, and prosperity, the conditions are favorable for the penetration of these forms of disorganization into the social structure.

### CORRUPTION IN STATE GOVERNMENTS

Although the peculiarly extreme social disorganization of urban slums provides the most convenient conditions for the basis of political corruption, since the populations of these areas are most easily controlled and exploited by urban political machines, there are occasions of corruption in governments of larger regions—of states, and sometimes of officials in the federal government. In some cases this is made possible in a state by virtue of the dominance of a metropolis in the state, so that the urban machine may extend its power over the state government as well. The relations of the Thompson machine in Chicago with the administration of Governor Len Small were close, and they permitted the re-election of Small after his conviction on a serious charge of mishandling of public funds. Small had organized a bank of his own, located in a room over a corner store in a small town, which contained one deposit which was reinvested elsewhere. The one deposit consisted of state funds, placed in the care of the bank without bearing interest. The interest on the reinvestment, of course, was all available as the profit of the little bank. The court did not jail Governor Small but merely required him to return the interest to the state. The vigorous support of the Thompson machine in Chicago was sufficient to re-elect him in spite of this exposure of his dishonesty. This control, however, of the state government by a city machine is not the usual condition in Illinois. Politics in the state outside of the city of Chicago is dominated ordinarily by farmers and small-town people who dislike and distrust urban politicians. The strength of this rural distrust of city people in itself may have its effects on the integrity of state governments, for it often furnishes a motive for the unconstitutional refusal of state legislatures to redistrict, as legally required from time to time, the political areas of the state. This "rotten borough" condition prevailed for years in Illinois and for the larger part of a century in Rhode Island and was a factor in the perpetuation of state political administrations whose actions fell short of the ideals of democracy.

Where urban corruption is extreme, however, and penetrates throughout the state, it may produce there on a larger scale many of the same conditions that have been described in the cities. Steffens claimed this to be the case with several states with which he was familiar in the early years of the twentieth century—Pennsylvania, Missouri, New York, Illinois, and Connecticut. In his exposé of conditions in Missouri, Steffens described the way in which the machine reduced the legislature, the courts, and the state officials to a system which was responsible to the special interests of bribers, corruptionists, and criminals and to the special influences of trusts, railroads, public service corporations, manufacturers, and even school textbook publishers. These people could buy laws from the legislature, and could buy interpretations from the courts, through the machine.[14]

The conditions in Democratic Missouri were found by Steffens to be duplicated by Republican Illinois. Here the chief concern in these days was with the operations which Yerkes, the traction and utilities magnate, employed to gain his aims, but Steffens found that the railroads, and big business in general, had also done their part to corrupt the political processes of the State of Illinois.

A different type of boss arises in states in which there is a large mass of poverty-stricken and uneducated voters, whose grievances are easily exploited by a candidate who knows how to make an appeal to them. The outstanding example of this process is furnished by the career of Huey P. Long in the State of Louisiana. This state had long been near the bottom in average standard of living, and conditions were made worse in the depression of the 1930's when cotton prices went below two cents a pound and money became a scarce commodity to most of the rural people in the region. In addition to this cause for discontent, the state had been dominated by a regime which favored certain of the larger business interests.

At the start of his career, Long was a salesman of patent medicines, and he soon developed a talent for charming prospective customers. Perhaps it was his success in appealing to people which suggested to him that he might do well in politics. He borrowed some money, acquired a quick legal education, and began his first campaign—for a position on the Louisiana Railroad Commission. He dressed in white and drove about the country meeting and talking

_____
[14] Lincoln Steffens, *op. cit.*, pp. 445–446.

to as many people as possible, paying particular attention to the poorest people in the remote sections—people who seldom if ever saw a political candidate. His appeal was personal and aimed at local prejudices. He denounced Wall Street and city politicians, and at the same time he gave out recipes. He pursued this campaign with great vigor, sometimes going for eighteen hours a day. When the time came for voting, his many new friends gave their support and elected him. He never forgot his obligations to these low-income people or the political power that could be obtained by gaining their support. These voters never lost faith in him throughout his long and spectacular career—they knew little of political theory or long-range considerations of general welfare, but they knew that Long was on their side and so gave him their loyalty.

Within ten years Long had achieved the governorship and the conquest of the state, and soon afterward he became United States senator from Louisiana and a national power. By use of his outstanding shrewdness and his willingness to use any method at hand to achieve his aims, he built up a personal dictatorship in Louisiana which was unique in American history. He packed the legislature and most of the rest of the state offices with his own henchmen and operated the business of the state by issuing orders to these men. Rivals or independents were crushed, or, in some cases, bribed. There was no finesse about these maneuvers—Long openly boasted that he bought legislators "like sacks of potatoes." When his men were slow to carry out his orders, he cracked the whip sharply and crudely, sparing no man's feelings. One commentator, discussing the process by which laws were passed, stated, "America has never seen anything more brazen or more slick. It is an object-lesson in the ease with which the form of democratic government can be twisted to serve the reality of one-man rule. The legislature meets, it pretends to initiate and enact laws, to scrutinize and debate them, and yet the operation has no more merit than it would have if these men moved in hypnosis."[15]

Long put through measures to increase his power, to punish his political enemies and other persons or organizations he did not like, and to benefit the underprivileged people who were the basis of his power. These aims were accomplished by a variety of moves. He had the legislature give him power to appoint schoolteachers. He punished a town where he had been pelted with eggs in a campaign appearance by removing their elected mayor. Another parish which

---

[15] Raymond Swing, *Forerunners of American Fascism*, New York: Julian Messner, Inc., 1935, p. 71.

had not supported him was penalized through a law which enlarged the local government board, enabling him to control it by the appointment of new members.   As a result of a feud with Tulane University, he built a greatly expanded plant at Louisiana State University at Baton Rouge, giving it the best of equipment and funds for a first-rate staff, as well as a superb stadium and football team. A new dental school established there is said to be a punishment for Loyola in New Orleans, where there already existed a good dental school.

Long disliked the Standard Oil Company, and he put through an "occupational tax" for refining oil.   This involved a new principle of taxation and was opposed by businessmen, who for some time kept him from applying the tax.   When Standard laid off more than 1,000 workers and mass meetings of protest followed, Long had an occasion for calling out his militia.   With the armed men in public view, Long took occasion to make a bargain with Standard whereby some of the tax would be remitted but the new taxing principle would remain.   He thus won his victory and had the new tax in operation as a threat to any other recalcitrant industries.

Although within the first few years of his power Long had increased the state debt from $11,000,000 to nearly $150,000,000, the tax burden was removed from the low-income group and measures were taken to improve their conditions.   Property of the value of $2,000 or less was made tax-exempt, thereby relieving about half of the white people, and nearly all of the Negroes, from taxes on everything except gasoline, tobacco, and liquor.   He arranged that school children would be furnished free textbooks, and gave his support to a campaign to stamp out illiteracy.   He built a large system of modern highways, giving remote sections better accessibility to cities. When the private owners of a toll bridge near New Orleans set too high a price, Long had a finer free bridge built parallel to it, getting his revenge and helping the poor at the same time.   He reduced power and telephone rates, doubtless for the same double satisfaction. The newspapers were punished for their opposition by means of a 2 per cent tax on gross receipts from advertising.

Long made use of armed bodyguards and when necessary employed the threat of their weapons to gain his ends.   On one occasion a group of bankers was held at gunpoint in a room until they agreed to conform with Long's desires.   The members of his own organization knew that he had a great variety of measures by means of which he could discipline them.   Severe as this discipline was, it did not extend to matters of manners or morals, which were not important to the dictator.   The president he installed in his favorite university embezzled state property and in time was made to serve a prison sentence for it.   Others of his henchmen displayed greed and in many cases doubtless profited without causing public uproar.   One of his men, the unofficial treasurer of the organization, was indicted for income tax evasion for neglecting to pay on $176,972 received in the years when Long was governor, and by 1935 eight of his men were involved in similar charges.   The men who ride to power on the coattails of such a dictator are not motivated solely by idealism.

Long's power spread to neighboring states and, during his period in the Senate, to even wider areas.   Through his skilled and bitter opposition to President Roosevelt and the New Deal, and through his "Share-the-Wealth" movement, with its slogan of "Every Man a King," he was able to gather the support of discontented persons over the nation, and, in the opinion of some observers, he was in reach of achieving a dictatorship over the nation.   The possibility was disposed of, however, by his assassination on September 8, 1935, allegedly at the hands of a young physician whose father-in-law had been wronged by the Long machine.

While Huey Long was unique in his talents, he was not the only man who aspired to demagogic power within a state.   In fact, during the same depression period there arose leaders whose tactics had a certain similarity to his.   In several of the states near Louisiana, where conditions were much like those of Long's territory, some of these men actually rose to power.   The two most conspicuous of these were Talmadge of Georgia and Bilbo of Mississippi. Both were talented, though crude, rabble-rousers, addressing their appeals primarily to the low-income uneducated people of remote rural sections, and both capitalized as heavily as possible on the racial tension in their states.   They were also like Long in their opposition to certain large interests and in their vengeful measures against the city dwellers, and particularly university people.

During his governorship, for example, Bilbo in one day removed the heads of the State University, the State College for Women, and the Agricultural and Mechanical College, at the same time having 179 professors and teachers discharged—all for political reasons. He put his own men, not qualified by experience or training, in charge of these institutions.   They included the director of public relations of a power company; a real estate salesman without a college degree; and, as members of an administrative board for the university, two dentists, a bank cashier, a physician, and three lawyers. Now, perhaps feeling that the university was his own, Bilbo took an interest in it and spent $2,000,000 on buildings.

For patronage Bilbo saw to it that much construction was undertaken. An enormous and luxurious new insane asylum was built, and he tried to get an $82,000,000 bond issue for road-building, but, not having the degree of power that Long enjoyed in Louisiana, he was blocked.

The career of Talmadge was somewhat similar, and both he and Bilbo were in and out of power after the day of Long. In 1946 they both won elections, primarily with an appeal based on the racial issue, promising to keep the Negro in subjection.

### CORRUPTION IN THE FEDERAL GOVERNMENT: TEAPOT DOME

Serious disorganization of the national government of the United States has never occurred, although minor scandals have touched members of it from time to time. The essential business of the nation has been carried out, not always without some waste, some errors, and some disputes, but without any near approach to a general breakdown. With all of the defects which thoughtful persons find in it, the national government has been more steadily successful than have the governments of cities and states in the areas of extreme disorganization.

The most serious national scandal in recent times, the affair known as the Teapot Dome Scandal, reached somewhat more near the top than have other such episodes and involved persons of importance, including members of the Cabinet itself and close associates of the then President, Warren G. Harding. It is possibly of significance that the events took place in the postwar decade, when there was something of a general letdown of morality and responsibility in the nation, and when a casual, pleasure-seeking frivolity became the spirit of the times. The public lost its alertness of supervision of national affairs, and the way was left open for corruption to steal in.

Following the reforms made by President Wilson, and the somewhat dictatorial control he was permitted to assume during the course of the war, the public was ready for a change. There was no interest in having another professor or "idealist" as a president, but rather some practical businessman who would let the country get "back to normalcy." Harry M. Daugherty, a lobbying lawyer from Ohio, sensed this atmosphere and early began to take personal charge of the candidacy of the Marion, Ohio, newspaper editor and United

States senator from Ohio, Warren G. Harding.   Harding was not regarded as a leading contender, there being half a dozen men whose chances appeared better, but Daugherty foresaw that the top candidates might kill each other off, as in fact they did, leaving the way open for his man as a "dark horse" candidate.   In fact, before the convention which nominated Harding, Daugherty made a prediction which became nationally famous for its close resemblance to the actual events.   He predicted, "There will be no nomination on the early ballots.   After the other candidates have failed, after they have gone their limit, the leaders, worn out and wishing to do the very best thing, will get together in some hotel room about 2:11 in the morning.   Some 15 men, bleary-eyed with lack of sleep, and perspiring profusely with the excessive heat, will sit down around a big table.   I will be with them and present the name of Senator Harding.   When that time comes, Harding will be selected, because he fits in perfectly with every need of the party and nation.   He is the logical choice, and the leaders will determine to throw their support to him."[16]   The public shortened this to the phrase "15 men in a smoke-filled room" and made no effective objection to this manner of selection of a candidate.

In the autumn election of 1920 the voters had a choice between the handsome, engaging, easy-going Harding and the "normalcy" he represented—which in later years came to appear to be irresponsibility—and another Ohio editor and politician, Governor James M. Cox, who identified himself with the ideals and aims of Wilson. Mark Sullivan, a close observer of the campaign, believed that the election of Harding was largely a result of the tired, disillusioned letdown of the public from the discipline and idealism of the war. He quotes Charles Willis Thompson as saying, "The people of the United States . . . did not vote for Harding; nor did they vote against Cox; in 1920 they did not vote for anybody; they voted against somebody; and the somebody they voted against was not a candidate; it was Woodrow Wilson."   A similar judgment from Franklin K. Lane is also quoted: "Cox will be defeated not by those who dislike him but by those who dislike Wilson. . . . This seems mighty unjust.   Cox, I think, has made a gallant fight; he is to be beaten because Wilson is as unpopular as he once was popular."[17] Perhaps in this deterioration of the public mentality lies the main cause of the Teapot Dome affair, for it is not to be imagined that the

---

[16] Mark Sullivan, *Our Times*, New York: Chas. Scribner's Sons, Vol. VI, 1935, p. 37. Sullivan condensed and paraphrased this account from quotations in *The New York Times* of June 13, 1920, and the Washington *Post* of February 27, 1921.
[17] *Ibid.*, p. 111.

politicians and businessmen did not sense such an atmosphere and plan to take advantage of it. In selecting a "normalcy" man, the voters unwittingly invited the predatory interests to make their plots against the public welfare.

It requires effort and a sustained resolution and dedication to public interest to make adequate scrutiny of the characters of the men who are to administer the affairs of a nation. A cynical, reactionary public, bent on making up time for pleasure postponed, does not take the time or energy to do this, nor to insist that the responsible elected officials do it. When men do not judge their officials by fundamental character, they do it on the basis of superficialities—appearance, membership in certain classifications, the recommendations of friends. The men in the "smoke-filled hotel room" were trusted by the Republican voters to have used good judgment in the selection of candidates, and the new president, Harding, was trusted to make the proper appointments. Harding in turn trusted his friends and judged men too hastily by their splendid appearances or attractive recommendations. There were many appointments made with little or no earnest consideration of the real qualifications of the candidates or the welfare of the nation and the world. A small-town Ohio political friend, whose highest previous position had been that of county sheriff, was appointed to the technically and legally exacting post of Director of the Mint. A former newsboy on his own paper, the Marion *Star,* who had later been a page in the Senate and then a flyer in the war, was made White House military aide. Instead of seeing the irresponsibility in such an appointment, his home-town friends interpreted it as a great exhibition of democracy. Another home-town friend, a homeopathic physician, was appointed to be physician to the President and was made a brigadier general in the Medical Reserve Corps of the United States Army. Harding's sister's husband, a missionary of the Seventh Day Adventist Church, was made Superintendent of Federal Prisons. Another friend from Marion, a small-town lawyer who had had a few months as head of a bank, was made Comptroller of the Currency, and later Governor of the Federal Reserve System.[18]

Two other appointments which later brought great trouble to Harding were based on friendship. On a vacation trip to Honolulu Harding had met a lively, breezy, joking go-getter named Charles R. Forbes. Forbes had risen from private to colonel in the war,

---

[18] Even Coolidge kept this man in office, and thus Harding's old friend held office all during the period which preceded the depression of 1929. He must therefore be held partly responsible for the policy which failed to meet the 1929 crisis.

and thus was qualified, in the opinion of Harding, to be head of the Veterans' Bureau.   Harding failed to uncover an earlier desertion in Forbes's army record, and of course had no suspicion that his vacation friend would turn out to be a crook.   While Forbes had been making Harding proud of the rate with which he had been getting veterans' hospitals built, he had also been having corrupt relations with contractors, and was involved in irregularities concerning the sale of excess supplies left over from the war.   When word of the matter began to travel about Washington, Harding called Forbes in and let him go abroad and resign while there.   A Senate investigation was begun, and was followed by the suicide of Forbes's closest assistant in the Bureau.   Forbes was later convicted and sent to jail.

The other friend was Albert Fall, a central figure in the Teapot Dome scandal to be summarized below.   Fall was a friend during Harding's Senate career and was a man of somewhat imposing countenance, western style, with the long, steady look and fierce dignity.   Harding wanted him to have the highest cabinet post, that of Secretary of State, but his party advisers objected, and Fall was with apologies made Secretary of the Interior.

In addition to these, Harding's close friends, Harry M. Daugherty, whom he appointed Attorney General in spite of lack of legal qualifications, and Jess Smith, who attached himself to Daugherty as unofficial aide, were also to fail in their responsibilities and contribute to the blackening of the Harding administration. Daugherty was later accused, indicted, and tried for faithlessness to duty; although acquitted, he was left with little reputation.   Smith became involved in bribery—in one case accepting more than $50,000 to use his influence with the Alien Property Custodian—and committed suicide, presumably in anticipation of exposure.

The tendency to judge men by their façades is best illustrated in the choice of Edwin Denby to be Secretary of the Navy.   As inauguration time drew near with no appointment yet in sight, Harding consulted Weeks, whom he had already appointed to be his Secretary of War, and Weeks thought of a Detroit lawyer and former congressman who had a good war record in the Marine Corps and who had a face that expressed power, poise, and dominance. According to Mark Sullivan, "In looks, Denby was the most adequate Secretary the Navy ever had. . . . He took the most impressive photograph of any man in public life (and how he liked to!). . . . His tragedy was that nature, after giving him features that would have fitted a Bismarck, had neglected to fill the space behind his features with Bismarck material."[19]  Without this high-minded stuffed shirt at the head of the Navy Department, it would have been difficult for the Teapot Dome affair to take place at all, for he had casually agreed, at the suggestion of the crooked Secretary Fall, to transfer the naval oil reserves in question to the Interior Department without knowing why and without obtaining any other advice.  He apparently did not have any idea what was going on, and he trusted Fall implicitly.

The central crime of the Teapot Dome affair was the bribery of Secretary of the Interior Fall to lease, at first in secret, certain oil reserves that had been set aside for the use of the Navy in any possible future wars.  The bribery was engineered by two oil producers, Edward L. Doheny, head of the Pan-American Petroleum and Transportation Company, and Harry F. Sinclair, head of the Mammoth Oil Company.  The arrangement first came to light through a letter written by a Wyoming oil man to a senator from his state, mentioning a rumor that certain governmental oil lands had been secretly leased to a private corporation.  The senator, John B. Kendrick, a Democrat, wrote to Fall asking for an explanation and, when Fall failed to reply, introduced a resolution in the Senate, calling for an investigation.  This brought out a reply from Fall, admitting the action and refusing to say more, hiding his refusal in the excuse of "reasons of national security."  A committee was appointed, with a Montana Democrat, Thomas J. Walsh, as chairman.

Walsh worked long and hard on the case, taking eighteen months for preparation before holding the first public hearing.  The first witness called, in October, 1923, was Fall himself.  Fall, bearing himself with boldness and apparent pride, bluffed through the hearing, claiming that all he had done was in the public interest, and that the secrecy of the matter was essential.  He had not called for bids because he knew he could get the best prices by the method he had followed.  He assured the committee that no sinister purposes were served by the action and that he had not personally profited in any way.  His denial was complete and absolute and convincing to many hearers.

Information, volunteered from scattered sources, came to Walsh, however, suggesting that Fall had recently become moderately wealthy, although he had shortly before been poor.  He had purchased a ranch in New Mexico adjacent to his own, and had

---

[19] *Ibid.*, pp. 295–296.

spent large sums in improving his property, the whole outlay amounting to approximately $175,000. Fall was called upon for an explanation and stated that he had borrowed the money from Edward B. McLean of Washington, D.C., a wealthy young heir to a newspaper fortune.

McLean acquired a sudden illness and fled to Florida, betraying himself by his anxious measures to avoid being summoned to testify. Eventually Walsh himself went to Florida and found that McLean had actually given Fall checks for $100,000, but that Fall had returned them unused. Fall's testimony was thereby shown to be untrue.

By this time Doheny had become panicky and tried to persuade Fall to return from his refuge in New Orleans and tell another story. When Fall failed to do so, Doheny appeared and stated that he loaned Fall the money out of pure friendship, claiming it was not a bribe for the oil leases. But the fact came out that Fall had initiated the matter of the money. Of course, the time connection between the "loan" and the leases was apparent, and so the story failed to convince. A few days later, on February 10, 1924, Fall was served with a subpoena and thus was forced to appear at last before the Senate Investigating Committee. His statement, a virtual confession, was to the effect that he declined to answer any questions on the ground that it might tend to incriminate him.

It took years of legal action to put Fall behind bars. The original indictment was set aside on a technicality in 1925. On a new indictment Fall and Doheny were acquitted of conspiracy to defraud the government. Next, Fall and Sinclair were tried on a similar indictment, and a mistrial was declared. A retrial resulted in acquittal in 1928. In 1929 Fall was put on trial for having accepted a bribe. This time he was found guilty and sentenced to a year in jail. It was July, 1931, however, before he began to serve his sentence.

Through legal action the leases were annulled. Neither Sinclair nor Doheny, however, was convicted of bribery, even though Fall had been jailed for accepting bribes. Sinclair, because of his refusals to answer questions, served two jail terms for contempt of court and for contempt of the Senate. Secretary Denby resigned his post in order to relieve the administration of embarrassment. A number of other high officials in the government suffered in public reputation by virtue of their proximity to these matters, and even those who were in no way suspected of being a part of the conspiracy were blamed for their silence. During the long period when the fraudulent actions were developing, the most honorable members of the cabinet, such men as Calvin Coolidge, Herbert Hoover, and Charles E. Hughes, never spoke out on the disturbing subject, although many persons have believed that it would be difficult for them not to have known or suspected that something highly irregular was going on.  Perhaps the standard comradely practice of "minding one's own business" is itself a reflection of the relatively carefree and irresponsible political atmosphere of the day.

From the panic of 1929 until after the end of the second world war the nation was almost perpetually in a state of crisis.  The importance of governmental action was highly visible to citizens, and high officials worked in the spotlight of public scrutiny.  Mistakes could be made, and were made, but the opportunity for the kind of corruption that creeps in during times of prosperity and public apathy no longer existed.  The President and every member of his family, and each member of the cabinet as well as others in high administrative posts, were subjected to constant inspection and comment by writers, radio commentators, and lecturers.  The public knew what card games they played, what night clubs and horse races they attended, what travel they undertook, who their friends were, and even more intimate details of their lives.  If an official purchased a house more pretentious than his salary would justify, the public learned of the source of the funds—the source being the estate of a former wife in one case.  No such land acquisition as that of Albert Fall could take place during this latter period without immediate publicity and informal newspaper inquiry.

During the second world war the sudden expansion of military and civilian organizations presented rich opportunities for illegal deals and graft.  These did not, however, penetrate high into the administration.  One congressman came under suspicion and developed a sudden strategic illness when called on to testify before a congressional committee, but most of the offenders in the case were persons whose integrity had always been low and who worked into the rapidly expanding war organizations when the urgency was so great that there was no time for complete investigation of the qualifications of all.  Certain businessmen, for example, borrowed letterheads and solicited and won large contracts from the government, although they had neither plant nor capital and not even any experience in the production of machinery.  The rapid expansion of the military services made it possible for certain persons of ability though low integrity to rise to high ranks, thus accounting for certain scandals of black market activity by officers and some other forms of graft and theft as well.   Here again, however, these practices did not penetrate to the top of the services, nor, in the individual instances, did any one offender long conceal his corrupt practices.

History does not repeat itself perfectly enough to insure that the period following the second world war must duplicate that after the first.   The very uncertainty of the public concerning the merits of the administration tends to prevent the complacency characteristic of the early period of Harding's administration.   The radio, the newsreels, the picture magazines, and the habit of travel have all brought Washington closer to the American home, and the voters retain their interest in the personal lives of officials.[20]

Corruption is probably kept in check also by the increasing number of organizations which find it to their interest to keep vigilant watch on the government.   Women's organizations, academic groups, labor unions, and others watch the behavior and voting records of congressmen and maintain contacts with and supervision over administration officials.   Such measures do not guarantee unity or infallibility, but they do make conspicuous any dishonesty and lack of ability and make it costly for an administration to retain officials who are unqualified in these respects.

It is possible, however, for decadence to appear by creeping into the society from the bottom—from among the large masses of the population.   The conditions favoring this are in certain respects analogous to those prevalent in the period following the first world war.   In addition to fortunes made by promoters, there was a prosperity among many laborers and farmers in both periods, along with a reaction against the controls, the disciplines, and the shortages of wartime.   Much of the free-flowing money, therefore, was applied in the pursuit of pleasure.   In the first year following the capitulation of Japan, race tracks in the United States did a record gambling business, in spite of high taxation, at the betting windows.   People of Los Angeles swarmed on a new and luxurious gambling ship that anchored off the shore for all-night business.   Resorts were jammed, in spite of the highest prices up to that time.

The wartime reaction against rationing and price-controls had been somewhat similar to the earlier experience with national prohibition of alcoholic beverages.   Many persons were unwilling to

---

[20] An important member of the administration, whose appointment had met with some resistance on the ground of his lack of qualification for the post, stated in the summer of 1946 that he could not be corrupt no matter how much he might wish, for he lived in a goldfish bowl of publicity.   If any temptation should arise, such an official would surely hesitate on considering the detailed, analytical, and critical inspection given by columnists and commentators to the financial activities of the members of President Roosevelt's family.

undergo the inconveniences and discomforts and sought means of evasion. Rationalizations arose as a matter of course, for most people do not like to face the fact of their own selfishness. The controls were said to be unnecessary, to be arbitrary measures of dictatorial members of the administration. Some persons claimed that in doing certain kinds of war work they were doing more than most others to further the war effort and were thus entitled to the small comforts of extra gasoline, sugar, coffee, and other scarce commodities. There was also the steadily increasing belief, probably half-true, that "everybody else is getting theirs, so why shouldn't I ?" The effect, however, of weakening the ability of government to carry out even the most essential controls over the economy probably lasts far beyond the original situation in which such noncompliance develops.

In the 1920's many sharp dealings of noncriminal businessmen, as well as certain practices that may properly be classified as "white-collar criminality" were justified by those who engaged in them on the same ground that everybody else cheats, and that it is therefore permissible to cheat too. The policy expressed in the phrase "Let's get ours, regardless of others," spreads to other classifications of the population. When labor groups perceive the sudden fortunes made in war profiteering, they use this as their justification for striking for higher wages. Certain veterans' organizations reach for all the benefits they can get. Food producers hold back their yields for higher prices, even if it means that the national economy is upset and populations of famine areas starve. Some manufacturers close their plants, however important to national recovery their products may be, until they can be assured of the profits they desire. The national economy becomes partially strangled in the conflict of opposing and uncompromising interests.

At the close of the second world war, the recognition began to arise and spread that it is increasingly perilous to national welfare, and even to the world-wide interests of humanity, for governments to confine their principal efforts to compromising the daily internal conflicts in a process of perpetual improvisation. New and fantastically destructive methods of warfare and increasing interrelations with other continents are insistent reminders that national foresight is indispensable to survival. Although the normal political processes of a democracy have not as a rule operated to force governments to take the long view in world affairs and have thus virtually prevented the United States from having either a stable foreign policy or any kind of long-range national planning, the hard lessons of the war and its aftermath have begun to force the government to look ahead, at least in a few respects.  The administration, supported by Congress, eventually gave indications of some willingness to commit the nation to certain stable international arrangements.  Perhaps even more significant is the altered policy of the traditionally conservative military services in supporting not only practical technological experiments but also, on a large scale, basic scientific research in universities.  Perhaps these are indications that some persons have come to a recognition that the only kind of national government we can afford in the future is one that is far more efficient and foresighted than ever before.

## SUMMARY

Political disorganization and corruption are at the same time consequences of and contributing factors to social disorganization. An efficient achievement of the collective will through democratic governmental machinery requires a certain degree of community of interest in the population as well as an adequate level of education or wisdom and a supply of relevant information.  In the transition from a preindustrial society to an urban civilization many of the conditions out of which governmental machinery evolved have changed.  In place of an informed electorate, there is a large mass of voters not only with little education or information, but even unassimilated into the culture of the nation.  There are also interest groups whose special demands lead them to place certain goals above the general interest.  There is a complexity of governmental problems which frustrates the process of intelligent understanding and voting.  Out of such conditions there grows a campaign technique based on showmanship, personal appeal, and private commitments to interest groups and an administrative process that is in varying degrees inefficient and criminal.  As the realities of this development become known to voters, there is a public loss of morale which is variously expressed in political indifferentism, cynicism, and even determination to exploit the corrupt processes to obtain legitimate goals.

It is noteworthy that the intertwining of general social disorganization and political corruption is so complex and intimate that direct reform crusades usually either fail entirely or have only temporary effects, while a general decline in the social disorganization itself permits political efficiency and integrity to increase automatically.

SELECTED REFERENCES

Gist, Noel P., and Halbert, L. A. *Urban Society*. New York: The Thomas Y. Crowell Co., 1941. Ch. 18, "The Organization of Politics and Government."

Gosnell, Harold F. *Machine Politics: Chicago Model*. Chicago: University of Chicago Press, 1937.

Gosnell, Harold F. *Negro Politicians*. Chicago: University of Chicago Press, 1935.

Lynch, Denis T. *"Boss" Tweed: The Story of a Grim Generation*. New York: Boni & Liveright, 1927.

Merriam, Charles E. *Chicago: A More Intimate View of Urban Politics*. New York: The Macmillan Co., 1929.

Salter, J. T. *Boss Rule: Portraits in City Politics*. New York: Whittlesey House, 1935.

Steffens, Lincoln. *The Shame of the Cities*. New York: McClure, Phillips and Co., 1904.

Wooddy, Carroll H. *The Chicago Primary of 1926*. Chicago: University of Chicago Press, 1926.

# Chapter 13

## DISORDERS OF MASS BEHAVIOR AND MOB VIOLENCE

### Mass Behavior and Social Disorganization

The relations between the members of a successful social organization are essentially cooperative and harmonious. Competition and conflict do occur, but they are kept within limits and do not destroy the operations of the basic institutions and processes. There is an indispensable sense of mutual confidence which allows each person to perform his role without fear of desertion by other members of the organization.

When the structure of mutual confidence weakens or falls apart, there is a tendency for behavior to lose much of its cooperative aspect and to become pluralistic—that is, each person seeks similar ends, but the collectivity does not pursue common ends. Under conditions of scarcity this pluralistic behavior becomes highly competitive and readily merges into panic. Panic thus reflects a general deterioration of the fabric of mutual confidence and so operates as to further destroy it.

The cooperation of group with group requires a similar mutual confidence and is subject to destruction by a process of panic. Race riots reflect the deterioration of confidence in the orderly cooperativeness of the races concerned, as well as of trust in the functioning of law enforcement machinery and other aspects of social organization which regulate harmony among groups. In a riot the groups are the panicking units—within such a group it is possible to have cooperation and discipline. It is a condition of disorganization in the larger society, however, when component groups no longer trust the ordinary mechanisms of cooperation and become involved in mutual violence.

Although mass behavior is individualistic in a sense and reflects a condition of disorganization in the society, it nevertheless is a form of collective behavior. The interaction is centrifugal in effect, rather than centripetal. Mass behavior is distinguished from crowd interaction in that the persons concerned in the mass are not necessarily gathered together in one place and are not necessarily in direct and reciprocal communication with one another. The mass is composed of individuals who are anonymous to one another and who do not evolve any structure of social relations.

Mass behavior is involved in panics, rushes, booms, fashions, fads, and crazes. In the collective process whereby persons become aware that many others are pursuing some particular aim or interest, a degree of irrational excitement spreads, leading others to increase the intensity of their efforts in the same direction. In its most intense forms, the excitement involved in mass behavior may approach that of the religious ecstasy of the orgiastic revival meeting or the frenzy of the lynching crowd, so that many members find themselves joining in the activities without previous intention and many experience a loss of self-control that is so impressive as to produce an illusion of control by some external and mystical agency. In lesser degrees of excitement the behavior has a spontaneity which makes it seem natural, and which for the time being protects the participants from indecision and from the operation of conscience.

## FORMS OF MASS BEHAVIOR

**Booms and Panics.**—Certain aspects of organized economic life are sustained by the system of mutual confidence mentioned above. An illustration of the principle is furnished by the example of an independent bank which is not protected by deposit insurance. Depositors entrust their money to the bank, knowing that the funds are reinvested, and risked to a certain extent, in properties not readily subject to liquidation. This means that not all of the depositors are able to withdraw their funds at the same time. Ordinarily, however, this does not disturb the persons who leave money in the care of a bank, for they assume that no great number of depositors will ask for their money at the same time. Such confidence is justified when conditions are normal, but on certain occasions depositors tend to lose confidence in one another and thus begin to fear the closing of a bank. The individual aim is then to reach the bank before the other persons, for the last few to ask for their money may find the funds exhausted. The rush is intensified by the knowledge that other persons are also rushing, and by rumors of a lack of adequate cash to pay demands or of other aspects of weakness on the part of the bank. When depositors see others moving toward the bank and see crowds gathering at the doors, the panic becomes general and acquires a momentum which is difficult to check, even in cases in which the bank is sound and solvent. The crowd does not draw back from its panic until confidence is restored in the bank's ability to pay, and in the willingness of depositors to leave their accounts in the bank.

In periods of economic tension, such as the early period of the great depression of the 1930's, events of a trivial order are sufficient to set off the hair-trigger responses of bank depositors. The death of a bank official, particularly if suicide is suspected, may encourage a rumor of embezzlement and therefore of shortages of funds in the bank, and thus lead to a run. A newspaper story of an attempted robbery may have the same effect. And if, in such times of declining values and freezing of assets, a number of banks in an area fail, a situation develops of tension so high that runs may start from stimuli so trivial that it may be difficult or impossible to account for their origin. Runs may thus spread from bank to bank, closing all the banks in a large area, and may then even sweep across to other areas like a rapidly spreading forest fire. In the winter of 1933 such a panic, originating in Detroit, swiftly closed the banks in the State of Michigan, then progressed to neighboring states and within a few more days to the entire nation, freezing billions of dollars in deposits and bringing the financial machinery of the country virtually to a stop. The banks were reopened after a nine-day national "holiday," ordered by the newly inaugurated President Roosevelt, and were strengthened by new legislation which included the insurance feature which has had the effect of making bank runs rare since that time.

Many other panics have a nature similar to that of the bank panic. A system of cooperation, built on an equilibrium of mutual confidence, is disturbed to a critical extent, and from then on the lack of confidence and the panic behavior intensify each other in a "vicious circle" process. Such a development is particularly likely to occur in situations where values are arbitrarily based on a general public enthusiasm unsupported by any kind of necessity, as in the case of the great tulip mania in seventeenth century Holland. Beyond a moderate value for decorative purposes, the tulip prices became at that time entirely artificial, supported only by an irrational collective demand which held the prices up and kept sending them higher. This enthusiasm was widespread in the population of the country. Men and women of all ranks and in all occupations neglected their ordinary tasks to indulge in the tulip trade. Many foreigners were caught in the contagious enthusiasm and sent their money into the tulip markets. Fortunes were made as prices went up to thousands of florins for some of the more precious bulbs. It was generally assumed that the passion for these flowers would be permanent, in spite of the entirely artificial character of the values. As long as the collective enthusiasm kept growing the values were maintained, but in time there arose and spread a recognition of the precarious position of those with large investments in tulips, and, shortly after a few persons began to liquidate, the panic spread over the whole tulip world. Many fortunes vanished suddenly, and rich men turned into beggars.[1]

Land booms, at their most lively development, may take a course somewhat similar to that of the tulip craze. One of the most spectacular examples in recent times was that of the Florida boom of the 1920's. As the prosperous postwar urban dwellers began to discover the pleasures of winter vacations along the southern beaches of Florida, the demand for land began to spread, and as prices rose the speculator began to take an interest. Word passed around the country, and before long people were going to Florida in some number, not merely for a vacation, but to make money through the buying and selling of land. The buying turned into a minor frenzy, and promoters did what they could to stimulate it. Buses, labeled with the names of subdivisions, brought prospective purchasers from other cities, and cars from many states crowded the highways, attracted by stories of rising land values and fortunes to be made. Free entertainment lured people to some areas. More enterprising salesmen even provided free trips to lively prospects. Prospective purchasers were given flamboyant welcome.

Word went about the country that persons might buy lots one day and sell them the next day at a substantial gain. One writer, who came to observe, caught the fever and on a "piker's purchase" made about $13,000 in a month. The pervading spirit of rapid gains proved almost irresistible. She later characterized the condition in the following description:[2]

Again and again I declared that I had no intention to buy, but nobody let me forget for an instant I was a prospect. As upon others, the power of suggestion doubtless worked on me. It is subtly flattering to be the implied possessor of wealth. The kingdoms of the world appeared to be displayed for my choice. To help me choose, I, like everyone else, was accosted repeatedly on Miami streets, offered free dinners and bus trips, besides a deal of entertainment, conscious and unconscious, by high pressure salesmen.

The boom bacillus thrives on prodigality. The price of good food brings many a prospect to the point of spending thousands. Two unusual concerns

---

[1] This and other such phenomena, including the "Mississippi Scheme," are described in C. Mackay, *Memoirs of Extraordinary Popular Delusions*, London: Routledge, 1852.
[2] G. M. Shelby, "Florida Frenzy," *Harper's*, Vol. 152, 1926. Quoted in Kimball Young. *Source Book for Social Psychology*, New York: Alfred A. Knopf, Inc., 1927, pp. 714–717.

rewarded only real purchasers *post hoc*. One gave them an airplane ride, the other a free soft drink.

On account of an inherited notion of conduct towards those with whom one breaks bread, I refused all such bait. On my independent investigations salesmen found me unusually inquisitive. One, trying to sell me a $3,500 lot, reproved me. "Those things don't matter. All Florida is good. What you are really buying is the bottom of the climate. Or the Gulf Stream. All you've got to do is to *get the rich consciousness*. There's the dotted line— you'll make a fortune."

Authentic quick-wealth tales, including innumerable lot transactions, multiplied astoundingly. They were not cases of twenty-five-dollar land proved worth one hundred dollars, but of prices which had pyramided high into the thousands. When I saw the sort of people who were making actual money my hesitation appeared ridiculous. I resolved to invest. I tried to assume an attitude of faith. . . . Searching continually for some deal to fit my modest purse, I found that the only ranch tracts priced within my reach were six or seven miles back in the Everglades. . . .

Among the places offered for sale to the above writer was a deep hole in a rock pit, priced at $1,000. But another unimportant-appearing lot which was offered at $60,000 was sold about a week later for $75,000 and about two weeks later for $95,000. "Imagine how I felt. . . . By risking $2,500 with faith I could have made $35,000 clear, enough to live on some years. Terror of an insecure old age suddenly assumed exaggerated proportions. Right then and there I succumbed to the boom bacillus. I would gamble outright. The illusion of investment vanished."

The mentality of the boom speculator, clearly visible in the above account, is made up partly of fear—fear that some one else will beat him to the easy profits. There is a recognition, perhaps not in the very center of attention, that the rapid rise of values cannot continue indefinitely. It does not necessarily matter if values of land, tulips, or other commodities reach a height so artificial that no possible use could justify the price. The value is there, to the speculator, as long as there are other persons bidding for the commodities. All of the others are bidding for the same reason, and the prices remain high as long as the collective enthusiasm endures. When a sizable break in this optimism appears, however, the panic process, which is similar to the boom process except that the race is in the opposite direction, gets under way. Now the fear is that other persons will sell first—it is a fear not merely of missing a fortune, but a more serious fear of being ruined financially. The descent is nearly always much faster than the climb and does in fact leave many stragglers penniless.

Such was the course of the Florida boom. The craze had spread far beyond the limits of the state, and some of the visible casualties were a thousand miles away. For years there remained an unintentional monument to the sky-high optimism of the Florida boom days, high on a mountain peak in North Carolina. There stood the framework of an unfinished skyscraper resort hotel, thrusting into the clouds from a small cleared area littered with bathtubs, waiting vainly to be installed for the tourists that never were to come.

In times of war, when shortages of many luxuries and even necessities develop, there arises in any population a tendency to acquire and to hoard such commodities. The acquisition becomes competitive and may take on the character of panic when conditions are favorable to it. During the second world war, a number of such buying and hoarding panics took place among the citizens of the United States, where at no time did there develop any severe hardships from lack of essential goods. One of the first of these took place in September, 1939, when, perhaps remembering the sugar shortages of the first world war, housewives began a rush for sugar, quickly emptying the shelves of grocery stores in the United States and Canada. The conditions at this time, however, were not such as to threaten a real shortage of sugar, and the panic was shortlived.

Later, following the Pearl Harbor attack and the news of the approach of many kinds of shortages and of rationing programs, a series of panic buying waves took place, directed toward various commodities. Persons bought clothing far in advance of needs—at an eastern private school for girls, for example, a rumor went about one afternoon that clothing was to be rationed, and that same day most of the girls in the school rushed to department stores to buy new coats, charging them to the accounts of their parents. Coffee and sugar panics took place, as it became apparent that the supplies would dwindle. Tires were hoarded by many, and gasoline by those who could arrange a means of storing it. In some cases there was no rational basis for advance buying, but in the excitement judgment deteriorated—one woman was known to purchase 75 dollars' worth of electric light bulbs. As the news leaked out that shoe rationing was imminent, crowds descended on shoe stores, buying any shoes that could be obtained, whether or not they were needed, or even could fit the purchasers' feet. The canned food panic however, reached the greatest extremes—one family in a Philadelphia suburb purchased a 40-year supply.

Human beings panic in the face of other dangers besides financial ruin and threat of shortage.   In wartime the panicky evacuation of areas threatened with invasion often becomes a serious problem to military transport, as roads are so crowded with refugees as to obstruct traffic.   In the second world war there were reports of deliberate measures to instigate such panics in order to cripple the efficiency of military movements.

Other panics may occur with less visible reason, particularly in times of tension and among persons whose information and education are insufficient to protect them against vague terrors.   A historian of the French Revolution has described a panic known as the "great fear."   In July, 1789, shortly after the time of the storming of the Bastille in Paris, a rumor went through the town of Gueret that "the brigands are coming."   No one knew who the brigands were, or why they should be coming.   Some believed the king had hired brigands to rob the peasants.   As the fear ran through the town, the men gathered for defense and the women fled from the town to hide in thickets and ditches.   Aid was sought from neighboring villages, and some thousands of men came into the town.   At one time the word came that 2,500 brigands were marching along the Soissons road, and the assembled men marched out to meet them.   A miller, encountered on the road, told them that Bouresches had just been sacked and set afire—but on arrival at that village the men found that the appearance of flames was merely the reflection of the sun on the roofs.   Another rumor of approach of the brigands was investigated, but it turned out to be a group of women, fleeing from the men in the belief that they were the brigands.[3]

A somewhat similar panic occurred on Hallowe'en Day in 1938, as a result of a broadcast by Orson Welles, consisting of a highly dramatic fantasy describing an invasion by strange creatures from the planet Mars.   The story was related in the form of special news bulletins and on-the-spot broadcasts, interspersed with interviews with witnesses, public officials, and commentators.   The program began with dance music, purporting to come from a hotel orchestra. Suddenly the music was interrupted with a special bulletin, mentioning the landing of a strange space ship in the fields near Lakehurst, New Jersey.   Highly dramatic announcements came in quick order —strange men were seen emerging from the space ship, equipped with fantastic weapons.   Other landings were reported.   Units of

---

[3] From H. M. Stephens, *A History of the French Revolution*, Vol. I, pp. 178–179.   Cited in E. B. Reuter and C. B. Hart, *Introduction to Sociology*, New York: McGraw-Hill Book Co., Inc., 1933, pp. 465–466.

the National Guard were said to be moving toward the scene and to be mysteriously exterminated by the strange weapons.

As the broadcast proceeded, persons ran to tell others by word of mouth and by phone. Some ran to the streets in panic. Others took to their cars to drive as far as possible from the place of the invasion. For some hours during the remainder of the evening many thousands of persons were engaged in panic behavior. It is estimated that about 1,000,000 were disturbed by the story. By the following morning, when newspapers and radio broadcasts reported the affair as a hoax, the excitement was ended.

The extremity of the emotions aroused is illustrated by some typical reactions, given in the words of those concerned:[4]

(A Newark filling-station operator)  My girl friend and I stayed in the car for a while, just driving around. Then we followed the lead of a friend. All of us ran into a grocery store and asked the man if we could go into his cellar. He said, "What's the matter? Are you trying to ruin my business?" So he chased us out. A crowd collected. We rushed to an apartment house and asked the man in the apartment to let us in his cellar. He said, "I don't have any cellar! Get away!" Then people started to rush out of the apartment house all undressed. We got into the car and listened some more. Suddenly, the announcer was gassed, the station went dead so we tried another station but nothing would come on. Then we went to a gas station and filled up our tank in preparation for just riding as far as we could. . . .

(Wife of a day laborer)  I was terribly frightened. I wanted to pack and take my child in my arms, gather up my friends and get in the car and just go north as far as we could. But what I did was just set by one window, praying, listening, and looking out to see if people were running. Then when the announcer said, "evacuate the city," I ran and called my boarder and started with my child to rush down the stairs, not waiting to catch my hat or anything. When I got to the foot of the stairs I just couldn't get out, I don't know why.

(A college senior)  One of the first things I did was to try to phone my girl in Poughkeepsie, but the lines were all busy, so that just confirmed my impression that the thing was true. We started driving back to Poughkeepsie. We had heard that Princeton was wiped out and gas was spreading over New Jersey and fire, so I figured there wasn't anything to do—we figured our friends and families were all dead. I made the 45 miles in 35 minutes and didn't even realize it. I drove right through Newburgh and never even knew I went through it. I don't know why we weren't killed. My roommate was crying and praying. He was even more excited than I was—or more noisy about it anyway; I guess I took it out in pushing the accelerator to the floor. I imagine having to concentrate on the driving held

⁴ Hadley Cantril, Hazel Gaudet, and Herta Hertzog, *The Invasion from Mars*, Princeton, N. J.: Princeton University Press, 1940, pp. 48–51.

me together somewhat. On Monday, after it was all over, and I started to think of that ride, I was more jittery than when it was happening. The speed was never under 70. I thought I was racing against time. The gas was supposed to be spreading up north. I didn't have any idea exactly what I was fleeing from, and that made me all the more afraid. All I could think of was being burned alive or being gassed. And yet I didn't care somehow whether I hit anything with the car or not. I remember thinking distinctly how easy it would be to get shot cleanly in a war. I remember also thinking there wasn't any God. My roommate was really praying and crying all the time. I thought the whole human race was going to be wiped out—that seemed more important than the fact that we were going to die. It seemed awful that everything that had been worked on for years was going to be lost forever. . . .

A study of the phenomenon, undertaken almost immediately, showed that most of the persons who accepted the simulated news broadcast as fact had not been tuned in at the beginning, when it was made clear that the program was to be a Hallowe'en scare story, or during the middle break, when again assurances were given that the whole account was fictional.[5]   There was internal evidence that the story was studio-produced, but those persons who were relatively uneducated, or who by virtue of their excitement were uncritical, missed the indications and gave way, while others perceived that only in fiction could a completely equipped sound truck, for example, be taken to a remote rural district in a matter of seconds, or would units of a National Guard be assembled, equipped, and placed on the scene within three or four minutes after the landing of the "Martians" was observed.

Some interpreters of the event considered that tension caused by the trend of events in Europe was partly responsible for the panic. Some persons fled, knowing an invasion from Mars to be improbable, but believing that an invasion from Germany by air was under way.

**Fashions, Fads, and Crazes.**—It is a characteristic of certain sections of modern populations, particularly of city people, to be subject to waves of enthusiasm for current popular novelties. The interest is not merely in novelty itself, but in the particular new things that are coming into vogue. A woman is willing to wear a costume that has a somewhat ridiculous appearance if she can be confident that within a short time many other women will be wearing similar clothing. There is in fact a type of individualistic

[5] *Ibid.*

competition among those persons who try to remain in the vanguard of fads and fashions. They try to differentiate themselves from the large crowd of passive style followers and race against one another to be among the first to adopt a leading fashion. Imitativeness is not a characteristic of this group, although it is important in the motivation of the lagging followers of fashion.

The psychology of style leaders bears a slight resemblance to that of the participants in booms and panics. It is important to them to be among the first, in order to reap the psychological rewards of being in the forefront of fashion, and it is almost as important to flee from a new style when it is assumed by the masses. Farther back in the procession, among the followers, the motivation is more purely sociable—persons adapt to styles to avoid being conspicuously traditional, rather than to be conspicuously original. At the most traditional end of the sequence there is even a considerable part of the population that is little affected by fads and fashions. In the most stable of isolated rural settlements there is no virtue in being different and no value is put on novelty for novelty's sake. In fact, in many of the most conservative religious sects, uniformity of costume and behavior is demanded by the sacred mores.

Style leadership then, and the frontier of fads and crazes as well, is found where traditionalism is weak and where social change is most rapid—in the large metropolitan centers. Paris, New York, and Hollywood have been centers of development of clothing styles for women—even those styles, such as the recently popular dirndl skirt of peasant women, which are inspired from other areas. It is among certain elements of the populations of such cities that the new styles are actually adopted. Some extreme styles are entirely confined to these populations. Others spread from the major centers to lesser centers, and on from there toward the more conservative regions of the country and the world. As new styles diffuse, the more radical elements tend to become modified, so that at the most distant limits of their diffusion only the fainter essentials of the novelty remain. Paris styles thus eventually reach Two Forks, Saskatchewan, but only after the passage of some time, and in a diluted form. They never reach the Old Order Amish of Lancaster County, Pennsylvania.

In its deliberate differentiation from tradition, faddishness symbolizes the secularization of swiftly changing societies. When historical motifs are adopted in modern styles, it is in the spirit of amusement at antique quaintness, or even in a spirit of ridicule of people of earlier periods. Extreme interest in fads and fashions also probably reflects in the persons involved a degree of unrest, a lack of a satisfactory or important role in society, leading to the placing of an emphasis on external and superficial aspects of personality. This accounts for the prevalence of faddish behavior in such circles as the childless wives of well-to-do city people, particularly of the class sometimes referred to as "cafe society." At the same time it accounts for the fact that certain persons, even those entirely modern in attitudes and knowledge and who are residents of large centers, but who are engaged in important and absorbing activities, may remain almost totally uninterested. It is not sacred traditionalism that accounts for the indifference to fads and fashions on the part of such persons as Marie Curie, Thomas Edison, Albert Einstein, and other creators and pioneers of modern civilization.

It is approximately as difficult for one person to create a new fashion or fad as it is to introduce a new word into the language. The act of invention is not as difficult as is the matter of putting it into circulation. Fortunes can be made from a single fad if an exploiter can control it from the start. The craze for miniature golf in the late 1920's both made and lost fortunes. An inventor who devised a surface made of crushed cotton-seed hulls reaped large profits, as did many land speculators and developers, but there were others who razed buildings or cleared off parking lots near the end of the public enthusiasm for the game, only to lose their shirts.

Fashion designers and inventors operate constantly to create new styles, and take the best steps they can to put them across, but of the many efforts that are made, only a small proportion succeed, and there is no science of the matter to account for the successes. Some efforts have been maintained for years in the face of failure. During much of the decade of the 1930's announcements appeared in newspapers that the styles of men's suits were to change, in the direction of an earlier fashion of tapered or "peg top" trousers. Since the early 1920's, however, when trousers became wide enough to enable men to remove them without first taking off the shoes, few males have been willing to purchase the narrower styles. Fashion tailors knew they would increase their earnings if they could make obsolete all the clothes in the closets of the American male, but they could not succeed in their efforts to change his tastes.

Faddishness varies with the times. In periods of prosperity and international tranquility, when peoples are more concerned with the pursuit of happiness than with the grimmer tasks of crises, conditions are favorable for eager pursuit of current rages. In times of war or severe depression, on the other hand, the rate at

which such developments occur appears to decline. In the prosperous postwar decade of the 1920's a series of spectacularly swift
rages followed one another in the United States, to an extent
which was not equaled during the following depression and war
periods. Skirts of women became spectacularly short then for the
first time. Women's hair was bobbed in a rapid revolution of
coiffure. Galoshes and cloche hats became all but universal for
women. Men took to silk shirts, then powder blue shirts, and
then to wide trousers. Bathing suits dwindled rapidly in size
for both sexes. New and revived games raged for a season or so,
sometimes providing ample profits for foresighted entrepreneurs.
Mah-jong, for example, required expensive sets, and, since it raged
particularly around the season of Christmas, the sellers cleared good
profits on gift sales. Other rage games of the period were cross-
word puzzles, ping pong, backgammon, contract bridge, jigsaw
puzzles, and the like. In addition there were many minor rages
that engaged the interest of particular sections or levels of the
population—face-lifting, knitting, bicycling, 18-day diets for reducing, tree-sitting by juveniles, dancing marathons, and "walkathons."
    Although the number and prevalence may have been somewhat
less than in earlier years, there were also in the 1930's a number of
similar fads. These included culottes (for women's sportswear),
Esquire costumes (for high-style young men and a few cafe-society
sports), such games as Handies, Monopoly, "Knock-knock," yo-yos,
and the like; and such assorted crazes as page-boy bobs, guppy
raising, charm bracelets, bubble gum, "Confucius say," the "Big
Apple" dance, jitterbugging, and zoot suits. During the early
1940's, with minds on the war, with shortages of materials and
labor, with the absence of a large proportion of young males, and
with other conditions contributing to the reduction of faddishness,
there was a minimum of such behavior.
    Few of these crazes can be said to be harmful in themselves.
They may be thought of, however, as symptoms of a sort of
collective frivolity which is a part of the causation of public apathy
toward important matters. Thus the carefree attitude may be a
factor in the lack of interest in international relations, in the neglect
of the ballot or the practice of voting frivolously, and in the sans-
gêne toleration of criminality and political corruption. The game
of bridge alone probably contributes to the above conditions in an
important degree by virtue of its demand on the time of its devotees,
if in no other way. For the bridge enthusiast, most social gatherings are dedicated to the game, at the expense of reading, conversa-

tion, or constructive activities. Time available for study is spent, not in acquiring political sophistication or in self-improvement, but in learning bidding strategy and other tricks of the pastime.

**Epidemics and Rumors.**—There is an account of an epidemic of nervous fits among young female workers in a Lancashire cotton mill in February, 1787.[6] It is reported that a girl put a mouse into the bosom of another girl who had a fear of mice. The latter was at once thrown into a fit, which possessed her for 24 hours and gave her violent convulsions. The following day, without the agency of mice, three more girls began to have similar fits, and the next day the behavior spread to six more, in the manner of a contagion. A true disease was suspected, the plant was closed in order to prevent the further spread of the fits, and a physician was summoned from a neighboring town. The fits continued to spread, however, and on another day three more were seized, and then the next day 11. Of the 24 in all, 21 were young women, two were ten-year-old girls, and one was a man who had become fatigued by holding the girls who were in their convulsions.

The epidemic was put to an end by the physician, who employed a portable electrical machine to shock the women. He then informed them that the complaint was merely nervous and had nothing to do with infection from the cotton in the factory. No further fits developed, and the matter was ended by holding a dance, after which the factory resumed its operations.

History contains accounts of a number of epidemics which begin suddenly, sweep a region quickly like grass fires in a field, and then vanish almost as abruptly. The dancing mania of the Middle Ages, in which persons apparently became caught in a mass frenzy which forced them to dance in a wild fashion until they fell from exhaustion, is said to have spread like a disease from Aix-la-Chapelle into neighboring regions of the Netherlands, France, and Germany. Its meaning was not understood, although some interpreted it as demonic possession and priests sometimes attempted cures by exorcism. The affected persons formed circles and danced wildly, hand in hand. Some were said to have had convulsions, and to foam at the mouth. Persons who came to observe, even unsympathetically, were said to have begun to twitch as the excitement possessed them, and then soon were dancing with the others. The numbers of the afflicted persons increased—at one time there were over a thousand

---

[6] Taken from *Gentleman's Magazine*, March, 1787, p. 268. Cited in R. E. Park and E. W. Burgess, *Introduction to the Science of Sociology*, Chicago: University of Chicago Press, 1924, pp. 878–879.

dancers in the city of Metz. Some persons left homes and employ-ment and formed bands of wandering dancers, thus spreading the contagion to other communities. The epidemic prevailed in the Rhenish cities for some four months before authorities were able to stamp it out.

Among the similar phenomena of medieval and modern times may be listed the pilgrimage epidemic of the eleventh century, the crusade epidemic that followed during the next two centuries, the flagellant epidemic from 1260 to 1348, the Black Death and the anti-Semitic mania of 1348, and the witchcraft mania from 1488 to the end of the seventeenth century. Although interpretations in each case cannot be made with the same ease with which modern phenomena are studied, it seems apparent that the readiness with which these early populations became swept into the wild contagions listed above reflects a sense of unrest, a feeling that something is deeply wrong, so that the collective definitions of the troubled situa-tion found ready acceptance, particularly among the unlearned and unsophisticated sections of the populations.

Rumors of a highly contagious sort thrive in the same kind of social circumstances. Where there is tension, apprehension, and a feeling that available information is incomplete, and where fervent wishes are involved, people are eager to hear, to believe, and to spread the trivial scraps of information that may explain, or foretell, important events. Not all rumors are pleasant in content—rumors of approaching disaster may spread panic. In the days following the Pearl Harbor attack in 1941, various rumors of sudden danger were spread among the population. The most spectacular was that of an approaching formation of enemy planes over the Atlantic, said to be a half-hour from Long Island. In Boston it was widely believed that the attack was coming that way, and many persons took to cellars for some hours.

Spy scares are common in times of war. Actual accomplish-ments of enemy agents furnish the basis of a belief in their almost universal presence, and of rumors concerning plots which in peace-time appear to be absurd. During the first world war the presence of German spies in various parts of the country was suspected on the basis of stories of overheard conversations in "harsh gutturals" and sometimes apparently on no more basis than nervous imagina-tion. In a small town in Iowa, a community without war plants or of any importance to the conflict with Germany, a rumor spread that one of the principal bakeries had been selling bread with ground glass inside—an action of enemy agents to destroy some of the civilian population. Similar phenomena occurred in the second world war, particularly in connection with the Japanese residents of Pacific Coast areas. The rapid assembly and confinement of these persons, even those with American citizenship, after the Pearl Harbor attack, is believed by some observers to be an indication that such panic had reached into the military organization.

Among the rumors that flourish on undernourished hopes are those of the death of a powerful enemy. In the first world war there were several rumors of the death of the leading German general, von Hindenburg. Later, in the middle 1930's, a similar story spread about Adolf Hitler and was reported in certain leading magazines, even finding acceptance by one of them. It was argued that Hitler was dead, and that a double, closely similar in appearance and voice, was used for the public appearances that were ostensibly being made by Hitler. In some versions there were several doubles involved. Scraps of evidence were cited in support of the belief, but it eventually died of neglect and implausibility. When Hitler himself died, at the close of the European part of the war, there was no resurrection of the old rumor, although certain new rumors circulated to the effect that he had escaped alive with Eva Braun and was presumably hiding somewhere—one rumor placing them in Patagonia.

A rumor of hope for salvation was observed among the natives of central Africa, by a visitor in the early 1930's—a man who was able to converse in the native tongue. The natives had found many aspects of their colonial status unsatisfactory, and were beginning to be somewhat restive under the dominance of foreign white imperialists. Word spread about that "Black America" was coming to save them. Many natives did not know what the term meant, and did not know anything about the United States or its Negro population. It was a mystical conception, but one which served as a basis of optimism. Although the origin of the rumor is not known with certainty, the possibility has been suggested that it may have been presented to the natives through the promises of Communist agitators. If so, it is only to be expected that the involved theory of Marxism would have to be reduced to a magical word before it would spread so easily among such primitive peoples.

Rumors arising from wishes may be not only those of hopes for good things, but of dreams of bad things for, or about, those to whom we are hostile. In periods of intense political controversy the conditions are favorable for malicious rumors concerning prominent participants in the conflict. During the long tenure of

Franklin D. Roosevelt in the presidency, personal dislike among certain members of the political opposition became so intense that there were many libelous rumors circulated about the country. These were particularly frequent near the times of elections, when personalities of candidates became favorite topics of discussion.

During the war years of the early 1940's a series of rumors was current concerning waste and special privilege on the part of high officials in the administration. A research project undertaken during this period in Syracuse, New York, found a number of such rumors current in this city and found a high proportion of the 537 persons interviewed to have accepted as true certain stories which were known by the investigators to be without foundation.[7] For example the most widely accepted rumor, that "A certain prominent government official has three cars and a large underground storage tank filled with gasoline for his own use" was believed by 44.5 per cent when it was mentioned to them by investigators as a rumor, although less than half of these persons had previously known of it. The rumor that "There is plenty of coffee in the United States. The big companies have cornered the market and are holding out for higher prices" was believed by 33.7 per cent. The story that "Gasoline storage tanks of the producing companies are so full of gasoline that ocean-going tankers are dumping their cargoes at sea" was accepted as at least partial truth by 13.5 per cent.[8]

Investigation of certain characteristics of those who partly accepted the rumors reveals something of the relationship to hostility toward the administration. There were significantly larger tendencies toward acceptance among those who held adverse attitudes toward the rationing program, those who had a lack of faith in their fellow Americans, those who felt that they had been inconvenienced by wartime sacrifices, and those who did not have a close friend or relative in a war zone. There were some smaller differences among classes based on occupation, sex, and age.

## Mob Violence

Lynchings.—The lynching pattern in the United States is a survival from frontier conditions, in which the lack of organized law enforcement furnished the motive for spontaneous and tem-

---

[7] Floyd H. Allport and Milton Lepkin, "Wartime Rumors of Waste and Special Privilege: Why Some People Believe Them," *Journal of Abnormal and Social Psychology,* Vol. 40, Jan., 1945.

[8] The figures on belief do not mean in every case complete acceptance of the rumor but at least some tendency to believe—wondering if it may be true, or believing that "there may be something in it."

porary teamwork for the handling of the occasional crisis of criminality. The horse-thief and the murderer were not allowed to go unpunished for the lack of legal machinery. Leading citizens organized a group from whatever persons were available and pursued the offender for the purpose of dealing out punishment. In some cases the forms of legal trial were employed; but as certain crimes, such as the theft of horses and cattle, became chronic, public temper increased and led to the shortening or omission of such formalities, particularly where there was no reason to doubt the guilt of the culprit.

Spontaneous actions when repeated eventually acquire patterns which take their places among the stable traditions. Thus the pursuit and hanging of horse thieves in the western range territory eventually became a standardized and conventional procedure. It was the expected action on the occasion of an offense, and there was little tendency to disapprove the measure, at least until legal machinery came to replace these actions of popular justice. Even then, the behavior tended to persist in regions in which a sense of crisis remained and in which legal machinery worked too slowly for popular temper.

Lynching of offenders is a pattern which, while not confined to southern regions of the United States, has tended there to persist longer and to find expression more often than elsewhere. The action is used primarily in cases involving some sort of threat to the pattern of race relations on the part of Negroes, although on occasions the lynching pattern may be applied to white offenders whose misdeeds are serious enough to shock the community. The lynching pattern in southern regions reflects a conflict between tradition and law; for the slow, patient, impartial processes of a trial, with all of the technical safeguards to the accused person, are considered to be too slow where outrageous crimes are involved and where the existing and partially sacred structure of society is threatened.

In view of the effects of the lynching pattern on the efficacy of law enforcement and on the community reputation elsewhere, it is considered by many citizens and officials who take the larger view of affairs to be a greater harm than good. The pattern receives its principal support from the less sophisticated and educated members of the region and from those who have not had the occasion to bear the greater responsibilities and to take the long-run view of the welfare of the region. Thus a lynching often involves not only hostility toward the victim but also a conflict with administrators of the law and with other community leaders.   The latter, contending in order to preserve legality, are handicapped in the conflict with adversaries who are not in any way concerned with maintaining the technical proprieties of the law.[9]

A lynching does not have, to the participants, the sole meaning of the punishment of the victim.   It is principally a gesture, a warning, to the people of whom he is a representative.   It demonstrates a determination to meet with quick and extreme measures any challenge to the existing pattern of race relations.   While the most intolerable challenge to this pattern is the crime of rape by a Negro man against white women, there have been many lynchings to punish other types of challenge—murder, fighting a white man, attempts to organize Negroes for rebellion, and even "talking back" to a white man.

**The Leeville Affair: an Account of a Lynching.**—The literature does not contain many satisfactorily complete accounts of lynchings, with detailed information on the composition of the mob, for participants are seldom willing to discuss or record any detail of the event, and nonresident observers are not encouraged to gather information.   In the case of the lynching at Leeville, Texas, however, a member of the community who witnessed much of the action has provided one of the most complete accounts of what appears to be a typical lynching.   If there is any departure from the usual action, it is largely in the matter of the extremity of the violence and the large amount of damage done by the mob.[10]

The events occurred in a Texas town of about 15,000, in the springtime of a year in the early 1930's.   The crime of the victim was the classic one—rape of a white woman.   The Negro, who worked as a laborer on the farm of a white man near the town of Leeville, appeared at the farmhouse one Saturday morning to collect his wages.   The farmer had gone into the town without leaving the money, and as his wife so informed the Negro, the latter left, disappointed and angry.   He soon returned with a shotgun, forced the woman into the bedroom, and assaulted her.   He then tied her

----

[9] In the prominent case in early 1947 of the lynching of a Negro man by a Greenville, South Carolina, mob, it developed that most of the leaders were taxi-drivers.   The victim, Willie Earl, had been accused of killing a driver.   The tendency of southern officials to more determined efforts at punishment of lynchers was illustrated in this affair, when both the judge and the governor moved firmly against the defendants.   When the jury set the taxi-drivers free, the United States Attorney General, Tom Clark, himself a southerner, threatened to find means of intervention.   Probably the last essential for success in such prosecutions will be the obtaining of juries willing to convict.

[10] The information is all taken from an article by Durward Pruden, "A Texas Lynching," in *Studies in Sociology*, Vol. I, No. I, Summer, 1936, published by the Department of Sociology, Southern Methodist University, Dallas, Texas.

up and left.   The woman soon freed herself and ran to the house
of a neighbor, from which the sheriff was telephoned.

The Negro was soon found and arrested.   The deputy sheriff
who made the arrest claimed that the Negro had fired at him.
According to the account, the Negro confessed, agreed to plead
guilty, waived all rights, and was taken to a jail, secretly, in a
town some miles away from Leeville.

For the next six days the affair was discussed in Leeville, and
collective anger began to rise.   On Monday night a small group of
men and boys loitered near the Leeville jail, and the following night
a larger crowd appeared.   They refused to disperse until the sheriff
allowed some of the leaders to go through the jail to see for themselves that the Negro was not there.   Discussion went on, however,
and during the week many exaggerated versions of the assault were
told on the streets.

On the following Friday, the day of the opening of the trial,
many persons from Leeville and the surrounding countryside
appeared at the court.   The judge refused to change venue, taking
no unusual measures beyond having four Texas Rangers present.
The Negro was brought in early in the morning, before the crowd
gathered.   During the long process of selection of the jury, the
crowd which gathered about the building and the halls became
larger and more belligerent.   A rumor, false but generally accepted
at the time, circulated through the crowd, to the effect that the
governor of the state had sent orders to the Rangers that they were
not to shoot any members of the crowd.   This increased the confidence of the members.   At about one o'clock, the woman who had
been assaulted was brought in an ambulance to the courthouse and
carried on a stretcher through the crowd and into the courtroom.
This was apparently an intentionally dramatic gesture.

At once the crowd turned into a wild and active mob.   The
courtroom was stormed.   Rangers, using drawn guns and tear gas,
drove them back several times.   The trial was stopped, as the judge
decided to change venue.   The Negro was locked in a fireproof
vault room.   Balked by this measure, the members of the crowd
decided to burn down the courthouse.   Windows were broken with
rocks, gasoline was thrown in, and about two-thirty in the afternoon
the building was set afire.

As firemen rescued persons from the second floor courtroom,
using ladders reaching to the windows, the crowd watched and
occasionally made objections to the rescuing of the judge, county
attorney, sheriffs, and Rangers, but made no serious attempts to

stop it.   The firemen were not allowed, however, to extinguish the flames.   The mob cut the hoses and sometimes attacked the firemen. The action merged into open warfare.

The Rangers, on leaving the scene, telephoned the governor for aid, and a small detachment of National Guardsmen was sent over from a neighboring town, arriving at about four o'clock in the afternoon.   Concluding that they were greatly outnumbered, however, they made no attempt to control the crowd and withdrew.   Two hours later a larger group of 52 soldiers from another city arrived and took measures to drive the mob away from the burning courthouse.   The mob, confident that the soldiers would not fire on them, fought the soldiers with rocks, bricks, broken bottles, and even chunks of dynamite.   A few members of the mob received bullet wounds, and a number of the soldiers were cut and beaten.   The soldiers retreated several blocks to the jail, and there made a stand, shooting into the air.

The mob withdrew and returned to the ruins of the courthouse in order to open the vault and get the body of the Negro.   It took from eight in the evening until about midnight to open a hole, with a torch and dynamite, and bring out the dead body.   A procession then formed, and the corpse was dragged behind a car to the Negro business district some blocks away.   The crowd sang, yelled, and sounded the horns of cars as it moved along.   When the heart of the Negro district was reached, the body was hung from the limb of a cottonwood tree.   The crowd then broke into a nearby Negro drug store, seizing furniture and furnishings for fuel, at the same time looting the store of money and other goods.   A fire was lighted under the body, and following the burning most of the crowd dispersed and went home.

A portion of the mob, however, continued the campaign of destruction.   Roaming through the Negro district they ransacked and burned many residences and business establishments of Negroes, including a hotel, drug store, two cafes, two barber shops, two dentists' offices, a doctor's office, two undertaking establishments, an Odd Fellows Hall, a Knights of Pythias building, a theater, a lawyer's office, a life insurance office, and a cleaning and pressing shop.   Their expressed intention was to "run all the damn niggers out of Leeville."

During this activity of the mob, the Negro residents took cover elsewhere.   Some hid with white friends and employers, others escaped to the country, in some cases hiding in ditches, ravines, or under houses and bridges all through the night.

The mob was finally dispersed by a larger group of 150 National Guards, armed with machine guns, rifles, side arms, and tear gas. By dawn the town, reinforced with still more troops that came early in the morning, was under control. Soldiers guarded the streets. Martial law was declared, and arrests were made. Tension remained, however, and rumors circulated that the mob would reassemble on the outskirts of the town at dark, attack the soldiers again, and complete the job of driving all of the Negroes out of town permanently by destroying all their dwellings. Still more troops were brought in, and no mob action took place. On some Negro dwellings warnings were attached, and one white employer was notified anonymously that he must discharge his Negro workers and employ whites in their places, but no other hostile actions occurred. Race relations, however, remained strained for many months, and there was much abuse and persecution of the returned Negro citizens for some time.

A military court of investigation went to work and eventually turned over 29 persons and a large amount of confidential evidence to the civil authorities. Public opinion did not, however, give adequate support to the law enforcement processes. A few prominent citizens spoke out against the mob—one prominent minister who censured the affair from his pulpit was visited by a committee of his church members and advised to avoid the subject if he wished to retain his position—but most others who presumably disapproved maintained a discreet silence. When the military court specifically invited public-spirited citizens to give confidential testimony, virtually none of the persons who are ordinarily presumed to be community leaders—businessmen, bankers, pastors, teachers, attorneys, college alumni—took this opportunity to cooperate. Most of the 64 persons who did give information were ordered to appear, and of these half or more were evasive, either from fear of retribution or from their sympathy with the actions of the crowd.

Eventually only 14 men and boys were indicted. These were taken to a jail in a large city south of Leeville, where a trial took place, after much delay on the part of the county attorney. The court, however, failed to find a jury of men who would agree to convict even if the defendants were proved guilty. The trial was then held in the capital city of the state, and, more than a year after the lynching, one young man, who had previously been involved with the law on other charges, was sentenced to a two-year term for arson. Even this brief sentence was not served in full, for a petition from Leeville citizens gained his release on an order from the governor, on the ground of illness of the prisoner's mother. The other 13 defendants were not put on trial.

The author of the study of the Leeville lynching was able to gather some information on 58 persons who took an active part in the mob. Of these, 19 were unemployed, 13 were common laborers, 8 were farmers, 8 were skilled laborers, and the remaining 10 were salaried persons, owners of small businesses, or miscellaneous in occupation. At least 11 of the most active members were known to have previous police records.

The acknowledged leader of the mob was a 40-year-old illiterate, with no regular profession. He did some cattle trading, and some bronco busting in rodeos. He drank a great deal, and was known to officers as a "rough and ready bully." He had been in trouble with the law several times as a bootlegger. He lived in a shabby part of town with his wife and young daughter, near some Negro shanties. He owned no property, and did not belong to a church. Although he lived largely on the earnings of his wife, who took in washing, he was described at the trial as a brave protector of womanhood. A few years after the lynching he was killed in a drunken brawl on a sheep ranch.

The boy who received the sentence lived with his widowed mother, who was a low-paid worker in a shirt factory. He had a record of truancy from an early age and of chicken and cattle stealing and had been in prison for these offenses. Another of the active men later became involved in a rape case. Others were a chronic drunkard, a hobo who slept in the city park and stole bread and milk from doorsteps for his breakfast, a feeble-minded boy 18 years old, and five high school boys who were said by school officials to be problem boys, "overgrown and hungry for notoriety."

The Leeville lynching is typical of the standard pattern in southern regions. In so far as information is available, it appears that the principal participants in such crowds are persons who are relatively detached from stable community life. They are the persons whose status is most in jeopardy when Negroes rise in position, and they are the ones who have the least to lose by violence. Public officials hesitate to interfere too strongly where there are large numbers of voters in this class, for to antagonize this section of the public would endanger their careers.

It appears evident that the orgiastic character of the mob violence presents a pleasurable opportunity for many members to feel important—perhaps noble—and at the same time to give uninhibited release to all of the minor irritations that have arisen in their relations with Negroes, and to a certain extent in recent years to serve as an answer or a challenge to outside Northern agitators who have encouraged Negroes to work toward a higher political and economic status.

The Race Riot.—When the power of two antagonistic races in a community becomes somewhat more evenly matched, the uneven conflict of lynching is not possible—instead the battle becomes a two-way affair and constitutes a riot, or a small-scale war. This becomes possible in northern regions, particularly in the large cities where major areas are populated by tens and hundreds of thousands of Negroes, which constitute the local majority. Losing the daily habit of deferring to white people in every respect, such Negroes react with collective violence when crowd action is taken against them. Two crowds in conflict are even more difficult to stop than one, and the equilibrium following the active fighting is more difficult to establish.

The Chicago Race Riot of 1919.—One of the most spectacular riots of modern times between the Negro and white races took place in Chicago soon after the first world war. Negroes had been imported to the city in large numbers to relieve the acute wartime shortage of labor in the large industries, and they were severely crowded in some of the worst slums of the city.[11] The Negro population in fact had more than doubled since 1910, growing from 44,000 to 110,000 in the decade. Their experience in the northern environment, however, did not live up to their expectations of freedom from race discrimination. Their efforts to live in, and enjoy recreation in, new areas were opposed by the whites already there. In some industries, the use of Negroes to break strikes led to antagonism toward them on the part of organized laborers. Added to this was a considerable amount of torment and persecution at the hands of gangs of young delinquent boys and of men who fought Negroes for the sport of it.

The atmosphere of racial tension was further increased by news of riots elsewhere. A number of minor conflicts had occurred, and two years before the Chicago riot a large and highly destructive riot in East Saint Louis had lasted for a week.

The Chicago riot also endured for a week. It involved the deaths of 38 persons and the injury of 537 others, and it made

---

[11] The material is taken from *The Negro in Chicago* by the Chicago Commission on Race Relations, published by the University of Chicago Press in 1922.

about a thousand persons homeless and destitute. Although both sides suffered, the toll in numbers was heavier for the Negro population.

The occasion for the outbreak had as its background a conflict over the use of lake-front beaches for swimming. These beaches were not part of the public park system but were used by persons who wished to enter the lake at their own risk. By a tacit understanding the Negro and white groups kept to separate areas—an area near Twenty-seventh Street being used by the Negroes, and an area near Twenty-ninth by whites. Both groups observed an imaginary boundary extending into the water.

On Sunday, July 27, 1919, at about four o'clock in the afternoon, a young Negro named Eugene Williams entered the water at the place used by Negroes and swam and drifted south into the water occupied by whites. At the same time, four Negroes entered the shore part where the whites were and went into the lake from there. White men ordered them away, and the four left but soon came back with other Negroes. A series of attacks and retreats, with stone-throwing, took place. Williams, remaining out in the water, held on to a log. Stones fell into the water near him. A white boy of about the same age swam toward him, and Williams let go the log, swam a few strokes, and then sank. There were no stone bruises on him—the coroner's jury later rendered a verdict of drowning, caused by fear of stone-throwing which kept him from the shore.

Several Negroes on the shore put blame on a certain white man and demanded of a white policeman that he be arrested, but without success. A crowd grew as persons dived for an hour or so for the body. Whispers and rumors circulated through the crowd. The Negroes said that the boy was stoned to death, and that the policeman had refused to arrest the murderer. Tension mounted as the Negroes massed together, and, when the accused policeman arrested a Negro on a white man's complaint, the Negroes mobbed the officer and the riot was under way.

A group of policemen were summoned to the scene. A Negro man fired into the group and was shot and killed by a Negro policeman who had also been sent to restore order. From then on the action took place at various places on the South Side. Many of the Negro men from Twenty-ninth Street stayed together and attacked such white men as they encountered—beating four, stabbing five, and shooting one. Meanwhile new crowds gathered as the rumors went about, and a general war without organization raged about the Negro districts.   White gangsters joined in the action and during the first night beat 27 Negroes, stabbed seven, and shot four.

On Monday morning people of both races went to work as usual, even to places where they worked side by side, but in the afternoon groups of white men and boys waylaid Negro workers returning home.   Groups gathered along streetcar routes, particularly at transfer points, to pull the trolleys from the wires, drag out the Negro passengers and subject them to beatings.   The actions were too numerous to be controlled by the police, and during the afternoon four Negro men and one white man were killed, and 30 Negro men were severely beaten.   Negro groups similarly assaulted whites, and one elderly Italian peddler and a white laundryman were stabbed to death and robbed by Negro groups.

When two white men, who had been shooting at Negroes from a speeding automobile, were injured and taken to a hospital conducted by Negroes, a Negro mob gathered outside of the hospital to make a demonstration.   Other Negro mobs stabbed six white men, shot five, severely beat nine more, and killed two others.   When a rumor went about that a white man in a certain apartment building had shot a Negro boy from a fourth-story window, a crowd of Negroes laid siege to the building.   A call for rescue went out, and about a hundred policemen, some mounted, appeared.   The mob demanded that they bring out the man who had been shooting, but a search by the police failed to locate him.   A brick was then thrown, hitting a policeman.   The police fired into the crowd, killing four and injuring many others.

By this time both races were in a panic.   Each race drew apart from the other.   Small bands roved about to terrorize and kill, many of these being boys and young men partly motivated by the excitement of the conflict.   Many cars went at high speeds through Negro districts with gunfire pouring out in all directions.   Negroes formed barricades and volleyed and sniped from ambush.   Their fear led them in many cases to fire at any motor vehicle they saw, without first establishing the intentions of its occupants.

At midnight on Monday all streetcar service ended because of a strike and was not resumed during the week.   On Tuesday, therefore, many persons walked to work, and there were more killings of those who had to pass through hostile territory.   Gang rioting increased, and one gang of white soldiers and sailors in uniform, joined by civilians, raided the downtown section of the city, killing two Negroes and beating and robbing several others.

Some property of white businessmen was wantonly destroyed at the same time.

Gangs roving in districts far to the south broke into the homes of Negroes, stealing and destroying furniture. Several houses were burned. On the West Side, where many Italians lived, a rumor circulated that led an Italian group to kill a Negro man.

The fighting continued through Wednesday, largely in the Negro district and areas immediately to the west, but at a slightly diminished rate. The militia, which had been held ready since Monday night, was finally called in by the mayor.

On Wednesday night and all day Thursday rain kept many persons at home and cooled tempers, but sporadic violence continued. On Friday only one injury was reported. But on Saturday, 49 houses in the neighborhood to the west of the Negro district, an area populated largely by Lithuanians, were set afire, destroying about $250,000 in property and rendering homeless 948 people. No further rioting took place after that day, and about a week later the militia withdrew.

Observers stated that, in each crowd involved in violence, there had been a large group of sympathizing onlookers, and a small active nucleus of persons who did the violent work. The active persons were mostly young men between 16 and 21. In the typical case from 4 to 25 would be active, while from one to two or three hundred would be looking on. In some cases a larger crowd would gather as the action proceeded, attracted by curiosity more than by sympathy with the actions of violence. It is probable, however, that their presence, as a responding audience, stimulated and encouraged the active members to do the fighting. In one case a Negro, being pursued by active white members, outstripped all others of the mob by climbing fences and hiding in a back yard. The few pursuers who succeeded in locating him lost their determination to harm him and left without striking a blow. The violence apparently required the support of the war cries of an excited mob.

The size of the supporting crowds apparently is a factor in the amount of violence committed by the active fighters. Thus many persons unwittingly contributed to the assaults merely by their presence. Inquiries revealed that a number of onlookers utterly lacked hostility toward the victims of the mob and were not aware of the fact that their presence added to the conflict. Interviewers recorded such statements as: "I didn't have any grudge against them [the Negroes]. But they [the mob] seemed to have it in for the colored people, That is all." "I followed the crowd, and I was in there because I was in there; they all bunched around and what could I do?" "I just wanted to see how things were getting along. We wanted to see what the riot looked like." "I was following the rest. I wanted to see what they were going to do." "When they started to grab them [the Negroes] in the lot, I rushed over directly to the conflict, by the colored men, thinking I would see more on that side."

For a period and to a degree impossible to measure, race relations were strained. Bitterness, distrust, and fear remained on both sides. Many white persons held a belief that Negroes were gathering stores of arms and ammunition for a future riot. Negro anxiety was perhaps even greater, and some of this group urged their fellow Negroes to carry arms and fight if attacked. It is probable that a permanent increase in hostility toward whites, and in political solidarity of Negroes, were among the effects of the riot.

**The Detroit Race Riot of 1943.**—The city of Detroit experienced a rapid industrial growth similar to that of Chicago and developed, some years later, a situation of racial tension closely analogous to that of 1919 in Chicago.[12]  Trends of the prewar period intensified rapidly during the period of the second world war and built up a set of racial tensions which were almost unprecedented in severity. Detroit had grown rapidly with the expansion of the automobile and other machinery industries and was already overcrowded before the war boom developed. From 1940 to 1943 approximately half a million new residents entered the city, of whom about 60,000 were Negroes. Among the whites who entered at the same time there were a large number from southern regions—Tennessee, Kentucky, and adjacent areas where there was at the time a labor surplus. These whites, competing for jobs and homes with Negroes, were unaccustomed to standards of cooperation in northern regions and were quick to resent the challenge to white supremacy as they had known it in their former regions of residence.

At the same time a pressure of collective resentment had been developing within the Negro group. Hopes of more favorable status, built up during the Roosevelt administration and intensified during the early period of the war, were adversely affected by practices of segregation in the armed forces and by the limitation of opportunities for promotion. Negroes expressed particularly strong resentment at the policy of the Red Cross, which stored Negro blood and plasma separately from white persons' blood. This latter policy

[12] Information on the Detroit riot is taken from Alfred McClung Lee and Norman D. Humphrey, *Race Riot*, New York: The Dryden Press, Inc., 1943.

was considered an unnecessary insult, for Negroes in general were aware of the scientific judgment that the blood plasma of the two races is not distinguishable and that no harm could result from using both types on any patients. Leadership within the Negro race, through such organizations as the National Association for the Advancement of Colored People, and through political and other figures, provided information on developments of this type and sustained a general alertness and sensitivity among the Negro population.

Physical friction between the races occurred in connection with use of inadequate facilities for housing, recreation, and transportation. These facilities had been inadequately developed and maintained during the depression of the 1930's and were inadequate even before the rapid war expansion added its crushing burden. The desperate housing crisis became the occasion of a brief conflict in February, 1942, when both white and Negro groups expected to occupy the homes in a new housing project known as Sojourner Truth Homes. Indecision of housing officials caused it to be promised to one group and then to the other in turn and back again. The final decision favored the Negroes, but on the day scheduled for occupation, a crowd of several hundred white persons attempted to keep them out with threats, beatings, and stonings.

Friction also developed in factories. In an automobile plant the promotion of three Negro workers to the assembly line led to the walkout of 3,000 workers. In general Negroes were employed in lower proportions than were whites and were placed in lower categories of work. A prominent Negro leader on one occasion accused officials of an automobile plant of actually encouraging rioting against Negroes.

The general social disorganization that is characteristic of urban slums and becomes particularly severe following periods of rapid growth was also observed in Detroit. Rates of delinquency, crime, and vice were high in the same kind of areas as in other cities, and there were large numbers of delinquent boys of both races who were susceptible to the lure of a fight.

The readiness for conflict of the Detroit population was further assisted by such organizations as the Christian Front, the Black Legion, and the Ku Klux Klan, which for some years had been organizing the population against Negroes, Jews, Catholics, foreigners, and radicals. These organizations left a residue of suspicion and false belief among the uneducated sections of the population. An illustration of resulting attitudes is furnished by a rumor in which it was stated that a battle was expected between Jews and

Negroes, and that the governor was preparing to send 15,000 soldiers.

When tensions and hostility are raised to the degree experienced at this time in Detroit, it does not require more than a trivial inter-personal conflict between members of the two races to start a large-scale riot. In the Detroit affair the fighting began on the evening of June 20, 1943, at Belle Island Park. It was the close of a hot and humid Sunday on which large crowds had sought recreation on the playground and beach of this large city park. It was estimated that some 100,000 persons were on the island, of whom about 85 per cent were Negroes. Irritations were inevitable, and four complaints of insult and injury were made to police by both Negro and white picnickers during the hours preceding the riot.

As is often the case, there were several versions of the outbreak. A newspaper reported that it started with a fist fight between a Negro and a white man. Another version held that a Negro baby had been thrown from the bridge by whites, and it was also held that a white baby had been thrown in by Negroes. Others believed that Negroes insulted or attacked white girls on the bridge, or in the water at the beach. The county prosecutor stated that the fight was started by a gang of teen-aged colored boys and girls who set out in the early evening to drive all whites from Belle Isle and began by beating a white boy, after which they attacked a man and his wife as the latter were eating a picnic lunch. Whatever the true version, it is unquestionable that there were many members of either race capable of starting a minor fight, and that at the particular scene it was almost certain that any small interracial fight would spread to a general riot, regardless of the merits of the original quarrel.

Within a short time hundreds were involved in the conflict. By 10:30 P.M. some 200 white sailors were fighting on the bridge with Negroes, and additional men of both races were entering the fight. The riot spread to the mainland and fanned out from there, becoming particularly severe in the Negro slum section. Small roving groups of both races were formed to pursue and beat up individuals or groups of the opposite faction. A Negro is reported to have shouted into a microphone at a night club, urging the Negro patrons to attack a group of white persons who "killed a colored woman and her baby at Belle Isle Park." At the same time a rumor circu-lated among the whites to the effect that Negroes had raped and killed a white woman on the bridge.

For a period during the night casualties were arriving at a leading hospital at the rate of one a minute. Negro groups stabbed a white man in the chest, fractured a policeman's skull, stopped a streetcar and stoned white factory workers, and others began to loot stores and to destroy property of white persons. White groups stoned the automobiles of Negroes and stood at the exits of certain theaters and beat the Negroes as they emerged from the shows. A police inspector reported to the commissioner that the situation was out of control, especially in the Negro slum district. During the next day the fighting continued, some of it on the main streets and in the downtown area, where gangs of young white men stopped and burned Negro cars and assaulted lone Negroes. Officials conferred, but a Negro request for federal troops was not granted, as the mayor and governor did not wish to declare martial law.

An eyewitness described one of the characteristic assaults as follows:[13]

There was an automobile burning on Woodward, and up a side street a Negro was being horribly beaten. Eventually the mob let the Negro go, and he staggered down to the car tracks, and he tried to get on a streetcar. But the car wouldn't stop for him.

The Negro was punch-drunk. There were policemen down the street, but they didn't pay any attention to him.

I started shouting, "Hey, copper. Hey, copper." And I pointed to the Negro in the middle of the street. The policeman finally took notice of me, but instead of going in the direction in which I was pointing he walked over to his parked scout car. Then two huge hoodlums began to slug the Negro, and he hung there on the side of the safety zone, taking the punches as if he were a bag of sand. That infuriated me, and I yelled even louder to the cops, all the time gesturing towards the Negro.

Finally the police started walking slowly toward the fight, which in the meantime had moved down the street. Then the crowd started pushing me around, but I kept moving and kept my fists up near my chest, and the crowd moved after the much tastier and more permissible Negro game.

Attacks were made on high school boys as they emerged from their school buildings. A typical incident is described by a witness:[14]

Jim was no more than out of the school yard when a white boy hit him in the stomach with a baseball bat. The Negro turned around and ran quickly to a parked car in which two women teachers were sitting. The teachers quickly let him into their car, but the driver in her excitement flooded the engine.

Meanwhile white rioters began to crowd around the car, and one who had an axe started to chop in the roof.

[13] *Ibid.*, p. 32. The witness is N. D. Humphrey, co-author of the book.
[14] *Ibid.*, p. 34.

Before the mob got too large to "make a break-through," the colored boy dashed for the school building. He entered it and locked the door. By this time a considerable gang had gathered on the front steps of the building, and the police were called to disperse the mob and take the boy to safety.

Downtown action was described by an observer who watched from a window high in an office building:[15]

Without being able to understand the cries, it was obvious that one in the mob would yell something like, "There's black meat! Let's get 'im!" Then the hoodlums would spill like quicksilver toward that unfortunate. The rioters, who immediately surrounded the victim, acted as though they were embarrassed and didn't know what to do in most cases. Hoodlums standing back in the gang would sidle toward the Negro and hit him from behind an unwilling shield.

Then the police would come with tear gas, and that particular demonstration would dissolve. But in a few moments you could see a leader running toward another Negro and gesticulating, and the quicksilver would begin to pour towards that new focus. One had an overpowering sense of irresponsibility, of Hallowe'en marauding at its worst. It was hard to keep from permitting the laboratory-table analogy to "get you," to convince yourself that somehow those were human beings and not small laboratory animals strangely different from guinea pigs.

The peak of the riot was reached early Monday evening, about 24 hours after its beginning. A large crowd of white people moved toward the Negro slum district in Paradise Valley and were checked on the edge of the district by police. As the mob kept trying to cross a boundary highway, surging back and forth, milling and shouting, shots came from a Negro hotel nearby. A policeman was wounded in the back as he came out of his car, and the Negro who shot him was instantly fired upon and killed. As more police arrived, general shooting from the hotel windows rained down. The police returned the fire and threw tear gas bombs. After some steady fire by about fifty police, shooting from the hotel windows ceased, but sniping commenced from an apartment building a block away, and the police turned their attack in that direction. Eventually the firing ceased, the crowd of about a thousand persons was dispersed, and officers entered the darkened building with drawn pistols. Dozens of Negroes were brought out and sent to hospitals and jails.

On the same day, in certain of the Negro districts, looting and destruction of property owned by whites was carried on by Negroes. Negro stores were not harmed—some were protected by signs indicating the race of the owner. A Negro reporter observed "men with

---

[15] *Ibid.*, p. 36. The observer is A. M. Lee, co-author of the study.

arms full of liquor bottles run from the building while, just a few doors below, two men carried a quarter of beef through the smashed open front of what, until Sunday night, had been a grocery store." Some gangs of looters are said to have engaged in destruction of property "as if they had gone berserk."[16]

Late Monday evening the governor requested and obtained from President Roosevelt a proclamation calling on military forces to quell the disorder, and the presence of the soldiers rapidly restored peace, except for slight disturbances that took place during the following days. Six thousand troops occupied strategic points in the city, and the civil authorities undertook the work of finding the origins of the riot and of administering justice. The population, however, remained nervous for some time, and there were rumors that fighting would recommence as soon as the soldiers left. One Negro woman stated that she had heard that white men were planning to wait until things were quiet and then to return and burn out the whole Negro district.

A week later, on Monday, June 28th, the governor removed restrictions on civilians, except for the ban on sales of bottled liquor. Federal troops remained for some weeks while National Guard men were trained to succeed them in maintaining order.

In the study that followed, it was apparent again in this riot that a large part of the active rioting crowd consisted of young persons, already somewhat delinquent or uncontrolled, who participated less from a particular grievance against members of the other race than from the general thrill of excitement of a fight. In the tense atmosphere some young boys appeared to be exceptionally suggestible and capable of impulsive actions outside of their normal inclinations. One boy, member of a group of four in their late teens, explained the shooting of an elderly Negro as follows:[17]

We didn't have anything to do. We were just bumming around. Bob ——— and Blackie ——— were in the poolroom. We wanted to see the fighting, but we didn't want to go where we would get hurt.

We had my gun along. It was my car. Aldo was driving. Someone—I don't know who—said: "Let's go out and kill us a nigger." We agreed that it was a good idea.

We drove around for a long time. We saw a lot of colored people, but they were in bunches. We didn't want any of that. We wanted some guy all by himself. We saw one on Mack Avenue.

Aldo drove past him and then said, "Gimme that gun." I handed it over to him and he turned around and came back. We were about 15 feet from

---

[16] *Ibid.*, p. 34.
[17] *Ibid.*, pp. 37–38.

the man when Aldo pulled up, almost stopped and shot. The man fell and we blew.

We didn't know him. He wasn't bothering us. But other people were fighting and killing, and we felt like it too.

A police officer described some of the rioters of a somewhat older age group: [18]

I recognized a lot of those fellows. We've had lots of trouble with them before. The whites that did most of the car burning on Woodward were from gangs of Italians, Syrians, and others who hang around bars and poolrooms, and in 'peacetime' pull false alarms and that sort of thing. Almost all of them have police records. And it was the same type of Negro who did most of the fire-setting in Paradise Valley.

The number of casualties was almost the same for the two races—the City Receiving Hospital treated 222 white persons and 211 Negroes during the first 24 hours of the fighting. Serious injuries were somewhat more numerous for Negro victims, however, and of the 17 deaths 14 were Negro. It is estimated that loss from property destruction amounted to approximately two millions of dollars. Other costs, not easy to estimate, include the expense of the Federal troops, the loss of production from increase of absenteeism in factories, and the cost of relief to sufferers.

**The Los Angeles Riots of 1943.**—In June, 1943, rioting that had a racial aspect broke out in the city of Los Angeles. The city contained a large Mexican-American population, only partly assimilated, and subject to a pattern of discrimination something like that directed against Negroes. The American-born children of this nationality group resented their low status among other native Americans, and at the same time did not wish to return to the culture and status of their Mexican-born parents. In this situation of cultural marginality they developed a pattern of symbolic revolt. Their style of clothing, elsewhere assumed by both Negro and white youth as an expression of rebellion against traditional ways, consisted of the "zoot-suit"—a costume involving exaggerated peg-top trousers, long loose coat, long watch chains, "ducktail" haircut, and other unconventional features. These *pachucos,* as they are locally designated, were particularly resentful of uniformed authority and made frequent gestures of defiance against police and members of the armed services. Some roving gangs made knife attacks on Navy men who went through the streets alone, with the result that gangs

---

[18] *Ibid.,* p. 81.

of soldiers and sailors formed to fight back. Newspaper headlines played up the incidents with sensationalism and kept the mob excitement at a high pitch for many days. There were fewer deaths and injuries than in the Detroit strike, but a longer duration of the conflict.

A Price Riot in Brazil.—In early September, 1946, a brief outbreak of violence in Rio de Janeiro developed suddenly and apparently spontaneously as a reaction against high prices and other aspects of the postwar economic deterioration.[19] Inflation had there, as elsewhere, put prices of many commodities out of reach of a large proportion of the population. As food prices rose, many slum dwellers searched through the scraps from the public markets, and through garbage collections, to avoid starvation. Hospitals were crowded with children of whom a high proportion were severe malnutrition cases. The economic basis of the nation was in bad shape. A coffee glut kept millions of tons in warehouses while many coffee farms had to be abandoned. Industrialization had not been sufficiently developed to yield a visible amount of relief. An enormous and expensive luxury hotel which was expected to attract tourists from all over the world remained virtually empty.

Tempers were quickened by a hot spell that reduced the volume of drinking water to an uncomfortably low level. Smells, insects, and skin diseases added to the irritation. The occasion for the beginning of the riot was the death of a seventeen-year-old high school boy who had eaten a tainted cream puff. A crowd of students attacked the shop that sold the bad food. The riot then broadened during the next two days into a general protest of the poor against profiteering establishments. Stores and motion picture theaters were wrecked, and pitched battles were fought against police. The riot was checked only through the declaration of martial law and the use of groups of special police in addition to soldiers. In response to the riot, to talk of a crusade against the black market, and to talk even of revolution, the president took measures to increase the food supply. Among merchants, however, there was discussion of even higher prices.

SUMMARY

Mass behavior is a collective reaction to a general sentiment that the existing order is not functioning in a satisfactory manner. Something is not going as it should, and a spirit of unrest conse-

---

[19] *Time,* Sept. 9, 1946.

quently pervades the population.  As the old ways, or the existing ways, are found wanting, attention turns to possibilities that are new, or at least different.

When the dissatisfaction concerns minor aspects of life, the restlessness may be expressed merely by a contagious interest in novelty.  Enthusiasm for fad and fashion does not exist in the successful periods of highly integrated societies, but develops in such populations as the secularized urban dwellers who live in socially unstable conditions in which traditions are weak and precedents do not fit.  Once attention becomes centered on certain forms of novelty, these become values in themselves, and those who are swept into the mass enthusiasm develop a mild form of panic in their efforts to be among the first to adopt the new things.

Booms and financial panics grow out of a sense of maladjustment in the economic order.  During a period of rising prices and therefore of depreciation of the value of currency, the persons who continue to rely on fixed income and on savings to provide for their present and future needs may acquire a sense of being left behind, of losing ground.  As others pass them by, achieving higher incomes or even fortunes through speculation, the uneasiness becomes more intense.  Stories and rumors spread through populations, alert to the conditions—tales of quick gains at small risk—until more and more become involved in the boom fever.  Once the decision is made to join in the rush, haste becomes important.  It is necessary to beat the crowds to the field of speculation, else the early arrivals will have skimmed the cream of the profits.  The sight of others who are also rushing adds to the haste, which then takes a panic character.

The financial panic is a similar rush in an opposite direction—toward getting rid of real values and putting property into liquid form.  The fall of prices makes money more important.  As the drop threatens banks and credit, it makes money more scarce, so that it becomes important to beat others to selling and to withdrawing money from banks.  Money, banking, and economic life in general rest on an integrated structure of general public confidence, and when this becomes substantially weakened, teamwork disintegrates and individuals rush, each for his own sake, to further his own interest in disregard of the welfare of others.

Political unrest similarly prepares the ground for such frights as the Martian scare or the "great fear," for local revolts, and for revolutionary movements.  Furthermore, the uncertainties that accompany the operations of warfare and the essential secrecy which leaves the population inadequately informed about the success or failure of military developments permit rumors to flow freely among the population. It was a public unsure of its knowledge of international developments that fled in fright from the Martian Invasion—many believed that it meant that the Germans had made a landing. The study of rumors during the war period showed the relations between distrust of the government and hostile rumors toward the administration. Panics of buying and hoarding also demonstrated the general sense that the social mechanisms of fair distribution of scarce goods did not have the confidence of the public—even those whose confidence held for a time tended to lose nerve as the panics, the price "chiseling," and the black market activities progressed. Some were thus reluctantly tempted to engage in activities which they themselves disapproved, swept in by a panicky fear of being left behind by the general rush.

Race rioting and lynching arise out of challenges to an existing pattern of race relations. In such an interracial system as has long existed in southern states the population is not fully aware of the sociological principles of the equilibrium of Negro-white relations, but most persons are aware that these relations are part of a total system, and that a challenge by Negroes to any aspect of race relations constitutes somewhat of a threat to the whole social system. The threat is not analyzed fully but is sensed by the less educated and sophisticated part of the white population as a disturbing force. Their uneasiness is made stronger by the vague realization that they, the low-income and relatively uneducated whites, would suffer the most obvious loss as Negroes made competitive gains.

It is this section of the southern white population, largely rural or small-town, low in income and educational status, that gives political support to candidates who exploit the race issue and which supports lynchings by active participation as well as by frustrating official efforts to enforce laws against such forms of violence.

A similar section of the northern urban population senses a threat when there occurs a mass invasion of Negroes into industrial areas. Negroes, as any other new entrants to the industrial system, supply a low-wage demand and thus act to depress wages in many large factories. In times of shortages and crowding, also, their competition for houses, places on public transportation vehicles, space in recreation areas, and the like, is also highly visible. Those who preceded the Negroes in such places do not view the newcomer solely as a human being in search of a satisfactory life, but as an organized competitor and a threat to their own status. The tendency toward organization for self-protection and for conflict among the Negroes intensifies the fear and generates an unrest that approaches a panic stage.   Relatively trivial incidents may at this point start an active riot.

Although the background of the riot may be the competitive situation described above, much of the active fighting is done by young persons who are more interested in the excitement and fun of the fight itself than in the pattern of race relations.   The outbreak of riot releases a pattern of criminality for more than ordinary free expression, as young delinquent boys seek victims to kill for the sport of it and participate in wholesale looting.   The role of the crowd apparently is to give encouragement and support to the smaller group of active, and probably largely criminal, fighters.

Since it is the explicit responsibility of government to preserve order in the population, and to solve potential conflicts by peaceful and legal means, any outbreak of mob violence must be interpreted as governmental inadequacy if not actual disorganization.   Studies of some of the major riots of recent years indicate that these were probably preventable if officials had been more alert and prepared to use prompt methods of control.   The use of soldiers and martial law quelled the riot in several instances, following the total failure of local police to stop the disorders.   In general, however, this drastic measure has not been relied upon in time, and a considerable number of the riots have virtually run their course before martial law was declared.   In part this hesitancy, as well as the reluctance to search vigorously and to prosecute and convict the rioters, reflects the responsiveness of the officials of government to politically powerful groups of voters who are to some extent in sympathy with rioters.

Martial law and special police methods are helpful in crises and apparently may curtail or even avert incipient riots.   But full public protection from the disorders of mass behavior depends largely on the general soundness of the political and social order, on the absence of the general failures that have been shown to underlie the mass unrest and the violent reactions.

## SELECTED REFERENCES

Blumer, Herbert.  "Collective Behavior."  Part IV in Park, Robert E., *An Out-line of the Principles of Sociology.*  New York: Barnes & Noble, Inc., 1939.
LaPiere, Richard T.  *Collective Behavior.*  New York: McGraw-Hill Book Co., Inc., 1938.
Park, Robert E., and Burgess, E. W.  *An Introduction to the Science of Sociology.*  Chicago: University of Chicago Press, 1921.  Ch. 13, "Collective Behavior."

# Chapter 14

## PROCESSES OF REORGANIZATION

### Change, Disorganization, and Reorganization

More ancient than history itself is the sense of alarm concerning the rate of social change, the failure of youth to respect the ways of elders, the disintegration of sacred traditions, and the degeneration of morality. From the beginning of history the normal conservatism of human beings has led many to deplore and to fear new inventions and forms of behavior made possible by them. Social disorganization thus, in a sense, began with change itself. Virtually every new element in a social order affects something in an existing system. Therefore it is inevitable that the long process of building civilization is accompanied by almost continuous processes of social disorganization.

During periods, and at places, involving exceptionally rapid change and disorganization, even forecasts of complete disaster become common. Those who are not aware of the possibility that new ways may be developed and may succeed in maintaining essential functions of the society tend to expect utter collapse of the social system and the end of civilization at an early date. Predictions of the downfall of civilization of course occur far more frequently than do actual complete disruptions. If impressions of the trend of history were based solely on the most pessimistic anticipations, it would be difficult to explain why mankind did not become extinct many centuries ago.

There is no reason, however, to doubt the constancy of the disorganization process in history. This process fails to destroy civilization because it is accompanied by various forms of reorganization. Man is a social being and does not prefer to live in a state of anarchy. As old standards and mechanisms disintegrate he finds various means to recreate system in social life. The processes of reorganization are doubtless as variable and as continuous as are those of disorganization.

### Revivals

One of the most obvious means for checking what appears to be a trend of disorganization is to attempt to return to old ways—to revive certain aspects of the cultural system which formerly operated successfully. Revivals vary in scope from a mild collective interest in a limited aspect of some early culture to a general effort to return to a whole system of bygone days. The former type of revival is by far the more common. A great variety of such limited efforts may be observed in modern times. Revival of folk arts persists in America today in the organized support of square dancing and the related antiquarian interests such as old-fashioned fiddling, early Colonial pastimes, furniture, architecture, and the like. The collections assembled at Greenfield Village by Henry Ford express this type of interest. Collections include McGuffey's Readers, themselves the subject of a brief sentimental celebration in the 1930's, and the little schoolhouse from Sterling, Massachusetts, where "Mary had a little lamb." Discovery and popularization of folk arts of minority peoples is a related phenomenon. Recent years have witnessed revivals of interest in early Pennsylvania Dutch art, glassware, furniture, and architecture, as well as the folk arts of early Quebec. In California native Americans have taken an interest not only in Mission architecture, but more recently in present-day Mexican folk arts, including glassware, dancing, cooking, and other crafts. While such concerns as these are not expected to solve all problems of modern social disorganization, their supporters usually claim that the expression of such interests does have a beneficial effect beyond that of mere recreation.

Architectural revivals vary from the reflections of ancient Greece and Rome in nineteenth century American homes and the current interest in Colonial and Georgian styles, to the more expensive and earnest restorations of entire settlements, as in Williamsburg, Virginia, where the pre-Revolutionary buildings were re-erected on their original sites and completely furnished in the original manner. The large and ambitious projects stand as symbols of a past which remains glorious in the minds of those who support them. Mussolini's restoration of ruins of early Roman structures was meant to arouse the modern Italians' pride in the greatness of the Roman Empire and to stimulate the nation toward new efforts at expansion.

Nationalistic revivals are expressed not only in architecture but also in other aspects of national heritages. The Irish have fostered the use of the ancient Gaelic language as a part of their movement toward nationalism. The Jewish effort to keep alive the Hebrew language has in part a similar meaning. Parallels may be found among peoples all over the world.

Religious revivals occur almost continuously in the United States to this day. Barnstorming preachers pass from town to town, camp meetings are held frequently in villages and rural areas, and religious proselyters of many denominations as well as those of the Salvation Army operate almost continuously on the transients of large cities. During the nineteenth century and before, some mass conversions and enduring organizations resulted from such revival efforts, but it is probable that the very thoroughness of the evangelistic coverage of the American population has reached the near limit of diminishing returns. In recent years the only spectacular gain by a religious movement has been that of an unconventional form of revival which was aimed at a section of the population relatively untouched by the old-fashioned revival meeting. This recent movement is the one variously known as the Oxford Group, Moral Rearmament, and Buchmanism.[1]

Dr. Frank N. Buchman, a former Lutheran minister from Pennsylvania, adapted the technique of conversion-to-Christianity to the manners of the upper social and educational classes. The highly emotional mass revival meetings had never had great success among these people, but Buchman learned at the leading English universities to approach persons quietly, discuss with them their personal attitudes toward religion, and achieve an unspectacular conversion or "change" in their lives. He developed techniques of spreading this form of conversion, sending teams to strategic places and holding house parties at which religion would be discussed, confessions made before small groups, and lives "changed" by conversion. Following this event, it was held that the person would be subject to direct guidance by God and that he would be expected to work actively to change others.

Buchman directed his efforts toward well-to-do persons and persons who were highly influential. At various times he sought and obtained cooperation from leading churchmen of various denominations and from many political, business, and intellectual leaders. His belief was that the persons at the top were of the greatest importance, and he once stated that the world would benefit through a fascist dictatorship if the leader could be converted to his principles. Although he never achieved his wish to "change" Hitler or Mussolini, he did enlist in support of his "Moral Rearmament" campaign a considerable number of persons of prominence and influence. In England these included Earl Baldwin, former Prime

---

[1] An analytical account of Buchmanism may be found in Hadley Cantril, *The Psychology of Social Movements* (New York: John Wiley & Sons, Inc., 1941, pp. 144–168). Most of the material in the present discussion is taken from this source.

Minister, some 25 peers in high government positions, and a large following of industrialists, journalists, and prominent athletes. In the United States he succeeded at various times in obtaining some cooperation or endorsement from such persons as Mayor LaGuardia of New York City, Henry Ford of the automobile industry, Joe DiMaggio in professional baseball, and Congressman Joseph Martin of Massachusetts. The degree of understanding of the movement by these supporters varies, but in some cases it is slight. Martin, for example, is reported in a news magazine to have endorsed it ". . . whatever it is. It's just like being against sin."

Part of the success of Buchmanism may be attributed to the use made of modern techniques of commerce. Slogans have been developed with efficiency approaching that of modern advertising practice.

An unknown but probably large proportion of those attracted to the movement has consisted of relatively successful but restless young persons who found their lives of business activity, golf, and cocktail parties empty. Following conversion at a house party, these persons found their lives to contain a new meaning, which they hoped would not only provide them with satisfaction, but also spread to operate as a general reforming influence in the country and the world. As the novelty wore off, however, and as the course of world events continued without showing any effects of Moral Rearmament, the movement failed to hold their interest. No organization was formed to hold the "changed" persons together—it was the intention that each would return to his own denomination and work from there, but few organized churches gave encouragement to the methods of this new group. Buchmanism was somewhat checked also by the disapproval, by conventional church people, of the group confessions at house parties, for in many cases these were reported to consist of a series of lurid descriptions of sexual license. Public expressions by Buchman such as the one mentioned above made persons of prominence less willing to lend their names to endorsement of the movement, and during the second world war it virtually disappeared from sight.

## SOCIAL MOVEMENTS

Many attempts to remedy conditions of social disorganization take the form of an effort to organize a permanent structure of social relations to deal directly with the undesirable conditions. Social movements, in fact, arise almost continually in a changing civilization.  They vary from small, short-lived organizations of limited scope to enduring and comprehensive revolutionary movements. They represent conscious and intentional collective effort to repair a social structure which appears to be disintegrating.  In their nature and their courses of development, they reflect the type of apprehension present in the population, the direction of collective desires, and other variable conditions.  Some begin quietly and grow steadily into large and enduring institutions, while others originate in a wave of collective excitement and enthusiasm and run through a course of settling down toward conventionality, and in some cases even to corruption and disintegration.[2]  Movements may be classified in various ways, but will be treated here under four headings: (1) unconventional or "crank" movements, (2) movements with limited objectives, (3) general reform movements, and (4) revolutionary movements.[3]

**Unconventional or "Crank" Movements.**—Among certain elements of the population in which the eagerness for a quick and simple solution of the troubles of civilization is not matched by a correspondingly high level of education, there occasionally arises a theory containing an easy remedy, often based on a single principle or practice.  Diet is a frequent element in such a theory.  It has been held by uneducated extremists, for example, that the practice of meat-eating is the cause of war, depression, great floods, and other major catastrophes.[4]  The obvious solution, therefore, is to enlist mankind in a great collective drive to eliminate the evils by this particular means.  To this exciting purpose men enthusiastically devote their fanatical energies, and often by their zeal and force of character persuade a number of bewildered persons to submit to their leadership.

An idea for such a movement may occur almost anywhere, but recruits are not as available in settled and conventional communities as in large cities where many socially detached and unsatisfied persons are to be found.  In general it is the largest cities which furnish the best ground for the expansion of these highly unconventional movements, but one city, Los Angeles, appears to be the most hos-

---

[2] An excellent sociological analysis of social movements is contained in Carl A. Dawson's and Warner E. Gettys's *Introduction to Sociology,* New York: The Ronald Press Co., 1948, Ch. 25, pp. 678–714.
[3] These overlapping and somewhat illogical categories are employed here because of their relation to the type and seriousness of the social disorganization to which the movements respond.
[4] Though based on inadequate knowledge, many such theories are not without rationalization.  Floods may be attributed to meat-eating, for example, through the importance of corn as food for hogs—corn-growing leaves the ground bare and permits rains to run off quickly, causing floods.

pitable of all.   Southern California is primarily a land of migrants, a goal for restless persons of many kinds from all parts of the country.   It contains a high proportion of old, isolated, dissatisfied persons.   Many are concerned about their health and originally sought the region in the hope of improving it.   Circumstances selected a population more inclined toward mysticism and superstition than toward intellectualism and science.   Such a population is susceptible to many kinds of social currents, including booms, panics, suicide waves, gambling crazes, and others.

A recent journalistic study of Southern California finds that this region has been a favorable place for cultism for a century.[5]   In 1841 there arrived in Los Angeles a quack doctor named William Money who founded what is said to be the first cult in the region. It was called "The Reformed New Testament Church of the Faith of Jesus Christ" and contained elements of both health and financial-success magic.   Characteristically he included among his prophecies a statement that San Francisco stood on a section of earth which would soon collapse into the hot interior and be destroyed.

In 1900 there was founded in San Diego a community centering about yogi elements.   Its leader, Katherine Tingley, who called herself "The Purple Mother," ruled the Point Loma Theosophical Community with despotism, but the colorful and splendid atmosphere of the community attracted many followers.   The forty buildings were in mixed architectural style, in which Egyptian and Moorish elements were conspicuous.   Amethyst Egyptian gateways, opalescent green domes, Greek theaters, buildings of as many as ninety rooms, hidden buglers announcing the arrival of visitors—all provided an appealing splendor.   New members were expected to present The Purple Mother with a sizeable "love offering," after which they partook of the life of agriculture, chicken-raising, and silkworm cultivation, accompanied by lectures on matters of theosophy by yogis in Greek costumes.   The number of adherents— presumably persons who yearned for splendor and felt lost in the complexity of modern life and who desired authoritarian domination—was stated by the organization itself to be 100,000, including members in other parts of the world.   The eccentricity of the movement was too much for more conventional California neighbors, however, and gossip spread, hinting at scandal.   In 1923 Mrs. Tingley deserted the community, following a judgment against her in an alienation of affections suit.

---

[5] Carey McWilliams, *Southern California Country*, New York: Duell, Sloan and Pearce, 1946, p. 251.   Much of the material on cultism in Los Angeles is taken from this work.

A somewhat similar community, Krotona, was founded in Los Angeles by Albert Powell Warrington, who came to the city in 1911. Krotona contained elements of Oriental mysticism, with a Greek theater, an occult temple, and a psychic lotus pond, all appealing to a culture-hungry population. For the health faddists there was a vegetarian cafeteria, and for self-development there were courses in music and drama, the human aura, and Esperanto. Enough writers and artists of various kinds were attracted to make Krotona something of a force in Los Angeles, and a number of books, as well as the Theater Arts Alliance, which became responsible for the Hollywood Bowl concerts, emerged from the activities of the members. A contemporary settlement at Ojai is an offshoot from the Krotona community. This latter spot has been referred to as the center of all esoteric influences in the region.

During the 1930's there arose in Southern California a cult which has been characterized as "the weirdest mystical concoction that has ever issued from the region."[6] Its founders, Mr. and Mrs. Guy W. Ballard, migrated from Chicago to Los Angeles in 1932. Ballard had been a paperhanger, stock salesman, and promoter and had once been indicted for an improper gold-mine promotion. His wife had been a professional medium and had edited a spiritualist magazine. Two years after arriving in California, Ballard issued a publication in which he claimed that an Ascended Master Saint Germain had appeared to him, offering him a cup of "pure electronic essense" and a wafer of "concentrated energy," after which Ballard was encircled by a great white flame. The fire served as a vehicle which transported him, together with the saint, all over the world, visiting ancient cities, buried cities of the Amazon, and places of natural wonders. Elsewhere they found gold, silver, and fabulous quantities of precious stones.

From the sales of the book the Ballards financed radio broadcasts, and as listeners became convinced of the authenticity of the Mighty I AM Presence a rich flow of "love gifts" began to come to them. A large tabernacle was acquired, from which lighted signs proclaimed the Presence. Soon a large number of I AM products were being profitably sold to the followers. There were various publications, with new mysteries and rituals, jewelry, cosmetics, and phonograph recordings. Sales and "love offerings" brought in over three millions of dollars. The cult spread to ten or more large cities all over the country and enrolled 350,000 converts—presumably among the relatively uneducated and dissatisfied persons who

---

[6] *Ibid.*, p. 262.

could believe and follow a leader of the most fantastic character as long as he furnished splendor, excitement, and the hope of mystical power.

Others have also discovered the easy money that comes to the promiser of great things. Arthur Bell, the organizer of Mankind United, was among those who made efficient use of such opportunities. Here again, the central elements were hidden, mystical, and unlimited power, together with a life of security, ease, and luxury. Bell announced in 1934 that he had discovered a race of supermen with metallic heads, living in the center of the earth. From them he had learned of a means of eliminating war and poverty. He promised his followers short hours of work, with early retirement on a pension, and homes with the latest automatic and electrical equipment, surrounded by landscaping, pools, waterfalls, athletic fields, and other luxuries. Members were expected, as is the case in many such cults, to present all their possessions to the leader at the time of joining. The grand benefits were promised as soon as 200,000,000 members had signed up. But meanwhile there were enough followers for Bell to acquire some large properties, and to enable him to indulge in showy luxuries.

Among Bell's unconventional claims were the possession of a destructive ray which was effective at ranges of thousands of miles, the ability to go into a trance and be transported at once to any place on earth, and association with seven doubles all capable of thinking as one. Referring to himself as "The Voice," Bell quoted the Bible and preached against capitalism and war. Following the Japanese attack on Pearl Harbor, he stated that the attack was really made by United States planes, disguised as Japanese, and that it had been ordered by the "hidden rulers of the world." This action resulted in a conviction of sedition and a sentence to five years of imprisonment.[7]

Following his setback during the war, Bell returned to operate the cult. His laundries, hotels, restaurants, canneries, mills, and other establishments are all operated by members, who work cheerfully for 12 hours a day for food, clothing, lodging, and expenses.[8] This oppressive working load is borne without protest by disciples who believe that they are thereby advancing the cause of the society of the future. Other persons of the region, unconvinced of the

---

[7] The conviction of Bell and his nine associates was later set aside by the United States Court of Appeals at San Francisco. The decision, however, was not made on the merits of the case, but on the ground that the defendants had been denied a fair trial because women had been excluded from the grand jury which indicted them.

[8] *Time*, May 21, 1945. pp. 20–21.

authenticity of "The Voice," characteristically regard the movement with suspicion and fear. Business interests fear the competition of his enterprises, which do not pay income tax. Bell charges even his personal expenses, including clothing and manicures, to "legitimate church expenses." Labor unions, alarmed at the low standards of work and reward, have attacked his policies and have sought legal methods to prevent the replacement, in businesses acquired by Bell, of salaried workers by his unsalaried followers. Bell's position on the matter is that his followers have no employer but God and that the government has no jurisdiction.[9]

Less unconventional movements may also find a large and eager following in Southern California. It was here that Aimee McPherson built her center, which at its height included a temple costing a million and a half dollars to build, a broadcasting station, and a large school for evangelists. Through magazine publicity she started an empire which consisted of 240 local churches affiliated with the temple. Her following is stated to have been composed largely of city residents of the lower middle class—shopkeepers, barbers, small businessmen, and the like. They were made to feel at home and were given a sense of purpose in life, as well as a sense of dignity, beauty, and importance, by the dramatic performances staged by their leader.

Not all strange or queer social movements originate in Southern California, but, since this region provides such a favorable home, some movements started elsewhere eventually find their enduring home here. Such is the case with Technocracy, a plan by relatively unsuccessful engineers and related specialists to govern the nation on the basis of technical scientific engineering, an arrangement in which engineers would hold an almost dictatorial control. Among the features proposed by a prominent founder was the abandonment of gold as a basis of currency and the substitution of units of productive energy, "ergs," which could be represented by certificates. Whatever chance Technocracy had to hold the serious interest of stable intellectuals was lost when a cartoon, effectively lampooning the movement, circulated over the nation.[10] A few faithful members, probably a selection of the less conventional and educated, remained with Technocracy as its headquarters were moved to Los Angeles, where it remained for some years in almost total obscurity.

The tendency of a movement to change its character, as its headquarters transfers its location, has been observed in other cases.

---

[9] *Ibid.*, p. 21.
[10] The drawing showed a hen proudly crowing, "Tech..Tech..Tech..Tech..NOCracy" as it finished laying an "erg."

It is possible that the change of location could be either cause or result of the alteration of content, or both together. An illustration of changes of this sort is furnished by the movement, New Thought, which had its origin in New England during the period when it was the home of intellectual ferment of many degrees of respectability. A student of the movement finds its origin in the teachings of P. P. Quimby, the mesmerist who collaborated with Mary Baker Eddy, and in the transcendentalism of Emerson and the Concord Group.[11] It developed into something distinct from either.

New Thought was not a church but a system of high-powered mental telepathy which members of various churches could practice. A central feature was the doctrine that all matter could be brought under the domination of thought. Evil was ignored, for man was held to be an "emanation of God," and by concerted communion with the "Supreme Power—Universal Presence—All Mind" men could partake of this mystical power and at the same time feel like "persons in an impersonal world."

New Thought became perceptible as a movement about 1890 and spread about the country, principally to large cities—New York, Chicago, Kansas City, San Francisco—until by about 1912 it had entered practically every city of note in Canada and the United States, except for the southern regions, where it did not appeal. In 1915 it found its final home in Southern California, where its most receptive followers resided. In this new scene, however, the emphasis turned somewhat away from communing with the All-Mind, and toward the economic aspect. New Thought became a get-rich-quick system, a something-for-nothing religion, or a new way to pay old debts.[12] Organizations grew rapidly, and in the early period of its Los Angeles phase there was established a University of Christ, a Southern California Metaphysical Institute, and a Metaphysics Library. A Metaphysicians' May Day Festival became an annual civic event.[13]

New Thought prophets encouraged a frank interest in economic success by telling their followers that "thoughts are things" and that any man could think his way to wealth. Through "personal magnetism" he could control others and "reap the lion's share of the profit." By "direct psychic influence" and the "power of the eye," involving the "magnetic gaze," he could gain any end. "Everything is yours," he was told, "if you only want it hard enough. Just

[11] Alfred Whitney Griswold, "New Thought: A Cult of Success," *American Journal of Sociology*, Vol. 40, Nov., 1934, pp. 309–318.
[12] *Ibid.*, p. 311.
[13] Carey McWilliams, *op. cit.*, p. 257.

SOCIAL DISORGANIZATION     [Ch. 14

think of that. *Anything.* Try it. Try it in earnest and you will succeed. It is the operation of a mighty law."[14]

One New Thought author told in a pamphlet how she had solved her income problem. She told herself:[15]

> I must claim wealth NOW. . . . Then I began to say, I AM *wealth*— I AM. I said it actually millions of times. . . . I took infinite pains to get into the *wealthy* attitude of mind over the spending of every five cent piece that went through my purse. . . . *Now* I was taking great pains to spend as the truly wealthy spend, with that sense of *plenty* always in reserve. . . . By little fits and starts more money came to me. My success grew by fits and starts.

Another testimonial to the power of thought was offered by Helen Wilmans. She told of going from farm to city, possessing only ten borrowed dollars. As her landlord proposed to eject her for failure to pay rent, she brought personal magnetism into play and informed him that the rent would be paid. In answer to his question regarding source of funds, she announced, on the spur of the moment, that she would start a paper, and that it would be a success before it was born. The result was a loan from the landlord of $20,000.

Unconventionality merges by small steps into illegality, and Miss Wilmans eventually came into conflict with the law, as have many other prophets of new systems. She was indicted by the government for fraudulent use of the mails, on the grounds that by claiming powers known to be impossible she was deceiving the public. She lost the profits from sales of her writings and died in poverty, but the movement did not die. It lives on, in fact, in other movements which have drawn elements from its ideology and symbolism. As McWilliams puts it, "theosophy and New Thought constitute the stuff from which most of the latter creeds and cults have been evolved."[16]

**Transition to Conventionality.**—The typical course of the highly unconventional movements of the type discussed above appears to be quick growth, luxuriant development of organization, and a turbulent career and short life, with certain of the principal elements capable of being taken over into new cults essentially similar in form and purpose.

---

[14] Alfred W. Griswold, *op. cit.*, p. 313.
[15] Elizabeth Towne, *How I Healed My Purse*, pamphlet, quoted in Griswold, *op. cit.*, p. 315.
[16] *Op. cit.*, p. 257.

Some religious  movements, beginning as highly unconventional cults, may, even after severe conflicts with nonbelievers, eventually find a basis of accommodation to the outside world and evolve toward conventionality as they become denominations.  This, in fact, has been the history of a number of respectable, stable, conservative Protestant denominations in the United States today.  The process of generation of sects of this type continues in modern times, and such groups may be observed in their early and freakish stages today, as well as in the various later stages of accommodation.

A messiah who believes, and who persuades a group of followers, that he is destined to save the world or a deserving section of it in his own lifetime, cannot escape unpopularity or persecution.  He is necessarily fanatic, and his followers are inevitably impatient with conventionality, law, and existing institutions.  The resentment of outsiders to the challenge of the believers is also inescapable.  During the lifetime of a messiah, often a brief period, the conflict between the cult and outsiders usually is intense, bitter, and irreconcilable.  After his death a change must occur in the movement, for there is never a successor with the same absolute authority—a fanatical messiah does not attract or permit to develop under him another like himself.  The absolute leader wishes only absolute followers, and can be succeeded only by a follower.  The successor to a dead messiah can only promise salvation sometime in the future—he cannot personally guarantee achievement of the goals in his own lifetime.  His best role is that of administrator and organizer.  In his regime the movement may take a shape that can endure, for patience and accommodation to other customs are more acceptable if the millennium is to arrive at an indefinite time in the future.

It sometimes is possible for the original prophet to take both roles, that of the fanatical messiah as well as that of the practical organizer and administrator, but, because of the essential conflict in these roles, it is only an exceptionally versatile leader who is able to make the combination.  Such a feat, however, has apparently been achieved by the Negro leader known as Father Divine.

**The Movement of Father Divine.**—During the 1920's and the 1930's a short, gentle-mannered, unimpressive Negro man known as Father Divine built a large and successful cult with members who literally regarded him as God.  His followers turned all their possessions over to him, lived in his "Heavens," and obeyed his commands.  They became so numerous that additional Heavens were acquired, as well as business establishments for employment of his people. In time the movement was large enough to constitute something of a political power, and candidates for public office were careful to seek the approval of Father Divine. At the same time there was, as usual, hostility on the part of the surrounding community, and certain difficulties arose with the law. Unlike many of the prophets of fanatical groups who lacked legal sense and were ruined by these conflicts, Father Divine showed indications of such sophistication that legal measures to alter his ways were generally unsuccessful. The explanation of his superior control of these affairs is to be found in his life history, which contains explanatory educational experiences.[17]

At about the turn of the century, the man who was to be known as Father Divine bore the name George Baker. He was about twenty-five years old and earned a modest living in Baltimore doing such work as lawn-mowing or odd jobs at the dock. He kept a cash reserve for jobless times and appeared to have little ambition. He was serious about religion, however, and regularly taught Sunday school and participated in prayer meetings, often speaking on the nature of God.

One day a visiting preacher, Morris, from a steel district in Pennsylvania made the claim, before the Baltimore congregation in which George Baker sat, that "I am the Father Eternal." He was ejected by his hearers, but Baker alone was impressed, took him to his (Baker's) home, and soon became a disciple. Morris had obtained his exalted conception of himself from a verse he read in the third chapter of First Corinthians. "Know ye not that ye are the temple of God, and that the spirit of God dwelleth in you?" Morris took this to mean him alone, not everyone who read the passage, and from then on claimed actually to be God. In a dream a voice had ordered him to go to Baltimore and save the people there, and it was while he was doing his best to carry out this mission, with little success, that he met Baker.

During their association Baker learned much from Morris, and in time he began to claim that he had been reborn and used the title "The Messenger." Morris tolerated this claim, but defined Baker's status as "God in the Sonship Degree" while he himself was "God in the Fathership Degree." At their small religious gatherings, Morris preached in the style that later was to become that of Father Divine,

---

[17] Facts taken from biographical "Profiles" in *The New Yorker*, June 13, 20, and 27, 1936, by St. Clair McKelway and A. J. Liebling. See also H. Cantril, *The Psychology of Social Movements*, New York: John Wiley & Sons, Inc., 1941; R. A. Parker, *The Incredible Messiah*, Boston: Little, Brown & Co., 1937; and J. Hosher, *God in a Rolls Royce*, New York: Hillman-Curl, Inc., 1936.

and it was from Morris that the latter learned the magic exclamation, "Peace, it's wonderful."

For a period Morris and Baker were joined by a disciple who called himself St. John the Divine Bishop, who had been a preacher with experience in various sects, including Pentecostal Holiness, Holy Rollers, Live Ever Die Never, and others. Bishop was a gifted and dramatic preacher and undoubtedly contributed much to the oratorical talent of Father Divine. He eventually broke from Morris and Baker, however, believing that anyone, not only Morris, is God. Baker parted from Morris soon after and went south alone, where he continued his religious work, but without great success. In Georgia he was tried for lunacy because of his claim to be God and was pronounced by a jury to be of "unsound mind," but not enough so to require commitment. The jury did, however, ask that he leave the state, which Baker did. Together with a few followers he slowly worked his way north, until in 1915 he arrived in New York.

Here Baker found opportunity to learn some practical matters concerning the discipline required within a cult, for he found St. John the Divine in difficulties with the latter's Church of the Living God. Since each member of this group, in accordance with their leader's teaching, was a God, social control was difficult. Baker and St. John the Divine did not cooperate much professionally, but did meet often for a meal to talk over their affairs. The disintegration of the Church of the Living God taught Baker a lesson, and he never allowed his own disciples to achieve a status near to his own or to challenge his authority.

Calling himself The Messenger, Baker developed a small meeting house in Brooklyn, which also served as a kind of employment agency, for he sought jobs for his followers and guaranteed the quality of their work. His following grew, and he began to house and feed the disciples, who accepted his claim to be God and obeyed his will. The sexes were put in separate rooms for sleeping, several persons to a room, for celibacy was required. All property and earnings were turned over to Baker, and he provided food, clothing, and other necessities. He made economical purchases of second-hand clothes and had a seamstress disciple make necessary alterations. Cooking was done by followers and so was inexpensive. Income therefore exceeded expenses, and the financial resources grew with increasing rapidity.

For a time the community inhabited a house in Sayville, Long Island, and while there Baker dropped his title of The Messenger,

and adopted the name Major J. Divine.   Shortly after he made it
Rev. J. Divine, and then Father Divine (God).   At Sayville new
members were slowly added, and the movement there found the
form in which it was soon to grow large and successful.   Members
became Angels, taking new and unworldly names, such as Faith
Sweetness, Hosanna Love, Flying Angel, Celestial Virgin, and
Wonderful Devotion.   They ate together at meals over which Father
Divine presided, blessing plates as they were passed, leading songs,
and talking to his followers.   Angels were expected to live virtuous
lives, to forget their pasts, and to trust completely in their leader.
Their adoration was freely and frequently expressed in such responses as "Thank you, Father!"   "Yes, Father, you are *so* wonderful!" and of course many variations on the basic, "Peace, it's
wonderful!"

Guests were welcome and were, for a time, served large and
delicious free meals.   Besides the Negroes who came for these were
a few whites, and some of the latter eventually joined the movement,
but no large proportion was ever white.   Since Father Divine
insisted that "Father will provide," he objected to life insurance
and required his followers to cash in any policies they owned and
turn the money over to him.   Since he claimed healing power, he
disapproved of doctors and medical treatments.   Death was unnecessary for those with complete trust in him, he claimed, and thus
only those who lacked the proper attitudes would die.   Some of the
latter were abandoned to pauper burial.

Many of the Angels acted as if they were living in a state of
ecstatic contentment.   For the dissatisfied followers there was severe
discipline.   Father Divine laid claim to awful wrath on certain
occasions and exploited his reputation for disciplinary purposes.   In
1931 he was arrested on a charge of being a public nuisance and was
convicted and fined $500 and sentenced to a year in jail.   The judge
died four days later, and to his followers it was clear that Father
Divine had struck him down.   On an appeal the conviction was
reversed—a result similarly exploited as an indication of supernatural power.   Father Divine's followers also attribute the death
of Will Rogers to some unfavorable remarks the latter made over
the radio, and the assassination of Huey Long to his refusal to see
a delegation from Father Divine.

The court action accelerated the growth of the movement, and
Sayville no longer seemed adequate as headquarters for a society of
more than 300 Angels, so Divine transferred his chief location to
Harlem in New York City, where it remained.   Here details of the

organization were adapted to requirements of its size—some charges were made for meals, not all members became Angels at once, but some persons who were not ready to turn over all their property to Father Divine could join with the status of Children.   As numbers grew, more branches, or Extension Heavens, were required, and by 1936, beside his principal Heaven, there were three apartment houses, nine private houses, over fifteen dormitory flats, and three meeting halls with dormitories above—all in Harlem.   Heavens were also established elsewhere, up the Hudson across from the Franklin D. Roosevelt estate, and in other cities even as far away as Los Angeles. Various business enterprises were also acquired.   These included restaurants, grocery stores, barber shops, cleaning and pressing establishments, a coal business, newspapers, and farms.

In his commercial dealings, as well as in his inevitable difficulties with the law, labor unions, and other business interests, Father Divine showed evidence of a degree of skill not ordinarily found in persons who believe they are God.   When one of his buses collided with a car, injuring its passengers, a court judgment of $6,152 was awarded against him, but it was found to be impossible to collect, for he had no property in his name.   All visible assets were in the ownership of his Angels.   His transactions were in cash, and attempts to trap him by sending checks were unsuccessful—these were returned with a slip stating, "Father will provide." Although he had not, at least until 1936, paid an income tax, the Bureau of Internal Revenue did not find a way to enforce collection.   Labor union interests brought pressure at one time to force compliance with the provisions of the Workmen's Compensation Act, but Father Divine made use of two powerful means of defense—he stated, through his attorney, that insurance of any kind was against the religious principles of the group, and he inspired a considerable gathering of his Angels to attend the court hearing and at frequent intervals shout, "Peace, it's wonderful."

The movement has also weathered scandals that ordinarily might destroy a religious group.   Angels have left the organization, revealing in their anger conditions of a scandalous nature, including sex irregularities of the leader, but without inflicting lasting harm on the movement.   While a majority of Negroes disapprove of Father Divine, holding that he presents a false impression of the race, there is a certain approval among police, who find that his followers tend to be law-abiding and orderly.   Employers often appreciate the quality of service given by Angels and Children, and landlords tend to be satisfied with the regularity of their rent payments.

The fundamental reason for the success of Father Divine's move-ment, however, would appear to be the existence of a considerable number of urban Negroes who remember a stable and secure life in earlier days and who find in this new organization a set of absolutes that in part restores these conditions. Their Father "provides," gives them wonderful "Peace," raises their self-esteem, and allows them close association with God.

**Jehovah's Witnesses.**—A religious movement of an entirely different character, but similarly opposed by more conventional persons and organizations, has thrived and grown to tremendous size in the face of difficulties. Jehovah's Witnesses are for the most part uneducated persons, but not, as in the case of Father Divine's followers, seekers of immediate heaven on earth. They are diligent workers, self-sacrificing in their earnestness to achieve their purposes.

The movement was started in 1872 by Charles Taze Russell, a Presbyterian, who organized a small class to study the Bible. His group, which took the name of Zion's Watchtower Tract Society, made their own distinctive interpretations of what they read, and these became the foundation of the movement. The central idea is taken from the 43rd Chapter of Isaiah, "Ye are my witnesses, saith Jehovah, and my servant whom I have chosen." On the basis of this, the members constitute a league of "witnesses"—going from door to door to tell of their beliefs. Along with this goes the program of publication, which by 1946 included a production of more than 1,500,000 books, 11,000,000 pamphlets, and 12,000,000 magazines annually. These materials, printed in 88 languages, are for the most part produced in a modern factory in Brooklyn, New York. "Witnessing" is also accompanied by the playing of phono-graph records at doors of homes, and by radio programs. The radio network reached the large number of 403 stations in 1933, but this was later reduced as a result of opposition from other religious groups.

The content of the movement is in general a Biblical fundamental-ism. The members find no justification for a church or a hierarchy of any kind in the Bible, and so take a stand against all organized religion. They do not believe in an after life, but expect that some time before 1984 there will be a Day of Judgment, on which all of the faithful will be resurrected to enter the Kingdom of God, and those then alive will simply go on living in this new condition. Their slogan is, "Millions now living will never die."

Along with opposition to churches goes a dislike for governmental authority. Members in various nations have refused to vote, serve on juries, salute national flags, or serve in armies. In the United States during the second world war over 4,000 Witnesses were jailed for refusing to serve in the armed forces or to be classified as conscientious objectors. They claimed that each member was a minister of the gospel. They held to this position in the face of severe intolerance, including beating, tarring and feathering, burning of their homes, expulsion of children from school, and other such measures. After the war, they opposed the United Nations, speaking of it as a world conspiracy which would soon bring down the vengeance of God.

The growth of this movement, in the face of such persecution, to the impressive size of about 500,000 members in the United States and nearly 3,000,000 in the world must be accounted for in part by the practical organizing sense of its leaders. The organization is in the charge of officers who are chosen by a board of directors. The latter group is elected annually by the votes of such members as have contributed at least ten dollars. The directors live at the headquarters in Brooklyn, where they issue instruction and interpretations of the Bible, operate the publications, the radio station, the foreign offices, the school for leaders, and the farms. The staff of the headquarters, called "headquarters servants," live in a building owned by the Witnesses and work for a nominal money income, having their needs met by other members.

Notable managerial efficiency was demonstrated at the 1946 convention in Cleveland, attended by over 75,000 members coming from all parts of the United States and many foreign countries. In advance of the opening, a group of members systematically combed the city, block by block, and located more than 60,000 rooms for the use of those to come. Others were cared for in tents and trailers at a camp outside of the city. A cafeteria was organized—and in a time of food shortages—which fed two meals a day to 50,000 people. Food was brought by the carload from out of town. The Witnesses had crews of cooks, carpenters, plumbers, policemen, doctors, nurses, mechanics, and barbers, all working without fees. They participated in mass baptisms in Lake Erie, lectures at the Municipal Stadium, and a general invasion of homes all over Cleveland, playing on doorsteps their portable phonographs and selling their publications.

High ability is also available for legal defense, for their attorney, a recent convert, has won a series of impressive court victories.

From 1941 to 1946 he had charge of more than 4,000 cases involving the movement, of which 35 were cases in the United States Supreme Court. Among the notable triumphs was the decision of the Supreme Court that three school children of West Virginia did not have to salute the flag if their principles were against it and another that the distribution of religious publications is to be protected as a part of the freedom of religion.

Jehovah's Witnesses cannot be accounted for solely by what the movement does for its members, although the promise of eternal life in the near future is surely a powerful attraction to those who can accept it. The movement imposes a discipline upon its members which tends to attract energetic and zealous fundamentalists rather than the merely lost and confused persons who drift into the Southern California cults. The Witnesses perceive the disorganization in their world today as a matter of corruption of church and state and throw themselves enthusiastically into the solution that appears obvious to them—the saving, before the Day of Judgment, of as many souls as possible.

**Secular Movements with Limited Objectives.**—Not all social movements rest on the belief that the existing order is hopeless and that the world is divided between the few who are saved and the many who are lost. There are many persons and organizations holding the belief that contemporary society is in general satisfactory, but that certain aspects are disorganized. The natural response is to build an organization that proposes to remedy the specific defect without overturning the whole order. Such movements are secular in character because they are limited, whereas sacred movements tend to embrace an entire social system. The number of such organizations in the United States today is far too great to list. As examples one may consider the various nationalist movements, racist movements, the labor union movement, the feminist movement, the temperance movement, the cooperative movement, various movements for calendar reform, and for international languages such as Esperanto, Volapuk, and Basic English, nudist movements, dress reform, Boy and Girl Scouts, Townsend Plan, Ham'n Eggs movement, the EPIC movement in California, such terrorist movements as the Ku Klux Klan, Black Legion, and the like, and many other varieties of organizations.

The course of such movements varies greatly. Some start quietly and grow into powerful organizations—many movements have even constituted strong political forces in the United States, e.g., the Granger Movement, Temperance, Free Silver, Every Man a King, and others. Some, like calendar reform and Esperanto, begin quietly and go through a slow, unspectacular life cycle, eventually dying of discouragement. Others start in spectacular fashion and then, like many religious sects, gradually become accommodated and respectable, and evolve into stable and conventional institutions. There are also attempts, like that of "General" Jacob Coxey, to start something, without ever actually achieving a durable organization. More than a half-century after his unsuccessful march on Washington of 1894, Coxey was still trying to start social movements. His 1946 interest was in the establishment of an international currency.

Movements with somewhat indefinite functions may discover purposes as they go along, and movements with one purpose at the start may add new ones, or alter the old, in the course of experience. The Boy Scout movement, for example, had its origins in several considerations. In England, Sir Robert Baden-Powell wished to do something to improve idle boys who opened gates for tips, engaged in minor mischief, and wasted their days and years. Remembering how useful young boys were as spies or scouts in the Boer War, he organized a movement with a considerable amount of military emphasis, even to the matter of spying (observation) as a desirable technique to be developed in the boys. In the United States, organizations of boys interested in outdoor life, woodcraft, Indian lore, and such matters became absorbed into the same movement. Uniforms designed to appear military, close-order drill, and a system of ranks and badges continue to reflect the Boer War inspiration; and camping, fire-by-friction, and other such activities remain among the vestiges of American frontier life. The merit badge program, however, has lately turned much of the Scout's energy toward the study of modern subjects—electricity, engineering, salesmanship, science, and the like. At the same time the religious content of scouting has greatly increased, probably largely as a result of the willingness of churches to provide meeting places and leadership.

It is not uncommon for an organization which has for objectives primarily the advancement of the interests of a minority of the society to enlarge its appeal by attempting to show that broad general benefits will come to the rest of the society if its purposes are achieved. Thus the feminist movement not only asked for rights and justice for women, but promised to introduce a new idealism in politics as soon as women were allowed to vote. Movements based

on pension schemes, primarily for the welfare of a limited category
of the population, are promoted by arguments of the general contribution to national prosperity that will be made by the expansion
of purchasing power.  Among the examples of this kind of expansion of function may be cited the Townsend Plan.

**The Townsend Movement.**—During the depression of the
1930's a considerable proportion of the population, having more
spare time than was available in days of virtually full employment,
and suffering from bewilderment and worry, undertook an increased
amount of serious reading, much of which dealt with economic
problems.  There was a great natural interest in the cause and cure
of depressions, and, by virtue of such reading and discussions between neighbors that inevitably followed, there was generated a new
mass of amateur economists.  Many of these persons developed
original schemes for ending or preventing depressions.  Most of
the ideas did not go beyond the stage of cracker-barrel conversation,
but the scheme invented by Dr. Francis E. Townsend caught the
enthusiasm of a particularly susceptible group, the elderly poor, and
rapidly grew to large size and became for a time a ponderous political
force.  Townsend himself was typical of his followers.  He had had
a hard and only moderately successful life in the Mid-West and had
migrated to Southern California in his later years, looking for the
same kind of happiness sought by hundreds of thousands of similar
migrants.  There, while in his sixties, unemployed and with a family
to support, he had an inspiration.  He proposed that the government
give to each person over sixty a monthly pension of $200, which the
latter would agree to spend entirely within thirty days, and that a
2 per cent tax on all business transactions be levied to pay the costs.[18]
This would support the aged in comfort and, according to an official
statement by Townsend and his co-founder, Robert E. Clements,
"provide an adequate plan of recovery from the devastating financial
depression which has so dreadfully afflicted us as a people."  It
would also "restore national prosperity without inflation, . . . provide
immediate employment for all . . . reduce crime . . . reduce taxes . . .
balance the budget."[19]  While this appeal was directed to all the
people of the country, the principal supporters of the Plan continued
to be found among the direct potential beneficiaries.  There were,
however, considerations that led to some support from other categories of the population.  Young persons, who would inevitably

---

[18] Chapter 7, in Hadley Cantril, *op. cit.*, contains a summary of the history of the Plan
and a psychological interpretation of its success.
[19] *Ibid.*, p. 171.

bear the load of support in the taxes they would pay during the earning period of their lives, would be presumed to be the most natural opponents, but there were many with aged parents to support. These saw the possibility of a burden being taken from them and a vision of their parents happy in a separate home.

The founders further appealed to youth by arguing that the pension scheme would allow many elderly persons to retire, thus making room for the advancement of ambitious young persons. There was unexpected support from other quarters, as interests of various kinds were attracted by certain aspects of the Plan. It is said that certain chain stores provided support, seeing in the proposal a means of lightening their tax burden. Other interests saw in the Plan a weapon which could help fight labor unions and radicalism. Townsend himself had no use for radicalism of the ordinary sort, was violently opposed to the New Deal, and even exchanged political cooperation with the most violent opponents of President Roosevelt. At the movement's 1936 convention in Cleveland, there were, beside the Townsend speakers, addresses from Gerald L. K. Smith, fascistic follower of Huey Long, and Charles E. Coughlin, both violently condemning Roosevelt. William Lemke, leader of an unsuccessful and fascistic nationalist Union Party, won Townsend's support by endorsing the pension plan.

The Townsend Movement developed in the course of its growth other functions of perhaps greater importance than any so far mentioned. As letters began to pour in during the early days of the movement, Townsend suggested to interested persons in other parts of the country that they organize Townsend Clubs in their own communities. These clubs sprang up all over the country, and, while support of the Plan continued to be their primary ostensible purpose, they did furnish a basis of social life for elderly persons and a cause in the service of which they could have almost a religious enthusiasm. The procedure at meetings generally included such exercises as speeches, songs of a fervent character—hymn-like, with a militant ring—games, and other social activities. The members were made to feel important, part of something big, and they enjoyed sharing these sentiments with one another.

While politically the Townsend Movement passed its peak as the difficulties of the depression of the 1930's began to pass—the passage of the Social Security Law and the decisive defeats of the candidates backed by Townsend, Coughlin, Smith, and Lemke were among the factors—there remained for years the small, quiet social gatherings in villages, towns, and cities all over the nation. Here the elderly

people still meet to discuss pensions, but the hopes for $200 a month
in their own lifetimes are not sufficient to account for their attendance.  The radical economic and political scheme became little more
than a tranquil social organization for lonely old people.

**Other Types of Social Movements.**—While it is almost inevitable that some changes in the functions of an enduring social movement take place in the course of its experience, there are some crises
which require abrupt change to put off the death of the movement.
The Anti-Saloon League, which took for its goal the passage of
national legislation for the prohibition of alcoholic beverages, virtually died of success after the passage of the Twenty-first Amendment.  This is the general danger to an organization which exists for
a purpose which can be completely achieved.  It would be expected
that this termination would be satisfactory to all, but such is not
always the case.  There is a certain sentimental reluctance of war-
riors to disband after having fought a good fight, and a tendency to
find a new fight and continue the association.  There is also a vested
interest in the bureaucracy of organizations which tempts them to
find some basis for a continued existence, thus relieving their officials
of the necessity of finding new employment.

During the later years of the prohibition period in the United
States, there arose an organization which took for its name the
Crusaders.  It purported to be an idealistic organization of young
persons who sought to end the prohibition amendment and thus to
reduce crime, political corruption, and other general evils.  While it
is not certain that any large membership ever was achieved, contributions came in from great numbers of persons, and the movement
became an influential part of the repeal pressure.  Repeal, however,
brought to this organization the same sort of crisis that prohibition
brought to the Anti-Saloon League.  There was again a danger of
dying from success.  A nucleus of officers and members, however,
remained to try to work out a new function.  The chosen purpose
was to rally a following of a native nationalist character somewhat
similar to the fascist pattern in European countries.  Contributions
were sought, and radio time was purchased for frequent speeches
by one of the new leaders.  The Crusaders now campaigned against
"Reds" and "foreigners" and sought support from "true-blue Americans."  This appeal did not succeed, however, and the movement
eventually disappeared from sight.  The nation was not ready for
fascism and had already turned down more forceful political leaders

of this type in favor of Roosevelt, who was during this period at the peak of his peacetime popularity.[20]

Local political reform movements face the same kind of difficulty. From time to time in the history of the large cities of the United States the corruption of political machines has become so offensive that the normally indifferent voting population has been willing to join crusades for reform. Many such movements have succeeded in turning the objectionable administration out of office and putting in the officials of the reform ticket. The most frequent history of such processes has been that the crusading organization virtually falls apart after the successful election, while the permanently organized machines lie in wait to capture the city at the next election. When a reform administration remains in office for more than one term, it becomes scientifically desirable to seek the explanation in some changes more fundamental than a crusading movement.

### THE REVOLUTIONARY PROCESS

When the disorganization within a nation becomes severe and general, it is harder to persuade a population that a particular limited secular movement could be adequate to correct all of the undesirable conditions. A more desperate sentiment tends to emerge—that nothing short of a radical and complete alteration of the government and the society will save the population from unbearable injustice and misery. To the extent that such a belief becomes general, the ground is prepared for revolution.

Within recent years there have appeared studies which constitute attempts to go beyond mere historical description and to account for revolutions as collective processes which have, to a certain extent, a natural life cycle.[21] Revolutions in different nations and at different historical periods vary in their details and may even take somewhat different courses, but there is presumed to be an underlying "ideal type" of process to which all tend to conform and which more nearly approaches a general description of revolutions than would any other account. At present, however, such analysis must be regarded as tentative, for future research may modify the conception of the revolutionary cycle to a considerable extent. The follow-

---

[20] One reason so few radio listeners ever heard the broadcasts for the Crusaders is that they were scheduled for the same period in which "Amos 'n Andy" was on the air.

[21] Lyford Edwards, *The Natural History of Revolution*, Chicago: University of Chicago Press, 1927; Clarence Crane Brinton, *The Anatomy of Revolution*, New York: W. W. Norton & Co., Inc., 1938. The present discussion is largely based on these two sources, which are notable for the extent to which sociological analysis is achieved.

ing stages represent approximations from our present incomplete knowledge.

**The Background of Revolutions.**—It is apparent that revolutionary movements do not come into being abruptly. Edwards states that it takes at least three generations to develop a revolution:[22]

> The reason why it takes at least three generations to develop a revolution is simple. When a given social institution begins to function badly the generation then alive, the first generation to suffer, can remember it when it functioned well and believe that it can be restored to useful activity by means of some minor reforms. This belief proves erroneous, but the second generation are brought up to hold it, and in any case they have heard the first generation tell personal experiences of the former successful functioning of the detrimental institution. So the second generation still love and venerate it, in spite of its increasing social inadequacy. The third generation experience continually greater frustration of their elemental wishes as the institution becomes more and more archaic. Since they find nobody who has had personal experience of its successful functioning, the harmful institution is sometimes destroyed by the third generation of those it harms. This, however, is very rare. Generally the third generation still have a strong attachment to the old institution, an attachment in part derived from tales of its former excellence, heard in early youth from grandparents and other elderly persons. In the great majority of cases it is in the fourth generation, or later, that the overthrow of the old institution occurs.

Brinton holds that the soil out of which revolutions grow is not the greatest misery, oppression, and helplessness of the masses.[23] On the contrary he asserts, as does Edwards, that there is often a period preceding a revolution in which the lowest classes have made notable gains in income and influence. Revolutions arise from dissatisfaction with the government itself, particularly with certain disorganized aspects of the economic functions of government. The people may be more prosperous than ever while their government is bankrupt. It is pointed out that in the English, French, American, and Russian revolutions taxation was an important issue in each case. The great complaint was not hunger, but injustice. The governments were not performing their functions as effectively as they should, and a sense of grievance arose. As Brinton states it:[24]

> Thus we see that certain economic grievances—usually not in the form of economic distress, but rather a feeling on the part of some of the chief

---

[22] Lyford Edwards, *op. cit.*, p. 17.
[23] Crane Brinton, *op. cit.*, Ch. 2, pp. 38–81.
[24] Reprinted from *The Anatomy of Revolution* by Crane Brinton, by permission of W. W. Norton & Company, Inc. Copyright 1938 by the publishers. P. 46.

enterprising groups that their opportunities for getting on in this world are unduly limited by political arrangements—would seem to be one of the symptoms of revolution. These feelings must, of course, be raised to an effective social pitch by propaganda, pressure-group action, public meetings, and preferably a few good dramatic riots, like the Boston Tea Party. As we shall see, these grievances, however close they are to the pocketbook, must be made respectable, must touch the soul. What is really but a restraint on a rising and already successful group, or on several such groups, must appear as rank injustice towards everyone in the society. Men may revolt partly or even mainly because they are hindered, or, to use Dr. George Pettee's expressive word, *cramped;* but to the world—and save for a very few hypocrites, also to themselves—they must appear *wronged.* Revolutions cannot do without the word "justice."

There is also a basis for discontent in what is perceived to be general incompetence of government. The machinery does not operate with efficiency, and its failures become apparent to the population in numerous ways. The government loses respect and authority.

Preliminary symptoms of revolution precede by some time the actual outbreak of violence. One of the earliest manifestations, visible also in the backgrounds of less extreme social movements, is an increase in general restlessness. It is at first undefined, and gets expressed indirectly in such behavior as wandering and travel, which in turn tends to increase the unrest by exposing the traveler to other systems of life and making him conscious of alternatives to his own society. Along with this restlessness there tends to develop a degree of cynicism, which may reduce moral standards and bring about a general increase in crime and unconventional behavior.

Another early symptom is termed the "balked disposition." According to Edwards:[25]

> People come to feel that their legitimate aspirations and ideals are being repressed or perverted, that their entirely proper desires and ambitions are being hindered and thwarted—they do not know how or why. Disappointment and discouragement become widespread. Work becomes unsatisfactory and monotonous to great numbers of people. Life itself becomes stale and objectless. Throughout society there runs a strong, though inarticulate, demand for new stimulation and fresh incentives. The unrest which has been previously unconscious or subconscious becomes in a measure objectified. People gradually realize that "there is something rotten in the state of Denmark." Still the degree of objectivation is slight. The dominant characteristic is mere discontent with the established routine of life—but this discontent begins to be contagious.

[25] *Op. cit.*, p. 30.

When the process approaches closer to the revolutionary outbreak, there is a tendency for articulate persons to give the situation
a degree of definition. Edwards refers to this as the "transfer of
the allegiance of the intellectuals." While formerly the bulk of the
publicists justified the old order, they now become converted to the
cause of the discontented masses; if not, a new group of publicists
arises and gains popularity. In France, for example, there were
eminent writers in 1700 who upheld the divine right of kings, but,
as Edwards points out, within two generations virtually all men of
intellectual distinction in that country attacked the conception as
false and ridiculous. Each of the major revolutions appears to
have had a forceful group of such publicists to give direction and
dignity to the cause.

The intellectuals or publicists do not necessarily perceive the
situation clearly at first. There is a tendency to write in anger and
to see the solution as a substitution of good men for bad. Edwards
calls this the "good-man" fallacy—that everything will be well again
if only the right king, pope, or ruler, can be found. It takes time for
them to discover that it is the social order itself that is at the base of
the trouble, and that more radical action is required. The intellectual influence grows to important size when there is concerted
attack on certain institutions by the bulk of the publicists, so that,
instead of diffusing their energies and spreading public attention,
they concentrate it on one weak spot by a powerful campaign of
exposures and attacks. At the same time there is a dramatization
of the worthy qualities of the revolutionary class itself. The revolutionists are shown to be important and are sentimentally linked with
great causes of other times. They gain in moral certainty, and
their indignation against the existing regime is intensified.

The campaign of the publicist may in part persuade even the
rulers of the old regime, so that they lose confidence in the justice of
their side and put up only a half-hearted defense. It is also possible, of course, for the attacks to harden the minds of oppressive
rulers so that even more severe and righteous repression is called
forth. It is contended, however, that the important role of the
publicists is to destroy the faith and self-confidence of the ruling
class and to weaken them for the attacks which are to come.

**The Outbreak of Revolution.**—When the preliminary processes
have run their course and the stage is set for the actual conflict, it
does not require more than a minor disorder or riot to set in motion
the irreversible progress of the active revolution itself. When the

population reaches a degree of heat in the preliminary stages, combustion appears to be spontaneous. An event such as the storming of the Bastille, the St. Petersburg riot, or the Boston Tea Party initiates this active phase. It is not necessary, however, that the people involved recognize at the time that the revolution has begun —only the events that follow make that certain. In time the mob action may become the symbol of the revolution, as in the case of the Bastille action, which symbolically remained as a national holiday.

Edwards holds that the role of mobs in revolutions is usually exaggerated in popular thought:[26]

> Mobs do play an essential part in certain revolutionary crises, but these crises are few and in some important revolutions they never occur at all. Even in the French Revolution, where mob action was most conspicuous, it played a decisive part only on five or six days during more than that number of years. In the Russian Revolution the mob was of importance only twice— in February and October of 1917. In the American Revolution mobs were never a decisive factor. The same is true of the Puritan Revolution. Only in the easily repressed peasant revolt did the mob figure to any great extent in the Protestant Reformation. Even then the mob had no decisive part in the outcome of the great struggle.

Furthermore, the spontaneity of the action may be misunderstood. The crowd has direction and is subject to some control and leadership. It is in fact the organization and direction of it that makes it as effective as it is. It often includes among its members not only the low-income masses and the criminals but men of reputation and influence. Paul Revere, for example, was among those who participated in the Boston Tea Party, and there were others of his class there.

Perhaps the most important accomplishment of the mob is that by its action it demonstrates the helplessness of the government. The revolutionists gain confidence, or even certainty of success, from the spectacular demonstration of the inabilities of the rulers. These inabilities are in some historical cases most extreme. Edwards presents the following examples:[27]

> If the commander of the Bastille had not been a spiritless imbecile, the Bastille could never have been captured. Two thirds of his garrison were more or less in sympathy with the populace. Louis XVI was repeatedly urged to replace De Launey with a competent commander and to man the fortress with reliable troops. Through sheer indolence and indecisiveness he neglected to do either. The grotesque blunderings and stupidities of which

---

[26] *Op. cit.*, pp. 100–101.
[27] *Ibid.*, pp. 105–106.

Charles I was guilty in his attempt to seize the five members of Parliament not only insured the failure of that criminal action but discouraged all his supporters and encouraged his enemies. The way the royal government mishandled the Boston Tea Party crisis was almost moronic. There were both military and naval forces available to protect the tea ships amply. No attempt was made to use these forces, though nearly everybody in Boston seems to have been aware that an attempt was to be made to destroy the tea. . . .

The czar Nicholas II may not have been an actual mental defective, but his handling of affairs at the outbreak of the revolution in March, 1917, strongly suggests it. In spite of the most urgent representations he kept troops in St. Petersburg who were known to be in sympathy with the people; he refused to appoint a government responsible to the Duma. He let himself get caught and separated from his loyal troops, and he let these troops in turn get caught at an impossible distance from the capital. He left the railroads in control of an official about whose revolutionary leaning he had been repeatedly warned. It is the exhibition of a man trying to rule an empire without brains enough to run a grocery store.

**Government by the Revolutionists.**—Encouraged to take control by the failure of the existing government to stop them, the revolutionary leaders must at once set out to carry on the most essential functions of a government. They must organize police and restore order, they must collect taxes and handle other affairs. There appears to be something of a tendency for the relatively moderate revolutionaries to take control for a time but, lacking boldness and decision, later to lose control to the more extreme faction. The latter tend to have more discipline, to be single-minded and ruthless, and to possess centralized authority and are thus able to push out the moderates. When this happens, the "honeymoon" period ends and the "reign of terror" begins. According to Edwards:[28]

The essential characteristics of the radical rule are physical and mental courage, boldness, determination, an absolute faith in the righteousness of their cause and in their own ability to govern, despite lack of experience. This enthusiastic boldness does more than enable the radicals to gain supreme power at the crisis of the revolution. It enables them to obtain the success of the revolution, because their boldness kindles a like boldness in the public. There is a general tendency in a revolutionary public, as in a peaceful one, to give a new authority a chance to prove itself. When the new authority is composed of men of real ability and of bold enthusiasm, it is able to carry the general body of the public along with it and to accomplish things which, looked at in the calm detachment of a later day, seem almost incredible.

---

[28] *Ibid.*, pp. 156–157.

The "terror" is not necessarily a time of disorder, but of tight control by force. The revolutionary government is in danger of failure from various directions—foreign intervention, vengeance of the ousted moderates, and counter-revolutionary forces. They lack ordinary experience in governing, and yet must succeed in order to save their lives. Force and severity are thus virtual necessities, as is audacity. To a considerable extent the "terror" may be intentionally staged. It may be understood as a dramatic mechanism to control by fear. The essentials are not death and destruction so much as the fear of death and destruction. Edwards explains:[29]

> The radical rulers employ the most terrible and menacing language in innumerable speeches. Their endless oratory abounds in the most fearsome pronouncements of the dreadful danger that everybody will incur who disobeys or revolts against the existing government. The impression is carefully created that everybody is being watched and that the least hostile move means instant death. The most sinister and frightful rumors of the omniscience and vengefulness of themselves are industriously circulated by the radical rulers through the agency of trusted subordinates. The scheme, in order to be successful, requires that all this alarmist eloquence be substantiated by a certain number of highly dramatic executions carried out in such a manner as to give the impression that they are enormously more numerous than is really the case. All the means for producing this effect are studied with as much care as Mr. Ziegfeld gives to his most elaborate theatrical productions.

An example of such a show is furnished by the destruction of Lyons in the French Revolution. The city had harbored a revolt, and an army was sent to conquer it. It was announced that the city was to be utterly destroyed, together with all of its inhabitants, that the ground was to be leveled and the very name of Lyons erased forever. Publicity was given in all cities where there were possibilities of revolt. After the taking of Lyons, there were mass executions totaling 1,684 persons—a small proportion of the population of the city, but these were done in such a manner as to give the impression that complete extermination was under way. Some persons were allowed to escape to tell others of the horror. Some buildings were wrecked before the eyes of witnesses brought in from other cities. The belief in the destruction of this large city was thus effectively spread over much of the nation.

Brinton refers to the period as a "reign of terror and virtue," pointing out the tendency for zealousness among extreme revolutionists. If the old order was bad, the new leaders are glorious. Furthermore the political change tends to become also a general

---
[29] *Ibid.*, p. 176.

cultural transition—reminders of the old order are repulsive, and novelty is the order of the day. Some of this spirit is reflected in the enthusiasm for renaming. In some cases this has involved personal names, elsewhere the calendar, and nearly always many cities and streets. No city bearing the name of a monarch of the old regime is likely to keep it after a revolution. Even such names as King Street or Queen Street, as in Boston, are subject to change to something more appropriate like the Federal and State streets of that city.

The new spirit often takes something of a "religious" character, with emphasis on morality, or even asceticism, and a general idealism. Lenin, for example, instructed his followers to keep accurate and honest accounts, manage economically, be honest, and keep strictest discipline in labor. Not only does discipline require a certain austerity within the population, but the presence of hardship and tragedy makes conspicuous pleasure inadvisable. Furthermore, since it is the opponents of the revolution that are held to be the sinners, the revolutionists must themselves react with virtue.

**The Return to Normality.**—Popular tension cannot be kept at high pitch indefinitely. With the ending of the reign of terror, events become so dull in comparison that the masses turn their attention to other affairs, and the revolution enters its final stage of quieting down. This has been termed the Thermidorean reaction, after the phase of the French Revolution in the month called Thermidor in 1794. There is a tendency for a dictatorship of the steady, calm type to emerge at this time. Control is as necessary as before, and since there is no high fervor to aid it, a strong-willed leader issues orders. As his control becomes effective, terror is no longer required for the general population, although it may still be unsafe for any rival to challenge the rule of the dictator. Certain old opponents, however, may be extended forgiveness and allowed to go free again, and old-order institutions like churches may be permitted to resume their normal activities.

The relaxation of the revolutionary fervor removes some of the restraints on pleasure, and permits the public to indulge itself to a somewhat greater extent than in normal times, as if to make up for years of dullness. Brinton describes this reaction in France, following the death of Robespierre:[30]

Dance halls were opened up all over Paris, prostitutes began operating "with their former audacity" (to quote a police report), well-dressed pros-

[30] Reprinted from *The Anatomy of Revolution* by Crane Brinton, by permission of W. W. Norton & Company, Inc. Copyright 1938 by the publishers. P. 262.

perous young men most unrepublicanly drunk began running about and cracking dour, virtuous Republicans over the head. These young men were the famous *jeunesse dorée,* a gilded youth with no illusions about a Republic of Virtue, and which would nowadays certainly be labeled Fascist at once. Both male and female costume had during the crisis period tended towards sobriety, the women being wrapped in flowing Roman robes and in more than Roman virtue. Now all was changed. The men's clothes became extremely foppish, with tight trousers, elaborate waistcoats, and stocks that mounted beyond the chin. The women's dressmakers were still classically inspired, but with a sure erotic sense they concentrated their efforts on the skillful revealing of the breasts. The *costume directoire* is an excellent symbol of the period.

During this period inflation sets in. Taxes are insufficient for expenses, and the governments characteristically resort to confiscation and to the printing of money. Speculators and profiteers arise, and with their new wealth achieve some success in corrupting officials. The nation begins to appear to be on the road to disorganization and failure, and often it becomes necessary to impose restraints on the process. Brinton states that there is often an alteration between moral restraint and moral looseness, finally arriving at an equilibrium of customs which differs by no great amount from the ways of their prerevolutionary ancestors. Edwards also agrees that the new order eventually arrives at a condition much like that of the old system which the revolution was supposed to eliminate. "The new, revolutionary principles are simply fitted into a place in the old scheme of things."[31] The revolution eventually comes to the completion of its cycle, not on any date which can be fixed precisely, but by the gradual melting away of its characteristic features. The normal processes of social change continue, and along with them the processes of social disorganization which make possible, though not inevitable, another revolution in the future.

**The "New Deal" as a Quasi-Revolution.**—In the midst of the depression of the 1930's, when the New Deal administration was in its most active phase of reform, there occurred an incident which raised the question in the minds of the public as to whether this new government was really revolutionary. A prominent educator of the public school system in a mid-western city was a guest at a small dinner in Washington, at which certain minor functionaries of the new administration were present. During the discussion a remark was made to the effect that "Roosevelt is just the Kerensky

---

[31] Edwards, *op. cit.,* p. 196.

of this Revolution," implying that a more severe phase was to follow, like the succession of Lenin after Kerensky in the Russian Revolution. The educator thought he was in the company of conspirators and raised an alarm at once in the newspapers. Subsequent inquiries revealed that the remarks were not meant seriously, that in fact there was actually some intention to tease the educator, and that there was no revolutionary plot. None of the persons involved were again prominent in the news after this event. The affair did, however, initiate some serious discussion about the character of the process in which the "New Deal" developed. It could hardly be called a revolution in the ordinary sense of the term, but it might be regarded as a social movement that fulfills the functions of a revolution in a nation which is so responsive to public will that old-fashioned revolutions from despotism are inappropriate and unnecessary.

Like revolutions, the New Deal descends from movements that can be traced back a century or more in American history. The farmers and workers who participated in the Populist, Greenback, Granger, and labor movements of the nineteenth century and the followers of William Jennings Bryan in the years about the turn of the century were in a sense the early members of the New Deal movement. After Bryan's repeated failures to gain the presidency, his leadership in a sense fell into the hands of Woodrow Wilson, who was elected on a platform of economic reform which was essentially that of these movements, and of the later New Deal. Wilson's title for his program, in fact, was the "Square Deal." Some of his supporters remained active to give support to Franklin D. Roosevelt in later years. Wilson's program was only half accomplished when it was interrupted by the first world war. In the postwar reaction, during the administrations of Harding, Coolidge, and Hoover, the movement was without effective leadership or political expression, but the dissatisfaction and the aims were still there, and by virtue of being dammed up by the long delay they sought more radical expression in 1933 than might have been the case if the process had not been interrupted.

There were no events such as the St. Petersburg riots or the storming of the Bastille, and no executions of tyrants. There was, however, a bitterness among many unemployed persons that might, if elections were not a part of our political system, have been the source of revolutionary violence. There was also a march on Washington by a bonus army which had to be sent away with bayonets and tear gas. President Hoover was not executed, but he was retired in a decisive and somewhat angry electoral process and for a time was inactive as a political influence. The transfer of office had its dramatic aspects—all banks were closed, the economy was near paralysis, groceries were being purchased with temporary scrip. In the inaugural address the new president emphatically promised action, some of it seemingly constituting vengeance (driving the money-changers out of the temple), and some novel and drastic recovery and reform measures.

The measures nearest to a "reign of terror" were probably the threats to "crack down" on those who failed to comply with the National Recovery Act. The administrator, Hugh S. Johnson, a tough old army general known as "Iron Pants," set a tone of harshness in his brief reign over the economic life of the nation. At the same time there was a new directness in the amounts of money spent for relief and public works, a sternness of reform of such institutions as the stock exchanges, and an attack on the Supreme Court for its opposition to the new measures. Frightened businessmen and conservatives actually took the process for a revolution and reacted in alarm, some calling for a "man on horseback" to take over the government, others making inquiries about moving to Canada or England.

There was exhilaration and fervor among the persons in and close to the leadership, and among the mass of followers. Opposition to the new cause was virtually sinful in their eyes, and Republicans were labeled with such characteristic epithets as "Bourbons" and "economic royalists." Measures of liberalism not required by the strength of the pressure of the electorate were pushed through on moral grounds. Among these may be mentioned the encouragement of women in politics, the advancement of Negroes, and the increase in the power of labor organizations. The moral certainty is symbolized in a remark attributed to Harry Hopkins, close friend and confidential adviser to the President as well as holder of various administrative offices. Hopkins is said to have promised, "We will spend and spend, tax and tax, elect and elect."[32]

During the early period of the New Deal administration, there rose to influence a number of officials who, by comparison with the traditional politicians of American history, might be called fanatics. Some of these, like Henry Wallace and Harold Ickes, had long had an interest in reform but little success in achieving it. By their nature they did not find it possible to win elections, but as appointees

---

[32] Hopkins denied making the statement, but in the minds of many supporters as well as opponents, it fairly symbolizes the character of the certainty and determination of the inner circle of the administration.

of a popular president they finally found expression for their special energies and interests.  In positions of sub-cabinet rank there was an especially large number of fervent young fanatics, sometimes referred to in the press as "Janissaries."  It was in this group that there may have been a hope that Roosevelt would eventually be succeeded by someone even more radical.

It is said to be a characteristic of revolutions that they "eat their own children."  Men who are for a time important in the inner circles differ with the top leaders and are cast aside and, if they remain stubborn, are executed.  The New Deal brought forth no executions, but high favorites were set aside from time to time.  Some, like Rexford G. Tugwell, took it in good grace and were rewarded with positions of honor though without influence.  Others, like Raymond Moley, Lewis W. Douglas, and Hugh S. Johnson, became intense or almost bitter critics of the movement in which they had for a time held high positions.

The New Deal was well into its period of calming down when the approach of war put it aside entirely.  The reform aims were not consistent with the necessities for large-scale production and organization for combat and were deferred to a later time.  There was thus no opportunity to observe the natural process by which this movement might have reached its final stage.  The matter of succession to leadership, however, probably developed in characteristic fashion.  It is an essential trait of the strong leader, whether dictator or president, to require loyalty of his associates.  Those who do not put their loyalty above everything else are soon banished from the inner circle.  The result is that, when the time comes to find a successor, there are no persons close to the top who are outstanding in their leadership qualifications.  The movement can either be captured by a relative outsider, or it can be put in charge of one of the steady and faithful followers of the strong man.

There is little doubt that the selection of Harry S. Truman to run as Vice President was made because of his long record of able and loyal service.  There had never been an indication of strong political leadership in his record, but rather a display of energy and initiative, as well as dedication to the national welfare, in his conduct of the affairs of the Truman Committee, which had saved the nation great sums by investigating war production and expenditures.  A man of this type does not hold the almost mystical authority over a mass of supporters and can hold only a fraction of the leadership power of the original head of the movement.  Thus as far as progress is concerned, the movement virtually comes to an end at the time of his accession, and in fact the combination of familiarity and almost boredom with the spirit of the movement, and the growing discipline and confidence of the opposition, permit the development of such a period of reaction as was shown in the Congressional elections of 1946, when the Republican Party recaptured both the House and the Senate and commenced at once to consider measures to alter policies on taxation, foreign trade, labor, and other matters which had been the concern of the late New Deal.

### MOVEMENTS OF THOUGHT

Among the processes by which some reorganization takes place in a changing society must be included trends of ideology or belief. The organization of practical philosophies is a cooperative affair and has continuity over many centuries.  Movements of thought are not closely similar in nature to the social movements examined previously in the chapter.  There is less of a focus of leadership and little tendency for persons to gather and to submit to discipline. Ideas, however, are developed, published, and taken up by others, who discuss and add to them, until a separate stream of thought is perceptible.  Occasionally this becomes clear enough to acquire a name, perhaps ending in —*ism*.  In some cases there is a distinguishable group of adherents who self-consciously proclaim their common beliefs and thereby constitute a "school of thought."

Opinions differ concerning the power of ideas in a practical world.  There are scholars who believe that movements of thought are the primary forces behind wars, revolutions, and other great political and social developments.  Others assign only a minor role to ideas.  Measurement is not at present attainable in such a question, but if, as Brinton stated, a revolution cannot do without the word *justice,* then the idea of justice, and the connotations it bears, must be considered part of the forces that make revolutions come into being.  It also seems clear that ideological wars have been fought, perhaps as frequently as any other kind.  The discovery and settlement of new continents has been connected with aspirations of national glory, freedom of worship, and other ideological conceptions.

No brief treatment of movements of thought could be adequate. It can only be indicated here that many ideologies that operate as factors in modern history are the products of long collective thinking.  The divinity of kings and the associated ideology of monarchy are inheritances from as far back as ancient Egyptian times.  Christianity is a long and complex process of thought which divides as well as unites nations in the world. Democracy as an ideology is not a recent American invention, nor is socialism or communism. Science itself, as a free, objective, methodical inquiry, is in a sense a movement of thought and was well under way in ancient Greece.

Races and nationalities tend to develop organized rationalizations of their past and myths to guide their future. The Zionist dream nurtured for so many centuries by Jews of Europe and America became a factor in bitter international controversy and strife in the twentieth century. The Italians' dreams of the past and perhaps future Roman Empire brought the world into trouble, and Italy into ruin, in modern times. The rational economic organization of Europe has been blocked, and remains so, by a complex of nationalist hopes all over the continent. In mid-century both India and China appear hopelessly divided by religion and ideology, with prospects of abundant bloodshed but not of early tranquility.

The spread of conceptions of justice, of the right of people to survive and to be free appears to operate to counteract some of the ideologies which threaten peace and stability. The "One World" conception, relatively new in comparison to political beliefs of modern times, played its part in the motivation of the United Nations, which constitutes one of the most important reorganization attempts in the history of the world.

### CONSERVATIVE DRAG AND REACTION

Ideas stimulate their own extension, and also opposition. Most movements of importance encounter organized opposition. Unorganized trends of thought stimulate a certain amount of discussion of a contrary point of view. Challenges to old customs are met by defenses, and new customs find explicit opposition. Reorganization processes in general work against a certain amount of such drag, which may delay their effects and in certain times and places produce organized reaction which puts a society back to an earlier condition, sometimes more than negating the attempted changes.

In Spain, for example, a progressive political movement developed so far during the middle 1930's that a relatively liberal democratic or socialist regime achieved power and set about to abolish the monarchy, extend the voting right to women, and carry out other standard measures of modern democratic regimes. The conservative clerical and military reaction, however, eventually produced the Franco rebellion, the civil war, and the reactionary dictatorship, putting Spain back to an earlier stage of political development.

In general the growth of fascism in Europe may be interpreted as a reaction against a rate of change too fast for nations to accept. It is true that often a majority of voters favored progressive government, but it is also clear that a fanatical and disciplined minority may succeed in taking over a nation and in destroying a large part of the movement toward progressive change.

In the United States there has developed in response to the labor movement an anti-labor opposition, in response to the feminist movement a small but articulate drive to put women back into the kitchen, in response to the extension of equality to Negroes a strong political reaction in certain southern states, and various other minor reactions of this type. Reorganization movements do not as a rule navigate in calm waters but generally pull against a dragging current, and often against rapids. There are many conditions, however, in which change holds greater attraction than the status quo, and the drag fails to check progressive movement.

## SUMMARY

Human society is not like a clock which, once wound, continues to run down until it stops. Disorganization accompanies change, but reorganization is also virtually continuous. New circumstances create new customs as well as destroying old. The processes by which folkways and mores are born were not abolished in prehistoric times but operate all the time.

Much reorganization, however, is conscious and intentional. Virtually all conceivable solutions to the problems of disorganization are tried by some persons or groups. Many seek the answer by a concerted return to the past, through revival of customs, arts, language, architecture, or religion or a reconstitution of the entire society of the earlier age. Others look toward novelty and try to devise solutions which attract followers who are congenial. One of the conspicuous aspects of an unsettled society is the number of unconventional social movements that continually arise. In the United States such phenomena are particularly prevalent among the indigent aged in the new regions of retirement. Any dissatisfied group, however, may be led into an organization, and the movements may be sacred or secular, may be inclusive or limited in their objectives, and may have a life of days or of centuries. The great crises tend to produce the largest movements, and revolutions constitute the most drastic means of reorganizing failing nations. Along with the actions go beliefs, and in opposition to both, reaction and counter-beliefs. In the long run, however, reorganization keeps pace with disorganization and man survives.

## SELECTED REFERENCES

Blumer, Herbert. "Social Movements." Ch. 22 in R. E. Park, *An Outline of the Principles of Sociology*. New York: Barnes & Noble, Inc., 1939.

Brinton, Crane. *The Anatomy of Revolution*. New York: W. W. Norton & Co., Inc., 1938.

Cantril, Hadley. *The Psychology of Social Movements*. New York: John Wiley & Sons, Inc., 1941.

Dawson, Carl A., and Gettys, Warner E. *Introduction to Sociology*. New York: The Ronald Press Co., 1935. Chs. 18 and 19.

Edwards, Lyford. *The Natural History of Revolution*. Chicago: University of Chicago Press, 1927.

LaPiere, Richard T. *Collective Behavior*. New York: McGraw-Hill Book Co., Inc., 1938.

Reuter, Edward B., and Hart, Clyde W. *Introduction to Sociology*. New York: McGraw-Hill Book Co., Inc., 1933. Ch. 29, "Public Behavior and Mass Movements."

# Chapter 15

## PROSPECTS OF STABILITY IN THE POSTWAR ERA

### WAR AS THE MAJOR THREAT TO STABILITY

While in the long run disorganization and reorganization may develop at about the same pace, there are certain times and places of severe disorganization that are dangerous to a nation or civilization. Our western civilization appears less likely to fall apart from gradual deterioration than to be extinguished in the sudden and severe peril of an ultra-modern world war. It is conceivable that a finish fight in which all of the most potent new weapons are employed without restriction might actually wipe out the populations of whole continents, for the few who survived the nuclear fission weapons, the diseases and poisons, and the destruction of supplies, materials, water supplies, and other necessities would hardly be able to reconstruct a system which could be called a civilization.

**Disorganizing Effects of Modern Warfare.**—Modern warfare is the greatest form of disorganization and has itself become a creator of many lesser types of disruption.[1] A most obvious casualty is international law itself—a crescive structure of organization among nations that arises slowly and laboriously in times of peace. Never of great or certain power, this beginning is always set back in wartime, as each belligerent party is accused by the other of violations. Without a functioning court to give definition to the law in the novel situations that inevitably arise in each new war, it is virtually certain that violations must arise. As Kirk points out, such regulations as the rules of contraband, formulated in regard to previous conflicts, become inapplicable in later wars that are total in character.[2] Such distinctions as those between absolute contraband, conditional contraband, and noncontraband no longer function, for the only effective blockade is total—all materials are war materials in modern warfare.

Warfare also retards or even sets back an intangible but important sense of world unity that tends to emerge from the trade,

---

[1] See Grayson Kirk, "Nationalism, Internationalism, and War," in Ralph Linton, *The Science of Man in the World Crisis.* New York: Columbia University Press, 1945, pp. 496–520.

[2] *Ibid.*, p. 497.

communication, and travel of peaceful days.  There is a conception that all peoples have common aims and viewpoints that are essentially human and decent and that cooperation based on such a sense of community is possible.  The effect of warfare is to cause people to doubt such a view.  Each nation perceives the enemy as immoral, or even inhuman.  During and for a time after each war there is a widespread wish to crush the enemy and to hold him down for an indefinite period.  Even the neutral nations are somewhat excluded from the category of those who honor right principles, for each fighting nation is convinced that its own aims are moral and that indifference or neutrality constitutes partial immorality.

A significant aspect of international integration is that produced by a number of organizations and agencies that have international memberships and objectives.  While it is difficult to measure the influence of any one of these, or even of their combined force, the very number of such organizations and conferences indicates their importance.  Kirk states that during the years 1910–1920 more than 1,800 meetings of organizations of such a character were held.[3]  War ends some, suspends others, and restricts the activities of the rest.  The Red Cross is about the only international agency that continues to function fully during the actual period of conflict, and even its activities do not imply any notable amount of cooperative spirit among nations.

Economic cooperation among nations is an important part of the solidarity that normally grows during times of tranquility.  Here again there is a sharp setback in wartime.  Many devices are used by each belligerent to cut off, as far as possible, the enemy's normal lines of trade.  The end of the period of active fighting does not necessarily mean a return to the earlier trade relationships, for the wartime readjustments remain to tangle the economic order for extended periods.  Where war has cut off a nation from an essential material, as in the case of the United States rubber supply, there arise substitutes which may remain in the postwar period to delay the re-establishment of old trade relations.  The synthetic rubber industry of the United States may be artificially retained, even if it incurs a loss, as a measure of national protection.  This and other emergency industries of wartime also create vested interests to exert powerful political force for protection.  The encouragement of western sugar-beet growers during the first world war led to such an expansion that the United States has, at cost to

---

[3] *Ibid.*, p. 498.

the consumer, "protected" itself against sugar from outside its borders ever since.

Further economic disorganization follows from the enormous war debts incurred by certain nations. These debts necessitate the maintenance of a favorable trade balance, which often means that trade cannot be permitted to find its natural channels but must be subject to drastic restrictions and controls. Britain in 1947 had virtually no choice but to limit imports to the absolute minimum and to deprive her own people of many types of goods in order to push exports to other countries. Without a drastic readjustment of international obligations there is no prospect of free trade among nations in this condition for many years to come.

War also fosters the development of nationalism, which operates as a force to oppose international cooperation. Populations become disillusioned concerning the motives of peoples of other nations and turn their loyalties to their own people. The general interest in humanity declines as the emphasis on the worth, the greatness, and the destiny of one's own nation increases. The pursuit of national self-interest inclines a nation to take measures that irritate its neighbors and act as destructive agents in international affairs.

**Public Opinion and Militarism.**—Despite the disorganizing effects of warfare on international efforts at cooperation, there is an important form of reaction against war that tends to produce a trend to reorganization. The misery of despoiled populations and of exhausted belligerents produces a general distaste among many for fighting as a means of obtaining national objectives. Large and powerful nations thus may learn what small and weak nations have long known—that there are other ways to show a love for one's own nation than by attacking others. As wars become larger and more destructive, there develops an expanding sentiment that the present conflict should be the last and that some form of international government must be devised to prevent the outbreak of the next, and inevitably the worst, war. The League of Nations became a war aim while the conflict of 1914–1918 was still in process. It did not survive because the lesson—the disillusionment with war as a way of gaining happiness—was not yet sufficiently widespread. There is little doubt that the second world war taught the lesson to additional millions more, but it remains to be seen whether the United Nations will be able to gain the influence required to prevent warfare.

In the times between wars, few populations would, if polled, directly choose to go to war for its own sake. Even as wars draw near, most people who are asked continue to say that they do not wish war. It is often the case, however, that public opinion insists upon governmental actions which greatly advance the probability of war. In the United States, for example, the public opinion polls repeatedly indicated, during the months and years preceding the Pearl Harbor attack, that something like 80 per cent of the population was opposed to war, but at the same time there were majorities in favor of such measures as discontinuing oil shipments to Japan, convoying American shipments to England, and similar measures which bore a relation to the process of becoming entangled.

Peoples who ardently seek political aims that can be achieved only by means of warfare tend to produce political leaders who either advocate war openly or, while protesting their aversion to warfare, undertake measures that lead to it. In the case of the latter type it may be that the leader earnestly abhors the idea of open conflict but is forced into actions by political pressures on the part of peoples who also do not want war. A leader who recognizes that the actions of his government are bringing his nation to certain warfare is usually forced to keep this knowledge from his people, for to admit that war is certain is to invite surprise attack at the enemy's earliest convenience. In order to keep the probability of war secret, a political leader must also withhold much information and interpretation concerning the actions of the government. Thus it is difficult for citizens to know the consequences of their own actions and expressions and to make intelligent choices. The people are free to choose, but they necessarily lack the essential knowledge, while the political leaders possess knowledge but not the freedom of choice. In this situation neutrality becomes a difficult status for a nation to maintain while other nations are at war. For small nations located in the main paths of wars neutrality may only mean submission to the first belligerent power to move into their territory.

**Militaristic Political Movements.**—Not all nations enter war by the process of drifting into it, as described above. There are nations that do not hesitate to advocate or to glorify war. In the present century Mussolini produced the most unabashed praises of warfare for its own sake, while Hitler and other fascist leaders took similar stands in varying degrees. The fascist nations also proclaimed aims which were intended to justify aggressive warfare. Their governments were constituted of agents of political movements which put their narrow interests above those of peace and international organization and law.  The force of such aggressive fascism is a product of movements which have a background in internal conditions of both political and economic disorganization, and the power of fascism is multiplied when the movement gains possession of the resources and the governmental and military machinery of a nation.

It is generally believed that a fascist government depends for its survival on the maintenance within its nation of a warlike spirit. In order to keep power, and perhaps to avoid losing their own lives, the leaders must keep up the sense of excitement and belligerency on which the movement is founded.  While it may be possible for such a movement to calm down in time, there does appear to be a strong inner necessity in most cases to keep alive the war spirit, and as long as this is done, the nation involved inevitably is a threat to general peace.

The greatest threat to international stability, therefore, appears to be the type of disorganization which fosters the growth of movements of militant fascism, so that they gain control of national governments.  Virtually every nation has sufficient internal disorder to permit some of its citizens to become disillusioned and to join conflict organizations, and some of the larger nations have at any time a considerable number of small and unimportant fascist movements.  In a nation which enjoys reasonably good political health such movements remain small and attract largely those persons whose general unconventionality leads them to be classified as part of the "lunatic fringe."  These organizations may be ignored or tolerated as long as they are small and not overtly destructive or criminal, but they are often stamped out rapidly if they attempt violence.[4]

It is the condition of disorganization within a nation that allows fascist movements to enlist masses of supporters and to grow beyond the "lunatic" stage.  While no such movement has gone far in the United States, it is significant that the highest development of pseudo-fascist organizations took place here during the dislocations of the 1930's.  It was also during this period that France had its Croix de Feu and the Cagoulards, and England had the fascist movement of Oswald Mosley.

---

[4] In late 1946 such a movement came to light in Georgia.  The "Columbians" constituted an imitation of Nazism, wearing uniforms, holding secret meetings, persecuting Negroes, and planning the capture of the United States government.  Exposure and indictment came within a few weeks after discovery of the organization, and virually no public sympathy or support was extended to the defendants.

**The Support of Fascism in Germany.**—In the early days of the Nazi movement, Hitler and his small group of cronies were regarded locally as unimportant members of the "lunatic fringe" and were virtually unknown outside of Germany. It appeared hardly worth while to take measures against them, except to put down riots and imprison the leaders when they misbehaved. Certain visiting publicists took note of the movement, but a frequent judgment was that no such eccentric organization would ever attract a large following in Germany.

While it is true that the Nazi movement did not reach power by means of winning an election, it was the size and desperation of the movement that permitted it to make such a nuisance of itself that a weary old Hindenburg finally permitted Hitler to become Chancellor and to make a rapid and irreversible consolidation of his hold on the nation. It is not necessary for a fascist movement to wait for a majority at the polls if its followers are determined and disciplined while its opponents continue to obey the rules of fairness. Illegal crises can be created, during the excitement of which the fascists may quickly take over all agencies needed to hold absolute power. It would appear, then, that the crucial matter that determines whether a whole nation becomes fascistic and warlike is the extent of the following that the small extremist movement can enlist among the population of the nation.

Extensive research in the backgrounds of the Nazi movement has shown the nature of its appeal to different sections of the German population.[5] It is also of interest that in general it was the same people who gave early support to the movement and, according to studies of the United States Strategic Bombing Survey (Morale Division), continued to have high war-supporting morale during the conflict.[6] In general the movement did not attract in large numbers the memberships of such large organizations as already possessed something of a political ideology—organizations such as the Catholic group and the socialist and communist parties. The appeal was greatest to the politically unorganized, and particularly to those whose previous position of integration was in the process of deterioration.

Most notable in providing mass support were certain rural areas where farming had retained its traditional character, with one-family farms on which dairying and hog-fattening constituted the principal

[5] See Hadley Cantril, *op. cit.*, Ch. 8, "The Nazi Party," and Charles P. Loomis and J. A. Beegle, "The Spread of German Nazism in Rural Areas," *American Sociological Review*, Vol. 11, pp. 724–734, Dec., 1946.
[6] Loomis and Beegle, *op. cit.*, p. 724.

activity.   In these areas traditionalism, familism, and primary group life predominated, but at the same time much of the land was of a poor character and the farmers' incomes were meager and insecure.   Then, during the late 1920's and early 1930's, price fluctuations in cattle added to the hardship and uncertainty.  As foreclosures increased, farmers took desperate measures similar to those taken by American farmers of the Mid-West during the 1930's and attempted by mass force to stop the sales.  The Nazi movement appealed to this population and in some areas rapidly won over virtually the entire population.  The fervor of the peasants' enthusiasm has been compared to that of American farmers for the various religious and secular movements that have risen in this country in times of rural hardship.

Significant support of the Nazi movement also came from a large number of salaried employees of the low- and middle-income groups. These people had suffered severely in the inflation of the middle 1920's, when any savings they may have had were wiped out and prices rose to a level that impoverished them.   At the worst of the inflation, money became virtually worthless.   It took some three to four billions of marks to acquire one American dollar.  Bills of small denomination were thrown on the pavement as utterly useless.   A peasant with a few potatoes was better off than a man with a basketful of money.   People with fixed salaries or savings had to survive by selling their possessions until they finally stripped themselves of belongings.   Their desperation was further intensified in class-conscious Germany by the recognition that ordinary laborers were gaining upon them and that their status of superiority was also being lost.

The economic uncertainties and political developments of the 1920's were also experienced as a threat by the landed aristocracy and by large industrialists, who saw in the Nazi movement a defense against disorder and socialism.  When Nazis sought advice and support from these groups the cooperation was often extended, and a few such groups provided important financial support for a time.   While these people were not threatened with hunger to the extent that low-income people were, they had a capacity for as much desperation, when faced with the loss of a family estate or loss of the control of a large industry and were therefore willing to try political measures that ordinarily would have been distasteful.

It is clear that the economic disruptions, including the inflation, and the political disorder in postwar Germany of the 1920's were interrelated and were in large part products of the recent warfare and defeat. A process of a "vicious circle" character is thus suggested—war and defeat producing extreme dislocations, which in turn produce movements of political extremism and warfare, and again further dislocation. It is apparent that the greatest hope of breaking the chain of causality would be through reorganization of economic and political relations in the postwar period. Such a task is possible in the modern world only through international cooperation, and it is to such problems that the efforts of the United Nations are addressed. It is not possible to predict, during the early stages of such a novel attempt at organization, the possibilities and the rate of success. Without success, however, it is unlikely that any kind of enduring stability between or within modern nations is possible.

### PROSPECTS OF INTERNAL STABILITY IN THE UNITED STATES

Internal stability within the United States, as stated above, must depend somewhat on the condition of international relations. At the same time, however, the degree of stability in the member countries of an international organization may be a factor in the success of the latter. It was internal dissension in the United States which caused this country to withhold cooperation from the League of Nations and thereby to destroy the League's effectiveness. On various other occasions this nation has abstained from international agreements on economic matters because of concern with its internal economic health. In a democratic country, furthermore, the degree of education of the population is a factor in the responsibility of its government. A disintegrated, corrupt, or demoralized population may force its political leaders to respond to short-run and segmental policies and to disregard the long view and the general view in international affairs. Thus internal conditions are of double importance—to matters of national health and to the success of international cooperation.

It has been shown throughout the previous chapters that certain aspects of internal instability and disorganization in the United States are in part consequences of conditions that are not necessarily permanent. In so far as the national character may be a product of the experience with an open frontier, it is clear that a change must inevitably be taking place. It is also certain that rapid population growth must soon complete its effects upon the society. While the Industrial Revolution may not have such a definite final point, some of the major readjustments to industrialization may in time reach a stage of virtual completion. It appears probable that certain forms of disorganization will diminish as the society has the opportunity to find an equilibrium in the more stable conditions that follow.

**The Passing of the Immigration Waves.**—During the century from 1820 to 1920 the growth of the United States population was mainly a result of the large amount of immigration from Europe. During the latter forty years of the period, when the bulk of this immigration came from southern Europe, the amount was especially large, and in 1907, the peak year, the arrivals totaled more than a million. The rate of this inflow exceeded the capacity of the nation to assimilate the newcomers. Large groups of foreign nationalities accumulated in industrial cities, often forming isolated communities in which many of their foreign culture traits, including language and costume, were for a time preserved. The association of certain of these populations with high rates of delinquency and crime, the vices, disorders of mass behavior, political corruption, and other forms of social disorganization has been analyzed in the foregoing chapters. An inevitable sentiment of antagonism arose in the native American population, and each immigrant nationality became the object of racial and cultural prejudice and discrimination.

Assimilation of foreign populations is relatively easy when the people come a few at a time and disperse among native peoples in settled communities. A large part of the stream of immigrants to America, however, consisted of persons recruited for common laboring tasks in the large and rapidly growing urban factories. The number of such entrants and the circumstances of their work and places of residence virtually cut them off from contacts with native Americans and left them to associate with one another until they could in time work their way out of the slums. Assimilation of the typical immigrant nationality ordinarily did not proceed far until the second or third generation. In the meantime, during the process of transition from peasant culture to urban civilization, processes of disorganization took severe effect.

The European sources of immigration to this country changed from Sweden, to Germany, Ireland, Italy, Poland, and other countries—each having a period of maximum flow. When the Irish were newcomers, their rates of disorganization were high, but as they learned to qualify for more rewarding occupations and learned the ways of their adopted country, they moved out of the slums and gradually progressed through the immigration cycle. The slums which they abandoned retained their old character, however, with the new nationalities that succeeded them. Thus the disorganization long remained constant in the area, although the condition was temporary for any one nationality.

During the early 1920's an accumulating political sentiment against the immigrant found expression in legislation to limit the amount of inflow and to set quotas for various countries. The quotas favored northern European countries against the southern, since the representatives of the latter regions were at the time in the disorganized phase of their cycle. The total to be admitted in any one year was 153,000, but since some of the nations did not fill their quotas, the actual immigration has remained below that figure since the time of the legislation. During the depression of the 1930's immigration fell to a low point and emigration for a time actually exceeded it. For the whole decade of the 1930's the net loss by migration was about 47,000 persons. The period of rapid immigration was over.

While laws are always in theory subject to change, there is no indication that the people of the United States are likely to favor, in the predictable future, the reopening of immigration on a large scale. The increasing power of organized labor operates as a force to keep out large numbers of competitors for jobs. Disillusionment that follows two large wars fosters a sentiment opposed to entertaining large groups of immigrants and the customs and ideologies they would import. The high birth rates of certain regions, particularly India, and the consequent population pressure and starvation are more likely to promote a defensive reaction against admitting excess populations than to arouse a sympathetic attitude. There is thus little reason to believe that the United States will gain further appreciable population through migration. Future immigrants will be few in number and highly selected.

The distribution by age groups of the foreign-born populations in the United States in 1940 shows the largest concentration in the ages from forty-five to sixty years. Below the age of forty-five the proportion becomes rapidly smaller in each five-year age class, with a very small number below the age of twenty-five. By the end of the century this group will have virtually passed out of the population, with only slight replacement by the small numbers of immigrants now admitted. This fact should permit the development of a cultural homogeneity that has not been possible since the early nineteenth century and should in various ways contribute to cultural stability in general.

**The Fall of the Birth Rate and the Aging of the Population.** —At the same time that the United States population growth was being slowed by the virtual cessation of immigration, it was also showing the effects of a decline in the national birth rate. During the early years of the twentieth century this nation passed through the readjustment which comes to industrialized modern nations— a change from a condition of high birth rates and high death rates to a condition of low birth rates and low death rates. Since the birth rates decline faster than the death rates in the later phase of the readjustment, the net reproduction rate tends to fall below the replacement level. This took place in the United States during the middle 1930's. In this period, although more persons were born each year than died, the net reproduction rate fell below the level which would have been adequate if the nation had not happened to have an excess proportion of females in the child-bearing ages at the time. As this abnormally large proportion of females disappears and is not replaced by a similar large group of young females, the same birth rate will no longer even equal the deaths in the country, and the population may then begin to decline. Estimates have placed the probable time of this stabilization or decline of the United States population at some time in the last quarter of the present century.

It is also forecast that the age composition of the population in the latter part of the century will be very different from that in the beginning of the century. The proportion of children and young persons will diminish, and the proportion of elderly persons will greatly increase. The average age of a stable population is much higher than that of a growing population, and conditions will be different enough to require certain cultural readjustments.[7]

Some of the effects upon society of the stabilization and aging of the population can be foreseen with confidence, while others are speculative. There are both unpleasant and beneficial aspects to the change. From the point of view of national pride, and perhaps from considerations of military power, it is to be expected that some efforts may be made to alter the trend and keep the population growing, even if it means an alteration in policy on immigration. It is likely that various measures, already in effect in some European countries, will be tried to increase the birth rate. As Ogburn and

---

[7] The basis of such predictions, and a well-organized study of their significance, is presented in *The Problems of a Changing Population*, Washington: National Resources Committee, 1938.

Nimkoff point out, the nation has always been adapted to conditions of rapid growth, and even a marked slowing of the growth acts like a decline.[8]   Since business is adapted to expanding markets and real estate values are based on expectations of future growth, the population slackening introduces a depressing effect.[9]   American optimism, connected with its record of rapid and continuous growth, is related to business daring and experimentalism.   Here bankruptcy may be borne with relative ease, since other opportunities are generally available, in contrast with such a stable country as France, where bankruptcy is a more serious tragedy.[10]

Many readjustments in business and government will be required. The use of real estate as an important basis of taxation will probably decline.   Goods for which demand is inelastic will face decreasing demand.   Production of clothing, toys, and other goods for infants and children will fall off, and the demand for schoolteachers will decline.   At the same time it is expected that there will be something of a boom in goods that appeal to the aged—books and magazines, radios, warm clothing, dogs and cats, and real estate in Florida and California.   Predictions have been made of an increase in esoteric cults, demands for security legislation, and political conservatism.[11]   Not all of these are certain of fulfillment, but it is probable that the effects of the aging will be general in character and important in their totality.

The cessation of growth may be expected to contribute to stability in further ways.   In the first place, if children are scarcer, it is likely that they will be more appreciated and valued.   Parents will provide better care, and negligent parents will be subject to greater pressures to provide for the general welfare of their children. Educational opportunities will be supplied more generally, and, with a stable and not too large school population to care for, there will be further impovement in educational systems.

The passing of the population expansion phase of our history will also reduce the speculative aspect of economic life—an influence that has worked in opposition to stability and long-range planning.   Few uses of land, buildings, or agencies could be viewed as permanent during the time of rapid growth of the economy.   The automatic

---

[8] William F. Ogburn and M. Nimkoff, *Sociology*, Boston: Houghton Mifflin Co., 1946. Chapters 15 and 16 provide an adequate discussion of modern population questions.
[9] Even the realization that some time in the future the growth of a city may cease is sufficient to make present alterations in the structure of real estate values.   For this reason, real estate and banking interests of an Eastern city recently attempted to remove from a city planning report an objective population analysis that indicated that the city growth would probably not continue beyond a few decades.
[10] *Ibid.*, p. 507.
[11] See Stuart Chase's article on population in the *Atlantic Monthly*, Feb., 1939.

profits that accompanied expansion were so pleasant that little could be allowed to stand in their way.

**Rural-urban Migration and the Growth of Cities.**—Industrial cities have not made their growth through natural increase. The urban birth rate, in fact, has long been too low to replace the population. It is migration, primarily of young adult workers, which has produced the long and rapid expansion of American cities. Part of this has been composed of immigration from abroad, but when this stream was cut off, the demands of industry in times of growth were such that population was drawn at the necessary rate from rural areas. Rural population is still available, largely because of the declining manpower requirements of farm life that is in process of mechanization. A long series of technical developments has reduced the need for farm labor. Among these are the harvester, corn-planting machines, tractors, machine plows, and recently the cotton-picking machine. The released labor does not necessarily migrate to cities—during the depression the rural unemployed stayed on the farms because cities offered no employment opportunities. But during times of industrial activity there have always been large cityward migrations from farming areas. The call of industry during such times may be so great that not only does it take off the excess of farm labor but it may even reduce the needed supply of farmers. The war boom of the 1940's not only reduced farm labor to a dangerously low point but in many areas virtually drained off the labor from many other occupations of low income and prestige. Domestic servants all but disappeared in some areas, and for years the supply of workers for restaurants, laundries, and similar types of business was inadequate. The crowding of such workers into the industrial cities was reflected in the many acute housing crises.

City growth in the United States is not over, and will not necessarily end at once as the natural increase of population ceases. The rural birth rate, though falling in recent years even faster than the urban birth rate falls, still remains higher, and for a time will be sufficient to supply a continuing rural-urban flow of population. Furthermore, the transition from one-family traditional farms to mechanized factory farms is far from complete. Tractors and other forms of machinery which have long been in existence have not come into their full use, and such machines as the cotton-picker are yet to have their principal effect. There are undoubtedly further improvements in mechanization to come, as well as an extension of the development of industrial methods to farming. There will eventually be a large number of farms which are not only mechanized but which apply factory methods of division of labor and specialization to great tracts of land. Laborers will be hired at wages, and all traces of the farm family type will be lacking in such enterprise. When such a trend has progressed to its limit, not only will the rural birth rates be as low as those in cities, but all excess population will have disappeared from farms, and the labor supply will be at the minimum required to operate the system. Unless some new source of population supply comes into view, there will be no further basis of city growth. Actually, most cities may cease to gain in population before such a point is reached, but it would be unsafe to predict such stability before the latter part of the twentieth century.

Permanent cessation of city growth is likely to have an almost revolutionary effect on certain aspects of American culture. Our civilization is a characteristically urban system, and in America urbanism has always meant the traits of rapidly growing cities. In general this country lacks experience with stable city life in the sense that it has long been known in slower-growing or stable countries of Europe and elsewhere.

The spatial arrangement itself of our industrial cities is to a considerable extent an expression of growth. Land use everywhere reflects the expectation of change. Even in the central business districts, where high land values force the construction of tall and expensive buildings, there is often a recognition of their impermanence. Buildings erected to last a century have in some cases had to be recognized as obsolete after two or three decades. Factories have had to be pushed out of the business district, homes have been displaced to receive the factories, and houses have had to make way for apartment buildings. The anticipation of such expansion from central regions outward makes it economically unwise to build for quality and permanence, and in certain borderline areas temporarily unwise to build at all. A considerable part of the physical deterioration of slum residences is attributable to the presence of high speculative land values in the path of expanding industry. To build a home or apartment building here would mean foregoing the chance of the greater gain that would result from an anticipated industrial sale, and even if an occasional builder were willing to do that, the occupants would soon find their new home surrounded by noisy, smoking, dirty factories. Even in the buildings that already stand in the pathway, it is in general not profitable to make improvements. Many landlords expect only to clear taxes on rentals in slum areas—they wait for the expected sale to make their gain. Tenants thus occupy deteriorated buildings, but at a rental which is too low to be profitable to an owner. The provision of private-profit slum-clearance housing runs into this difficulty, that there is no possibility of meeting in new houses the rent competition of such deteriorated buildings operated at a loss. And, although large numbers of families occupy such dwellings in the larger cities, it is safe to say that few of them do so by choice—most of these persons can afford no higher rent.

Governmental slum-clearance projects encounter opposition from those who have interests in the existing structure of urban land values. Plans to clear a slum and erect at government cost a permanent housing project imply the barring of industry from the immediate neighborhood and thus tend to reduce land values even at some distance from the new residences. Other permanent improvements of a nonresidential character may meet with similar opposition. An eastern industrial city in recent years faced a proposal to construct a broad bypass highway to form a loop about the central area, relieving the business streets from through traffic and permitting local traffic to escape the delays of downtown streets. Determined opposition came from representatives of the interlocking real estate, business, banking, and political groups. However convenient and attractive the improvement may be, they had the fear that it would imply or actually set a limit to the expansion of the central business district itself. The very recognition of such a limit would have immediate effects on the land values in and near the city center.

The contrast between construction for permanence and exploitation for as quick profits as possible may be seen in the comparison between certain of the older and more stable European cities and such rapidly growing industrial cities of America as Chicago or Detroit. In the former there are many evidences of building for permanence and of a sense of pride in appearance and harmony of buildings. A builder may believe that his structure will be a source of admiration a century or more after he builds it, and a man may improve his residence and grounds in the expectation that his grandchildren will enjoy the benefit. In contemporary America on the other hand, improvements are in general required to justify themselves in a short period of time, and expense for decoration and landscaping of a commercial structure is less appropriate when it cannot be certain what the use will be, or what the nature of its surroundings will be, after the passage of a few years.

Rapidly expanding cities also disrupt culture by virtue of the transition they impose on their new populations. A high proportion of the population of the larger cities is new to city life and is unable to settle immediately into a stable equilibrium. Not only is this illustrated by the severe forms of social disorganization like delinquency, crime, family disruption, and others, but also by various minor symptoms of disequilibrium. The way of life of the village and small town is unavailable, and the new urban dweller does not know how to find a satisfactory social life. Commercial recreation of various kinds is patronized but does not permanently satisfy—it in fact constitutes a minor form of vice in many cases. Urban populations do not have access to a ripe body of folk knowledge to solve for them the ordinary small crises that arise frequently and to help them in their social relations. They have no settled way of life and in many cases are unable, in a single lifetime, to devise a satisfactory one on their own initiative.[12]

It has been shown that control of children is relatively ineffective where the efforts of the family are not supported by a cooperating primary group in the neighborhood. Furthermore, adult behavior tends to deteriorate in some respects when the relation to surrounding dwellers is anonymous. Thus a large part of urban populations—those in apartment buildings and apartment hotels—are, by virtue of the physical isolation and mobility of their dwellings, detached from a supporting social order. Neighborhood life is difficult to establish in apartment-house districts of high mobility and heterogeneity, and the resigned urban dweller eventually learns to prefer his isolation from neighbors. The resulting deterioration of conventionality reacts back as a further isolating factor. The normal processes by which neighborhoods are spontaneously formed are continually frustrated by the mobility, much of which is based on the fact of continuous growth of the city.

All indices of social disorganization are lower in the outlying residential and suburban districts than they are in the apartment-house and slum areas of the cities. Since the former districts are at least in part inhabited by groups which migrated from slum to apartment house to a residential neighborhood, it is clear that a certain amount of stability in social life is re-established in the new

---

[12] Not all immigrants are new to city life. A large proportion of immigrant Jews have a background of centuries of urban life in conditions of hardship and thus possess cultural solutions to many of the conditions they encounter in American cities. They do not escape all of the troubles and may suffer from some difficulties with which they have no previous experience. But where they preserve their own culture, as in the ghetto life of the orthodox Jew, they are somewhat protected from the delinquency and crime, alcoholism, vices, venereal diseases, and related mental disorders which occur with such frequency among slum dwellers lacking in previous experience with urbanism.

situation.  This stability is particularly well developed in the suburban areas populated by single homes of moderate size in which
the residents are also the owners.[13]

The suburban community is not in all respects a transplanted
small town.  Most of its inhabitants have migrated outward from
the city and are two or more generations removed from village life.
The resemblances to small-town social life are more the result of
analogous conditions.  The suburbanite who owns his home tends to
live in the same place for many years and to be surrounded by neighbors who have similar permanence of location.  Unlike the barrier
walls of urban apartments, the boundaries of suburban yards expose
persons to their neighbors.  Privacy here, in the degree that is
available to the apartment dweller, is impossible.  While in the city
the parking of a car and the entrance of a visitor to a building may
not reveal which of fifty or more families is receiving a caller, there
is no such uncertainty in a colony of single homes.  The eyes of the
suburban housewife turn to the window when a strange car draws
up next door.  If the visitor is a man with a physician's kit, her
interest frequently becomes active and she telephones to inquire, to
offer aid, and perhaps later to inform other interested neighbors.
Such activity fosters sociability and cooperation.

The recent migrant to suburbs, accustomed to the anonymity of
the city, may at first feel uncomfortable in such an atmosphere of
supervision, and even actively resent the lack of privacy.  He comes
to realize, however, that the people next door will be his neighbors
indefinitely, and that unpleasant words or quarrels will remain to
embarrass him for years.  He has not the ready escape of the city
dweller, and thus comes in time to recognize the necessity of
entering into the spirit of the primary community.  The positive
values of neighborliness may be dramatized if he encounters troubles
and receives many offers of aid, both large and small, from his
neighbors.[14]  Furthermore, as the passage of time makes him
accustomed to this style of life, the new suburbanite usually comes
to prefer it and to enter into the same kinds of relations with new
neighbors that come out from the city.

---

[13] In some such suburbs the residents form community associations to promote neighborliness and to handle problems they have in common.  In these groups it is common to find an
informal distinction drawn between the renter and the owner.  The former is looked upon as
less committed to the general community welfare.  It is the owner who has the important
stake in keeping up the condition and value of his property and who sees the interconnections
of his own interests with those of his neighbors.

[14] Among the common services observed by the author in such communities are such
things as the offer of food, even ready-cooked hot meals, in cases of sickness; the care of
children when parents are away; the reception of parcel deliveries, mowing of lawns, and
shoveling of sidewalks for persons who are unable to take care of these tasks; and even blood
donations for neighbors in case of need.

New organizations emerge in residential suburbs to integrate further the social life of the community. Parent-teachers associations or mothers' clubs at the schools become in part neighborly and gossip meetings. Bridge clubs form among housewives and extend the networks of interacquaintance. Churches, less sectarian in character than village churches, become social centers which make their members and visitors conscious of the social fabric of the community. Other less formal circles and cliques grow up spontaneously, so that all who enjoy social gatherings have ample opportunities to partake of them. To the extent that acquaintanceships have long duration, conversations at such gatherings tend to form about personal matters, and the spread of anecdotes and information about mutual acquaintances insures that few secrets remain private for long within the community.

Such conditions produce a powerful pressure toward conformity with general standards of expected behavior. These are not necessarily the standards of the rural village—there is less emphasis on church-going, for example, and less objection to the use of alcohol—but they are of a sort that produces responsibility in the person and stability in the community. Persons whose behavior is intolerable in the light of the standards may be frozen out by intentional and organized ostracism or may even be visited by a committee and asked to move. In such cases a local social order has developed. Judging from the general success, both occupational and social, of the children of suburban dwellers, it is an order which is capable of reproducing itself over the generations. Unlike the relatively traditional and sacred order of the rural village, it is adapted to modern conditions. It is probably the aspect of the modern social order which has the least to fear from the future, for it may be said to have solved to a certain extent the problem of living in modern urban civilization. This may be the real "brave new world."

The residential and suburban dwellers of the cities, therefore, represent in a sense the end product of a cycle of adaptation to the Industrial Revolution. In the transition from an agricultural society to an industrial civilization, populations have streamed from farm to factory, living in urban slums, in apartment-house districts, finally passing through the disorganizing transitional stages and emerging into the stable residential communities where the new equilibrium has emerged. At the present time no great proportion of the population has gone all the way through this process. But the stream continues to flow, and for some time to come will flow, in such a direction. Except for a brief period during the depression of the

1930's the farming areas have been losing population by migration, and the central areas of the cities have also been losing. The outlying residential areas and particularly the suburban areas outside of the city limits have had the most notable gains.[15]

It is not assumed that all of the population must live in suburbs before a stable culture can be regained. Certain aspects of a similar stability may penetrate even an apartment-house district of a city. Home ownership occasionally develops here in cooperatively owned apartment buildings. In certain such dwellings there have emerged networks of interacquaintance and developments of neighborliness and community spirit much like that of the suburbs. Something of a similar community life may develop even in the homes of low-income workers, where conditions facilitate stability and acquaint-anceship. Illustrations may be found in certain of the government-built housing projects for low-income urban populations.

It appears evident, then, that social disorganization is connected with urbanism not at all because of the inevitable nature of city life, but as a consequence of the transition from a traditional folk society. There is reason to expect that the completion of the cycle of urban growth will in time allow a large part of the population to evolve a stable equilibrium and to have a social organization that will function in urban society.

**Technological Developments and Social Stability.**—While inventions have been important in forcing the great change known as the Industrial Revolution, and hence the growth of great cities and the social disorganization that develops in them, there are other inventions that may serve to advance the achievement of a new equilibrium. It is not often possible to forecast with certainty the particular effects of any invention, but speculations concerning certain general consequences of the advancement of technology may be of some value.

Power and machinery continue to increase in amount and to be applied to more uses, both in industry and in other places. Not only are the traditional sources of power from coal and water increasing, but there is the unknown potentiality of atomic power to add to the total. Machine technology may be expected to continue the long-time trend of reduction of manual tasks, particularly those involving little or no skill, and perhaps in time to approach the abolition of the occupational class of common laborer. In fact, machinery has

---

[15] This material is presented in National Resources Committee, *Population Statistics* (*3. Urban Data*), Washington: U. S. Government Printing Office, 1937.

for some time been altering the occupational structure of the population and will almost surely continue to do so.[16]

Mechanization of industry carries with it a level of wages somewhat higher than prevails in factories using unskilled labor and thus tends not merely to displace unskilled labor but to abolish a whole class of low-wage occupations. It is to be expected that the resulting general increase in standard of living will contribute in various ways to cultural stability. Furthermore, the economic pressure to keep expensive machinery in operation as steadily as possible may operate as a pressure for employers to provide continuity of employment, which in turn should reduce residential mobility and therefore allow even the urban communities of the working populations to develop some stable organization.

An important development of recent decades has been the growth of agencies of mass communication. Although printing is centuries old, the enormous circulation of books, magazines, and newspapers, is relatively recent. Research on the effects of mass reading is too new to have produced ripe fruit, but it is safe to say that the cumulative effects of exposing millions of persons, day after day or year after year, to the particular biases that may appear in the Chicago *Tribune,* the New York *Daily News, Time,* the *Reader's Digest,* and other leading publications are important both culturally and politically.[17] Perhaps the most important influence of the press, however, lies in the fact that the very amount of reading is a contributing factor to general intelligence. The reading habit in time becomes persistent, so that the person who has acquired it develops a general appetite for printed matter and tends to absorb a considerable amount of information that he would not otherwise have. As a reading population the United States people are probably only beginning to come of age. The effects will be more visible in the future than in the past.

The motion pictures, with weekly audiences of many millions, unquestionably have far-reaching effects. Among the most impressive must be the influence toward standardization of concepts, ideas, and tastes. Unwittingly millions of movie-goers are persuaded, by the prestige of the leading actors and the splendor of the settings, to admire certain types of character, certain styles of clothing, and

---

[16] Ogburn and Nimkoff (*Sociology*, p. 335) show that in the half-century from 1880 to 1930 the percentage of farmers in the United States declined from 34.9 to 15.8 and farm labor shrank from 8.9 per cent to 5.6. Wage earners declined from 37.9 per cent to 30.4. The most notable gain was in the proportion of low-salaried workers—3 to 14.6 per cent. A *Fortune* article in November, 1946, forecast the completely automatic factory, which would of course force many more into personal service and professional occupations.

[17] A useful general work on the subject is Douglas Waples, B. R. Berelson, and F. R. Bradshaw, *What Reading Does to People,* Chicago: University of Chicago Press, 1941.

certain themes in interior decoration and architecture. History, far more impressive and memorable in color movies than in schoolbooks, becomes transformed into mythology. Foreign lands and peoples are stereotyped, not necessarily at present in an unfavorable light, but at least in an oversimplified manner. Certain comforting though necessarily safe principles are spread, such as the notion that the wrongdoer always receives a definite punishment. Even science, though simplified and distorted in many cases, is presented to audiences in palatable fashion, woven into plots of romance and adventure. A series of films on psychoanalysis, for example, has popularized certain of the leading conceptions of Freud without emphasizing the theoretical structure of his system.

Standardization of culture through the influence of the films is perhaps most visible in the matter of clothing fashions. In the early period of sound pictures, for example, Clara Bow wore for one film an outfit consisting of a short skirt, blouse, and suspenders. The film was popular, and almost as fast as the clothing could be produced and put on the market, high school girls over the country rushed to affect the same dress. No figures are available, but it may be that sales of this type of dress exceeded ten millions. Since then Hollywood styles have had so many effects on the national dress for both men and women that the movie colony may be said to be the national style capital and to be taking from Paris the claim of being the world center of fashion. Even persons who never attend motion pictures are affected, for virtually all clothing available in stores carries reflections of Hollywood influence.

In similar though perhaps less obvious and measurable ways, the films impose standard speech traits, folkways, and even moral concepts on their audiences. They may be an important influence in reducing local variations of culture within the United States, both by presenting standardized forms of speech, dress, and manners and also by presenting in a somewhat comical light the local ways of peoples from the South, the West, New England, and the like. Similarly the contrast between farmer and city dweller is reduced by the common experiences and influences imposed on them by the films.

Radio has effects comparable to those of the films and of reading matter. By presenting to national audiences a fairly uniform standard of pronunciation it reduces localisms of speech, and by providing a common fund of information and entertainment it unifies American culture. The educational function is also potentially great. Some of the largest audiences on record are those that have listened, at the same moment, to the "fireside" chats of the President. These speeches, carefully written and delivered, are the products of a collaboration of active and learned men and present the essentials of foreign and domestic policies in the clearest terms that their authors can devise. As the custom becomes older and is perfected, the isolation of the President from the voters will doubtless be greatly reduced. Perhaps in time a steady bridge of communication will be developed between other important officials and the public.

Cultural unity appears to be promoted to some extent by the mere fact of common possessions. While the intellectual or moral contributions of certain popular celebrities—Joe Louis, Jack Benny, Bing Crosby, and Fibber McGee and Molly—may be unimportant, they do serve as topics of conversation and matters of mutual interest to persons of diverse ages, regions, occupations, and educational classes. The development of the national network, with its costly nation-wide broadcasts, is recent enough not to have had its full effects. New kinds of programs are still in process of development and have the potentiality of increasing the hours spent each week at the radio as well as the numbers of persons acquiring the practice.

The effects of television will probably be similar to those of radio and the motion picture, since the former combines the characteristics of the latter instruments. The perfection of color television may be expected to increase its appeal, and the development of satisfactory programs, which may take some years, will eventually build an important mass audience. Although films may be used to supply some television programs, a part of the potential fascination of the new device lies in the possibility of seeing events as they occur. Radio audiences have shown a preference for spontaneous programs in which "anything may happen," and television offers the additional advantage of seeing unpredictable current events.

In the earlier days of radio there were suggestions that this device would counteract trends of family disorganization by bringing the various members of each family together again in the home each evening. This effect, however, does not appear to have been as important as foreseen, nor is it to be expected that mere proximity in an audience is the condition that produces family solidarity. It is probable that the greatest effects of agencies of mass communications are to be found in the general relations of the population to one another rather than in primary group life.

Modern technology may introduce a significant additional contribution to cultural unity and stability through the mechanization of household tasks and the further liberation of women.  In our civilization women have traditionally been less active than men in the wider circles of social activity, partly because of the pattern of male dominance but also partly because of the necessities of house-keeping work.  Although progress in reduction of this work through labor-saving inventions is a century or so old, the transition from kitchen to public affairs is far from complete.  Only a minor proportion of housewives has so far been able to make use of a large part of household machinery and improvements; others must wait for further rise in standard of living.  The additional income required to take advantage of all available modern aids to household efficiency is considerable for most of the population, and so the availability of the new technology must come gradually.  Further developments in technology are to be expected, in such directions as the design of houses that are more convenient and easy to care for, electrical removal of dust from air and consequent lightening of cleaning tasks, rapid electrical cooking, and the like.  The house-wife of the future, of middle income or higher, may expect to have a considerably greater amount of time than at present, and will almost surely use part of it to participate in activities outside of the home.  The child-bearing function may prevent the full achievement of the degree of domestic independence available to males, but the difference between the public roles of the sexes will be diminished.[18]

Effects of Increase in Education.—While illiteracy in the United States has long been reduced to an insignificant proportion of the population, education at higher levels is a matter of recent decades.  High school enrollment entered its period of rapid growth as late as 1910, when there were less than a million pupils enrolled in high schools in the whole United States.  The numbers more

---

[18] It need not be assumed from the above discussion that all effects of new inventions are in the direction of reorganization and stability of culture.  There are inventions which may be primarily disorganizing in their effects, as well as many which may have effects in both directions.  The automobile, for example, has in many ways both weakened and strengthened the stability of social organization.  It is not generally possible to forecast the consequences of any particular new device.  It is recalled that a prominent business adviser predicted, during the early days of the 1930 trailer craze, that within a few years a majority of the population would live in trailers, that the land value structure and tax system would be destroyed, and that many other forms of disorganization would result.  It turned out, however, that persons living in trailers usually tried to get out of them and into a house as soon as it could be arranged.

Machines are, of course, often directly perilous.  The rate of automobile accidents, as well as particular incidents of crashes, furnishes illustration of this.  In California, early in 1946, a line of cars rushing down a six-lane highway passed through a cloud of smoke from a burning garbage dump.  In the tangle, 25 cars were wrecked or damaged and 13 persons were injured.  Mankind in the mass has not yet learned to proceed cautiously when powerful machines are involved.

than doubled in the next decade and again in the following decade, and by 1940 the enrollment was approximately six and a half millions. This constitutes a spectacular change in the mental qualities of the population. In general the younger half may be considered much better educated than their elders. The effects of such educational gain may take another half-century to be fully felt, for not until nearly all of the older and uneducated population dies off, to be replaced in all age levels by those with superior education, will the transformation be complete. It can safely be predicted, therefore, that, barring unforeseen circumstances, the second half of the present century will witness steady improvement in the intelligence of the United States population.

A surge into the colleges of considerable importance, though of smaller size, took place in the 1920's, during which the enrollment grew from half a million to slightly over a million. During the middle 1940's, after the termination of the war, government provisions for veterans' education produced another sudden expansion of colleges, enabling large numbers who normally would not have had the opportunity to get a taste of education on this level. By the fall of 1946 the number enrolled reached approximately a million and a half.

Education beyond the college level did not reach a large number until the 1920's, when graduate schools entered a period of rapid expansion. Between 1918 and 1940 the total graduate student body in the United States grew from 14,406 to 54,584. In approximately the same period the number of graduate schools offering the Ph.D. degree increased from 46 to 96, and the number of Ph.D. degrees awarded annually increased from 562 to 3,526. The growth is expected to reach new high levels in the late 1940's. Here again, the full effects of such developments will not be felt for a half-century, during which the lesser educated population will gradually be replaced by those with more developed minds.

It is not possible to specify all of the ways in which such a great alteration in the information and intelligence of a population may affect the general stability of the social order. It is probable that almost every aspect of life will be influenced in some way or another—perhaps in some cases in an unidentifiable manner. On the other hand, some influences will be quick, definite, and obvious. Many aspects of health and disease and of accidents are directly related to the amount of general knowledge in the population. Not only is it expected that rates of morbidity and of injuries and deaths from accidents will be reduced, and the life span thereby lengthened, but a very large amount of waste in useless remedies as well as expense of hospitalization and other care should be eliminated.

Formal education should facilitate the process of occupational upgrading which is expected to accompany further mechanization of industry and farming. Fewer unskilled laborers of farms and factories will be needed, and these will have to be educated up to higher occupational levels. More clerks, managers, and profession-ally trained persons will be produced by the educational processes available.

The potential effects of a high level of education in the population on political processes are of great magnitude. An utterly ignorant population is incapable of sustaining democratic forms of govern-ment and almost inevitably is led by a dictatorship.[19] Voting requires intelligence and information and needs to be sustained by a reading habit not only of current news, but of background information and general knowledge. The extent to which this is so is impressively suggested in public opinion surveys, in which responses are classified by educational levels of the persons inter-viewed.[20] In a series of inquiries undertaken after the end of the second world war, it was found that important political issues are viewed differently by those of various levels of education, and that, high as is the present educational level, there is much to be gained from an increase.

It was found late in 1946, for example, that only 21 per cent of a random sample of United States adults were capable of giving a correct definition of the Bill of Rights. The population does not appear, however, to have a general awareness of the importance of improvement in the educational system. Less than a third of those with only grade-school education had suggestions to make when invited to do so, though 86 per cent of college-educated persons offered suggestions.

Persons of lower education have less appreciation of civil liberties —they are far more disposed to forbid newspaper criticism of

---

[19] A condition close to absolute zero in political intelligence was found in certain countries visited in 1946 by Norman Corwin, who recorded and later broadcast his interviews of the man on the street in these lands. In Cairo, the typical workingman did not know, in 1946, who had won the recent world war—some said that Hitler won it. Most never read a news-paper, saw a motion picture, or traveled to another town. They knew nothing of how they were governed, and held no political opinions. Many expressly disclaimed interest in politics, and some even expressed a general fear of having such an interest or of having any contacts with police or other officials. Many refused to answer questions, and on some occasions when Corwin recorded street interviews, crowds gathered to watch in mixed fear and anger. Open expression of opinion, recorded by machine, was novel and frightening.

[20] The information is taken from various issues of *Opinion News* and of *Reports*, pub-lished by the National Opinion Research Center, University of Denver, Denver, Colorado

government.  They are also much less active in their attention to their government—less than one sixth as many persons with a grade-school education write to their congressmen or other officials than do persons with college education.

Persons of low education are in general less informed and less tolerant regarding racial and national minorities.  For example, only half as many grade-school respondents as college-educated persons were correctly informed about the nature of Negro and white blood composition.  Similarly, in their attitudes toward American people of Japanese descent persons of lower education showed greater hostility and misunderstanding.  More than twice as many, for example, believed that the average American Japanese was disloyal, as did the college-educated persons.  College-educated persons were also far more disposed to send food and other aid to populations abroad.

The technicalities of foreign trade are not well understood by the majority of the United States population, but polls indicate that an increase in education should improve this condition.  Persons of low education were less inclined to consider that the United States is better off when foreign countries are also prosperous.  Similarly the subject of foreign relations is less well understood by persons with only a grade-school education—these showed a greater inclination in late 1946 to believe that the disputes between the United States and Russia were serious enough to warrant war.  Furthermore, the same group is somewhat more inclined than the college-educated group to be quick on the trigger, for the former favored in greater numbers the sudden initiation of atomic warfare on the suspicion that some other nation might be planning an attack on us.

Faith in international cooperation varies by educational classes and is lower in the classes with less education.  Distinctly fewer grade-school persons than college-educated persons believed that the United Nations could ever become strong enough to prevent wars.  When asked what they might personally do to help prevent wars, 73 per cent of grade-school-educated persons had no suggestions, while only 41 per cent of college-educated persons were lacking in proposals.

The relation of low educational status to political instability has also been suggested by the character of the support given to corrupt urban political machines and by the followings of such extremists as Huey Long and Gerald Smith.  If, by the end of the present century, the potential supply of adherents to such unconventional political movements is reduced to a small proportion of their present number, even the statesmen of the major parties will not be forced to make the concessions hitherto necessary to head off further growth of the movements.

In somewhat similar fashion it is to be expected that a more educated population would be less susceptible to the attractions of extreme social movements of the type described in Chapter 12. It is also probable that even such normal organizations as political parties, labor unions, and the like will achieve greater stability, efficiency, and responsibility as the educational level of the population, and therefore of their own membership, increases.

Since certain forms of personal disorganization, particularly the vices, can be shown to be somewhat related to deficiencies in intelligence or education, the expected educational advance should also reduce this class of difficulties. In general it should contribute in a variety of ways to both personal and social reorganization.

## Summary

The greatest threat to the social order, as the situation appears in the middle of the century, is the possibility of a third world war in which destructiveness of an order hitherto unknown would come into play. Since there is a technical possibility that an entire continent could be made uninhabitable, there is little question of the threat to social organization or to civilization itself. Even a limited war holds the promise of severe and dangerous disruptions of the social organization within and between nations. The principal hope of avoidance of such disaster is generally believed to lie in the evolving machinery of international cooperation, which is expected to develop into effective international government.

Internal stability within the United States, if war can be prevented, appears to be possible. It has been shown that some of the most important factors in the prevalent forms of social disorganization are of a temporary character. The filling up of the land area, the immigration of masses of laboring population, and the transition from agricultural to industrial society are all near the stage of completion, and their disorganizing effects should diminish within the next few decades. The possibility is thus visible that this country will achieve a relatively homogeneous population which will become successfully adapted to the new circumstances of an urban culture and which will, by normal sociological processes, work out a new general social equilibrium to fit this culture.

The handicaps of high death rates have been greatly reduced, and further progress is in prospect. Advances in technology and in industrial organization promise further increase in the general standard of living and in opportunities for the extension of activity other than income-earning. A part of this wealth and time will be spent in increasing the educational level of the population, which in turn promises to contribute to stability in a variety of ways.

Attractive as the above possibilities may be, they do not promise an automatic progress toward earthly paradise. There remain threatening conditions in other lands besides the United States— conditions such as political rivalry, population crises, racial antagonisms, and others—and there is also the possibility that new kinds of danger to civilization, hitherto unknown, may emerge. There is nothing inevitable about improvement. Perhaps the most encouraging factor, however small in present importance, is the growth of the recognition that social disorganization has causes that are intelligible and that possibilities of control increase with the development of sociological wisdom.

SELECTED REFERENCES

Cantril, Hadley. *The Psychology of Social Movements.* New York: John Wiley & Sons, 1941. Ch. 8, "The Nazi Party."
Furnas, C. C. *The Next Hundred Years.* New York: Reynal and Hitchcock, 1936.
Kirk, Grayson. "Nationalism, Internationalism, and War." In Ralph Linton, *The Science of Man in the World Crisis.* New York: Columbia University Press, 1945.
National Resources Committee. *Population Statistics (3. Urban Data).* Washington: U. S. Government Printing Office, 1937.
Ogburn, William F., and Nimkoff, Meyer. *Sociology.* Boston: Houghton Mifflin Co., 1946. Chs. 15, 16, and 26, "The Distribution of Population," "The Growth of Population," and "The Social Effects of Inventions."

# AUTHOR INDEX

# SUBJECT INDEX